"Who is this tremendous personality who speaks to the whole church with a voice that expects no challenge or dispute? Who appeals to no authority but that of God, knows no superior but the Lord Himself, quotes examples only from the great ones of the Old Dispensation, instructs, chides, encourages, denounces with a depth, an energy, a fire, second to none in the whole range of sacred literature?"

R. St. John Parry, *St. James*, p. 73

JAMES
The Man and His Message

by

JAMES B. ADAMSON

GRAND RAPIDS, MICHIGAN
WILLIAM B. EERDMANS PUBLISHING COMPANY

To

My Father and Mother,
My Wife Jean,
and
Fiona, Jennifer, and Wendy
WITH GRATITUDE

255 Jefferson Ave. S.E., Grand Rapids, Mich. 49503

Printed in the United States of America

Library of Congress Cataloging-in-Publication Data

Adamson, James B.
James: the man and his message.

Bibliography: p. 489.
Includes indexes.
1. Bible. N.T. James—Criticism, interpretation, etc.
I. Title.
BS2785.2.A23 1988 227′.9106 86-16240
ISBN 0-8028-0167-6

Contents

Preface

The Epistle of James has been termed the riddle of the NT and until now has defied solution. Written for interested laypersons and busy pastors as well as for scholars, this study is neither a definitive discussion of all aspects of the problem of the Epistle nor a verse-by-verse commentary on the text itself but rather an exposition of its essential message. As the title suggests, this book emphasizes the relevance of James for us today.

Admittedly, many authors disparage this Epistle as the rambling effusion of some indeterminate scribbler without plan, purpose, or authority. Some, too, appear to be unduly dogmatic in their conclusions. Joseph B. Mayor, for example, declared, "It is now generally recognized [or words to that effect] as being the earliest portion of the New Testament." Still others, such as Martin Dibelius, see the church in James as "a curious and unlikely mixture of an original freshness and at the same time an undeniable decay." "It is unthinkable," wrote H. C. Kee and F. W. Young, "that James, the brother of Jesus, could have written this book." More recently Kenneth G. Phifer asserted: "The apostolic authorship by the brother of Jesus has been widely abandoned." Such diverse views leave little room for dogmatism but plenty for healthy discussion and vigorous debate.

This book is an independent sequel, complement, and companion to *The Epistle of James* (NICNT, 1976), with which it should be read. In that volume we discuss critical and exegetical matters to which this book occasionally refers. Both works are in substantial agreement on the major issues, being based initially on the Ph.D. thesis submitted to the University of Cambridge, undertaken at the suggestion of C. H. Dodd, pursued later under W. L. Knox, and completed under the wise and gracious supervision of C. F. D. Moule. They are, we believe, the first sustained effort in English in this century since J. B. Mayor to establish unequivocally the authenticity of the Epistle as the oldest extant uninterpolated document of early first-century Christianity.

On one question there can be no disputing—the sheer modernity of the Epistle. Martin Luther was nearer the truth than he knew when he called it "a really dangerous book." The explosive teaching of this fiery testament offers a unique possibility for church renewal. "A fervent attention to such seemingly harmless epistles as I John and James," wrote Peter Rhea Jones, "could actually bring off a renewing of the Christian life. There will be a recurring temptation to tame the powerful social message of this flaming letter, to domesticate it and calm its biting, all too relevant message into palatable terms. If the message of James is allowed to go out unmuffled, it will rattle the stained glass windows."[1] Ageless in its appeal, James's message, which is essentially a layman's manifesto, is particularly relevant to the urgent practical, ethical, and social issues before the church and the world today, especially in the Third World with its theology of liberation. The Epistle is filled with what Karl Barth called "God's unconditional and passionate concern" for the poor.

As in many similar works, frequently cited commentaries and related works are listed by author's name and page only. Fuller bibliographical information can be found in the lists following the Abbreviations and our Concluding Reflections.

I wish to record my deep gratitude to Professor F. F. Bruce, without whose guidance, practical help, and constant encouragement this book would never have been written. He read the book in manuscript form and offered invaluable advice, criticism, and inspiration.

To my late friend and teacher P. B. R. Forbes I also owe an enormous debt of gratitude both for his influence on my life and thinking and for his help and guidance in my study of the Epistle of James. To him I owe innumerable insights. Finally, I wish to thank my wife Jean not only for her extraordinary patience and indulgence but also for her diligent and careful reading of the proofs. I have drawn great strength from her understanding as well as that of our daughters Fiona, who helped to prepare the indexes, Jennifer, and Wendy. To them and all who helped me along the way, I express my warm thanks.

J.B.A.

1. "Approaches to the Study of the Book of James," *RevExp* 66 (1969): 426.

Introduction

"Those who have managed to read James on its own terms discover in it a writing of rare vigor and life, which interprets the 'faith of our Lord Jesus Christ of glory' (2:1) in a manner both distinctive and compelling."

L. T. Johnson, *The Writings of the New Testament* (1986), p. 453.

The novelist Upton Sinclair once read the opening verses of the last chapter of the Epistle of James to a crowd of clergymen and suggested that the words came from a woman terrorist agitator. The ministers were furious at the nerve of the author and declared that the rebel ought to be deported.[1] Much of James's teaching is hard to handle, especially by middle-class Christians in our society for whom it could even be "inflammatory."[2] By setting the poor at odds with the rich who are called "oppressors," James seems to encourage class struggle.

Controversy has always dogged the Epistle. Martin Luther called it a "really dangerous and bad book";[3] he threatened to thrust it out of the Bible and someday use it to heat his stove.[4] In 1542 he said: "Up to this point I have been accustomed just to deal with and interpret the Epistle of James according to the sense of the rest of Scripture. For you will judge that none of it must be set forth contrary to manifest Holy Scripture. Accordingly, if they will not admit to my interpretations, then I shall make rubble also of it. I almost feel like throwing Jimmy into the

1. J. D. Douglas, "Grovelling Among Trifles," *British Weekly* (February 6, 1976): 13.

2. See K. G. Phifer, "Expository Articles: James 2:1-5," *Interpretation* 36.3 (July 1982): 278.

3. See, e.g., H. H. Kramm, *The Theology of Martin Luther* (1947), pp. 111ff.

4. *LW*, XXXIV, 317.

stove, as the priest in Kalenberg did."[5] Both Eusebius in the ancient Greek Church and Jerome in the Latin Church accepted its authenticity; but in the Syrian Church, Theodore of Mopsuestia (among others), following the tradition of that church, excluded the Epistle of James (and other "Catholic Epistles") from the canon. Such rejection is consistent with the fact that even till the latter half of the second century it was not in the canon; and, indeed, it was not known. (Does this suggest, it is conjectured, a possible date of composition?) Eusebius voices the current reservations when he says the Epistle is "disputed" and has not been mentioned or quoted by many writers.[6]

These misgivings, which lay dormant from the early part of the fifth century through the Middle Ages,[7] were revived with the rebirth of biblical scholarship at the Reformation, and the name and stigma of Luther's condemnation have, unfortunately, never ceased to be linked with our Epistle. There are now some clear signs that James may be vindicated as in fact (after Jesus) the oldest and best authority on the earliest phase of Christianity, when many of the Jews, for a short but appreciable period, recognized Christianity no less than their traditional Judaism as part of their national religion.

We are aware—and few will dispute the fact—that of all the work undertaken by NT scholars, the least satisfactory is that done on the least popular Epistle of James. Whereas the Gospels, the Pauline Epistles, and other parts of the NT have been the object of endless research, this much maligned little book has received the greatest (and least deserved) neglect.

The evolution of the history of the interpretation of the Epistle of James follows three stages and these to some degree correspond to similar stages in the modern study of Jewish Christianity, where we discern at least three distinct phases:

1. From the 1830's the Tübingen School with its excessive emphasis on the contrast and even enmity between Paul and James, often exalted James at the expense of Paul. This was later effectively challenged, notably by Zahn and especially by the Cambridge scholars J. B. Lightfoot, B. F. Westcott, and F. J. A. Hort. Recently, S. G. F. Brandon, H.-J. Schoeps, and others, with limited success, have tried to revive the Tübingen thesis.
2. From the 1880's the *Religionsgeschichtliche* School dominated NT

5. Paul Althaus, *The Theology of Martin Luther* (1966), p. 81, n. 31, explains: "The pastor of Kalenberg used the wooden statues of the apostles for firewood when the countess came to visit." For a fuller version, see *LW*, XXXIV, 317, n. 21.

6. *Hist. Eccl.* 2.23.24f.

7. Meinertz, pp. 203ff.

study generally and that of Jewish Christianity in particular, stressing the genealogical relation of Greek philosophy to NT theology; and finally,

3. From the 1950's, the Scrolls and Nag Hammadi texts have not only confirmed the existence of Early Jewish Christianity but also radically changed our entire approach to this subject.[8]

Turning to the Epistle of James we also find three stages of modern criticism:[9]

1. The first phase begins in 1826 with de Wette, who rejected its apostolicity because of its good Greek and for other reasons.[10]
2. Next, de Wette was followed in 1831 by F. C. Baur[11] and the Tübingen School, who saw the Epistle as a forgery, specifically composed to combat Paul, Paulinism, and even Gnosticism—positions that have been held with appropriate variations up to the present day; thus, for example, S. G. F. Brandon spoke of "the author's assumption of the masque of James, the great antagonist of Paul."[12]
3. The third phase came at the end of the century, when the pendulum had swung violently in the opposite direction: two French and German scholars, Louis Massebieau (1895) and Friedrich Spitta (1896), working independently about the same time, proposed the novel view that the Epistle was originally a Jewish work that was later slightly Christianized.[13] Although this theory won few supporters—sometimes they suggested the most bizarre variations, positing, for example, a Jacob allegory[14]—by stressing the Jewishness of James, it naturally, even if indirectly, strengthened the traditionalists' argument.

Roughly speaking, commentators in English were split on the question of value and authenticity. While J. B. Mayor's magisterial commentary on the Epistle of James was a watershed and is still an indispensable tool,[15] he wrote before ossuary inscriptions, papyri, and

8. For details see, e.g., R. N. Longenecker, *The Christology of Early Jewish Christianity* (1970), pp. 4ff.

9. See M. Dibelius, *James* (1976), p. 56.

10. *Lehrbuch der historisch-kritischen Einleitung in die kanonischen Bücher des Neuen Testaments* (1826). See also Meinertz, pp. 252f.

11. "Die Christuspartei in der korinthischen Gemeinde, der Gegensatz des petrinischen und paulinischen Christenthums in der ältesten Kirche," *Tübinger Zeitschrift* (1831): 61-206; also *Paul: The Apostle of Jesus Christ*, 2nd ed. rev. by E. Zeller, tr. A. Menzies, II (1875), 297ff. See also Meinertz, pp. 254f.

12. *The Fall of Jerusalem and the Christian Church* (1951), pp. 238ff.

13. See our discussion of the Epistle as a Christianized Jewish document (pp. 106f.); also Mayor, pp. cxiiff.; Meinertz, pp. 262ff.; Dibelius, pp. 21f.

14. See our later discussion, pp. 106ff.

15. *The Epistle of St. James* (^{3}1913).

various rabbinic, Nag Hammadi, and Qumran writings had become available, and his approach was therefore too narrowly classical. To some extent, later commentaries, including Dibelius's stellar study, have filled this need.[16] Less helpful, however, are those attempts to treat the Epistle as merely another example of Jewish Hellenistic wisdom, parenesis (a term that really has little distinctive meaning), or any other single literary type.

The influence of Luther also persists here, for, thanks to him, writers still tend to disparage both the authenticity and quality of the Epistle, most of them even denying any plan in its structure, and few of them finding anything of doctrinal interest in its theology. Even a cursory glance at its contents is enough to show that it is almost completely confined to one theme, "Faith and Works"—true faith expresses itself in action. For James the Christian life-style is truly the way of "faith."

This Epistle has always suffered comparative neglect and disparagement because of its paramount merit, namely, its simplicity, which furnishes little food for theological erudition and controversy. On this point, the verdict of J. H. Ropes is worth considering:

> When we make a comparison with the Apostolic Fathers, the positive traits which give definite character to the thinking of every one of them are all lacking in James. . . . Indeed, James exhibits not one distinctly marked individual theological tendency which would set him in positive relation to any of the strong forces either of the apostolic or of the post-apostolic period. His simple-minded and robust emphasis on the power and duty of right fundamental choice and of right action and his way of describing his religion as God-given "law" are the two most distinctive ideas in the epistle.[17]

Even the notorious imputations of heresy on "Faith and Works" arise from a misunderstanding of what it says on that subject.

On the other hand, its very simplicity has helped to vindicate its true place in the history of nascent Christianity, on which recent discoveries have thrown so much valuable light. Indeed, it has been noted that "the chief interest of the Epistle of James is in its evidence of the way the nature of Christianity was understood by this author, his readers and, maybe, by those who accepted his work as a part of their scrip-

16. E.g., those of Ropes, Mussner, Laws, Davids, and Scaer, to mention only a few besides Dibelius. A detailed investigation of later interpretations of the Epistle of James is outside the scope of this present work. Quite adequate post-Reformation treatments may be found, e.g., in Huther, pp. 21-30. Schammberger (pp. 7-32) traces the development of German Criticism beginning, strangely enough, not with de Wette but with Kern (1835), and continuing to Schlatter (1943); see also Meinertz, pp. 237ff.; Ropes, pp. 104ff.; and Wessel, pp. 25-43.

17. P. 37.

ture."[18] Its historical interest is likewise limited to the struggle of dawning Christianity to survive the opposition and infiltration of Judaism and paganism, for example, in Rome, Colosse, and, naturally, in the capital of Judaism itself; but we must defer this matter for later consideration. For the present, let us recognize that James is primarily concerned with the most vital question of his religion, the reality of Christ and his impact on our lives.

Further difficulty has been caused by the relation of the Epistle to Judaism; for this writing, like a novel by Sir Walter Scott, seems to have an assured footing on both sides of the border and could build an important bridge in any possible rapprochement between Christian and Jew, church and synagogue. "Again and again," wrote Hort, "the wild dream of a Christianity without Judaism has risen with attractive power. But the Epistle of James marks in the most decisive way the continuity of the two Testaments. In some obvious aspects, it is like a piece of the Old Testament appearing in the midst of the New."[19] To the Christian, therefore, who has sought to part Christianity from its parent Judaism and thus to sever the NT from its roots in the OT, this book has been a thorn in the flesh, a constant fear, and a target for criticism. This fear has in no way been allayed by those who have contended that the book is not only anti-Christian in the sense of anti-Pauline, but even intrinsically un-Christian in that its author was a Jew who had merely reedited an older Jewish document.

Marcionism is ever with us; and in the attitude of the many who have denied, on the grounds of its Jewishness, the right of the Epistle of James to a place within the Christian tradition, we see a rebirth of this ancient heresy.[20] Here again Martin Luther and the stigma of his judgment, unfortunately, have always haunted our Epistle. While conceding that Luther was sincerely motivated in his condemnation and while recognizing that, like all spiritual pioneers, he was driven to be prejudiced by his Reforming purpose, we are persuaded that by stressing that Paul was the only valid representative of Christianity, Luther, like Marcion, did a serious injustice to biblical theology in general and the Epistle of James in particular.

18. Laws, pp. 1f.

19. *The Epistle of St. James* (1909), p. X.

20. Martin E. Marty wisely suggests that "Christians need the constant reminder that they are grafted on to Judaism and to the experience of God's ancient people: Jesus was a Jew. They need the counsels and piety of the Old Testament. They need the attention to the details of living practical God-pleasing lives. In the Letter of James, which despite its good Greek breathes the spirit of Jewish Christianity, these themes live on. Here the Old Testament is reappropriated, grasped once more, given a second life and a new stamp of approval" (*Good News in the Early Church* [1976], p. 62).

The present work explores in greater depth matters sometimes merely touched on in our Commentary but proceeds from the same firm conviction that the author of the Epistle is James the Lord's brother, who, after his conversion, rose to the leadership of the Jerusalem Church, was one of the three "pillars," and was killed by an illegal act of the high priest Ananus II against the wishes of "the Jews," whose more responsible leaders denounced the high priest. Everything that is said in this book is to be understood in the light of this hypothesis.

We believe that the author of the Epistle is James the Lord's brother and that the Epistle is correspondingly important in its exposition of the Christian life and faith. This deduction rests on several (inevitably overlapping) considerations of thought, style, structure, and other evidence. Yet over against the evidence of the early apostolic content of the Epistle must be set the various arguments against its authenticity, and these must also be given due weight and serious examination.

Whether the Epistle of James is by James the Lord's brother or by someone else can be decided only on the basis of a study of the Epistle itself—the final court of appeal. It is our intent in this study to interrogate the Epistle and allow the author to speak for himself, for, as Adolph Schlatter[21] wisely noted, "It does not make any sense to compare James with Paul (or, we would add, with anyone else) before at least James has been understood." Seldom indeed has James been allowed so to speak; more often than not, time has been wasted in searching for all sorts of hidden clues and motives. Thus the Epistle is said to be anti-Pauline, polemical, political, ascetic, Ebionitic, anti-Gnostic, and even a letter to the twelve tribes of Israel. Certainly, as long as the Epistle of James is used simply to show whether it emanated from James the Lord's brother or from an obscure alternative source, its true nature, origin, and purpose will remain an enigma.

Nothing but a thoroughly inductive approach to this Epistle will suffice, and this is the method adopted throughout this book. When all literary and similar problems are taken into account, the most important work is still to be done: to take the book as a whole and humbly submit to the task of learning its lessons for today. This is why the church has valued and studied it since early days.[22] "If the Epistle is 'of straw,' then there is within that straw," J. G. Herder once observed, "a very hearty, firm, nourishing but as yet uninterpreted and unthreshed grain."[23]

21. For reference see B. S. Childs, *The New Testament as Canon: An Introduction* (1984), p. 434.

22. See C. H. Dodd, *The Interpretation of the Fourth Gospel* (1953), pp. 290, 355.

23. *Briefe zweener Brüder Jesu in unserem Kanon,* in *Herders sämmtliche Werke,* ed. B. Suphan, VII (1884), p. 500, n. 2.

The interpretation of the Epistle of James, therefore, is no purely scholarly, intellectual process, but primarily prayerful, pastoral, and practical. As J. B. Lightfoot reminded us, all true theology belongs to the street and the marketplace, for "after all is said and done, the only way to know the Greek Testament properly is by prayer."[24] Permitting our author, therefore, to speak relevantly from his own pastoral concern and from his own age and environment, we shall seek to let the Epistle itself shed light on these subjects.

The study is divided into four parts: the Book, the Message, Value, and Concluding Reflections. We begin with the most vexing and controversial aspects, that is, its Author, Purpose, Plan, Form, Style, and History. The second and main division deals with the Message of James, namely, his relation to Jesus and Paul, his social and economic thought, and his teaching on Faith, Trial and Temptation, God, Wisdom, and Salvation. Following this are a discussion of the Epistle's abiding worth and, as a kind of epilogue, a short summary of our findings. All the evidence—literary, social, didactic, and theological—points to the belief that the Epistle of James comes from a nascent, pre-Pauline period in the early church about or probably before A.D. 60, or even as early as A.D. 40.

Our principal aim, however, is to present the Epistle's present-day challenge. We sincerely believe that few things would do more to revive the flagging faith of many modern Christians than a conscious attempt on their part to take James seriously. "That autograph letter," says Thomas Carlyle of Cromwell's letters, "it was once all luminous as a burning beacon, every word of it a live coal in its time—that letter!"[25] This is also a superb description of the Epistle of James, though penned almost two thousand years ago. In this book we meet none other than James the Apostle and the Lord's brother, a towering personality of the early church, who speaks with extraordinary power and force, and indeed "instructs, chides, encourages, denounces with a depth, an energy, a fire, second to none in the whole range of sacred literature." If we are wise, we shall listen carefully to James the man and his message and then apply it to our daily lives.

J. B. A.

24. G. R. Eden and F. C. Macdonald, eds., *Lightfoot of Durham* (1932), p. 14.

25. *Oliver Cromwell's Letters and Speeches*, I (1885), 68.

Abbreviations

AB	Anchor Bible
Ant.	Josephus, *Antiquities*
ATR	*Anglican Theological Review*
b.	Babylonian Talmud
BAG	W. Bauer, W. F. Arndt, and F. W. Gingrich, *A Greek-English Lexicon of the New Testament* (1957)
BDB	Brown–Driver–Briggs, *A Hebrew-English Lexicon of the Old Testament* (1951)
Bib	*Biblica*
Bib Or	*Bibliotheca Orientalis*
BibSac	*Bibliotheca Sacra*
Bl–D	F. Blass–A. DeBrunner, *A Greek Grammar of the New Testament and Other Early Christian Literature* (ET by R. W. Funk, 1961)
BJRL	*Bulletin of the John Rylands University Library*
BSF	*Biblische Studien*, Freiburg
BST	The Bible Speaks Today
CBQ	*Catholic Biblical Quarterly*
CBSC	Cambridge Bible for Schools and Colleges
EGT	Expositor's Greek Testament
EQ	*Evangelical Quarterly*
ERE	*Encyclopaedia of Religion and Ethics*, ed. J. Hastings (1908)
ET	English Translation
EThR	*Études Théologiques et Religieuses*
Ex	*Expositor*
ExpT	*Expository Times*
GNB	Good News Bible (Today's English Version)
GNC	A Good News Commentary
HDB	*Hastings' Dictionary of the Bible*
HDCG	*Hastings' Dictionary of Christ and the Gospels*

Hist. Eccl.	*Ecclesiastical History*
HNT	Handbuch zum Neuen Testament
HTKNT	Herders Theologischer Kommentar zum Neuen Testament
HTR	*Harvard Theological Review*
HUCA	*Hebrew Union College Annual*
IB	*Interpreters' Bible*
ICC	International Critical Commentary
IDB	*Interpreter's Dictionary of the Bible*
ISBE	*International Standard Bible Encyclopedia* (Vols. I, II, III, IV), 1979-88, ed. Geoffrey W. Bromiley
JB	Jerusalem Bible
JBL	*Journal of Biblical Literature*
JBR	*Journal of Bible and Religion*
JE	*Jewish Encyclopaedia*
JQR	*Jewish Quarterly Review*
JR	*Journal of Religion*
JSS	*Journal of Semitic Studies*
JTS	*Journal of Theological Studies*
KEK	Kritisch-exegetischer Kommentar über das Neue Testament (founded by H. A. W. Meyer)
KJV	King James Version, 1611 (Authorized Version)
LQR	*London Quarterly Review*
LS	H. G. Liddell and R. Scott, *Greek-English Lexicon*, rev. by H. S. Jones (1940)
LW	*Luther's Works*, I-L, gen. ed. H. T. Lehman (Philadelphia, 1958-75)
LXX	Septuagint (Greek Old Testament)
M.	Mishnah
Midr.	Midrash
MM	J. H. Moulton and G. Milligan, *Vocabulary of the Greek Testament* (1930)
MNTC	Moffatt New Testament Commentary
NCB	New Century Bible
NEB	New English Bible
NICNT	New International Commentary on the New Testament
NIDNTT	*New International Dictionary of New Testament Theology* (Vols. I, II, III), 1975-78, ed. C. Brown
NIGTC	New International Greek Testament Commentary
NIV	New International Version
NovT	*Novum Testamentum*
n.s.	new series

NT	New Testament
NTC	New Testament Commentary
NTD	Das Neue Testament Deutsch
NTS	*New Testament Studies*
OT	Old Testament
PG	J. Migne, *Patrologia graeca*
PL	J. Migne, *Patrologia latina*
P46	Chester Beatty papyrus
R.	Rabbah (midrash Rabbah)
RB	*Revue biblique*
RevExp	*Review and Expositor*
RHPR	*Revue d'histoire et de philosophie religieuses*
RHR	*Revue de l'histoire des religions*
RSV	Revised Standard Vision
RV	Revised Version
SB	Sources bibliques
S–B	H. L. Strack and P. Billerbeck, *Kommentar zum Neuen Testament aus Talmud und Midrasch* (1922-28)
SBLTT	Society of Biblical Literature Texts and Translations
SBT	Studies in Biblical Theology
SJTh	*Scottish Journal of Theology*
SNTS	Society for New Testament Studies
SNTSM	Society for New Testament Studies Monographs
ST	*Studia Theologica*
StEv	*Studia Evangelica* I, II, III = *TU* 73 (1959), 87 (1964), 88 (1964)
SWJT	*Southwestern Journal of Theology*
TDNT	*Theological Dictionary of the New Testament* (ET I-X, 1964-1976)
TDOT	*Theological Dictionary of the Old Testament* (ET I-V, 1974-86)
ThBl	*Theologische Blätter*
ThLB	*Theologisches Literaturblatt*
ThLZ	*Theologische Literaturzeitung*
ThWNT	G. Kittel and G. Friedrich, eds., *Theologisches Wörterbuch zum Neuen Testament* (1930-79)
ThZ	*Theologische Zeitschrift* (Basel)
TNTC	Tyndale New Testament Commentaries
TR	Received Text
TU	*Texte und Untersuchungen zur Geschichte der altkirchlichen Literatur*
Vulg.	Latin Vulgate Version

WBC	Word Biblical Commentaries
WH	B. F. Westcott and F. J. A. Hort, *The New Testament in Greek* (1881)
ZKG	*Zeitschrift für Kirchengeschichte*
ZNW	*Zeitschrift für die neutestamentliche Wissenschaft*
ZTK	*Zeitschrift für Theologie und Kirche*

Commentaries

The books in the following list of frequently cited commentaries and related works are generally cited simply by author's name and page(s).

Adamson, J. B., *The Epistle of James,* NICNT (1976).

Barrett, E., *Will the Real Phony Please Stand Up?* ([2]1984).

Beasley-Murray, G. R., *The General Epistles,* Bible Guides (1965).

Beyschlag, W., *Der Jakobusbrief,* KEK (1888).

Blackman, E. C., *The Epistle of James,* Torch Bible Commentaries (1957).

Blanchard, J., *Truth for Life* (1986).

Bryson, H. T., *How Faith Works* (1985).

Burdick, D. W., *James,* The Expositor's Bible Commentary, XII (1981), 161-205.

Cadoux, A. T., *The Thought of St. James* (1944).

Cantinat, J., *Les Épîtres de Saint Jacques et de Saint Jude* (SB) (1973).

Cedar, P. A., *James, 1, 2 Peter, Jude,* The Communicator's Library (1984).

Cranford, L. *James Diagramed* (1984).

Davids, P. H., *The Epistle of James,* NIGTC (1982).

Davids, P. H., *James,* GNC (1983).

De Ambroggi, P., *Le Epistole Cattoliche Di Giacomo, Pietro, Giovanni E Guida* (La Sacra Bibbia) (Rome, 1957).

de Wette, W. M. L., *Kurzgefasstes exegetisches Handbuch zum Neuen Testament,* 3 vols. (1841-48).

Dibelius, M., *Der Brief des Jakobus = James. A Commentary on the Epistle of James,* Hermeneia (1976).

Doerksen, V. D., *James* (1983).

Easton, B. S., *The Epistle of James,* The Interpreter's Bible, XII (1957).

Gaebelein, F. E., *The Practical Epistle of James* (1955).

Gaugusch, L., *Der Lehrgehalt der Jakobusepistel* (1914).

Grünzweig, F., *Der Brief des Jakobus,* Wuppertaler Studienbibel (1973).
Haar, J., *Der Jakobusbrief* (Praktische Schriftauslegung) (1971).
Hauck, F., *Der Brief des Jakobus,* NTD (1926).
Hoppe, R., *Der theologische Hintergrund des Jakobusbriefes,* Forschung zur Bibel (1977).
Hort, F. J. A., *The Epistle of St. James* (1909).
Hubbard, D. A. *The Book of James: Wisdom That Works* (1980).
Huther, J. E., *Critical and Exegetical Handbook to the General Epistles of James, John, and Jude* (1887).
Kent, Jr., H. A., *Faith that Works. Studies in the Epistle of James* (1986).
Kern, F. H., *Der Brief Jacobi* (1838).
Kistemaker, S. J., *James and I-III John* (1986) in New Testament Commentary, by W. Hendriksen and S. J. Kistemaker.
Knowling, R. J., *The Epistle of St. James* (1904).
Krutza, W. J. and Di Cicero, P. P., *Living That Counts: A Study Guide to the Book of James* (1972).
Laws, S., *A Commentary on the Epistle of James,* Black's New Testament Commentaries (1980).
Lenski, R. C. H., *The Interpretation of the Epistle to the Hebrews and of the Epistle of James* (1946).
Manton, T., *An Exposition of the Epistle of James* (1693; reprint 1968).
Martin, R. A., and Elliott, J. H., *James, I, II Peter, Jude,* Augsburg Commentary on the New Testament (1982).
Marty, J., *L'Épître de Jacques, Étude critique* (1935).
Marty, M. E., *Good News in the Early Church, 1, 2 Timothy, Titus, James, 1, 2 Peter, 1, 2, 3 John and Jude,* in Today's English Version (1976).
Massebieau, L., "L'Épître de Jacques est-elle l'oeuvre d'un Chrétien?" *RHR* 32 (1895), pp. 249-93.
Mayor, J. B., *The Epistle of St. James* ([3]1913).
Meinertz, M., *Der Jakobusbrief und sein Verfasser in Schrift und Überlieferung* (1905).
Meyer A., *Das Rätsel des Jakobusbriefes* (1930).
Mitton, C. L., *The Epistle of James* (1966).
Moffatt, J., *The General Epistles,* MNTC (1928).
Moo, D. J., *James,* TNTC (1985).
Motyer, J. A., *The Message of James,* BST (1985).
Mussner, F., *Der Jakobusbrief,* HTKNT ([5]1987).
Oesterley, W. O. E., *The General Epistle of James,* Expositor's Greek Testament, IV (1910).
Ogilvie, L. J. *Making Stress Work for You* (1984).

Parry, R. St. J., *A Discussion of the General Epistle of St. James* (1903).
Plummer, A., *The General Epistles of St. James and St. Jude*, Expositor's Bible (1891).
Prime, D., *From Trials to Triumphs* (1982).
Reicke, B. I., *The Epistles of James, Peter, and Jude*, AB (1964).
Rendall, G. H., *The Epistle of St. James and Judaic Christianity* (1927).
Rendtorff, H., *Hörer und Täter* (Die urchristliche Botschaft) (1953).
Roberts, J. W., *A Commentary on the General Epistle of James* (1963).
Robertson, A. T., *Studies in the Epistle of James* (1915).
Ropes, J. H., *The Epistle of St. James*, ICC (1916).
Scaer, D. P., *James, the Apostle of Faith* (1983).
Schammberger, H., *Die Einheitlichkeit des Jakobusbriefes im antignostischen Kampf* (1936).
Schlatter, A., *Der Brief des Jakobus* (1956).
Sidebottom, E. M., *James, Jude, 2 Peter*, NCB (1967).
Sloyan, G. S., *Hebrews–James–1 and 2 Peter–Jude–Revelation*, ed. G. Krodel, Proclamation Commentaries (1977), pp. 28-47.
Spitta, F., *Der Brief des Jakobus*, Zur Geschichte und Literatur des Urchristentums, II (1896), pp. 1-239.
Stevenson, H. F., *James Speaks for Today* (1966).
Strauss, L., *James, Your Brother. Studies in the Epistle of James* ([2]1967).
Tasker, R. V. G., *The General Epistle of James*, TNTC (1956).
Thurneysen, E., *Der Brief des Jakobus* (Basel, [3]1959).
Vaughan, C., *James: A Study Guide* (1969).
Von Soden, H., *Die Briefe des Petrus, Jakobus, Judas*, Hand-Commentar (1891).
Vouga, F., *L'Épître de Saint Jacques*, Commentaire Du Nouveau Testament, Deuxième Série, XIIIa (1984).
Weiss, B., *Die Katholischen Briefe*, KEK ([6]1900).
Wiersbe, W. W., *Be Mature* (1978).
Windisch, H., *Die Katholischen Briefe*, HNT 15 (1951).

I. THE BOOK

"The Epistle of James can take its natural place, alongside other literature in the process of formation in the second decade of the Christian mission, as the first surviving document of the church."

J. A. T. Robinson, *Redating the New Testament* (1976), p. 139

1. Author

"Without doubt James claims to be written by him. Even if the letter is not authentic, it appeals to this famous James and the weight of his person as authority for its content."

W. G. Kümmel, *Introduction to the New Testament* ([2]1975), p. 412

Section One

On the question of authorship there has been great misunderstanding and disputing. We shall discuss first the case for authenticity and then possible difficulties, real or imagined.

A document as straightforward as the Epistle of James might seem to be beyond scholarly debate. Containing five brief chapters of simple prose covering daily topics, this letter with its robust ethical message has a unique appeal to ordinary Christians. Technical examination might therefore seem superfluous. Yet critical issues such as nature, origin, author, purpose, and date are nowhere more vigorously debated than here. "There is no writing in the New Testament," said E. F. Scott, "on which critical opinion has varied so widely as on this Epistle."[1] Few NT books pose so many questions. This "strangely mixed Jewish/Christian, good Greek/Semitized Greek" work is truly a "riddle," the odd man out, perhaps the biggest riddle of the New Testament[2]—and a host of riddles spring from it.

Nevertheless there are certain indisputable facts. The letter is catholic, not individual, in its appeal. It is a vehicle of "ecumenical

1. *The Literature of the New Testament* (1932), p. 210.

2. A. Meyer; *The Cambridge History of the Bible*, I: *From the Beginnings to Jerome*, eds. P. R. Ackroyd and C. F. Evans (1970), p. 265; also R. A. Martin, *James* (1982), p. 12.

Christianity" addressed to those "of the Dispersion" (1:1), and there is no hint of any personal bond between the author and his readers, the picture of both being equally colorless and indistinct.[3] Some have held that its contents were mainly inherited ("a book of popular slogans"), like an anonymous broadcast or a collection of unrelated broadcasts aimed at different classes of people (see 4:13ff.; 5:1ff.).[4] But even if the audience were fictitious, the substance is fitted to their feigned character. On its variety, however, Luther exclaims, "What a chaos!"[5] A staccato abruptness marks the Epistle, and the tone sometimes rivals the severity of an OT prophet. The aim is the building of the Christian church, not the compiling of a Christian encyclopedia.

Commentators cannot agree in placing this Epistle anywhere on the Christian map, although admittedly—and here in part lies the Epistle's uniqueness—the differing views are not due to differing conceptions of Christianity.[6] Some affirm that the Epistle is basically Jewish, written by a thoroughly Hellenized Palestinian Jew, our James or another,[7] an unknown Galilean,[8] or even a pre-Christian Jew.[9] "The Epistle of James," wrote R. V. G. Tasker, "is outside the main development of Christianity . . . and is the most intensely Jewish of all the Christian documents given to the world."[10] Some argue that it is essentially Hellenistic in its origin and thought,[11] or possibly Egyptian,[12] as it is

3. Moffatt, p. 3; G. A. Deissmann, *Bible Studies,* tr. A. Grieve (^{2}1903), p. 53.

4. Dibelius, pp. 5ff. Similarly, G. Bornkamm: "More than any other epistle, that of James largely takes over ethical instruction without altering it or adding Christian content" ("Formen und Gattungen," *Die Religion in Geschichte und Gegenwart,* II [1958], col. I, pp. 1004-05).

5. *LW,* XXXV, 397.

6. M. Goguel, *The Birth of Christianity* (1953), p. 373, n. 4.

7. So Mayor, Rendall, Cadoux, Mitton, and Metzger. For a fuller, though incomplete, list of this and other positions on dating James, see Davids, Table I, p. 4.

8. Elliott-Binns, pp. 45ff.

9. C. J. G. Montefiore, *Judaism and St. Paul* (1914), pp. 34-44 (Ropes, p. 31). See K. Kohler's article "The Epistle of St. James," *JE* 7 (1904): 68-70; also Massebieau, Spitta, and A. Meyer.

10. *The Old Testament in the New Testament* (1940), p. 125. According to Hort, p. x, "In some respects the Epistle of James is like a piece of the O.T. appearing in the N.T."; but, he adds, "it is truly of the N.T. too." See H. C. Kee and F. W. Young, *The Living World of the New Testament* (1960), p. 318; Schlatter, pp. 29ff.

11. See Dibelius, Patrick, W. L. Knox, Davids, and others.

12. See Kennedy, pp. 37-52; Moffatt, p. 1.

preeminently in its language.[13] J. H. Ropes, for example, argued for a Christian teacher of "an admirable type of Christianity, but one of extraordinary intellectual isolation . . . in some half-Hellenistic city of Palestine" who wrote in a period of quiet sometime before the Bar Cochba revolt, A.D. 132-139.[14] Others see it variously as an anti-Zealot tract written in the time of Domitian (A.D. 81-86),[15] a product of "early Catholicism,"[16] or an anti-Gnostic polemic dated as late as the first half of the second century.[17] Still others find traces of Stoic influence.[18] Compounding the problem is what has been called the Epistle's "peculiarly undated quality."[19]

Many scholars hold that while the possible range of James's education should not be underrated, it is hardly likely that he would possess the wide culture, the acquaintance with classical literature, or the vernacular and literary Greek. "Perhaps our accepted picture of James and of other members of his family," observes F. F. Bruce, "is not as accurate as we imagine; it is based on very inadequate information."[20] The question of the expertise of James's Greek and his use of the LXX, diatribe, and parenesis is also a problem and is discussed elsewhere. But most of those who stress the Hellenistic quality of the Epistle of James would ascribe its origin to the Greco-Roman world, and even Rome itself,[21] rather than to Palestine, while rejecting the traditional view. H. Köster, for instance, still holds that the Epistle is an important witness to the continuing tradition of the Jerusalem Church in the Hellenistic world.[22] Such scholars are almost all agreed in denying that it

13. E.g., the hexameter (1:17) is allegedly from an unknown Greek poet; "the wheel of nature" (3:6) is a supposedly Orphic expression; and "Father of lights" (1:17) has a Hermetic affinity. See C. H. Dodd, *The Interpretation of the Fourth Gospel* (1958), p. 14; for James's Greek view of the law, see also Dodd, *The Bible and the Greeks* (1935), p. 39. For alleged late Gnostic congruences, see Schammberger, Pfleiderer, Windisch, Schoeps, and others.

14. P. 49. For similar dating, see Dibelius, p. 67; A. E. Barnett, "The Letter of James," *IDB* (1965), p. 795.

15. B. I. Reicke, *The Epistles of James, Peter and Jude* (1964), pp. 6f.; M. J. Townsend, "James 4:1-4: A Warning against Zealotry?" *ExpT* 87 (1976): 211-13.

16. W. Marxsen, *Der "Frühkatholizismus" im Neuen Testament* (1958), pp. 22ff.

17. H.-J. Schoeps, p. 343; see also notably Schammberger, who finds Gnostic catchwords in 1:18, 25; 2:20; and elsewhere, especially chs. 3 and 4.

18. E.g., M. Jones, *The New Testament in the Twentieth Century* (1914), p. 316; M. O'R. Boyle, "The Stoic Paradox of James 2:10," *NTS* 31.4 (1985): 611ff.

19. C. E. B. Cranfield, "The Message of James," *SJTh* 18.2 (1965): 185.

20. *Peter, Stephen, James and John* (1979), pp. 96, 113.

21. So Streeter, Reicke, Laws, and others.

22. *Introduction to the New Testament*, II (1982), 157.

is by our James, and they find the address, "to the twelve tribes of the Diaspora," as well as its general excellence unintelligible.

The Epistle is not in evidence in the Apostolic Age, and indeed was among the last of the NT books to be admitted into the canon. Till then its history, if any, is scanty and obscure. Origen (about A.D. 230) believed the author to have been James the Lord's brother, but he has found little support, especially among later commentators; on this there has been much talk and, with few exceptions, little sense. It is certainly hard to see why a letter from such a great Christian figure as James, the Bishop of Jerusalem, first lay in obscurity for two centuries and then came to be admitted to the canon. This matter is dealt with later in this chapter and elsewhere.[23]

All these questions are subordinate to the final question, Who wrote the Epistle of James?

OPENING SALUTATION

The first important clue to the author's identity is found in the opening salutation: "James, a bond slave of God and the Lord Jesus Christ, to the twelve tribes of the Dispersion, salutation." The concise but studied balance of the sentence is exactly like James's style in the rest of the Epistle. If it were a later addition[24] (and this is to ignore the semantic connection *chairein . . . charan,* 1:1-2), it is well adapted to the rest. Whether or not a later addition, "the simplicity of the majestic self-designation"[25] shows that the James clearly intended is *the* James, who of all the NT Jameses is referred to without further comment; only later do we find significant elaboration.[26]

23. See especially ensuing discussions, pp. 38ff., 47ff., 147ff., 487ff.

24. If the superscription be detached (it is said) any resemblance to a letter disappears. Exclaimed B. W. Bacon: "Imagine the mode of delivery!" (*The Making of the New Testament* [1912], p. 118); see also Elliott-Binns, pp. 47f.; A. Harnack, *Chronologie,* I (1897), 487; E. J. Goodspeed, *The Story of the New Testament* (1940), p. 10; Blackman, p. 25; also B. H. Streeter, who suggested that the ascription was "prefixed in the second century by some Alexandrian scholar" (*The Primitive Church* [1953], p. 191).

25. W. G. Kümmel, *Introduction to the New Testament* (1966), p. 290; see also Windisch, p. 3.

26. E.g., "James the righteous for whose sake heaven and earth came into being" (*The Gospel according to Thomas,* logion 12. *The Nag Hammadi Library,* ed. J. M. Robinson [1977], p. 119); "the brother of God" *(adelphotheos)* (A. Trollope, *Liturgy of James,* p. 25); "the Lord and Bishop of the Holy Church" (*Epistle of Peter* I.1 in E. Hennecke, *New Testament Apocrypha,* II [1963], 111, cited with others by, e.g., M. Hengel, "Jakobus der Herrenbruder—der erste 'Papst'?" in

The highest claim that James makes (and its Greek position is emphatic) is that he is "a servant" *(doulos)*—a thoroughly Hebrew rather than Greek idea,[27] setting the author in the best Semitic tradition as a true "son of the prophets,"[28] who, like some rabbis,[29] regarded themselves as slaves of God *('eḇeḏ YHWH)*. If it is true, as Hort suggested, that the translation "slave" "lays the whole stress on a subordinate point . . . the mere absence of wages or the right to depart,"[30] it is well to remember that for the Jew, if not for the Greek, there was nothing servile in the relation of man to God, the Heb. *'eḇeḏ* being "strictly correlated with the verb *'āḇaḏ,* to do service, homage, or religious worship, a word which is sufficiently elastic to cover the service which a son does for his father, as well as that which a master requires from a slave."[31] In the OT the word is used widely not only of prophets and rabbis, but also of individuals like Moses,[32] Joshua,[33] David,[34] of Israel as a whole,[35] and very often of God's "worshippers,"[36] and even nonworshippers (e.g., Nebuchadnezzar);[37] in the NT the term is an apostolic title of honor.[38]

James had become Christ's convert and his worshipper, and therefore his "servant." James uses this title "not only because of a keen awareness of the prophetlike authority belonging to him, but also," as

---

Glaube und Eschatologie: Festschrift für Werner Georg Kümmel zum 80. Geburtstag, eds. E. Grässer and O. Merk [1985], pp. 75ff.; J. J. Scott, Jr., "James the Relative of Jesus and the Expectation of an Eschatological Priest," *Journal of the Evangelical Theological Society* 25.3 [Sept. 1982]: 324ff.; Mussner, pp. 4-7; also J. A. T. Robinson, *Redating the New Testament* [1976], p. 129); or even simply "the Just" or "brother of the Lord." That he does not even call himself "apostle," but merely "servant," suggests not only that he was sure of himself and his authority, but also that he realized with his Lord that "the greatest among you must be your servant" (Mt. 23:11). See also Jude 1. Also J. A. T. Robinson, *Can We Trust the New Testament?* (1977), p. 68.

27. *Pace* W. Bousset, *Die Religion des Judentums im neutestamentlischen Zeitalter* (1903), pp. 113ff.; R. Reitzenstein, *Die hellenistischen Mysterienreligionen* (1910), pp. 66, 78; K. H. Rengstorf, *doulos, TDNT,* II, 276f.

28. E.g., Am. 3:7; Jer. 7:25.

29. E.g., Gamaliel, Johanan B. Zakkai. See Schlatter, p. 87.

30. P. 2. Cf. H. St. J. Thackeray, *Grammar of the Old Testament in Greek,* I (1909), 8.

31. W. R. Smith, *The Religion of the Semites* (1972), p. 69.

32. Josh. 14:7; Ps. 104:26.

33. Josh. 24:29.

34. 2 Sam. 5:8; 7:4.

35. Jub. 23:30; Ps. Sol. 12:7; 17:23; Sifré on Num. 15:41.

36. E.g., Ps. 34:22; see also Lk. 2:29; Acts 4:29; 16:17.

37. Jer. 25:9.

38. See Dibelius, p. 66.

Scaer observes, "because he is aware of the self-degrading attitude in which his Brother offered the atonement. James is now not only one who has accepted the results of the atonement by faith, but one who with Jesus has assumed a servant position."[39] Since a servant cannot serve two masters, this word emphasizes that service to Christ is also service to God. By combining the two James is saying (with John) that the work of Christ is also the work of the Father,[40] and thereby avoiding, or at least reducing to the minimum, possible offense to the monotheistic Jew, converted or not.

Of the conceivably relevant bearers of the name James in the NT, the most important are the following:

1. James the Lord's brother, head of the Jerusalem Church.[41]
2. James the Apostle, son of Alphaeus, one of the Twelve.[42]
3. James the Apostle, son of Zebedee and Salome, executed by Herod Agrippa (c. A.D. 44).[43]
4. James the Less, whose mother was Mary the wife of Clopas and whose brother was Joses or Joseph.[44]
5. James, the father (brother?) of Judas, one of the Twelve; the latter may be the same as Thaddaeus or Lebbaeus.[45]
6. Jude . . . brother of James, in the identification of the purported author of the Epistle of Jude.[46]

Jerome held that 2, 4, and 5 were identical, taking 5 as brother, this last being an assumption for which there is no justification.[47] Many hold that the James of the Epistle of James is known neither in the NT nor in any discoverable history; "James" may have been his real name or a pseudonym. Erasmus favored this latter view, citing the absence of the name "apostle" in the opening verse and lack of Hebraisms in the Epistle itself.[48] Hort suggests that the early church may have confused

39. Pp. 26f.

40. Jn. 5:17; 9:4; 17:4.

41. Acts 12:17; 15:13; 21:28; 1 Cor. 15:7; Gal. 1:19; 2:9, 12.

42. Mt. 10:3; Mk. 3:18; Lk. 6:15; Acts 1:13.

43. Mt. 4:21; 10:2; 17:1; Mk. 10:35; 13:3; Lk. 9:54; Acts 12:2.

44. The Gk. *ho mikros* may better be translated (*pace* Jerome) "the Little" (Mt. 27:56; Mk. 15:40; Jn. 19:25; see also Mk. 16:1; Luke 24:10; Ropes, p. 60).

45. Lk. 6:16; Acts 1:13; see also Mt. 10:3; Mk. 3:18.

46. Jude 1. There is no significance in the reading *Iakōbon* for *Leuei* in Mk. 2:14 D and other manuscripts. See F. C. Burkitt's article, "Levi, Son of Alphaeus," *JTS* 28 (1926-27): 273f.

47. *Against Helvidius* 13ff. (Migne, *PL*, XXIII, 195).

48. See Ropes, p. 25. On pseudonymity, see further below, pp. 9f.

1 and 3 in the above list.[49] The latter was an important apostle, but there is no evidence or likelihood that he wrote the Epistle.[50] The claim of James son of Alphaeus is so weak and speculative that of notable Protestant scholars only Calvin supported it. Mitton held that the second and third suggestions can probably be ignored, and we agree, though we do not share his difficulty with a date before A.D. 44.[51]

The final option, that this was some unknown person with the true or pseudonymous name James, raises far more difficulties than the first. If a Shakespearean play is said to be not his but just as good, the question arises, Who of the writers of that time was capable of writing it? Who of the known writers of his time was able to write the Epistle of James if *the* James did not write it? Is there any good reason for believing that the Epistle of James emanated from any other center than Jerusalem, or any other period than that of the metropolitan and religious dominance of which she lost most in 70, and the rest in 135? And at the right time and place, who but our James could write the Epistle of James?

If it was not by him, its brilliant and authoritatively apostolic author lived and died in impenetrably ignominious and anonymous obscurity, "as one nameless man among the many."[52] It is difficult to understand why a forger should have been content with such a simple addition when he could have chosen to elaborate his authority in more sophisticated ways not only in the opening signature but also throughout the work. Indeed, the Epistle of James is significantly free of later legendary accretions,[53] or attempts to exalt James above the

49. *Judaistic Christianity* (1904), p. 62. *The Gospel according to the Hebrews* (see Ropes, pp. 68f.) may imply that James was one of those present at the Lord's Supper. F. Kattenbusch, however, suggested that the vision was really to James the Apostle—a special privilege since he was to suffer martyrdom (art. "Die Vorzugstellung des Petrus und der Charakter der Urgemeinde zu Jerusalem," p. 329, n. 1 in *Festgabe von Fachgenossen und Freunden Karl Müller* [1922]). See also the Corbey MS, which says in the postscript that the Epistle was written by James the son of Zebedee (*explicit epistola Jacobi filii Zebedaei*) (J. Wordsworth, *Studia Biblica,* I [1885], 123) and the statement in the Apostolic Lists that James the son of Zebedee preached the gospel to the twelve tribes of the Dispersion (J. Weiss, *The History of Primitive Christianity* [ET 1937], II, p. 743, n. 4). Dante also confuses James and the Son of Zebedee (*Paradiso* 25.17f.).

50. But even this view has had its (few) supporters, especially from the Spanish Roman Catholic Church—and notably Isidore of Seville (c. 636)—who claim him, St. James of Compostella, as patron saint.

51. Pp. 222ff.

52. Dibelius, pp. xii, 18, 19 n. 51; for a long (partial) list of those advocating pseudonymity, see Davids, p. 4.

53. From the middle of the second century, in addition to matter that lies behind the *Pseudo-Clementine Homilies* (see Elliott-Binns, pp. 52f.), a new inter-

other apostles.[54] Again, nowhere does he insist, like the Apostolic Fathers, on impeccably pure doctrine, refusing to make this a sine qua non of salvation;[55] in fact, James denounces credalism per se, for (as he says) even the demons are impeccably orthodox.

Puzzling enough in an early document, the absence of doctrine in a later pseudonymous work is quite inexplicable. Understandably the Pastoral and Petrine Epistles claim apostolic sanction since they are written to combat heresies of a later time; but, we may ask, "Why produce a non-polemical Jewish-Christian Epistle that is not even taking the position of the Judaizers but simply giving a call to 'practical religion'?"[56] Besides, we should expect more explicit reference to Paul and his position, as well as stress on "the unique and unrepeatable status of the writer as the brother of the Lord himself."[57]

If the whole Epistle is later than the date of James, it is hard to understand why such a thing would be written at such a date. Any man owning or assuming the name James[58] who wished to foist his letter off on the public would have made it plain which James he was pretending to be, and, as Mitton shrewdly observes, "those who favor the pseud-

---

est seems to have been taken in St. James, notably in the works of Hegesippus, *Gospel according to the Hebrews*, and other apocryphal or heretical writings. On these numerous legends and traditions, intriguing but usually fanciful and inauthentic, see, e.g., Hengel, *art. cit.*, *Glaube und Eschatologie: Festschrift für Werner Georg Kümmel zum 80. Geburtstag*, pp. 75ff.; Scott, Jr., *art. cit.*, *Journal of the Evangelical Theological Society* 25.3 (Sept. 1982): 325ff.; R B. Ward, "James of Jerusalem," *Restoration Quarterly* 16.3, 4 (Third and Fourth Quarter, 1973): 180ff., especially 183-90, for an extensive treatment of Nag Hammadi material on James; Ropes, pp. 64-74; also T. Zahn, *Introduction to the New Testament*, I (ET 1909), 140.

54. See the *Pseudo-Clementine Homilies* and the *Gospel according to the Hebrews*, cited in the previous note; also, notably, *Pseudo-Clementine Recognitions*, 1.44.

55. See Ropes, p. 37.

56. Robinson, *Redating the New Testament*, p. 130.

57. Ibid., p. 130.

58. See Jerome, "and even this is claimed by some to have been published by someone else under his name, and gradually, as time went on, to have gained authority" (*On Famous Men* 2); Ropes, pp. 52, 45. On the deplorably weak case for "honest pseudonymity"—the weakest in the NT—see Robinson, *Redating*, p. 129; D. Guthrie, "The Development of the Idea of Canonical Pseudepigrapha in NT Criticism," *Vox Evangelica* 1 (1962): 4ff. For the other side, see K. Aland, "The Problem of Anonymity and Pseudonymity in Christian Literature of the First Two Centuries," *JTS* n.s. 12 (1969): 44; L. R. Donelson, *Pseudepigraphy and Ethical Argument in the Pastoral Epistles* (1986); Dibelius, pp. 18ff.; Laws, pp. 38ff. On this problem in Jewish literature, see L. Jacobs, "How Much of the Babylonian Talmud is Pseudepigraphic?" *Journal of Jewish Studies* 28 (1974): 46-59.

onymous explanation must be able to provide an explanation why James of Jerusalem seemed a better choice than either of the two apostles of that name."[59] Certainly it seems unlikely that the attribution to a little-known person like James Panther, for example, or a disciple of James the Just, would have ensured the book's survival.[60] If, as we have said, there is a Shakespearean play that we think is not his but is nearly as good, we have to face the question, Who of the known writers of his time apart from Shakespeare could have written it?

Similarly, who do we think was able to write a work of the Epistle of James's quality? If we assign the Epistle of James to his period of Christianity, he would be the only possible answer to the question, "Who wrote the Epistle of James?" *Prima facie,* nobody seems better qualified in every relevant way to have conceived and executed the Epistle thus. Since it is hardly conceivable that the church accepted the signature arbitrarily, the most logical explanation is that the man who composed the document was James—*the* James of Jerusalem; and this is the most plausible interpretation of the first part of the opening salutation.

We have stated our belief that the name in the opening verse of the Epistle of James is really that of James the Lord's brother. Now it is our duty to try to interpret the rest of that verse in the atmosphere of thought that plainly characterizes the mind of the Epistle of James and its author.

J. H. Ropes[61] points out the affinities of the Epistle of James both in style and method to the Hellenistic diatribe[62] and in its deeper roots of thought[63] to the Jewish Wisdom literature. We must now interpret and evaluate the meaning of "the twelve tribes of the Dispersion" in relation to the thought thus admitted to be prominent in the author's mind.

Who are "the twelve tribes of the Dispersion"? The phrase has been variously interpreted.[64] We submit that it means the Jewish people

59. P. 229.

60. See Reicke, p. 4; also H. J. Lawlor, *Eusebiana* (1912), pp. 35ff.; Ropes, p. 67.

61. Pp. 10ff.

62. See p. 15 *ad init.*

63. See pp. 16f.

64. It has been taken to refer, e.g., to (1) unconverted Jews, implying a later Christianized ascription (e.g., A. Meyer, p. 123); (2) the Jewish nation (e.g., Mayor, p. cxliii); (3) Gentile Christians (see 1 Pet. 1:1), perhaps of the third or fourth generation (e.g., H. von Soden, *The Books of the New Testament,* pp. 470f.); (4) Christian Jews (e.g., Hort, p. xxv; Davids, p. 64); (5) the church as the new Israel (e.g., Ropes, pp. 125ff.; B. W. Bacon, *An Introduction to the New Testament* [1900], p. 464; Moffatt, p. 6; Mitton, p. 17; and Laws, p. 48). (6) Some have taken

as a whole and is not to be limited to "extra-Palestinian Jewish Christians."[65] If James had wished so to limit the application, he could have made this clear in the Greek.[66] We see no reason to believe that James did not intend "the twelve tribes of the Dispersion" to include both Christian and non-Christian Jews outside Palestine. Since the twelve tribes stand for "the integrity of the nation Israel,"[67] and since the rabbis regarded the Jews as representing all Israel, "the twelve tribes" as an exclusive title fits them admirably.[68] We do not think that the phrase necessarily excludes the Jews living in Palestine or even Jerusalem.[69] But there is no need to press this point.[70] We do not think Gamaliel[71] was alone in his comparatively temperate tolerance; we would rather believe that the very striking scarcity of the name of Christ in the Epistle of James is one result of the prohibition recorded at the end of Acts 5:40 (*q.v.;* see also Acts 15:26).

We see no reason to believe that James did not intend "the twelve tribes of the Dispersion" to include both Christian and non-Christian Jews outside Palestine, and possibly within Palestine (see Acts 17:1-4). In the sequel (vv. 5-9) we notice a (here not very effectual) assault by non-Christian Jews; but the attitude of those persecutors must not make us shut our eyes to the temperate element in non-Christian Jewry, as in Gamaliel (see Acts 17:1-4, already cited). Verse 2, "as his manner was," speaks volumes for the tolerance of the traditional Jews of Thessalonica and the other places visited by Paul as a missionary for Jesus. So we see no reason why James should not have included non-Christian Jews as well as (his main concern) Christian Jews in the Epistle of James.

We believe that our interpretation of "the twelve tribes" best fits the content of the Epistle as a whole. It has been suggested that the phrase is to be taken symbolically of "Israel in its fulness and complete-

---

1:1 as a gloss (e.g., A. C. McGiffert, *History of the Apostolic Age* [1897], p. 585; J. Moffatt, *Introduction to the Literature of the New Testament* [1911], p. 473, n*). On the "circular" nature of the problem, see K. L. Schmidt, *diaspora, TDNT,* II, 102; also Robinson, *Redating,* p. 122.

65. *Pace,* e.g., Hort, J. Marty, Beyschlag, Selwyn, Davids, and others.

66. Ropes, p. 124.

67. Ropes, pp. 119, 124.

68. See Acts 26:7; also Justin Martyr, *The Dialogue with Trypho* 126.

69. *Pace* Ropes, p. 127.

70. Frankly we would like more positive evidence that "No time after the crucifixion is known to us when a Christian teacher could expect a respectful hearing for a didactic tract from both converted and unconverted Jews in the dispersion at large, or would have felt such responsibility for the general moral instruction of all diaspora Jews alike as this writer shows" (Ropes, p. 127).

71. Acts 5:34-40: "his speech persuaded them" (v. 40, NIV).

ness,"[72] that is, the church composed of Jewish and Gentile Christians. The members of this true Israel were in exile from their heavenly home.[73] The difficulty with this view is that it has no real parallel in primitive Christian usage, except possibly in Mt. 19:25; cf. Rev. 7:4; 14:1. That the church should displace "Israel after the flesh" was a natural development,[74] but it is a strange designation for Christians. Indeed, Ropes himself admits that the symbolic interpretation he defends is "not strictly symbolical"[75]—and the application of the technical "of the dispersion" to Christians separated from their heavenly home makes it still more difficult.

The "symbolical" view, if at all possible, could fit only a later and more advanced stage of Christianity than the whole tone of the Epistle of James seems to indicate. The Epistle of James seems to us to reflect in every way one of the earliest stages after the death and resurrection of Christ when for a very brief period the church was composed exclusively of believing Jews,[76] one of the earliest stages of the most earnest expectation of the "end of this world." It also seems to reflect one of the earliest stages, and the most Jewish milieu, of the propagation of the gospel, in a sphere of thought and nationality in which the Gentilization of Christianity is hardly if at all relevant. Our view is quite in keeping with the obviously early date of the Epistle of James and the probability that this is an open pastoral letter written by James the Just, a Jewish teacher or "rabbi" (3:1), and one who is concerned with the spiritual well-being of the flock.[77]

Further, even if an early or late Christian could be expected to address his audience, Christians in general, as the twelve tribes of God, which we will for the moment admit as possible though not very probable, it seems paramount that in so doing he must not try to stand in both worlds of thought at once. If he has a new spiritual meaning and application for the term "twelve tribes" he must not immediately give it a description, "of the Dispersion," which at once ties us down again to the historical application of the term to the Jews in the old, restricted, physical and national sense of those under the covenant.

Ropes himself has:

72. See Ropes, p. 125 *ad fin.;* Hort, p. 2; Parry, p. 84.

73. Dibelius, p. 66.

74. See Gal. 6:16; 1 Cor. 10:18; Rom. 9:6ff.; 1 Pet. 2:5, 9; 4:17; also Justin Martyr, *The Dialogue with Trypho* 123.

75. P. 120.

76. See Robinson, *Redating,* p. 122.

77. See, e.g., D. J. Moo, *James* (1985), p. 36; V. D. Doerksen, *James* (1983), p. 10, and others.

> This is one of the fundamental thoughts of Luke and Acts as well as the Epistle to the Hebrews, where everything pertaining to the old national religion is shown to belong also (only in the reality, not the shadow) to the new religion.[78]

For our present purpose we would underline the words in the parenthesis. "Of the Dispersion" *(en tē diaspora)* is a phrase belonging to the physical aspect, not the spirituality of the new religion. The absolute use of the term occurs here only in the NT. The force of the article, omitted in 1 Pet. 1:1, shows that the term is still nontechnical and is used concretely, as Ropes says, "of the Jews so dispersed."[79] What he means by "so" is obvious in the context; what follows, "or even of the districts in which they were dispersed," is correct enough, but the result in this verse of James is practically the same. The phrase does indeed "belong to the physical": its meaning is mortal, terrestrial, ethnic, material, and geographical, and has no more spiritual, celestial, or eternal significance than the regular Jewish diaspora;[80] in fact, the distinction is not relevant here.

In our view, James uses "of the Dispersion" of the physical, the old religion, the old Jewry. To him Christianity is not a new religion but the consummation of the old; and we shall never see the OT and the NT as the unity they really are unless we manage to grasp what we take to be the truth about, and preached by, James.

James was not "a Jewish Christian";[81] he was a Christian Jew. "Christian" is the adjective, "Jew" the noun—the thing that he was—and leadership of Jews in particular, not of Christians in general, was his clear goal: "a servant of God, and of the Lord Jesus Christ." Note that this "signature description" occurs in the opening of none of Paul's Epistles except that to Titus. Contrast the formula that Paul, with slight variations, generally adopts. But, of course, the opening of the Epistle of James is in close harmony with the opening of the Epistle to the Hebrews (not by Paul). So James, Christian that he has become, is essentially a Jew, as Jesus in the flesh on earth not only was a Jew but most emphatically said: "Do not think that I have come to abolish the Law or the Prophets; I have not come to abolish them but to fulfil them" (Mt.

78. P. 120.

79. P. 120.

80. Jas. 1:1. On "Judaism in the Diaspora: Gentiles and Judaism," see G. Vermes, F. Millar, M. Goodman, and E. Schürer, *The History of the Jewish People in the Age of Jesus Christ,* III, 1 (1986), 1-176.

81. Ropes, p. 17 *ad fin.:* see Laws, pp. 36f., however, who argues that James would neither call himself a Jew nor "retain the practice of Judaism as the framework of his life."

5:17f., NIV).[82] In Acts 21:20-26 we see how anxious Christian Jews were for the maintenance of their old law over Jews, and how the Christian Council was eager to convince them that the hold of the law over Jews, Christian or non-Christian, was not to be endangered.

With due diffidence we venture to assert that the main advance of Christianity on the Jewish faith (apart from Christ) was in its belief in human immortality, a belief already held by some Jews, and now regarded by Christian Jews as essential to their faith. It is clear from Acts 5:17f., 34-39, that the main opposition to infant Christianity arose precisely in regard to this doctrine, an opposition that was pressed home by the Sadducees, as well as by the high priest Gamaliel, a Pharisee who was only a temperate sceptic. So, according to Acts 22:30 and 23:10, when Paul is put before the Jewish Council he apologizes for unwittingly reviling the high priest and expressly accepts the Jewish law on that point as binding on himself.

The sequel (23:6-9), however, is illuminating: those of the non-Christian Jews who were Pharisees made common cause with Paul when he proclaimed himself a Pharisee, the son of a Pharisee, and asserted that the bone of contention between himself and the Jews who were persecuting him was "my hope in the resurrection of the dead" (NIV). In 24:14-21 Paul asserts that he is orthodox in all the requirements of the Jewish law but in addition indulges in a newly assured belief in the resurrection of the dead. In 25:1f. the high priest again is the instigator of action against Paul; and again in 25:7f. Paul maintains that he has kept all of the Jewish law, and also all of Caesar's law. Similarly, before Agrippa (ch. 26) he repeats his claim that he is scrupulously obedient to the Jewish law, but also believes in the resurrection of the dead (26:5). In 26:12-20 he adds an account of his mission to the Gentiles and its origin, and in v. 21 the result: "that is why the Jews seized me in the temple courts and tried to kill me" (NIV).

Thus besides the doctrinal antipathy of some Jews (the Sadducees) there was also the racial jealousy of some others against the Gentiles. In Acts 6:9-14 we see how some non-Christian Jews, with the high priest and Council, vented their spleen on Stephen, the chief of the seven Jews (one a proselyte) chosen to minister to the Gentile Christians in Jerusalem at a time when a great number of the priests there had become Christians. Stephen himself (Acts 7:51-53) boldly asserted that Christ is the true, and rejected, consummation of the law. But he refused to repudiate his incorrigible brothers; he began his defense by calling

82. See also Jn. 14:1-10, where his dearest words of comfort are founded on the old Jewish faith in God.

them "brothers and fathers," and his dying words were "Lord, do not hold this sin against them" (NIV). However wronged, a good Jew never forgot the bond of brotherhood between Jew and Jew.

The distinction we make between Jewish Christianity and both Judaism and Pauline Christianity is important and especially needs clarification in respect of *Christology.* It was their commitment and allegiance to Jesus as *Messiah* that distinguished the Jewish Christians from their Jewish brothers and sisters, and made them more than mere protesters or sectarians, a distinction made crystal clear from the very beginning by virtue of the sacraments. From Pauline Christianity also they were palpably distinct in at least three ways:

1. In their intrinsically Jewish heritage, for example, in patterns of thought, and in understanding the OT, rather than that special training in which Paul was reared (and almost ruined);
2. In their distinctive way of thinking on practical and historical, rather than academic or philosophical, lines; and
3. In their idea of the church as the true Israel, which shaped much of their thinking on the Christian's attitude to the Jewish Torah.

The Christianity of the Jerusalem Church can only be understood within the context of unity and diversity—unity in their devotion to Jesus as Messiah and Lord; diversity in at least three ways:

1. First-century Jerusalem was a pluralistic society, bearing marks of foreign influences and ideologies, and no longer uniformly Pharisaic.
2. Judaism has always been more a code of observances than a code of doctrine. Paraphrasing Augustine, W. D. Davies puts it thus: "Observe the Law and believe what you like."[83] Much of this freedom of diversity continued on into the early Jewish Christian church.[84]

83. "Torah and Dogma: A Comment," *HTR* 61 (1968): 88-90, cited by R. N. Longenecker, *The Christology of Early Jewish Christianity* (1970), p. 7, n. 14, to whom I am indebted, here as elsewhere, in this area.

84. It is appropriate at this point to define what we mean by (A) "Early Jewish Christianity" and (B) NT "Jewish Christian" books.

(A) *"Early Jewish Christianity"* here means

1. *Chronologically,* the first Christian century, i.e., A.D. 30-132, and particularly the apostolic period of that century;
2. *Theologically,* early Christians with Christian concepts and expressions stemming from Semitic roots and from Judaism in particular; and
3. *Territorially,* early Christianity focused on Jerusalem or that regarded (in fact or in ideal) the Jerusalem Church as its "Mother Church," and worked to keep the active ministry of that (Jerusalem) Church from perishing.

3. Though the first Christians all acknowledged a common Lord in the details of doctrine and practice they would be heterogeneous as, for example, they had been in nationality and religion—Pharisees, Hellenists, Zealots, Samaritans, and others.

We believe, therefore, that in his address "to the twelve tribes" James is consciously writing as a Jew of his day to Jews of his day, not to later Jews,[85] nor to an overwhelmingly Gentilized people of God. We see no evidence that James had given up hope that the Jews would be converted to Christianity or that the paternity of Abraham "our father" (Jas. 2:21) would be extended symbolically to the Gentiles as in Gal. 3:7; there is no more analogy between these two passages than there is between a testamentary device and a proposition of Euclid. The attempt to interpret 1:1 as a piece of mystical symbolism designating Christianity at large seems inappropriate to James's mind, work, and office just as the effort to make *telos* in 5:11 mean the death or resurrection of Christ; and we cannot see any likelihood that James would plunge headlong into that fantasy of transfiguration in the opening signature and address of his Epistle.

Consider the prominence, the traditional Jewish prominence, given to God, without prejudice to Christ (1:1; 5:8, 12-15, 16-21, 26f.), before James turns in full faith to Christ (2:1), and then reverts to God (2:19-25; 3:9 [and probably 17]; 4:4-10, 11f., 13-17 [especially 15]; 5:1-6 [especially v. 5, and in the prophetic tone of the whole passage], 7f., 9-11, 14f., and finally the example of Elijah [5:16-18]). Here at least the incarnate Jesus Christ does not displace the Father, as sometimes

---

(B) Among *the "Jewish Christian" books of the New Testament* are the Gospels of Matthew and John, the Epistle to the Hebrews, the Epistles of James, John, and 1 Peter, the Book of Revelation, and perhaps 2 Peter and Jude. These are closer ideologically and doctrinally to a nonconformist type of Judaism found at Qumran than to any other group yet known. Within this category falls the Epistle of James. An important Jewish-Christian writing, this letter reflects a Jewish-Christian background, comes from one who is perhaps still in the synagogue, and is addressed to Jewish Christians or to potentially interested Jews of Palestine-Syria or the wider Diaspora. Quite possibly the Epistle of James represents "the extremest example within the New Testament of Judaistic Christianity." See C. F. D. Moule, *The Birth of the New Testament* (1962), p. 166; Longenecker, *The Christology of Early Jewish Christians*, pp. 18ff.; J. Daniélou, *A History of Early Christian Doctrine Before the Council of Nicaea*, I: *The Theology of Jewish Christianity*, tr. and ed. J. A. Baker (1964), 7ff.; R. A. Kraft, "In Search of 'Jewish Christianity' and its 'Theology': Problems of Definition and Methodology," *Recherches des sciences religieuses* 60 (1972): 81-92.

85. See Daniélou, *A History of Early Christian Doctrine Before the Council of Nicaea*, Vol. I: *The Theology of Jewish Christianity*, 7ff.

happens in some brands of Christianity. James knows full well that Jesus did not come to earth to supplant but to supplement the Father, and did not come to supersede but to increase the force of God's OT lessons to the Jews and to extend the scope of their operation to the Gentiles.

The address of the Epistle of James, then, is a significant clue to its authorship, origin, and date. The Jews of the Diaspora were for the most part within tolerable traveling distance from Jerusalem. Coming in for some feast(s) they trebled its population, and the Jewish hierarchy levied the half-shekel, "a sort of Peter's pence," on Jews of the Dispersion as well as on those of Palestine. The address is, as it were, from the center of a circle to its circumference, *not* from an unmapped unit of a formless spread to the rest of its particles. It is not anything like "James, from one wanderer to the rest." We must not underestimate, as we are apt to do, the strength of the bond between the Jew and his homeland, wherever he might be domiciled.[86]

We interpret the term "Diaspora" in James in the light of the missions, mentioned by Paul in 1 Cor. 9:5, of the Lord's brothers to their fellow Christian Jews outside Palestine. As the "quasi-encyclical" letter (written, we are sure, by James) to Antioch, etc. (Acts 15:23) was to Gentile Christians there and thereabouts, so the similar quasi-encyclical to the Jewish Christians was, we believe, to those Jews who had been visited or influenced by the various missions such as are mentioned in Acts. After being converted these Jewish Christians had voluntarily or under persecution scattered from, for example, Jerusalem to other places (mostly, may we guess?, in Asia Minor—but why not, e.g., Cyprus?). This diaspora, of course, is of a different context and significance from the scattering of the Jews generally, since, of course, many of them had been in dispersion for countless generations.

We also consider it the most natural thing in the world for James, "Bishop of Jerusalem," "Pope" (or whatever we may style him), to talk *viva voce* to his charges in and around Jerusalem and to think it also his duty to write a missionary letter, possibly when he became "Bishop"[87] but certainly while his obviously precarious life lasted, to the Jews of the Dispersion, in whom he certainly had no less spiritual interest than they had in coming up for the feast(s), or the temple officials had in collecting the half-shekels from them.[88]

86. See Philo, *Flaccus* 46. On this and related questions, see J. N. Sevenster, *Do You Know Greek?* (1968), Part IIA, "The Diaspora," pp. 77ff.

87. On this, see our remarks, pp. 112f., 117.

88. See Sevenster, *Do You Know Greek?*, p. 79; also J. Jeremias, *Jerusalem in the Time of Jesus* (1969), p. 167; J. Klausner, *Jesus of Nazareth* (1925), p. 304.

JAMES THE LORD'S BROTHER

If then there is nothing bogus about the letter, to whom can it be ascribed without great difficulty except to James, the head of the Jerusalem Church? Who else would have come more naturally to write it? Who else would have written it to those hearers with such stern and loving authority? In whose lifetime but his was the need of that letter felt?

The simple identification, "James," and the comprehensive address, "to the twelve tribes of the Dispersion," point clearly enough to the head of the Jerusalem Church, the greatest of those bearing the name "James," the Lord's brother. Since the other theories of homonymity or pseudonymity are even more disputable, let us here consider James the Lord's brother as at least the most probable author of the Epistle.

Initially a member of the household of Nazareth, then later at Capernaum, the Lord's brother (Gal. 1:19) was reared a Palestinian Jew of Galilee.[89] The precise physical relationship of James to Jesus, though important, has little relevance to the problem of his relationship to the present Epistle. Until shortly after the resurrection he was an unbeliever, and he was probably, like his brothers in general, hostile to the mission of Jesus, though it is entirely possible that the reported antipathy within the Holy Family, for example, in Mk. 3:31-35 (where they are not indifferent to Jesus but Jesus to them), has been exaggerated, owing perhaps to a desire, such as is sometimes perceptible in Acts, to minimize the part of the brothers, including James, in the first propagation of the gospel after the resurrection. At that stage, certainly no hostility is apparent. The picture in Acts itself (1:14) is one of harmony and unity between Mary the mother of Jesus with her sons and the rest of the apostles: "they all joined together constantly in prayer" (NIV). It has also been conjectured that the family of Jesus, with James at its head, for some time held a leading position or "caliphate" in the church as the Founder's kin.[90]

89. On his relationship to Jesus, opinions differ: (1) some say he was one of the children born to Mary and Joseph after the birth of Jesus (Helvidian theory); (2) others say he was not a brother but a cousin of Jesus; this Hieronymian theory is required by the doctrine of Mary's perpetual virginity; (3) still others say he was Joseph's son by a previous marriage (Epiphanian theory). The theory has no bearing on our subject. See Ropes, pp. 57ff.; F. V. Filson, *Pioneers of the Primitive Church* (1940), pp. 155ff.; J. J. Gunther, "The Family of Jesus," *EQ* 46 (1974): 25-41; J. W. Wenham, "The Relatives of Jesus," *EQ* 47 (1975): 6-15; Bruce, *Peter, Stephen, James and John*, pp. 87f.

90. See Dibelius, p. 13, n. 32 for references; also C. H. Dodd, *Studies in the Gospels* (1953), p. 19; Elliott-Binns, pp. 60f.; F. F. Bruce, *The Epistle to the Galatians*. NIGTC (1982), pp. 99, 120ff.

Almost as enigmatic as the Epistle of James is the figure of James himself, especially his apparently sudden introduction in the Acts of the Apostles, where having been appointed c. A.D. 41 or more probably during the Herodian persecution, c. A.D. 44,[91] he appears as the head of the Jerusalem Church during the imprisonment of Peter (12:14ff.), later presides as undisputed president of the Council, and plays a key role in the admission of the Gentiles (15:13-21). In his final appearance, James and all the elders welcome Paul when he comes to Jerusalem with the collection (21:18ff.). Here he is again seen as clearly "first among equals" among the elders, his authority is unchallenged, and Paul almost reverently defers to him as a "pillar apostle" (Gal. 2:9; see also 1 Cor. 15:7).

At the eye of the storm in these turbulent times, James the Lord's brother, known also as "the Just" and "the Bulwark,"[92] emerges as a devout lifelong Nazirite[93] and powerful Jewish-Christian apostle,[94] a unique mixture of saint and OT prophet,[95] strangely like the Teacher of Righteousness, who might well have formed a bridge between Galilean Christian Nazirites and the Qumran Covenanters.[96] Possibly a priest

91. See Bruce, *Peter, Stephen, James and John*, p. 91; W. L. Knox, *St. Paul and the Church at Jerusalem* (1925), p. xiii; but also F. J. Foakes-Jackson and K. Lake, *The Beginnings of Christianity*, I (1920), 24f. See also Josephus, *Ant.* 14.8.2; Acts 11:27-29; Gal. 2:1-10.

92. See R. H. Eisenman, *James the Just in the Habakkuk Pesher* (1986), pp. 10, 43, 66; H.-J. Schoeps, "Jacobus *ho dikaios kai* Ōblias," *Biblica* 24 (1943): 398ff. with references. For further discussion see our remarks, p. 49, n. 60.

93. Eusebius, *Hist. Eccl.* 2.23.5f.

94. See 1 Cor. 15:7; the apocryphal *Gospel According to the Hebrews* cited by Jerome, *On Famous Men* 2; Hennecke, *New Testament Apocrypha*, I, 165; see also W. Schmithals, *The Office of Apostle in the Early Church* (1969), esp. pp. 64ff. for an important discussion.

95. See T. C. Baird, *Now Let it Work* (n.d.), p. 3.

96. See, e.g., Eisenman, *James the Just in the Habakkuk Pesher*, pp. vii and throughout; *Maccabees, Zadokites and Qumran: A New Hypothesis of Qumran Origins* (1983), pp. xiif. and throughout; I am indebted to Dr. Eisenman for kindly sharing his earlier paper, "James as Righteous Teacher" (SBL, 1977), where he reaches the more cautious conclusion that James was *a* teacher of righteousness, though not necessarily *the* teacher of righteousness. On attempts to discern references to James the Just in the Qumran literature, especially the Habakkuk *Pesher*, F. F. Bruce is skeptical. In a personal note he says, "I once made an intensive study of the Habakkuk Scroll and found no allusion to James there"; also M. Black, *The Scrolls and Christian Origins* (1961), p. 82. More striking than any similarities are the fundamental differences reflected in the teaching and practice of the communities each led (see Laws, p. 11). For a synopsis of other possible identifications, see Vermes, Millar, Goodman, and Schürer, *The History of the Jewish People in the Age of Jesus Christ*, III, 1, p. 436, n. 7.

himself with access to the sanctuary,[97] James would naturally sympathize with the poorer clergy against the Sadducean aristocracy: the climax of his wrath is against a brood of the sort that flourished in, and on, Galilee.[98] While remaining thoroughly Jewish after his conversion and apparently a faithful adherent of the Torah—but certainly neither an ally of the Judaizers[99] nor a zealot of the ceremonial Torah[100]—nevertheless by his breadth of vision James is able to sympathize with the problems of the Gentiles, does not insist on their circumcision, and appears in every way anxious to cooperate with Paul in his efforts to evangelize them.[101] On his excellent relations with Paul and the Gentiles, we must speak at some later time;[102] it is a subject on which there could scarcely be greater or more prevalent misunderstanding.

The picture of James at the Apostolic Council and especially his speech fit in nobly with his Epistle: he is the unchallenged head of the Jerusalem Church, presides with dignity and authority, and drafts the Apostolic Decree. It has been pointed out that "the Jerusalem Church could not have promulgated it without James's approval. That it was actually promulgated on James's initiative, as Luke records, is entirely credible. Luke himself appears to have regarded it as a masterpiece of statesmanship."[103] His precedence in office and dignity is obvious in his speech (Acts 15:13-21), as it is in Gal. 1:19, when on his visit to Peter, Paul yet paid—as, we submit he felt bound—his visit of duty and courtesy to James, whom he certainly regards as an apostle.[104] He is aptly called "the Amos of the New Testament" both for his character and for his heritage from not only the thought but also the style of Amos,[105] as in the short, grave, balanced, vivid, and simple speech in

97. See below, p. 245, n. 99; also B. I. Reicke, *The New Testament Era* (ET 1969), p. 215, n. 7.

98. See Jas. 5:4.

99. See S. G. F. Brandon, "The Death of James the Just. A New Interpretation" in *Studies in Mysticism and Religion,* presented to G. Scholem (1967), pp. 57-69.

100. See Eusebius, *Hist. Eccl.* 2.23 and, for a critical evaluation, Ropes, pp. 64ff.; see also H. Kemler, *Der Herrenbruder Jakobus bei Hegesipp. und in der frühchristlichen Literatur* (1966).

101. See G. Kittel, "Die Stellung des Jacobus zu Judentum und Heidenchristentum," *ZNW* 30 (1931): 145ff.; Elliott-Binns, pp. 59ff.

102. See our discussion, pp. 195ff.

103. See Bruce, *Peter, Stephen, James and John,* p. 93; see also Laws, pp. 39f.; Scaer, pp. 34f.

104. See Bruce, *Peter, Stephen, James and John,* p. 89.

105. D. A. Hayes, "The Epistle of James," *International Standard Bible Encyclopedia,* III (1929), 1562.

Acts 15:13-21 (nearly all of which is from the prophets).[106] The citation from the prophets is characteristic of the author of the Epistle of James, and the authoritative *krinō* here (as often, meaning to give judgment, decide, not merely to vote or opine) indicates his authority in the church. In the sequel there is not a hint of even a formal vote of confirmation of James's decision itself; the apostles and elders at once address themselves to the promulgation and dissemination of his decision. In the letter the quality of the Greek equals that of the Epistle of James in vocabulary and force of style.

To me at least, it seems obvious that not only is the Epistle of James by James the Lord's brother but equally, and partly on the same grounds, the letter in Acts 15:23-29. A priori who else would be likely to write the letter but James (or others at his dictation or from his original)? J. B. Mayor emphasizes the "remarkable agreements" between the 230 words of James's speech in Acts 15:23-29 and the Epistle of James,[107] facts that tend to make us (with Oesterley)[108] "recognise the same mind at work" in both, for example, in the Hellenism of the final *errōsthe*, which in the NT occurs again only at the end of the letter from Claudius Lysias to Felix (Acts 23:30).

Yet such evidence is cumulative, for though these parallels in themselves do not prove the identity of the two speakers, they do have "a certain force when added to the other favourable arguments."[109] Among other things we may note a similar fondness for the OT,[110] plus several significant verbal parallels.[111] It is significant that even after re-

106. For an excellent discussion of James's "biblical exegesis" at the Council of Jerusalem, see Bruce, *Peter, Stephen, James and John*, pp. 93ff.

107. P. 111. See J. Jervell, *Luke and the People of God* (1972), p. 190, especially for the authoritative *egō krinō* (Acts 15:19).

108. P. 392.

109. Mitton, p. 231.

110. See Jas. 2:23, 25; 3:11, 17; Acts 15:16-18, 21.

111. Analysis of the vocabulary and style of the speech's 230 words shows (1) verbal congruences: e.g., the epistolary *chairein*, elsewhere only in Acts 23:26; the pregnant *onoma;* the repetitive *adelphos* with *agapētos*, Jas. 1:16, 19; 2:5; Acts 15:25; *tērein*, Jas. 1:27//*diatērein*, Acts 15:29; *episkeptesthai*, Jas. 1:27; Acts 15:14; *epistrephein*, Jas. 5:19f.; Acts 17:19; (2) idiomatic congruences: *to kalon onoma to epiklēthen eph' hymas*, Jas. 2:7//*ep' hous epikeklētai to onoma mou ep' autous*, Acts 15:17; the unique *akousate adelphoi mou*, Jas. 2:5//*andres adelphoi akousate mou*, Acts 15:13. These delicate Greek verbal and idiomatic nuances, together with their OT affinities (Jas. 2:23, 25; 3:11, 17; Acts 15:16-18, 21), seem too numerous and striking to be coincidental, or to be seen simply as "the common accidents of speech" (so Spitta, p. 43; A. H. McNeile, p. 209; Laws, p. 39). In response to the view that a pseudonymous James inserted "authentic" fragments of James's idioms and expressions to give his work credence, Guthrie is skeptical, noting that this is "generally contrary to pseudepigraphic evidence" (*New Testa-*

dactional revision, compression, and perhaps even literary construction, James's speech should within such short compass have such vital linguistic links with the Epistle of James. We are quite prepared to concede that Luke may have composed the version of the speech James doubtless made on that occasion; but we think the style is that of James himself.[112] In the substance of the speech in Acts we definitely see *the* James of the Epistle of James.

In our chapter on *Style* we shall discuss his command of expressive words as a clue to his identification with James the Lord's brother. As Ropes remarks:

> Especially in his figurative language, the writer shows his command of well-chosen and *expressive* [our italics] words. The vivacity, simple directness, and general effectiveness of his style are conspicuous even to the reader of the English version.[113]

To me at least, convincing evidence that the letter in Acts is by the same author as the Epistle of James is to be seen in the use, here only in the NT, of the word *anaskeuazontes* in Acts 15:24—a point we will mention again. The convincing literary fingerprint of the Epistle's style in the letter of Acts 15:13-29 is this same word. The originality and forcefully expressive use of a word—whether it be an uncommon word, or an uncommon use of a common word—are superlatively marked here. As *kataskeuazein* means "to furnish with gear *(skeuē),*" so *anaskeuazein,* its opposite, means "to dismantle, disfurnish," as in the "Displenishment Sales" that used to be held on the breaking up of a Scottish farm.

Now, as we have said, it is a priori most probable that the Council's letter in Acts 15 would—at least in part—be drafted by James. We do not think the importance of his position or his importance in that

---

ment Introduction: Hebrews to Revelation [1966], p. 67; also pp. 39, 754; see also "Epistolic Pseudepigraphy," *New Testament Introduction: the Pauline Epistles,* pp. 282, 284). For another, less favorable, view, see Laws, p. 39.

112. We believe that Luke may have been like, e.g., Thucydides, who put speeches in the mouths of his generals and politicians, as he himself says: "Keeping as far as possible the general tenor of what was actually said" (*Peloponnesian War,* Bk. 1, sec. 22). For the view that James's speech is not authentic, see, e.g., E. Haenchen, *The Acts of the Apostles* (1971), p. 448. The position of F. F. Bruce is probably very near to ours. See *The Acts of the Apostles* (1951), pp. 18-21; "The Speeches in Acts—Thirty Years After," in *Reconciliation and Hope,* ed. R. J. Banks (1974), pp. 53-68; and *New Testament Development of Old Testament Themes* (1968), p. 79; see also R. C. Worley, *Preaching and Teaching in the Earliest Church* (1967), pp. 43ff., 160f.; D. E. Aune, *The New Testament in Its Literary Environment* (1987), pp. 124ff., 155f.

113. P. 24.

position can be doubted: Gal. 1:19 and 2:9 are not without significance. The use of *anaskeuazō* to signify the shattering upset or havoc on the minds of the Gentile Christians at the proposal to require them to be circumcised[114] is characteristic of the style of the Epistle of James and one of the most conspicuous features of that style. Anyone who has experienced the upheaval, not to say havoc, of spring-cleaning displenishments will recognize the force and aptness of this (the only occurrence in the NT) figurative use of *anaskeuazō* intensifying the already forceful picture of *etaraxan.*[115]

The clinching proof inherent (as we think) in the quite convincing oddity of *anaskeuazontes* cannot be ignored. The choice of this far from trite Greek word for the upheaval and perturbation of mind in these Gentile converts is, as it were, a fingerprint of the vivid and resourceful vigor of the style of the Epistle of James.[116] The word is characteristic of James's incisive, vivid, rare, almost OT "metaphors" and of his rabbinic thought and language. We maintain that "the cultivated Greek"[117] of *anaskeuazontes* is from the same hand as wrote the Epistle of James; that is, they are both by that James to whom Luke attributes the speech to the Council.

To us the evidence seems quite conclusive that the author of the Epistle of James and the writer of this *anaskeuazontes* in the Council's letter are the same man; and, given all the evidence, who could that be but James the Lord's brother? The attitude of James at the Council of Jerusalem is not that of his men in Gal. 2:12, and it was not only permissible and natural but also a duty for the first Bishop of Jerusalem and the Christian Jews to send such an Epistle as the Epistle of James to his fellow-Christian Jews, not only in Palestine but also in their many great centers elsewhere.

THE EPISTLE OF JAMES

So far we have examined the Epistle's opening address and the NT pic-

114. Vulg. *evertentes animas vestras* is better than KJV or RV "subverting your souls."

115. Vulg. *turbaverunt vos verbis.*

116. In ch. 1 alone we can compare v. 6, *klydōni,* in the NT only here and in Lk. 8:24; v. 11, *kausōni,* in the NT only here and in Mt. 20:12; Lk. 12:55; v. 14, *exelkomenos* in the NT only here; *kai deleazomenos,* in the NT only here and in 2 Pet. 2:14 and 18; v. 22, *paralogizomenoi,* in the NT only here and in Col. 2:4; v. 23, *esoptrō,* in the NT only here and in 1 Cor. 13:12; v. 26, *thrēskos,* in the NT only here; v. 26, the verb *chalinagōgein,* in the NT only here and in 3:2; v. 27, *aspilos,* in the NT only here and in 1 Tim. 6:14; 1 Pet. 1:19; and 2 Pet. 3:14.

117. Cited by E. Haenchen, *The Acts of the Apostles* (1971), p. 452.

ture of James, especially his speech, finding in both ample support for the traditional view of authorship. The final court of appeal, however, is the Epistle itself. Naturally a late date would eliminate the possibility of James the Lord's brother; if the Epistle is early he is clearly the strongest and perhaps the only candidate. The problem of the identity of the author must, I suppose, be approached through a study of the Epistle of James itself.

Let us now briefly consider how the contents of the Epistle seem to date it within the lifetime of James, the first leader of the church at Jerusalem.

The Epistle includes rich farmers, merchants, and financiers as well as the distressed and oppressed poor. The two classes are found in sharp contrast in a period of comparative quiet, free travel, and arrogant wealth, which ended in the Jewish War and the fall of Jerusalem in A.D. 70, of which catastrophe the Epistle contains no mention (understandably so if it had not yet happened).[118] Nor is there any hint of "a permanent breach with Judaism desolated by national defeat, such as marks the Epistle of Barnabas."[119] Allusions to blasphemy and judicial harassment (2:6) recall the actions not of the Roman state (e.g., persecutions of Domitian or Trajan), but of the Jewish Sanhedrin; and these, we agree,[120] "do not go further than anything described in Acts 8:1, 3; 9:2 (compare 26:10); 11:10—in fact, not as far."

Further, Jas. 1:9-11 chimes admirably with the first period of Christian "communism" (Acts 2:44ff.; 4:32ff.): "abasement" in 1:10 is apt enough for the abnegation of the rich man who gives his wealth to the common stock, and so doing would well take him out of the mischief of 1:11b. The Epistle may well be earlier than A.D. 50. Certainly, if he wrote later than A.D. 66-70, James could hardly have dwelt on a social cleavage that no longer existed. The loss of Jewish rank and riches also meant the loss of power to oppress. No loss of power is apparent in his Epistle; the opposite, rather, is the case (2:6; 5:1ff.).

The position, emphasis, and vehemence of its reprobation of the corrupt rich (but we must not forget people like Joseph of Arimathea) confirm our early dating of the Epistle of James. Probably there never was a time when many of the world's poor were not suffering from the wickedness of many of the rich. But we suggest that never could that wickedness have been so rampant, even under a regime of atheistic plu-

118. See W. L. Knox, *St. Paul and the Church of Jerusalem*, p. 23, n. 49; Davids, p. 63.

119. Robinson, *Redating*, p. 120.

120. Robinson, *Redating*, p. 122; see also D. Guthrie, *New Testament Introduction: Hebrews to Revelation*, p. 87.

tocracy, as under the godlessly perverted "theocracy" of Israel in the days of Jesus and James. That age, not the period between the Jewish Calamity of A.D. 70 and the final ruthless clearance of the Jews from Judea after their last desperate insurrection in 134-135, is the period to which it seems most reasonable to ascribe the Epistle of James.

There is no evidence, proof, of even probability for ascribing it (as some do) to the second or even mid-third century. It has been described variously as "decadent," "curiously dry," "lacking in missionary zeal and vitality," "antidogmatic," "Ebionitic," reflecting an "early Catholic stage," a "blanched Christology," a "relapse or loss of early love," "a curious and unlikely mixture of an original freshness and at the same time an undeniable decay," and a "sober vapid moralism" after its struggles with Paul or the Gnostics—in sum, the least Christian book in the NT.[121] There is no evidence for the hypothesis, which the whole tenor of the Epistle of James, from its very opening doctrine, refutes. The initial "count it pure joy" is scarcely the language of decadence—and certainly *not* of martyrdom[122]—but rather of buoyant faith—a faith that faces suffering with joyous abandon, suggesting a young, vigorous church of the first days.

The sins James denounces—snobbery, oppression, strife, self-righteousness, hypocrisy, greed, worldliness—are common enough today but also flourished in the first century.[123] The dew of its birth was still on the infancy of Christianity, and that birth was in one of the most corrupt and degenerate epochs of Judaism. J. A. T. Robinson observes:

> There are no signs of heresy or schism, as are inveighed against in the later Paul(ine) and the Johannine Epistles; no marks of incipient gnosticism, whether speculative or even, as we might expect in this Epistle, moral (with the tell-tale swing between asceticism and licence), such as is characteristic of Jewish Christianity in the latter half of the New Testament (Colossians, the Pastorals, the Epistles of John, Jude and II Peter).[124]

121. See, e.g., Dibelius, p. xl; Knowling, p. lix; H. A. A. Kennedy, *The Theology of the Epistles* (1919), p. 222; Moffatt, *An Introduction to the New Testament*, p. 471; E. F. Scott, *The Gospel and Its Tributaries* (1928), p. 97; M. Goguel, *The Birth of Christianity* (1955), pp. 394f.; Schammberger, Schoeps; and many others. On this, with the supposed "lack of missionary concern," see Davids, p. 18; for especially trenchant criticisms, see Parry, pp. 72f.

122. *Pace*, e.g., E. Beyreuther and G. Finkenrath, "James 1:2 comes close to teaching Christians to rejoice in martyrdom" ("Joy," *NIDNTT*, II [1976], 361).

123. See Mitton, p. 233; Ropes, p. 41; Mayor, p. 41.

124. *Redating*, p. 123. In a footnote he adds: "Allusions to gnostic tendencies have been seen, e.g., in the antithesis between the true and false wisdom (3:13-

Moreover, the sins are more Jewish than Gentile; for example, there is no reference to immorality, drunkenness, slaves and their masters, idolatry, or meat offered to idols.[125] The lack of provision for the instruction of Gentiles has been held against the authenticity of the Epistle. It is, however, expressly addressed to Jewish Christians, and emphasizes the law of liberty for all Christians without forbidding circumcision to any Christian Jews. Nevertheless, they are well warned that it takes more than circumcision to make an earnest Christian. Nor do we see any evidence of a later date (e.g., so K. Aland[126]) in the fact that James refers to healing by the "elders" of the church, whereas in 1 Cor. 12:30 that power is exercised by no one class of Christian. In sum, the theological, like the economic, evidence suggests a date before A.D. 70 or even before A.D. 50, when the good Christian Jew could set out to be a good Jew, with an ethical ideal shared by Jesus and the prophets.

One unique aspect of the Epistle of James is its didactic content, affording unsurpassed evidence of the infancy of the Christian religion. On the Judaizers and their debate over Gentile admission the Epistle is silent, from which it has been inferred that James composed his letter either before the controversy arose (c. A.D. 40-50) or after it had ceased. This silence is seen as proof against the popular mediating date c. A.D. 60.[127] Nor is there any mention of dietary and ceremonial law, slavery, relations with heathen masters, and other typical Gentile problems. But the argument from silence should not be pressed. In a letter sent to these addressees the question of Gentile admission would hardly arise in any case; the Gentile mission was outside their purview.[128] Certainly for James Christianity is neither un-Jewish nor anti-Jewish; he has no sense of "we" and "they" as found in writings c. A.D. 90-150; nor, as we have hinted, like the Epistle of Barnabas, the Didache, and Justin Martyr, does he present salvation as a "new law" *(nova lex)* or a pure spiritual

---

18), in the word *psychikē* (3:15), and the use of *teleios* (1:4, 17, 25; 3:2). but none of these need imply anything more than can be found in the Jewish Wisdom literature or in Philo or, for example, in 1 Cor. 2:12-14; 15:44ff." See particularly Ropes, pp. 36f.

125. See T. Zahn, "Die Soziale Frage und die Innere Mission nach dem Brief des Jakobus," *Zeitschrift für kirchliche Wissenschaft und kirchliches Leben,* 10 (1889): 102.

126. "Der Herrenbruder Jakobus und der Jakobusbrief," *ThLZ* 69 (1944): 97-104.

127. So Mitton, Cadoux, Hort, and others.

128. I owe this insight to F. F. Bruce.

"nomism" *(nomismus),*[129] a conception fundamentally incompatible with the unity James saw equally in original Judaism and its integral consummation, Christianity.[130] Baseless, too, is the view that James was "a fanatic" whose sole idea was that "Jerusalem, the O.T. *Civitas dei,* must become the holy city of the new and true people of God, the Christian center of the growing Church."[131] To James, Christ is the long-promised Messiah, whose Torah is perfect, and whom he hopes Israel will yet acknowledge.

The use of the Greek *Christos,* first as an appellative and then as a proper name (and as the root of the name of their religion in the ancient world) shows how basic and central Messiahship was for the early Jewish Christians. Jewish expectation is much more interested in the Messianic Age, and what God is to do in it, than in the person or persons he is to use in bringing about that Age and accomplishing his purpose therein; but the early Jewish writings on the Final Age do contain some thought and mention of a personal Messiah.[132] The belief in Jesus as Messiah was shared by all first-century Christians, Jewish or Gentile; but it obviously owed much to the force of early Jewish Christian thought. In Acts Messiahship is prominent in the early presentation of Jesus; thus Peter in Acts 2:31; 2:36; 3:18; 3:20; 4:26; 5:42; Philip, 8:5, to Samaritans; Paul, 9:22; 17:3; 18:5, to Jews of Damascus, Thessalonica, and Corinth; Apollos to Jews at Corinth, 18:28, and others. In Acts *Christos,* used singly or in "Jesus Christ" or "Christ Jesus," is always an appellative, and used only in addressing a Jewish audience (except, *possibly,* by Philip, to Samaritans, and, notably, by Paul before

129. So Dibelius, p. 25; W. Marxsen, *Introduction to the New Testament* (1968), p. 230. For the *nova lex* in Tertullian and later writers, see H.-J. Schoeps, *Paul: The Theology of the Apostle* (1961), pp. 267f.

130. Knowling, p. lxii; Robinson, *Redating,* p. 120.

131. E. Stauffer, *New Testament Theology* (1955), p. 34.

132. The Hebrew word *māšîaḥ* in the OT and other early Jewish literature is used of a person or persons to whom God has given a special call or special mission, e.g., an anointed king of God's people, a priest, prophet, or patriarch, and even Cyrus as doing a specific task within God's purpose (Isa. 45:1). By the first century B.C., perhaps earlier, the word had become a *terminus technicus* for the Anointed One who would be God's deliverer in the last days (Dan. 9:25-26a). In the Qumran writings, e.g., 1QS 9:11; 1QSa 2:14, 20; 11QMelch. 18, we find "The Anointed One of Israel and Aaron" and the like, and, in what seems an absolute use, "the Messiah." But the idea differed extensively as to the portrayal of the promised Messiah. Of the spiritual and national hopes of pre-Christian messianic expectations the most popular was that of a political and nationalistic deliverer, and even a military leader, and to this notion was linked the title "Son of David"; in NT times the "Son of David" concept dominated details and discussion. See K. H. Rengstorf, "Jesus Christ" *(Christos), NIDNTT,* II, 334ff.

Agrippa II). Perhaps it was not yet a proper name; certainly the evidence is that in Acts *Christos* is usually employed as a title. It is so elsewhere in the NT in addressing Jews; except perhaps in Mt. 1:1, 18, all the 14 uses indicate a title or designation, not a name.

The Epistle of James is "a production of primitive Jewish Christianity, in which Christ's religion is conceived as the fulfillment of the perfect law."[133] Earlier we showed that there is no need to adopt a "symbolic" interpretation of Jas. 1:1. James is addressing Jews in Jerusalem and throughout the Dispersion, converted and unconverted, at a time when Christianity was still simply a Jewish sect.

Helpful on this point may be the comparative study of sects within early Christian Palestinian communities. At least seven sociological phenomena seem to be shared by the sects and those early Jewish Christians, including, we believe, those addressed by James. Applying these seven criteria, in convenient summary form, to his Epistle, we find significant similarities.[134] Thus the community (1) is apocalyptic (5:7f.); (2) commands and demands total commitment (1:6f., 22f.; 2:14ff.; 3:13f.; 4:7, 17); (3) is a voluntary organization (1:25; 2:12; 5:19f.; note the striking use of "brother" [1:2, often]); (4) offers love and acceptance within the community (1:27; 2:8, 14ff.; 3:1f.; 5:9f.); (5) preaches nondiscrimination (2:1ff.; 3:9); (6) rejects the view of reality claimed or implied by the establishment (1:20; 2:5f.; 4:13f.; 5:1ff.); and (7) emerges out of protest (1:1). Unlike later NT writings, for example, 1 Peter, which had long separated from the Jewish synagogue, the Epistle of James significantly gives no hint whatever of any such break.

James's Christianity is only the culmination of Israelism (the religion of Abraham) and Abraham's (the Jewish) line, and of God's earlier dealings with mankind before there were any Jews. We fancy that Paul (Saul) the persecutor regarded Christians as on much the same footing as the Pope of his day regarded Luther. It was some time before the Christian Jewish "heretics" were expelled from the synagogues. We believe the Epistle of James belongs to the period when Christians still met in the "synagogue" (2:1), which we think means building rather than "gathering"[135]—recalling the days when, as in the early chapters of Acts, the Christian movement is still a sect of Judaism.[136]

133. R. H. Charles, "Eschatology," *Encyclopedia Biblica,* ed. T. K. Cheyne and J. S. Black (1914), p. 1377.

134. See J. H. Elliott, *A Home for the Homeless* (1981), p. 74.

135. See Adamson, p. 105; D. Guthrie, *New Testament Theology* (1981), p. 781, *pace* Davids, p. 108.

136. Robinson, *Redating,* pp. 119ff.; see also his important remarks on "the absence of any clear-cut frontier between Christianity and Judaism," with impres-

But to say[137] that the primitive church order, especially the silence on bishops, points to a place other than Jerusalem and to a later date based on geographical isolation seems unlikely. The synagogue organization appears to be simple, primitive, and above all Jewish:[138] there is social equality (2:1ff.); prayer,[139] praise,[140] and confession of sin[141] are encouraged (5:13f.); and in the case of "trouble" (*kakopathia*, v. 13) and "sickness" (*astheneia*, v. 14), [142] the elders[143] are to be summoned to pray over, lay hands upon, and anoint the patient with oil (5:14). "Anointing is a symbolic act by which demons are cast out," writes W. Brunotte;[144] "The healings performed by the disciples or elders of the church were accompanied by anointing, and took place in the context of preaching and prayer. Healing, and therefore anointing also, came to be seen as a visible sign of the beginning of God's reign. The quasi-magical misunderstanding of anointing is, however, held firmly in check, especially in Jas. 5:13ff., by the importance attached to accompanying prayer." Specifically, the officials named are "teachers" (3:1) or "elders" (5:14), all officials of the Jewish synagogue, contrasting with the elaborate, hierarchical ministry of bishops, deacons, and others developed in later Christian literature (e.g., 1 Cor. 12:28; Eph. 4:11; Did. 13:2; 15:18, et al.).

Absent, too, are specific references to organized worship, a monarchical episcopate, and the sacraments: swearing, healing, confession, prayer, and conversion of the lost dominate James's so-called final

---

sive arguments from silence in relation to the Epistle of James. For similar remarks, with different conclusions, see B. S. Childs, *The New Testament as Canon: An Introduction* (1984), p. 434. Also Eusebius, *Hist. Eccl.* 7.24.6.

137. See Moffatt, *Introduction to the Literature of the New Testament*, p. 464; *General Epistles*, MNTC (1928), p. 1.

138. See further below, pp. 277f. L. Coenen, "Church" *(ekklēsia), NIDNTT*, I, 304.

139. See our forthcoming discussion, pp. 449f.

140. See K. H. Bartels, "Song" *(psalmos), NIDNTT*, III, 672.

141. For these three ideas, confession of sin, the prayer of repentance, and the praise of God, theologically all closely associated in Judaism, see D. Fürst, "Confess" *(homologeō), NIDNTT*, I, 345.

142. On the difference between the two words, see B. Gärtner, "Suffer" *(paschō), NIDNTT*, III, 719-25; H.-G. Link, "Weakness" *(astheneia), NIDNTT*, III, 993-96.

143. On the NT "elder," see G. Bornkamm, *presbyteros, TDNT*, VI, 651-83; also L. Coenen, "Bishop" *(presbyteros), NIDNTT*, I, 192-200. On visiting the sick, see S-B IVa, 573f. See our remarks, pp. 449f.

144. See, e.g., Moo, pp. 179ff.; "Anoint" *(aleiphō), NIDNTT*, I, 119-21; H. Schlier, *aleiphō, TDNT*, I, 230-32; also M. Goguel on "Unction for the Sick" and "The Imposition of Hands," in *The Primitive Church*, pp. 371-85.

"Manual of Discipline" (5:12-20). And for some time before the synagogues were among the chief centers from which Christianity was disseminated, Paul, coming to a new mission field, regularly went to the local synagogue (Rom. 7:1; 1 Cor. 7:18; Gal. 2:13; Phil. 3:2; Col. 4:1). These few places, chosen at random, show the early importance of Jewish Christians, and some of the texts also show the difficulties (and indeed hostilities) between Jewish and Gentile brothers in Christ.

This Jewish approach to infant Christianity is only one of the many inevitable marks of the contemporary nature of the Epistle of James. Most notable of the ample evidence is its conception of Christianity as consummation, a consummation for all humanity of God's historic promises and favors to Israel. James appeals to the Jewish law and God the giver (2:9-11; 4:11f.), and there is "not a hint that the Christian message represents anything but its fulfilment."[145] Thus it is natural that many of the doctrines, exhortations, and illustrations (e.g., his basic monotheism, 2:19) that pervade the Epistle come from the OT; such personalities as Abraham, Rahab, Job, Elijah, and the prophets (2:21ff.; 5:10f., 17) together get more mention than Christ. Abraham is simply described as "our father" (2:21); contrast Paul, who of necessity must add "according to the flesh" (Rom. 4:1).

In our opinion, the Epistle of James reflects a pre-christological, almost pre-crucifixion stage, containing "the simplest expression of Christian consciousness, still untouched by complex dogmatic reflections,"[146] as it must have developed with original freshness in the circle of Jews who believed in the Messiah. This freshness is vividly seen in the sayings of Jesus of which the author's mind seems to be full. Evidently uniquely Jacobean but never actual Gospel quotations (contrast, e.g., Did. 15:3f.), the *verba Christi* were apparently still fluid, circulating orally and not yet crystallized into their Synoptic forms. The Kingdom is still prominent, and there is no question of disappointment over a delayed parousia (which, of course, was to begin in Jerusalem). This strong, vivid, and unquestioning belief in a speedy return, within the lifetime of the readers of the Epistle, points to an early date for the Epistle of James, in contrast with the outlook of the Pastorals, which reflect "a second stage" when "the sense of the speedy Parousia of the Lord passed away."[147]

Let us now turn to the vexed problem of faith and works and the

145. Robinson, *Redating*, p. 121.

146. See Elliott-Binns, p. 46; G. V. Lechler, *The Apostolic and Post-Apostolic Times*, I (1886), 291f.

147. W. Lock, *The Pastoral Epistles* (1924), p. xv.

supposed conflict between James and Paul (a matter to be discussed more fully later). Here again we find evidence of the Epistle's early origin. Luther condemned this Epistle as contradictory to Paul on the power and duty of faith, on which, says Luther, James had learned that Christians strongly insisted, so he decided he must oppose them and insist on works alone;[148] and so (according to Luther) James does. There is in fact no difference between the religion of James and that of Paul in their doctrine of the Christian spirit and the Christian conduct in which it must be expressed.

The main difference between Paul and James is that, without the least disparagement of the essential importance of "works," Paul seems to enjoy going more elaborately than James into theologizing. James, with his home background and "fundamentally laic practical piety,"[149] can often take in stride what leads Paul into abstract argument. Jesus is present throughout the thought of the Epistle of James, but is named "Christ" only twice (1:1 and 2:1). The teaching of James is as simple as his Master's, that the relation of humans to God is a moral one, a way of life, and by obedience to God humans can attain to true life. "Like his Master he speaks with authority: he does not cite authorities—not even that of his Master."[150] Nothing is said of the Holy Spirit or of the life, death, and resurrection of Jesus (so prominent in early apostolic teaching[151] and in James's conversion[152])—almost suggesting a pre-resurrection theology of a devout Jew. His ethics, too, are in the simplest and most dynamic form and represent a primitive point of view akin to the Synoptics and before the influence of Paul. The doctrine of God is central: he alone is named in reference to regeneration, justification, repentance, and prayer. Tyndale, like many others, thought that James does not lay "the foundation of the faith of Christ";[153] for James that faith came not in argument but in his life's experience.

Any polemic in the Epistle of James, therefore, is not against Paul, who says the same thing as James on this matter, and more in 1 Cor. 13. Even those[154] who argue for a post-Pauline context admit that the opponent (2:18) is a caricature of Paul. Pauline influence is less discern-

148. *LW,* LIV, 424.

149. Dibelius, p. 48.

150. Robinson, *Redating,* p. 125.

151. See 1 Pet. 1:3.

152. 1 Cor. 15:7.

153. "The Prologue upon the Epistle of James" (1526), *The Work of William Tyndale,* edited and introduced by G. E. Duffield, I (1964), 161. See Mitton, p. 222, for Tyndale's and John Calvin's judgment.

154. See Childs, *The New Testament as Canon,* pp. 436, 440.

ible here than in any other NT book of like length, and the entire discussion of faith and works seems to rule out a deliberate attack on Paul. In truth, this so-called "doctrinal separation from Paul," in our opinion, suggests, rather than prevents, an early date.[155] The situation envisaged is pre-Pauline, Judeo-Christian, and essentially ethical. Thus the theory that the Epistle is a blast against a corrupt formalized Paul or ultra-Paulinism,[156] written *after* Paul, is improbable.

The polemic, therefore, is yet another clue to the dating of the Epistle of James. It is addressed to the Christian Jews of the Diaspora, and we suggest that here is evidence of their attitude to Christianity in the early Apostolic Age. After the fall of Jerusalem the attitude of Jewish converts loomed much smaller on the horizon of Christian evangelism than here in the Epistle of James or in Gal. 2:12f.

A clue to the understanding of the Epistle may be found in the increasing conservatism that seems to have marked the Jerusalem Church.[157] From James it appears that too many of them continued to trifle not only with the old Jewish law but with any religious law. They would understand it well enough since, as James points out, it was part of their own old law; but many of them were bent on ignoring it, as many of them had been on ignoring the old law: theirs had been, and still remained, a selfish, not a social, attitude to religion. In their basic doctrine of the *limitations* of the law for salvation, James and Paul are in complete agreement, though, like some Christian churches, they differ in their exposition of that truth. The differences in Paul's theological explanations of that fact are no proof that the Epistle of James is post-Pauline or that it does not reflect the attitude of the Jerusalem Church; and in structure there is a striking, though little recognized, affinity between their Epistles.

Thus the didactic content of the Epistle of James also suggests a date in the lifetime of James before A.D. 70, possibly (as Mayor thought[158]) before the Jerusalem Council (c. A.D. 40-50). But all sides have tended to exaggerate the significance of a silence on circumcision, which is by no means as complete as is usually imagined by those who scarcely realize what James means in ch. 2 in putting the Christian "law

155. So W. G. Kümmel, *Introduction to the New Testament* (ET 1966), p. 291; see also Ropes, p. 35.

156. G. Eichholz, *Jakobus und Paulus, Ein Beitrag zum Problem des Kanons* (1953), pp. 36ff.; R. H. Fuller, *A Critical Introduction to the New Testament* (1966), p. 153.

157. Bruce, *Peter, Stephen, James and John*, p. 98.

158. P. cxxii; also his article "Epistle of James," *Dictionary of the Bible*, ed. J. Hastings, II (1901), 543-48.

of liberty" above "the law." His admonition takes much of its force from the contemporaneous question—the freedom that Paul had difficulty in getting some of his Galatians to enjoy.

CONCLUSION

If, as we have seen, the economic data point to the conclusion that the Epistle must be dated before the fall of Jerusalem, the didactic data suggest a similar conclusion. All the evidence leads us to think that the Epistle emanated from a pious Jewish group at Jerusalem led by James the Lord's brother—a group that, linked with ordinary people of deep and simple piety, carried on the tradition of Israel. Imbued with a healthy Hebraic respect for righteousness, they could not, even while embracing the gospel, accept that gospel without continuing to reverence the Jewish law.

We are convinced, therefore, by the economic and didactic evidence that the Epistle must be dated very early, before the Jerusalem Council, perhaps even earlier (c. A.D. 40-45), making it probably the earliest literary product of the Christian church.

Section Two

"It is certainly no longer possible to assert with complete confidence that James of Jerusalem could not have written the good Greek of the epistle, since the wide currency of that language in Palestine is increasingly appreciated. . . . Yet other familiar objections still seem to hold good."

S. Laws, *The Epistle of James* (1980), p. 40

There is clearly a strong case for authenticity, but some difficulties remain.

A few may resent what they feel to be an infringement of Paul's title of pioneer of Christian literary evangelism, but most of us will be content to yield to a better claim if it can be established.

The common disparagement of the Epistle of James as not being the work of James the Lord's brother arises from three notions:

1. the substance and the form are too bad;
2. the Greek is too good to have come from a peasant of Galilee; and
3. the Epistle was late in being received into the canon.

1. We have tried to show that Luther's and modern attacks on its alleged displacement of faith from its doctrine of Christianity are completely unjustified and that the Epistle of James is entirely in agreement with Paul on the function and value of faith and works. It is a perfect proto-apostolic match, from the Jewish standpoint, of Paul's presentation of Christ to the Gentiles, without any of the (we do *not* say unnecessary or unjustifiable) elaboration and refinements that appeared very soon in the Christian religion and its theology.

Another evidential fact may be mentioned, namely, the form of the Epistle of James. Hitherto many critics have tended to deny that it has any form. But we have shown elsewhere that it has the same structure as all but the extensive and the few very short Epistles of Paul. James was a Christian evangelist and probably wrote an evangelical Epistle before Paul was even a Christian. Which is the more probable, that James modeled the form of his Epistle on the typical Pauline Epistle, which, for example, 1 Corinthians is not, or that Paul took his typical pattern from James, whom he may have revered? And if the pattern really came from some suggestion in the service of the synagogue, as it almost certainly did, who was the more likely to take it first, the elder and senior James from the Jewish synagogue to the Jewish-Christian synagogue, or Paul to his antinomian congregations?

2. It is sometimes said that James the "Galilean peasant" could not possibly have had the skill in Greek composition, literature, and thought that we find in the Epistle.[1] It is also said that "the epistle presents a test case of whether a non-literary lower-class Palestinian in the period before 70 could or would have spoken or written such good (though still limited and Semitic) Greek."[2] This point may appeal to a post-Reformation Englishman, but not to a Scotsman[3] or a Jew. The quality of the Greek is second only to that of Hebrews.[4] Its "rugged, homely simplicity" is akin to that of A. E. Housman in the preface of

1. Initially by de Wette, then by many others, e.g., Weizsäcker, McNeile, Ropes, Kümmel, and Köster. See also J. Sevenster, *Do You Know Greek?* (1968), pp. 9ff.; A. R. C. Leaney, "Greek Manuscripts from the Judean Desert." *Studies in New Testament Language and Text,* ed. J. K. Elliott (1976), pp. 283-390; G. Vermes, F. Millar, M. Black, and E. Schürer, *The History of the Jewish People in the Age of Jesus Christ,* II (1979), 74ff.; yet, see the wise caution in Sevenster, p. 80, n. 283.

2. J. A. T. Robinson, *Redating the New Testament* (1976), p. 133.

3. Beasley-Murray, p. 19; and, as R. Newton Flew pointed out in personal conversation, this is also true of the Welsh.

4. Mayor, ch. IX; Mitton, p. 227.

his *Juvenal.*[5] This ignorant fiction of Galilean illiteracy is now little more than a legacy of the "Dames Schools" in England. It may not have the ease and fluency of native Greek and it does not betray "a wide knowledge of Classical Greek,"[6] but it is superlatively good.[7]

On this point there is weight in Rendall's remark: "It is time surely to disregard the figment of Galilean illiteracy."[8] He names Philodemus, Meleager, and Theodorus, all from Galilee, and Josephus, long its administrator and one who had learned Greek, adding:

> It is not sufficiently recognized that the Jews were the most literary of all Mediterranean nations—far more than the Greeks. . . . The LXX marks the Jewish adoption of Hellenism and it rapidly became the manual of the synagogue and the whole Dispersion west of the Jordan.[9]

Galilee was studded with Greek towns,[10] Nazareth, James's hometown, being open to Greek influence.[11] Greek was taught and studied in Jerusalem[12] where many, even among the lower classes, were bilingual;[13] see, for example, the speeches of Stephen and Paul in Acts.[14]

5. *D IVNII IVVENALIS SATVRAE* "Editorvm in VSVM EDIDIT A E HOVSMAN" (1931). The first preface was written in 1905 and appears on pp. V to XXXVI. The second, dated 1931, continues on pp. XXXVII to LVII.

6. W. Patrick, p. 208.

7. H. A. A. Kennedy, "The Hellenistic Atmosphere of the Epistle of James," *Ex* 2 (1911): 38.

8. Pp. 38ff.; see also Vermes, Millar, Black, and Schürer, *The History of the Jewish People in the Age of Jesus Christ,* II, 49f.; G. Dalman, *Jesus-Jeshua* (1929), pp. 1ff.; J. Goldstein, "Jewish Acceptance and Rejection of Hellenism," in *Jewish and Christian Self-Definition,* II, ed. E. P. Sanders with A. L. Baumgarten and A. Mendelson (1981), 64ff. and esp. 67, for six suggested characteristics of Hellenism.

9. See further Robinson, *Redating the New Testament,* p. 134; also for the spread of Hellenism, Vermes, Millar, Black, and Schürer, *The History of the Jewish People in the Age of Jesus Christ,* II, 29ff.

10. S. Freyne, *Galilee: From Alexander the Great to Hadrian, 323 B.C.E. to 135 C.E.* (1980), pp. 101ff., 138ff.; G. W. Thatcher, "Galilee," *HDCG,* I (1906), 624.

11. G. A. Smith, *Historical Geography of the Holy Land* (1895), p. 433.

12. E.g., b. Soṭa 49B for rabbinic references; see also, e.g., S. Lieberman, *Greek in Jewish Palestine* (1942), pp. 23f.; T. Zahn, *Introduction to the New Testament,* I (ET 1909), 63; J. N. Sevenster, *Do You Know Greek?, passim;* A. W. Argyle, "Greek Among the Jews of Palestine in New Testament Times," *NTS* 20 (1973): 87ff.; M. Hengel, *Jews, Greeks and Barbarians* (1980), pp. 110ff.

13. E.g., Lieberman, *Greek in Jewish Palestine,* pp. 30ff.; Robinson, *Redating,* p. 133, n. 46.

14. See Acts 6:1f.; 22:2; also J. Young, "Language of Christ," *HDCG,* II (1908), 4; R. O. P. Taylor, *The Groundwork of the Gospels* (1946), pp. 94f.; J. Weiss, *The History of Primitive Christianity,* I (1937), 165ff.

Permanent,[15] not temporary,[16] Jewish "Hellenists" and residents of Jerusalem almost certainly knew Greek (and perhaps *only* Greek) better than anyone else at that time[17] and bear eloquent witness to the penetration of Hellenism into Jewish Palestinian circles.

Ignorance of Greek was not a *prima facie* probability in the status James indisputably attained as leader after the resurrection.[18] It is difficult to see how a leader like James could lead effectively without being able to speak to his constituency.[19] The "secretary hypothesis"[20] raises more problems than solutions: there is no evidence that James employed a secretary (contrast Silvanus, 1 Pet. 5:12), and if he did, how he operated. Nor is it helpful to assume that James dictated his text; to say that he expected his secretary to create the text from a few notes presumes a secretary more brilliant than the author, a most unlikely presumption.

We take the quality of the Greek as actually supporting the ascription of the Epistle to James the Lord's brother. Tasker argues quite soundly: "There would seem to be no real ground for supposing that an intelligent artisan living in Galilee in the first half of the first century could not have acquired skill in the use of the Greek language."[21] It should be remembered that James resided at Jerusalem till martyred thirty years after the resurrection, was in frequent contact with Jewish and Gentile Christians from outside, and was almost certainly bilingual,[22] often speaking and debating publicly in Greek, and so developing skill in the language. "Add to all this that James must have been a man of quite extraordinary intelligence and ability to have risen so quickly to the position he achieved. What might have been improbable

15. Acts 2:5; 14:1ff.

16. See Lk. 24:18.

17. See P. F. Esler, *Community and Gospel in Luke-Acts* (1987), pp. 136ff.; Zahn, *Introduction*, pp. 34ff.; Sevenster, *Do You Know Greek?*, pp. 16ff.; H. M. Smith, *The Epistle of James*, p. 14; C. F. D. Moule, "Once More, Who Were the Hellenists?" *ExpT* (1958-59): 100-102; J. A. Fitzmyer in *Studies in Luke-Acts*, eds. L. E. Keck and J. L. Martyn (1966), pp. 237f.; W. D. Davies, *The Gospel and the Land* (1974), p. 269; M. Hengel, *Between Jesus and Paul* (1983), pp. 2ff.; F. F. Bruce, "The Church of Jerusalem in the Acts of the Apostles," *BJRL* 67.2 (Spring 1985): 644f.

18. Including Paul's in Gal. 1:19.

19. Mitton, pp. 227ff.; Robinson, *Redating*, p. 134; Sevenster, *Do You Know Greek?*, p. 16 (with Zahn's arguments).

20. So, among others, Mussner, Kittel, Kümmel, Mitton, Beasley-Murray, and Bruce; for details, see Sevenster, *Do You Know Greek?*, pp. 10ff.

21. P. 29, cited by Mitton, p. 228; but see the doubts of, e.g., Davids, p. 11, and others.

22. See Schlatter, p. 84.

for a more ordinary person is not so improbable to one of his unusual calibre."[23]

3. Last of all, and of another nature, are the unanswerable questions why the Epistle of James disappeared so long and why, after its final emergence, it remained so long outside the canon, neglected, if not rejected.[24] These two facts may not be due to the same causes; for example, its apparent lack of theological content may be what made it seem unworthy of canonical dignity. Incidentally, it must not be overlooked that inasmuch as the early church *was* sensitive to date and authorship, in the final analysis the very doubts about James's canonicity pointed in its favor. "The mere fact," notes Brooks, "that the Church critically examined James at the point of apostolicity and antiquity and then approved it speaks well for its authenticity."[25] Christianity soon fell under Pauline and Gentile philosophical influence, and whereas Paul's theological Epistles won ready acceptance, James's practical Epistle could not.[26] Its original handicap may be that it appealed, if at all, only to Jewish Christians, or that it lost all its prestige and authority after the fall of Jerusalem and the decisive rupture between Judaism and Christianity.

We can easily understand why Christianity, divorced from Jewry, took little and late interest in the Epistle of James, especially since the Epistle is, more than any similar NT work, keyed to the expectation of an imminent, almost immediate, "apocalypse," that is, an end of the present age. Moreover, if we remember the disparagement that has attended the Epistle of James *after* it was received into the canon, it is not so hard to see why it was so late in being admitted to that canon. This, however, does not explain satisfactorily why both Josephus and Hegesippus preserve traditions of James and why he appears to have been highly honored by the Ebionites, who, however, show no knowledge of this or any other writing by him. We should, therefore, offer some explanation of this phenomenon.

What made a book canonical? The impetus to canonicity started in the local congregation, without its having any idea of forming a canon and, at first, a New Testament. Each congregation would cherish, for example, its letter from Paul, and these would later be collected and organized by the church. B. H. Streeter once suggested that each of the

23. Mitton, p. 228.

24. See pp. 147ff., 165f. for a discussion of the Epistle's canonical adventures.

25. J. A. Brooks, "The Place of James in the New Testament Canon," *SWJT* 12.1 (1969): 53.

26. On this, see H. F. D. Sparks, *The Formation of the New Testament* (1952), p. 129.

four Gospels was preserved and subsequently canonized through the support of an influential church.[27] The history of the conservation and canonization of the Epistle of James may well have followed along these lines. In the Western Church the Epistle of James is first mentioned by Hilary of Poitiers (c. 366). But Mayor points out: "While the Churches of Rome and Carthage long doubted the canonicity of the Epistle of St. James, it was acknowledged from a very early period by the Churches of Jerusalem and (probably) of Syria."[28] The reason probably was that the Epistle was held to be connected with James, the first leader of the Jerusalem Church, and was therefore regarded as apostolic and authoritative in the Jewish world. Such a link seems to be at least suggested in the opening allusion to "James."

Increasingly we have become convinced that this Epistle is intimately associated with James the Lord's brother, whose death by martyrdom may well have provided the initial stimulus toward its preservation. The most logical reason for the name "James" in 1:1 is that the one who composed, or was vitally connected with, the document was *the* James of Jerusalem. If the document had been forged, we should expect a more sophisticated effort to stress his authority.[29]

We note the emphasis laid by Schmithals on the missionary activities of the Lord's brothers, including, we must surely assume, James himself, although this may be disputed.[30] Furthermore, we have already mentioned the earliest spread of the gospel, not from Jerusalem but from the Galileans, from whom the Christians got their first name, and, as Paul's persecution showed, not least noticeably in the region of Damascus. Now it is *possible* that parts of James's speeches in his evangelical work were remembered by some of his hearers and orally transmitted to their descendants, and that, say, about A.D. 80-130, a fine Greek scholar, carefully preserving the proto-apostolic spirit and carefully avoiding any

27. *The Four Gospels* (1925), pp. 500ff. For other criteria of canonicity, both external and internal, e.g., apostolicity, catholicity, orthodoxy, and established usage, see B. M. Metzger, *The Canon of the New Testament* (1987), pp. 75ff., 252ff.; H. Y. Gamble, *The New Testament Canon* (1985), pp. 67ff.; also J. A. Sanders, *Canon and Community* (1984), pp. 33ff.

28. P. li.

29. On the vexed problem of pseudonymity, see further the previous discussion, pp. 28ff. *The Pseudo-Clementine Homilies* and later apocryphal books vie in exalting James at the expense of the other apostles. See S. Brown, *James: A Religio-Historical Study of the Relations between Jewish, Gnostic, and Catholic Christianity in the Early Period through an Investigation of the Traditions about James the Lord's Brother* (1972).

30. See, e.g., F. F. Bruce, *Peter, Stephen, James and John* (1979), p. 98; also contrast, e.g., F. V. Filson, *Pioneers of the Primitive Church* (1940), pp. 174ff.; R. P. Martin, *New Testament Foundations*, II (1978), 359.

doctrinal anachronisms, fashioned these scattered items into the Epistle's present magnificent structure, Greek.[31] But even if it is possible, such a theory is hardly plausible, being born of the same school that accepted Luther's tragic misrepresentation of both the doctrinal and literary ("What a chaos") quality of the Epistle of James, and that almost idolized Paul while paying scant heed or respect to James.

Further, no historical facts support that theory, whereas some do argue against it. The long-prevalent refusal to take James of the Epistle of James at all seriously springs partly from a quite false opinion active through many centuries that James is not at one with Paul on the importance of faith. Some, notably S. G. F. Brandon, have argued (wrongly, we believe) that a much more potent animus against James and the Epistle may have been started and perpetuated by NT Scripture itself, suggesting, in turn, that the true history of the first relations of the Jews to Christianity contained in Acts needs fresh evaluation.

According to Brandon, there are two reasons why the story of Acts achieved credibility: (1) there is no rival account; and (2) it is so vivid and dramatic.[32] The aim, he says, was to propagate, not Christianity as such, but a partisan account of the beginnings of the Christian church, particularly by a biased handling of James the Lord's brother. That James was the leader among the Christians at Jerusalem is witnessed by Paul (Gal. 1:19; 2:9; see also 1 Cor. 15:7), but never by Acts treating the same period. Acts suddenly introduces a James of unique status in the Jerusalem Church, but he is not identified as a brother of Jesus (Acts 12:17). He is obviously not the apostle James, son of Zebedee, whose execution is already recorded in Acts 12:2. Equally discrediting to Acts is the similar mention of James without further identification (15:4ff.), giving his decision against circumcision for Gentiles after Peter, Paul, and Barnabas had spoken. In his third and last appearance in Acts (21:18), James is clearly the head of the Jerusalem Church, but Acts says nothing about the circumstances of this appointment or about any of James's antecedents or relationships that might explain it. This silence, Brandon says, can only be deliberate.

To be sure, it could be argued that Acts wished to suppress any record of a dynastic principle, a sort of caliphate, that appeared in some sense or form in the first days of the Christian movement.[33] But such an

31. On the "secretary hypothesis," see, e.g., Beasley-Murray, p. 19; also above, n. 20.

32. "The Death of James the Just: A New Interpretation," in *Studies in Mysticism and Religion*. Festschrift for G. Scholem (1967), pp. 57-69.

33. S. G. F. Brandon, *Jesus and the Zealots* (1967), pp. 274-76; see also K. L. Carroll, "The Place of James in the Early Church," *BJRL* 44 (1961): 49ff.

objection, on principle, cannot explain why Acts gives only these three brief cryptic references to James. The reason, Brandon thinks, is possibly twofold: that probably James was personally objectionable to the author of Acts, and that certainly when he wrote late in the first century for Gentiles, the disappearance of the Jerusalem Church in the Jewish catastrophe of A.D. 70 gave the new, dominant Gentile Christian church the incentive and opportunity to hide this Jewish bishop and his Jewish church, so far as was possible, from the memory of their religion. The extent of its silences in its presentation of James and the emphasis of its anti-Jewish polemic make it appear "that James represented an aspect of the original Christian movement in Judaea which the author of Acts preferred not to record."[34]

Brandon goes on to doubt (without taking the responsibility of denial) whether the Council of Jerusalem ever took place, and, if it did, whether James sided with Paul in the dispute and decided against requiring circumcision for Gentiles: "However that may be, when Paul visited Jerusalem, for what proved to be the last time, James very astutely demanded that Paul should prove his Jewish orthodoxy by participating in the ritual discharge of the Nazirite vow undertaken by four members of the *Urgemeinde*. Paul was placed, designedly so, in a dilemma, the outcome of which proved fatal to his mission. Accordingly, despite the obvious intention of Acts to present an idealized picture of the beginnings of Christianity, it is evident that James, as the leader of the Jerusalem Church, was closely identified with the maintenance of Jewish orthodoxy and the ritual practice of the Temple, and as such, he was hostile to Paul."[35]

Personally, I cannot believe that James was hostile to Paul. I cannot believe that James designedly put Paul into a dilemma (over the Nazirites' vow): I think it was just a sop to placate the non-Christian Jews of Jerusalem, exactly as Paul (Acts 23:5-6) quotes the law, apologetically, against himself—even Paul's "antinomianism" is tempered by expediency. Accepting the Epistle of James as written by James, I take its second chapter as evidence that James had no more than conformity to give to the law; his enthusiasm was solely for the Christian law of love and liberty.

Our other sources on James are twofold and mutually contradictory, agreeing only on his high repute in Jerusalem. Our concern here is to establish the reason for his execution. The earlier account is that of Josephus (*Ant.* 20.197-203), who states that on the death of Festus

34. Brandon, *art. cit.*, in *Studies in Mysticism and Religion*, p. 61.
35. Ibid., p. 60.

in 62 and before his successor as Procurator arrived in Judea, Ananus, who had recently become high priest, after legal process executed James "the brother of Jesus called Christ" *(tou legomenou Christou)*[36] and some others by stoning for offenses against the Torah *(paranomēsantōn katēgorian),* although the exact nature of the infraction is obscure. It may be that James's attitude in the Trophimus incident would savor of treason in the eyes of strict orthodox Jews, giving Ananus the adequate legal pretext he wanted,[37] or it may be that if, as Ananus probably thought, James's sympathies appeared to be with the Zealots, this would give him another motive, leading him to believe that he could act with impunity since Rome would surely understand and protect him.[38]

Whatever the charge, James was found guilty and put to death by stoning. Those who were most fair-minded *(epieikestatoi)* and most diligent in respect to the Torah *(tous nomous)* secretly petitioned (Herod) Agrippa II, who had appointed Ananus high priest, to restrain him from any more such outrages, and some went to meet the new Procurator, L. Lucceius Albinus, to protest that the session of the Sanhedrin that condemned James had been invalidly convened without the Procurator's consent. As a result Ananus was severely rebuked by Albinus and was deposed from the high priesthood by Agrippa II.

The consequences of James's death were swift and cataclysmic: Josephus, cited by Origen, thought that the fall of Jerusalem was a direct consequence of the death of James the Just, "who was a brother of Jesus who was called Christ, since the Jews killed him who was a very righteous man."[39] Vespasian immediately laid siege to Jerusa-

36. Sometimes translated "so-called" or "alleged," thus implying doubt. Here we take *legomenos* at face value to mean what it says, "called." See G. Vermes, F. Millar, and E. Schürer, *The History of the Jewish People in the Age of Jesus Christ,* I, *Excursus II—Josephus on Jesus and James* (1973), 430f.

37. Acts 21:27-29. See also R. P. Martin, "The Life-Setting of the Epistle of James in the Light of Jewish History," in *Biblical and Near Eastern Studies: Essays in Honor of William Sanford LaSor,* ed. G. A. Tuttle (1978), pp. 98, 101 n. 8. For the intriguing possibility that James's execution was opposed by the Pharisees, see E. P. Sanders, *Jesus and Judaism* (1985), p. 404, n. 55.

38. See F. F. Bruce, *New Testament History* (1971), p. 354, n. 3; G. H. Stevenson and A. Momigliano, ch. 25, "Rebellion Within the Empire," *Cambridge Ancient History,* X (1963), 854.

39. *Against Celsus* 2.13 (Migne, *PG,* XI, 824). Origen's reference to Josephus is puzzling since Josephus himself does not expressly link the fall of Jerusalem with James's death. It has been suggested that through lapse of memory he may have written "Josephus" by mistake for "Hegesippus." See Eusebius, *Hist. Eccl.* 2.23.11-18. For this suggestion and discussion, see further Vermes, Millar, and Schürer, *The History of the Jewish People in the Age of Jesus Christ,* I, 430,

lem,[40] and with its fall in A.D. 70 the Jerusalem Christians fled to the obscurity of Pella.[41]

This reference to Jesus implies some previous reference to him, but *Ant.* 18 has none, and so doubt has been cast on the text there and consequently also on the present passage in *Ant.* 20. Brandon conjectures that in 18 Josephus described Jesus as a political messianic pretender *(goēs)* so offensively that some substituted the present text, probably toward A.D. 300. On this conjecture, Brandon proceeds to guess what view Josephus would have given of James if he had not confined himself to the reserved and neutral account extant in *Ant.* 20. His sympathies at least appear to be with James and the party whose protests, and their effect, are there recorded.

Brandon quotes Josephus, *War* 4.318-25, describing Ananus's death at the hands of the Zealots as depriving the Jews of "the leader of their salvation" *(hēgemona tēs idias sōtērias)*, since otherwise he would have been able to lead the nation back to its allegiance to Rome and so have prevented the catastrophe of A.D. 70. Brandon also calls the account given by Josephus of the protests of those who objected to Ananus and the other diligent cherishers of the Torah "vague descriptions," and he attributes this alleged vagueness to Josephus's sympathy for Ananus.

Brandon's theory seems a little strange. On the previous page he remarks that the issue of need for the Procurator's authority for convoking the Sanhedrin has been much debated;[42] if Josephus's sympathies here were with Ananus in the matter of the death of James, he would scarcely have failed to give some hint that the technical point was disputed. But Brandon himself candidly says, "His next statement, however, suggests that, *whatever these charges were, they were unfounded*" (my italics).[43] Incidentally, we beg leave to repeat here our suggestion that the word Brandon translates "the most fairminded *(epieikestatoi)* of the citizens" really means, as often elsewhere, "the most righteous"; and at this mention of the Torah *(tous nomous)* we think that Josephus was aware of the not infrequent significance of the

---

n. 1 and our remarks with rebuttal, which immediately follow, p. 44 For an analysis of the contradictory data, see G. W. H. Lampe, "A.D. 70 in Christian Reflection," *Jesus and the Politics of His Day,* eds. E. Bammel and C. F. D. Moule (1984), pp. 167ff.; R. M. Grant, "Eusebius, Josephus and the Fate of the Jews," SBL 1979 Seminar Papers, II, 73ff.

40. Eusebius, *Hist. Eccl.* 2.23.18, quoting Hegesippus. See the previous note.

41. See further p. 193, n. 67.

42. *Art. cit.*, in *Studies in Mysticism and Religion,* p. 62, n. 19.

43. Ibid., p. 6.

adjective[44] implying a righteousness or uprightness in *spirit* and not confined to formal keeping of the letter of the law, a distinction we have already tried to do our best to clarify.

Origen, commenting on the death of James, says that Josephus, while acknowledging the righteousness of James, refused to accept Jesus as the Messiah. He also asserts that Josephus recognized the fall of Jerusalem in A.D. 70 as divine punishment for killing the righteous James. But though, as we have just seen, the extant text of Josephus in the passage above could reasonably be interpreted as testifying to the innocence of James, it contains no indication that Josephus thus connected the death of James with the fall of Jerusalem. Hegesippus does so, but Origen was not so stupid as to confuse him with Josephus.

Now our extant text (much disputed) of Josephus does *not* deny the Messiahship of Jesus, and it has been conjectured that Origen's complaint, mentioned above, induced some Christian scribe to delete the original text with the denial in Josephus and substitute the text we now have. In that case, why did he not also insert in Josephus's mention of the death of James something explaining the fall of Jerusalem as the result of that death?

Brandon offers an answer that, he claims, "could elucidate other problems which the present version of Josephus' account of the death of James raises."[45] He conjectures that the original text of Josephus actually did contain something so connecting the fall of Jerusalem with the death of James, something later cut out by a Christian editor. Why did a Christian editor do that? For a reliable answer, we should need to know exactly what Josephus originally wrote. "This knowledge is unfortunately lacking to us"; all he says we know for certain is that Origen's text of Josephus for this passage differed from what we now have. This is where Brandon remarks that the extant text of Josephus is vague about the charges against James and the identity of those who protested against Ananus's action: Brandon conjectures that the original text gave both the reasons for Ananus's action and the identity of his opponents.

Brandon thinks that Josephus was bent on showing that the calamitous Jewish revolt against Rome was the work of extremists, in particular the Zealots, and that their sedition was opposed by the priestly magnates, headed by Ananus. From about A.D. 59 there was a grave divergence between the higher Jewish clergy, who for the sake of their power and wealth looked to Rome, and the lower clergy, the ordinary priests, and Levites *(clerus minor)*,[46] who supported or at least had much

44. See Liddell and Scott, s.v.
45. *Art. cit.*, in *Studies in Mysticism and Religion*, p. 65.
46. See Jeremias, *Jerusalem in the Time of Jesus*, pp. 145ff., 98, 108.

sympathy for the Zealots. After some rebellious violence by these lower clergy, the high priests deprived them of their tithes, their only source of income. The refusal of the lower clergy to do the daily temple sacrifice for the emperor and the Roman people (A.D. 66) sparked the revolt, and in the ensuing conflict they were effectively reinforced by the Zealots; when the Zealots won control of the city and the temple, a new high priest was elected by the ancient custom of drawing lots, not by Roman or Herodian appointment. In the fighting Ananus perished.

As between the social and moral interests represented by the two sides, the NT leaves no doubt where Christian sympathies lay. Nevertheless, they followed the teaching of Jesus, "render unto Caesar. . . ." There is no ground for supposing that Jesus or James ever advocated or condoned political revolt or bloodshed. Yet, just as the Romanist party made Jesus a scapegoat for popular Jewish animosity against the Romans and the power and greed of the higher clergy, so it is possible and even probable that Ananus welcomed the opportunity of the procuratorial interregnum to destroy the successor of Jesus in the leadership of what he considered a pestilential sect, which went on proclaiming its firm belief in the imminent return of the same Jesus.

According to Hegesippus, James's influence was so great that the Jewish leaders were put in fear, because the whole people *(pas ho laos)* were expecting Jesus to come as the Messiah;[47] the Jewish leaders, therefore, in the hope that James would help them to quiet the people and persuade them not to err about Jesus, proceed publicly to interrogate James about Jesus.[48] "When he proclaims his belief in the imminence of the parousia of Jesus, and the crowd enthusiastically greet his attestation with the political salutation, 'Hosanna to the Son of David,' the Jewish leaders hurl him down from the battlement of the Temple and he is beaten to death where he fell: and thus he suffered martyrdom."[49]

"What kernel of fact may lie behind this tale cannot be discerned."[50] However, it is at least significant that the issue turns on James's alleged public attestation of his belief in the imminence of the parousia, and that the Jewish authorities were prompted to their alleged action by popular excitement of a messianic character centered on Jesus.

47. Eusebius, *Hist. Eccl.* 2.23.10.

48. Ibid., 11.

49. Ibid., 18.

50. *Art. cit.*, in *Studies in Mysticism and Religion*, p. 69. For further thoughts on the (in)credibility of Hegesippus, see Eusebius Pamphili, *Ecclesiastical History*, tr. R. J. Deferrari, "The Fathers of the Church," gen. ed. R. J. Deferrari, I (1953), 126; also later in our discussion, p. 221, n. 74.

Josephus likewise tells of mounting politico-religious tension and messianic expectancy in the period immediately preceding the revolt of A.D. 66. Thus in the fantasy of Hegesippus, there may not impossibly be a grain of historical truth in the messianic background in which Ananus's action against James is set.

I personally find it extremely hard to believe that the author of Acts and his contemporary Gentile Christians so desperately desired to eclipse all these and similar facts simply for fear that the Roman authorities and the Roman and Greek world in general might think Christianity was once infected and was still infected with the sedition for which they *remembered,* and with which they associated, the Jews. Nothing could hide, and Christians have never tried to hide, the fact that their Jesus was executed by the Romans for sedition.

We suggest that for the Jews, early Christians often had an animosity that went deeper than politics: we think it may have been predominantly racial and, to a certain extent, sectarian (as between Jewish and Gentile Christian). The non-Christian Jews in Palestine were evidently willing to live on terms with Christian Jews. The relations between them were delicate, as when Paul thought that fear of the non-Christian Jews there might make the Christian Jews reject Paul's offering (Rom. 15:31), lest, if they accepted, they might be identified with his "antinomianism."

Nor can we believe that Luke "pretends" or deliberately distorts his sources; in fact, Luke was very well informed (see Lk. 1:1-4). He does insist, moreover, that the new movement was launched by Galileans (Acts 2:7), who nevertheless made Jerusalem their base. And it was in the Jerusalem Church that James exercised his authority, Galilean though he was. Every time, too, that James is mentioned in Acts, he is a leading figure in the church.[51] If he is not explicitly said to be one of the Lord's brothers, his inclusion among them in Acts 1:14 is implied. There is no reason why Luke should feel hostile to James unless (as some think)[52] James and his fellow elders deliberately decoyed Paul into a snare in Acts 21:23f.

If it is true that in Acts James seems to be brusquely introduced, sometimes in the briefest and most tantalizing way, this is not because Luke is necessarily embarrassed or disenchanted with the Lord's brother or the Jerusalem community. This same argument could well apply to Peter, who suddenly disappears from the scene, as well as some

51. See Bruce, *Peter, Stephen, James and John,* pp. 86ff.

52. Brandon, *art. cit.,* p. 69. This view is discussed and refuted by Bruce, *Peter, Stephen, James and John,* pp. 108f.

of the other apostles who are not mentioned at all. Nor in the case of James do we attribute to Luke any sinister ulterior motive or subtle theological bias. Writing as a Gentile to Gentiles, he is interested in the Jerusalem Church only as it relates to the wider story of the church's mission to the Gentiles and to the whole world. So he is limited not only by space but also by this overriding purpose, which does not allow him to divert his readers' attention to James. Since Luke must focus his attention on Paul and his mission to the Gentiles, he therefore deliberately downplays the role of James and the Jerusalem Church.[53]

Between Christian Jew and non-Christian Jew, unless the Christian Jew, like Paul, *apparently* preached downright antinomianism, the bond of race and, to some extent, religion remained strong, stronger than between Christian Jew and Christian Gentile; and between non-Christian Jew and Christian Gentile, the existing gap was widened, if possible, by the latter's religion. Not many of the non-Christian Jewish magnates seem to have been like Gamaliel (Acts 5:34-39; contrast vv. 17, 18, and 40); and in the next chapter (6:1ff.) the attitude of the Christian Jews to the Christian *Hellenistai* is indisputably arrogant. It was not just a matter of serving tables of the poor of the Christian *Hellenistai* (with latent fear, perhaps, of the question raised in Acts 11:3ff.); the seven deacons were evangelists (see v. 8, and the whole story of Stephen), and the contemptuous or at least tactless granting of permission for their institution is the first sectarian cleavage to afflict the Christian church. The persecution of the Gentile Christians at Jerusalem was bound to strengthen any already active racial animosity in its victims. We suggest, therefore, that the eclipse of James and his Jewish Christian evangelism and his Jewish Christian church is not really due to thought of the Jewish revolt against Rome or fear of being tainted with the odor of Jewish sedition, but to the age-old animosity of Gentile against Jew, here specifically embittered by the arrogance of the Jewish Christians to their Gentile fellow-Christians, and the attitude of the Christian Jews that had split the Christian church and left Stephen, without their support, to his death.

Here, in short, is the key to our so-called "riddle of the Epistle of James": Jewish Christianity crashed with the crash of Jerusalem and of the Jewish state and nation (that slight exaggeration may even serve the truth), and the Gentile Christianity that survived and prospered would know little of the Epistle of James and probably care less for it or for the Jews. The Gentile Christian church seems to have retained no great love or loving memory for the Jewish nation or the Jewish Christian

53. See R. P. Martin, *art. cit.*, in *Biblical and Near Eastern Studies*, p. 98.

church; and in due course its Christian public took no care to cherish the Epistle of James, which, with its address to the Jews of the Diaspora, is a witness to the early evangelization of the Jews outside Palestine. Paul did not long survive A.D. 62, and with the death of James the original link between Judaism and Christianity ended.

Though in cast of mind James was thoroughly Jewish (if less Hellenic than Paul), that was not at all the reason for the eclipse of the Epistle of James and the reign of Paul's Epistles in the Christian church. As we have said, the reason for the eclipse of the Epistle of James was the crash of Jewish Christianity along with the Jews themselves and their city and temple and the indifference or hatred of even Christian Gentiles in the following centuries.

Why did this Epistle come to be almost lost to Christianity? A prior and more important question, however, ought to be asked: why was the Epistle eventually included? To this the short answer is: *It proved its value in the life of the church.* "It is not the mere fact that James began to be used," observes Brooks, "but the significance of that fact which is most important. The book made its own way because it proved to have spiritual value. It met definite needs in the lives of individual Christians and their Churches."[54] Modern Christians, including even those most vigorous advocates of "salvation by faith alone," now accept the book without demur, mainly for the same reason: it is highly "multivalent,"[55] that is, capable of saying different things to different people at different times, and has stood the test of time. But we can surmise why James did not easily get into the canon. It is doubtful that the neglect was entirely accidental or that the letter was actually forgotten by its recipients; yet the manuscript may have lain unnoticed and uncopied for a number of years, especially if the recipients were a relatively small group of Christians, especially Jewish Christians.

We must remember the really fundamental difference between the two categories of Jewish worshippers, one believing both the traditional Judaism and the new Christianity with its Christ and the other stoutly clinging to the old Judaism but vehemently abhorring the new Christianity and its Christ. This is significant especially if it is true (as we may argue[56]) that James is writing (as a rabbi, in fact, in our view) to his own people, the *Jews* (1:1), in the plain sense of the word, who are Christians, or may be toying with the idea of Christianity, or at least are in need of his message.

54. *Art. cit., SWJT* 12.1 (1969): 51; Metzger, *The Canon of the New Testament,* p. 253.

55. On this, see Gamble, *The New Testament Canon,* p. 22.

56. For our discussion of this, see pp. 18, 52, 110ff., 468ff.

The Epistle was penned in the days when Christianity and synagogue were not yet divorced, when Jerusalem was still as Jesus knew it and was, further, still the center of Christianity as a religion and as an organization (see Gal. 2:1-10). During the (sadly brief) survival together of these two categories, finally shattered by the fall of Jerusalem in or about A.D. 70, Jewish Christianity succeeded in preserving and propagating Christian doctrine, the Epistle of James, and (for some time at least) the personal ministry of James. But in the calamities about A.D. 70 Jewish Christianity and Jewish Christian writings had little or no "public" interested in preserving them, as did the "public" that was not so completely lacking among the Gentile Christians.

The lack of exposition of "theology," especially Christology, would certainly tend to lower the Epistle's value, at least in the eyes of some.[57] Peter's sermon in Acts 10:34-42 might have pleased James, but some of the followers of Paul (but not Paul himself) would find it sadly inadequate. Indeed, even now many NT scholars are very reluctant to believe that the Epistle of James is in harmony with Paul and the truth. Christianity soon became "Paulinized" and "Gentilized" and "theologized" and had little time for a little practical Jewish-Christian book, reflecting perhaps an odd type of Galilean Christianity,[58] written by James the Lord's brother (and even this identity was questioned)—not that the Epistle of James is at odds with Paul, or that the early church ever so regarded it. Indeed, we may concur that "if the book was known at all, the mere fact it was ignored is an indication that it did not provoke controversy of any kind."[59] The Epistle of James tacitly implies, or just tacitly requires, acceptance of much that Paul feels it necessary to *expound,* and so Paul endears himself to the theologian, the Gentile theologian, as the Epistle of James never could.

Our reading of the New Testament clearly shows that only one James in the early church was in a position of authority corresponding to that which is indicated in this Epistle, namely, James, the apostle and brother of Jesus. He rose to unquestioned leadership in the Jerusalem Church, and, as his title "Protector of the people and Righteousness"[60]

57. See A. F. J. Klijn, *An Introduction to the New Testament* (1967), p. 150.

58. See, e.g., Elliott-Binns, *Galilean Christianity,* pp. 43ff.

59. Brooks, *art. cit., SWJT* 12.1 (1969): 52.

60. Eusebius, *Hist. Eccl.* 2.23.7. For a discussion of the difficult "Oblias," meaning "Protection," "Pillar," or "Bulwark" with literature, interpretation, and possible emendations, see, among others, Dibelius, pp. 15f., nn. 36, 37; Mussner, p. 3, nn. 5, 6; Ropes, pp. 64f.; R. H. Eisenman, *James the Just in the Habakkuk Pesher* (1986), pp. 10, 43, 66; *Maccabees, Zadokites, Christians and Qumran* (1983), pp. xv, 48, 52, 74 with Qumran parallels, "Shield," "Fortress"; also

implies, was its most formidable defender, especially among the poor. With his death, however, that defense disappeared, and disaster soon ensued.

The martyrdom of James almost certainly destroyed Jewish Christianity to all intents and purposes[61] and, soon afterward, the fall of Jerusalem led to the devastation of Palestine. Even between these two incidents the non-Christian Jews would almost certainly try to see to the destruction of any copies of the Epistle of James found in Palestine or its neighborhood. Obviously the Epistle of James was suppressed for the same reason that James was killed,[62] and was spurned by the Jews as the work of a Christian martyr.[63] At any rate it is clear that, compared with the Pauline epistles, abnormal difficulties attended the survival of copies of the Epistle of James, and it is no surprise that our first sure contact with it is through Origen in Alexandria.

After the final fall of Jerusalem and the other developments of Christianity, we can easily understand why Christianity, divorced from Jewry, took little interest in the Epistle of James, especially since this Epistle is, more than any similar NT work, keyed to an expectation of an imminent, almost immediate end of the present age. In these circumstances the Epistle of James was bound to "go scarce" after the original tincture of Jewish Christians disappeared (after A.D. 70) from their short-lived mixed teaming in daily life with the non-Christian, intransigent, unblended, Mosaic devotees of Judaism and only Judaism. We do *not* think it at all strange that for a few centuries a few copies of the Epistle of James turned up, but *only* in odd corners of the Christian world. What is strange—and truly gratifying—is that the Epistle of James, despite all doubts and questionings, was eventually welcomed into the canon.

It is, we think, indisputable that no nation has excelled the Jews in cherishing, collectively and individually, grateful memories of their friends and benefactors, especially among their own people. We venture to conjecture with some confidence that (whatever his exact relationship in the Holy Family) James would share a lively and grateful

---

M. Hengel, "Jakobus der Herrenbruder—der erste 'Papst'?" in *Glaube und Eschatologie: Festschrift für Werner Georg Kümmel zum 80. Geburtstag* (1985), p. 78, n. 28.

61. For what constituted "Jewish Christianity" after A.D. 70, see J. Daniélou, *A History of Early Christian Doctrine Before the Council of Nicaea*, Vol. I: *The Theology of Jewish Christianity*, tr. and ed. J. A. Baker (1964), 7ff.; Laws, pp. 36f.; with our previous discussion, pp. 16f.

62. See W. Schmithals, *Paul and James* (ET 1965), p. 107.

63. See J. H. Moulton, "James," *Peake's Commentary* (1931), p. 903.

memory of the friends of the sojourn in Egypt,[64] and we think that the Galileans who carried Christianity into Syria did not stop at that, but, not necessarily in person but with the same zeal they had shown in Syria, organized the promotion of the gospel in Egypt no less than elsewhere in the Diaspora. We also venture to conjecture that copies of the Epistle of James did not fail to reach Alexandria, which, though in the Diaspora, was, as the last footnote indicates, almost a little Jerusalem.

After the martyrdom of James, the propagation and existence of Jewish Christianity soon came to an end, but it is not historically impossible or even canonically improbable that some copies of the Epistle of James survived in Egypt and eventually came to the knowledge of Origen in Alexandria.[65] Initially accepted in Egypt and there preserved as the authoritative word of the head of the church at Jerusalem and cherished during his lifetime and no less after his martyrdom, his epistle was perhaps employed as a *vade mecum* by catechists and evangelists.[66] In Syria, too, the words of James would be reverenced, quoted (as in the early *Epistles to the Virgins*), and carefully preserved in the archives of that church.[67] Though theoretically available to Christendom, in reality its circulation was extremely narrow, confined to a tiny segment of the surviving Jewish Christian church. With its passage to Egypt and discovery by Origen, it gained a new lease of life: papyrus fragments like P[20] point to its wider circulation. Incidentally, we have wondered whether it would be possible to extend Origen's argument even further than he seems to have cared to push it. He and other good judges after him were convinced that the Epistle was of outstanding quality, beyond doubt (as they thought) worthy to be called "apostolic."

Who else could have written this epistle? One of his contemporaries? A later master of Greek style and Hebrew religion, and Christianity? Even less likely. The argument from silence might be pressed as strongly for James's authorship as it has been pressed against it. Indeed, it is psychologically possible that he may have deliberately chosen *not* to mention that he was the Lord's brother.[68] (A strong advocate might

64. See the important note in E. H. Plumptre, "A Discussion of the General Epistle of St. James," CBSC (1909), p. 64.

65. See Davids, p. 7, n. 23.

66. On the collection of the Epistles of Ignatius, see K. Lake, *The Apostolic Fathers*, I (1914), 280. Some of James's speeches and letters may have been taken by Jewish Christians to Pella after the fall of Jerusalem, but for some unknown reason were not preserved. See Eusebius, *Hist. Eccl.* 3.5.3; Brandon, *Jesus and the Zealots*, pp. 208-17, 306-08; J. L. Teicher, "The Damascus Fragment and the Origin of the Damascus Sect," *Journal of Jewish Studies* 2.3 (1931).

67. Ropes, p. 94.

68. See G. E. Ladd, *A Theology of the New Testament* (1974), p. 589.

well say that silence is the *only* argument against saying our James wrote the Epistle of James.) But after the end of Jewish Christianity, on the martyrdom of James and the fall of Jerusalem, what reason had anyone, above all a fine Greek scholar, for taking, as some believe, unconnected elements of the evangelism of Jewish Christianity, or even a perfect Aramaic Jewish Christian Epistle—not to mention a pre-Christian Testament of Jacob, combining both Judaism and Christianity in ch. 2, redacting and turning it into such excellent—or indeed any—Greek, under the name of "James"?

CONCLUSION

We can see no alternative but to accept James as the author of the Epistle of James and as a master of Greek. The notion that he could not possibly have had such a knowledge of Greek is merely part of the delusion that he was neither a good Christian nor a good partner with Paul, not skilled in any language or culture. Even if James was not, as we believe he was, a rabbi or at least a teacher, there is neither evidence nor presumption that he was not a master of Greek; witness, for example, the letter in Acts 15:23ff.

We believe that the Epistle of James is by a Christian Jew like James, written for Christian Jews, of a date that would fit in with James, in a very good style that has perceptible affinities with the literary style and personal character of James in his speech to that Council and the Council's letter, which we think he wrote, thoroughly in keeping with his office as "Bishop of Jerusalem" and with the typical structure of the Epistle as very often followed by Paul for the early Christian church. To the question why this Epistle was so long in being received into the canon, there is a simple answer: "When in doubt, do nothing."

2. Purpose

"The Epistle is a masterpiece of virile and devout simplicity. . . . The mind of the author is oriented mainly towards the practical. . . . The Christian tradition which it inherits, undoubtedly well-nurtured on the profound truth of the primitive Gospel teaching, has become detached from the framework of the life of Jesus and condensed into a 'wisdom from above,' which is stimulated by the hope of the Second Coming and which has to affirm itself in deeds in a sanctified life, worthy in every respect of the 'honorable name' it claims."

Jacques Marty, *L'Épître de Jacques* (1935), pp. 270f.

Unlike most of the NT epistles, the Epistle of James was written for a considerable number and variety of congregations. The style and language indicate that the whole of the Epistle is by one man, but the exceptionally self-contained detachability of the second half, highlighted in 3:1 and 5:19f., gives something unique to the structure of the Epistle. In this connection the summary *(Table 1)* on page 54 may be helpful.

Since we are emphasizing the difference between the two halves of the Epistle, we wish to point out immediately the element of rural thought on which, like the rest of the Bible, the whole of the Epistle of James is founded: James, like the OT prophets, is at home with nature. We need not catalogue the evidence of the first part of the Epistle. The following words from ch. 3 of the second part speak for themselves: v. 2, bridle; 3, bits, horses; 4, ships, fierce winds, small helm; 5, a little member; 5, 6, a fire; 7, tamed; 8, deadly poison, fountain; 12, fig, olive, vine; 18, fruit.

Suppose, as is entirely possible, that James, as president of the Jerusalem Council, for his own reasons had to write an encyclical to fit two (not necessarily conjunct) periods and two different types of audience. What would he do?

We suggest that possibly, or even probably, he might compose a two-part pastoral missive for "those of the Jewish Dispersion." The first half would be like that of the Epistle of James, intelligently effective in itself and partly critical but not so in the extreme; but if he wished to aim a diatribe at the shocking defects and devices of one of those groups, he would put it into the second half, and, after the manner of a wise pastor—and here we note the parallel with 1 Peter[1]—would refrain from prescribing that the circular be read aloud in full to each of the synagogues in the Dispersion.

TABLE 1

SUMMARY OF THE EPISTLE OF JAMES

I.	1.	*Signature*
	2.	*Trials can teach us patience.*
	5.	*Wisdom can be got by prayer.*
	9.	*Lowly, rejoice in being exalted in Christianity; rich,* per contra.
	12.	*Welcome trials, for prospect of reward; temptation comes not from God but from human lust.*
	16.	*God is the sole source of good, and only of good; the Christian is the firstfruit of his creation.*
	19.	*Be swift to hear, slow to speech and to wrath; practice meekness.*
	22.	Do *God's word; don't just let it in at one ear and out at the other.*
	26.	*An unbridled tongue makes our Christianity a sham; true Christianity is Christian love and Christian pureness of life.*
II.	1.	*No respect of persons, please, in disparagement of God's poor and God's law.*
	10.	*To break one of his laws is to break all.*
	12.	*In God's law, a law of liberty, mercy is paramount—in God's judgment and in our claim to mercy.*
	14.	*Faith and works.*
	21.	*Instances of the foregoing.*
	25.	*Christian works are indispensable in the life of Christian faith.*
III.	1.	*Don't be many of you rabbis; your professional tool, the tongue, is (among other faults) a world of evil.*

1. On the possibility that all of 1 Peter was written and sent by the same writer but with instructions that two different forms (1:1–4:11; 5:12-14 and 1:1–2:10; 4:12–5:14) be read to two different segments of the church, see, e.g., with other theories, C. F. D. Moule, "The Nature and Purpose of 1 Peter," *NTS* 3 (1956): 1ff.; see also L. W. Barnard, "The Epistle ad Diognetum. Two Units from One Author," *ZNW* 56 (1965): 130-37.

	6.	*Of pernicious ambivalence.*
	13.	*Instead of delighting in conceited rivalries of learning, study and practice Christian meekness and kindness.*
IV.	1.	*A vehement condemnation of lust.*
	4.	*and worldly ambition.*
	7.	*A call to repentance.*
	11.	*Don't speak ill of another.*
	13.	*Boast not yourself of tomorrow.*
V.	1.	*The coming doom of the present rich.*
	7.	*Be patient till the coming of the Lord.*
	9.	*Be patient with one another.*
	12.	*Swear no oath.*
	13.	*In affliction, pray; in joy, sing psalms; in sickness, seek the prayers of the elders.*
	16.	*Likewise (with the sinner's confession) in sin; on the prayers of the righteous, remember the precedent of Elijah.*
	19.	*The teacher's reward.*

We venture to suggest that James may not have required or even expected both halves of the Epistle of James to be read to every one of his congregations: in composition either half is potentially complete, and they are composed for two very different kinds of audiences, one of which we here, for present purposes only and with respect, not depreciation, label "rural" and the other "sophisticated" (the difference is clear in our two summaries of the respective contents). In our opinion, nothing in the passage from ch. 1 would seriously discompose the most staid member of the average Jewish Christian synagogue of the Dispersion either by its tone or by its substance; on the other hand, we think an orthodox Jew could resent the tone in every verse of the second, and the substance in every verse except possibly v. 7 and the last two.

Nothing is too obvious to escape human notice. The popular epistle familiar to the average Christian, mainly Paul's Epistles, was addressed to one locality, even if it contained more than one Christian congregation. James had a very different task: he had to meet the needs and tastes of a large congregation, or at least a considerable number of congregations. There were differences, of course, even between Paul's "audiences." He says some rather unpleasant things to the Romans, at least in some of the chapters; and in Galatians he has to break his otherwise standard custom of beginning with thanks to God for some aspect of his audience's progress or condition—in fact, he can find nothing in his audience to be thankful for, and so he duly lets them have the full force of his invective.

The difference between the two halves of the Epistle of James far exceeds that between the pleasant and the chastening passages of Romans or Galatians. In these two, however the tone varies, the reader always feels that the same congregation is being addressed. Contrast Jas. 1:12-21 and 4:1-10, as set forth in the accompanying *Table 2*. If we had not had the evidence of the text we might reasonably have hesitated to believe that the second half of the Epistle of James was part of the same Epistle as the first:

We scarcely need to point out the strong OT Jewish element in the second half of the Epistle of James. Speaking only for myself, I am most struck by the use of the verb "howl" in 5:1, here only in the NT and, as we were bound to expect, in a passage of prophetic, not evangelical character. The rich here denounced need not be taken to be present in the listening congregation any more than the nations and people are present in Isa. 34:1. James is here using a common OT method of comforting the afflicted by predicting—in effect, promising—the fall of their enemies and oppressors; he proceeds in exactly the same way as Isaiah, in which the comprehensive curse of ch. 34 is immediately followed by the sublime comfort of the next chapter. The technique of Jas. 5:1-6 takes us back at once to the OT and the synagogue.

TABLE 2

JAMES 1:12-21

12. *Happy is the man who with constancy endures trying assaults of evil; for when (upon trial) he has been approved, he will receive the crown of life, which God has promised to those who love him.*
13. *Let no one under trying assaults of evil say, "My trial by assault of evil comes from God." For God is invincible to assaults of evil, and himself subjects no one to assault of evil.*
14. *But each man is tried by assault of evil by his own lust, as he feels the pull of its distraction and the enticement of its bait.*
15. *Then his lust having conceived gives birth to sin; and when sin is full grown it brings forth death.*
16. *Make no mistake, my beloved brothers (I'm not arguing, I'm telling you):*
17. *Every good gift, yes, every perfect gift, is from above, coming down from the Father of lights of heaven, whose nature (unlike those lights) suffers neither variation of orbit nor any shadow.*
18. *He of his own wish begot us by the Word of truth, for us to be a kind of firstfruits of his creation.*
19. *Wherefore, my beloved brothers, let every man be swift to hear, slow to speak, slow to wrath:*

20. *for a man's wrath (or "anger") does not express in action the righteousness of God.*
21. *Wherefore strip off all filthiness and prodigality of vice, and with meekness accept the implanted word (implanted by those who have preached the gospel to you), which is able to save your souls.*

JAMES 4:1-10

1. *What is the source of wars and fightings among you? Is it not in this, in your lusts, which make war in your members?*
2. *You lust, and have no satisfaction; you covet and you envy, and you cannot get your desire; so you fight and war: you have not, because you do not ask.*
3. *When you ask, you do not receive, because of your corrupt asking, in order that you may spend it on your lusts.*
4. *Adulteresses, do you not know that friendship with the world is enmity with God? Anyone who has chosen to be a friend of the world becomes an enemy of God.*
5. *Or do you suppose that it is an idle saying in the scriptures that the spirit that has taken its dwelling in us is prone to envious lust?*
6. *But he gives grace that is yet stronger: and so it says, God sets himself against the haughty, but gives grace to the humble.*
7. *So enlist under God: fight the devil, and he will flee from you.*
8. *Draw near to God, and he will draw near to you. Clean your hands, sinners, and purge your hearts, you double-minded.*
9. *Repent, and mourn and weep; let your laughter turn to mourning and your rejoicing to dismay.*
10. *Humble yourselves before God, and he will exalt you.*

Let us here consider one aspect of the question whether the Epistle of James as now printed originated in the form of a single, complete letter, or as two missives, the first now appearing as Jas. 1–3, and the second as Jas. 4–5. The basis for following the latter view may be a supposed break in style and thought between the first three chapters and the rest. We here wish to offer some facts that, we believe, point in the opposite direction.

First, let us notice the realistic (but not necessarily pessimistic) opening (1:2f.), followed by the sort of tone that for brevity we will call "hostile" (1:6-8 inclusive as well as in all the discussion that follows). 1:10f. is on the rich (here, naturally, a noticeable priority). Then comes a cautionary, not yet hostile, mention. But after this, "hostile" can be applied to discussions of lust (1:13-15), wrath (1:19f.), filthiness (1:21), hearers, but not doers of Christianity (1:22-24), the sham religion of the unbridled tongue (1:26), snobbish partialities (2:1-4), oppression of the poor by the rich and their blasphemy dishonoring Christ (2:5-7), the sin of snobbery (2:9), the sin of the pitiless (2:12, 13), faith without works (2:14-26), the undisciplined tongue (3:1-12), arrogance (3:13), envy and strife (3:14-16), base and selfish lusts (4:1-5), slander and presumption of evil in another (4:11f.), counting of chickens before they hatch (4:13-15), those who *know* but don't *do* (4:17), the indictment of the rich (5:1-6), and personal quarrels (5:9). Thus, of a total of 108 verses, 69 can be designated by the word "hostile." All these warnings help to furnish clues to the twin problems of unity and purpose; in short, the Epistle is a "book of warnings."

Now there is a calculated unity within the Epistle of James, one that combines chs. 1–3 with 4–5, just as in a pair of shoes there is the combined unity of left plus right. In this picture of the unity of James, we must try to remember its unique character. Unlike the other NT Epistles, it is "at home" not only with one "audience," that is, the Jews, who are actual or prospective Christians, but also with impenetrably encrusted *anti-Christians* who may be good citizens, and with godless hedonists and greedy materialists who seek nothing but pleasure (ch. 4) or wealth (ch. 5:1-6). In chs. 1–3 James addresses the first of these two types; in chs. 4–5:6 he denounces the other, returning to the first type only with the final comfort of 5:7-18 and the authoritative 5:19f.

The Greek proves that one man is the author of the whole of the Epistle of James. Even the "self-contained" second part, with its uniquely highlighted opening and close, points to something unique in the composition of this Epistle. Did James wish to provide a "bifocal" edition from which the widely scattered receivers could choose the mild or the bitter to suit their flocks? Did he, in his position of authority and awareness of varied standards in various localities, send one version to one and the other to another?

We cannot say; we do not know of any way of deciding whether James sent both halves to each "addressee" or sent only one half to many of them (e.g., for baptismal or catechetical purposes), and the other half (or perhaps both) to unconverted Jews or perhaps to the extreme Judaizers, especially those of the notorious "James party" (Gal. 2:12). But the document does indicate something to the intelligent reader, for example, why there are duplicate treatments of one topic in Jas. 1:12-21 and 4:1-10, or why the theme of works concluding ch. 2 did not need all the elementary detail of 5:12-18; and it lends at least a little color to our association of some of the substance in the Epistle of James with some of Paul's message to the Colossians.

However attractive our thesis (and we believe it has merit), it cannot be proved and we choose not to press it, except on one important point, the structure of the Epistle: the Epistle of James, dividing at the end of ch. 2:26–3:1 for convenient regular (we mean frequent or occasional) reading within the service pattern of the synagogue of the time, exactly parallels the equally proto-apostolic practice of Paul (e.g., end of Eph. 3—actually a doxology) in his Epistles of a similar length.

Here, we submit, is evidence that the two features we have noted in the typical apostolic Epistle, namely, an approximately standard length and a standard division into two (or sometimes more) installments of approximately standard length, most probably arise from practices James and Paul knew in their worship before they became Christians. The selective, not comprehensive, scope of the contents to which James limits his Epistle is precisely in keeping with the (free, not rigid) pattern of the Jewish synagogue.[2]

For James and Paul salvation is linked with *hªlāḵāh*,[3] the way of life—in a word, "faith and works." Thus we ought not to be surprised that the keynote of Teacher James's thought is Torah or law, which he equates with salvation, and that 2:8, "If indeed you fulfil the sovereign law, according to the Scripture, 'Thou shalt *love* thy neighbor as thyself,' you do well," does no less justice to *agapē* than Paul does in 1 Cor. 12:31 and the following chapter. It is important to recognize in the plan of the whole and of many of its parts the influence of those conditions that led James and Paul to compose their Epistles in what we have called installments.

We also think that James took over from the synagogue the wide notion of Torah (not to the detriment or prejudice of Torah in the narrower technical sense, or Pentateuch). That is why we now prefer to translate *word* of salvation rather than gospel of salvation, where the Greek so allows. It gives a proper widening to the horizon. Both *logos* ("word") and *nomos* ("law") have a primordial place in our religion, long before the actual incarnation and the story thereof. In and long before NT times Jewish religious education was traditional, partly ritual in content, and oral in method. Its subject matter was, they held, *wisdom,* embodied above all in priests, parents, and teachers, and inculcated by them most notably in (1) Passover instruction (e.g., Ex. 12–24); (2) synagogue assembly (e.g., Lev. 17ff.), and (3) the rabbinic schools (e.g., Ecclus. 1–7).

2. See R. C. Worley, *Preaching and Teaching in the Earliest Church* (1967), pp. 57ff.

3. For a discussion of its OT theological use, see F. J. Helfmeyer, *hālakh, TDOT,* III (1978), 392ff.; also K. Koch, *derekh, TDOT,* III, 270ff.

Torah (or "law"), as the correlative of *ḥoḵmāh,* "wisdom," signifies "direction"—not imperious dictation but guidance for human conduct or *hᵃlāḵāh,* "walking." This "law" originates in God and gives the human father a godlike status among the elders of his tribe. Likewise, when teachers had achieved a professional status, we find them assuming a father-son-like relationship as the basis of their authority.[4] At first, as in Proverbs and Ecclesiasticus, the pupils seem not yet to have used books, but in the NT reference is made to the written "law," which the pupils now study.

There were also oral catechisms like the *Mandates* (i.e., Commandments) of Hermas. These consist mainly of Jewish catechetical material closely akin to passages in James, Ephesians, and the *Two Ways,* as well as the Dead Sea Scrolls (e.g., the Manual of Discipline). The Sermon on the Mount is a typical transcript of such material as it was originally taught by the elders of the Christian community, a new form of the oral "law" of Israel to which constant reference is made in Matthew (as in 5:17ff.; 7:12).

Ecclesiasticus is typical of the teaching of the rabbinic schools. It does not touch on the specifically priestly Torah concerning sacrifice, clean and unclean, and other such matters;[5] the subject is "the fear of the Lord" and the dutiful righteousness it nourishes in the genuine believer. This resembles the ancient Greek view of law as *a way of life,* where "eunomy," perfection of law, is regarded as the salvation of the community. So Hesiod preaches to the Greeks, and so the Hebrews also teach.[6] As in Dt. 17:14-20 and Zech. 9:9, the material of Ecclus. 1–7 on "the fear of the Lord" is used again and again in later writings, "especially in the *Two Ways,* the *Mandates* of Hermas, and the Epistle of St. James." While it is true that "James does not present a staccato roster of apodictic commands, one must infer from his sermonic, midrashic mode a larger number of strong recommendations for right conduct."[7] In short, the subject of the Epistle of James, too, is "the fear of the Lord" and dutiful righteousness as *a way of life* (i.e., *hᵃlāḵāh*).

Old Jewish piety, like much old pagan piety, as a rule looked only to this world for rewards and punishments; but already before the NT period some Jews at least had ideas of rewards and punishments as well as of good and evil spirits at war in the universe at large and in the human

4. See P. Carrington, *The Primitive Christian Catechism* (1940), pp. 4ff.; also R. P. Martin, "Haustafeln," *NIDNTT,* III, 928ff.; D. E. Aune, *The New Testament in Its Literary Environment* (1987), pp. 196f.

5. Ibid., p. 9.

6. G. Ebel, "Walk" *(hodos), NIDNTT,* III, 936.

7. P. Sigal, "The Halakhah of James," *Intergerini Parietis Septum* (1981), p. 338.

soul. In the NT these latter ideas appear most strongly in Paul but quite clearly in Peter, and their best monument is the *Testaments of the Twelve Patriarchs,* written in Hebrew in Palestine about 100 B.C., and in Greek no later than the second century A.D.[8] The Greek version, notwithstanding recognizable Christian additions, may fairly, says Ropes, "be accounted a monument of Hellenistic Judaism contemporary with James."[9]

That statement, though not so intended by Ropes, supports our view of the authorship of the Epistle of James, and is best so interpreted. He quotes a few other statements on compassion, peace, humility, envy, anger, arrogance, and other virtues and vices; in the *Testaments of the Twelve Patriarchs* the chief interest in law (called "The Word of Truth," Test. Gad 3:1; compare Jas. 1:18) is on the side of moral precepts, but all the parallels only illustrate the common background of high Jewish morality in which both the *Testaments* and James (and Hermas) share. That, however, is no ground for denying that James wrote our present Epistle and made use of these common themes. The Hebrew common moral tradition, "the right way" of Gen. 24:48, or the most natural, the most human, and the most Godlike way of human life, was no less apposite and even necessary for James than it would be for a modern evangelist. It is significant that 1 Pet. 1:16, Rom. 5:3f., and Jas. 1:2 not only present forcible parallels in their substance but also point to the leading place given to the right way in their respective Epistles.

After discussing certain neo-Levitical material in Paul and showing that Paul seems to be working on an early form of Christian Torah involving a taboo on Gentile sins, baptism, the reception of the Holy Spirit, and consecration in a holy community characterized by love, Philip Carrington proceeds to examine the *Four Main Points* of the primitive Christian catechism.[10] These motifs, which are conveniently represented by the Latin words *Deponentes* (putting off evil), *Subiecti* (submit yourselves), *Vigilate* (watch and pray), and *Resistite* (resist the devil), occur in four of the Epistles (Colossians, Ephesians, 1 Peter, and James) and also partly in Hebrews and even in the Sermon on the Mount. Other words associated with the pattern are also mentioned—*logos* (word), *epithymia* (desire), *stephanos* (crown), *prosōpolēmpsia* (re-

8. See Ropes, p. 20; also H. C. Kee, "Testaments of the Twelve Patriarchs (Second Century B.C.)," *The Old Testament Pseudepigrapha,* ed. J. H. Charlesworth (1983), pp. 775ff., and article, "The Ethical Dimensions of the Testaments of the XII as a Clue to Provenance," *NTS* 24.2 (1978): 259-70, esp. 269f. for speculation on date and place of origin.

9. P. 20.

10. *The Primitive Christian Catechism,* pp. 31ff.

spect for persons), and *teleios* (perfect). The point is that when these writers follow analogous patterns, this is due not to literary borrowing but to the use of a common catechetical source. With his materials, Carrington—followed notably by Selwyn[11] but also by others—constructs a formula of catechesis to prepare converts for church membership. This, he suggests, was a standard pattern, based on Jewish Torah and especially on the Holiness code of Lev. 19.

The Epistle of James, unique in its emphasis on teaching *(didachē)* as distinct from preaching *(kērygma)*, offers an excellent test of the catechesis thesis. Essentially a brief compendium of Jewish Christian ethics, it seems admirably suited for instruction of new converts—catechesis that Carrington thinks reflects a baptismal Torah of the school of James the brother of Christ.[12] Further, if we accept B. R. Halson's theory, the Epistle may be regarded as "a collection of catechetical material for use in the Christian Churches, emanating from a particular 'school' of catechists."[13] The material preserved and used by this school has been cast in the mold of the Wisdom tradition as a conscious attempt to use a teaching form with Jewish antecedents yet with an "international flavor" suitable for use in the Hellenistic world. Both content and style reflect its use along these "Christian Wisdom" lines.

The common pattern, setting forth the new Torah of Christ or the way and walk of Christian sanctification as similar to the law of OT holiness, is found in very much the same order in James, though perhaps less clearly than in the other Epistles.[14] If the pattern apparently has only a small place in the Epistle, closer examination reveals more than at first sight. The main ideas occur in the same order as usual, which can hardly be accidental and does not seem to be due to literary dependence. The pattern, which is especially discernible in chs. 1, 3, and 4, extends only to 4:11, the rest of the Epistle being of a different nature.

In essence Carrington's theory does not appeal to us so much as the evidence he has collected. Even though he states his theory with caution and expressly refrains from postulating a single *Ur-catechism*

11. See Selwyn, pp. 363ff. For an excellent summary of the code and catechetical theories, see W. Munro, *Authority in Paul and Peter* (1983), pp. 3ff.

12. *The Primitive Christian Catechism,* p. 78.

13. "The Epistle of James: Christian Wisdom?" *StEv* IV = *TU* 102 (1968): 312f.

14. Carrington, *The Primitive Christian Catechism,* pp. 4ff.; see also M.-É. Boismard, "Une Liturgie Baptismale dans la Prima Petri II—son Influence sur l'Épître de Jacques," *RB* 64 (1957): 161-83; G. Braumann, "Der theologische Hintergrund des Jakobusbriefes," *ThZ* 18 (1962): 401-10.

(a current original document),[15] we are not convinced that the hard core of early Christian agreement on doctrine in the apostolic circle of teachers was as organized as he implies. The conclusions he draws from the parallels sometimes ignore the principle of the fortuitous. It would therefore be hazardous to think of the catechetical material as a single whole or even as a number of small manuals on different themes. But the facts he adduces, that is, the parallels themselves, do suffice to prove a hard core of agreement on certain fundamentals of Christian teaching.

This "core of agreement" is very clear in the Epistle of James, although, as we have said, there are some variations and omissions (e.g., *Haustafel; Vigilate;* Gentile sins). This, of course, is to be expected, suggesting that James was nearer to the source of catechesis than to its mainstream. As "Bishop" of Jerusalem James was faced with the necessity of instructing the Jewish converts in Jerusalem and the Diaspora in the Christian Way. The first-generation Christians would be faced with a bewildering array of new theological and organizational problems that, if left unsolved, would mean the end of the young church. In response to this crisis James wrote his pastoral letter, and perhaps for the first time the early church had to deal not with an OT writing but with a new type of authoritative document.[16] Here we have a rare insight into the beginnings of the NT. James's task was made even more difficult by the attitude of the Jewish authorities, especially on the Christian interpretation of the Jewish Torah.

James therefore had to evolve his own baptismal "catechism," based primarily on the prophets and Jesus rather than other NT *Haustafeln,* to suit this specific situation and its peculiar needs. The source of early tradition and the model of interpretation was not catechesis, missionaries, or polemics, but Jesus himself; and his early parousia was confidently expected. With the early Christians the center of force was in Jesus, not in the church. The first Christians needed some time to develop and organize their creed, as Jesus had predicted (John 16:12f.; 14:26; 15:26; 16:14). Therefore these early statements of James must be understood in the light of both "hard-core kerygma" and of particular circumstances and requirements in real-life situations.

Even Carrington, in our opinion, scarcely sees clearly enough this important truth, namely, that it was not catechesis that built up the Epistle of James as we have it now. The Epistle of James as we have it

15. *The Primitive Christian Catechism,* p. 25; see also D. Daube, *The New Testament and Rabbinic Judaism* (1956), p. 125.

16. See Scaer, p. 22.

came from the pen of James, who in his own teaching contributed (no doubt very largely) to the items and order of that common stock of Christian essentials upon which (stock) other NT Epistles noticeably draw: James is *not* the fruit of an indeterminate period of agglutinative effort resulting in a series of heterogeneous elements with no unity of form or thought. In our view, the Epistle of James, though distinctive, is an excellent example of a primitive Christian catechism.[17] The four main points (except for *Vigilate*) as well as the keywords *(logos, epithymia, stephanos, prosōpolēmpsia,* and *teleios*) are there,[18] as are common but less prominent themes such as warning against temptation, prayer for wisdom and endurance, and the law of love.

Carrington warns us that he is not outlining a complete catechism, which would necessarily be fuller. One would expect, for instance, that, as the Pliny parallels show, a manual of instruction for catechumens would give a larger place to faith in Christ.[19] But that the pattern as he extracts it is there, and is probably derived from some baptismal manual (though probably oral, not documentary), seems in accord with the evidence.

Many of the elements of the Epistle of James, on this view, fall into place, so that the work has fresh meaning. "The Epistle," Calvin comments, "is a rich source of varied instruction, of abundant benefit in all aspects of the Christian life. We may find striking passages on endurance, on calling upon God, on the practice of religion, on restraining our speech, on peace-making, on holding back greedy instincts, on disregard for this present life. . . ."[20] The pattern begins in a manner reminiscent of the Jewish rite of proselyte baptism by warning the convert of the possibility of trial, though linked to the specifically Christian idea of rejoicing and triumphing in it. This is followed naturally by an exhortation to heroic endurance and unwavering faith, coupled with a prayer for wisdom, this last being especially appropriate since it would

17. See Jas. 1:23, where the term "hearer" is especially appropriate for catechumens; see also Mt. 5:21, 24, 33 *et saepe;* Jn. 12:34, where the verb is used in a technical sense, like *šᵉma'* (imperative) or *šāma'* (perfect) in rabbinic literature referring to the acceptance of a halachic tradition. See also O. A. Piper, "John and the Didache of the Primitive Church," *JBL* 64.4 (1947): 437; W. Bacher, *Die exegetische Terminologie der jüdischen Traditionsliteratur,* I (1899), 189-91; W. Mundle, "Hear" *(akouō), NIDNTT,* II, 172ff.

18. Carrington, *The Primitive Christian Catechism,* pp. 55ff.

19. Ibid., p. 11.

20. *A Harmony of the Gospels of Matthew, Mark and Luke,* Vol. III, *and the Epistles of James and Jude,* tr. A. W. Morrison, eds. D. W. Torrance and T. F. Torrance (1972), p. 259.

probably precede periods of teaching.[21] The references to the struggle with the evil *yēṣer* and the reward of the crown of life lead to the dramatization of wisdom and truth in the creative word.

Such ideas—the Word of God as a creative power with the associated conception of the struggle in the world and in the soul of man, the stripping off of evil and putting on of good, the contrast between true and false faith, as well as wisdom, the duty of joy, the need of endurance, humility and maturity, good works, submission to God, and stern resistance to evil—are all peculiarly appropriate to the instruction of converts for baptism and are especially close to the older type of Jewish piety (and to the terminology of the Synoptic Gospels) that focused largely on this life and emphasized humility, prayer, and steadfastness.

Catechesis therefore offers a fresh explanation as to why the Epistle of James was written, and it is thus well worth further independent investigation. We shall show that the Epistle contains reflections of early Christian catechesis as developed under James, with some examples of the method that are rarely or never paralleled in other NT Epistles.

NEW LIGHT ON THE PARALLELS

If James and the other NT writers knew and employed a common stock of catechetical material, this would shed light on the old problem of NT passages that we will here call "parallel,"[22] though the relation does not always appear as close as it is. These can be ascribed mainly to a common catechetical origin in the infancy of Christianity, arising not simply from arbitrary personal borrowing but from the force of a common stock circulating among the early Christians, for example, a *traditionelle Motivgruppe* or an early Christian "master theme" *(Grundthema)* such as "joy in suffering" in 1 Pet. 1:6//Rom. 5:3//Jas. 1:2.[23] Carrington shows that although James has two phrases that agree verbally with Peter, namely, "various temptations" and "the testing of your faith," he also has one phrase, "works patience," that is found in Romans and not in Peter.[24] The word "hope," present in both Romans and James,

21. Carrington, *The Primitive Christian Catechism,* p. 59.

22. On the problem of literary relationships, see almost any good work on the Epistle of James or NT Introduction; e.g., Mussner, pp. 12ff., 33ff.; Mayor, pp. lxxxivff.; Ropes, pp. 21ff.; Dibelius, pp. 26ff.; Schlatter, pp. 43ff.; Rendall, ch. IX, pp. 96-102.

23. See Mussner, p. 64; also Hoppe, pp. 18f.; Davids, pp. 65f.

24. *The Primitive Christian Catechism,* pp. 23ff. See also Boismard, *art.*

is lacking in Peter. Further, both Paul and James employ the phrase "knowing this," the so-called "imperative participle,"[25] in such a way as to suggest that they are about to introduce a well-known saying, implying that both of them are borrowing older catechetical formulas based perhaps on primitive Christian hymnody or baptismal liturgy. The variations that frequently occur, as in these three texts, are a very strong point in Carrington's case.

This hypothesis therefore gives almost the only and certainly the best explanation of the wealth of similarities[26] in James, Peter, and, as we shall see, Paul,[27] and is in fact confirmed by the independence in their variations from one another. As Parry wisely remarks: "The connection need not be direct. . . . It may be due to . . . some teaching or document unknown to us."[28] Although there is a close similarity between James and 1 Peter[29]—and it has been held that James borrowed from Peter[30] and vice versa[31]—the parallels show remarkable independence. Nowhere is this more clearly seen than in the ethical and religious background of the two Epistles. Whereas Peter exhibits the paschal and priestly strain, derived from Judaism, James reflects "a rabbinic school of the type of Ecclesiasticus, transfigured by the *torah* of the Sermon on the Mount."[32] While the same thoughts occur in the same sequence, they are set in entirely different backgrounds and the final impression is quite different.

Examination shows that these formulas would not naturally be picked out as leading thoughts; nor can they be attributed to the literary influence of either writer. Yet, as further consideration confirms, the

---

cit., RB 64 (1957): 162ff.; also T. W. Leahy, "The Epistle of James," *The Jerome Biblical Commentary,* ed. R. E. Brown, II (1968), 371.

25. D. Daube in Selwyn, pp. 467ff.; also Daube, *The New Testament and Rabbinic Judaism,* pp. 90ff.; W. D. Davies, *Paul and Rabbinic Judaism* (1948), p. 329; see Mussner, p. 32, n. 4, for further reference.

26. Carrington, *The Primitive Christian Catechism,* p. 28.

27. See our discussion, pp. 225f.

28. P. 57; see also Dibelius, p. 30, who postulates dependence on a common parenetic tradition.

29. E.g., Jas. 1:1//1 Pet. 1:1; Jas. 1:2//1 Pet. 1:6; Jas. 1:3//1 Pet. 1:7; Jas. 1:10f.//1 Pet. 1:24; Jas. 1:18//1 Pet. 1:3, 23; Jas. 4:6//1 Pet. 5:5; Jas. 4:7//1 Pet. 5:6; Jas. 4:7//1 Pet. 5:8f.; Jas. 5:20//1 Pet. 4:8. See Mayor, pp. ciiff.; Selwyn, pp. 365-466; Davids, pp. 26f., 15.

30. E.g., Moffatt; B. Weiss; see also Selwyn, p. 463.

31. E.g., Mayor, Zahn, Spitta, A. Meyer, Sidebottom, and notably Schlatter, p. 73, who held not only that Peter knew and borrowed from James, but also that this ensured its preservation by the Greek church.

32. Carrington, *The Primitive Catechism,* p. 28.

formulas rise at the same stage of thought, following one another in a predetermined order;[33] and both writers employ virtually the same vocabulary and appear to derive their teaching from a common Jewish catechetical source.[34] Hence when we have similar references in James and Peter, it is not permissible to assume that they have borrowed from each other, unless in each instance the context implies or suggests some special relationship. To express this in another way, we must leave more room than hitherto for the influence of a common stock of catechetical material on James's teachings.

So this approach has the merit of simplicity, and is in line with the arguments of form and later criticism. Certainly it simplifies the entire question of authorship, eliminates the hypothesis of literary borrowing with its problems of plagiarism,[35] and explains the apparently poor or limited use the borrower makes of the NT books he is supposed to know. Each author used his catechetical sources in his own creative way for his own distinctive purpose. Significantly James makes no mention of the problems of Gentile converts and their relation to the Law of Holiness,[36] to which Paul frequently alludes. This would appear to point to a type of Christianity neither Pauline nor Johannine, but with a strong Jewish emphasis on duty and obedience to the Torah, reflecting the essential teaching of the church at Jerusalem. Even the controversy about faith and works is not so much theological as simply ethical.

NEW INVINCIBILITY

Turning now to the content of the Epistle, we are struck with the way James begins. The pattern bears some resemblance to that of Jewish rites for the baptism of proselytes; witness, for example, the term "brothers"[37] in v. 2: "Deem it nothing but an occasion for joy, *my brothers,* whenever you encounter trying assaults of evil in their various forms." Likewise, as the old Jewish religion had to endure persecution, so must the Christian, and this persecution confirms the parallel so often mentioned by the early Christian teachers between the Old Israel and

33. Ibid., p. 29; also p. 44.

34. Ibid., p. 54.

35. F. F. Bruce, in a personal note, writes: "I am not sure that the ancient world was conscious of plagiarism as a problem as we are; nevertheless, your argument for a common drawing on a body of catechetical material is probably right."

36. Carrington, *The Primitive Christian Catechism,* pp. 78, 36.

37. See S-B II, 76ff.; H. von Soden, *adelphos, TDNT,* I, 147ff.

the New;[38] but the trouble goes deeper than religious persecutions and includes all the moral, spiritual, and eschatological dangers that may come in our ordinary life.

James's call to rejoice (1:2) reflects the authentic NT attitude toward *peirasmoi,* exemplified in parallel passages like 1 Pet. 1:6f. and Rom. 5:3-5. These point to a common tradition of "eschatological expectancy"[39] (*Vorfreude,* lit. "foretaste of joy"), rejoicing over ultimate deliverance and peace, found in later Judaism,[40] including Qumran (e.g., 1QS 10:17), but more especially to the unique teaching of Jesus on moral joy in suffering (see Mt. 5:11; Lk. 6:22f.). In the Epistle of James *peirasmoi* does not seem to refer to general religious persecution (in this instance, "Persecution Code" is a misnomer[41]). In this connection 1 Cor. 10, especially vv. 1-13, is important; there Paul is speaking of the ideas James expresses by *dokimeion* and *dokimos,* and of *peirasmos* (vv. 13f.). For "approval" Paul uses *eudokēsen:* they all had the initial advantages of baptism, etc., but not all won approval; they succumbed to (the *peirasmoi* of) their lusts.

We are therefore inclined to think that the validation of Christianity in Jas. 1:13 and 1 Pet. 1:7 is contemplated as the result of withstanding not only *peirasmoi* from without, such as Ropes mentions,[42] but also, and perhaps primarily, those from within; hence the emphasis on these in the sequel (e.g., Jas. 1:21-25; 2:14; 3:13; 1 Pet. 1:13-16, 25; 2:3, 11). To restrict *peirasmoi* in Jas. 1:2, as Ropes does, seems to us to divorce the exordium from the rest of the Epistle. Moreover, in our opinion, the Epistle of James is more closely related to Rom. 2:5-11 than it at first seems; this passage contains, besides other

38. See b. Yebamoth 47a; also D. Daube, *The New Testament and Rabbinic Judaism,* p. 117; A. Cohen, *Everyman's Talmud* (1932), p. 60; R. Schippers, "Persecution" *(thlipsis), NIDNTT,* II, 807f.

39. J. Thomas, "Anfechtung und Vorfreude," *Kerygma und Dogma* 14 (1968), 183ff. See also Dibelius, pp. 74f., on the literary relationships of Jas. 1:2-4; Hoppe, pp. 18f.; Davids, pp. 65f.; U. Falkenroth, C. Brown, "Patience" *(hypomenō), NIDNTT,* II, 775.

40. J. Thomas, ibid.; W. Nauck, "Freude im Leiden: Zum Problem einer urchristlichen Verfolgungstradition," *ZNW* 46 (1955): 68; C. G. Montefiore and H. Loewe, *A Rabbinic Anthology* (1938), pp. 541ff.; Mussner, p. 64; E. Beyreuther, G. Finkenrath, "Joy" *(chairō), NIDNTT,* II, 357.

41. See Selwyn, pp. 441, 450; Ropes, p. 133. For the unlikely view that James is addressing "Christians who are being lured back into the full communal life of the Jewish culture from which they have begun to be cut off abruptly by a persecution that reached a cutting edge with the stoning of Stephen," see Scaer, p. 43.

42. P. 133.

points of interest and affinity, two fairly rare words, *eritheia* (five times in Paul, two in James, but nowhere else in the NT) and *prosōpolēmpsia* (three times in Paul, once in James, but nowhere else in the NT; but see *prosōpolēmpteō* in Jas. 2:9 and *prosōpolēmptēs* in Acts 10:34).

We also think that *hypomonē* in Jas. 1:3f. no less than *hypomenei* in Jas. 1:12 includes temptations; and *hypomonē* in Jas. 1:4 seems indistinguishable from that of Rom. 2:7, both in its *activity* and (if we match Jas. 1:2 with Jas. 1:2ff. as suggested) in its *reward*. Even 1 Pet. 1:7—praise, honor, glory—is reminiscent of Rom. 2:7—glory, honor, immortality; and in 1 Pet. 1:6 *peirasmoi* (we think) include temptations. The *dokimeion* in both Peter and James is of wide scope, based on Christian conduct in general, not only in adversities; the eschatological *peirasmoi* in 1 Pet. 4:7 are verbally and (we think) deliberately distinct from the *poikiloi peirasmoi* of 1 Pet. 1:6 (where, we think, the meaning is comprehensive).

Mayor's note on *dokimeion* indicates the difficulties of the conventional text.[43] We have already proposed an emendation that removes these,[44] makes sense of v. 3, and is more in keeping with James's thought in general. His main thought surely is that constancy in enduring wins final approval; this not only brings v. 4 in line with v. 3, with constancy at work in both, but it also brings v. 4 in line with all the assaults of evil of v. 2. It also avoids the improbable assumption that *dokimeion* does not have the same meaning here as in 1 Pet. 1:7. We think the dative *hypomonē* is clearly right. Certainly the nominative *hypomonē* (with *katergazetai* of course as a middle deponent) gives the same sense, and the order is such a few times in James; but our feeling is very strongly for the dative with the passive verb—"is accomplished by 'endurance.'" We have never been happy with the usual view that in James *dokimeion* means "testing, to find out if you pass or fail" while in Peter the same word means "approval," "approbation," that is, passing the test. But unless so translated, James would make no sense: the argument would be wrecked. Now, however, with the dative *hypomonē* we get the same meaning for *dokimeion* in both James and Peter, both referring to the successful outcome of the test, *approbation*, not mere probation (for probation may end in rejection).

Like all ethical catechisms, the Epistle of James is marked by a highly developed "psychological pneumatic dualism,"[45] indicative of

43. P. 33.

44. See also our discussion, p. 317, n. 48.

45. Carrington, *The Primitive Christian Catechism*, p. 82; J. I. H. McDonald, *Kerygma and Didache* (1980), pp. 77, 85, 95.

the gulf between the pre- and postbaptismal life and the choice of "the two ways." The spiritual benefits and rewards of the one are constantly contrasted, sometimes chiastically, in the present and the future, with those of the other; thus while the Christian can rejoice even in the midst of trial, the happiness of the rich will soon end. After discussing the unregenerate life of the double-minded in the light of the *yēṣer,* James works out the contrast between the evil *yēṣer*–"sin"–"death" syndrome and its opposite, namely, "endurance"–"approval" ("perfection")–"life" (1:12-15),[46] products of the good *yēṣer,* now exhibited in the life of the Christian regenerated by the Word; note 1:15 and 18 where the antithesis extends even to *semantic* parallelism, recalling Rom. 6:23, "the wages of sin is death, but the gift of God is eternal life." The life of lust and anger must now yield to a life of gentleness, love, and service—all of which have a bearing on the Levitical Law of Holiness.[47]

This dialectical contrast between the "two ways" of life and the "two spirits" of truth and falsehood is further heightened by the allusion to "hearers" and "doers" and the two kinds of faith, the one dead and the other living, which in turn leads to the ambivalence of the tongue, the two types of water, one sweet and the other bitter, with their corresponding fruits, and the two types of wisdom with their fruits. "As a call to conversion employing the *topos* on envy," writes L. T. Johnson,[48] "we see that James 3:13–4:10 is organised according to sharp

46. Mussner, p. 88. See also our discussion, p. 341.

47. For a general discussion, see L. T. Johnson, "The Use of Leviticus 19 in the Letter of James" (*JBL* 101 [1982]: 391-401). After isolating seven passages in Leviticus, in which James "engages in halachic midrash," Johnson goes on, pp. 399ff., to suggest with some credibility that James's systematic use of Lev. 19 may be similar to the late rabbinic tradition concerning the role of this chapter as a summary of, or counterpoint to, the Decalogue, to be read now in the Jewish Christian synagogue.

48. "Friendship with the World/Friendship with God: A Study of Discipleship in James," in *Discipleship in the New Testament,* ed. F. F. Segovia (1985), pp. 168f. Commenting in a valuable separate article on Jas. 3:13–4:6, L. T. Johnson shows how the discourse moves by means of rhetorical questions in 3:13, 4:1 (two), and 4:5 (two), each of which is followed by exposition or accusation, and then goes on to say: "In 3:13-14, an initial contrast between a wisdom from above and bitter jealousy is explained by a second set of antithetical statements in 3:15-16 (*ouk estin . . . alla,* and *hopou gar . . . ekei*), and 3:17-18 then resumes, with an emphasis on *eirēnē,* the thematic opposition established by 3:13: true wisdom is manifested in mild and peaceful behavior. The second set of rhetorical questions forms a sharp antithesis to 3:17-18, and returns to the bitter jealousy of 3:14-15, now explicitly seen not only as a cause of *akatastasia* but of wars and battles." Johnson then goes on to show how accusations rather than exposition follow these questions, followed by an explanation of why their requests are refused (4:3), with

contrasts. The most obvious is that between the attack and the command, between the indictment and the exhortation. The reader is told to replace one way of life with another. Corresponding to this contrast is another between two measures of reality, which derive from different sources and lead to different actions." The false wisdom as to origin is from beneath; as to nature is "of the earth, of this life, of the devil"; and as to outcome results in jealousy and faction, confusion, and every evil; the true wisdom as to origin is from above; as to nature is characterized by seven virtues, yielding all the fruits of the Spirit; and as to outcome yields the fruit of righteousness. The idea of divine wisdom and its pacific nature leads, by way of contrast, to a treatment of the hedonistic, materialistic spirit at work in society. This leads James to address such hearers, not as faithful "brothers," but as unfaithful "adulterers." Do you suppose it is an idle saying in the Scriptures that the Spirit that has taken its dwelling in us is prone to envious lust?" (4:5).[49] The "friendship of God" and the "friendship of the world" are contrasted (4:4), just as "Jesus" and the "devil" are contrasted in Mt. 4:1 and the "Spirit" and the "flesh" in Gal. 5:17.

Theologically interpreted, the flesh is the sinful self, and "the world," "this age" (*aiōn houtos*), the total kingdom of evil, is to be understood in the Johannine and Qumranic sense of "a radical ethical dualism."[50] "God" and "his Kingdom" *(basileia tou theou)* and the "world" are in tension, mutually incompatible and irreconcilable. Each of us, then, must deliberately choose one or the other as a friend: "Anyone who *has chosen* to be a friend" (4:4; see 1:18 for the same but contrasting idea of divine and human *choice* with their correspondingly contrasting results). To be a "friend of the world" is ipso facto to be an "enemy of God," hostile to what is best and holiest, and to align oneself with the devil. This is why James finally has to emphasize that the "world" is evil (1:27; 3:6). In baptism our catechism renounces the world, the flesh, and the devil. But final resolution of this dualistic dilemma awaits the Second Coming.

---

another rhetorical reminder of the irreconcilability of the two friendships (4:4), the climax of the indictment being reached in 4:5, 6. While Johnson admits that the rhetorical drift may seem obscure, he correctly concludes: "The whole exposition comes down to the validity of the scriptural witness. Is all that the Scripture says in vain?" ("James 3:13–4:10 and the *Topos Peri Phthonou*," *NovT* 25.4 [1983]: 333).

49. On this difficult verse, see Adamson, pp. 170f.; see also below, pp. 330f. For further antitheses, see pp. 406f.

50. Dibelius, p. 220; see also Spitta, p. 117; 1 En. 108:8. See L. T. Johnson, *art. cit., Discipleship in the New Testament*, pp. 172ff.; H. Sasse, *kosmeō, TDNT*, III, 894f.

Though persecutions (which are said not to be in James's mind) and adversities are trying aggravations for the believer, they do not differ essentially from the assaults of evil, however sweetly some of these assaults are disguised. It may be asked what "desire" (*epithymia;* Jas. 1:14) has to do with affliction and adversity. Does not *epithymia* relate only to things like stealing and lechery? No. The answer is suggested in 2 Tim. 4:10, where Paul says near the end of his life, "Demas, because he loved (*agapēsas*) this world, has deserted me" (NIV). Not only persecution but also physical infirmity and illness induce people to renounce Christ; in such circumstances, however, the many heroes of the faith have stood fast.

The dangers from fleshly lusts, false teachers, and the like are obviously present in the minds of James, Paul, and Peter, as are those from poverty, oppression, sickness, or foul weather. "For we are all guilty of many sins," says James (3:2); in a similar vein Heb. 12:1 puts "every sin to which we cling" (*tēn euperistaton*) with "let us run with patience" *(di' hypomonēs trechōmen).* The notion that "temptations from within . . . could not be a subject of rejoicing" (so Ropes) is in conflict with the practice of, say, those Corinthian Christians who courted the temptations of sex for the pleasure and benefit of withstanding them; from 1 Cor. 7:36-38, however, it appears that they sometimes became incontinent. But whatever the theological significance of *peirasmos,* one's practical attitude is all-important—endurance brings joy and life while yielding brings pain and death.

In 1:8 and 5:16, James places opposites such as lust and the Christian life on parallel lines; in like manner he contrasts death in 1:15 with salvation in 1:21 and the futile in 1:8 with the effectual in 5:16 in the cases of the "double-minded" *(dipsychos)* and the "righteous" (*dikaios*).[51] The moral maxim and gnomic style of 5:16b on the effectual prayer of the "righteous" (*dikaios*) are exactly parallel to 1:8 on the ineffectual prayer of the "double-minded." Already in the Dead Sea Scrolls there is evidence that the Jews had early developed a philosophy of the "double-minded" (*dipsychos*) as the opposite of the righteous. As we shall see,[52] it now seems plausible that James knew the word *dipsychos* from writings using this word, possibly an apocryphon (Lightfoot conjectured the Book of Eldad and Modad[53]) or some early commentary on Num. 11:26-29.

51. See Kee, *art. cit., NTS* 24.2 (1978): 265.

52. See pp. 269ff.; also pp. 323f.

53. See G. Vermes, F. Millar, M. Goodman, and E. Schürer, *The History of the Jewish People in the Age of Jesus Christ,* III, 2 (1987), p. 783; also "Eldad and Modad (Prior to the Second Century A.D.)," A New Translation and Introduction

The NT frequently condemns pagan life as offering too little resistance to temptations of even the grossest sort; but Jas. 1:21 shows that in this respect some of the earliest converts, to whom this Christian Epistle is (1:1) addressed, may have been little better than some unconverted Gentiles: "Wherefore, my beloved brothers, . . . strip off all filthiness . . . and with meekness accept the implanted Word, which is able to save your souls." "Stripping off" *(apothemenoi)* is another imperative participle,[54] used literally in Acts 7:58 but metaphorically here as elsewhere in the NT. James is probably thinking of baptism, in which the candidate strips off his clothes, thereby symobolizing repentance and cleansing from sin.[55] In 2:2 "dirty" *(ryparos)* is literal; in 1:21, however, "dirt" *(ryparia)* is metaphorical, meaning not any particular physical dirt, for example, of the ears,[56] but morally dirty living, "uncleanness of life" (*akatharsia;* see Col. 3:5)—and this the convert must give up. It is thought[57]—we think with little justification and no proof—that "the Epistle of James shows a certain tendency to return to a concept of purity already discarded by Paul and John, in that it describes self-denial in the face of a sinful world as pure and undefiled religion (Jas. 1:27)." The Gk. *ryparian* is just a stylistic novelty for the more usual *akatharsian,* and in line with the rather novel "prodigality of vice."[58]

---

by E. G. Martin, *The Old Testament Pseudepigrapha,* ed. J. H. Charlesworth, II, 463-65.

54. See n. 25 above.

55. Not here, but in most of the NT occurrences, the corresponding word "putting on" *(endyō),* as of clothes, comes a verse or two later, e.g., Eph. 4:24 (22 and 25). On *apothesthai* ("strip off") LS cites *Iliad* 3.89, put off armor; Herodotus 4.78, put off dress; Euripides, *Helen* 367, *ap. komas,* i.e., cut off hair in mourning; Thucydides 1.77, *ap. ton nomon,* i.e., disregard law; Pseudo-Demosthenes, *Oration* 42.32: *Against Phaenippus, ap. rathymian,* put off sloth; Plutarch, *Coriolanus* 19, *ap. orgēn,* put off anger. These instances show the literal and metaphorical uses of *apothesthai.* In the latter, virtues are often likened to clothes that must be stripped off. James would be familiar with the OT allusion to "filthy rags" (Isa. 64:6). For the same idea, that "As soiled garments can be cleansed, so the Israelites, albeit they sin, can return by repentance unto the Lord," see Ex. R. Beshallah 23.10; also b. Shabbath 153a. J. Jeremias, *The Parables of Jesus* (1954), p. 131, n. 35, commenting on Midr. Ecclesiastes 9.8, where the white garment symbolizes fulfilling the commandments, good works, and the study of Torah, notes: "This does not differ materially, but is the rabbinical commentary on the word 'repentance.'"

56. S. Zodhiates, *The Behavior of Belief* (1970), p. 105.

57. See H.-G. Link, J. Schattenmann, "Pure" *(katharos), NIDNTT,* III, 107.

58. Beza obviously preferred *sordes,* "dirt," to *immunditiam,* which in form and meaning rather suggests *akatharsian* (*mundus* = *katharos*); e.g., "blessed are the *pure* in heart" *(Beati mundo corde).*

"Dirt" is a common Jewish expression for sin;[59] and while James himself gives no hint of the nature of this "dirt," later (4:8) he speaks of cleansed hands directly after attacking "lust" and "friendship of the world," that is, idolatry (4:1ff.). James's use of the unusual "wickedness" *(kakia)*, which may be derived from traditional Jewish matter, may point to a catechetical source, since it "comes at the same point in each document and nowhere else in the New Testament."[60] But his approach is uniquely his own, for unlike Paul and Peter who give long lists of vices, James does not specify the sins to be renounced. He concentrates on the dangers of wealth and speech and keeps to his customary binary form; the only place where he has a list is in the stylistic climax at 3:15, 17.

Next, with ten sharp commands, James reminds his readers of their immediate duty: "enlist," "fight" (4:7); "draw near," "clean," "purge" (v. 8); "grieve," "mourn," "wail," "change" (v. 9); "humble" (v. 10). Escape from this "wickedness" or rebellious state may be found through humble submission to God, rejection of the world with its lusts, resistance to the devil, and sincere, heartfelt repentance. James is especially succinct regarding the devil (4:7); contrast, for example, Eph. 6:11f.: "Fight the devil, and he will flee from you." This picture of the devil fleeing and powerless, a far cry from the all-powerful being of popular belief, intrigued St. Ignatius of Loyola, who notes well that, when unresisted, the devil becomes an entirely different creature. He says, "No wild beast on earth is more fierce than the enemy of our human nature."[61]

Ropes paraphrases Jas. 4:7 thus: "Take a bold stand in resisting temptations to worldliness sent by 'the prince of this world' (Jn. 14:30) and you will be successful."[62] Here James may be recalling—and urging his readers to emulate—Christ's own example of submission and resistance in temptation (Mt. 4:1ff.; Lk. 4:1ff.). He now stresses the need for reverence and repentance. Our attitude to God, in contrast to "the proud" (and the devil), must be one of submissive awe. The numinous verb *engizō*, "draw near," usually of God's drawing near and of his salvation to us, but here only in the NT (except Heb. 7:19) of our responsive approach to God but in a way deeper and surer than in the LXX,[63]

59. See S. Schechter, *Some Aspects of Rabbinic Theology* (1909), pp. 233f.; Oesterley, p. 432.

60. Carrington, *The Primitive Christian Catechism*, p. 49.

61. *The Spiritual Exercises*, tr. A. Mottola (1964), pp. 131f.; see also our remarks, pp. 436ff.

62. P. 268.

63. H. Preisker, *engys*, *TDNT*, II, 331; also W. Bauder, H.-G. Link, "Near" *(engys)*, *NIDNTT*, II, 55.

underlines the gulf that separates the sinner from a holy, transcendent God. The one act involves the other: "Draw near to God, and he will draw near to you. Clean your hands, sinners, and purge your hearts, you double-minded" (4:8). "The purifying of hands and hearts by the *dipsychoi* in 4:8," says L. T. Johnson,[64] "corresponds to *hagnē* and *adiakritos* in 3:17. Fleeing the *diabolos* in 4:8 matches the *daimoniōdēs* in 3:15. The *pneuma* God made to dwell in us in 4:6 contrasts with the *psychikē* in 3:15. The lowliness and sorrow in 4:9-10 oppose the arrogance and boasting of 4:6 and 3:14, *katēpheia* nicely balancing *hyperēphania*." Again the aorists are decisive, indicating the completeness of the approach with its priestly and ritual overtones but referring here to self-denial and ethical purification showing perhaps "a certain tendency to return to a concept of purity already discarded by Paul and John."[65] Impurity excludes God's presence from the community. Repentance, therefore, is the first step to fellowship with God.

Now follows the triple command: "Repent and mourn and weep; let your laughter turn to mourning and your rejoicing to dismay" (4:9).[66] James is not calling us to a life of gloom; he is not against joy but against the sinful pleasures that the converts sought in the past. It is not necessarily sinful for a Christian to smile. The final warning is against the almost universal and ineradicable human temptation toward vanity and pride (4:10). While there is no command to "watch" *(vigilate)* as in 1 Peter and the other Epistles, its substance at least is implicit in the preceding call to purity.

James shows his familiar Jewish heritage in setting forth that duty, but his presentation of it is fresh and effective, pointing, we believe, to a primitive Christian baptismal liturgy. Like the "spiritual sacrifices" of Peter (1 Pet. 2:5), the "pure worship" of James (Jas. 1:27)[67] is probably another form of the individual "reasonable service" of Rom. 12:1, based, no doubt, on Mal. 1:11, which is familiar in apostolic literature in the period when Christianity was still part of Israel. References to "the Father of lights" (1:17) and "the firstfruits" (1:18) recall two Jewish

64. *Art. cit., NovT* 25.4 (1983): 334; also *Discipleship in the New Testament,* p. 179, n. 22.

65. See H. Ringgren, *ṭahar, TDOT,* V, 294ff.; R. Meyer, F. Hauck, *katharos, TDNT,* III, 421-25; H. Baltensweiler, "Pure, Clear" *(hagnos), NIDNTT,* III, 101; H.-G. Link, J. Schattenmann, "Pure" *(katharos), NIDNTT,* III, 102-8, especially 107; also M. Newton, *The Concept of Purity at Qumran and in the Letters of Paul* (1985), pp. 36ff., 73, 79ff.

66. For weeping in connection with repentance, see V. Hamp, *bākhāh, TDOT,* II, 119.

67. Carringotn, *The Primitive Christian Catechism,* p. 63.

festivals, Succoth and Omer, which may indicate that "the Church had not yet abandoned the hallowed customs of the Jewish calendar and its agricultural associations."[68]

The other liturgical echoes, such as prayer (1:5ff.; 4:2ff.; 5:15), "the crown of life" (1:12), "God the Father" (1:27),[69] ushers and seating arrangements (2:1ff.), "the honorable name" (in baptism) (2:7), passing the peace (2:16), the creed (2:19), cleansing of hands (4:8), singing (5:13), anointing (5:14), and confession (5:16), also have a distinctive Jewish flavor, strongly suggesting that early period when church and synagogue shared a common worship. James, however, is at pains to distinguish between genuine "worship" and mere ceremonial observance (1:26f.), and emphasizes that mere ritual without good works is equivalent to self-deception (1:22). Indeed, the entire Epistle is a protest against "vain religion" and as such is aimed at discouraging all kinds of formalism, not least that in worship; caring for orphans and widows is the test of moral and spiritual purity. So to care is to show that one is "unstained from the world" (1:27) and is really "shorthand language for meeting covenantal obligations."[70]

On the sequence of thought (in short, the logic) of Jas. 1:19-21—indeed, of 1:12-21—we prefer now, on reflection, to emend 1:19 to read: "Wherefore, my beloved brothers. . . ."[71] This emendation, if correct, would forge an even stronger link between this verse and those before. Having spoken of the new birth, James now shows the difference it makes in conduct, specifically mentioning *the peaceful disposition* (vv. 19f.): living, as indicated in 1:4f., worthily of that privilege and destiny will bring salvation. The introductory "wherefore" *(dio)*[72] in v. 21 does not simply connect this verse with the immediately preceding verses, and the parallel "putting off" *(apothemenoi)* passages are quite illuminating in their homiletic conjunction of the themes of chaste and peaceable living.

68. A. Cabaniss, "The Epistle of Saint James," *JBR* 22 (1954): 28; see also M.-É. Boismard, *art. cit., RB* 64 (1957).

69. Ropes, p. 184.

70. L. T. Johnson, *Discipleship in the New Testament,* pp. 173, 181 nn. 40, 41, 42, 43. See W. F. Lofthouse, *Ethics and Atonement* (1906), p. 6; also Mitton, p. 15; Davids, pp. 101f.

71. See *Excursus A: James 1:19—A Suggested Emendation,* pp. 86f.

72. *dio* (lit. "because of which") means "wherefore" or, if English style prefers, "therefore." The connection, as most commentators (but see Mussner, p. 101) rightly perceive, is with the entire preceding section 1:12-20, i.e., "Therefore, because of what is said in 1:12-20, give up your unclean life, etc." This advice, which is of a comprehensive and general nature, is for everybody and not merely for preachers and their preaching: against Scaer, p. 63.

In the same way peace (and forgiving love) in Rom. 12:18-21, especially v. 21, coupled with civic obedience and duty in 13:1-7 and with brotherly love in 13:8-10 ("Love is the fulfilling of the law" is the equivalent of "wrath does not express in action the righteousness of God," Jas. 1:20), leads up to 13:11-16, famous in the story of Augustine's conversion. Strife and envy have their inevitable place in the list, but it is mainly concerned with profligate indulgence in lusts (see Jas. 1:21); thus Paul adds "put on" to the familiar metaphor, "put off." The practical code begins at 12:1, connected by "therefore" (12:1) to the Divinity passage, especially 11:22-38. Note the moral logic linking 11:22 (NIV): "provided that you continue in his kindness. Otherwise . . . ," and 12:1, "therefore . . ."; note also how 12:1 is immediately preceded by the comprehensive Divinity verse, 11:36. Paul's phrase is paralleled, in thought and art, in Heb. 12:1 (NIV): "Let us throw off everything that hinders, and the sin that so easily entangles." So the exhortation in 12:2, resumed at 12:12, enjoins first peace (v. 14), then holiness (i.e., purity) (also v. 14); in v. 16 chastity reappears, along with worldliness, as in the case of Esau. This order of (a) peace and (b) purity appears again in Eph. 1:19-21. The order is reversed in Eph. 4:19-26; Col. 3:5-8; also 1 Thess. 4:1-8, 9-12 and 5:5-11, 13 *(eirēneuete).*

We need not expatiate on the Divinity chapter of Ephesians (ch. 3, esp. vv. 9-20). It is more detailed than James's Divinity statement (1:16-18). Note Eph. 3:17 and its "epitome," that "Christ may dwell in your hearts by faith . . . that you may . . . know . . . , filled to the measure of all the fulness of God" (NIV). Note also the *immediate* transition to "his power that is at work within us" and to the practical, beginning again with, "then, I urge you . . ." (Eph. 4:25). Here "putting off" repeats the verb of v. 22. Also observe that the Divinity verse (about the "new self . . . created to be like God in true righteousness" (v. 24, NIV); compare "born of God" by the "Word of truth," Jas. 1:18) is immediately followed by *dio,* "therefore," introducing a practical code, just as 1:18 led at once to the practical directive of 1:19, 21. Here the moral logic in Ephesians and in the Epistle of James is obviously the same.

The same sequence is found in 1 Peter, where the Divinity theme of 1:1-12 leads on, by "wherefore" *(dio),* to the practical directive of 1:13-16; then in vv. 17-25 the author reverts the Divinity theme (note esp. v. 23; see Jas. 1:18 again) but immediately, at 2:1, he returns to practical directives, which continue to 3:12 (some come later). Notice also how the practical directive at 2:1 turns from the Divinity theme of 1:25 with "therefore . . . rid yourselves of all malice" (NIV) *(apothemenoi oun pasan kakian),* which is very close to Jas. 1:21, "Wherefore strip off all filthiness and prodigality of vice" *(dio apothemenoi pasan ryparian kai perisseian kakias).* This is the ubiquitous moral logic of Christianity, namely, that the *data* of faith entail its *facienda.* All these *apothemenoi* passages show a definite, recognizable concord about basic conduct following conversion. This common concord seems to throw a satisfying light on much that commentaries have sometimes left obscure, reaffirming in particular that the Epistle of James is definitely Christian and not simply a Jewish document with Christian touches.

From the "need for repentance" James inevitably proceeds to "the impulse thereto," namely, through acceptance of the divinely implanted impulse toward repentance. There is no need here to speculate on the meaning of this: "implanting" is here what grammars call a "pregnant construction," indicating both God's offer and the individual human person's acceptance thereof, thus effecting completion just as human birth completes impregnation. This Christian doctrine of regeneration is put concisely in Eph. 2:10, a verse that (as we believe) contains the ingredients of Jas. 1:18-22 (NEB), for example: ". . . created in Christ Jesus to devote ourselves to the good deeds . . ." (that was part of "the Word of God"). Even "the gift of God" in Eph. 2:8 chimes with Jas. 1:18, "by his own set purpose" *(boulētheis),* Eph. 4:20-25 repeats the Christian argument in fuller form but is still parallel with James, and v. 25 emphasizes Christian fellowship using the same train of thought as in 1:9f. Then vv. 26f. resemble James on anger and endurance under *peirasmos* by the devil (1:19f., 14, et al.). Eph. 4:24 is very close to Jas. 1:18, and "strip off" in Eph. 4:22 chimes with Jas. 1:21 on "filthiness and vicious excess," where we almost hear *(sotto voce)* "after your former practice," reminding us of the transformation to be wrought by the gospel at work in human life and constantly at war with sin.

As Ropes says, *logos* here means the Christian gospel.[73] Of the

73. P. 166. The relation of James's use of the *logos* to the Johannine *logos* is intriguing, since it appears as a Christian christological title only in the Johannine writings and is widespread in the religious writings of Greece and Iran. John's use of the term, and James's also, probably owes most to the statements on the Word in early Jewish writings on the Word, Wisdom, and Torah, where the reference is to the autonomous Word of God. It is not known when Wisdom and Torah became associated with the Word. The concept of Wisdom as a preexistent and personal entity is common in Jewish Wisdom literature, notably in Prov. 8:22-26 and Wis. 7:26. For the rabbis the Wisdom of God was the Torah, which they describe as preexistent, firstborn, the agent of creation, life, light, and truth. It is not here implied that the use of the *logos* in John's Prologue or, less likely, in James's Epistle stems directly from an earlier Hymn to Wisdom; but the coincidence is striking, and the religious language and thought of Jewish-Christianity in Asia Minor undoubtedly owed much to the Greeks. Further on this, see, e.g., G. Fries, B. Klappert, "Word" *(logos), NIDNTT,* III,108ff.; also our discussion, pp. 379f.

three objections Ropes cites and rejects, the second and third seem without force.[74] The first is not consistent with a proper view of the sequence of thought in the whole of this passage, the logic of which, and the phraseology seen in this and the other *apothemenoi* parallels, is definitely as Christian as anything in Paul (e.g., Rom. 11:36 immediately preceding 12:1). In fact, this passage displays exactly that harmony with the characteristic and fundamental tenets of primitive Christianity that we should expect if Acts 2:42 has any meaning at all. Further, we cannot see that it reflects any epoch except that of the primitive apostolic beginnings of Christianity, especially its baptismal catechesis. Both as history and theology, the *logos* and all the rest of Jas. 1 stand firmly within the four corners of, for example, Acts 6.

There is no better commentary on the *logos* in Jas. 1 than Acts 6:2, 4, and 7. That *logos* signifies both certain facts, the evidence for them, and their antecedents and no less infinite consequences and implications, as we see in Acts 2:22-40, summed up in v. 42 cited above. That the Torah was an expression of divine truth was a basic Jewish belief. Thus the midrash on Ps. 25:10 reads, "All your ways are grace and truth." "Grace" means God's acts of love, and "truth" means Torah. For James, too, "truth" means the Word or Torah, the truth revealed by Christ in his life and teaching, especially the Christian Torah of love. This notion of another, final interpretation of the Mosaic Torah by the Messiah, which pervades our Epistle (1:21, 25; 2:8, 12), is in turn linked with the idea of Israel as the children of the Torah.

By this Word God has chosen to renew Israel by bringing forth the Christian church, which, like Israel, is "the firstfruits of his creation" (Jas. 1:18). "Receive" in this context means "really accept"; not just "hear" and "disregard" or "reject" but accept with both the privilege and the duty thereof. In the battle with evil, and especially lusts, the Christian's weapons are repentance, the gospel, and good works.[75] We must resist lust, bring forth the fruits of repentance, and wholeheartedly welcome the implanted Word of truth. By God's grace, therefore, we shall overcome the assaults of evil and win the salvation of our souls.

In common with the apostles, James urges that acceptance of the Word be shown in a new cleanness of life (1:21), and that is precisely

74. For a fuller discussion, see pp. 394ff.

75. Significantly, perhaps a similar pattern is found in Judaism, where repentance, Torah, and good works are said to be effective against the *yēṣer;* e.g., "If God has created the *Evil Yezer,* he also created the Torah as a spice (remedy) against him" (b. Baba Bathra 16a). See Schechter, *Some Aspects of Rabbinic Theology,* pp. 313ff. for further details.

what the wicked world hates (see 2 Tim. 3:12, NEB). Tit. 2:11f. well expresses the moral principle and duty of salvation in Christ, and 2 Pet. 2:14, 17 illustrates the danger, which includes false teachers, whose mischief is not simply that of false theory but of a wicked life (2 Pet. 2:19-22; 3:3). In the Apostolic Age it was indeed hard to be a Christian, and we repeat that the hardest test was not from Nero or hostile Jews but from the corrupt world with its hatred and contempt of those who by baptism bore the "name" of Jesus (2:7).[76] A sensual life of the kind here indicated by James is the opposite of the Christian ideal of brotherhood, and of the peace that is one of the prime essentials of that ideal. James knows full well that none of us can attain the perfection of unblemished righteousness and virtue; but with God's help a genuine Christian can and must strive *toward* that ideal. None of the NT apostles excels James in Christian sympathy and care for weak or errant brethren.

G. R. Beasley-Murray observes that the closing words of the Epistle of James convey an impression of revealing the thing that is nearest to his heart: "If a brother falls into sin, you know that he who brings him back to the right way will save a soul from death and hide a multitude of sins."[77] It is not hard to think of the author of the Epistle as the brother of the Lord.

James does not report the coming of the gospel, nor does he ignore it. Rather, he makes it the key to human life here and hereafter, as he makes perfectly clear in 2:8. The primitive Christians had difficult problems to solve, for example, in worship, in the logical relationships with old Jewish law, sacred and secular, and in the characteristic code of Christian life; indeed, "no other book of the New Testament concentrates so exclusively on ethical questions."[78] Yet it is wrong to say that "for all its intensity James hardly rises above the level of a manual of moral instruction."[79] James's morality springs from his theology. He is not indifferent to Christian doctrine but presupposes it. His religious theme is Christianity as a way of life, as Judaism had been since Moses. Conduct, not theology, was the paramount test for both the old Jew and the new James. Religion is paramount in human life, but only because

76. See F. Mussner, "Die Tauflehre des Jakobusbriefes," Hansjorg auf der Maur und Bruno Kleinheyer, eds., *Zeichen des Glaubens, Studien zu Taufe und Firmung*, F. S. Balthasar Fischer zum 60. Geburtstag (1962): 61-67; Hoppe, p. 85. For another view, see Laws, pp. 19f.

77. P. 40.

78. W. Schrage, "Ethik des Neuen Testaments," *Grundrisse zum Neuen Testament*, IV (1982), 266.

79. Blackman, p. 32.

life is paramount in religion. And surely there can be no great harm in teaching that it took the Jewish Christians some time to realize the fuller meaning of Christ. Palm Sunday was just another of our rebel demonstrations, and the crown of thorns signified not spiritual agony but political derision. Given the political conditions (exquisitely explosive) of the ministry of Jesus, it was surely necessary for him and the apostles to concentrate on *didachē* ("teaching") not *kerygma* ("preaching"), on ethics not theology, least of all the theology of an incarnate God.

Whatever the reason, James, like the extracanonical book called the Didache, does in fact concentrate mainly on conduct. His view of God is an essential, but tacit, basis for his way of life, and rather than an example of "how the gospel came to be moralized in over-reaction against the Pauline *kerygma*"[80] it seems to be clearly the most primitive Christian apostolic *hᵃlāḵāh* ("way of life") we possess. This distinction between *kerygma* (proclamation) and *didachē* (teaching) is of prime importance: the former was concerned mainly with efforts to win the hearers to Christ, the latter—of which the Epistle of James is a superb example—with efforts to inculcate the way of life required of the truly faithful believer. Yet, be it noted, James's preoccupation with *didachē* is not to the exclusion of *kerygma*. This important point, it is suggested, is sometimes obscured to some degree by James's "calculated indirectness" of style.[81] But preaching *is present* in this Epistle, and in sustained prophetic fashion in the last two chapters, although as sometimes happens, preaching merges almost imperceptibly with teaching in the body of the Epistle, suggesting that "teaching" was more than ethical instruction but included proclamation of "Jesus Christ the God of glory." This may mean that the once firm distinction between teaching and preaching requires revision.[82]

There is accordingly a right way of life for us. The OT, and much more consistently the NT after the incarnation and the crucifixion, reveals God not as a ruthless Dictator but as an active and compassionate partner in human life. "I have come that they may have life, and have it to the full" (Jn. 10:10, NIV). No one, except Jesus in the Gospels, excels James in his proclamation of that truth.

The bond of sacred (or indeed secular) partnership is *faith,* and

80. For a thorough discussion and literature, see McDonald, *Kerygma and Didache*, pp. 1ff.; also K. Wegenast, "Teach" *(didaskalia)*, *NIDNTT*, III, 769ff.

81. Beasley-Murray, p. 12; see also R. P. Martin, *New Testament Foundations*, II, 364f.

82. On this see, e.g., R. C. Worley's discussion of C. H. Dodd's theory of *kerygma* and *didachē* in "Preaching and Teaching in the Primitive Church," *McCormick Quarterly* 20.1 (1966): 12-25.

James declares our duty to show that faith by our endurance, that is, both our steadfastness against the assaults of the devil and all the other enemies of our soul and our steadfastness in our religious belief and, not a jot less, in its standard of conduct.

In his ethical and catechetical interpretation of religion among the Jews, James displays a loyal mind of his own. He appears to belong, says L. Goppelt,[83] "to a stream of early Christian tradition that stretched from Matthew's Gospel to the Didache and further to the regulations of the Syrian Church. In this Syrian-Palestinian tradition one tried to restate what it meant to be a Christian through regulations for living and thus to portray it in empirical terms." He goes on to say, without offering any proof, that this way of doing things stood in tension with the conventional parenesis in the Pauline realm. We have, we think, sufficiently emphasized that Judaism is essentially a *way of life* (witness, e.g., the doctrinal freedom of the Sadducees, who knew no resurrection [Mt. 22:23]), and that correspondingly the Epistle of James is conspicuously a moral code for Christians, akin to Pseudo-Phocylides and other Jewish ethical literature.[84] The nearest modern equivalent might be the "catechism" that used to be taught in our Sunday Schools. But in primitive Christianity adults no less than their children had to be taught the Christian faith, and Carrington, perhaps not superfluously, remarks that he is not attributing to James anything as elaborate as, for example, a modern sectarian "Authorized Cathechism" (such as the Westminster Shorter Catechism). James concentrates rather on the difference that genuine acceptance of Christ must make in any human life.

The contents of such a catechesis seem to have been adapted to current Christian needs, but evidence of a common basis of belief is to

83. *Theology of the New Testament,* II, 207f.

84. This ancient poem, a product of Hellenistic Judaism written in Greek hexameter lines, contains a series of aphorisms, many of which at least in form resemble those in the Epistle of James. To cite only one example: line 144 reads "Look from how tiny a spark a forest's expanse can be kindled." See also Dibelius, p. 4 and throughout his commentary; Carrington, *The Primitive Christian Catechism,* p. 9; B. S. Easton, "Pseudo-Phocylides," *ATR* 14 (1932): 222-28 for introduction and English text; P. W. van der Horst, *The Sentences of Pseudo-Phocylides* (1978), p. 4; L. T. Johnson, "The Use of Leviticus 19 in the Letter of James," *JBL* 101 (1982): 392ff., on the use of Lev. 19 in Pseudo-Phocylides; also Vermes, Millar, Goodman, and Schürer, *The History of the Jewish People in the Age of Jesus Christ,* III, 1 (1986), 687-92; P. W. van der Horst, "Pseudo-Phocylides (First Century B.C.-First Century A.D.)," *The Old Testament Pseudepigrapha,* ed. J. H. Charlesworth, II, 565-82; G. Klein, *Der älteste christliche Katechismus* (1909), p. 57, on the *derek 'ereṣ* literature in relation to the catechetical process in general and the Epistle of James in particular.

be seen in the general sequence of contents and (within reasonable variations) in a common vocabulary. The Epistle of James is indebted to a similar catechetical stock, prevailing pattern, and basic moral ideas and vocabulary as Paul, Peter, and others, though with sufficient variation due to James's individuality and purpose.

One obvious value of the Epistle of James is that it contains information about the obscure but extremely important period of Jewish Christianity about which the NT, apart from the Gospels and the Acts, is so strangely silent. "Written less than one generation after the salvific events," wrote Scaer, "James reflects the theological tensions of the early Church as it lived between its still vivid memory of Jesus and its anticipation of His early return as the world's judge."[85] We agree.

In this Epistle, we suggest, we reach a lower stratum of Christian life than elsewhere in the NT except in some of the sources that lie behind the Synoptic Gospels. So we are entrusted with an instrument with which we may penetrate more deeply into the history of the Jewish Christian community, a history in which agreement is often no easier to achieve than in secular history.[86] We must constantly remember that we are dealing with a formative rather than a more settled stage of Christianity, a stage when its leaders were less apt to be "tied to the book." We have seen that that outlook and those ideas in the Epistle of James are intensely Jewish in tone—so much so that some regard it as originally a Jewish writing into which a few Christian phrases have been interpolated. It is certainly closer to the OT than any other NT book and suggests a very primitive type of Christianity, a Christianity whose theological implications are there but have not yet been fully worked out, as have those of the Pauline Epistles, Hebrews, or the Fourth Gospel.

Is the Epistle, then, possibly a deliberate effort by a Christian Jew to reconcile Christian and non-Christian Jews? Attractive in this connection is the hypothesis that the Epistle of James was, in part at least, an appeal via ethics rather than doctrine to non-Christian Jews by James the Lord's brother, the one Christian leader whom the Jews respected, thus building a bridge between Judaism and Christianity.[87] This would explain the silence on the scandal of the suffering Messiah and other distinctively Christian doctrines, as well as the indirect rather than direct quotation of the sayings of Jesus. There is, indeed, a Judaic tone to the Epistle, and while it has three OT illustrations of endurance, it is sig-

85. P. 22.

86. See Selwyn, p. 459.

87. See C. F. D. Moule, *The Birth of the New Testament* (1962), p. 166; G. C. Martin, "The Epistle of James as a Storehouse of the Sayings of Jesus," *Ex* 4 (1907): 45-55. See also our remarks, p. 67.

nificantly silent on the example, death, and resurrection of Christ; also, unlike Peter, James scarcely mentions the name of Christ.

On the other hand, the Jewish Torah on which the catechism is based does appear to be baptized into the teaching of the Sermon of the Mount.[88] "The School of Catechists which preserved the material," wrote Halson, "is to be connected with James of Jerusalem, and we may even speculate that the use of the Wisdom form originated with him. The members of the School may have been scattered in one period following his martyrdom in Jerusalem. Such a thesis provides an explanation for some of the puzzling features of the Epistle. If it is true that we have here catechisms set in a particular 'mold,' we have an explanation for the apparent absence of specifically 'Christian' features."[89] The "words of Christ" *(verba Christi)* constitute the code of this original Christian community, representing a new Law of Holiness and perhaps, as Carrington says, in the first instance, "a transcript of the baptismal torah of the school of James the brother of the Lord."[90]

Originally circulated in the Diaspora as the authoritative pronouncement of the Lord's brother and thoroughly saturated with the words of Jesus, the Epistle of James would naturally be cherished and almost certainly employed as a primitive baptismal liturgy for catechetical purposes among Jewish Christians until and almost certainly after the death of James. The Jewish Hellenistic teachers in Jerusalem (Acts 5–8) would use this unique Jacobean material in accordance with the necessities of their own fellowship and possibly accommodate it to their own state of development.

CONCLUSION

Apart from its intrinsic worth, James's Epistle would be of great practical value. But how was it preserved?

Thus far we have glanced at the Epistle in the context of the Jewish Christian synagogue and suggested that, like Paul's Epistles, it may originally have been delivered in such a setting. But the answer to

88. This projection of the evangelic strain in the Epistle of James partially reflects the contribution of the early founders of Jewish Christianity, which M. Goguel described as an attempt "to develop the feelings and experiences which, directly or indirectly, had been implanted in them through the impression made on them by Jesus' person and teaching" (*The Life of Jesus* [1933], p. 585; see also Selwyn, pp. 358f., Essay II on *verba Christi* in catechesis).

89. B. R. Halson, "The Epistle of James: Christian Wisdom?" *StEv* IV = *TU* 102 (1968): 308-14.

90. *The Primitive Christian Catechism*, p. 70.

this further question is dependent not only on the form of synagogue worship but also on the form of synagogue instruction. It is axiomatic that the Jewish teacher in the NT period did not commit his teachings to writing. The disciple of a teaching rabbi was compared to a "plastered cistern which loses no water"[91] and trained to recollect and transmit his exact words. Undoubtedly the first Christians transmitted their *didachē* in the same manner; and it is unlikely, if our research has been accurate, that the Epistle of James was treated differently. The teaching incorporated in the Epistle of James is compact, terse, and picturesque, written in easily remembered language and given by the self-designated teacher, James himself.

We may well imagine that the Epistle of James was heard with the same eagerness that marked the hearers of the rabbinic *hᵃlāḵāh*. But while "the *hᵃlāḵāh* of James is pietistic and partakes of the quality of Qumran," Sigal correctly observes, "it is nevertheless also proto-rabbinic because of James's long period of pragmatic leadership in Jerusalem, where he was distant from the monastic and pietistic ambience of Qumran and alienated from those circles that were part of the large Essene and Qumranite movements."[92] The position James held as head of the Jerusalem Church would in itself guarantee an attentive hearing. It may indeed be that the material was memorized in the first place by mnemonic devices, for example, catchwords.[93] In such a teaching tradition, great care would be exercised to guarantee accurate preservation. This was certainly true in the synagogue instruction; and, we surmise, there would be no less concern for the same policy in the primitive church and especially in a metropolitan center like Jerusalem.

The original *Sitz im Leben* of the Epistle of James must therefore be traced to Jerusalem, where it was first composed as a letter by James the head of the Jewish Christian church and preserved for baptismal parenesis by his disciples and his congregations. Palestinian Christianity, especially the orthodox section of the Jewish Church, apparently lacked literary incentive; for this we must look to Hellenistic influence. In the case of James, we believe that this specific incentive was supplied by the Greek element of the Church at Jerusalem, which, despite its exodus after Stephen's death, would still persist to some degree: this would be the immediate cause of the preservation of the Epistle. We have already seen that it was admirably suited for catechetical purposes,

91. M. Aboth 2.10.

92. *Art. cit., Intergerini Parietis Septum* (1981), p. 339.

93. See L. Finkelstein, "The Early Rabbinic Traditions," *HUCA* 16 (1941): 115; also *Proceedings of the American Academy of Jewish Research,* VI, 200ff.

and now it would almost certainly be used in the regular baptismal instruction of the Hellenistic converts. The exigencies of church life and the needs of the converts would call for the conservation and reemphasis of this Jacobean *didachē*. The fact that it was written in Greek and associated with the Hellenists suggests that it may have found a home in some center like Pella, Caesarea, or Antioch in northern Palestine or Syria until it was rescued and taken to some such center as Egypt.

Such a document would undoubtedly be cherished during and after the lifetime of James, whose authority certainly extended far beyond Jerusalem to Jews throughout the Dispersion. Ultimately, this would lead to its entrance into the Hellenistic Christian stream of tradition, mainly through baptismal catechesis, and this is the basic clue to its ensuing history. So preserved, the Epistle is inextricably bound with the fortunes of the Greek wing of the Jewish Christian church.

Excursus A

JAMES 1:19—A SUGGESTED EMENDATION

Following most of the MSS,[1] our versions read *iste* and translate "Know you," "Know this," or something similar. If so read, *iste* must be imperative, as Ropes (p. 168) says. But we reject this reading, for it is hopelessly weak, and—abruptly used without any explanation such as a *hoti* clause or *touto*—is without parallel in James (or, we believe, the NT). The next *iste* is thus impossible. The citations of its only other NT occurrences in Ephesians and Hebrews show how it can be used. Hort's idea that "Know you" is just the positive of "Make no mistake" is unfounded. The latter, as it has been pointed out, is a regular introduction to a quotation or maxim in the NT, not an exhortation: "Make no mistake" would have been out of place here. Mayor takes it as indicative—a reading that is equally impossible: we cannot make out Mayor's reference to Jas. 1:20. His references from 1 John do not touch the point, they have an object or clause, and they do *not* come in an abrupt belch such as the commentators give in James.

Further, this reading obscures the logic of James's thought. In Jas. 1:16 *mē planasthe* is taken up in sense in the following sentence. But "Know" (or even "Know this") and "let every man . . ." are not connected, and "Know" (without "this") is not James's way of referring to what he has just said. The

1. See, e.g., B. M. Metzger, *A Textual Commentary on the Greek New Testament* (1975), p. 680; R. Hill, *An Overview of the Discourse Structure of James* (1978), pp. 6ff.

reading of the Antiochian group of MSS may be "a characteristic emendation," but with *iste* such an emendation was obviously needed, and whether as traditional or an emendation, *hōste* is as valuable (subject to a limitation we will presently mention) as the Peshitta reading at 3:6 (Ropes, p. 234, penultimate paragraph). It develops the argument at 1:19 in a manner worthy of James. The confusion of the MSS at 1:19 on *de, kai,* or the omission of any conjunction suggests that the Antiochian reading is more than an emendation: when *hōste* was corrupted to *iste* the temptation to add *de* or *kai* to *estō* was obvious. The use of *hōste* as an illative conjunction with the imperative is regular enough in the NT. Phil. 4:1, *hōste, adelphoi mou agapētoi,* which concludes the argument of Phil. 3:15-20, is a good parallel to Jas. 1:19, *hōste, adelphoi mou agapētoi,* which concludes 1:12-20.

Further, we believe there was a special reason why *hōste* was misread as *iste*. We believe *hōste* itself originated as a gloss or substitution for *hothen* ("wherefore"). This word is not so common in the NT, though it appears in Mt. 14:7, Acts 26:19, and not infrequently in the Epistle to the Hebrews. It will be remembered that only in the Epistle to the Hebrews (if at all) does the NT approach Classical Greek (*Kunstprosa,* "euphonic prose") more closely than in the Epistle of James.

Here we think the Epistle of James used *hothen* followed by *dio,* exactly as the Epistle to the Hebrews has *hothen, adelphoi hagioi* followed by *dio* in 3:1, 7. It is curious that *katanoēsate Iēsoun* in Heb. 3:1 and the message in 3:7-13 are very close to that of James in our present passage, 1:19-21. The word *hothen,* not uncommon in Demosthenes, is nevertheless supplanted by *hōs* in Pseudo-Demosthenes, *Oration* 49.40: *Against Timotheos* in MS A. The best MS is S; by far the next best is A, but it has the weakness of making the text easier for the schoolboy. The sentence runs: "One of your relatives or friends would have been bound to know *from what source* Philondas procured the money to pay the shipmaster the fare."

In James the meaning is less literal, but it seems someone thought it would be easier. "Wherefore, my beloved brothers, . . ." seems quite excellent to us.

3. Plan

"Suppose James had been writing this Epistle to read it, or have it read, into a microphone to go out on the air. I imagine, in the ignorance of my complete inexperience, that he would write it so that it could be divided up into convenient little sections, each fairly intelligible by itself and nicely typed, as it were on its own separate sheet but all adding up to a coherent and integrated whole. Could I do this for you, with the Epistle of James? It ought to be possible, for, in principle, that is precisely what James was aiming at."

P. B. R. Forbes, "The Structure of the Epistle of James," *The Evangelical Quarterly* 44.3 (1972): 149

It has wrongly but commonly been denied that there is any unity or plan to the composition of the Epistle of James. "James," wrote Martin Luther, "throws things together so chaotically that it seems to me he must have been some good, pious man who took a few sayings from the disciples of the apostles and tossed them off on paper. Or it may perhaps have been written by someone on the basis of his preaching."[1] Here is a hint of the conjecture that the Epistle of James is an incomplete compilation of older sayings based on a better collection, perhaps sermonic, a view that repeatedly recurred to Luther and others.

Most critics (there are some notable exceptions)[2] suggest that the work is loose in structure[3] and has no unity or methodical train of

1. *LW,* XXXV, 397. More recently, H. F. Stevenson delivered a similar verdict: "No Epistle in the New Testament is more disjointed than James" (*James Speaks for Today* [1966], p. 29).

2. For references see Dibelius, p. 6, n. 22; worthy of mention are Cladder, Motyer, Johnson, Parry, Francis, Forbes, Davids, and others.

3. Laws, p. 6.

thought,[4] but is rather a "handful of pearls,"[5] a diffuse and disconnected anthology of loosely connected preexisting sayings,[6] Wisdom logia,[7] Islamic *ahadith,*[8] or even independent sources,[9] flyleaves of prophetic addresses,[10] an "ethical scrapbook,"[11] or a literary mosaic of a somewhat artificial character, having definite resemblances to the Wisdom books, diatribe, and especially parenesis.[12] There is no sustained or progressive chain of argument or even instruction, so far as *they* can discover—the writer is continually indulging in apparent digressions. There are many detached and isolated sayings that seem to bear no relation to their context; and the whole composition lacks continuity of thought and is badly arranged and set forth. In a word, the book is "planless." Some have relented and suggested a plan—but not for the Epistle per se but rather, with some degree of plausibility, for the social situation that produced the Epistle.[13] The book is a rubric of warnings against social injustice, and this is the unifying force.

But significant progress has been reported in this entire area of structure. After analyzing the Epistle, a team of scholars from the International Linguistics Center, Dallas, for example, discovered a definite, discernible structure, with all the marks of an artist's meticulous care[14]—findings that, in most instances, however, we had already anticipated.

4. W. G. Kümmel, *Introduction to the New Testament* (^{2}1975), p. 284. For an excellent summary of various opinions, see D. E. Hiebert, "The Unifying Theme of the Epistle of James," *Bibliotheca Sacra* 135 (1978): 221ff.

5. E. J. Goodspeed, *An Introduction to the New Testament* (1946), p. 290. See also our discussion below, pp. 100ff.

6. C. von Weizsäcker, *The Apostolic Age of the Christian Church,* II (ET 1895), 27ff.

7. T. Y. Mullins, "Jewish Wisdom Literature in the New Testament," *JBL* 68 (1949): 338.

8. E. F. F. Bishop, *The Apostles of Palestine* (1958), p. 178.

9. Oesterley, pp. 466f. See also Ropes, p. 228, on the belief that Jas. 3:2-12 is based on a written tract.

10. J. E. Symes, "The Epistle of James," *The Interpreter* 9.4 (1913): 406-13.

11. A. M. Hunter, *Introducing the New Testament* (1946), p. 96.

12. E.g., Dibelius, pp. 1ff., "The Literary Genre of the Letter of James."

13. See, e.g., P. U. Maynard-Reid, *Poverty and Wealth in James* (1987), pp. 11, 105 n. 50; P. R. Jones, "Approaches to the Study of the Book of James," *Rev Exp* 66 (1969): 431; A. S. Geyser, "The Letter of James and the Social Condition of His Addressees," *Neotestamentica* 9 (1975): 25-33; also Mussner, p. 57.

14. J. O. Ekstrom, "The Discourse Structure of the Book of James" (1975); C. Rountree, "Further Thoughts on the Discourse Structure of James" (1976); "Discourse Analysis of James" (1976); R. Hill, "Overview of James" (1978); K. Torakawa, "James 1–2" (1978); R. Hill, "James 3–5" (1978); R. Hill, "Displays of Paragraph Constituent Level for James 3–5" (1978).

We believe, and propose to show, that, far from being formless, the Epistle is built on a carefully constructed, harmonious pattern, the product of a single powerful mind.

CATCHWORDS

G. R. Beasley-Murray asks, "Is there a plan in this writing?" Then he states, without acceptance but also without decisive denial, the view of "most critics": "Paragraphs are linked by catchwords, so causing the topics to be connected and developed apparently in purely accidental fashion."[15] The examples given are "rejoice" (1:1), followed by "joy" (1:2) and "lacking" (1:4f.); 3:18 closes the paragraph with a reference

15. The catchwords on which the critics, as reported by Beasley-Murray, p. 16, base their view of James as an amiable wanderer are in fact almost confined to the beginning of the Epistle, to the first section in our analysis of its structure. We think that all of them except those in that first section are included in the list below, and almost none in the list is on the same footing as catchwords in the full sense alleged by the critics as clues to James's procedure in composing his letter.

1:12-14:	*peirasmois*	+	4:2:	*aiteisthai*. See below.
14:	*epithymias*	*	11:	(*katalaleite* +
15:	*hamartia*	*		(*krinōn*
				(*nomon*
19:	*orgēn*	+	5:9:	*krithēte* +
21:	*logon*	+	11:	*hypomenontas**
26:	*thrēskos*	+	17:	*brexai;* insignificant
2:8-12:	*nomon*	+	19:	*epistrepsē*
14-26:	*erga*	+		
17:	*karpōn*	*		

+ not a *bridge* as 1:3f., but a *beginning.*
*not a *bridge,* but an *end.* The critics speak as if these were like 1:3f. and 1:21f.

Notes on the above list.

2:8-12—the word occurs often in this passage: see *peirasmos,* etc. (1:11-14), and *erga* (2:14-26).

4:2—this certainly is a repetition signifying not a transition to a new topic but the coherence of unity of thought in an organized climax, very much like 1:2-8 or as in the list of differing but kindred sins of 4:1-3. On examination it will be found that almost all or all of the above, except in 1:21, serve for continuity only, not, like *hypomonēn* in 1:2, as preludes to a point such as in 1:4, *hē de hypomonē.* My little Bagster's *Greek and English New Testament* indents for a new paragraph at 1:2, 5, 9, 12, 16, 19, 22, 26; at 2:1, 10, 12, 14, 21, 25; at 3:1, 7, 13; at 4:1, 4, 11, 13; and at 5:1, 7, 9, 12, 13, 16, 19. "Candidates" are underlined. 1:2—see *chair. char.* valid in 1:5 in the first section. 1:22—admitted, uniquely. 2:10, 12, 25—in organized, not haphazard, discourse. 4:1—semantic, not haphazard link peace/war. Only that in 1:21f., we think, can be verified. 2:8-13 and 14-16 are not really parallel; their breaks do not carry anything really new.

to those who make peace, and 4:1 asks where wars and fighting originate. It is *therefore* (my italics) generally felt that the author had no plan in mind when he began his letter and that he wandered amiably as he reproduced the popular religious and ethical ideas of his day.

Let us say at once that, apart from the cases just mentioned, there is in the whole of James only one other example in which "paragraphs are linked by catchwords" and in which the second introduces a really new point, namely, 1:21f., where "the engrafted Word" at the end of one paragraph is caught up in the next paragraph, beginning "But be doers of the Word, and not hearers only. . . ." Nobody could say that these points are "connected and developed apparently in purely accidental fashion," or that that is true of the transition from peace to war in 4:1. In 1:5, likewise, we think that wisdom in righteousness is not irrelevant in a summary, as we take it to be of the day-to-day position and needs of the Christian, which we believe is the theme of 1:2-11. In 2:9 the thought of law, already mentioned in 2:8, passes on into 2:10ff. But this continuation does not really introduce a new point, nor is it wandering; rather, it states the arguments for the charge made in v. 9.

The whole passage, vv. 8-13, is a continuous unity and as far as could be from anything "developed apparently in purely accidental fashion"; and the same is true of the paragraphs beginning at 2:21 and 25 within the coherent unity of vv. 14-26, with many repetitions of the word "works" and some other words. In 4:2, "ask," recurring twice in v. 3, is another good example of the use of these unifying repetitions; it comes toward the end of the climax built up in 4:1-3. 5:9 is linked to the previous verse, but not by a catchword; the link is the common thought of the parousia, expressed differently in the two verses and more vividly, of course, in the latter: James is not really the wanderer that critics see reflected in the Epistle of James. The best example of this unifying technique is in the opening verses of the Epistle.

Let us look at this first section, 1:1-11. As to the opening salutation, we would neither maintain nor deny (though we incline to the latter) that the conjunction of the verb of greeting and the noun for joy in vv. 1 and 2 respectively is anything more than accidental. But we hold that in vv. 2-11 James is deliberately trying to summarize the day-to-day situation of the Christian. Writing, as he does, with a plan, he shows that the variety of points mentioned in the opening section are invested with unity, and that, more than by anything else, by the use of those catchwords, which have so impressed the critics who apparently have read no further in the Epistle, he here achieves the unity that both as apostle and artist he deemed essential for his opening sentences. In the rest of his letter the problem is easier.

Verses 2 and 3 are linked by the semantic and grammatical connection between "consider" and "realizing," vv. 3 and 4 by "patience," and within v. 4 "perfect" work leads to the next point, "that you be perfect." "Lacking" at the end of v. 4 leads to "be lacking" in wisdom in v. 5; and "let him ask" leads into v. 6, which begins with the same word and adds "nothing wavering," which is immediately followed by "For the waverer" with exactly the same word in the Greek. Following this are vv. 7 and 8. Mark the artistry. In v. 7, as hardly ever happens in the Epistle of James, there is scarcely any art at all, either in form or in force, any more than in, for example, "That's the man from whom I get my newspaper." But in v. 8 you feel at once the force of James's brilliant invention, the word "*dipsychos,*" and even the word for man in v. 8 belongs to a higher style than that in v. 7. The adjective for "unsettled," in the NT only here and in 3:8, is likewise of the higher style, and forcible. It is noteworthy that in 1:20 the weightier word for man follows the lighter, used in the previous verse; and although v. 19 is very carefully balanced, v. 20 is far superior in force, brevity, and sentiment.

In the next section, "Contents and Coherence," we shall see how James returns to where he began. Here, too, he starts with "joy" and ends with "Let him [poor or rich] exult" in his reward. But the unconverted rich will find no joy in his.

For the sake of completeness we will mention the other repetitions in the Epistle of James: 1:12 (tempting), 19 (wrath), 26 (pious), 3:2 (falling), 4:11 (speaking ill, judging, law), and 5:9 (being judged). There are no bridges from topic to topic: they come in the beginning of the new topic of the paragraph, for example, piety in 1:26. There remain 1:14 (lust), 15 (sin), 3:17 (fruits), 5:11 (endure), 17 (rain), and 19 (convert). These all come at or toward the *end* of a paragraph, completing it, and not at all taken up in the next; indeed, in 5:19f. the Epistle ends.

The critics speak about catchwords as aids to the amiable wanderer. There are almost *no* catchwords in the rest of the Epistle, and those in 1:6 (or 2:6) are elements in a consummate little piece of architecture, continued otherwise, but with no less unifying art, to the end of the section (v. 11)

CONTENTS AND COHERENCE

(1) In our view, every principle and theme in the rest of the Epistle of James is repeated, expanded, or derived from 1:2-18, on the Christian mind (what are we to believe and feel?), and 1:19-27, on Christian conduct (what are we to do?). There is more unity of thought in James than we sometimes suppose.

Welcome trials: they strengthen faith and perfect the Christian character.

But how can we conquer them? With God's help—who gives godly wisdom to the person who has the humility to ask for it, and the faith to make his prayer effectual. With human help—in unity of Christian brotherhood, in which the poor are no longer mere "lower orders" and the rich put off the false worldly superiority and arrogance of wealth.

For what reward? *Life*—for those who love God and not the world.

Is resistance to temptation really necessary? Do not believe the doctrine that temptation comes from God and so does not need to be resisted but may be indulged. That is not the way of *life*, but of lust, sin, and *death*. God is altogether and always good, and the source of all good. He begot us with the *verbum-ratio* of righteous truth,[16] not of lust, sin, and death, in order that of all his creation we Christians, becoming *teleioi*, "fully ripened" (v. 4), might, like the firstfruits of a harvest, be hallowed to him.

For that reason, namely, that God's good purpose ordains for us the way of right and life, we have a duty of conduct. The account of this begins with v. 19; that conduct is working out of the engrafted Word or perfect law of liberty (vv. 21, 25), the Word of truth (v. 18).

We must now show how the rest of the Epistle is related, as we have said, to the first chapter.

Jas. 2:1-13 returns to the theme of 1:9f., the proper relations of rich and poor in Christian society and the Christian congregation. Respect of persons (2:1) and despising the poor (2:6) constitute a denial of Christian brotherhood, the essential theme, we believe, of 1:9f. as of 1:25, 2:12f., and 2:8 and the implication of the rule of 1:27; it is also a breach of the rule of wholehearted consistency in 1:6-8, as 2:4 indicates.

Jas. 2:14-26 is plainly an elaboration of 1:21ff., "Be doers . . . and not merely hearers."

Chapters 3 and 4 are so closely related as to form almost a unity. Now it is one mark of James's style, as of much other oratory, to round off a paragraph by coming in full circle to the point with which it began: 3:13-18 is an obvious example, beginning and ending with the duty of good works as part of true wisdom. So here James begins the former and ends the latter of these two related chapters with the same warning, namely, the responsibilities of advancement in knowledge (3:1 and 4:17).

Jas. 3:1f. is an application of 1:19, "slow to speak"; 3:13-18, of

16. Ropes, p. 213, last line.

the same verse, "slow to wrath"; and 3:3-12 is related to 1:26 on the duty of bridling the tongue. 3:13, 15, 17 indicate the special application to teachers of the directions against wrath (in 1:19, as already mentioned) and of the directions to humility and good works, as in 1:21f.; on "pure" in 3:17 see 1:21; on "peaceable," "gentle," "easy to be entreated" see 1:27 and 2:13; on "good fruits" see 1:22; on "unwavering" see 1:6; and "without hypocrisy" is close to 1:22, 26.

Jas. 4 continues the topic of strife, addressing now not only the "teachers" of 3:14 but also the rest of the brothers who commit a similar sin: James ascribes strife to the worldly lust of covetousness (see 1:14f.). Boaz Cohen points out that Jews and Gentiles have held that the breaking of the Tenth Commandment leads to trespassing all the commandments:[17] he cites among other references Pesiḳta Rabbati 107a, b, and Seneca, *Moral Epistles* 8.9.

4:6-10 is closely akin to ch. 1. Thus 4:6 and 1:5 both speak of God's liberal grace to the meek and humble; see also 1:21. The second half of 4:8, on purity, harks back to 1:21, 27, and "sinners" and "double-minded," in the same verse, to 1:15 and 6-8. The humble repentance of 4:9f. is akin to that of 1:21, and the concluding promise of 4:10 is not far from that of 1:21, "which is able to save your souls."

James now turns to another sin of the tongue, censorious condemnation of a fellow-Christian (4:11f.). Exactly as in 1:26, this failure to bridle the tongue is a form of self-righteous pride; so is the self-confident boasting of 4:13-16.

4:17, as we said above, returns in full circle to the teacher and the responsibilities of his privileges in wisdom.

In 5:1-6 the diatribe against the rich renews those of 2:1-13 and 1:9-11. We think it is characteristic of James that he begins and ends his chapters of censure (and, indeed, invective) (2:1–5:6) with the same theme, the rich, balanced around the intervening unity of the related chs. 3 and 4.

It also seems characteristic that, after the pattern of some Jewish homiletical,[18] Hellenistic,[19] and even Qumran[20] literature, the Epistle

17. *Law and Ethics in the Light of the Jewish Tradition* (1957), p. 14.

18. For examples, see I. Bettan, *Studies in Jewish Preaching* (1939), pp. 260f., 214.

19. On the final formula, eschatology, summation, prayer, oath, and pagan wish, see Francis, pp. 110-26. Davids, pp. 24ff., 29, uses this article effectively to develop his own thoughts on "Structure."

20. On this and the apparently elaborate and carefully articulated pattern of some Qumran writing, see D. L. Beck, *The Composition of the Epistle of James* (1973), summarized in Mussner, pp. 247ff.

ends with sympathetic encouragement of the faithful to endure. 5:7-12 resembles 1:2-4, and 5:9 is quite relevant to this theme: we know how prone we are to blame our associates for our difficulties. 5:12 belongs to the theme of bridling the tongue (1:19, 26); but we think it is especially related to the circumstances of the fraud of the rich and their oppression of the poor through the courts of law (2:6).

It is significant that, generally, the early preachers concluded their homilies with words of comfort and hope. At times they turned their attention to the glories of the Messianic Age, when oppression and sorrow would no longer plague their people. Occasionally they mused on the happier state in the world to come, when the spirit, freed from the shackles of the body, would engage in higher activities and rejoice in pleasure divine. Not infrequently they would invoke God's blessing on Zion and reiterate their faith in its speedy redemption. In all these they sought to emulate the prophets of old, who closed their messages in a hopeful, inspiring way, despite the severity of their indictment of the people's conduct (Pes. K. 18, 19). After mentioning this in a personal note, O. S. Rankin also points out that at the end of the polemical poem *Zichron Nizzachon de Rabbi Lipmann* (Middle Ages) appear the words:

> *O God, make haste to send a Redeemer,*
> *And mayst Thou declare: "I am the Lord your God."*

5:13-18 may fairly be regarded as expanding the ideas of the first chapter—the fatherhood of God, the brotherhood of Christians, faith, prayer, and salvation—not with upbraiding but with forgiveness. The last injunction in these verses, "Confess your faults . . ." (again characteristically), balances the example at the end of the first parenetic section, about the man who thinks he is religious, boasts, and deceives himself—almost in the language of "The pride of your heart has deceived you" (Obad. 3, NIV) or the familiar, "If we say that we have no sin, we deceive ourselves, and the truth is not in us; but if we confess our sins, he is faithful and just to forgive us our sins, and to cleanse us from all unrighteousness" (1 Jn. 1:8f., KJV).

The last two verses of the Epistle (again characteristically) close the circle by returning to the first verse. In the first verse James "signs on"; in the last sentence he "signs off," saying (not in these exact words, of course) "I hope I have done some of you—and myself—some good." This is *not* a frivolous suggestion of ours, but is in accord with some remarks of Ropes, "Final saying on the privilege of being instrumental in the restoration of an erring brother to the way of truth. . . . It forms a fitting conclusion and gives the motive of the whole tract. . . . Various examples of such erring have occupied the attention of the writer throughout his Epistles *(sic).*"[21]

(2) We have said that in our view Jas. 1:9 ("Let the brother . . .") relates to Christian brotherhood. The usual interpretation is that the poor brother should glory in his present moral progress and the promise of future bliss in heaven, and the rich should glory in the worldly tribulation that is or soon will be his lot in the flesh.[22] This is not satisfactory. As to the poor, this view does not differ perceptibly from what, in vv. 2-4, James has already told *all* the brothers to do, that is, to rejoice in their moral progress toward perfection; and worldly impoverishment, if it comes to the rich brother (we are sure that the reference here is not to the rich unbeliever), is as much within the meaning of *peirasmoi poikiloi* ("manifold or divers trials or temptations") as the hardships of the poor. "Let the poor glory in being lifted up by God, and the rich in his come-down to bankruptcy" makes no sense in religion or rhetoric. It is common knowledge, as 2:5 indicates, that God exalts the poor.

Why does he not exalt the rich? See 4:6: "God sets himself against the *haughty,* but gives grace to the humble." It is not hard to understand that in the ancient world, as in ours, the besetting sin of the rich is arrogance. As a rule, it is only by an act of humility, by putting off this arrogance, that a rich person can become a Christian, as is clear from 4:10: "Humble yourselves before God, and he shall exalt you." It need hardly be said that in this passage (4:1-10) James is addressing some of the richer sort of people. The poor, then, are to glory in being lifted up, by their call to the Kingdom; the rich are to glory in their lowering, in their humbling of themselves, in having put on humility instead of arrogance, and so having made themselves fit to receive the grace of admission to that same Kingdom.

It is obvious that this frame of mind, if sincere, is the only thing that can make Christian society a true brotherhood; anything else lets in at least snobbery, and, beyond that, covetousness and every other sin. Except in our interpretation of 1:9 we do not think anyone would question the relation we have maintained as existing between the first chapter and the rest of the Epistle. "Ch. 2 is more original and less a repetition of current Jewish ideas than any other part of the epistle."[23] It seems to me that that is why the kernel of its thought (as we believe 1:9 *is* the kernel of its thought) appears so soon and so conspicuously in the first chapter.

21. P. 313.

22. E.g., as in Ropes, pp. 145 and 146 *ad fin*. See also W. Grundmann, *tapeinos, TDNT,* VIII, 1-26; our further discussions, e.g., pp. 324ff.

23. Ropes, p. 185.

The very use of the word *"brother"* in 1:9 seems to be deliberately designed to strike, as it does, the note of equality and love. On the common use of the vocative plural, "Brothers," Ropes writes: "It is a form appropriate to a member of a strictly defined society, such as the Jewish or Christian brotherhood, addressing other members whom he recognises as equals. This characteristic distinguishes the Christian parenetic literature from the OT Wisdom Literature."[24]

We believe that the interpretation we have given, instead of leaving 1:9-11 without contact in the Epistle until 5:1-6, unites both of these passages with the passage on snobbery in 2:1-13 and that on lustful avarice in 4:1-10. Since the fourth chapter is unified with the third, as we have said above, we now see throughout the Epistle that unity and coherence which do so much to give this work its characteristic power on the other topics too.

The thought of humbleness and of its opposite, pride, dominates and unites the entire Epistle. It begins, as we think, in 1:10, "Let the rich man glory in his abnegation of the pride of worldly wealth, a wealth which after all comes to nothing." (There is no need for the rich Christian to abdicate his wealth itself, if he can make his possession and use of it compatible with Christian humility. The world needs the conversion of the poor, but even more it needs the conversion of the rich. With their wealth they could do great work for the Kingdom.)

The code of conduct begins with meekness (1:19-21). 1:22, 26 reprobate a vanity of self-deception that is synonymous with pride, as are the vanity of snobbery and contemptuous treatment of the poor in 2:1-13; Christ is not the Lord of that sort of glory. No different is the vanity of faith without wisdom (3:14, "glory not . . ."). In 4:1-10 the life of greed and lust is but the pride of the flesh: God resists the proud (v. 6); the remedy is humility (v. 10) or submission (v. 7). 4:11f., "Who are you, that you pass judgment on your fellow?" is a return to the theme of presumptuous pride. In 4:13-16 we again meet pride, this time in a kindred form of self-confidence; as v. 16 says, "You vaunt yourselves in your bragging; all such vaunting is wicked." The "woe" of 5:1-6 is not parenetic; it shows up in more detail the "surfeit" *(koros)* and "arrogance" *(hybris)* of the rich, and their approaching punishment. Nothing could be more Greek than James's doctrine of the far-reaching (we might almost say comprehensive) scope of the sin of *hybris,* the pride and arrogance common but not confined to the prosperous and powerful of this world.

J. H. Ropes says, "Cf. 1:19, 23-25, 26, a section which seems to

24. P. 132.

be in mind in this summarising exhortation."[25] This is true, but the truth seems to go a little further. 1:19-21 is the kernel of the entire code of Christian conduct; then from 1:22 to the end of ch. 3 we have a continuous and coherent unity of argument, expounding the meaning of the requirement summarized in 1:19-21. The gist of the argument (1:22 to the end of ch. 3) is that the Christian's faith must be wholehearted, not half-hearted, partial, and wavering. It is no wonder that 2:4 speaks of wavering in a way that reminds us of the same warning given in 1:6-8 with reference to the first Christian act mentioned in the Epistle, the act of prayer in 1:5. (For, surely, prayer, like worship, is an act as much as the giving of alms.) Be doers (1:22) of the Word (1:22, 25), of the work of the law of liberty. Do not be like the man of 1:26, for he is like the Pharisee in Luke 18:9-14 who was satisfied with himself and said so without any reticence of humility; indeed, that Pharisee seems the very sort of man for whom the word "religious" *(thrēskos)* might have been invented.

Chapter 2 continues the train of thought. Wholehearted faith forbids favoring the rich and despising the poor. "If indeed you fulfil the sovereign law acording to the Scriptures, 'Thou shalt love thy neighbor as thyself,' you do well"; we cannot believe that this is, as Ropes says, a reply to a supposed excuse, namely, that the Christian is required by the law of love to one's neighbor to attend to the rich man and to disparage the poor.[26] Whatever we may think of the lawyer's question, "Who is my neighbor?", the suggestion that the poor of the assembly of Christians do not count as neighbors is too absurd to put into the mouth even of the snobs as a serious religious argument.

James does not say that all Christians make these false class distinctions. The argument proceeds quite cogently without the assumption of such an excuse, and runs like this: "If you keep the law of love, by treating the poor no less well than the rich, your conduct is right; but if you favor the rich and despise the poor, you are in sin, and are convicted by the law, that is, the law as a whole, through your transgression of the rule mentioned in 2:9, the rule of loving your neighbor. Therefore you ought to try to keep the whole Christian law, *not* omitting the rule of loving your neighbor, so that after a life of merciful conduct (to the poor, among others) you may be judged by the law with the benefit of mercy to those who have shown mercy."

"You have had only contempt for the poor" (2:6) cannot possibly be taken as meaning that James alleges that all Christians or Christian

25. P. 201, on 2:12.
26. P. 197 *ad fin.*

societies whom he is addressing do commit this sin; it applies only to those whose conduct is as in the case supposed in the "if" clause beginning in 2:2. There must have been Christians who behaved otherwise—in fact, as in the case supposed in 2:8.

Having thus dealt with inadequate doers, James completes the argument—begun, as we saw, in 1:22—by refuting those who think doing is not necessary. This topic is capable of fuller treatment, but for the moment this is enough to show the continuity that runs from 1:22 to the end of the third chapter.

CONCLUSION

Summing up our discussion of the doctrine and unity of the Epistle of James, we have found clear evidence of a strong and pervasive if subtle unity. In this Epistle all the essential principles of Christianity appear, expressly or by necessary implication, in 1:2-18, on the Christian mind, in 1:19-27, on its expression in a corresponding Christian life. The temptations that we are all bound to encounter in our earthly life can, with the help of God and Christian brotherhood, become exercises in overcoming them by our endurance.

That endurance is required not only against other sins but also against those of many of the magnates of wealth and power, as we see in Jas. 5:6,[27] and against those of the renegades who claim that temptation, since it comes from God, need not be resisted. That doctrine leads not to eternal life but to lust, sin, and death. God's purpose offers us the right way of life, a way that is described first at 1:18, that can easily be traced in 2:14-26 and in the twin chs. 3 and 4, and that culminates in 5:19f. with a characteristic return to the dominating thought introduced in the first chapter, a tribute to true Christians, to the rich who help the poor and to the steadfast who aid their wavering brothers and sisters in Christ.

27. The suffering of the righteous poor was often regarded in Jewish thought as equivalent to judicial murder. For close parallels in thought and language see, e.g., Ecclus. 34:20f. (NEB): "To offer a sacrifice from the possessions of the poor is like killing a son before his father's eyes. Bread is life to the destitute, and it is murder to deprive them of it. To rob your neighbor of his livelihood is to kill him, and the man who cheats a worker of his wages sheds blood." See also Adamson, p. 188, and our forthcoming comment, p. 244.

4. Form

"The position held by James in the early church compels one to expect writings from him; the head of the mother-church of Christendom would, of all people, be the most obvious one from whom one would look for communications of one kind or another to daughter-churches. Still more within the natural order of things would be an Epistle of a general character—something in the form of an encyclical—addressed not to any particular local church, but to the whole body of believers."

W. O. E. Oesterley, *The General Epistle of James,* Expositor's Greek Testament, IV (1910; reprinted 1983), 389

Dubbed "a coat of many colors,"[1] the Epistle of James, says Ropes, is a letter only in its first verse.[2] What then is its literary type? Let us examine six notable answers to this question, and then offer our own.

REARRANGEMENT

Authors have given various labels to describe the shape of the Epistle: (1) an incoherent and unstructured "ethical scrapbook" of five small homilies, "Temptation," "Rich and Poor," "Faith and Works," "Use and Abuse of the Tongue," "Patience and Prayer,"[3] (2) a mosaic of fragments *(disiecta membra)* containing a hypothetical ecclesiastical midrash plus an anonymous commentary on an original Jacobean nu-

1. E. W. Bauman, *An Introduction to the New Testament* (1961), p. 147.

2. P. 6. See B. S. Easton, p. 9; also R. Funk, *Language, Hermeneutic and Word of God* (1966), p. 255; N. Dahl, "Letter," *IDB Sup.*, pp. 538ff.; S. K. Stowers, *Letter Writing in Graeco-Roman Antiquity* (1986), pp. 17f.; D. E. Aune, *The New Testament in Its Literary Environment* (1987), pp. 14f., 158ff., 222ff.

3. J. A. Findlay, *The Way, The Truth, The Life* (1940), pp. 159ff.; see also A. M. Hunter, *Introducing the New Testament* (1946), p. 97.

cleus;[4] (3) an essay (3:1-18) by an Alexandrian scribe, the remainder mostly by the original anonymous Jewish-Christian author;[5] (4) either an original collection of prophetic addresses, like the Shepherd of Hermas[6] or loosely connected preexisting sayings;[7] (5) a collection of three types of Genizah fragments (not a letter) that came from Pella or even Jerusalem, chs. 4 and 5 probably emanating from James;[8] and finally (6) a literary piece requiring transposition (e.g., Moffatt places 4:11f. after 2:26)[9] or even "transmutation" by an anonymous redactor (e.g., the "two-tiered hypothesis").[10]

Such conjectures—arbitrary, subjective, and without manuscript support—are mutually contradictory, prompting the question: why trouble with a redactor at all?[11] The account we offer of the structure of the Epistle is sufficient, we submit, to refute them all.

WISDOM BOOK

Much of James's ethical teaching can be found in the Wisdom books. The Wisdom writers praised such virtues as industry, honesty, humility, patience, marital faithfulness, parental discipline, filial obedience, guarded speech, kindness to animals, and returning good for evil. Their standards are primarily prudential. Essentially, the rewards of the wise are a good reputation, length of days, peace, and prosperity. Such similar Wisdom themes as wealth, pride, and the brevity of life pervade our Epistle. These, coupled with James's gnomic style, shrewd insights into human life and nature, expressed in pithy, often picturesque language, and especially the identification of "wisdom" with "righteousness," are said to make the Epistle of James "a NT wisdom book" *(Weisheitslehre);* yet his warm pastoral approach is far removed from the detailed sage of the proverb *(māšāl),* and as far as wisdom is concerned he is much closer to the teaching of Qumran. Mussner lists the parallels with the

4. Oesterley, p. 408.

5. Von Soden, p. 176; *The Books of the New Testament,* pp. 463ff.

6. J. E. Symes, "The Epistle of James," *The Interpreter* (July 1913): 406-13.

7. C. von Weizsäcker, *The Apostolic Age of the Christian Church,* II (ET 1895), 27ff.

8. W. L. Knox, "The Epistle of St. James," *JTS* 46 (1945): 10-17.

9. Pp. 45f.; *An Introduction to the Literature of the New Testament* (1911), p. 463.

10. Davids, Mitton, Mussner, and others.

11. For searching criticism of the redactional approach, especially by Davids, see H. A. Kent, Jr., *Faith that Works* (1986), pp. 22f., 157; and further our "Concluding Reflections," pp. 483f.

Wisdom books, especially Ecclesiasticus (with Jas. 1:5-8) and Proverbs;[12] only in Jas. 4:6 and Prov. 3:34 is the debt direct.

James knows his Wisdom books thoroughly, but he does not offer cut-and-dried rules for conduct. Doubtless he generally approved the moral approach of the Wisdom books, even though his own thought went far beyond them. The ethic of James represents an entirely different point of view; that difference is Jesus Christ, for the wisdom of James is simply the wisdom of Christ.

ARAMAIC ORIGINAL

F. C. Burkitt held that the Epistle of James was "a free rendering of an original Aramaic discourse," rescued by the new Church of Jerusalem in Aelia Capitolina, "rather like a new purchaser that has bought the Old Manor House, who after a while begins to collect old family portraits and souvenirs."[13] Sometimes cited at this point is the analogy of *The Jewish War* of Josephus, which was originally written in Aramaic and then translated into Greek.[14]

This theory, though attractive since it would date the Epistle before the fall of Jerusalem and the death of James, to whom the Epistle is traditionally ascribed, has never received much support because of lack of evidence. The textual variants of Codex Corbeienses can be explained without it, and the free translations therein "do not at all imply any other original than the current Greek text in a form much like Codex Vaticanus."[15] Again the Greek, which is excellent, does not read like a

12. P. 68; Mayor, pp. lxxviff., lxxif.; A. Plummer, p. 573; and R. Leconte, *Les Épîtres Catholiques* (1953), p. 10. Less notable are the parallels with the Book of Wisdom, especially its Palestinian half (e.g., Wisd. 9:6 et al.), sometimes taken (unconvincingly) as proof of the Epistle's Jewish origin (see Ropes, p. 19; R. H. Charles, *Apocrypha and Pseudepigrapha* [1913], p. 524; Dibelius, p. 106).

13. *Christian Beginnings* (1924), pp. 65ff.; see also J. Wordsworth, *Studia Biblica* (1885), pp. 136ff.; J. M. Faber, *Observationes in Epistolam Jacobi ex Syro* (1770.4); Mayor, p. ccxxxiii, n. 1; S. C. Agourides, "The Origin of the Epistle of St. James," *The Greek Orthodox Theological Review* 9.1 (1963): 70, 72. One ancient writer thought that James first translated Matthew's Gospel from Aramaic into Greek (*Synopsis Scripturae Sacrae;* see Migne, *PG*, IV, 432). For the Greek text, see Mayor, p. ccxxxvii, n. 1.

14. "May it not be permissible to inquire whether some books of the New Testament have been subjected to similar literary revision, and, though Hebraic in origin, have been Graecized almost beyond recognition? The Epistle of James, for example, reads in English like an Old Testament prophecy, and in Greek like a well-written *diatribe*" (F. J. Foakes-Jackson, *Josephus and the Jews* [1976], p. xiv).

15. Ropes, p. 27.

translation; nor are there any cases where such an original appears to have been misunderstood.[16] Also inexplicable on the hypothesis of an Aramaic original are the alliterations and the paronomasia, as well as acquaintance with the LXX and Greek meter and expressions. Moreover, there is no proof of Torrey's contention that the Aramaic Christians at Jerusalem were so anxious to transcribe their tradition.[17] Finally, and most significantly, there is no word of the alleged original even from the Edessene scribes of the Syriac versions. We think therefore that this theory may safely be rejected "as an example of desperate expedients."[18]

DIATRIBE

The Epistle of James, especially 3:1-11, is said to have affinities with the Hellenistic diatribe,[19] the popular ethical address invented by Bion (c. 280 B.C.) and popularized by Seneca and Epictetus. For our purpose this is still a valid literary form.[20] These "causeries" often contained real or imaginary dialogue between philosophers or rivals, whose moral tone on occasion is alleged to recall that of James. Comparable literary techniques are also cited, for example, rhetorical questions (2:4, 14-16; 3:11f.; 4:4), frequent imperatives (throughout), dialogue (2:18f.; see also 5:13f.), terse questions and answers (4:1f.; 5:13f.), objections anticipated and answered (2:8, 14), and stock formulas.[21] Appeals to his-

16. See D. G. Lyon and G. F. Moore, eds., *Studies in the History of Religions* presented to C. H. Toy (1912), pp. 283ff.

17. *The Origin of the Gospels* (n.d.), pp. 237ff.

18. Mayor, pp. cclxff.; Zahn, p. 118; Tasker, pp. 36f.; B. W. Bacon, *An Introduction to the New Testament* (1900), p. 160; Moffatt, *An Introduction to the Literature of the New Testament*, pp. 474f.

19. Ropes, pp. 1-18 with literature cited; Hauck, pp. 16f.; Mussner, p. 29; J. I. H. McDonald, *Kerygma and Didache* (1980), pp. 39ff.; R. Scroggs, "Paul as Rhetorician: Two Homilies in Romans 1-11," in *Jews, Greeks, and Christians. Essays in Honor of William David Davies*, eds. Robert Hamerton-Kelly and Robin Scroggs (1976), pp. 270ff.; H. Thyen, *Der Stil der jüdisch-hellenistischen Homilie* (1955); A. Wifstrand, "Stylistic Problems in the Epistle of James and 1 Peter," *ST* 1 (1947): 178; Aune, *The New Testament in Its Literary Environment*, pp. 200ff.

20. See, however, Davids, pp. 12, 23.

21. E.g., *mē planasthe* (1:16), *iste* (1:19), *ti ophelos* (2:14), *theleis de gnōnai* (2:20), *blepeis* (2:22), *orate* (2:24), *idou* (3:4f.; 5:4, 7, 9, 11), *age* (4:13; 5:1), *ou chrē* (3:10), *dio legei* (4:6). Other examples of rhetorical devices are paradox (1:2, 10; 2:5), antithesis (1:26; 2:13, 26; 3:15-18; 4:12), apostrophe (4:13–5:6), personification (1:15; 2:13; 4:1; 5:3f.), and irony (2:14-19; 5:1-6). For a full discussion of these and other points, see S. K. Stowers, *The Diatribe and Paul's Letter to the Romans* (1981), pp. 79ff.; Aune, *The New Testament in Its Literary Environment*, pp. 200ff.

torical examples such as Abraham, Rahab, Job, and Elijah, linked sometimes with harsh address, for example, in 2:20 and 4:4, are also linked with the diatribe, *Ō talaipōre, mōre* (Lat. *stulte,* "you fool").

But these stylistic congruences are not to be pressed too far, any more than the radio or TV technique that is often paralleled in Christian sermons of today. In substance our Epistle clearly owes nothing to the diatribe. Its ideas, ethics, and "worldview" *(Weltanschauung),* so far as they are shared by the serious pagan, do not come from that source,[22] nor does James use any of the Aristophanic license with which the Hellenistic diatribe was regularly diversified. Moreover, James's use of experience (3:5), analogy (2:14-17), and figures of speech, especially his striking Hellenistic metaphors (3:1-6), are much more simple, limited, and conventional.[23]

To sum up, whereas the diatribe is an entirely Hellenistic product, the Epistle of James is fundamentally and perpetually Semitic and biblical:[24] the stylistic similarities between James and the diatribes are obvious enough, but, like those between synagogue sermons,[25] they are mainly superficial. It is even more obvious that the Epistle as a whole is not a diatribe.[26]

PARENESIS

Martin Dibelius drew attention to literary parallels between the Epistle of James and the Greek "protrepticus" or parenetic tract, stressing such common features as association by catchwords *(Stichworte),* lack of coherence, and typical didactic eclecticism *(Eklektizismus).*[27] Parenesis

22. Ropes, p. 16.

23. Ibid.

24. R. Bultmann, *Der Stil der Paulinischen Predigt und die kynisch-stoische Diatribe* (1910), pp. 3f.

25. See Wessel, pp. 73ff.; *ISBE,* II, 961f. For a summary of the main parallels, see Davids, pp. 12, 23, 58 n. 157; and, with cautions, Stowers, *The Diatribe and Paul's Letter to the Romans,* pp. 39-41.

26. J. Marty, p. 240; Dibelius, pp. 120ff.

27. Pp. 1-10. For a development of Dibelius, with further insights and examples, see Stowers, *Letter Writing in Greco-Roman Antiquity,* pp. 91ff.; L. G. Perdue, "Paraenesis and the Epistle of James," *ZNW* 72.3-4 (1981): 241-56; H. S. Songer, "The Literary Character of the Book of James," *RevExp* 66.4 (1969): 379ff.; also his commentary, *James.* Broadman Bible Commentary 12 (1972). The Greek term *parenesis* embraces a large variety of compositions, aptly defined as "exhortation or rather moral instruction with a dash of exhortation" (so A. M. Hunter, *Paul and His Predecessors* [[2]1961], p. 62; see also McDonald, *Kerygma and Didache,* pp. 69ff., 87ff.). They professed no originality but were "later prose

has at least two further important characteristics: 1. The writer, the recipient's friend or moral mentor, recommends (or in contrast rebukes) certain types of conduct on the basis of this relationship; 2. he usually borrows from such sources as Judaism, Greek mysticism (1:18), Stoicism (1:21), Orphism (3:6), and Gnosticism (3:15). Dibelius described the content as general warnings expressed in collections of literary units *(topoi)*[28] or isolated apothegms, admonitory and hortatory with their "conventicle-ethic" *(Konventikel-Ethik),* characterized by internationalism and interconfessionalism, usually of a practical but impersonal, though relational, nature, and not all directed to one class of reader.[29] It has been suggested that the Epistle contains "instruction given by a teacher at a time when he is either separated from his audience (a parenetic letter) or is about to leave them because of increasing age and approaching death, an address, later modified into an epistle."[30]

In our view, the single most difficult problem besetting "parenesis," besides its atomistic approach, is its social setting, which in the nature of things is hard to determine. Conscious of this, some have tried to argue that "the primary function of parenesis is socialization," which they define (somewhat vaguely, in our opinion) as "the comprehensive and consistent induction of an individual into the objective world of a society or sector of it." It is conjectured (without evidence) that there may have been links between such Greek collections of maxims *(Gnomai)* and Jewish and even Christian influences including, according to Dibelius, the Epistle of James.

But whatever points of resemblance (e.g., moral injunctions) the Epistle of James may have to such a collection of proverbs, these throw

---

representatives of the poetical tradition of gnomic literature seen in Theognis and in the now lost Phocylides, and are the precursors of the useful florilegia and gnomic collections of a later time," represented as early as the fourth century B.C. in Greek works like Isocrates, *To Nicocles,* and Pseudo-Isocrates, *Speech to Demonicus* (Ropes, p. 18; also with literature for discussion and the text of Pseudo-Phocylides, see B. S. Easton, "Pseudo-Phocylides," *ATR* 14 [1932]: 222-28). See, too, Islamic *ahadith* (E. F. F. Bishop, *The Apostles of Palestine* [1958], p. 178).

28. For a discussion of the *topos* in Hellenistic philosophy see E. Milobenski, *Der Neid in der griechischen Philosophie* (1964), and for its wider use in the NT see L. T. Johnson, "James 3:13–4:10 and the *Topos Peri Phthonou,*" *NovT* 25.4 (1983): 334ff., especially n. 33; also pp. 328ff. for penetrating criticism of Dibelius's atomistic approach; Aune, *The New Testament in Its Literary Environment,* pp. 32f., 172f..

29. See Songer, *art. cit., RevExp* 66.4 (1969): 384; McDonald, *Kerygma and Didache,* pp. 70ff. Yet, it is worth noting, as S. K. Stowers reminds us, that "a seemingly random series of precepts or virtues may actually provide an implicit pattern of character" (*Letter Writing in Greco-Roman Antiqutiy,* p. 95).

30. Perdue, *art. cit., ZNW* 72.3-4 (1981): 246f., 251.

no light on the nature, origin, date, situation, or authorship of the Epistle. They prove no more for this claim than do those similarly cited by others for the claim for the diatribe. According to Dibelius, the distinctive feature of the Epistle of James—that which classifies it as parenesis *(paränese)*—is that its teaching is neither coherent nor specific and is by no single author. This is contrary to our belief in the unity of the Epistle and its being from the hand of James the Lord's brother and therefore not a counterfeit collection of disconnected maxims by an unknown compiler (c. A.D. 80-130), who, like the other apostles, was an editor rather than an author and followed what C. H. Dodd called "some common model"[31] (though curiously, in his treatment, Dodd does not include the Epistle of James). The two types are as dissimilar in form and spirit as, for example, Lord Chesterfield's *Letters Written to his Son* and a sermon by John Wesley.[32] Any theory that reduces the Epistle of James to a series of ethical generalities and its author to a mere compiler is, in our opinion, quite unsatisfactory; this claim, therefore, must be rejected on the same grounds as those for the diatribe.

ALLEGORY

Lastly, let us consider as seriously as possible Arnold Meyer's suggestion that, apart from its few obviously Christian elements, which he believes to be later additions—for example, 1:1; 2:1 (name of Christ); possibly 5:7f. (parousia); 5:12 (swearing); and 5:14 (presbyters)—the Epistle of James was a pre-Christian Testament of Jacob;[33] for some of these supposed Christian elements (e.g., the parousia) he says good rabbinic parallels can be cited. Others before and since have held the same opinion.[34] Meyer's originality was in his views of the literary form and fundamental purpose of the Epistle, matters that merit serious and more extensive consideration.[35]

31. *Gospel and Law* (1951), p. 19, n. 3.

32. Ropes, p. 18. See also Agourides, *art. cit., The Greek Orthodox Theological Review* 9.1 (1963): 68f.

33. *Das Rätsel des Jakobusbriefes* (1930).

34. Spitta, pp. 1-239; Massebieau, pp. 249-83. See A. Meyer, p. 113, n. 1 for further references; also M. Gertner, "Midrashic Terms and Techniques in the New Testament. The Epistle of James; a Midrash on a Psalm," *StEv* III = *TU* 88 (1964): 463; "Midrashim in the New Testament," *JSS* 7 (1962): 267ff.; "Terms of Scriptural Interpretation," *Bulletin of Oriental and African Studies* 25 (1962): 1-27. On this improbable hypothesis, see Mussner, pp. 58f.; Laws, p. 10, n. 1; I. Jacobs, "The Midrashic Background for James ii:21-3," *NTS* 22 (1976): 457-64.

35. For reviews of A. Meyer, see O. Cullmann, *RHPR* (1932): 178-84; M. Dibelius, *Theologische Rundschau*, Heft 4 (1931): 207ff.; G. Kittel, *Deutsche*

According to Arnold Meyer, the Epistle of James is basically Semitic and follows the scheme of the typical Jewish allegorical tract that was familiar to the circle of Philo and others. As Jacob the patriarch, "God's servant" (Gen. 32:10; Isa. 41:8), did of old, so our James (i.e., Hebrew "Jacob") counsels the twelve tribes of the Diaspora through their eponymous founders, whose names, according to Meyer, are concealed, each in due order, in the text of the Epistle. He rests his theory on an exhaustive examination of the patriarch stories in Genesis, the Testaments of the Twelve Patriarchs, the writings of Philo, and the patristic "book of names" known as *Onomastica*.[36]

In Gen. 49 Jacob characterizes each of the twelve tribes with the vice or virtue that peculiarly distinguished it, and this characterization played a large part in later Jewish tradition; thus in the Testaments of the Twelve Patriarchs Reuben reproves fornication; Simeon, envy; and so on. It is a fact that the noncanonical work with which James has most parallels is the Testaments.

These are striking, but no literary dependence can be proved: they "do not go further than to exhibit a common background of high Jewish morality in which both the Testaments and James (and Hermas) share."[37] Meyer seeks to prove the presence of the traditional pattern, descended from Gen. 49, by what he sees as a series of puns or similar "double entendre" based on the Hebrew meaning of the twelve tribal (and three other ancestral) names.[38] Besides these, he finds allusions to

---

Literaturzeitung 53 (1932): 50ff.; and H. Seesemann, *ThLZ* 56 (1931): 318b-21. For relevant material see H. Windisch, *Die Katholischen Briefe* (^{2}1930 and ^{3}1951), and E. Fascher, A. Jülicher, *Einleitung* (^{7}1931), pp. 203ff. And for the view that the Epistle could contain Christian elements rather than Jewish allegory, see A. Farrer, *A Study in Mark* (1952), pp. 320, 348ff.; G. Hartmann, "Der Aufbau des Jakobusbriefes," *Zeitschrift für Katholische Theologie* 66 (1942); F. Hauck, *Die Katholischen Briefe*. NTD 3 (1937); Thyen, *Der Stil der jüdisch-hellenistischen Homilie* 9.16; R. Bultmann, *Theology of the New Testament*, II (1955), 143, 163; Tasker, pp. 34ff.; Easton, pp. 9-12; W. Marxsen, *Introduction to the New Testament* (1968), pp. 228f.; J. B. Polhill, "The Life-Situation of the Book of James," *RevExp* 66 (1969): 373f.

36. I.e., a type of literature patterned on names of the famous, like the Twelve Patriarchs. The Greek word means "relating to or connected with a name or names, or naming, consisting of, or dealing with name . . . book of names." S.v. "onomastic(on)" (*The Oxford Universal Dictionary* [1955], rev. and ed. C. T. Onions, p. 1371).

37. Ropes, p. 21.

38. As follows: 1:2, *chara*//Isaac, *yiṣḥāq;* 1:4-12, *peirasmos*//Jacob, *ya'*^{a}*qōḇ;* 1:4, *hypomonē*//Rebekah, *riḇqāh;* 1:18, *aparchē*//Reuben, *r*^{e}*'ûḇēn;* 1:19-20, *orgē*//Simeon, *šim'ôn;* 1:27, *thrēskeia*//Levi, *lēwî;* 2:5ff., *basilikos*//Judah, *y*^{e}*hûḏāh;* 2:12f., *krisis*//Dan, *dān;* 3:17ff., *eirēnikē*//Naphtali, *nap̱tālî;* 4:1, *polemoi*

Jacob's encounter with the angel at the brook Jabbok, and to other characters in the Jacob story, including Esau and Rachel; he also believes that the twelve sons of Jacob occur in their proper order in accordance with the traditional pattern.[39]

Arnold Meyer's hypothesis is that, contemporary with Philo and written between Antioch and Caesarea probably under the influence of the Essenes in the Hellenistic synagogue, the Testament of Jacob, now known as the Epistle of James, was revised and redacted, doubtless at Caesarea, and issued in an abbreviated Christian form between A.D. 80 and 90; that from Caesarea the book went to Rome, where 1 Peter, 1 Clement, and Hermas are its first witnesses; and that subsequent canonical recognition was ensured by ascribing to it the authoritative name of James.

If any such theory were true, it might provide a pattern if none other existed, as we maintain one does, in the Epistle; but even at face value this theory has scarcely any bearing on the question of pattern.[40] The strength or weakness of Meyer's case rests on the Jewish parallels he adduces in each instance. These parallels—which we may call "Meyer's Keywords in James"—are artificial connections with the names (or with incidents in the lives) of the sons of Jacob as mentioned in the Testaments of the Twelve Patriarchs or Gen. 49. In the Epistle of

---

kai machai//Gad, *gāḏ;* 5:1-6, *plousioi*//Asher, *'āšēr;* 4:7, *misthos* and *geōrgos*//Issachar, *yiśśāḵār;* 5:12, *(mē) omnyete*//Zebulun, *z^eḇûlûn;* 5:15f., *energei ho Kyrios* and *iathēte*//Joseph, *yôsēp;* 5:20, *thanatos*//Benjamin, *binyāmîn.*

39. See Table, A. Meyer, pp. 282ff.

40. In our opinion the idea that James is referring to, or guided by, names or incidents in the patriarchal narratives is artificial, unreal, and worthless, exhibiting a credulity that is almost incredible. But that is not all, for A. Meyer does not seem to be perfectly impartial in fixing the keywords. Issachar, e.g., is identified by the keyword *geōrgos* (Jas. 5:7), and the Test. Iss. mentions the *husbandman* and his valuable work. But there the meaning of Issachar's name is given as reward *('śāḵār).* If James had seen that, why did not he also adopt this meaning—or does 5:4 belong to Issachar? If so, how do we explain the disorder in the mention of Asher (according to Meyer) in 5:5, coming between 5:4 and 5:7? If James is regarded as carefully selecting words that referred to individual sons of Jacob, how can we explain this placing of his references out of order? Again, Issachar appears ninth in the list in James as seen by Meyer, but he was the fifth son of Jacob according to the Testaments of the Twelve Patriarchs. If James had been studying the Testaments at all at the time he wrote, and working on the basis supposed by Meyer, there is no good reason for his suddenly departing from the order. Some of the alleged allusions, e.g., to Zebulun, also are unbelievably farfetched. Further, according to this reasoning, why does not *emphytos logos* also allude to Leah (Meyer, p. 263); and why does *chalinagōgein* (Jas. 3:2) belong to Naphtali, but not Levi (Jas. 1:26)?

James, these keywords do not betray the least connection with the personages and would not have maintained their spontaneity if they had been selected and inserted as part of a mechanical scheme in the mind of the author. Nor is it clear why James should select and insert them where he did. If our Epistle were an original Testament we should expect the allusions to be represented throughout the whole writings, but this is not so, for there are notable omissions, namely, Levi and Zebulun.

Certainly Arnold Meyer "seems vastly to have underestimated the contributions of the Christian editor."[41] It is far easier to conclude that "there is no sentence which a Jew could have written and a Christian could not,"[42] and to view the writing as produced by a Jewish Christian of the early period spontaneously stressing those qualities of life that seemed basic to him, but unconcerned at this stage with any question of a distinctively Christian terminology. Clearly, too, the Epistle's ethical strength springs from the gospel, and not least from the very words of Jesus himself.

If the author of the original work was writing a midrash or using a pattern, as Meyer suggests, this does not account for the fact that he—contrary to the usual custom of allegorists—omits every one of the tribal names.[43] This objection has all the more weight in that the author of the work does not hesitate to mention other OT names such as Rahab and Job. Even if the first thoughts of the Epistle—joy in *peirasmos* and endurance—were consciously taken from the pattern of the tribal pedigree Isaac, Jacob, and Rebekah, and even if wrath takes its place in the traditional order in 1:19f. after firstfruits in 1:18, this has no bearing on the cardinal topics of wisdom and prayer in 1:5 and faith in 1:6, or the lesson for the rich and the poor in 1:9-11. Wrath in 1:19-21 does not belong to the pattern of either the preceding verses (17f.) or the following (22-25). In fact, the pattern and cohesion of the whole passage (1:16-27) come not from "firstfruits," or "wrath," or being "religious," but from

41. Easton, p. 10; see also Davids, p. 6, n. 14. On the other hand, it is equally difficult to imagine a Christian writer taking over the obscure Jewish allegory and leaving it so obscure—without even the assistance of an allusion to the key names. There seems to be no point in keeping the secret so dark. Notes Martin E. Marty: "The enterprise is a bit too arcane, too cute, too ingenious. Would James not have 'tipped us off' that he was writing in such code? Does not such a style deny the patent sincerity and simplicity of the author?" (*Good News in the Early Church* [1976], p. 65).

42. Ropes, p. 33; also p. 37 where he notes "the entire absence of allegory" in James.

43. Tasker, p. 36, n. 1; also p. 34 on the "argument from silence"; see also Laws, p. 11, n. 1.

"the Word of truth" (v. 18).[44] In the 108 verses of the Epistle tribal allusion can be imagined in about 21 verses. The fatal objection to Meyer's theory is not that in 87 verses there is no echo of any patriarchal name, but that in the successive stages of the development of the pattern—a conspicuously coherent pattern—such patriarchal echoes, if any, have no structural significance at all.

To sum up: Arnold Meyer's allegory theory is not only elaborately bizarre, but it is actually too ingenious.[45] Most commentators reject Meyer on essentially the same ground—the total improbability of such a simple and straightforward writing being based on such an incredibly abstruse scheme.[46]

Our examination of these six theories shows that while they explain a few literary features, none is really satisfactory. So we must propose our own solution.

A PASTORAL EPISTLE

In seeking to name the category to which the Epistle of James belongs, we should keep in mind that inevitably it shares even some of its best qualities with works of a somewhat different character. Thus it has often been likened to a sermon or even two sermons, "sermon-letter," or homily[47]—"that unique creation of the Jewish spirit"—[48] suggesting "the pulpit rather than the desk,"[49] and the product of a Jewish-

44. As is the case of 2:14-26.

45. P. Feine, *Theologie des Neuen Testaments* (1951), p. 390; Agourides, *art. cit.*, *The Greek Orthodox Theological Review* 9.1 (1963): 70f.

46. E.g., Davids, pp. 3ff.

47. So, originally, M. Luther, *LW*, XXXV, 397, who argued that someone unknown wrote the Epistle from James's homilies. See *The New Oxford Annotated Bible* (1973), p. 1469; *The New Jerusalem Bible* (1985), p. 1993; Moffatt, *Introduction to the Literature of the New Testament* (^{2}1900), p. 462; J. W. Bowman, *Hebrews, James, 1 and 2 Peter.* The Layman's Bible Commentary (1962), pp. 94ff., 98. Embraced notably by Kistemaker (two sermons); Jülicher (penitential sermon); Harnack (homiletical mosaic by unknown teacher, c. A.D. 120); Feine (transcribed homily to Jerusalem Church by the Lord's brother); others include H. A. A. Kennedy, J. Weiss, H. F. D. Sparks, T. W. Manson, Moffatt, Goodspeed, J. Marty, Leconte, Barth, Henderlite, Motyer, Wessel, Davids, Moo; see also V. Taylor, *The Atonement in New Testament Teaching* (1946), pp. 43f.; C. F. D. Moule, *The Birth of the New Testament* (1962), p. 30, n. 2; p. 166, n. 2.

48. I. Bettan, *Studies in Jewish Preaching* (1939), p. 3; see also Wessel, pp. 73-89; *ISBE*, II, 962; Aune, *The New Testament in Its Literary Environment*, p. 202.

49. T. W. Manson, *Companion to the Bible* (1939), p. 118.

Christian preacher *(daršan)*[50] steeped in the OT prophetic tradition. Instead of dealing conjunctly with his subject, the *daršan* selected one aspect, stressed it for the moment, and then moved on to the next subject, often using catchwords, a homiletic device known as "the stringing of pearls" *(ḥarûṣîm)*.[51]

Impressed by certain similarities in form between the Jewish sermon *(d^erāšāh)* and the Epistle of James, we may, like William Barclay,[52] compare sections of *topoi* (passages) in the Epistle to pearls loosely strung on a single thread, like Wordsworth's poems of 1831.[53] Employing the familiar Haggadic catchword system, James can move rapidly and rhythmically[54]—and apparently casually—among his varied themes,[55] speaking, it has been held,[56] to certain specific groups within

50. Although very few first-century Jewish sermons have been preserved for us as sermons, i.e., as independent pieces of literature, nevertheless we possess everal midrashic collections, which have been edited and compiled over a period of about a thousand years. The literature on Jewish preaching is meager and often inaccessible; but see L. Zunz, *Gottesdienstliche Vorträge* (²1892); I. Elbogen, *Der jüdische Gottesdienstliche in seiner geschichtlichen Entwicklung* (1924); Bettan, *Studies in Jewish Preaching;* two monographs by A. Marmorstein, "The Background of the Haggadah," *HUCA* 6 (1929): 183-204, reprinted in his *Studies in Jewish Theology* (1950), pp. 1-71; also "Synagogue Sermons in the First Three Centuries," *London Quarterly Review* (1916): 227-40; J. Heinemann, art. "Preaching" (in the Talmudic period), *Encyclopaedia Judaica,* XIII (1971), 994-98; G. Vermes, F. Millar, M. Black, and E. Schürer, *The History of the Jewish People in the Age of Jesus Christ,* II, 453; Thyen, *Der Stil der jüdisch-hellenistischen Homilie,* pp. 14-17; McDonald, *Kergyma and Didache,* pp. 43ff.

51. McDonald, *Kergyma and Didache,* pp. 44f., 54; A. Edersheim, *The Life and Times of Jesus the Messiah,* I (1903), 445-50. Similarly, Bettan, *Studies in Jewish Preaching,* p. 192, notes that "the midrashic homilies abound in excellences of various sorts. . . . but these appear like sudden flashes, brilliant but sporadic, illuminating the theme for a brief moment but seldom furthering its logical development. They are not climaxes in a thought; they are sparks escaping from the rock when the darshan's hammer falls heavily upon it." See b. Sanhedrin 34a.

52. Pp. 30ff.; also R. Henderlite, "The Epistle of James," *Interpretation* 3 (1949): 465; Moffatt, *Introduction to the Literature of the New Testament,* p. 462; J. Knox, *The Fourth Gospel and the Later Epistles* (1945), p. 121.

53. See Songer, *art. cit., RevExp* 66.4 (1969): 384.

54. On the obscure rabbinic use of rhythm, see A. Wendel, *Das Israelitisch-Jüdische Gelübde* (1931), p. 149; S. Krauss, *Talmudische Archäologie* (1910-12), III, 78, 86; also b. Sanhedrin 99a. On rhythm in the Epistle of James, see, among others, Jas. 1:1f.; Mayor, p. ccxxvi; also Dibelius, p. 35; P. B. R. Forbes once expressed to me the view that James's strong sense of rhythm suggests the qualities of a musician.

55. On the varied themes of Jewish sermons, see Marmorstein, *art. cit., London Quarterly Review* (1916): 233ff.; also Zunz, *Gottesdienstliche Vorträge,* pp. 349ff.; Wessel; Davids.

56. A. Cabaniss, "A Note on Jacob's Homily," *EQ* 47.4 (1975): 219-22. See

the church, including both pastors and their flocks. Such casualness, however, is deceptive, for we find not only a unifying motif, as in Jewish sermons,[57] but also a closely knit logical structure with a single theme—"faith without works is dead."

It was not surprising that James, as "Bishop" of Jerusalem, should talk to his charges in and around Jerusalem as well as the other Palestinian churches in Galilee (Acts 9:31), Judea (Gal. 1:22), and Samaria (Acts 8:4-8), and also show interest in the Jews of the Diaspora. Scripture does not say if James married (see 1 Cor. 9:5), though we believe this is unlikely, leaving him free, like Paul, to leave Jerusalem to do missionary work. Here again, however, Scripture is silent. Whether the Palestine or Diaspora churches were founded personally by James or his evangelists and exiled members (Acts 8:4) or through his considerable contacts with Diaspora Jews visiting him in Jerusalem is of little consequence; we cannot believe that "these believers had less need of close pastoral oversight than their brethren who had come out of paganism."[58] Indeed, because James's Jewish converts faced persecution from both Jew *and* pagan, it can be argued that their need for pastoral care was at least twice as great as that of Paul's converts—and being well aware of this, James, as a good bishop, would be in constant communication with them. It is recorded, for instance, that James sent messengers from Jerusalem to Antioch to investigate the matter of Gentile freedom (Gal. 2:12). We believe that James was the first to commit his message to writing instead of depending on word of mouth, though, says Scaer, "as with many pioneers his role was forgotten and when revived, it was misunderstood."[59] If, as is scarcely credible, he wrote only brief notes,[60] it would be possible, but not historically probable, that these might be strung together in a later century, incorporating (though this is also unlikely) some specimens of his preaching.

This would mean, as some have held, that the Epistle of James was never a letter but was in fact a homily;[61] in this respect it was like 2 Clement, which is clearly a homily but almost immediately took rank

---

also Scaer, pp. 32f., for the novel but unlikely view that the Epistle is aimed primarily at the clergy.

57. For examples of the unifying principle in Jewish sermons, see Bettan, *Studies in Jewish Preaching*, pp. 196ff., 214ff., 239, and especially his comments on the Jewish preachers' imitation of Cicero's oratorical structure.

58. So E. F. Harrison, *Introduction to the New Testament* (1971), p. 382, but see also p. 388 and our relevant remarks, pp. 196ff.

59. P. 137.

60. See J. S. Stevenson, "St. James's Sermon Notes," *ExpT* 24 (1903): 44.

61. See above, n. 47.

as an Epistle. According to Sanday, "Early Christian Epistles often hover between the idea of a letter and a homily."[62] But is it at all likely that any such process of generation could have produced the masterpiece that the Epistle of James demonstrably is?

We submit that the best bridge between us and the Epistle of James is not diatribe, parenesis, or any other specific type of protreptic composition to which the Epistle of James may show certain points of resemblance or even obligation, but some of Paul's comparable Epistles, such as Galatians or, above all, 1 Corinthians. It seems hard for many to think of Paul and James without glorifying Paul as a theological thinker and belittling James as merely an admirable practicing and counseling Christian.

It is *prima facie* unlikely that one who could write on Christianity with such force and could write Greek with such distinction as James produced only the Epistle, which, probably as the result of the attitude of Gentile Christianity to him and his Jerusalem Church after the misfortunes of both, is (apart from the Council's letter) all that has survived. Suppose that Paul had written only 1 Corinthians. It is four times as long as the Epistle of James, but in spite of that, in 1 Corinthians—as will easily be seen from a synopsis—theory, credal doctrine, theology, spiritual thought, and originality are proportionally much more outweighed by considerations of practice and conduct than in the Epistle of James. For the proper apperception of that truth, the synopsis deserves to be studied with some care.

After the opening "signature," greetings and compliments, and a reminder of Christ's expected early coming (1:1-9), the rest of 1 Cor. 1 consists of castigation or chastening admonition on sectarian disputes and other unworthy conduct among the Corinthian Christians (reported by Chloe, 1:11). The same trend of rebuke dominates chs. 2, 3, 4, 5, and 6, for example, 2:12-14, 3:3, 4:7, 5:1, and 6:1. 1 Cor. 7:1-17 is devoted to Christian marriage as a prophylactic (vv. 2, 7, 9) against the sin denounced in 6:18-20; 7:18f. deal with circumcision (in practice), vv. 19-24 with slavery and freedom (in practice), and vv. 25-40 with virginity, male celibacy, abstinence in marriage, mourning, rejoicing, and buying (in practice), always remembering that "the time is short." Ch. 8 (the whole chapter) is on Christians and the pagan meat market. 9:1-14 assert the minister's right (see v. 14) to "live off the gospel"; vv. 15-27 confess Paul's inability (in practice) to avail himself of that right.

1 Cor. 10:1-14 castigates idolatry, fornication (again), tempting Christ, and grumbling, and vv. 14-33 again deal with idolatry and pagan

62. *Inspiration* (1893), p. 25.

provision markets and assert a Christian's duty of consideration for others even in what his conscience does not forbid. 11:1-16 has to do with headgear and hair length on men and women, vv. 17-19 with split congregations, and vv. 20-24 with profane gorging at Communion. 12:1-31 is on spiritual gifts and the right Christian attitude in having or not having one. 13:1-13 stresses that gifts of prophecy, tongues, and knowledge are partial and temporal, but that Christian love is perfect and eternal. According to 14:1, prophecy is to be preferred to the gift of tongues, vv. 2-28 castigate vanity in those flaunting the gift of tongues in church, vv. 29-33 set forth similar restrictive rules for prophesying, vv. 34f. tell women to keep silence in church, and vv. 36-40 enjoin the use of gifts in church in decent order and in the proper manner.

1 Cor. 15:1-11 presents Paul's summary of the gospel—salvation through Christ—how He died for atonement, was buried, rose again, was seen by Peter, by the Twelve, by the 500, by James, by all the apostles, and finally by Paul; according to vv. 12-55, Christ's resurrection is denied by some, but Paul vindicates its truth; lastly, vv. 56f. summarize his Christian theology and v. 58 emphasizes the necessary congruent Christian transmission. Following this are other personal information and messages.

We could not pray for a better illustration of what we mean by "a Pastoral Epistle." Further, though it seems to have received less than due attention from some theologians, the evidence of 1 Corinthians cannot be omitted from any true picture of Paulinism with impunity: we must not ignore 1 Cor. 13, where Paul expressly gives the practice of Christian love *(agapē)* priority over Christian faith, with an emphasis and sincerity unexcelled by anything in James and evoked by much the same circumstances and needs (see 1 Cor. 1:11, "I hear from Chloe . . ."; 5:1, "I hear reports that . . ."; or 7:1, "Concerning the things whereof ye wrote unto me . . ."). We do not mean to imply that James necessarily had before him written questions, requests, or reports from or about his flock of Jewish Christians (though no sceptic has yet denied that James could read), or that the substance of his considerations might not differ somewhat from that of those forced upon Paul; quite probably James is responding, at least in the main, to oral reports and his own observation in his care of his Jewish Christian converts and congregation.

We suggest that the Epistle of James has an ad hoc character and purpose, though with a somewhat wider encyclical audience in view than Paul had immediately under his censure in 1 Corinthians. We believe that Jas. 2:1-9 is as person-specific to its hearers as the invective in 1 Cor. 11:17-22 against gorging at Communion; in that censure (1 Cor. 11:21f.), just as in Jas. 2:1-9, we note how the rich were being allowed to flaunt the poor: "You shame its poorer members" (NEB). For the Epistle of James, like those of Peter, John, and Jude, "Catholic" is "an exceedingly deceptive misnomer," for affinities to Qumran show them to be Jewish compositions primarily circulated among Jewish Christians. Their Essene elements may not have been exclusively Essene but "may go back to earlier Jewish sects whose literatures have been lost: we do know, however, that little of this material is in Rabbinic sources which reflect later Pharisaism in its development from the time of Christ onward."[63] It is no disparagement of James to insist that his Epistle, like those of Paul, had a comparatively limited "target"; at the same time, of course, the needs of their congregations must partly coincide with those of Christians in all ages and everywhere, a fact that gives their letters a general and permanent appeal.

In the light of these analogies, we should have no difficulty in recognizing the Epistle of James as a quasi-prophetic address of pastoral encouragement and, no less, of pastoral rebuke, proceeding from an unquestioned right of pastoral vocation and authority. Written in Greek, terse and lively, limpid and pure, passionate and powerful, graphic and volcanic—unparalleled in the rest of the NT—his words shine with an incandescent quality. His scorn is devastating.

Swift, vivid, brusque, energetic, exclamatory, sometimes even minatory, poetical and rhythmical, blending pure Greek with Hebraic fervor, James's essentially brief nonperiodic sentences are better formed and more rhythmical than any (except perhaps 1 Cor. 15) in the NT. (We have just seen that in a matter of even more weight, Paul's 1 Corinthians comes closest to the Epistle of James.) In some sentences Mayor detects "a highly poetical imagination," "a volcanic energy," and "something of the Miltonic 'organ-voice,'" noting, too, that "in its rugged abruptness, in the pregnant brevity of its phrases, in the austerity of its demand upon the reader, in concentrated irony and scorn, this Epistle stands alone among the Epistles of the New Testament."[64]

Here, says Theodor Zahn, is a preacher who speaks like a fiery prophet, not overly concerned with life's mysteries but rather with the immediate problems of Christian conduct.[65] Since James is more akin to the OT and his style is a revival of the OT prophetic tradition, it is difficult to conceive of a writer with such an outlook deliberately seeking foreign models in addressing people of his own race.

63. R. N. Longenecker, *The Christology of Early Jewish Christianity* (1970), p. 21, especially the quotation from W. F. Albright, n. 48.

64. Pp. cclix, ccxxviii, and cclix.

65. *Introduction*, I, 111, 116. See R. V. G. Tasker, *The Old Testament in the New Testament* (1940), p. 126.

All that we can say of this compact, rugged, energetic writing—distinguished by polished rhetoric, often abrupt, full of passionate ejaculation, colloquial turns, and "I-you" appeals, aphoristic and prophetic, showing a fondness for invention but little quotation, love of pun, assonance, and alliteration as well as parallelism of words and phrases—is that it is the style of a NT prophet, a prophet who is versed in Jewish method and steeped in the literary traditions of both the Jewish and Hellenistic world.[66] Besides sharp antithesis,[67] there is paradox,[68] irony, seriousness and not flippancy,[69] and dialogue.[70] The illustrations are more limited than those of the diatribe, and, in characteristically Jewish and un-Greek fashion, the Epistle ends eschatologically.[71]

Though popular and hortatory—its 108 verses contain more than 54 imperatives—the Epistle reveals a more serious moral purpose than the typical Greek address; it is certainly not *spoudaiogeloion* ("jest blended with earnest") but rather the work of a genuinely Christian preacher, a Jew of Palestine, whom we are convinced is James the Lord's brother.

Elsewhere we have explained why we think the author was James the Lord's brother; other views, of course, have sometimes been held.

CONCLUSION

We suggest, therefore, that we should approach the Epistle of James as the first "Papal Encyclical," carefully remembering, of course, not to equate James with the Pope of later Ebionite fantasy ("Papst der ebjonitischen Phantasie").[72] Relying primarily on postcanonical testimony, especially that of Hegesippus, the pseudo-Clementines, and Eusebius-Jerome Canon, A. A. T. Ehrhardt and others[73] traced the doctrine of

66. See Dibelius, p. 37.
67. E.g., 2:13, 26.
68. 1:2, 10; 2:5.
69. 2:14-19; 5:1-6.
70. 2:18f.; 5:13f.
71. See McDonald, *Kergyma and Didache*, p. 46.
72. So T. Zahn, "Bruder und Vettern Jesu," *Forschungen Zur Geschichte des neutestamentlichen Kanons und der altkirchlichen Literatur*, 6 (1900): 280, cited by M. Hengel, "Jakobus der Herrenbruder—der erste 'Papst'?" in *Glaube und Eschatologie: Festschrift für Werner Georg Kümmel zum* 80. *Geburtstag* (1985), p. 71; see also H.-J. Schoeps, *Paul, The Theology of the Apostle in the Light of Jewish Religious History* (1961), p. 67.
73. *The Apostolic Succession* (1953), pp. 29ff., 35ff., 62ff.; J. J. Scott, Jr., "James the Relative of Jesus and the Expectation of an Eschatological Priest," *Journal of Evangelical Theological Society* 25.3 (Sept. 1982): 325ff.; S. G. F.

apostolic succession to the circle around James, who (they thought) was regarded as the first archbishop of Jerusalem and the high priest of the new Israel, sometimes even in an eschatological and messianic context. As President of the Sanhedrin of the new Israel, James would exercise supreme jurisdiction over the Christian synagogues of Palestine and the Diaspora, as well as the apostles; and, of course, this included Peter. Even those who accept the official Roman Catholic view of Peter's priorities and power as Vicar of Christ would (surely?) admit that these priorities and powers are not immediately and consistently visible in practice from the day of ascension or in the lifetime of the apostles. Indeed, if anyone deserved the title of "Pope" in the primitive Christian hierarchy, it would be James, not Peter.[74] We must also avoid carefully any suggestion that the title "Pope" or "Bishop" implies any elaborate ecclesiastical polity in a church as yet not separate from Judaism.[75]

In suggesting that we approach the Epistle of James as a "quasi-encyclical," we do not mean to imply that the circle of churches for which it was written (1:1) is as large as that to which a Papal Encyclical is addressed or that the authority claimed for it is identical with that of a Pope; we only mean that it was written—perhaps at his installation,[76] in response to Jewish Christian pilgrims visiting Jerusalem at festival time[77] or at some other appropriate occasion—by James the Lord's brother, an apostle of unsurpassed prestige among Jewish believers in Christ, and intended to be read to all their congregations.

But there is an important difference: the Epistle of James, we believe, was meant for regular, or at least frequent, reading in the churches; and, a point of fundamental importance, its scope concerns the Christian religion in general and not, as may be the case with Papal Encyclicals, some more limited aspects or problems of faith and conduct. It is highly probable that at least during the life of James, the first "Papacy" was at Jerusalem and the first "Pope" was James, the most

---

Brandon, *Jesus and the Zealots* (1967), pp. 122ff.; K. L. Carroll, "The Place of James in the Early Church," *BJRL* 45 (1961): 49ff.

74. A view also expressed by R. Newton Flew in a personal conversation; see also his *Jesus and His Church: A Study of the Idea of the Ecclesia in the New Testament* (1938), p. 184.

75. For similar cautions, see M. Hengel, *art. cit., Glaube und Eschatologie*, pp. 103f.; Schoeps, *Paul, The Theology of the Apostle in the Light of Jewish Religious History*, pp. 67f., 86f.

76. For this attractive, if unprovable, suggestion, see E. H. Plumptre, *A Discussion of the General Epistle of St. James* (1909), p. 23.

77. See C. L. Mitton, p. 9; R. P. Martin, *New Testament Foundations*, II (1978), 364.

influential and respected leader of Christianity in the dawn of "the Way."

No doubt we all tend to read history backwards, but surely anyone who cares to assert that God destined for Peter all the priorities and powers of, say, Sixtus V may yet, not inconsistently, admit that there was an early stage in Christian history (a stage to which the Epistle of James belongs) when the center of Christianity was still at Jerusalem and its leading influence was the Apostle of Jerusalem. At this stage some Christians still believed that the Second Advent was not indefinitely remote but immediately imminent, and the Jews were still fighting a vigorous, though losing, battle to have their principles and practices recognized as essentials of Christianity. Until it became clear (and it was not yet clear in the lifetime of James) that Jewry was going to reject Christianity, the Jews had priority in Christianity; at this time Christianity was as much a Jewish sect as Pharisaism.

The Epistle of James comes from the center and head of the Christianity of its day and speaks with the pastoral authority of its source. And the soul behind it all is, as it were, the soul of a Christian Isaiah or Ezekiel, not concerned with the saying of a statutory creed, or the slaying of a statutory lamb, or the swaying of a statutory censer, but (like Ezekiel and the other prophets) with sincerity in life, with walking in God's way.

Such an encyclical, in our opinion, could have only one author: the brother of the Lord. The burden of proof must rest with those who say otherwise. All that we know of James the Lord's brother from the NT and later tradition points to a man of final authority and unique character, champion of the poor and prophet of righteousness. Only this man, we submit, could have penned and circulated such an Epistle.

5. Style

"In his commentary J. B. Mayor has investigated the Greek of James exhaustively even in many points that need no investigation and that net us very little. The mode of thought found in James is more important. He employs simple language to express his thought. This is thought to be due to his Jewish type of mind; yet there are good writers in all languages who express themselves in simple instead of complex, involved sentences. Character and type of mind have not a little to do with one's form of language."

R. C. H. Lenski, *The Interpretation of the Epistle to the Hebrews and of the Epistle of James* (1946), pp. 511f.

Sydney Smith, a famous nineteenth-century canon of St. Paul's, once pointed out that you do not need to be a hen in order to be qualified to criticize an egg. We do believe, however, that an estimate of James's style in Greek must be founded on some knowledge of Greek style. You might describe a woman's style of cooking by mentioning that she makes the appetizer herself, that her recipe for soup appears elsewhere only in her mother's cookbook, her recipe for salad only in Mrs. Beeton's, her recipe for the main dish only in Julia Child's, and her recipe for the dessert only in Betty Crocker's: what we want to know is the manner in which she uses them and with what effect. So we will not begin our discussion with lists of the rare and unique words in James but rather with the main aspect of James's style, the ways in which he employs his resources of vocabulary and grammar to create an effect. Incidentally we see no reason to believe that "James's grasp of Greek is limited."[1]

Thus the basic question is, What power does the author demon-

1. Davids, p. 10.

strate in his use of Greek? J. B. Mayor speaks of James's Demosthenic skill *(deinotēs),* "energy, vivacity, vividness,"[2] and points out that "whatever James says, he says forcibly," "with no slight rhetorical skill"; moreover, he regards this as most essential in James, the first thing to look for. In our opinion, the word "power" or "force" *(dynamis)* is the most useful name for this paramount quality of style; and this sums up the total impact of our Epistle.

MERITS

Of the many great merits of James's style the main ones are *freshness* and *force, balance* and *brevity.* Its chief features are power, seen in its vividness, force (not far below that of Demosthenes himself), and versatility in form, combining studied balance with a rich variety very different from the uniformity, not to say monotony, of pattern to be seen, for instance, in the first chapter of Ecclesiasticus. Verses 3, 9, 11, and 12 resemble a chain of four links, and v. 2, one of three links. The last verse, 30, is quite exceptional in that it does not display bipartite balance, which appears quite simply as in v. 29, or more elaborately as in v. 20 or v. 27. Balance itself seems to have been innate in the earliest literature of both Hebrew and Greek;[3] but passages like 2 Chr. 28:15 show that there could be exceptions.

In James, a brief glance will detect not only an immense advance in the variety of structure of his sentences and his choice and use of words, but even more the range of thought and imagination from which these spring. On this count, and some others, his third chapter has only a few equals among all the NT epistles. This contrast in structure is exemplified by a comparison of James and Ecclesiasticus. In Ecclesiasticus bipartite balance holds almost a monopoly, while in James the reader will immediately detect an immense advance in the variety of the structure of the verses.

2. P. cclxii.

3. Brevity and balance are almost innate in OT Hebrew and in apocryphal and NT Greek. The tale of Creation could scarcely be told more concisely than in Gen. 1. Even narrative often falls into bipartite equipoise, as in 1 Sam. 16:14. Quite often, not only in narrative, a third portion is poised as it were on the center of the seesaw, e.g., in Gen. 1:10: "And God called the dry land earth, and the gathering together of the waters called he seas; and God saw that it was good." In the Epistle of James the third element is sometimes a participle, as in 1:22. But 2 Chr. 28:15, with its ten predications in a simple chain, reminds us that Hebrew narrative can be poured out as simply without any pattern or balance as a story in Greek in Hellanicus. See Mussner, pp. 30ff.

Balance, we must remember, need not entail correspondence in grammar, or parallelism, even antithesis, in meaning. Sometimes there is such correspondence: "Short rede, good rede"; "More haste, worse speed." On the other hand, one of the balancing units may be grammatically dependent on the other; for example, we might say, "Bad crow, bad egg." (The Greek proverb says, "Of bad crow, bad egg.") The two balancing elements may be grammatically inseparable in other ways: "The chariest maid/is prodigal enough. . . ." "Something is rotten/in the state of Denmark." One should not pause in uttering these two last examples, but they do demonstrate a clear poise of semantic balance. Of course there is often a pause, for the ordinary reasons, in the utterance of balanced composition, as in *Hamlet* 2.2, "O what a rogue . . . of eyes and ears." (See *Table 1*.)

Mayor stated that the Epistle of James contains 140 simple sentences, with two subordinate clauses; only two (2:2-4 and 4:13-15) exceed four lines in a printed NT and could be called periodic sentences; and throughout there is no elaboration of structure.[4] This in itself makes for a vivid and energetic style. A principal clause and a subordinate clause often balance, as in Jas. 2:26 where they balance in more than one point; or a subordinate clause (*hoti*, "that") balances a principal clause, which itself is balanced in two halves, as at 2:20.

One may receive a fair impression of James's brevity and balance by comparing it with Portia's speech on mercy (see *Table 1*). Besides the general resemblance in pointed balance and grave brevity, Portia's argument and subject have close affinities to Jas. 2:8-13. Her six short predications, 46 words in all, followed by one of 23 words, then by four of 34 words in all, and finally by three of 21, 19, and 29 words respectively, are curiously reminiscent of some of James's passages. Even the slightly longer sentences, which sometimes conclude phases of his argument, show resemblances (see 3:6 or 1:25; in 1:22-24 there are seven predications in seven and a half lines, and in 1:25 one in five lines).

4. P. cclvi. One of the best evidences of style is the use of logical particles, which are so frequent and often so necessary as to be employed almost unconsciously. James's use of *kai* is worth noting here, for it is both flexible and comprehensive. It has been said that the greatest invention of the Greeks was the use of *men* and *de*. The fact that James never uses them (though in 1:10, 13; 2:11 it is assumed) certainly does not mean that he lacked that sense of balance which the particles achieve. Here and there James conforms more strictly than any other writer to classical usage; see, e.g., *omnynai* with accusative (5:12) and *age* with the plural (4:13), as well as *chrē* and *eoike*. A writer whose Greek was that of the LXX and the *koine* cannot fail to exhibit numerous departures from strict classical usage; Mayor, p. ccxlii, thought that the most serious was the use of the genitive of quality.

We see two stylistic patterns intrinsically interwoven. In Portia's speech, they are (1) the rhythmic scanning of the lines of verse with each other (into which we shall not enter here) and (2) the juxtaposition of the main idea, or kind of affirmation, on the one hand, and its follow-up phrase on the other hand (which follow-up phrase may take the form of an attribution to the main idea or affirmation, or it may take the form of a logical consequence of the main idea or affirmation). Thus the juxtaposition of (1) and (2) produces a kind of rhythmic balance.

The following, therefore, is an effort to illustrate the balance. Note that the parentheses indicate unnecessary stylistic additions (i.e., padding for the rhythm) and that the underlining serves only to call the reader's attention to points of importance in thought, clarifications of meaning, *not* necessarily or usually to emphasis in speech.

TABLE 1

BALANCE IN PORTIA'S SPEECH ON MERCY (A THEME DEAR TO JAMES) IN *THE MERCHANT OF VENICE* 4.1

AFFIRMATION	*ATTRIBUTION OR LOGICAL CONSEQUENCE*
The quality of mercy is not strained;	*It droppeth as the gentle rain from heaven upon the place beneath.*
It is twice blest;	*It blesseth him that gives and him that takes.*
'Tis mightiest in the mightiest;	*It becomes the throned monarch better than his crown.*
His sceptre shows the force of temporal power,	*The attribute of awe and majesty, wherein [i.e., <u>force of temporal power</u>] doth sit the dread and fear of kings;*
But mercy is above the sceptered sway;	*It is enthroned in the hearts of kings;*
	It is an attribute of God himself,
And earthly power doth then show likest God's when mercy seasons justice:	*(Therefore, Jew, though justice be thy plea, consider this:)*
	That in the course of justice [i.e., <u>judgment according to law</u>], none of us should see salvation [i.e., relief from injustice].

We do pray for mercy, — *And that same prayer doth teach us all to render the deeds of mercy.*

I have spoken thus much to mitigate thy plea, — *Which (if thou follow,) this strict court of Venice must needs give sentence 'gainst the merchant there.*

Here now *Hamlet* 3.1:

To be or not to be,
That is the question:

Whether 'tis nobler — *in the mind to suffer*
the slings and arrows — *of outrageous fortune*
Or to bear arms — *against a sea of troubles*
and by opposing — *end them.*
For who would bear — *(here the balance is obvious)*
—when he himself — *might his quietus make*

with a bare bodkin ?
Who would fardels bear

to grunt and sweat — *under a weary life,*
but that the dread — *of something after death,*

the undiscovered country,

from whose bourn — *no traveller returns,*

puzzles the will

and makes us rather bear — *the ills we have*
than fly to others — *that we know not of.*

Many of the sentences are simple in the technical sense of having no subordinate clauses, and even the rest exhibit no real complexity. This in itself makes for a vivid and energetic style. His short sentences seem "to quiver in the mind of the hearer from the swiftness with which they had been launched."[5] But even in the formal greeting—the simplest sentence of all—we have an indication of the care, balance, brevity, and weight that characterize this Epistle.

James
of God, and of the Lord Jesus Christ, servant,
to the twelve tribes that are of the dispersion,
Joy!

For the present let us concentrate on ch. 1 (see *Table* 2) and study the kaleidoscopic variety in its sequence (vv. 1, 6, 8, 11, 13, 14, 16, 18, 19, 20, 21, 22, 25, 27).

5. F. W. Farrar, *Early Days of Christianity* (1882), p. 319.

The following are simple sentences:

1. address and salutation;
6. participle in both halves;
8. most simple and forceful;
11. chain of five, tone of prophets;
13. chain of four;
14. has twin participles;
15. careful bipartite;
16. introductory address;
18. participle plus infinitive construction;
19. tripartite, with adjectives;
20. maxim, short and weighty;
21. elaborate;
22. pair plus third;
25. participles, elaborate;
27. balanced definition.

Subsections end at:	4	8		15	25	
sections end at:			11	21		27

Throughout the entire Epistle conjunctions indicate subordination.

The balance of James's style is obvious throughout,[6] and there are many examples of great delicacy. As a result the Epistle reads almost like a prose poem. We have just cited 2:20 and 26. Later, in a separate excursus *(Excursus B)*, we shall discuss the famous hexameter of 1:17. Consider now 1:9-11(see *Table* 2):

TABLE 2

JAMES 1

1. *James, of God, and of the Lord Jesus Christ, servant, to the twelve tribes that are of the Dispersion, Joy!*
2. *Deem it nothing but an occasion for joy, my brothers, whenever (on each occasion when . . .) you encounter trying assaults of evil in their various kinds.*
3. *You must realize that your approbation is accomplished by constancy in endurance.*
4. *But let that constancy perfect its work, so that you may be perfect, and complete in every part, lacking in nothing (but able to withstand any kind of assault of evil by which you may be tried).*
5. *But if any of you is lacking knowledge (of God's way and will), let him ask of God, who gives it to all as a simple (unconditional) gift and chides not (the petitioner for previous ignorance).*
6. *But let him ask in faith, with no halting between two opinions. For the man who halts between two opinions is like a tossing sea, beaten with winds and blasts.*

6. See, e.g., F. F. Bruce, *The English Bible* (1970), p. 110 on Jas. 1:19 as an illustration of KJV "prose rhythms." He notes the use of critic feet (long, short, long): "Swift to hear/slow to speak/slow to wrath." For an early, interesting attempt to arrange the Epistle in verse form, see H. J. Cladder, "Die formale Aufbau des Jakobusbriefes," *Zeitschrift für katholische Theologie* 28 (1904): 295-330.

7. *Let not that (sort of) man imagine that he will get anything from the Lord.*
8. *A man who is of two minds is unsteady in all his ways.*
9. *(In the equality of Christian brotherhood) let the brother of humble degree exult in his being made high,*
10. *and the rich (brother) in his being made low: for he (in his being-only-rich) shall pass away like the flower of the grass.*
11. *For the sun arises, with the scorching wind, and parches the grass, and the flower among it falls off, and the beauty of its appearance perishes: so he who is (only) rich shall wither in his ways.*
12. *Happy is the man who with constancy endures trying assaults of evil; for when (upon trial) he has been approved, he will receive the crown of life, which God has promised to those who love him.*
13. *Let no one under trying assault of evil say, "My trial by assault of evil comes from God." For God is invincible to assault of evils, and himself subjects no one to assault of evil.*
14. *But each man is tried by assault of evil by his own lust, as he feels the pull of its distraction and the enticement of its bait.*
15. *Then his lust having conceived gives birth to sin; and when sin is full grown it brings forth death.*
16. *Make no mistake, my beloved brothers (I'm not arguing, I'm telling you):*
17. *Every good gift, yes, every perfect gift, is from above, coming down from the Father of lights of heaven, whose nature (unlike those lights) suffers neither the variation of orbit nor any shadow.*
18. *He of his own wish begot us by the Word of truth, for us to be a kind of firstfruits of his creation.*
19. *Wherefore, my beloved brothers, let every man be swift to hear, slow to speak, slow to wrath:*
20. *for a man's wrath (or "anger") does not express in action the righteousness of God.*
21. *Wherefore strip off all filthiness and prodigality of vice, and with meekness accept the implanted Word (implanted by those who have preached the gospel to you), which is able to save your souls.*
22. *But be doers of the Word and not merely hearers of it, deluding yourselves.*
23. *For if anyone is a hearer of the Word and not a doer of it, he is like a man observing the face of his mortal, physical birth in a mirror.*
24. *For he observes himself, and is gone, and immediately forgets what he was like.*
25 *But he who has bent over to look into the perfect law of liberty, and has stayed by it, since he has not been a hearer who forgets but a doer who acts, he shall be blessed in his doing.*
26. *If anyone among you thinks he is devout, and is one who does not bridle his tongue but deludes his own heart, this man's devoutness is vain.*

27. *Devoutness pure and undefiled in the sight of God the Father is this, to visit the fatherless and widows in their affliction, and to keep oneself unspotted from the world.*

Here, apart from the obvious features, one may note the opening joy of *kauchasthō* ("let . . . exult") (v. 9), balanced by the melancholy *pareleusetai* ("shall pass away") (v. 10); notice also the subtle inversion of order of noun and verb in *kai exēranen ton chorton* ("and parches the grass") and *kai to anthos autou exepesen* ("and the flower among it falls off") (see Isa. 40:7 LXX) and the parallel form and rhythm of the two predications at the end, the last with an even more melancholy clang, *maranthēsetai* ("shall wither") (v. 11).

EXAMPLES OF BALANCE (2:18; 3:13-18)

Another, and more complex, example of balance is James's use of dialogue in 2:18, where he introduces (we believe) a sympathizer and counterquestion to prove his point: "Indeed one will say: 'You claim to have faith, and I have works. Let me see your faith without your works, and through my works I will let you see my faith.'"

This notoriously difficult and apparently contradictory *crux* really harks back to v. 14: "If somebody says he has faith, but produces no works." James first says: "In practice that is useless, in fact dead *(nekra)*." Then he continues, in effect: "But useless or not, I challenge you [the man of v. 14] to prove it *exists,* if there are no works to show for it."

Now James never (and this is significant) says in first person singular: "I tell you. . . ." *Erei tis* in effect is very near it, and *tis* is an objector not to James but to the man's saying in v. 14. To the man making such a claim without works James obliquely sums up his own argument:

> "One may put it like this (by way of challenge that the challenger knows cannot be met), in effect:
> You claim to have *(echeis)* faith; I have works.
> I can prove my faith by my works.
> But come now, show me, I defy you, to prove to me the existence of your faith without works, for of course you can't do it."

Direct speech rather than a question makes the discussion more vivid.

To sum up:

1. *Alla* ("but") is adversative, but it refers to v. 14.
2. *Erei tis* ("one will say") is a sympathizer with James, although not

necessarily a monotheistic Jew (Mayor, Zahn) or non-Christian moralist (Haupt).

3. *Sy* ("you") is addressed to *tis* ("one") of v. 14.
4. *Egō* ("I") is *tis* ("one"), the sympathizing speaker.

The balanced vividness of this dramatized reply is typical of James's style and taste, and the use of "one" when he might well have written "I would reply" is paralleled by his modesty in the last sentence of the Epistle, where he might well have said, "I hope I have done some good." Ropes has no reason to say, "Further, the introduction of an ally, representing the same point of view, is wholly uncalled for. . . ."[7] We think that anyone familiar with James's art will see that "You believe" of 2:19, which introduces the conclusion of the paragraph (we mean the conclusion that completes vv. 19 and 20) deliberately, rondo style, returns to the beginning of the paragraph and the beginning of the speech (of objection) contained in that paragraph, that is, to the words "You claim to have faith"; the return is even clearer in the Greek, where the noun at the beginning and the verb introducing the conclusion are cognates. We would put a colon, not a full stop, at the end of v. 19; but we would not want to attempt to organize a consistent system of punctuation for Greek.

As further proof (if such be needed) of the balance, artistry, and coherence of our Epistle, we cite Jas. 3:13-18:

---

13. *Who among you is a man of wisdom and knowledge? Let him by his way of life show his works accordingly in meekness of wisdom.*
14. *But if there is bitter jealousy and faction in your hearts, glory not in your lies against the truth.*
15. *This wisdom is not one descending from above, but is of the earth, of this life, of the devil.*
16. *For where there is jealousy and faction, there is confusion and every evil.*
17. *But the wisdom from above is first pure, then peaceable, humane, yielding to persuasion, full of mercy and good fruits, undivided in mind, untainted with hypocrisy.*
18. *And the fruit of righteousness is sown in peace by those that cultivate peace.*

---

7. P. 214 *ad init.*; also Dibelius, Laws, Davids, and others. The balance in this dialogue is even clearer in the Greek: *theleis de gnōnai ō anthrōpe kene*. If this were spoken, you would hear the force of contempt in *ō anthrōpe kene*, balanced in *chōris tōn ergōn, nekra.* For an excellent discussion of the entire passage, see Gary M. Burge, "'And Threw Them Thus on Paper': Recovering the Poetic Form

Contrary to those who regard it as a detached fragment inserted later,[8] we believe that 3:18 is integral and climactic to James's entire argument. The particle *de,* unless it is a later addition, would appear to suggest some such connection. Even more significant, however, is the corresponding connection in thought within the passage itself, a connection that Hort, not surprisingly, firmly grasped. So he writes here of James's expository and rhetorical method and skill:

> It is as though St. James feared that the force of the one comprehensive word *eirēnikē* might be lost in the additional cognate epithets; and so returned to it with a fresh expansion for the emphatic close of the paragraph. *Karpos dikaiosynēs* in like manner catches up the *mestē karpon agathōn.*[9]

The point could be carried further.

To illustrate the formal scheme of 3:13-18:

T indicates *true*; A_1 "from above" *(anōthen);* W_1 wisdom (true, "from above" [*anōthen*]); R_1 righteousness; R_1 E righteous works; P_1 peace; F_1 good fruit; T_1 etc. will indicate the opposite of T_1 etc.

13. *(True, "from above" [anōthen]) wisdom must bear fruit in righteous*
T_1 A_1 R_1E
behavior, in peace.
P_1

14. *Animosity is a mind of vanity and lies, not wisdom.*
P_2 T_2 W_2

15. *It is a mind not "from above" (anōthen) but "devilish" (daimoniōdēs).*
Not A_1 but A_2

16. *Animosity produces evil behavior.*
P_2 F_2 R_2E

17. *(True) wisdom from above is a mind of many (named) virtues,*
(T_1) W_1 A_1 R_1
including peaceableness, and is full of the seed of good fruits.
R_1

18. *Peaceableness nurtures these virtues of mind into righteous behavior.*
P_1 F_1 R_1 R_1E

---

of James 2:14-26," *Studia Biblica et Theologica* 7 (1977): 31-45; also J. G. Lodge, "James and Paul at Cross-Purposes? James 2, 22," *Bib* 62 (1981): 200f.

8. On the unity of this passage, its relationship to the entire Epistle, and especially James's expository method and rhetorical skill, see, e.g., Hort, Mussner, Laws, Davids, Lodge; in contrast, see, e.g., Dibelius, J. Marty, and others. On the "double catalogue" *(doppelkatalog)* of 3:13-17, recapitulated in 3:18, see E. Kamlah, *Die Form der katalogischen Paränese im Neuen Testament* (1964), pp. 183f.

9. P. 87.

Notice that the three verses in the center (14, 15, and 16) are given to the *mala,* and the three (13, 17, and 18) embracing them are given to the *bona.* The "rondo" begins with v. 13 and closes with the repeat of v. 13 in vv. 17 and 18. Verse 17 enumerates the many virtues compendiously called "righteous behavior" *(kalē anastrophē)* in v. 13, and repeats the requirement of "meekness" *(praÿtēs)* merely named in v. 13 in a full predication that the "righteous behavior" *(kalē anastrophē)* of v. 13, called the "fruit of righteousness" *(karpos dikaiosynēs)* in v. 18 and the fruit with which the truly wise mind is *potentially* filled in v. 17, can be realized only by those who, having had the peace-loving *mind* to receive the seed, do so receive the seed, and then foster it to fruition by keeping the *work* of peace. Godly wisdom has a seed that only peace-loving minds can receive; and only if they continue in the *work* of peace can the seed grow and ripen into righteous conduct.

Notice also that v. 18, besides completing (with v. 17) the repetition of v. 13, is antithetically parallel to v. 16, which, with the other medial v. 15, completes the characterization of false wisdom. Compare also the parallelism between vv. 15-16 and vv. 17-18.

(a) The devilish mind (v. 15), in strife, works evil (v. 16).

(b) The truly wise mind (v. 17), in peace, works good (v. 18). Finally, notice the chiasmus in vv. 16 and 18.

Strife produces evil.

Righteousness is produced by peace.[10]

So much, then, for *brevity* and *balance;* we have discussed balance more carefully because brevity speaks for itself. Now we must further examine the quality of James's style, or its *freshness* and *force.*

A letter may be, inter alia, a narrative of recent events or little more than philosophic reflection on these events; it may resemble a one-sided conversation about the writer's or the reader's personal interests; or again it may be almost an oration.

Paul seems to prefer the conversational letter, James the oration; only rarely does the passion of Paul's Christianity overmaster his usual epistolary tone, for example, in 1 Cor. 15:20-57. The style of the Epistle of James is genuinely and skillfully rhetorical. Ropes rightly emphasizes this on pp. 6-18 of his excellent study, where he insists (mistakenly, we believe) that only in the first verse is it really an epistle at all; in all the rest its analogy (he argues) is to be found chiefly in the Greek diatribe, a genus fundamentally oratorical in character. "The flashes of

10. On chiasmus in James and the Bible, see Lodge, *art. cit., Bib* 62 (1981): 200f., esp. n. 15; G. Marconi, "La struttura di Giacomo 2," *Bib* 68 (1987): 250ff.

irony which break through St. Paul's splendid vindication of his apostolic authority in the Second Epistle to the Corinthians," observes Mayor, "seem passionless and pale, contrasted with the volcanic energy which glows beneath the denunciation of St. James."[11] If anything in what follows introduces a comparison of Paul and James, it is not to disparage either of them, but to help us understand the art of the Epistle of James, one of the greatest (and least admired) literary masterpieces of the NT.

The difference in style between Paul's Letters and the Epistle of James is due mainly, we suggest, to the difference in the degree of intimacy between the writers and the Christians they were respectively addressing, and (what is perhaps more important) due also to the difference between Paul's Gentile converts, novices to OT and NT religion, and James's Jews. The latter should have been at least twice as far as the former on the path to Christ.

Paul's Letters, though no doubt capable of edifying Christians of all times and places, were written specifically for localized groups of converts—the Corinthians, for example, or the Galatians; James, writing expressly for Jews "of the Dispersion," is contemplating what he might then have called a worldwide target, and an eternal message is the result. For while Paul only rarely addresses a comprehensive danger, the Epistle of James is thoroughly comprehensive and eternal in its appeal.

Paul's usual method in his Epistles is personal, like that of many short religious or moral talks over radio or TV. In contrast, the only word we are able to offer for the style of James is "episcopal," a term chosen to suggest a considerable number of hearers or readers not unlike the full audience of a one-time cathedral sermon. The difference between the contemplated targets of James and Paul can scarcely be exaggerated; *res ipsa loquitur.* Paul, writing letters for known Christians at known addresses, adopts a personal approach and a personal technique; James, writing a catholic circular for an unlocalized public, uses a more formal and cultured method, which we may safely call rhetorical—genuinely and skillfully so—provided we realize that it is not in any sense more rhetorical than a sober letter to a religious periodical or to a leading newspaper. The difference between Paul's congregational approach and James's catholic approach has consequences, literary and theological, that deserve further attention.

The style of the Epistle of James, as we said earlier, is genuinely and skillfully rhetorical.[12] Even without his speeches in Acts, it is self-

11. P. cclix.

12. On the rhetorical elements, see Mayor, pp. ccxlixff.; Mussner, p. 29;

evident that Paul, the prince of missionaries, was an expert in public speaking. But in his letters, apart from a few passages such as 1 Cor. 15, the art of rhetoric is scarcely noticeable; the general style is conversational, and nothing seems to be more lacking in architecture than, for example, Eph. 1:2-14. In Acts Paul's speeches resemble Stephen's and are not very different from James's speech in 15:13-21. The outstanding skill in the composition of the last sentence in Acts 15:13-21, however, is well matched in the Epistle of James. James must surely have drafted the Council's letter in Acts 15:23-29.

Whatever the reasons, then, Paul used an epistolary style in his letters; but James, if anything, intensified his effort in the Epistle of James. The consequences are obvious. Some can be measured. An epistolary style is normally prosaic; exceptionally it may become rhetorical, for example, in exhortation, entreaty, or consolation—and Paul in his letters studiously keeps down any tendencies to rhetoric. Pharisaism (we speak without irony) is a highly intellectual way of loving God and your neighbor, and we think it left a mark.

Even in the opening rhapsody of Eph. 1:3ff., whether "heart" or "mind" be read in v. 18, the mention of "eyes" emphasizes the intellectual aspect of the matter under discussion; in the same way, "wisdom and prudence" and "having made known" (vv. 8 and 9). Eph. 2:8-22 is almost as intellectual as theological lectures on doctrine are said to be. Again in 4:13, we read of the unity of the faith and of the knowledge of the Son of God; and the intellectualization of ethics is plainer still in 4:17f. *(q.v.)*. Likewise Phil. 3:8-15 is keyed to knowledge and the mind. In contrast to the intellectual bias of Paul's Letters, especially in their exposition of doctrine, rhetoric, which predominates in the Epistle of James, by its very nature cultivates an appeal to the emotions no less than to the intellect—an appeal no more necessarily insincere than an appeal to the reason.

CHARACTERISTICS

The intellectual epistolary style, as in Paul, normally employs plain prose and plain reasoning: as a rule it is not noticeably colored with emotion, an effect regularly characteristic of poetry and, both in prose and poetry, most commonly seen in (1) imagery, (2) vocabulary and grammar, and (3) the studied use of adjectives.

W. H. Wuellner, "Der Jakobusbrief im Licht der Rhetorik und Textpragmatik," *Linguistica Biblica* 43 (1978): 5-66. L. G. Gieger, *Figures of Speech in the Epistle of James: A Rhetorical and Exegetical Analysis* (1981).

(1) Hort discerned in such use of imagery an outlet for James's "great suppressed energy,"[13] not in a "mist of dubious symbols" but by way of giving a Hogarth-like force and clarity to his teaching.[14] Many, or even most, of James's images may come from an older stock, but the choice he has made of them is itself personally significant and sometimes may give new life to an old expression.[15] Among the images in our Epistle are these: the restless sea (1:6 and 3:4), the withering grass (1:16f.), the bridle (3:3), the rudder (3:4), fire (3:5f.), fountains (3:11), fruit trees (3:12), trading (4:13), mist (4:14), farming (5:4, 7), and childbirth (1:15).

We may also include references to such OT figures as Abraham, Rahab, Job, and Elijah, as well as the short parable (e.g., 1:23); the latter is akin to and almost indistinguishable from the image. See *Excursus C: The Waverer (1:6)—An Example of Style.*

(2) As for vocabulary and grammar, James writes the easy, accurate, "mellifluous,"[16] literary *koine* Greek of his period as well as any other NT author, and better than most of them.[17] He is closer to standard classical prose than any other NT writer, with the best Greek in the NT except perhaps (and not always) the author of the Epistle to the Hebrews.[18] We cannot here give details of grammar and vocabulary except

13. P. xxxiii.

14. See A. J. Gossip and J. F. McFadyen, *The General Epistles.* The Study Bible (1930), p. 2.

15. See S. T. Coleridge, "Christabel," Preface, *The Portable Coleridge,* ed. I. A. Richards (1978), pp. 105f.

16. See B. W. Bacon, "The Doctrine of Faith in Hebrews, James and Clement of Rome," *JBL* 19 (1900): 12.

17. See Ropes, p. 24: "There is less occasion than in Paul or in the Synoptic Gospels to turn from the ordinary grammars to the colloquial Greek of the papyri for illustrations of strange expressions. Some instances occur of . . . good Greek style . . . unique, or very rare, in the NT. . . . The relation of the style, on its Hellenistic side, to the diatribe has already been discussed (pp. 12-16)." For an almost microscopic approach of somewhat limited value, see C.-B. Amphoux, "Vers une description linguistique de l'Épître de Jacques," *NTS* 25.1 (1978): 58-92.

18. For this view, see, e.g., Mayor, p. ccxliv; Mussner, p. 26; J. H. Moulton and W. F. Howard, *The Grammar of the New Testament Greek,* II (1929), 20, 27; Dibelius, p. 34; J. Cantinat, *Les Épîtres de Saint Jacques et de Saint Jude* (1973), pp. 12f.; Ropes, p. 24; A. Wikenhauser, *New Testament Introduction* (1958), pp. 482f.; G. A. Deissmann, *Light from the Ancient East* (1927), p. 235; G. Salmon, *A Historical Introduction to the Study of the Books of the New Testament* (1894), p. 134; Patrick, p. 298; H. G. Meecham, "The Epistle of St. James," *ExpT* 49 (1937): 183. For less favorable views (e.g., Schleiermacher, Davidson), see Mayor, p. cclv; W. L. Knox, "The Epistle of James," *JTS* 46 (1945): 13; A. T. Robertson, *A Grammar of the Greek New Testament,* p. 123.

for a few typical examples of James's power and frequent originality in the use of adjectives, which often seem to be standard Hebrew thoughts in almost literally equivalent current Greek.

Ropes remarks that there are few Hebraisms; of grammatical Hebraisms, only the use of the genitive of a noun to serve for an adjectival meaning occurs—in *akroatēs epilēsmonēs,* "hearer of forgetfulness" for "forgetful hearer" (1:25).[19] In 2:4, "judges of pernicious discriminations" is not a Hebraism. To the other examples that Ropes considers he himself (very rightly) declines to accord any certainty. He also mentions many "correct but slightly unhellenic"[20] biblical phrases such as *eis ta ōta Kyriou Sabaōth* (5:4), *proïmon kai opsimon* (5:1), and *makarios* (1:12), all of which seem to be good examples of Hebrew thought in almost equivalent ordinary current Greek.[21] *Polysplanchnos,* "plenteous in compassion" (5:11), a word compounded from two ordinary Greek words to render one of the several Hebrew compounds of "bowels," as in "bowels of compassion," is an illustration of the same originality as *dipsychos* and the like for traditional religious or ethical thoughts.[22]

Furthermore, the Epistle contains about 570 words, of which 63 to 73 are found only in the Epistle and nowhere else in the NT.[23] The number of notes like "only here in the NT" indicate the freshness of the style, and, very often, its force. In 1 Peter, Galatians, and Ephesians, which are not, or not much, longer than the Epistle of James, the comparable figures are 63, 34, and 43 respectively. All but about 25 of the words are in the Greek Septuagint, with which James was inevitably and thoroughly familiar through the synagogue.[24] The following seven

19. P. 26. See also W. F. Howard's valuable article in Moulton and Howard, *The Grammar of the New Testament Greek* ([3]1923), II, 413f.

20. On this Ropes also refers to J. H. Moulton, *The Grammar of the New Testament Greek,* I (1908), 10f., "Prolegomena."

21. See Oesterley, pp. 394ff.; Schlatter, p. 78; J. H. Moulton, II, 446, "Prolegomena"; Mussner, pp. 30ff.; J. Chaine, *L'Épître de Saint Jacques* (1927), pp. xciff.; Davids, p. 59; also K. Beyer, *Semitische Syntax im Neuen Testament* (1962), pp. 296ff.

22. *dipsychos.* This word should be added to the six (*bryō,* etc.) in Ropes, p. 25 *ad fin.,* as is clear from his note at p. 143 on 1:8 (for Ropes's six Mayor has 17; but the texts vary).

23. See R. Morgenthaler, *Statistik des neutestamentlichen Wortschatzes* (1958), p. 177; also Dibelius, Mussner, Mayor, Chaine, Ropes, Davids, and the other commentaries.

24. See A. Wifstrand, "Stylistic Problems in the Epistles of James and Peter," *ST* 1 (1947): 182.

words, all in the Classical Greek literature, are used only by James in biblical Greek: "double-minded"[25] (1:8), "pious"[26] (1:26), "daily"[27] (2:15), "sea creature"[28] (3:7), "gush"[29] (3:11), "yielding to persuasion"[30] (3:17), and "dismay"[31] (4:9).

James also shows a marked fondness for compounds such as "with a gold ring"[32] (2:2) and "full of deadly venom"[33] (3:8); technical or semitechnical words such as "variation"[34] (1:17), "implanted"[35] (1:21), "rudder"[36] (3:4), "the circling course of creation"[37] (3:6), and "of this life"[38] (3:15); picture words such as "howl"[39] (5:1) and "merciful"[40] (5:11), and especially words from fishing, for example, "blow"[41] (1:6), "entice by bait"[42] (1:14), "sea creature"[43] (3:7), "salty"[44] (3:12); and from farming, for example, "the necessities of life"[45] (2:16), "gush"[46] (3:11), "rust"[47] (5:3), and "reap"[48] (5:4). His invention of new words is probable, but not verifiable in any given instance.

With regard to his neologisms we must remember that their apparent novelty may be due only to the absence of writings in which they had previously been used; many words once reckoned to be purely biblical, or used in biblical Greek with a special sense, have turned out to be ordinary *koine* Greek, for example, "unspotted"[49] and "affliction,"[50] both in 1:27. G. Adolf Deissmann laid it down as a principle that "When a word is not recognizable as a Jewish or Christian new formation, we must consider it as an ordinary Greek word until the contrary is proved";[51] so, too, BAG condemns the assumption that such words are biblical.[52]

The following words are apparently used in our Epistle for the first time: "merciless"[53] (2:13), "blow"[54] (1:6), "untemptable"[55] (1:13),

25. *dipsychos.*
26. *thrēskos.*
27. *ephēmeros.*
28. *enalios.*
29. *bryō.*
30. *eupeithēs.*
31. *katēpheia.*
32. *chrysodaktylios.*
33. *thanatēphoros.*
34. *parallagē.*
35. *emphytos.*
36. *pēdalion.*
37. *ton trochon tēs geneseōs.*
38. *psychikos.*
39. *ololyzō.*
40. *polysplanchnos.*
41. *anemizō.*
42. *exelkō.*
43. *enalios.*
44. *halykos.*
45. *epitēdeia.*
46. *bryō.*
47. *katioō.*
48. *amaō.*
49. *aspilos.*
50. *thlipsis.*
51. *Light from the Ancient East,* p. 78; Dibelius, pp. 36ff.
52. P. xvii.
53. *aneleos.*
54. *anemizō.*
55. *apeirastos.*

"shadow"[56] (1:17), "devilish"[57] (3:15), "merciful"[58] (5:11), "to have respect of persons"[59] (2:9), "filthiness"[60] (1:21), "bridle"[61] (1:27; 3:2), "with a gold ring"[62] (2:2). In the case of James we must reckon not only with their invention but also with their fresh, vivid, and forceful use, which is the mark of the expert craftsman; he shows the same striking ability in the use of rare words.

In 1:15 the reason for the unusual "brings forth" *(apokyei)* after "gives birth to" *(tiktei)* is stylistic, without any other gravity as in the verb in 1:18; likewise in 1:8 and 1:18 the reason for *poreiais* and *hodois* is purely stylistic; the compound in *apo* is suggested, we think, to avoid repetition of the same word; and James has a distinct taste for alliteration and assonance; for example, he chooses a rare verb at the end of 1:6 to match the last word for the sake of assonance. As often happens in literature, the word, *apekyēsen* in the aorist, is not long in recurring (1:18; see also *anōthen* in 1:17; 3:15, 17). The commentators can suggest no acceptable meaning but think it is synonymous with *tiktei.*

James's genius in the forceful use of words is matched in the Council's Letter in Acts 15:24, which, on similar evidence of the bold imagery of "displenishment"[63] as well as natural probability, must be taken to have been drafted by James. Like about 73 out of 570 words in the Epistle, *anaskeuazein* occurs nowhere else in the NT. This picture is absolutely in keeping with the familiar and vivid metaphors that make the author of the Epistle of James the Pericles of the NT.

(3) Another prominent characteristic of James's rhetorical style is a lavish and varied use of adjectives. Rhetoric aims at suggestion as well as argument or instruction; in this it partakes of some of the nature of poetry and uses some of the same technique that serves poetry. The most obvious element in that technique is the use of adjectives: in the first seven lines of Milton's *Lycidas,* there are eleven adjectives (see *Table 3*). Prose of the ordinary sort tends to shun adjectives, but rhetoric multiplies them. James's adjectives speak volumes. Comparing the Epistle of James with Ephesians and Colossians (together 2¼ times as

56. *aposkiasma.*
57. *daimoniōdēs.*
58. *polysplanchnos.*
59. *prosōpolēmpteō.*
60. *ryparia.*
61. *chalinagōgein.*
62. *chrysodaktylios.*
63. *anaskeuazontes.* On the writer's command of expressive words as a clue to his identification with James the Lord's brother, see Ropes, p. 24; also above, pp. 23f., 133ff.

long as the Epistle of James), we find, as we might expect, more adjectives in James than in the two Pauline letters together.

TABLE 3

MILTON, *LYCIDAS*

Yet once more, O ye laurels, *and once more, ye myrtles brown*
with ivy never sere,
I come
to pluck your berries *harsh and crude,*
and with forced fingers rude
shatter your leaves *before the mellowing year.*
Bitter constraint *and sad occasion dear*
compels me
to disturb *your season due.*
For Lycidas is dead, *dead ere his prime,*
Young Lycidas, *and hath not left his peer.*
Who would not sing for Lycidas? *He knew, himself, to sing,*
and built the lofty rime.
He must not
float upon his watery bier
unwept
or welter to the parching wind
without the need *of some melodious tear.*

N.B. The object of this English extract is to show how to approach the Greek style of the Epistle of James: particular attention is directed to Milton's lavish use of adjectives.

	No. of adj.	*No. of occurrences*
Ep. Jas. (8 pp.)	*75*	*122*
Eph. (11 pp.)	39	59
Col. (7 pp.)	29	53
Eph. and Col. together	*68*	*112*

As the table shows, adjectives are more than twice as frequent in James. It must be recognized, of course, that Paul is second to none in his feeling for adjectives when they suit his purpose. James, referring to the manifold trials and temptations of the Christian life, uses the adjective *poikilos* in 1:2; Paul, speaking of the manifold wisdom of God, uses the intensified *polypoikilos* in Eph. 3:10; and just before this, in 3:8, he uses *ton anexichniaston plouton* for the unsearchable riches of Christ. Usually, however, his purpose does not call for such eloquently moving adjectives.

The power of adjectives is evident throughout the Epistle of James. In ch. 1 the following occur (see *Table 2*): *pasan,* "utter joy" (v. 2); *poikilois,* "trials and temptations of an endless variety" (v. 2); *teleion,* "perfect fruit (or work)" (v. 4) (we take liberties in these quasi-translations in order to bring out some of James's force); *teleioi,* "that you may be perfect" (v. 4); *holoklēroi,* "complete in all parts" (v. 4); *haplōs* (adv., not adj., but of kindred interest to us here), only here in the NT, "God gives unquestioningly" (v. 5); *dipsychos,* in the Bible only in the Epistle of James, twice, "the man of divided mind" (v. 8); *akatastatos,* only here in the NT, "unstable" (v. 8); *pasais,* "all" (v. 8); *ho tapeinos* and *ho plousios,* used as nouns, not without feeling, for the man of low estate, of the "lower orders," and "the rich man" (vv. 9-11); *makarios,* "how happy and blest" with all the feeling of the Hebrew equivalent (v. 12); *dokimos,* "approved and accepted for salvation by God" (v. 12); *apeirastos,* "God is inaccessible to temptation" (v. 13); *agapētoi,* "beloved brothers," in James not yet just a way of speaking (vv. 16, 19); *every good* gift, *every perfect* boon (v. 17); *swift* to hear, *slow* to speak, *slow* to wrath (v. 19); *emphyton* (used proleptically) for "the implanting of the Word" (v. 21); "the *perfect* law" (v. 25); *makarios* (v. 25); *thrēskos* (only here), "punctiliously religious" (v. 26); *mataios,* "vain and futile" (v. 26); *kathara kai amiantos,* "pure and immaculate" (v. 27); and *aspilon,* "undefiled" (v. 27). In v. 14 *idias* combines with *hekastos,* "each . . . his own individual lust."

Doublets occur in participles as well as in nouns, for example, in v. 6 *ad fin.*, v. 14 *ad fin.*, v. 21 *ad init.*, and v. 17 *ad fin.* But in ch. 1 we notice pairs of adjectives only at the beginning, "perfect and complete" (v. 4), and at the climax, where "pure and immaculate" is reinforced with "before God and the Father" (v. 27). 1:2-8 is a marvel of art; James put all his skill into it. Note, for example, the alliteration in v. 2 *ad fin.* (with the initial *p* in *pasan,* its first word);[64] note also the pivoting of *peirasmois* and its adjective *poikilois* on the verb *peripesēte.* The only parallels are in 2:8 (noun first), 3:13 (adj. first), 4:6 (adj. first), and, with the verb "to be," 4:14, 5:11 (in this, adj. first), and 5:17; James, the master stylist, does not debase his art into artifice.

CONCLUSION

Both in substance and in language, the Epistle of James is alive with the personality of its author. In this chapter we have dealt with the sec-

64. On this feature of James's artistry, especially its frequency and variety, see Mayor, pp. ccliiiff.

ond of these two elements, namely, language, observing that few sentences are anything but brief. Of its other merits, the most striking are balance and variety, freshness and force. James also seems to have shared the contemporary fondness for inventing new words. But in recent years, many words once thought to have occurred only, or with a special sense, in biblical Greek have been discovered likewise, and likewise used, in ordinary contexts. At present, however, it seems that at least ten words were used for the first time in our Epistle.

We must recognize not merely the novelty or variety of such words but still more their fresh, vivid, and forceful use, which is the mark of the expert craftsman in language. He can convey strength in a phrase. This characteristic originality and force are matched, as we have seen, in the Council's Letter (which seems, on this evidence as well as natural probability, to have been drafted by James) in Acts 15:24, especially in the bold imagery of displenishment in *anaskeuazontes,* a verb that occurs nowhere else in the NT. This we consider one very strong ground for identifying James of the Epistle with James of the Acts. The bearing of this identification on questions of the author, date, purpose, situation, destination, and importance, not to mention the character and quality, of the Epistle of James will be obvious.

Excursus B

JAMES 1:17—HEXAMETER AS AN ASPECT OF STYLE

The commentators point out that the first half of v. 17 may be construed in three ways:

1. We prefer to take *anōthen* ("from above") as the predicate, with *katabainon* ("coming down") as an explanatory expansion, punctuated *anōthen estin, katabainon, . . .* and to translate as in the KJV and the RV: "every good gift is from above, coming down . . ." This is what Ropes also does,[1] quite rightly.

2. Following the Syriac Version, some take *estin* and *katabainon* together and translate: "and comes down." The effect is to make *anōthen* unnecessary and disjointed. Nor is the parallel 3:15—sometimes cited in sup-

1. P. 160.

port—really relevant, for there, as Hort points out, "the participle is adjectival or qualitative . . . while here a statement of fact is required."[2]

3. Hort himself favored the solution of Thomas Erskine, who makes the predicate consist of *agathē* and *teleion,* that is, "every giving is good and every gift perfect from above (or from its first source), descending . . ."[3] This view, however, is to be rejected because it assumes, as Ropes says, that *dosis* and *dōrēma* contain in themselves the idea of a *divine* gift—which is an impossible assumption.[4] If it is admitted that *dosis* and *dōrēma* are per se general, that is, any sort of gift, but particularized and restricted to *divine* gifts by the word *anōthen,* that is, if the clause is construed thus: "Every gift and every present from above is good," we reply that the Greek *cannot* be so construed.

Further, the Erskine-Hort view gives *anōthen* a meaning that, as Ropes rightly observes, "it can hardly have." The context does indeed require the sense "Every divine gift is good," but that is not to be obtained by giving words impossible meanings but rather from the whole passage: "God is the only source of all good, and he *never varies,*" that is, "He *never sends evil.*" Any notion that "any gift is a good gift" in the Gk. *dōron d' hoti dō tis epainei* and the Lat. *noli equi dentes inspicere donati*[5] ("Don't look a gift horse in the mouth")—quoted by Ropes and supported by H. Greeven, although Greeven gives no authority for it[6]—is quite irrelevant to James here. Probably he is quoting partially from a passage—perhaps pagan—with a thought really relevant and nearly similar to his own thought. We suggest, for example:

> "Every good gift, yes, every perfect gift
> is from Zeus, coming down from above to men,
> good and bad, who dwell upon the earth."
>
> *Pasa dosis agathē, kai pan dōrēma teleion*
> *ek Dios estin, anōthen ep' anthrōpous katabainon,*
> *esthlous ēde kakous, hoi epi chthoni naietaousin.*
> (see *Odyssey* 6.153)[7]

Elsewhere we have mentioned the (important) stylistic antecedents of

2. P. 27.

3. *The Unconditional Freeness of the Gospel* (^{3}1829), pp. 239ff.

4. P. 160.

5. Jerome, *Preface to the Ephesians* 3.537f. (Migne, *PL,* XXVI, 7).

6. "Jede Gabe ist gut," *ThZ* 1 (1958): 1-13. We all know: *Quidquid id est, timeo Danaos et dona ferentes* ("I fear the Greeks even when they bring gifts"); *echthrōn adōra dōra k' ouk onēsima* ("Gifts from enemies are no gifts and no good"); and *kakou gar andros dōr' onēsin ouk echei* ("A wicked man's gifts bring no benefit").

7. This conjecture, with comment, I owe to P. B. R. Forbes.

1:8, 20.[8] Here we have an actual hexameter,[9] made by lengthening the second syllable of *dosis* under the ictus, which could be done by inserting *t'* after *dosis* (see 3:7), although there is no manuscript evidence for it:

Pā́să dŏ/sī́s ăgă/thḗ kaī́/pā́n dō/rḗmă tĕ/leī́ŏn.

The hexameter may be from a lost Hellenistic poem (Ewald), a Sibylline book (Spitta), a Palestinian formula (Schlatter), or a Christian hymn. We do not know. We have continued with the sort of lines that the style and thought would naturally produce in Greek, believing that the obvious, almost inevitable, continuation is as we have it at the beginning of the second line. The thought is a commonplace in Greek poetry, especially in hexameters (so *Iliad* 1.63; see also *Odyssey* 1.33 and 40). Since James gives us two keywords, *anōthen* and *katabainon*, the line makes itself.

The third line is more open to doubt, at least in details. Investigation of the style, however, suggests that, as "Zeus" was balanced by mention of "earth," very likely "all" in connection with gifts will somehow be balanced by "all" in connection with men. What we have written for the third line is suggested by *Odyssey* 6.189 and 153. Mt. 5:45, it may be said, is no news to the Greek.

Now obviously James had to expurgate Zeus; thus he quite properly joins *anōthen* with *esti*, but not so effectively as was done in the suggested original, where it fits better with *katabainon* and gains force from the preceding mention of Zeus. James knows his business: he does relax the pressure somewhat with *anōthen*, but he more than compensates for the relaxation with the intensely forceful description of God that he attaches to *katabainon;* thus he ends the sentence as he began it, in his highest mood. In the suggested original there is a (characteristically Greek) relaxation of force and tension at the end.

Our verses, admittedly, are purely conjectural. James may have started from some quasi-Judaistic verse or verses such as we find in Pseudo-Phocylides: *anōthen esti, katabainon* may be his prose statement of *ouranothen katabainei*. For other NT verse quotations, see the iambic

8. See Adamson, pp. 59f., 78f.

9. See H. Fischer, "Ein Spruchvers im Jakobusbrief," *Philologus* 50 (1891): 377ff.; W. H. P. Hatch, "Note on the Hexameter in James 1:17," *JBL* 28 (1909): 149ff.; H. Greeven, *art. cit., ThZ* 1 (1958): 1-13; Mussner, p. 90, n. 4; Dibelius, p. 99, n. 156; C.-B. Amphoux, "A propos de Jacques 1:17," *RHPR* 50 (1970): 127-36. Literary coincidence is also a possibility. Quite unconsciously many prose writers, e.g., Dryden, Carlyle, and Dickens, can drift into poetry; see also W. Pater's poem "Mona Lisa," ll. 1-4, which actually purports to be a prose passage (*Oxford Book of Modern Verse* [1892-1935], p. 1). For a writer as skilled in Greek as James, it would be perfectly simple to lapse into meter. James obviously would not consciously compose a verse in his Epistle; he could *consciously* quote one, or *unwittingly* (by accident) write one.

measure of Lk. 5:21; Acts 17:28; 1 Cor. 15:33; Tit. 1:12; Heb. 12:13; and possibly (but not likely) 2 Pet. 2:22.[10] Now compare:

A: Every gift and every boon;
B: All things good and all things perfect.

A: *Pasa dosis kai pan dōrēma* . . . (not meter);
B. *Pan ti' agathon kai ti' teleion* . . . (not meter).

Or even,

B. *Pan agathon kai pan teleion* . . . (not meter).

Clearly B carries far more of the force of the line as given by James than A. So, obviously, in James's line the adjectives, *pasa, pan, agathē,* and *teleion,* carry far more force than the two nouns; in addition, the order reinforces the comparative strength of the adjectives, balanced and pivoted as they are upon the nouns: *pasa dosis agathē,* etc. The use of two different equivalent words is dictated simply by the convenience of the meter. To use a similar example: *Pas gar anēr agathos kai pas anthrōpos alēthēs.* The two nouns are very rare, especially *dōrēma,* which is poetic (see Rom. 5:16). The other noun, *dosis,* common in Ecclesiasticus and appearing three times in Philo but still rare, is found in the papyri in financial transactions (see Phil. 4:5).

Hort does not regard those nouns as synonyms, and he quotes Philo to show how he frequently prefers to use *dōrea* and also how he places *dōrea* and *dōron* above *dosis* and *doma* (see *On the Cherubim* 84 [*dōra* and *domata*]; *Allegorical Interpretation* 3.196 [contains *dōra* and *domata*]). Ropes, however, refuses to regard them as other than synonymous, declaring that "no special distinction is intended, the repetition being solely for rhetorical effect."[11] This is correct. There is *no* significant difference between these two nouns, any more than in the merely stylistic variation of Jas. 1:19f.

For the moment we will call this mode of expression "diplology." Tautology is the common term, but (a) that is almost a suspect word and (b) we are not committing ourselves to the view that the two halves are exactly identical in meaning. Diplology is common in Classical Greek, especially oratory, and in Hebrew literature, and it pervades James: "Tossed by winds and blasts" (1:6); "Feeling the pull of its distraction and the enticement of its bait" (1:14); and "Perfect and whole, lacking in nothing" (1:4), where a doublet is redoubled. As in these examples, diplology often goes with balance and even

10. See E. L. Hicks, "Traces of Verse in Prose Writers," *Classical Review* 4 (1890): 49; see also R. Renehan, "Classical Greek Quotations in the New Testament," in D. Neiman and M. Shatkin, eds., *The Heritage of the Early Church: Essays in Honor of the Very Reverend Georges Vasilevich Florovsky* (1973), pp. 17-45.

11. P. 159.

exact symmetry; but these may occur without diplology in the sense of virtual tautology; see, for example, 1:15.

Now "good" *(agathē)* and "perfect" *(teleion)* may be near tautology, but they are certainly not the same. "As 'good' *(agathos)* expresses the character of the gifts, derived from the Giver, so 'perfect' *(teleios)* expresses the completeness of their operation when they are not misused" (Hort). The two adjectives are frequently found together; for example, "as the result of the gifts showered upon him from above Isaac shewed himself good and perfect *(agathos kai teleios)* from the outset" (Philo, *On Dreams* 1.162). "Perfect" is sometimes higher than "good." If "good" means and is known to mean "truly good," it gains nothing from "perfect"; the truly good is perfect, like God. But when we say "Every good gift," how do we know that the man in the pew understands "good" in that divine sense? He may be thinking of a serenade, or of a sermon.

So, to leave less room for ambiguity and error, we say "good and perfect." (It was only to give the flavor of poetry that we added "yes" in our translation above—with, we are sure, no harm to the effect.) In the history of style diplology has often been useful, even necessary, in a sentence; but as a mere ornament for academic display it has been no more than vain repetition.

Excursus C

THE WAVERER (1:6)—AN EXAMPLE OF STYLE

"But let him ask in faith, with no halting between two opinions. For the man who halts between two opinions is like a tossing sea, beaten with winds and blasts." (Jas. 1:6)

The same unique quality of style is evident in the image of the wavering doubter (probably based on the Sea of Galilee). The doubter here inclines first toward one alternative (say, to believe in prayer) and then toward the opposite alternative, and never is able to settle upon either: he is in constant vacillation, but to no avail. In this he is like the Lake of Galilee, a sea of waves blown by the wind.[1]

Two questions arise: Does James mean a wave or the sea, and to what

1. See Gen. 49:4; Ecclus. 33:2; Eph. 4:13f.; Mt. 11:7; also the rabbinic doctrine *kawwānāh,* which speaks of Israel as a wind-tossed lily (Lev. R. 23.5). The reference to the wind-tossed wave has been taken as referring to "the doctrinal directionlessness of Christian pastors" or, more specifically, to Peter walking on the water. See Scaer, pp. 43f., 100. But both these suggestions are unlikely. Certainly we do not find any hint of an "anti-Petrine polemic" in the Epistle.

extent is it disturbed? *Klydōn*[2] is a strong word and refers to more than a "ripple." It can mean "wave," but on consideration we think that here it means an expanse of storm or at least swelling sea,[3] with emphasis, as Ropes observes, rather "on size and extension than on separateness and succession (*kyma*), hence often used in a collective sense."[4] Hort indeed says that *klydōn* always means rough water, noting that "in the tideless Mediterranean even a slight rufflement would be noticed in contrast with the usually level calm."[5]

We cannot believe, however, that James presents his "rough water" as fanned by soft breezes or gentle zephyrs. For that reason we cannot accept Hort's attempts to minimize the force of these aerial disturbances. It is true, as Ropes points out, that the point of comparison is the ordinary instability of the heaving sea,[6] but it is not true that this excludes the possibility of "the unusual violence of a storm."[7]

The first verb, *anemizō*, is rare,[8] and describes any movement of the wind, perhaps implying here, as Hort thinks, "gentler motions of the air." "Fan" itself is used with fiercer applications than we find in a lady's drawing room and what Hort calls "only the kind of blast proper to a fan." In Greek the cited texts use the verb in connection with war, fire, flame, strife, faction, and boiling fish: there is no reason to doubt that James here implies a considerable degree of agitation. *Ripis* and *ripizō* are used of bellows as well as fans, and James here (as well as in other texts) is quite likely drawing his metaphor from bellows.

Indeed, it is entirely possible that we have here another allusion to local life in Palestine, possibly to the winnowing of wheat. E. F. F. Bishop points

2. From *klyzō*, "to wash over," found in Homer and the dramatists with the meaning "wave," "billow," twice in the NT (here and in Lk. 8:24), and nine times in the LXX for the Heb. *seʿārâ*, the Arab. *saʿera* meaning "excite," "inflame," "be mad." See D. Y. Hadidian, "Palestinian Pictures in the Epistle of James," *ExpT* 63 (1952): 227f., who sees an allusion to the sudden storms of the Lake of Galilee—a view too hastily dismissed, we think, e.g., by Laws, p. 57, as "farfetched."

3. As, e.g., Sophocles, *Oedipus Tyrannus* 1527; see also Demosthenes, *On the Embassy* 136; M. Aurelius, *Meditations* 12.14; Philo, *On the Sacrifices of Abel and Cain* 13, 90; *On the Confusion of Tongues* 32. There are a few other analogies (e.g., 23, 25), but only in 32 do we find *salos* and *klydōn (tois salō kai klydōni chairousi)*. The two nouns occur together in each of the passages cited from *On the Sacrifices of Abel and Cain* (with *salos*, "the rolling swell of the sea") and *On the Creation of the World* 63 (with *kymatōsis*, "stormy and broken by waves"); Wisd. 14:5; Lk. 8:24.

4. P. 141.

5. P. 10.

6. P. 142.

7. P. 142; see also p. 11.

8. Found only here in the NT in the sense of the classical *anemoō*, but also in the scholium on Homer, *Odyssey* 12.336 and J. Moschus, *The Spiritual Meadow* (Migne, *PG*, LXXXVII, 3044a).

out that James lived less than a day's walk both from the Lake of Galilee and the Mediterranean Sea, and knew how the Sea of Galilee could be whipped up into foam-crested waves, quite oblivious of their direction.[9]

We have seen that James was at home with Greek. In his discussion of 1:6 Hort admits (but calls "exceptional") the use of *ēnemōmenos* with the meaning of "violent."[10] One must realize, however, that Hort's intent is to deny the meaning "storm" in James's simile, and to this end he embraces every sophistry, arguing that *ripizō* means a fan—whether fan or bellows does not, in fact, matter at all—and so could not kick up a storm, that the Mediterranean presents a "usually level calm," and that here "a slight rufflement of its waters" will do.

But it is not true that *ripizō* is confined to the blast produced by an actual fan. A metaphorical fan can be as big and forceful as the metaphor suggests, as when we say that in the Great Fire of London or Chicago the flames were fanned by a high wind. The metaphorical uses of *ripizō* cited by Liddell and Scott imply *vigorous* action. Nor is there anything mild about *anarripizō* in Philo, *On the Giants* 51: "*the fierce mysterious storm* in the soul, *whipped into fury* by *the wild blast* of life and its cares."[11] *Ripis* is simply an instrument (bellows or fan) for producing a *ripē*, or current of air.[12] On a lady's brow the current would be gentle; from the fire cooking fish it would be vigorous;[13] and the same is true of the cited uses in war, strife, and the like.

9. *Apostles of Palestine* (1958), p. 184; also Rendall, pp. 37f.; Hadidian, *art. cit., ExpT* 63 (1952): 228.

10. *Anthologia Palatina,* ed. F. Dübner, XIII (1864-72), 12.

11. Quoted by Ropes, p. 142 *ad init.* but apparently ignored by Hort.

12. Liddell and Scott (8) have *ripidion,* diminutive of *ripis:* (1) a small bellows (with citation), (2) a small fan (with citation); *ripizō,* to blow up or fan the flame;//*ripis,* a fan;//*ripisis,* blowing with a bellows or fan, the air of a fan, etc. The usual word for bellows is *physa,* commonly plural, *physai;*//*ripē,* the swing or force with which anything is thrown, Lat. *impetus:* used of javelins, stones, spears; of the sweep or rush of Boreas, the north wind; *ripai kymatōn anemōn te,* of waves and winds; metaphorically of gusts of passion; of a terrifying storm sent from Zeus; the rush of fire; of a man (*Iliad* 8.355); of thunderbolts, and hail; of love; also of the buzz of a gnat's wings and of the lyre's quivering tones; of twinkling light of stars; of the blinking eye (1 Cor. 15:52); of the aroma of wine.//*euripos:* "any strait or narrow sea, where the flux and reflux is violent: esp. the strait which separated Euboea from Boeotia where the ancients believed that the current changed seven times a day (modern observers concur in representing it as very variable, in consequence probably of the action of the wind through the straits)" . . . "proverb of an unstable, wavering, weak-minded man, *pleious trapomenos tropas tou Euripou*" (doing more turns, i.e., more changeable, than the Euripus) cited from Aeschines, *Oration* 3.90: *Against Ctesiphon,* and similarly Aristotle *(Ethics* 9.6.3 [1167b]).//*Euripistos,* unstable, occurs in Cicero. This last word, and the proverbial use of *Euripos,* sufficiently indicate the familiar Greek tradition to which James's present simile belongs (depicting the waverer).

13. See LS, *s.v.*

We cannot possibly exclude, but neither do we here insist upon requiring, the extreme set up by Hort, that is, "the *prima facie* notion of billows lashed by a storm." All that is necessary is a real wind, a vigorous wind, not any slight rufflement; and there is no objection to "billows" or "lashed" unless we insist gratuitously on pressing these words to mountainous size and hurricane ferocity. *Klydōn* is not *cheimōn:* it *can* come in a tempest, as in that which wrecked Odysseus's ship—*apo toichous lyse klydōn tropios,* "the surge loosened the sides from the keel"—but I think that what James has in mind is the more normal, but quite vigorous, action of the winds exemplified in the naval battle off Naupactus cited in Thucydides 2.84.[14]

It is of paramount importance that we perceive that the essence of the similitude is not in the mere disturbance in the soul of the waverer, but in the fact that just as the sea is swept now by this wind, now by that, so the waverer's mind (not that that is the name to call it by) is carried this way and that, exactly as in Eph. 4:14 where we find this same combination of wave-roughened seas and varying winds. Ropes, who cites Eph. 4:14, nevertheless writes: "The point of comparison is the ordinary instability of the heaving sea, not the unusual violence of a storm. The sentence is made less forcible through the excessive elaboration of the figure."[15] We agree with this use of the words "ordinary instability" and "not the unusual violence," but that is not the sole point of the comparison.

The elaboration is not excessive; in spite of it Ropes has missed the point of the winds. Although he cites Eph. 4:14 he seems not to have read beyond *klydizomenoi.* The winds speak of inconstancy of direction, as the history of *euripos* and the use of *euripistos* remind us; and (characteristically) James drives home the point in the almost tautological 1:8, where *dipsychos*

14. "The Athenians, formed in line, sailed round and round them, and forced them to contract their circle, by continually brushing past and making as though they would attack at once, having been previously cautioned by Phormio not to do so till he gave the signal. His hope was that the Peloponnesians would not retain their order like a force on shore, but that the ships would fall foul of one another and the small craft cause confusion; and if the *wind* should blow from the gulf (in expectation of which he kept sailing round them, and *which usually rose towards morning),* they would not, he felt sure, remain steady an instant. He also thought that it rested with him to attack when he pleased, as his ships were sailers, and that an attack *timed by the coming of the wind* would tell best. When *the wind came down,* the enemy's ships were now in a narrow space, and what with the *wind* and the small craft dashing against them, at once fell into confusion: ship fell foul of ship, while the crews were pushing them off with poles, and by their shouting, swearing and struggling with one another, made captains' orders and boatswains' cries alike inaudible, and through being unable for want of practice to clear their oars *in the rough water,* prevented the vessels from obeying their helmsmen properly. At this moment Phormio gave the signal, and the Athenians attacked" (R. Crawley's *Everyman's Translation,* p. 157).

15. P. 142.

and *akatastatos en pasais tais hodois autou,* respectively, are virtually synonymous with *diakrinomenos* and *klydoni . . . . ripizomenō*. Commentators[16] cite Jude 13 for its (partial) relevance; but if the above is correct, we will see the same partial relevance in Jude 12.

The point of comparison in James here is strictly *not* "the ordinary instability of the heavier sea," as Ropes thought,[17] but the unsettled behavior of the waves under the perpetually varying winds that keep driving them now in one direction and perhaps the next day in another, like the man hesitating before a choice—and perhaps never making it at all.

The sentence, says Ropes, is made less forcible through the excessive elaboration of the figure.[18] The elaboration is *not* excessive; it is typical of the author's skill. Since the action in this scene proceeds from the winds, they naturally figure prominently in the script.

16. E.g., Mayor, Ropes, and others.
17. P. 142.
18. P. 142.

6. History

"Though this epistle were refused in the old time, and denied of many to be the epistle of a very apostle . . . methinketh it ought of right to be taken for holy Scripture. For as for that place for which haply it was at the beginning refused of holy men, as it ought, if it had meant as they took it, and for which place only, for the false understanding; yet if the circumstances be well pondered, it will appear that the author's intent was far otherwise than they took him for."

William Tyndale, "The Prologue upon the Epistle of James" (1526), *The Work of William Tyndale,* edited and introduced by G. E. Duffield, I (1964), 161.

The point of greatest significance in the history of the Epistle of James is its origin from James the Lord's brother. Nevertheless its literary and canonical history have been affected by needless disparagement of its authority.

THE WESTERN CHURCH

Not even the name of the Epistle appears till the year 180, and none but Hilary of Poitiers (died 366) indicates any knowledge of it until the time of Jerome: apparently possible earlier congruences are more commonplace in Jewish-Christian thought,[1] but are a priori no less likely to be

1. E.g., supposed OT resemblances, especially to Abraham and Rahab, in Clement (c. 96) are insignificant and better explained by literary association than borrowing; *pace* F. W. Young, "The Relation of 1 Clement to the Epistle of James," *JBL* 67.4 (1948): 339ff. D. A. Hagner, *The Use of the Old and New Testaments in Clement of Rome* (1973), pp. 251f. A. Geyser, *The Letter of James in Rome* (1981), p. 5. See *The New Testament in the Apostolic Fathers by a Committee of the Ox-*

borrowed from James than from the pundit's choice, the Shepherd of Hermas (c. 150). Indeed, in James the Greek language used is sometimes the more selective among the alternatives employed; and we reject the trite view that the Epistle of James is a formless collection of trash. There are some small congruences in language and thought between James and Hermas. Sometimes these are only separate ideas or expressions, as in *Vis.* 3.1.6, which reminds us of Jas. 5:1.[2] But his condemnation of the rich extends only to those who boast of and in their wealth. More important are the parallels in *Mand.* 9 and Jas. 1:5-8 on faith, prayer, and doubt, and especially their common use of "double-minded."[3]

After thoroughly examining this unusual word and its cognates, O. J. F. Seitz and others found that James derived it, as did 1 and 2 Clement and Hermas—and we may add the Dead Sea Scrolls—ultimately from the Jewish concept of the *yēṣer.*[4] They maintain that neither James nor Hermas was dependent on the other, but that each drew from a common source and betrays knowledge only of that source. We find much force in this argument. Yet, especially in view of the parallel to Jas. 4:5 in *Mand.* 3.1, "the spirit which God caused to dwell in this flesh," we are not fully persuaded that we can entirely exclude the possibility that somehow a copy of the Epistle of James may have already reached Rome and been read by Hermas.

On the other hand, there is evidence to support the suggestion that Irenaeus (Bishop of Lyons, c. 180-190) knew the Epistle of James. He cites the words "He believed God, and it was imputed to him for righteousness; and he was called the friend of God" (*credidit Deo, et reputatum est illi ad iustitiam, et amicus Dei vocatus est*),[5] which is clearly a verbatim quotation from Jas. 2:23. The citation in Tertullian, "Whence

---

ford Society of Historical Theology (1950), pp. 137f.; Ropes, p. 87; A. Meyer, pp. 69ff.; Mussner, pp. 35f.; W. G. Kümmel, *Introduction to the New Testament* ([2]1975), p. 285; Laws, pp. 16, 21.

2. For other slight and commonplace parallels see, e.g., *Vis.* 2.2.7 and Jas. 1:12; *Sim.* 8.6.5 and Jas. 2:6; *Sim.* 6.1 and Jas. 5:5.

3. See Laws, pp. 22f.; A. Meyer, p. 62; and others who argue for literary dependence. But they fail to explain some discrepancies, e.g., why Hermas has *distazein* for *diakrinesthai* (Jas. 1:6)—the former was common in Rome for "to doubt"; why he omits the prayer for wisdom for his more congenial theme, the teacher's need of "understanding" *(synesis)*; and why he does not have the simile of the wave but only that of uprooting. See B. M. Metzger, *The Canon of the New Testament* (1987), pp. 66f.

4. For references see Adamson, p. 61, n. 52.

5. *Against the Heresies* 4.16.2. For background, see J. Quasten, *Patrology*, I (1960), 288ff.; also B. Altaner, *Patrology* (1960), pp. 150ff.

was Abraham accounted 'a friend of God' if not on the ground of equity and righteousness (in the observance) of a natural law?" (*unde Abraham amicus Dei deputatus, si non de aequitate et iustitia legis naturalis?*),[6] is much less certain. Significantly, too, Tertullian in his discussion of the temptation clause of the Lord's Prayer[7] argues that it is not (as in James) "lust" but the devil that tempts us. If Tertullian had read Jas. 1:12ff. he could hardly have ignored it. Similarly "law of liberty" is in harmony with Irenaeus's "law of liberty" (*libertatis lex*), but that does not prove dependence any more than many other formal parallels: "the demons shrink in fear" (*daemones reformidant*) is an uncommon expression, and may have been borrowed from Jas. 2:19.[8]

Even much later, neither Cyprian (died 258) nor Lactantius (died c. 320) betrays knowledge of the Epistle of James. An Arabic scholium on the commentary by Hippolytus of Rome (died c. 235) on Rev. 7:4, in which Jas. 1:1 is cited and James is confused with Jude, is the work of a later scholiast; otherwise this would have been the first citation of James as Holy Scripture in the West.[9] The simile of withering leaves—"things that bloom for a little" (*maranthēsetai*)—sometimes cited from Hippolytus[10] is too trite to prove a knowledge of Jas. 1:11 or 4:14; nor may we take it for granted that his prophecy of the world's coming woes is derived from Jas. 5:1,[11] or that his mention of God's efforts to recall the sinner from the error of his ways is based on Jas. 5:19f.[12] In the later Roman schismatic Novatian (c. 250), in *The Trinity,* ch. 8,[13] Abraham appears again as the friend of God, but neither this nor the unchangeability of God comes from the Epistle of James, which he never quoted. We conclude that neither the African nor the Roman Church up to the time of Augustine knew the Epistle of James or ascribed any importance to it.

In the West the earliest quotation is in Hilary of Poitiers (died 366), who, while in Asia Minor, wrote his treatise *The Trinity* (c. 360) against the Arians, who had quoted (inter alia) Jas. 1:17 in connection with God's

6. *An Answer to the Jews,* ch. 2.

7. *On Prayer,* ch. 8.

8. Of the two phrases quoted from *Against the Heresies* 5.1.1, (1) "doers of his words" *(factores sermonum)* is neither necessarily nor probably borrowed from Jas. 1:22, where "hear" and "do" are contrasted, not paralleled, as in Irenaeus. And (2) "the firstfruits of creation" *(initium facturae)* differs fundamentally in meaning from the Greek in Jas. 1:18. See A. Meyer, p. 11, n. 8.

9. Dibelius, p. 32.

10. *Commentary on the Prophet Daniel* 3.6. See A. Meyer, p. 14; also Altaner, *Patrology,* p. 186.

11. *Commentary on the Prophet Daniel* 4.12.

12. *On Christ and Antichrist,* ch. 3.

13. Migne, *PL,* III, 925.

unchangeableness: "With whom there is no change" *(apud quem non est demutatio)*.[14] From this we may deduce that the Epistle of James was known to the Arians but not necessarily to the church in the West, which is silent. The unique form of his "change" *(demutatio)* may mean that Hilary made an independent translation from the Greek.[15]

Next in the West to cite James is Ambrosiaster (c. 380), who, commenting on Gal. 5:10, uses the phrase "spoken by James the apostle in his letter" *(dicente Jacobo apostolo in epistola sua)*.[16] The popes of the period are silent on the Epistle of James, and the list of Catholic Epistles taken by Lucifer of Calaris (c. 371) into Sardinian exile does not contain James or 3 John. While Ambrose (died 397) does not quote it, his "rich in faith" (*locuples in fide*) in the *Commentary on the Gospel of Luke*, 8, 13[17] may echo Jas. 2:25.[18] The argument from silence, however, must not be pressed too far: in spite of its absence from the Muratorian Canon and the pervading ignorance or neglect of the Epistle of James in the West, knowledge of the Epistle was now gradually filtering in from the Greek world, as is proved by the translations and occasional quotations that were being made.

In Africa, Augustine, following the canon of Jerome,[19] accepted the Epistle of James, placed it last in the Catholic Epistles, and tried to write a commentary on it,[20] quoting a Latin translation, rather like the Vulgate, 389 times;[21] it was "not an accurate translation"[22] but, as he

14. *The Trinity,* 4.8. See *Saint Hilary of Poitiers. The Trinity* (1956), tr. S. McKenna, "The Fathers of the Church," gen. ed. R. J. Deferrari, XXV, 97; Migne, *PL,* X, 101.

15. So Vulg.: *transmutatio;* Corbey: *permutatio.* But see Priscillian, *Tractate* 1, pp. 26, 21; Ropes, p. 101.

16. A Souter, *The Text and Canon of the New Testament* ([3]1954), p. 175 and *Study of Ambrosiaster* (1905), p. 197; see also Hort, p. XXIX; Altaner, *Patrology,* pp. 457f.

17. Ropes, p. 101.

18. A comparison of the ff. version—*pauperes saeculi, divites in fide*—with the Vulg.—*pauperes in hoc mundo, divites in fide*—appears to corroborate this.

19. *Christian Instruction* 2.8.13. *Writings of St. Augustine. Christian Instruction,* tr. J. J. Gavigan, "The Fathers of the Church," ed. R. J. Deferrari, IV (1974), 71. Later in Africa the translation most used was that of Fulgentius of Ruspe (died c. 533), but it was superseded by the Vulgate. See A. Meyer, p. 15, n. 4; also P. Bergauer, *Der Jacobusbrief bei Augustinus und die damit verdunenen Probleme der Rechtfertigungslehre* (1962).

20. *The Retractations* 2.58. See Migne, *PL,* XXXII, 643f.; also *St. Augustine: the Retractations* 60, tr. M. I. Bogan, "The Fathers of the Church," ed. R. J. Deferrari (1974), pp. 186f.

21. J. Wordsworth, *Studia Biblica,* I (1885), 128.

22. *The Retractations* 2.58.

implies, "all he could get." A reputable Latin translation including the Epistle of James was made about 350, and this gave the earliest indication of its recognition, later influencing similar versions, for example, the Corbey MS, the pseudo-Augustinian Speculum, and finally the Vulgate itself.

In Spain the numerous quotations in the tractates of the heretic Priscillian, Bishop of Avila (died 385), show that he had a translation like the pseudo-Augustinian Speculum[23] and which Chromatius of Aquileia (386-406) quotes from a translation of his own Jas. 1:12 and 1:15.[24] It appears again in a ninth-century manuscript of a fifth-century collection of noncanonical writings.[25] The *Liber Comicus* (before St. Ildefonsus, c. 650) has a mixed text, comparable to that of another Spanish manuscript, P.[26]

The next key witness is Jerome, who published his Vulgate in 383, in which, despite ancient doubts, he included, with Jude, the Epistle of James as by the Lord's brother[27] and which he quoted 128 times.[28] His translation, however, did not completely displace other versions, and many of Italian, African, or Spanish origin survived for a time, for example, the Bobbio palimpsest, and indeed interpolated some of their readings into Vulg. manuscripts. Rufinus, the monk of Aquileia (c. 330-410), knew our Epistle, and like his contemporary Philastrius, Bishop of Brescia (383),[29] included it in his canon; he also interspersed his Latin translations of Origen to this effect.[30]

23. See Mayor, pp. cclxxxiv, 3-27; also Meinertz, p. 151.

24. *Tractate on St. Matthew* 14.7; 9.1 (Migne, *PL,* XX, 327ff.).

25. Wordsworth, *Studia Biblica,* pp. 115ff. For references to the Epistle of James in the works of lesser Spaniards like Paul Orosius (c. 415) and his contemporary Bachiarus, see Meinertz, pp. 151ff.; *Paulus Orosius,* tr. R. J. Deferrari, "The Fathers of the Church," L (1964); also *Iberian Fathers,* I, 2, tr. C. W. Barlow (1969). See Altaner, *Patrology,* pp. 280ff., 435.

26. A. Meyer, p. 17, n. 3. James the son of Zebedee, St. James of Compostella, is a patron saint in Spain and regarded as the author of the Epistle of James. See Isidore of Seville, *The Life and Death of the Fathers,* which consists of biographical studies of 86 biblical personalities. We read: "James, the son of Zebedee . . . wrote to the twelve tribes scattered among the nations, and he also preached the Gospel to the people in Spain and places in the West" (71.125). See Migne, *PL,* LXXXIII, 151; also Meinertz, pp. 212f.

27. *On Famous Men* 2.

28. Wordsworth, *Studia Biblica,* p. 128.

29. *The Book of Diverse Heresies* (c. 385-391), ch. 60 (Migne, *PL,* XII, 1111ff.). For the text, see Souter, *The Text and Canon of the New Testament,* p. 202.

30. *Commentary on the Apostles' Creed* 36. See M. J. Rouët de Journel, *Enchiridion Patristicum* ([18]1953), 1344 (Migne, *PL,* XXI, 374); also F. X. Murphy, *Rufinus of Aquileia* (345-411) (1945), pp. 179ff. In *The Book of Faith* (c. 413-428),

In spite of this growing interest, the result of an increased interest in Greek orthodoxy, the Epistle failed to receive authoritative recognition (e.g., in the Cheltenham or Mommsenian Canon and at Carthage in 369) until the third and fourth Councils of Carthage (397 and 419), on Augustine's insistence, admitted it to the Western canon.[31] The findings of the Third Council of Carthage on the books of the Bible repromulgated those of the Synod of Hippo (393). This canon, which was also accepted by the Donatists and by Pope Innocent in a letter to Exsuperius of Toulouse (405),[32] was thus now in line with that which Athanasius and Gregory Nazianzus made for the Orthodox Greek Church.

Henceforth the Epistle of James was firmly established in the Western Church, and this process was consummated on April 8, 1546, when the Council of Trent in its canonical decree (*decretum de canonicis*) formally declared the Epistle of James to be Holy Scripture, a "sacred and canonical" book, an absolute article of faith, and sealed by an Anathema.[33]

THE EASTERN CHURCH

a. The Syrian Church

The Syrian Church was a generation later than her Roman sister in recognizing the Epistle of James. A ninth-century manuscript notes that until 400, the only accepted NT Scriptures in the Syrian canon were the Gospels, Acts, and Paul's Epistles.[34] There is no evidence of any Syr-

---

for long wrongly attributed to Rufinus of Aquileia but almost certainly written by the Pelagian Presbyter Rufinus of Syria, we also read of "the Apostle of James in his Epistle" on the tongue (Jas. 3:9). See M. W. Miller, *Rufini Presbyteri Liber 'De Fide'* (1964), pp. 84f., 163; Migne, *PL*, XXI, 1135; Altaner, *Patrology*, p. 441.

31. On the genuineness of this canon, see Souter, *The Text and Canon of the New Testament*, pp. 195, 196; Metzger, *Canon of the New Testament*, pp. 237f.

32. For the text, see Souter, *The Text and Canon of the New Testament*, p. 210, based on C. H. Turner, "Latin Lists of the Canonical Books," *JTS* 13 (1911-12): 78-82. Ropes, pp. 102f., also notes that Cassiodorus (c. 544) had "a copy of the NT prepared, 'a second ancient translation' *(secundam antiquam translationem)*," i.e., as it was *before* Jerome's revision and containing the Epistle of James. See *The Institutions*, chs. 8, 13 (Migne, *PL*, LXX, 1120, 1124); also for the text Souter, *The Text and Canon of the New Testament*, pp. 213f.

33. For the text and discussion, see B. F. Westcott, *The Canon of the New Testament*, pp. 484ff., 590; also Souter, *The Text and Canon of the New Testament*, pp. 171, 218ff.; Metzger, *Canon of the New Testament*, pp. 246f.

34. See A. S. Lewis, *Studia Sinaitica*, I (1894), 11-14.

iac translation until the Peshitta. *The Doctrine of Addai* (c. 390-430) forbids the reading of any other books in the church of Christ because "there is not any other in which the truth which you hold is written, except these books."[35] Neither Aphraates in his *Discourses* (337 and 344) nor Ephraim (died 373), who was reputed to have visited Greek areas, refers to any Catholic Epistle. Though Ephraim may have known a few sayings (e.g., 2:17; 5:17) through his Greek contacts, other alleged parallels (e.g., "the Father of lights" [*'abbā' d'nahire*], 1:17; the duration of the drought, 5:17) do not prove literary borrowing.[36]

Not till the fifth century, before the Syrian schism, was a new NT Syrian translation commissioned by Rabbula (Bishop of Edessa, 411-435), who was influenced by John of Antioch. In the Greek Church the Epistle of James was given the primacy accorded by Rome to Peter and his Epistles. Based on a comparison of the Old Syriac version (which almost certainly did not contain James[37]) with the Greek text in Constantinople, the Peshitta almost invariably conforms in text, contents, and order to the Greek manuscripts: after the Gospels, Acts, and the Pauline Epistles come the three Catholic Epistles headed by the Epistle of James.

So Antioch, the Greek-speaking Syrian capital and a vital bridge between the Greek and Syrian Church, led to the inclusion of the Epistle of James in the Peshitta. Both Ignatius, the first Bishop of Antioch (martyred c. A.D. 115), and Bishop Theophilus (died c. 181-191) are silent on the Epistle of James. Ignatius's quotation "God resists the proud"[38] simply proves that he knew Prov. 3:34.[39] No evidence of the Epistle's position survives in the third century,[40] while in the fourth (c. 325) only two of the Catholic Epistles, 1 Peter and 1 John, were recognized as apostolic; but their leader, Diodorus of Tarsus (died 394), though recognizing them, seems not to accept or know the Epistle of James. His

35. See Souter, *The Text and Canon of the New Testament*, pp. 208f.; T. Zahn, *Grundriss der Geschichte des neutestamentlichen Kanons* (1901), p. 45; Altaner, *Patrology*, p. 78.

36. See W. Bauer, *Der Apostolos der Syrer in der Zeit von der Mitte des IV Jhs. bis zur Spaltung der syrischen Kirche* (1903), p. 48; Ropes, pp. 96f.; also our remarks, p. 357, n. 52.

37. So F. F. Bruce, in a personal note.

38. *Letter to the Ephesians* 1.5.3. For similarly slight and inconclusive parallels, see Mayor, pp. lxxiiif.

39. *Pace* Meinertz, p. 63. See also Mayor, p. lxxii. Equally worthless are the two alleged parallels (Jas. 1:17; 2:18) found in Theophilus's *To Autolycus* 1.1, 2. See R. M. Grant, "The Bible of Theophilus of Antioch," *HTR* 61 (1947): 185.

40. For the conjecture that the revised NT of Lucian of Antioch (died 311) contained the Epistle of James, 1 Peter, and 1 John, see Ropes, p. 99.

pupil, Theodore of Mopsuestia (died c. 428), rejected all Epistles except those of Paul; but the fragments of Apollinarius, Bishop of Laodicea (died 390), not only show that he recognized 1 Peter and 1 John, but also contain comments on Jas. 2:6f. and 8. There is no trace of the Epistle of James in either the *Didascalia* or the *Apostolic Constitutions,* parallels in the former to, for example, Jas. 1:12; 2:1-3, 19 being more apparent than real.

Doubts lingered especially among the Nestorians and the non-Greek Churches; witness the testimonies of Cosmas Indicopleustes (c. 545), Paul of Nisbis (died 571), Theodore bar Koni, and others cited by Ropes, who notes that in Eastern Syria "the adoption of James into the canon was tardier, and down almost to modern times a vivid recollection was preserved of the doubtful position of James."[41] But this period of partial or complete rejection of the Catholic Epistles by Antioch and the Syrian Church at last ended in definite acceptance not only of 1 Peter and 1 John, but also of the Epistle of James; and it seems clear that this was due mainly to John of Chrysostom (died c. 407).

The importance of Chrysostom lies, first, in his identification of the author of James as James the Lord's brother, literally "God's brother" *(adelphotheos).*[42] Elsewhere he speaks of James as Rabbi,[43] Bishop of Jerusalem, and a great and wonderful person,[44] but not as an Apostle.[45] (This view of authorship Eusebius had already heard [without conviction] in Caesarea.[46]) Secondly, he led the successful fight for the three principal Epistles of the three great Pauline authorities, namely, the Epistle of James, 1 Peter, and 1 John.[47]

That this selection was made by the Church at Antioch in the time of Chrysostom is proved by his *Synopsis of Sacred Scripture,*[48] written

41. Pp. 97, 100.

42. *Homilies on Penitence* 9 (Migne, *PG,* XLIX, 343). For a complete index of quotations from James in all the works of Chrysostom, see R. A. Krupp, *Saint John Chrysostom, A Scripture Index* (1984), pp. 251f. See also A. Meyer, pp. 26f.; Meinertz, pp. 166f. for references.

43. *Commentary on the Epistle to the Galatians* 2.9. See *Commentary on Galatians and Ephesians* (Oxford, 1895), p. 34 (Migne, *PG,* LXI, 641).

44. *Homilies on the Acts of the Apostles* 46 (Migne, *PG,* LX, 321).

45. *Homilies on the First Epistle to the Corinthians* 21 (Migne, *PG,* LXI, 172).

46. *Hist. Eccl.* 2.23.24f.

47. See *Commentary on the Epistle to the Galatians* 1:19; 2:9 (Migne, *PG,* LXI, 632, 641). For his comments on the Epistle of James, see *Fragments on the Catholic Epistles* (Migne, *PG,* LXIV, 1040ff.).

48. Migne, *PG,* LVI, 313f. For discussion and text, see Westcott, *The Canon of the New Testament,* pp. 450, 552f.; Zahn, *Geschichte des Kanons,* II, 1, p. 230.

at least under Chrysostom's influence and including specifically "Three of the Catholic Epistles." His pupil Severian, Bishop of Gabala (died after A.D. 408), likewise on the authority of the Fathers, rejected 2 and 3 John, but accepted 1 John as well as 1 Peter and the Epistle of James,[49] as did Polychronius, Bishop of Apamea in Syria (died c. 428) and brother of Theodore of Mopsuestia, who speaks of James as "one of the apostles."[50] Similarly, Theodoret of Cyrus (died c. 458) quotes Jas. 4:8 and 5:13,[51] and in his didactic poem *Iambics for Seleucus* of 333 trimiters, Amphilochius, Bishop of Iconium (c. 370), notes that "some say we should accept seven (Catholic Epistles), some only three, one of James, and one of Peter, and one of John,"[52] while Isidore of Pelusium (died c. 440) called the Epistle "divine writing."[53] The Diocesan Congress of Antioch show that these three—but only these three—Catholic Epistles were recognized in its jurisdiction at that time.[54]

b. The Greek Church

i. Alexandria. Although both Eusebius[55] and Photius[56] say that Clement of Alexandria in his *Outlines (Hypotyposes)* annotated the Catholic Epistles, there are at least three good reasons for thinking that Clement did *not* recognize the Epistle of James as either apostolic or canonical:[57]

1. The *Outlines (Hypotyposes)* translated by Cassiodorus (died 570)[58] include only 1 Peter, Jude, and 1 and 2 John; and he himself says Clement annotated only four Catholic Epistles, which Cassiodorus

49. Migne, *PG,* LVI, 424. A. Meyer, p. 27, n. 6. For background, see Quasten, *Patrology,* III, 484ff.

50. Ropes, p. 99. For Theodore's influence on Junilius the African's canon (*The Divine Law,* ch. 6), see Westcott, *The Canon of the New Testament,* pp. 451f., 552f.; also Souter, *The Text and Canon of the New Testament,* pp. 172, 214f.

51. *The Interpretation of the Song of Solomon* 1.3.2 (Migne, *PG,* LXXXI, 152); *The Interpretation of the Psalms* 26.6 (Migne, *PG,* LXXX, 1053). See Quasten, *Patrology,* III, 536ff.

52. For discussion and text, see Westcott, *The Canon of the New Testament,* pp. 453f., 565f.; also Zahn, *Geschichte des Kanons,* II, 1, pp. 212f., esp. 219, lines 60f.; Migne, *PG,* XXXVII, 1593ff.

53. *Letters* 4.226 (Migne, *PG,* LXXVIII, 1321).

54. Bauer, *Der Apostolos der Syrer,* p. 66.

55. *Hist. Eccl.* 6.14.1.

56. *Bibliotheca,* Cod. 109 (Migne, *PG,* CIII, 384).

57. See A. Meyer, pp. 43ff.; also Metzger, *Canon of the New Testament,* pp. 131ff.

58. *The Institutions,* ch. 8. See Westcott, *The Canon of the New Testament,* pp. 362f.

names as 1 Peter, 1 and 2 John, and James—wrongly, since the extant translation contained Jude but not James.[59]

2. In his commentary on Matthew[60] Origen gets his information on Jude from Clement's Introduction to the Epistle of Jude in the *Outlines (Hypotyposes)*. Since he says of James only that he was the brother of Jude and son of Joseph, it appears that neither from Clement nor from anyone else did Origen hear of our James as the author of the Epistle.
3. Clement makes few, perhaps no, allusions to the Epistle of James.[61]

Arnold Meyer seeks to explain, unconvincingly in our opinion, the apparent contradiction by emphasizing that the *Outlines (Hypotyposes)* are in fact an incomplete commentary on the Catholic Epistles. But in conclusion he admits that even if his belief in Clement's ignorance of the Epistle of James is correct, that ignorance, so soon before Origen, is itself astonishing.[62]

Origen (c. 255) is the first to champion the authenticity of the Epistle of James, to quote it as Scripture,[63] and to name the author as (an unspecified) James, whom he sometimes calls "apostle."[64] The omission of the Epistle of James (and Jude) from his list of canonical epistles is probably due to his restricting that list to apostles whose title was not, like that of James and Jude, in dispute, though apparently at the time of that list Origen himself sometimes gave that title to James.[65] His strategy is not to defy the existing canon rule as a matter of law, even when he is doing his best to get it changed.

59. See A. Meyer, p. 43, n. 3.

60. *Commentary on Matthew* 10.17 (on 13:55f.) (Migne, *PG*, XIII, 877). See Westcott, *The Canon of the New Testament*, p. 369, n. 2.

61. The alleged allusions to (1) the second birth (in baptism) in *Paedagogus* 1.6.45 (see Jas. 1:18) and to (2) the prohibition of swearing in *Paedagogus* 1.6.44 (see Jas. 5:12) are both probably due to common origin rather than literary borrowing (see, however, *Biblia Patristica*, ed. J. Allenbach and others, I [1975], 254f.).

62. P. 48. On Clement's silence, see also Westcott, *The History of the Canon of the New Testament*, pp. 361f., esp. p. 363, n. 8. See also Migne, *PG*, IX, 397.

63. *Commentary on John, Frag. 6*. See A. E. Brooke, *The Commentary of Origen on S. John's Gospel*, II (1896), 216. Other formulas include "It is written"; "James writes"; sometimes "James the Apostle says"; "James says"; or simply "he says," "it was said," or "according to the saying." All tend to confirm that he believed he was quoting Scripture. See Ropes, pp. 92f.; Mussner, pp. 38f.; Dibelius, p. 52. For an index of Origen's citations from James, see *Biblia Patristica*, ed. J. Allenbach and others, III (1980), 457f.

64. See Ropes, pp. 92f.

65. See A. Meyer, pp. 45ff.

In the meantime Origen feels quite free to express his personal opinion; for example, on Jas. 1:17 he remarks, "which I think is said by the Scripture,"[66] that is, "which I personally think has as much right to be in the canon as any of its present contents." Similarly, commenting on Jas. 2:26 he says that he is "one of those who accept the passage"[67] as being as spiritually valid as regular Scripture. With his usual patient deference he had previously referred to this verse as "in what circulates" *(en tē pheromenē)* as the Epistle of James,[68] but he spares no effort to vindicate his personal opinion vis-à-vis the present canon. Enunciating the canon as he saw it ought to be, Origen included the Epistle among the canonical books, linking it on the one hand with the OT trumpets at Jericho[69] and Isaac's well diggers,[70] and on the other with the Apostle James and other officially accepted NT writers such as Peter and Jude,[71] and it was this canon that the church finally accepted and ratified.

Origen, however, does not seem to know or care which James wrote the Epistle of James. In ascribing the Epistle of Jude to the Lord's brother Jude[72] he is silent on Joseph and Simon,[73] and on the oldest brother James he simply quotes Paul in Gal. 1:19. In view of his reference to the Epistle of Jude it is difficult to understand his silence on the Epistle of James, unless indeed he ascribed it to a James other than the Lord's brother.[74] Like Clement, Origen embraced the view that James was not both Mary's and Joseph's son.[75] We may conclude then that in the time of Origen the Epistle of James was already "in circulation" and widely read, but as yet it was not recognized in Rome and Antioch.[76]

66. *Commentary on John. Frag. 6.* See note 63 above.

67. *Commentary on John* 20.10 (Migne, *PG,* XIV, 591). Brooke, *The Commentary of Origen on S. John's Gospel,* II, 46.

68. *Commentary on John* 19.23 (Migne, *PG,* XIV, 569). Brooke, *The Commentary of Origen on S. John's Gospel,* II, 32. The term *pheromenē* here does not mean "reputed" in the sense of "disputed," "falsely so called," or "generally accepted" but "known under his name," "current," or, as we prefer, "in what circulates." See Meinertz, p. 107, n. 3; and, with examples, A. Meyer, p. 39, n. 4.

69. *Homilies on Joshua* 7.1. See Origène, *Homélies sur Josué* (1960), tr. A. Jaubert, p. 195; Migne, *PG,* XII, 857.

70. *Homilies on Genesis* 13.2 (Migne, *PG,* XII, 232).

71. *Homilies on Joshua* 7.1. See Origène, *Homélies sur Josué,* p. 196, n. 1; Migne, *PG,* XII, 857; Metzger, *Canon of the New Testament,* pp. 139f.

72. *Commentary on Matthew* 10.17 (Migne, *PG,* XIII, 877).

73. *Commentary on Matthew* 10.17 (ibid.).

74. See A. Meyer, p. 41, n. 1, on the interesting but unreliable Latin translation by Rufinus of a note on the Epistle to the Romans.

75. *Commentary on John. Frag. 31.* Brooke, *The Commentary of Origen on S. John's Gospel,* II, 244.

76. Origen's influence is seen in his pupil and admirer, Gregory Thauma-

The Alexandrians logically held that the apostolic quality of an author had to be proved by the apostolic quality of his Epistle. In this approach to the Epistle of James a high valuation of the Letter itself is fundamentally indispensable, and, apart from the numerous quotations,[77] it is testified

1. in the commentaries of Alexandrians like Cyril (died 444), Didymus (313-398), and Eusebius of Alexandria (5th or 6th century),[78] and
2. in their translations of the Epistle of James into Egyptian and Ethiopic, of which some are still extant today. From the third century there is a Greek papyrus, P^{20} (α 1019) or Princeton Oxyrhynchus Papyrus 1171, and this contains Jas. 2:19–3:19; and from the fourth and later centuries flow the Greek commentaries and Greek translations.

The Epistle of James is now established in the canon, and the point to be settled next is the order of the Catholic Epistles. In the early fourth-century Alexandrian *Catalogus Claromontanus* the order is Peter, James, and John.[79] In section 8 of his Easter Festal Letter of 367 Athanasius settled the order—James, 1 and 2 Peter, 1, 2, and 3 John, and Jude;[80] he also settled the status of James as an apostle and consequently that of his Epistle as apostolic, thus qualifying for inclusion in the canon.

ii. Asia Minor. After receiving his education in Palestine, Gregory of Nazianzus (died c. 390), together with his friend Basil the Great, launched a campaign to promote the scholarship of Alexandria and especially of Origen. Both embraced the canon of Alexandria and Caesarea in the form of verse and with all the seven Catholic Epistles in the order that later became fixed, namely, James, 1 and 2 Peter, 1, 2, and 3 John, and Jude.[81] Gregory's cousin Amphilochius, as we have seen, has the

---

tourgos (died c. 270), who seems at home in the Epistle when he writes: "for it is clear that every perfect good thing comes from God" (see Jas. 1:17, *Fragment quoted in a Catena;* B. F. Westcott, *The Canon of the New Testament,* p. 392, n. 1). Origen's opponent, Methodius of Olympus (died 311), also knew, accepted, and quoted the Epistle of James, which he once confused with Paul (but in fact Rom. 5:2f. agrees with Jas. 1:2f.). See Meinertz, pp. 128f.; J. W. Trigg, *Origen* (1983), pp. 12f.

77. Meinertz, pp. 161ff.

78. See A. Meyer, p. 49.

79. For the text, see Souter, *The Text and Canon of the New Testament,* pp. 194f.

80. For the text, see Souter, *The Text and Canon of the New Testament,* pp. 196f.; Westcott, *The Canon of the New Testament,* p. 456, n. 3; Zahn, *Geschichte des Kanons,* II, 1, pp. 203ff.; Altaner, *Patrology,* p. 319.

81. Zahn, *Geschichte des Kanons,* II, 1, pp. 216ff.; Meinertz, pp. 188f.

same seven in the same order, and his younger brother Caesarius (died c. 368) speaks of a "divine voice" from the "divine James."[82]

The Cappadocians, however, adopted the Epistle of James not through any love of it but in order to conform with Alexandria—quotations from it are rare;[83] the identity of James is disputed, and he is never called an apostle.[84] According to Bishop Theodotus of Ancyra (c. 431), Christ chose James and Jude, the two sons of Joseph, who as his servants wrote to all the world to be his apostles, that is, to write apostolic (and so canonical) Scriptures.[85]

For the ascetic monk Marcus Eremita (died after 430) of Ancyra, who was theologically close to Antioch, the Epistle is canonical, written by James "the holy Apostle."[86] The 59th canon of the Council of Laodicea (Phrygia, A.D. 363) contained the seven Catholic Epistles, headed by James.[87] On a crucial visit to Constantinople in 379 Jerome met Gregory of Nazianzus, came under his spell,[88] and revised his canon to agree with that of Gregory.

Rome now accepted all the seven Catholic Epistles, including for the first time the Epistle of James and giving it first place among the seven in the Vulgate. This is really the consummation of Origen's labors in Alexandria and Caesarea.[89]

iii. Palestine. Palestine Christianity had two centers, Jerusalem and Caesarea; at first the church was composed of Jewish Christians, with some speaking Aramaic and others Greek. After the fall of Jerusalem, however, the Hellenistic group prevailed and Christianized Jews were absorbed in the Christianized pagan congregations; thus the Christianized Jewish education and tradition became extinct. (Is not this at least one important reason why the Epistle of James, the *Jewish* vessel of *Jewish* Christianity, nearly vanished?) From Hegesippus (late 2nd century) Eusebius preserved much information on Christian Jerusalem and the Hebrew and Syriac Gospels, as well as important data about the

82. *Dialogue* 3, *Question* 140; *Dialogue* 1, *Question* 2 (Migne, *PG,* XXVIII, 857, 140.

83. A. Meyer, p. 36.

84. So Gregory of Nyssa (b. 335), *Sermons on the Resurrection of Christ* 2 (Migne, *PG,* XLVI, 648).

85. See Meinertz, p. 191.

86. *On Penance* 5 (Migne, *PG,* LXV, 972).

87. Though augmented later, this list reflects good Asia Minor tradition. See Westcott, *The Canon of the New Testament,* pp. 431ff.; for the text, see Souter, *The Text and Canon of the New Testament,* p. 178; Metzger, *Canon of the New Testament,* p. 312.

88. *Against Jovinian* 1.13; *On Famous Men* 117. For more details, see J. N. D. Kelly, *Jerome, His Life, Writings and Controversies* (1975), p. 70, n. 8.

89. A. Meyer, p. 37.

life and death of James the Lord's brother.[90] But apparently Hegesippus is silent about any Epistle by any James.[91] We can only conclude that Eusebius found no mention or knowledge of the Epistle of James in Hegesippus, and that the Catholic Epistles were as unknown (canonically) in Jerusalem as in Antioch.

In fourth-century Caesarea, however, the influence of Origen was now at work. He was the first to ascribe the Epistle of James to an author named James, but with no other designation than that of apostle, a term that, including his own case, Paul had already extended beyond the Twelve. Origen's example inspired Eusebius likewise to press for the inclusion of the Epistle of James into the canon: he declares it among the "disputed" books *(antilegomena),*[92] and is not certain ("it is said")[93] that it is by James the Lord's brother; on the other hand, he is certain that it is "apostolic" *(Ho Hieros Apostolos),*[94] the first of the seven Catholic Epistles,[95] and part of Holy Scripture.[96] His principle, which he took from Origen, is a form of *res ipsa loquitur;* the *majority* of the churches in his day, despite ancient objections, in fact let it be read as canonical.[97]

This intermediate status of de facto use before official inclusion in the canon is exemplified for the period after Origen but before Eusebius in the pseudo-Clementine tractate *Epistle to Virgins,* written in Palestine or southern Syria (3rd century) and to be read with Holy Scripture. This includes selections from the OT, the Gospels, and Paul and,

90. E.g., *Hist. Eccl.* 2.23.3f. See also Ropes, pp. 64ff.; Dibelius, pp. 14ff.

91. Eusebius had a great interest in the history of the canon; he even promises to give a true account of the views of the ancients on the NT and especially on the disputed books (*Hist. Eccl.* 3.3.3). When he speaks of Josephus's account of the martyrdom of James, it is significant that he immediately names him as the probable author of the Epistle of James (*Hist. Eccl.* 2.23.25). Indeed, Eusebius tells us that for Hegesippus the canon was the law, the prophets, and Christ (*Hist. Eccl.* 4.22.3); compare "the sacred Scriptures and the Lord" (Photius, *Bibliotheca,* Cod. 232 [Migne, *PG,* CIII, 1096]).

92. *Hist. Eccl.* 3.25.3; *Antilegomena* is not to be taken in a pejorative sense, i.e., "suspected," but as meaning "not yet universally accepted." See Plummer, pp. 15ff.; also Cornely "The entire reason for the arrangement of Eusebius (his canon) is simply historical" (*Introductio,* I, 184).

93. *Hist. Eccl.* 2.23.25; *legomenē* (3.25.3).

94. *Commentary on the Psalms* 56.2 (Migne, *PG,* XXIII, 505). On his view of James's relation to the original apostles, see *Hist. Eccl.* 1.12. See also Meinertz, p. 154, n. 5.

95. *Hist. Eccl.* 2.23.25.

96. *Commentary on the Psalms* 100.5 (Migne, *PG,* XXIII, 1244).

97. *Hist. Eccl.* 2.23.25; 3.25.3. The Syriac version, which reflects specific Syrian wishes, changes "in most" to "in many" churches (E. Nestlé, *Texte und Untersuchungen,* VI.2.68). See also Meinertz, p. 154, n. 5.

less frequently, some of Acts, 1 Peter, the Epistle of James, and Hebrews. But the extracts from the Epistle of James give neither his name nor the title of apostle; indeed, a verse from Paul, 1 Cor. 12:19, has set against it the text of Jas. 3:1f., the earliest undisputed *(die früheste einwandfreie)* quotation from the Epistle,[98] with the note: "They do not pay attention to this that he is saying."[99] The omission of the name in these quotations, however, is quite common, and here it in no sense excludes James. The value the compiler sets on the Epistle of James is clearly very high.

For the generation after Eusebius we have the record of Cyril, the young Jerusalem presbyter (c. 348), that the seven Catholic Epistles, headed by James, are now in the canon and, at last, so used in Jerusalem;[100] he freely quoted it as Holy Scripture[101] written by the Lord's brother, Bishop of Jerusalem, not one of the Twelve.[102] The same canon is given by Epiphanius, Bishop of Salamis in Cyprus (c. 315-403).[103] James is an apostle in the Pauline sense:[104] he is usually quoted as "the holy James,"[105] and his Epistle as "Holy Scripture" just like Paul's.[106]

From Palestinian scholarship of the fifth and sixth centuries, fragments remain of a *Commentary on the Epistle of James*[107] by Hesychius, monk, presbyter, and Bishop of Jerusalem (died 433): he also quotes the Epistle often as "God-inspired Scripture"[108] by "James,"[109] whom he calls "the brother of the Lord"[110] or "the apostle,"[111] but as a leading

98. *Epistle to Virgins* 1.11.4 (Dibelius, pp. 51f.).

99. *Patres apostolici,* ed. F. X. Funk, rev. F. Diekamp, II (^{3}1913), 19f.

100. *Catecheses* 4.28; also 14.15, 21 (Migne, *PG,* XXXIII, 492, 844, 852f.); also *The Works of Saint Cyril of Jerusalem,* tr. L. P. McCauley and A. A. Stephenson, "The Fathers of the Church," gen. ed. R. J. Deferrari, LXI, 1 (1969), p. 133; 2, pp. 41f., 46; also Quasten, *Patrology,* III, 362ff.

101. *Catecheses* 13.8 (Migne, *PG,* XXXIII, 784); *The Works of Saint Cyril of Jerusalem,* LXI, 1, p. 279; 2, p. 264. See also Meinertz, p. 157, n. 2, for other examples.

102. See n. 100.

103. *Refutation of all Heresies* 76.5 (Migne, *PG,* XLII, 560); Meinertz, p. 155, n. 1); Metzger, *Canon of the New Testament,* pp. 209f., 311.

104. *Refutation of all Heresies* 66.19 (Migne, *PG,* XLII, 57).

105. *Refutation of all Heresies* 31.34 (Migne, *PG,* XLI, 540).

106. *Refutation of all Heresies* 77.27; 31.34 (Migne, *PG,* XLII, 681; XLI, 540).

107. Migne, *PG,* XCIII, 1389. Meinertz, pp. 159f.; A. Meyer, p. 35.

108. *Commentary on the Psalms, Frag.* 50:7 (Migne, *PG,* XCIII, 1201).

109. Commenting on Jas. 5:10 (Migne, *PG,* XCIII, 1389).

110. Commenting on Jas. 3:2, *Temperance and Virtue* 2.24 (Migne, *PG,* XCIII, 1520).

111. Commenting on Jas. 4:17, *Temperance and Virtue* 2.26 (Migne, *PG,* XCIII, 1520).

rather than an original apostle.[112] The Epistle of James, therefore, is apostolic, written by James the Lord's brother, the leader of the apostles and the brightest star in the apostolic firmament.[113] Palestine therefore at least cherished and fostered the love for the Epistle of James that had been generated there by Eusebius, himself inspired by Origen of Alexandria.

* * * * *

After its authenticity was recognized by these early church councils, the Epistle of James remained unchallenged until the Protestant Reformation, when Luther spoke disparagingly of it as "an Epistle of straw"[114] and "deuterocanonical," a view that de Wette (1826) revived and that, unfortunately, tended to influence, consciously or unconsciously, every modern commentator on the Epistle.

Though Luther shared the erroneous view of other Protestants and Catholics that the Epistle was *universally* rejected by the early church,[115] this was not a decisive factor. He thought highly of it,[116] praised it, and considered it a good book[117] with many good sayings,[118] by a good, honest man, some Jew or other,[119] probably the son of Zebedee,[120] not the Lord's brother, whose Epistle contained not a syllable of Christ and nothing distinctively Christian.[121] "It is the office of a true apostle to preach of the Passion and resurrection and office of Christ," says Luther.[122] But the Passion of Christ, in Luther's estimation, means as little to James as his resurrection or his Spirit; and though he may have softened his view toward the end of his life,[123] his scornful remarks

112. *Sermon on James, the Brother of Jesus, and on David, Christ's Father,* Photius, *Bibliotheca,* Cod. 275 (Migne, *PG,* CIV, 241f.; also XCIII, 1480).

113. See previous note.

114. See F. Mussner, pp. 42-47; A. Meyer, pp. 4ff. For a discussion of Luther's *life-long* negative attitude towards the Epistle of James, see W. J. Kooiman, *Luther and the Bible* (1961), pp. 110ff., especially p. 226, n. 2.

115. See, e.g., the opinion of Richard Simon (1638-1712), one of the earliest scientific, biblical commentators. Not long after he sharply condemns Luther's obvious exaggeration "the ancients didn't acknowledge this letter as one of the Catholic epistles" (*LW,* XXXV, 395; LIV, 425). See *Histoire Critique des principaux Commentateurs du Nouveau Testament* (Rotterdam,1693), ch. 46, pp. 684-99. See also Meinertz, p. 217.

116. *LW,* XXXV, 395.

117. *LW,* XXXV, 395.

118. *LW,* XXXV, 397.

119. *LW,* LIV, 424.

120. *LW,* XXXV, 397.

121. *LW,* LIV, 424.

122. *LW,* XXXV, 396.

123. See C. E. B. Cranfield, "The Message of James," *SJTh* 18 (1965): 182, n. 6. It is also worth noting that "never, even at the height of his criticism of the

about "the ravings of James,"[124] "the Epistle of straw,"[125] and "its jumble of words"[126]—to mention only a few—are hard to forget.

For Luther, the style of the Epistle is not that of a typical inspired apostle of Christian salvation,[127] and so he placed it with other "deutero-canonical"[128] books like Jude, Hebrews, and Revelation (does not the inclusion of the theologically rich Hebrews raise further doubt about Luther's judgments on the canon?) at the end of the first edition of his German NT translation in 1522 with no numbers in the Table of Contents. His basic grievance is that James teaches justification by works and "nothing about faith, only mere law,"[129] thus contradicting Paul and his doctrine of justification by faith, leading him to prefer an epistle by Judas Iscariot if he "promoted" *(treiben)* Christ.

This means that in the end Luther would have the Epistle of James removed from the Bible because he detected in it nothing distinctively Christian but rather an unorthodox spirit alien to Christianity. The grace of God in Christ was the only thing that Luther recognized as decisive for salvation; to him the Epistle of James was worthless. But this is clearly a purely subjective judgment based on Luther's intuition[130] (or, we might say, prejudice) rather than sound historical criticism.[131]

Luther's doubts were obviously shared and echoed[132] by Erasmus,[133] who cautiously held that the Epistle might be by another James since it lacked true apostolic grandeur *(apostolica majestas et gravitas)* and dignity of style and was not Hebrew enough to be by James the first Bishop of Jerusalem. But despite his own doubts and his awareness of

---

Epistle of James, did Luther omit it from his editions of the Bible" (Metzger, *Canon of the New Testament*, p. 281, n. 29).

124. *LW*, IV, 134.

125. *LW*, XXXV, 362. In fairness to Luther, however, we must note his *comparative* use of this term (T. M. Lindsay, *The History of the Reformation*, I, p. 462, n. 1).

126. *LW*, LIV, 425.

127. See Dibelius, p. 54, nn. 217, 222.

128. For a somewhat defensive explanation, see R. C. H. Lenski, *The Interpretation of the Epistle to the Hebrews and of the Epistle of James* (1946), p. 514; see Ropes, p. 108; F. F. Bruce, *Tradition: Old and New* (1970), p. 148. For a sympathetic view of the Epistle by a modern Lutheran, with "an attempt at a defense" of Luther, the Lutherans, and James, see Scaer, esp. ch. 15, pp. 138ff.

129. For details see Dibelius, p. 56, n. 232.

130. See Spitta, p. 239.

131. See Dibelius, p. 55; also p. 56, n. 229.

132. Dibelius, p. 54, n. 217.

133. *New Testament Annotations* (1519), p. 523. See A. Meyer, p. 7, n. 2. On his *Annotations*, see A. Rabil, *Erasmus and the New Testament: The Mind of a Christian Humanist* (1972), p. 115; also *Collected Works of Erasmus*, New Testament Scholarship, ed. R. J. Sider (1984), pp. xxxff.

the attitude of the early church, he disapproved of fostering a distaste for the divinely inspired James. Among other Catholics, the Epistle had both its detractors (e.g., the very learned 16th-c. polemicist Cajetan,[134] Luther's opponent) and its defenders (e.g., Philipp Mencel and his unusual Latin "Poem on the canonical Epistle of St. James which Luther called a straw Epistle" [1591]).[135]

Much more important than Erasmus's own view was his reference to that of fourth-century Jerome: "He (James) wrote only one Epistle, one of the seven Catholic Epistles, which is said to have been written by someone else and published under his (James's) name, but in course of time gradually achieved canonization."[136] Though Jerome himself did not reject the Epistle's traditional authority or canonicity—and, unlike Luther,[137] he did not imply the previous universal rejection of the early church—his view, unfortunately, had an adverse effect on Luther and his followers.[138]

Outside Germany, the story was very different: reformers like Calvin, Zwingli, Beza, Knox, and others seem to have had no difficulty with the Epistle. The refreshing sanity of John Calvin on this matter is a welcome change. Calvin is a much more balanced interpreter of the Epistle (and, we think, of the whole NT) than Luther. In his *Commentary on the Catholic Epistles* (1551), he retains the Lutheran order and is cautious about the author's identity, but declares: "If James seems rather more reluctant to preach the grace of Christ than an apostle should be, we must remember not to expect everyone to go over the same ground—I am fully content to accept this Epistle, when I find it contains nothing unworthy of an apostle of Christ."[139]

Significant, too, is the testimony of William Tyndale. In his NT translations (1525, 1534) he also followed Luther's order, placing James at the end, and though he complains that "it does not lay the foundation of the faith of Christ," he also says that it calls upon men "to keep the law of God, and maketh love, which is without partiality, the ful-

134. See M. Meinertz, *Luther und der J. B.* (1904), pp. 217ff. On his doubts concerning extreme unction (Jas. 5:14), see T. de Vio Caietanus, *The Epistles of Paul and of the Other Apostles to the Greek Truth . . . Explained According to the Literal Sense*, 207G and 212B (1532), cited, in his broader discussion, by G. Hennig, *Cajetan and Luther* (1966), p. 179.

135. See Dibelius, p. 56, n. 233.

136. *On Famous Men* 2.

137. See n. 115 above.

138. E.g., Althamer, Andreas, Bugenhagen, Musculus, and L. Osiander.

139. *A Harmony of the Gospels Matthew, Mark, Luke, and the Epistles of James and Jude*, tr. A. W. Morrison, p. 259 in *Calvin's Commentaries* (1972), eds. D. W. Torrance, T. F. Torrance. See Meinertz, pp. 232f.

filling of the law, as Christ and all the apostles did . . . and hath also nothing that is not agreeable to the rest of the Scriptures." Thus he concludes: "Methinketh it ought of right to be taken for holy Scripture."[140]

In 1546 the Roman Catholic Council of Trent officially decreed the Epistle both apostolic and canonical; and as the Confessions of the other branches of the Protestant Church show, the question of canonicity was moot by the end of the sixteenth century.[141]

All the doubts of the Reformation and thereafter, however, merely reflect those of the ancient church, and this calls for a fresh study of its canonical history.

CONCLUSION

Till Origen, the Epistle of James was in obscure "circulation"; with him its known history began and also its struggle to become Holy Scripture. To get into the canon, it had to reckon with at least three forces in historical development:

1. People's addiction to their old heritage;
2. their passion to have what other churches, especially the big churches, had; and
3. the determination of the authorities to give the flock only apostolic Scriptures.

(1) The first factor kept the Epistle of James out of all churches for a time and out of the Syrian Church till the fifth century.[142] The canonical history of James shows a strange similarity to a strangely dissimilar early Christian document, namely, the Epistle to the Hebrews. In spite of strange and chequered histories and a period of obscurity, both managed to survive.

(2) The second worked for its admission, especially under the impetus of Origen's appreciative enthusiasm in Alexandria, and under the influence of Greek Orthodoxy, which extended at last even to the Roman and the Syrian Churches.

(3) The third, the sense of responsibility in the church leaders, made admission difficult for any new additions to the canon and especially hard for the Epistle of James.

140. "The Prologue upon the Epistle of James" (1526), *The Work of William Tyndale,* edited and introduced by G. E. Duffield, I (1964); also *The New Testament of Tyndale* (1934), ed. N. H. Wallis (1938), p. 161.

141. See Metzger, *Canon of the New Testament,* p. 247; Ropes, p. 109.

142. See J. S. Siker, "The Canonical Status of the Catholic Epistles in the Syriac New Testament," *JTS* 38.2 (1987): 311ff.

The fate of such an obviously Jewish writing would be linked with that of Jewish Christianity, and as the church became predominantly Gentile, the Epistle of James would become neglected. 1 Peter got into the canon on the basis of its name, 1 John on its kinship with the Gospel, and Jude on the certainty with which, although without a tradition, Clement and Origen felt they were able to identify its author; the Epistle of James, however, had no advantages of that sort. It was not at that time damned as anti-Pauline on the topic of faith and works, as antiestablishment when the church was growing wealthier, or as deficient in dogmatic theology: the trouble simply was that it could not, so to speak, produce its passport.

The Epistle of James won its place on its merits, recognized by Origen, Eusebius, Athanasius, Gregory of Nazianzus, and Chrysostom without knowing or asking for its author's particulars of identification; and the politic Roman and Syrian Churches finally accepted it as one of their measures to align themselves with the Greek Orthodox Church.

II. THE MESSAGE

"The Epistle of James may be the oldest book in the New Testament, but its message is as fresh as tomorrow morning."

Homer A. Kent, Jr., *Faith that Works. Studies in the Epistle of James* (1986), p. 15

"The ordinary English reader of the Epistle of James is troubled by few doubts as to its authenticity. There is an air of rugged freedom about it, of interest in practical ethics and the poorer classes, that recalls the Synoptic Gospels rather than the other New Testament Epistles. Theological dogma and sacerdotalism are conspicuous by their absence."

F. C. Burkitt, *Christian Beginnings* (1924), p. 65

"Luther was right in applying the criterion 'whatever promotes Christ (was Christum treibet) *is apostolic,' but wrong in not recognizing that the Epistle of James also 'promotes Christ' by its practical application of the Sermon on the Mount."*

Bruce M. Metzger, *The Canon of the New Testament* (1984), p. 244

1. James and Jesus

"For James there are no thousands of ifs and buts, but only the clear and simple demand for help, for forgiveness, for patience, for eschatological fulfilment of one's whole life. So it matches the teaching of Jesus as it is given to us especially in the Sermon on the Mount. To give heed to James is to give heed to Jesus. Both deal with the realization of the Word. Thus the Epistle of James belongs to those writings in the New Testament which in quite a special way urge and teach Christ."

F. Mussner, *Der Jakobusbrief* ([5]1987), pp. 52f.

The Relation of the Epistle of James to the Synoptic Tradition

The aim of this chapter is to show that the Epistle of James is a faithful and not inferior witness to the traditions of the teachings of Jesus that are more fully present in the Synoptic Gospels. After discussing briefly the vocabulary of the Epistle, we will consider two main topics: (1) the occurrence and form of some maxims of the Christian faith and Christian conduct as they appear in the Epistle and the Synoptic Gospels, and (2) the thought and outlook reflected in these Scriptures, especially the Epistle.

Perennial interest attaches to the problem of the relationship between the Epistle of James and the Synoptic tradition. This has been explained by different scholars in different ways. Some, for example, point to the possibility of a common milieu and tradition. Thus after noting that the words of Jesus crop up in the Epistle of James more than in any other document outside the Synoptics, W. D. Davies affirms that "in the milieu from which James drew his materials, the words of Jesus were in the air, so that, as a living and formative tradition, they moulded the life of the Christian community both directly by supplying, on occasion, specific *hᵃlāḵāh*, as at Jas. 5:12, and indirectly by supplying a climate and a norm for a Christian moral awareness."[1]

Even a cursory reading of the Epistle reveals the strong affinity that many of its sayings bear to the sayings of Jesus in the canonical Gospels—an affinity that has been noted by nearly every commentator on our Epistle. "The words of James, like these words of Jesus," notes Henderlite, "come in sharp, hammer-like blows! The imperatives are categorical and not hypothetical."[2] Martin Dibelius appears to downplay the significance of the Gospel parallels, but concedes a threefold similarity:

1. The Epistle of James and the sayings of Jesus share a similar literary heritage since both contain parenesis, made up of apparently disconnected sayings.
2. The two share a similar style seen in their use of short, pointed imperatives and fixed groups of metaphors; soil and plants (5:7; 3:12), moths and rust (5:2f.), watching and waiting (5:9), "adulteresses" (4:4), and the appeal to the prophets (5:10, 17f.)—all these recall the language of our Lord. Finally,
3. The two share the same general convictions in ethics and theology; for example, both praise the poor and the merciful but condemn the rich and their materialism.

"In both places," Dibelius writes, "we breathe the atmosphere of an ethical rigorism whose pithy injunctions warn against the world and a worldly attitude, and exhort to peace, meekness and humility. We gaze here into the realm of prayer which rejoices in the granting of its request, and of faith which works miracles."[3] To be sure, this opinion is not held unanimously. Occasionally a scholar has sought to prove that all the resemblances are purely coincidental, probably deriving from a common Jewish background. This has been true of men like Friedrich Spitta, Louis Massebieau, and Arnold Meyer, who, advocating the pre-Christian Jewish origin of the book, were forced to dismiss the possibility of its connection with Christian sources. Their contention, however, sprang from a priori considerations rather than from a strictly objective appraisal of the facts.

J. B. Mayor, at the other end of the scale, asserted that the Epistle

1. *The Setting of the Sermon on the Mount* (1964), pp. 402, 404; see also Schlatter, p. 19; Davids, p. 9, n. 30.

2. "The Epistle of James," *Interpretation* 3.4 (1946): 467.

3. P. 28.

of James preserved within its short compass of only 108 verses more sayings of Jesus (57 parallels with Matthew, 11 with Luke, and three with Mark) than are contained in all the NT Epistles put together[4]—an assertion that, if correct, would be sufficient to invest this NT writing with unique value. J. B. Mayor and other commentators have given impressive lists of echoes (*Anklänge*) of such parallel passages. If we are now inclined to be more sceptical, finding many of them accidental, far-fetched, or fanciful and others explicable by the postulation of a common Jewish (especially Wisdom) source, enough evidence remains to show an undoubted and striking similarity—a similarity that, on examination, fully corroborates Hort's verdict on this matter. "The style (of the Epistle of James)," he writes, "is especially remarkable for constant hidden allusions to our Lord's sayings, such as we find in the first three Gospels."[5] If we lack teaching about Jesus, we are given here the teaching of Jesus—and who can put a price on this?

This aspect of the study of the Epistle of James has been a fruitful field for speculation. Hans Windisch, indeed, compared it with the classic problem of the relationship between James and Paul, declaring that "the problem 'Jesus and the Epistle of James' appears almost more difficult and more puzzling than the familiar problem 'Jesus and Paul.'"[6] In part the problem arises because James *internalized* the teaching of Jesus rather than reproduced it mechanically.[7] Some have seen an affinity of context as well as form between our Epistle and the Synoptic sources, declaring that the groundwork of the former was the Sermon on the Mount.[8] Perhaps it was this that gave rise to the intriguing tradition that James translated the Gospel of Matthew from Hebrew into Greek.[9]

In a stimulating article, W. L. Knox drew attention to the curious,

4. P. xliv; see also C. C. Ryrie, *Biblical Theology of the New Testament* (1982), p. 137; A. Ritschl, *Die Entstehung der altkatholischen Kirche* (^{2}1857), p. 109; R. Patry, *L'épître de Jacques dans ses rapports avec la prédication de Jésus* (1899), *passim;* G. Kittel, "Der Geschichtliche Ort des Jakobusbriefes," *ZNW* 41 (1942): 84ff.; R. Hoppe, pp. 119ff.

5. P. xxxiii.

6. Quoted by G. Kittel, *art. cit., ZNW* 41 (1942): 64.

7. R. Wolff, *The General Epistles of James and Jude* (1969), p. 4.

8. Thus C. F. Schmid observed: "James not only agrees in numerous separate passages with Matthew's gospel, which (passages) appear to be but the echo of the discourses of Jesus with reference to the moral life in God's Kingdom, but also in that great body of precepts which Matthew gives as a whole, the Sermon on the Mount, which in its whole spirit, may be looked upon as a model of the Epistle of James" *(Biblical Theology of the New Testament* [1870], p. 364).

9. See p. 102, n. 13.

and perhaps significant, structural similarity between the Epistle and the Sermon on the Plain in Luke's Gospel, pointing out that the opening beatitudes and final exhortation in the Epistle correspond to the initial beatitudes and closing exhortation in the Lucan version of the Sermon.[10] This may be purely coincidental, or it may reflect a recognized form of primitive Christian preaching, familiar to both James and Luke. To be sure, these reminiscences (like those in the other NT Epistles) are given without narrative context and with neither quotation nor identification marks and, as a careful examination shows, are not confined to the so-called "Sermon on the Mount."

We cannot review all the theories of those who have dealt with this problem. One thing is clear: these similarities between James and the sayings of Jesus are by no means so plain as to warrant the assumption that they are direct quotations, perhaps because James, like the other apostles, somehow felt direct quotation was inappropriate, and in some instances perhaps handled them with relative freedom.[11]

The resemblances, or reflections, have been explained in various ways. The traditional explanation, given by Kittel and others,[12] is that they are vivid, fluid reminiscences of an eyewitness, suggesting a first period when the sayings had not yet become fixed and crystallized. Less conservative critics postulate an early written source, maintaining, either, like Von Soden, that James had (what he calls) a "Synoptical Lexicon" (*das synoptische Lexicon*) before him, which he interwove into his Epistle,[13] or, like Carl von Weizsäcker, that James knew and used an Ebionitic version of the Sermon on the Mount.[14] After E. J. Goodspeed,[15] Massey H. Shepherd simply suspected that James, of late date (probably c. A.D. 100), knew, but did not possess, the Gospel of

10. "The Epistle of James," *JTS* 46 (1945): 16.

11. See O. A. Piper, "Gospel (Message)," *Interpreter's Dictionary of the Bible* (1962), p. 446; also D. L. Dungan, *The Sayings of Jesus in the Churches of Paul* (1971). A clue to the editorial activity of James, Paul, and others in relation to the words of Jesus may be found in the Talmud: "A person should *study* the Torah (first) and then *explain* it" (b. Abodah Zarah 19a); "Let a person first *learn* and after *penetrate* that which has been learned" (b. Shabbath 63a). See, with comments, D. C. Allison, Jr., "The Pauline Epistles and the Synoptic Gospels: The Pattern of the Parallels," *NTS* 38 (1982): 21ff.

12. *Art. cit., ZNW* 41 (1942): 88ff., where he distinguishes three separate stages of *logia* transmission, on which see the cautions of Davies, *The Setting of the Sermon on the Mount*, p. 404. See also Mayor, p. xliv.

13. The second essay of the volume, *Theologische Abhandlungen* (1892), p. 135, dedicated to C. von Weizsäcker on his seventieth birthday.

14. *The Apostolic Age of the Christian Church*, II (1895), 30.

15. *An Introduction to the New Testament* (1937), p. 291.

Matthew, having heard it read in church;[16] while Eduard Lohse found links with the independent type of sayings of Jesus peculiar to the Didache.[17]

Free quotation and independent use of our other existing Gospels is another alternative that has been urged—though but rarely, since such a theory would compel an almost impossibly late date for the Epistle. Finally, while some critics have contended that the sayings of James resemble those of the Gospel of Matthew,[18] others have maintained their affinity with Luke[19]—and one modern writer has even found literary and theological links with the Gospel and Epistles of John, leading him to believe that the Epistle was earlier than the Gospel and directly influenced it.[20] This, if true, is a strikingly radical claim.

In our present study, we propose to investigate the problem, dealing with the relationship between the Epistle of James and the Synoptic tradition from the point of view of vocabulary, expression, thought, and outlook.

SECTION ONE

We analyzed the linguistic relations between James and the Synoptics in the following manner. Using W. Bauer, W. F. Arndt, and F. W. Gingrich, *A Greek-English Lexicon of the New Testament,* and a good concordance, we drew up three tables containing (a) those words that were peculiar to James and Luke-Acts and used nowhere else in the NT; (b) those words that were characteristic of James and Luke-Acts—by which is meant that they occurred in James and the Lucan writings but

16. "The Epistle of James and the Gospel of Matthew," *JBL* 75.1 (1956): 47, 107.

17. "Glaube und Werke—zur Theologie des Jakobusbriefes," *ZNW* 48 (1957): 1-22.

18. Shepherd, *art. cit., JBL* 75.1 (1956): 47; Mussner, pp. 47-52.

19. F. C. Grant, "Method in Studying Jesus' 'Social Teaching,'" in S. J. Case, *Studies in Early Christianity* (1928), p. 264.

20. Scaer draws attention to resemblances between the Epistle of James and the Gospel of John, noting, e.g., "the Word of truth" (Jas. 1:18) and "the Word" (Jn. 1:1) and "the Truth" (Jn. 14:6). See also "the Wisdom from above" (Jas. 3:15) and "He who comes down from above" (Jn. 3:31); the incarnate *Shechinah* (Jn. 1:14); and "the Lord Jesus Christ, our Glory (the *Shechinah*)" (Jas. 2:1). Scaer also argues that James anticipated and influenced "the incarnational language" of John, who was directly dependent on James (pp. 60ff., 107). But rather than attribute direct literary dependence to either, we believe that each knew and tapped the same sources. See also P. Ewald, *Das Hauptproblem der Evangelienfrage* (1980), pp. 58ff.; Mayor, pp. lxxxviiiff.; Davids, p. 41, n. 121 and p. 26.

not in Matthew or Mark, although they may occur elsewhere in the NT; and (c) those words that were peculiar to and/or characteristic of James and Matthew and Mark respectively. Naturally several words characteristic of Mark were duplicated in Matthew; we tabulated these separately for the sake of accuracy. "L" indicates Luke's special source.

TABLE 1

WORDS FOUND ONLY IN JAMES AND LUKE–ACTS

Word	*James*	*Luke*	*Acts*		
1. *anaptein:*	3:5	12:49	28:2		L
2. *apotelein:*	1:15	13:32			L
3. *atmis:*	4:14		2:19		
4. *bradys:*	1:19	24:25		*bradyploein* Acts 27:7	L
5. *gelan: gelōs:*	4:9	6:21, 25			
6. *eleos poiein:*	2:13	1:72			
		10:37			L
7. *helkein:*	2:6		21:30		
8. *epiblepein + epi:*	2:3	1:48			
		9:38			L
9. *esthēs*	2:2f.	23:11	1:10		
			10:13		
			12:21		L
10. *euthymein:*	5:13		22:22, 25	*euthymos* Acts 27:36	
11. *ephēmeros:*	2:15	1:3, 8(N)			L
12. *katadynasteuein:*	2:6		10:38		
13. *katerchesthai:*	3:15	4:31			
		9:37	*saepe*		
14. *klydōn*	1:6	6:24			
15. *lampros:*	2:2f.	23:11	1:10		
			10:13		
			12:31		L
16. *makarizein:*	5:11	1:48			L
17. *oiktirmōn:*	5:11	6:36			
18. *homoiopathēs:*	5:17		14:15		
19. *peripiptein:*	1:2	10:30	27:41		L
20. *pēdalion:*	3:4		27:40		
21. *poreia*	1:11	13:22			
22. *hypodechesthai:*	2:25	10:38			
		19:6	17:7		L

TABLE 2

WORDS USED BY JAMES AND LUKE–ACTS THAT DO NOT OCCUR IN EITHER MATTHEW OR MARK

Word	*James*	*Luke*	*Acts*	*Other NT Books*	
1. *hagnizein:*	4:8		21:24, 26		
			24:18	Pet.; Jn.	
2. *adikia:*	3:6	13:27	1:18		
		16:8f.	8:23	Jn. (3); Paul (10);	
		18:6		Heb. (2); Pet. (2)	L
3. *akatastasia:*	3:16	21:9		Paul (3)	
4. *anthrōpinos:*	3:7		17:25	Paul (4); Pet. (1)	
5. *antitassesthai:*	4:6				
	5:6		18:6	Paul (1); Pet. (1)	
6. *deēsis:*	5:16	1:13			
		2:37		Paul (12); Heb. (1);	
		5:33		Pet. (1)	L
7. *dioti:*	4:3	1:13	13:35		
		2:7	18:10		
		21:28	20:26		
			22:13		L
8. *dialogismos:*	2:4	5:22			
		6:8			
		9:46f.		See Mayor, p. lxxxiv.	L
		24:38			
9. *ekdechesthai:*	5:7		17:6	Jn. (1); Paul (2);	
				Heb. (2)	
10. *eniautos:*	4:13		11:26	Jn. (4); Paul (1);	
	5:17	4:19	18:11	Heb. (4)	L
11. *enōpion:*	4:10	25 times	13 times	Luke uses the phrase	
				enōpion tou kyriou (2)	L
				Jn. (35); Paul (18);	
				Heb. (2); Pet. (1)	
12. *herpeton*	3:7		10:12		
			11:6	Paul (1)	
13. *echthra:*	4:4	23:12		Paul (4)	L
14. *zēlos:*	3:14, 16		5:17	Jn. (1); Paul (10);	
			13:45	Heb. (1)	
15. *zēloun:*	4:2		7:9	Paul (8)	
			17:5		
16. *hēdonē:*	4:1, 3	8:14		Paul (1); Pet. (1)	
17. *thrēskeia:*	1:26f.		26:5	Paul (1)	

Word	*James*	*Luke*	*Acts*	*Other NT Books*	
18. *eidenai:*	1:19		26:4	Paul (1); Heb. (1)	
	(W.H.)				
19. *leipein:*	1:4f.	18:22			
	2:15			Paul (2)	
20. *machesthai:*	4:2		7:26	Jn.; Paul	
21. *mataios:*	1:26		14:15	Paul (3); Pet. (1)	
22. *metatrepesthai:*	4:9		2:20	Paul (1)	
23. *mēn:*	5:17	1:24, 26,	7:20	Jn. (6) Paul (1)	L
		36, 56	18:11		
		4:25	19:8		
			20:3		
			28:11		
24. *moichalides:*	4:4	18:11		Paul (1); Heb. (1)	L
25. *hopoios:*	1:24		26:2	Paul (3)	
26. *parakyptein:*	1:25	24:12		Jn.; Pet.	
27. *poiētēs:*	1:22f.,		17:28	Paul (1)	
	25				
	4:11				
28. *stērizein:*	5:8	9:51	18:23	Paul (6); Pet. (2);	
		16:26		Jn. (1)	
		22:32			L
29. *tapeinōsis:*	1:10	1:48	8:33	Paul (1)	L
30. *teleioun:*	2:22	2:43	20:24	Jn. (9); Paul (1);	
		13:32		Heb. (9)	L
31. *timios:*	5:7		5:34	Paul (1); Heb. (1);	
			20:24	Pet. (2); Jn. (6)	
32. *toinyn:*	2:24	20:25		Paul (1); Heb. (1)	
33. *tryphan:*	5:5	7:25		Pet.	
		(noun)			
34. *hyetos:*	5:18		14:17	Heb. (1); Jn. (1)	
			28:2		
35. *prosōpolēmpsia:*	2:1		10:34		
	2:9		(adj.)		
	(verb)			Paul (3)	
36. *hyperēphanos:*	4:6	1:51		Paul (2); Pet. (1)	L
37. *hypomonē:*	1:3f.	8:15		Paul (16); Heb. (2);	
	5:11	21:19		Pet. (2); Jn. (7)	
38. *hypotassein:*	4:7	2:51		Paul (23); Heb. (5);	
		10:17, 20		Pet. (6)	L

N.B. For our present purpose we have grouped the Johannine Epistles and the Apocalypse collectively under "Johannine"; Ephesians and the Pastorals are grouped under "Paul." This is done simply for the sake of convenience.

TABLE 3

WORDS USED BY JAMES, NOT IN LUKE, BUT WHICH ARE USED BY:

(a) Matthew

Word	*James*	*Matthew*	*Other NT Books*
1. *melos:*	4:1	5:29f.	
2. *mestos:*	3:8-17	23:28	Jn.; Paul; Pet.
3. *teleios:*	1:4, 17,	5:48	Jn.; Paul
	25; 3:2	19:21	
4. *phorein:*	2:23	11:8	Jn.; Paul

(b) Mark

Word	*James*	*Mark*	*Other NT Books*
1. *damazein:*	3:7f.	5:4	
2. *thermainesthai:*	2:16	14:54, 67	Jn.
3. *orphanos:*	1:27	12:40	Jn.
4. *pēgē:*	3:11	5:29	
5. *synergein:*	2:22	16:20	Paul

(c) Matthew and Mark

Word	*James*	*Matthew*	*Mark*	*Other NT Books*
1. *enochos:*	2:30	5:21f.	3:39	Heb.; Paul
		26:66	14:69	
2. *stephanos:*	1:12	27:29	15:17	Jn.; Paul
3. *phthonos:*	4:2	27:18	15:10	Paul

The results of the linguistic analysis can be summarized as follows:

(a) Words peculiar to:	
James and Luke–Acts	22
James and Matthew	1
James and Mark	2
James and Matthew and Mark combined	0
(b) Words characteristic of:	
James and Luke–Acts	38
James and Matthew	3
James and Mark	3
James and Matthew and Mark combined	3

(c) Total of such words in:	
James and Luke–Acts	60
James and Matthew	4
James and Mark	5
James and Matthew and Mark combined	3
(d) Total of such words in:	
James and Luke–Acts, Matthew, and Mark	72
James and Luke–Acts Tradition	60
James and Matthew–Mark Tradition	12

From this it is plain that at least 80 percent of such words in James are Lucan. The remaining 20 percent are divided fairly evenly between Matthew and Mark. Such a proportion, it need hardly be urged, is not without interest.

So far we have seen that James stands closer in vocabulary to Luke than to either Matthew or Mark. The matter cannot be left there, however. We must ask whether we can examine this linguistic relationship more closely. With a view to answering this question, we listed in Tables 1 and 2 the words that were peculiar to, or characteristic of, Luke. We did not include any that appear only in Acts. The number of such words was 37. We then counted the appearances of these words in the sections of Luke that it is safe to say are drawn from "L."[21] The total here was 25.

For the sake of clarity, we present the results thus:

Words common to James and Luke–Acts	60
Words common to James and Luke alone	37
Words common to James and Luke	25

It will be apparent at once that the words common to James and Luke are predominantly from among the peculiarly Lucan material in the Gospel—25 out of a total of 37, or almost 70 percent. The percentage may indeed be even higher since in estimating this figure we have preferred to err on the conservative side; but even so, 70 percent is a notable proportion.

21. In the present study, we assume the identification of passages from L given in E. E. Ellis, *The Gospel of Luke* (1974), pp. 25ff.; B. S. Easton, *The Gospel according to St. Luke* (1926), p. xxiii; see also I. H. Marshall, *Luke: Historian and Theologian* (1970), p. 62.

SECTION TWO

In vocabulary, therefore, the Epistle of James clearly stands much closer to Luke than to either Matthew or Mark. We could say much more on vocabulary; now, however, we must try to show the importance of the Epistle of James in providing evidence of the earliest available form of some of the sayings of Jesus. The kinship of these sayings in James with those in Luke and Matthew is obvious.

We are well aware that it is better to quote the relevant pericopes in Greek, especially when discussing the "earliest form" of dominical sayings; one needs *exact* linguistic information. Translations can be inadequate, even misleading. But for the convenience of the general reader, we have chosen to take this risk and quote from the NIV. Usually the texts speak for themselves:

James 1:5: If any of you lacks wisdom, he should ask God, . . . and it will be given to him.
Matthew 7:7: Ask and it will be given to you.
Luke 11:9: Ask and it will be given to you.

James 1:9f.: The brother in humble circumstances ought to take pride in his high position. But the one who is rich should take pride in his low position.
Matthew 23:12: Whoever exalts himself will be humbled, and whoever humbles himself will be exalted.
Luke 14:11: Everyone who exalts himself will be humbled, and he who humbles himself will be exalted.

James 1:17: Every good and perfect gift is from above, coming down from the Father of the heavenly lights.
Matthew 7:11: How much more will your Father in heaven give good gifts. . . !
Luke 11:13: How much more will your Father in heaven give the Holy Spirit. . . !

James 1:21: Accept the word planted in you. . . .
Luke 8:8f.: Other seed fell on good soil. . . . The seed is the word of God.

James is probably recalling the same parable given and expounded in Luke.

James 1:22: Do not merely listen to the word. . . . Do what it says.
Matthew 7:24: Everyone who hears these words of mine and puts them into practice.

Luke 6:46ff.: Why do you call me, "Lord, Lord," and do not do what I say? . . .

The thought here is essentially that of Matthew and Luke—the test of reality in religion lies in action—and we may well have another unrecorded saying of Jesus.[22] We cannot tell: equally possible is common Jewish influence.

James 2:5: Has not God chosen those who are poor in the eyes of the world to be rich in faith and to inherit the kingdom he promised those who love him?
Matthew 5:3: Blessed are the poor in spirit, for theirs is the kingdom of heaven.
Luke 6:20: Blessed are you who are poor, for yours is the kingdom of God.

Clearly James is alluding to our Lord's blessing on the poor, probably reflecting the Aram. *'ᵃnāwîm,*[23] and approximately in the form in which it eventually stood in Luke. Matthew alone has ". . . in spirit"; James agrees with Luke in making it unqualified, and has the dative of the person judging, "poor in the sight of the world,"[24] in contrast to the locative construction,[25] which is found in Matthew. Our author alone explicitly makes the blessing a promise for the future. The form in Luke may be earlier than that in Matthew, though James is independent of each.[26]

James 3:12: Can a fig tree bear olives, or a grapevine bear figs?

Matthew 7:16: Do people pick grapes from thornbushes, or figs from thistles?

22. For this, see, e.g., Origen, *Homilies on Genesis* 2.16 (Migne, *PG*, XII, 174).

23. See G. Kittel, *art. cit., ZNW* 41 (1942): 85f.; M. Black, *An Aramaic Approach to the Gospels* (1967), p. 156.

24. *tous ptōchous tō kosmō:* the inferior readings have "poor in the world," "poor of the world." For a discussion of James's use of the *dativus commodi* and other datives, see C. F. D. Moule, *An Idiom-Book of New Testament Greek* (^{2}1959), pp. 45f., 204; J. H. Moulton, *A Grammar of New Testament Greek,* III: N. Turner, *Syntax* (1963), 238.

25. *hoi ptōchoi tō pneumati.*

26. See H. Riesenfeld, *The Gospel Tradition* (1980), pp. 12ff.; also Black, *Aramaic Approach,* pp. 187f. For a discussion of the form and significance of the macarism in Mt. 5:3 and the view that it is "a mixed form of a complicated sort," with a toned down economic emphasis, see H. D. Betz, *Essays on the Sermon on the Mount* (1985), pp. 26ff.

No derivative connection can be assumed in these two quotations of the same piece of ancient proverbial wisdom.

James 3:18: Peacemakers who sow in peace raise a harvest of righteousness.
Matthew 5:9: Blessed are the peacemakers, for they will be called sons of God.

The author of the Epistle of James is (no doubt consciously) repeating the thought, but does not here profess to be repeating the words, of his Master. It may well be that "peacemakers" *(tois poiousin eirēnēn)* in James and "peacemakers" *(hoi eirēnopoioi)* in Matthew represent variants of the same Aramaic root; both appear to be linked with purity, in James with pure wisdom and in Matthew with the pure in heart. Nevertheless, the similarity is primarily one of thought rather than words.

James 4:9: Grieve, mourn and wail. Change your laughter to mourning and your joy to gloom.
Matthew 5:4: Blessed are those who mourn, for they will be comforted.
Luke 6:21, 25: Blessed are you who weep now, for you will laugh. . . . Woe to you who laugh now, for you will mourn and weep.

Here the wording of the Epistle is almost identical with that of the Lucan woe.[27] Both use "laugh" *(gelan),* a word used only in Luke and the Epistle of James and nowhere else in the NT, and both use the verb here in the second person. The style and compass of Mt. 5:4 are in accord with its context, vv. 5-10.

James 4:3: When you ask, you do not receive.
Matthew 7:7f.: Ask and it will be given to you. . . . For everyone who asks receives.

James 4:17: Anyone, then, who knows the good he ought to do and doesn't do it, sins.
Luke 12:47f.: That servant who knows his master's will and does not get ready or does not do what his master wants will be beaten with many blows. But the one who does not know. . . .

27. The "woes" are peculiar to Luke's version of the Sermon on the Mount. Luke's special material seems to have overlapped the source from which it came. It is generally agreed, too, that at many points Luke preferred this version (see Streeter, *The Four Gospels* [1936], pp. 209f.). There are signs that he knew more of L than he actually used. Note the sudden breaks in Lk. 6:27-39ff. with the corresponding passage in Matthew (5:43ff.; 7:1ff.).

The main thought here is the same. Both should be compared with (a) the saying about the man working on the Sabbath day (Lk. 6:5f.) preserved in Codex Bezae, and (b) the wording of extracanonical versions, for example Origen's quotation of Lk. 12:47 in Jerem. 16.7.

James 5:1-6: Now listen, you rich people, weep and wail because of the misery that is coming upon you. Your wealth has rotted, and moths have eaten your clothes. Your gold and silver are corroded. . . .
Luke 6:24ff.: But woe to you who are rich, for you have already received your comfort. Woe to you who are well fed now, for you will go hungry. Woe to you who laugh now, for you will mourn and weep. Woe to you when all men speak well of you, for that is how their fathers treated the false prophets.

The general background and eschatological thrust are the same: they contain words both of comfort and threat. If, as has been suggested,[28] the Lucan woes are not original to Jesus' teaching, then both pericopes may represent commonplace sayings of Jewish (e.g., 1 Enoch) and early Judeo-Christian homiletics. If, on the other hand, we grant the genuineness of the Lucan woe, can we exclude (in view of the foregoing parallels with the sayings of Jesus) the possibility that James is directly indebted to Jesus? It is also conceivable that the saying in James reflects the Lucan form mixed with current Jewish ideas.

James 5:17: Elijah was a man just like us. He prayed earnestly that it would not rain, and it did not rain on the land for three and a half years.
Luke 4:25: There were many widows in Israel in Elijah's time, when the sky was shut up for three and a half years and there was a severe famine throughout the land.

There is an interesting concord between the Epistle of James and Luke in another field—in two deviations from our OT record of Elijah: (a) in the OT there is no mention of Elijah's *praying* either for drought or for rain (1 Kgs. 19:11; 18:1, 41); (b) the forecast of rain in 1 Kgs. 18:1 is in the third year of Ahab's reign, and that is not three years and six months from his declaration (17:1) that there would be no rain "these years." Luke also gives the same period of three years and six months, denoting the period of suffering before divine deliverance. He is probably following the same Jewish tradition as James.[29]

Finally, the saying in Jas. 5:12 (not actually occurring in Luke)

28. W. Manson, *The Gospel of Luke,* MNTC (1930), p. 66.

29. See S-B III, 760f.; C. J. Hemer, "Number" *(eniautous treis kai mēnas hex), NIDNTT,* II, 688.

seems to go back more closely to Jesus than does the version of Mt. 5:37:

James 5:12: Above all, my brothers, do not swear—not by heaven or by earth or by anything else. Let your "Yes" be "Yes," and your "No," "No," or you will be condemned.
Matthew 5:33ff.: "Do not break your oath, but keep the oaths you have made to the Lord." But I tell you, Do not swear at all: either by heaven, for it is God's throne; or by the earth, for it is his footstool; or by Jerusalem, for it is the city of the Great King. And do not swear by your head, for you cannot make even one hair white or black. Simply let your "Yes" be "Yes," and your "No," "No"; anything beyond this comes from the evil one.

Elsewhere we have given reasons for ascribing the Epistle of James to the Lord's brother, whose qualifications may justly be inferred from (among other evidence) his appointment to lead the Jewish Christians after the ascension. To illustrate the merits of his reflection of the teaching of Jesus one may compare Jas. 5:12, "No swearing," with Mt. 5:33-37 in the "Sermon on the Mount." Whether that "Sermon" ever took place, on "Mount" or "Plain," and whether it is a real unity or a compilation as the break in style and treatment after v. 16 and the improbability of vv. 17-19 ever being used as a prelude to vv. 21-43 strongly suggest, may remain open to doubts; but Jas. 5:12 certainly gives a better and less ambiguous presentation of the teaching of Jesus.

Luke omits the saying on oaths—an omission that is probably due to his Gentile bias. "It is generally considered," wrote Massey Shepherd, "that this parallel presents the strongest single case for the dependence of James upon the Gospel, despite the fact that *James does not actually quote the Gospel and apparently reflects a more primitive tradition than the Gospel.*"[30] Most commentators, therefore, are inclined to regard this verse as the strongest piece of evidence for James's familiarity with the teaching of Jesus as it was handed down in the oral tradition, though a few (e.g., Spitta, Arnold Meyer, Von Soden) are content to dismiss it as nothing more than a commonplace of Jewish ethics. The general tendency, however, is to take it as a *verbum Christi;* its abrupt introduction, apparently as a genuine quotation, lends strength to this view.

The general thought is the same in both James and Matthew: the use of oaths is forbidden. Moreover, there is a striking verbal similarity, though it must be admitted that James's version is slightly different

30. *Art. cit., JBL* 75.1 (1956): 106f. (our italics).

from that of Matthew. This is clear from a comparison of the first half of each saying:

James: Do not use oaths, whether "by heaven" or "by earth" or by anything else. . . .
Matthew: "Do not break your oath," and, "Keep the oaths you have made to the Lord." But I tell you, Do not swear at all: either by heaven, for it is God's throne; or by the earth, for it is his footstool, or by Jerusalem, for it is the city of the Great King. And do not swear by your head.

Less marked but certainly no less significant are the divergences in the latter half of the sayings, which literally translated are:

James: Let your yea be yea, and your nay be nay, that you may not come under judgment.
Matthew: But let your word be "yea, yea" or "nay, nay"; whatever goes beyond that comes from evil.

Sophie Laws distinguishes at least seven important differences between the two versions:[31]

1. James uses correct Greek with the accusative case for things sworn by; Matthew, reflecting Semitic idiom, has *en* with the dative.
2. In addition to James's "by heaven" and "by earth," Matthew has "by Jerusalem" and "by earth," which may reflect the evangelist's own interest in the topic; see Mt. 23:16-22, where there is "an attack specifically in Jewish terms on 'avoidable' formulae, and Matthew may be conscious that the forms he quotes in vv. 34-36 would similarly be thought of as not binding."[32]
3. Unlike James, Matthew does give a theological explanation for the proscription of oaths.
4. Whereas Matthew has the classical imperative *estō,* James prefers the colloquial *ētō.*
5. James's version, with the definite article (*to nai nai* and *to ou ou*), conveys the idea of honest speaking; Matthew's, without the article, that of plain speaking.[33]

31. Pp. 222f.

32. P. 222.

33. The reading *ho logos hymōn* found in some cursives of James is clearly an early harmonistic interpolation. The phraseology of Matthew and James should be carefully compared. For James's *to nai nai kai to ou ou* Matthew has the slightly different rendering *nai nai, ou ou,* suggesting that James is here following the precanonical tradition, prior to and independent of Matthew. Against this we must set C. C. Torrey's view that mistranslation of Matthew's Aramaic original explains the

6. James ends on an eschatological note; Matthew with a ruling that "anything more than this is evil."
7. Unlike Matthew, James, as usual, does not attribute the saying to Jesus—although, in our opinion, he was well aware of his source.[34]

How can we explain these significant congruences and contrasts? Priority may be assigned to either version, depending on interpretation and point of view, although literary borrowing on either side is unlikely. "If the instruction goes back to Jesus," observes Laws, "it would originally have been given in a Jewish context and very probably with just such a polemical thrust as Matthew presents; James's presentation could be a simplification of the tradition as it passed outside the area of purely Jewish concerns, and his form of the alternatives might reflect the accommodation of it to the popular theme of truth-telling."[35] It seems safer, however, and less speculative to affirm that we have in James and Matthew an authentic saying of Jesus that had crystallized from the same oral source in two separate and independent forms.

The sophisticated repetition of "you have heard . . ." in Mt. 5:21, 43, so different from the repetition of the simple "Blessed . . ." in vv. 3-11, is unlike Christ's usual approach to the "multitude" (5:1), and it imports into vv. 33-37 an ambiguity about which Christians are not fully agreed. Does v. 33 introduce an extension of the old law as in vv. 21f. and 27f., or an abrogation (partial or complete) of an old rule as in vv. 38f. (complete) and 43f. (partial)? The commonest view is that Mat-

---

deviations; so James's translation is correct, while Matthew's is corrupt *(The Four Gospels* [^{2}1947], pp. 11, 291; T. W. Manson, *The Sayings of Jesus* [1949], p. 159). While Torrey's suggestion appears attractive, for two reasons at least we believe that James and Matthew represent two separate versions of the same saying: (1) where, as D. Daube showed, the rabbinic parallels for Matthew deal with "the proper mode of making binding declarations, those for James have honesty for their theme" (*BJRL* 29 [1945-46]: 69); and (2) Justin Martyr, *The Apology* 1.16; Clement of Alexandria, *Stromateis* 5.99; 7.50; Ps. Clem. *Homilies* 19:2; 3:55; and Epiphanius, *Refutation of all Heresies* 1.44 (Migne, *PG*, XLI, 268) all are identical with our author in "Let your yea be yea, and your nay be nay." Daube thinks that Matthew's text represents an earlier version than that of the Epistle of James. But it seems safer to suppose that behind both lies a primitive logion that Matthew elaborates one way and James another. See also J. Schneider, *omnyō, TDNT,* V, 182; Dibelius, pp. 297ff.; Davids, p. 190.

34. *Pace* Laws, p. 13. L. T. Johnson, "The Use of Leviticus 19 in the Letter of James," *JBL* 101.3 (1982): 397, sees a verbal allusion here to Lev. 19:12. We are inclined, however, to think that the Leviticus influence was secondary, the Mathean saying of Jesus on swearing being certainly the immediate, primary, and obvious formative factor in Jas. 5:12.

35. Pp. 223f.

thew here means that besides scrupulously keeping our solemn vows to God we must show him reverence by not profanely besprinkling our ordinary talk with needless and careless oaths; as Paul indicates, many Corinthians almost made Communion a profane feast. We submit, however, that Jas. 5:12 is concerned only with enjoining habitual patience and restraint in our talk as in the rest of our daily behavior, and the whole unit 5:7-12 is devoted to this.

Here, then, James gives us a better (because it is clearer and better coordinated) view of the actual teaching of Jesus. In the Epistle of James as a whole, which was written to impress upon Christian Jews how they should prepare in mind and deed for the judgment of the Second Advent, we must recognize the same merit as in this climactic pericope 5:7-12, which, with its kindred topic, prayer (vv. 13-18), ends, as it began (1:2-8), the Epistle of James.

SECTION THREE

Turning now to a matter of primary importance, let us observe how faithful James is to the teaching of Jesus as presented in the Gospels of (especially) Matthew and Luke, and how this has a bearing on the origin of the Epistle of James.

James's Epistle has been described as a republication, with adaptation to existing conditions, of the teaching of Jesus, not "in any mechanical way, but with a real understanding of the point of view from which our Lord proclaimed his teaching, which would make it an evangelistic or pre-evangelistic tract."[36] G. Currie Martin advanced an interesting hypothesis that attempted to harmonize the two extreme dates for the origin of the Epistle.[37] He thought James the Lord's brother might have made a collection of some early sayings of Jesus his brother, which were read in the gatherings of his followers, combined with reminiscences of the earliest applications of these sayings to the thought and need of the first disciples.

When Jerusalem was destroyed and the Christians fled, this manuscript may have been taken with them as one of their most valued possessions. As time passed, these words became mingled with many other teachings and reflections until finally they came to form a short treatise

36. D. Guthrie, *New Testament Introduction* (1970), p. 744; see also G. C. Martin, "The Epistle of St. James as a Storehouse of the Sayings of Jesus," *Ex* 4 (1907): 45-55; J. H. Moulton, "The Epistle of James and the Sayings of Jesus," *Ex* 4 (1907): 45-55; and "James," *Peake's Commentary* (1931), p. 903; Rendall, pp. 88ff.; see also our suggestion, pp. 83ff.

37. *Art. cit., Ex* 4 (1907): 45-55.

on practical conduct. Church leaders recognized its value and circulated it among the churches, giving the name of James to it, because they knew that James the head of the great Jerusalem Church was in a way responsible for it. Thus the lateness of the book's appearance can be accounted for and the evidence of its early source preserved. How many unwritten sayings of Jesus or *agrapha* it contains is hard to tell.[38]

If there were no Gospels, much would still be known about the teaching of Jesus from the Epistle of James. We find so much similarity between Jesus and James that no other explanation than direct knowledge of the latter is adequate; indeed, it is attractive to imagine "the two spending their boyhood under the same roof, seeing life lived simply, learning together to express deep meanings of the most fundamental and yet commonplace terms of everyday experience."[39] The reminiscences that are scattered here and there in the Epistle are even more impressive for not being direct references to tradition, for they reveal how thoroughly the mind of James was controlled by the mind of Christ. This resemblance, however, is seen not only in the tone and spirit that characterize the two, but also in their similarity of expression and elemental analogies. Nor is this hard to understand, for if James, like Peter, was the representative custodian of the collective apostolic memory,[40] what would be more natural for him than to share his unique remembrances of his brother in his own way by this Epistle before the memory faded.

Even a cursory study of the Epistle reveals a terse, vivid beauty, flaming ardor, pungent and incisive utterance, love of nature, and smell of "full fields" *(odor agri pleni),* that is unique to the Gospels. "The Epistle of James," declared Deissmann, "will be best understood in the open air beside the piled sheaves of the harvest field; it is the first powerful echo of the still recent synoptic-books."[41] Both the substance of the teaching and the halakhic method of its presentation remind us of the discourses of Jesus—so much so that we are almost persuaded that Jesus himself is speaking in the Epistle, as indeed, at some points, we believe he is.

In both James and Jesus, morality is grounded not in social obligation nor in virtue for virtue's sake but in the righteousness of God. James attacks a faith without works, as also, most notably of all the Gospels, does Matthew: compare and contrast, to cite only one example,

38. For extensive discussion and parallels, see Mayor, p. lxxxiv; also Schlatter, p. 19.

39. R. Henderlite, *art. cit., Interpretation* 3.4 (1949): 467.

40. W. R. Farmer, *Jesus and the Gospel* (1982), p. 58.

41. *Light from the Ancient East* (ET 1927), p. 248.

the respective wording of the parallels on saying and doing (Mt. 7:21; Lk. 6:46). Both give the highest place to love *(agapē)* and its moral imperative, brotherhood, the righteousness of God *at work* in human society. Religion is not that of a prescriptive creed, but of character and service. We see no evidence for the belief that the "Epistle of James falls flat after Q" or that "his interesting experiment (of accepting the ethical teaching of Jesus without its theological background) cannot be called a success."[42] On the contrary, as Renan remarked, "when James speaks of humility, of patience, of pity, of the exaltation of the humble, of the joy which underlies tears, he seems to have retained in memory the very words of Jesus."[43] Both condemn the same vices and prize the same virtues: on the one hand, pride, anger, faith betrayed, and presumptuous judgment; on the other, humility, kindness, pity, gentleness, peace, and mercy.

Nowhere does the Epistle show a closer affinity with the Synoptic record than on the subject of law, which James twice paradoxically calls "the law of liberty." Originating probably in the Jewish-Christian diaspora, the phrase is clearly messianic and probably refers "chiefly to those collections of Christ's sayings, such as the Sermon on the Mount (Mt. 5–7) and the Discourse on the Plain (Lk. 6:20ff.), which were regarded as the rule of life."[44] Obedience to this law brings release from the yoke of Jewish legalism with perfect freedom and blessedness to those who do it (1:25; 2:13). "The echoes of the Sermon on the Mount have often been noticed," says Rendall, "but what especially concerns us is to observe how deeply St. James has entered into that part of the Sermon which we examined at the outset—the true manner of the fulfilment of the Law."[45] The Epistle presents the idealization of Jewish legalism as under the transforming power of the Christian motive and life. The Epistle of James shows a distinct verbal connection with the Gospel of Luke, especially in the Beatitudes,[46] but in its presentation of religion it is nearer to the Gospel of Matthew.[47]

Affinities may be traced between James and Matthew (1) in vocabulary, for example oaths (Jas. 5:12//Mt. 5:33-37), "righteousness"

42. J. A. Findlay, *The Way, the Truth and the Life* (1940), pp. 158f.

43. *L'Antéchrist* (1873), p. 54, quoted by Knowling, p. xxi.

44. H.-H. Esser, "Law" *(nomos), NIDNTT,* II, 449.

45. P. 66.

46. Shepherd, *art. cit., JBL* 75.1 (1956): 43f.

47. A comparative examination of Luke's doctrine of law bears this out. See S. G. Wilson, *Luke and the Law* (1983), especially pp. 103ff., for a summary of his teaching in the Gospel and in the Acts; also P. F. Esler, *Community and Gospel in Luke-Acts* (1987), pp. 118ff.; and for Matthew see R. Mohrlang, *Matthew and Paul* (1984), pp. 7ff.

(Jas. 1:20; 3:18//Mt. 3:15; 5:6, 10, 20; 6:1, 33; 21:32), "perfect" (Jas. 1:4//Mt. 5:48; 19:21), "church" (Jas. 5:7//Mt. 16:18; 18:17), and "parousia" (Jas. 5:7//Mt. 24:3, 27, 37, and 39); and (2) in content, for example beatitudes on the poor (Jas. 2:5//Mt. 5:3), merciful (Jas. 2:13f.//Mt. 5:7), and peacemakers (Jas. 3:18//Mt. 5:9); anxiety for tomorrow (Jas. 4:13f.//Mt. 6:34); and ambitious teachers (Jas. 3:1//Mt. 23:8). These affinities in vocabulary and content are said to point to a special relationship between James and Matthew.

Yet these similarities need to be carefully evaluated. Some, it is true, may be due simply to a common ethical background, for example "righteousness" or "perfect"; and both mention "church" and "parousia," common quasi-technical terms, although Matthew, unlike James, also contains the other distinctive terms, "regeneration" *(palingenesia)* (19:28) and "end of the age" *(synteleia tou aiōnos)* (24:3; 28:20). Significant differences of interpretation, emphasis, and setting, however, can be observed in their respective sayings, notably those dealing with poverty, mercy and peacemaking, overanxiety or overconfidence for the morrow, the warning on teachers, "good gifts," and even the saying on oaths *(q.v.)*. Certain important differences can be seen in the way each speaks about riches: whereas James is hostile, Matthew is more conciliatory. Even more striking perhaps is James's more conciliatory attitude toward Judaism, the Jewish people per se, and the Jewish Torah in particular.

These similarities and differences are both extremely significant and hardly accidental. "Their characteristic concerns," notes Laws, "are so dissimilar that they must be seen as employing their common material in different situations."[48] Yet these parallels, even with their differences, are most impressive, especially when taken cumulatively. It can hardly be doubted that while Matthew and James employ their material in different ways for different purposes, the two show no literary interdependence but appear to be tapping—each in his own way—a primitive precanonical Gospel source.

In his *Studies in Matthew* (1930), B. W. Bacon claimed that Matthew interwove the sayings in Q into five sections, while including material from Mark. His model was the five books of Moses, so he outlined a new Torah which superseded that of Moses.[49] The Pauline ap-

48. P. 15; see also A. Feuillet, "Le sens du mot Parousie dans l'Évangile de Matthieu," in *The Background of the New Testament and its Eschatology,* eds. W. D. Davies and D. Daube (1956), pp. 261ff.

49. For a thorough discussion of Bacon's analysis, with alternatives, see e.g., J. D. Kingsbury, "The Form and Message of Matthew," in *Interpreting the Gospels,* ed. J. L. Mays (1981), pp. 66f., esp. p. 67, n. 5.

proach to Christianity is entirely alien to the Gospel of Matthew: its author still thinks in terms of law, though revised. While not explicitly quoting Jesus, James gives us "a revised and authoritative ethic, derived from the teaching of Jesus, and, as in Jesus, expressed in a revaluation of the Jewish Law."[50] It is also sometimes overlooked that James's discussion of faith and works (2:14-26), which is usually related to Paul's doctrine of justification, fits in exactly with the teaching of Matthew, especially the climactic "hearing and doing" (Mt. 7:21, 26), the Parable of the Two Sons (Mt. 21:28ff.), and the Parable of the Last Judgment (Mt. 25:31ff.).[51]

Both Matthew and James see in their doctrine—the doctrine of Jesus—the essential features of true Judaism; indeed, as Childs[52] notes, "in a manner paralleled to Matthew's Gospel, James understands the entire Old Testament from a Christian perspective with Christ being its true interpreter." That is doubtless why each presents his religion as law. But whereas Matthew sees it as a "new Torah" and at some points can be definitely anti-Jewish (e.g., Mt. 20:1-16; 21:28-32, 33-34; 22:1-14; 28:15), James is wholeheartedly interested in promoting a Christianity uncritical of and firmly grafted on Judaism, a Christianity still in its ill-fated infancy.

James also matches the Gospels in social teaching. In fact, he is particularly rich in this sphere, dealing with many aspects of the problem. But like Jesus (e.g., Luke 12:14), he nowhere sets himself up as the propounder of a "social gospel":[53] his teaching, like that of Jesus, has social and economic implications, but the appeal in both cases is essentially religious. The individual Gospels, especially Matthew and Luke, display a notable variation of emphasis that is most evident when they are apparently reporting the same saying; it cannot be denied that Luke expresses a more intense sympathy with the poor and a sharper antipathy to the wealthy classes.

Probably, as F. C. Grant thinks, the Lucan version is literally nearer to the word of Jesus than that of Matthew;[54] and it is clear that

50. Rendall, p. 66. E. J. Goodspeed thought that these affinities with Matthew (and the Didache) pointed to Antioch as the probable place of origin for James (*Introduction to the New Testament* [1937], p. 395); also Ropes, p. 39.

51. See Shepherd, *art. cit., JBL* 75.1 (1956): 45; P. Sigal, "The Halakhah of James," *Intergerini Parietis Septum* (1981): 338f.

52. B. S. Childs, *The New Testament as Canon: An Introduction* (1984), p. 437.

53. See T. Zahn, *Skizzen aus dem Leben der alten Kirche* (1894), p. 50; see Mayor, p. cxxxiii.

54. "Method in Studying Jesus' Social Teaching," in *Studies in Early Christianity*, ed. S. J. Case, p. 264. Comparison with the Qumran writings, especially the Thanksgiving Scroll, however, shows that Matthew *is* also interested in the so-

in this field the Epistle of James is linked in the closest possible fashion with Luke. One may clearly trace a common pattern of thought, turning on the contrast between riches and poverty, with the corresponding ideas of humiliation and exultation, throughout James and Luke. The contrast between rich and poor had long colored Jewish thought and language, till in the late OT period poverty had come to be synonymous with piety.[55]

The poverty–piety and wealth–wickedness identification is common to James and Luke (but absent from Matthew),[56] and the same affinity has been noted, from another angle, by Moffatt: "There is (in James and the Gospel of Luke) the same fusion of Wisdom ideas with Logia of Jesus."[57] Here Moffatt means ideas about riches and poverty, pride and humility, patience and trustfulness such as are found in the Wisdom literature and in James and Luke, indicating that both here agree in giving prominence to a strain in the teaching of Jesus that reflected this outlook.

This agreement between James and Luke is of immense value in determining the origin of the Epistle of James. It is psychologically probable that the sayings about wealth and poverty that the two authors found in their sources had special interest for them, and that they were led not only to emphasize them, but unconsciously perhaps to sharpen them: hence the "more lively pauperistic-apocalyptic strain" found in both Luke and James.[58]

Though the rhetorical form is far different from that of the Gospel pericope, the coincidences of language are striking. "But," remarks

---

cial side of Christ's gospel, though less so than Luke. See, e.g., P. U. Maynard-Reid, *Poverty and Wealth in James* (1987), p. 33.

55. See Dibelius, p. 41.

56. ". . . it would look as if the author of James had read Q in the version known to Luke" (B. H. Streeter, *The Primitive Church* [1953], p. 173).

57. *Introduction to the Literature of the New Testament* (^{3}1918), pp. 435ff. B. W. Bacon takes note of this point when he writes: "The type of ethical thought exemplified in James has been called Ebionite (Hilgenfeld). It is clearly manifest in the humanitarianism of Luke also. But with the possible exception of the prohibition of oaths, there is nothing which ought to suggest the epithet. The strong sense of social wrongs, the impatience with tongue religion, the utter ignoring of ceremonialism, the reflection on the value and significance of 'life' are distinctive simply of the 'wisdom' writers. Like these, our author holds himself so far aloof from current debate of ceremonial or doctrine as to escape our principal standards of measurements as regards place and time" ("The Epistle of James," *Encyclopaedia Britannica*^{11}, XV, 146). See C. S. Dudley and E. Hilgert, *New Testament Tensions and the Contemporary Churches* (1987), pp. 55ff.

58. Dibelius, p. 44; E. Bammel, "The Poor and the Zealots," *Jesus and the Politics of His Day,* eds. E. Bammel and C. F. D. Moule (1984), pp. 120ff.

C. H. Dodd, "the point to be noted is that these parts of the Epistle, like the gospel *pericope,* reflect a well-marked attitude or frame of mind, characterized by an acute sense of the miseries of an oppressed class, and by the expectation of a *peripeteia* (reversal of conditions)."[59] There can be no doubt that the materials in both Gospel and Epistle have been determined by the needs of the early church, and reflect the social and economic life of Palestine at that time. The situation is thoroughly Jewish, almost certainly going back to the beginnings of the Jerusalem Church and Jewish Christianity.

This limited resemblance between James and Luke confirms other evidence on the authorship of the Epistle, and in turn is reinforced by the appreciable difference between the eschatological teaching of James and that of the Synoptics, as in Jas. 5:1-11 and Lk. 12:22ff. Some scholars—for example, C. H. Dodd, in personal conversation—think they find here in Luke a rhetorical and overemphasized homiletical transformation of some simpler saying of Jesus; but it is hardly probable that, with the aim usually attributed to it, the Gospel of Luke would without authority perpetrate any such transformation: Lk. 12 appears to be a faithful record rather than a rhetorical exaggeration. The reason the Synoptic Gospels—even that of Luke—do not have the same immediacy and urgency in their predictions of the end of the world is this, that James's expectations of the Second Coming of Jesus were still part of "present conditions." Matthew's Gospel, with its unique teaching on the final judgment and its detailed descriptions, also contains clear witness to this.[60] Future and unrealized, the eschatology of Matthew and James is rooted in Jewish soil,[61] clearly reflecting the mind of Jewish Christians in Palestine who, believing deeply in the future eschaton, forsook everything and formed the nucleus of the Jerusalem Church.

CONCLUSION

We have found clear evidence that the Epistle of James is unique in that "the words of Jesus break through more often than in any other document outside the Synoptics, while at the same time they are subsumed under a single principle, the law of love,"[62] indicating that the author

59. *More New Testament Studies* (1968), p. 5, with his discussion of *peripeteia* in secular thought. See also Esler, *Community and Gospel in Luke-Acts,* pp. 164ff., esp. 189ff.

60. See G. Barth, "Matthew's Understanding of the Law," in G. Bornkamm, G. Barth, and H. J. Held, *Tradition and Interpretation in Matthew,* tr. Percy Scott (1963), pp. 58f.

61. See Davids, p. 39.

62. Davies, *The Setting of the Sermon on the Mount,* p. 402.

was familiar with a pre-Synoptic tradition he knew to be thoroughly accurate and authentic. He carefully chose a number of these sayings, wove them into the fabric of his Epistle, and, knowing that they would have special meaning for his readers, freely used them to reinforce his teaching on certain topics such as the value of trial, the need of wisdom, the generosity of God, the royal law of love, hearing and doing, faith and works, the parousia and the end time.

While much of the Epistle coincides, both verbally and conceptually, with the interests of the Gospel of Matthew on the one hand and Luke on the other, it is obviously independent of either, containing material similar in vocabulary, style, and thought to one of the special Synoptic sources. We found a particular affinity with "L." Many of the sayings in the Epistle would, it is true, be perfectly at home in pious Judaism; nevertheless, as J. H. Ropes points out, our author has more in common with those who in the "twilight period" put the sayings of Jesus then "in the air" into forms that later became sources for our Gospels,[63] which in turn suggests a very early date for the Epistle. The material has almost vivid Jewish coloring and, we believe, came straight from James the Lord's brother, one of the greatest men of early Christianity, who stood in the stream of preliterary tradition as the guardian of the *ipsissima verba* of Jesus.[64]

Here we have the earliest fruits of an authentic apostolic memory as well as an intimate filial relationship, for clearly "James had learned all the sayings of Jesus by heart—so he continually asks how what Jesus said is relevant to his day. The Epistle is his answer."[65] Thus James's paramount purpose, here as elsewhere and always, is practical. This is perhaps why he does not directly quote any of the sayings: they act like a prism through which the OT is now to be interpreted;[66] and we can imagine how a letter written by James, respected as one of "those who had been with Jesus" and saturated with the words of Jesus, would be treasured by the Jewish Church, not only for its own sake but also for its abiding ethical value—a value that, in our opinion, more than compensates for its alleged theological silences. After the fall of Jerusalem, his material was perhaps taken to Pella[67] and thence to a congenial place

63. P. 39.

64. See Hauck, p. 12.

65. Davids, "So What?" *New College Berkeley Notes* 5.2 (1983): 1.

66. For this metaphor, see B. S. Childs, *The New Testament as Canon: An Introduction* (1984), p. 437.

67. On Pella and the last days of the Jerusalem Church, see, e.g., G. Lüdemann, "The Successors of Pre-70 Jerusalem Christianity: A Critical Evaluation of the Pella-Tradition," *Jewish and Christian Self Definition,* I, ed. E. P.

where it was preserved, later incorporated in the NT canon, and thus eventually came to be known as "the Sermon on the Mount among the New Testament Epistles."[68]

Sanders (1980), 161ff.; S. Sowers, "The Circumstances and Recollection of the Pella-flight," *ThZ* 26 (1970): 305ff.; B. C. Gray, "The Movements of the Jerusalem Church during the First Jewish War," *Journal of Ecclesiastical History* 24 (1973): 1ff.; J. J. Gunther, "The Fate of the Jerusalem Church," *ThZ* 29.2 (1973): 81ff.; F. F. Bruce, *New Testament History* (1969), p. 356. See J. J. Scott, *The Church of Jerusalem, A.D. 30-100* (1969), for full bibliography; G. Vermes, F. Millar, M. Black, and E. Schürer, *The History of the Jewish People in the Age of Jesus Christ*, I (1973), 498, n. 65; II (1979), 145ff., esp. 148, n. 330. For the theory that the flight to Pella is a late legend, see S. G. F. Brandon, *Jesus and the Zealots* (1967), pp. 208-16; and further, M. Simon, "La Migration à Pella: légende ou réalité?" *Recherches de science religieuse* 60 (1972): 37-54.

68. M. Dods, *An Introduction to the New Testament* (1902), p. 191.

2. James and Paul

"God revealed himself through human personalities. There was a James and a Paul. What a difference there is between the Epistle of James and that to the Galatians. Yet there is a perfect harmony between the two, although that harmony is not human, but divine."

Karl Barth, *Eternity* 35.4 (April 1984): 20

The apostle Paul is an important witness to the primacy of James.[1] We will now examine one aspect of the relation between these two. The interpretation and valuation of the Epistle of James have long been confounded by a dominant theory of stark hostility between James and Paul, especially on the question of faith and works, a theory that is not far from suggesting that for Paul, faith alone, and for James, action alone, is of any avail for Christian salvation.

This view is like asking which blade in a pair of scissors is most necessary, or as if, in the normal person's walking, Paul said, "It is only the left leg that does it," and James, "It is only the right."[2] Elsewhere we have shown that theologically this is not so. Yet Paul does give most of his space, as it were, to "Don't forget the left leg," and James does give much of his space, as it were, to "Don't forget the right leg" in Christianity. It is now our task to consider recent attempts to explain how this (perfectly legitimate) difference is mainly due to the different situations and circumstances in which Paul and James, each in the best way possible, were working for the same gospel and the same Christ.[3]

1. E.g., Gal. 1:19; 2:9, 12; 1 Cor. 15:7.

2. See C. S. Lewis, *Mere Christianity* (1970), p. 127.

3. What immediately follows is based on the relevant evidence and conclusions of the study by W. Schmithals, *Paul and James* (1965), an extremely important book that gave me a really new feeling about the Epistle of James as one of

By an unfortunate misunderstanding, conflict is often supposed to exist between James and Paul on the question of faith and works in salvation.[4] In the traditional Jewish religion the essence of a person's relation and duty to God is *obedience*, not forced and compulsory, but willing obedience: this is so at the beginning of the OT and right on to the Christian crisis of Acts 5:29-32 (where the word is twice used with decisive emphasis). Genuine filial obedience, religious or merely human, is normally inconceivable unless it habitually exercises both heart and hand; the same is true of the question of faith and works. But circumstances may well require a speaker or writer to emphasize wholly or mainly one aspect of this twofold duty.

DECISIVE CIRCUMSTANCES

In *Paul and his Converts*, F. F. Bruce very pertinently reminds us that Paul in his Epistles constantly had to adapt himself to the situation before him, and to cope at the same time with some who thought that the gospel released them from all ethical inhibitions and others who in the name of their religion wanted to introduce an austerity that would have banished Christian liberty altogether. "We have to bear all this in mind if we are to understand the arguments he employs now on this side and now on that"[5]—what they mean, and why he uses them rather than others.

So, too, we must try to see the Epistle of James in the light of its circumstances. If the Epistle of James is concerned with matters of conduct rather than doctrine, it should be so interpreted. If, in what he says about faith and its value and function in the Christian life, James agrees (as he does) with Paul, we cannot complain if he does not go into that as fully or as philosophically as Paul sometimes does in his Epistles: neither James nor Paul professes to be expounding the whole of Christian theology and practice in a single letter.

For the Gentiles Christianity needed a different presentation from

---

the very rare documents of primitive Jewish Christianity, as close as, or even closer than, anything in Paul to the mind of Christ and the places and people he knew and loved.

4. E.g., "There can be no doubt that James 2:14ff. is inconceivable without the preceding activity of Paul" (W. G. Kümmel, *Introduction to the New Testament* [1965], p. 288). A few, e.g., Guthrie and others, take the opposite view—that Paul is responding to James. For full details, see Dibelius, pp. 174ff.; but on Dibelius, Eichholz, Via, and others, see also J. T. Sanders, *Ethics in the New Testament* (1975), pp. 115ff.

5. *Paul and his Converts* (1962), p. 17.

that required in the instruction of Jewish converts, to whom it could be, and was, offered not as a change of religion but as the glad fulfillment of a promise, in which they had long believed, from a God in whom they had long placed their faith. James does not say, as he might reasonably have said, that the higher morality of (say) Jerusalem as compared with Corinth was the fruit of God's Torah—the guiding instruction of his law, not the rabbinical details; and he might have said that the ordinary Jew's obedience to the old law was in itself an act of faith, a son's faith in his Father. Paul did not have this way of access to the pagans. In fact, however, James, like Jesus, found that the law with its host of rabbinic details destroyed the spirit and was thus a hindrance rather than a help, and that the Jews who were its adherents were a greater menace to the Christians in Palestine than the pagans were to Paul among the Gentiles.

The relationship between Paul and James is an aspect of the relationship of the Hellenistic churches founded by Paul to the primitive Jewish-Christian church in Jerusalem, and that is only one—though very significant—instance of the total relationship of Jewish Christianity to Gentile Christianity in the period before A.D. 70. For this, apart from the Epistles of Paul and James, the only important document is the account of the martyrdom of Stephen given in Acts 6:1–8:3.

In our approach to the Epistle of James we must realize how seriously the conditions under which James had to work among the Jews differed from those attending Paul's missions to the Gentiles. In the Jerusalem Church there was a split between the *Hebraioi* and the *Hellenistai;* and presently all these *Hellenistai* were scattered, but the *Hebraioi* as well as their leaders remained unmolested by the animosity of the non-Christian Jews.

To have roused such a bloody persecution of the *Hellenistai,* their doctrine must have been thought (by the non-Christian Jews at large) to strike at the very roots of traditional Judaism. It cannot have been simply that Stephen and his like spoke against the temple and the law. Criticism of these, and of the details of the law, was neither new nor rare, and did not lead to persecution. In view of Gal. 2:9 and 1:23, it is very unlikely that it could have arisen merely on the grounds of a mission that told the Gentiles to disregard the Jewish law: a non-Christian Jew did not need to care if they did.

We must therefore conclude that Stephen and his group declared the law as a whole, including circumcision, to be abolished by Christ both for Jews and Gentiles, as Paul also did. This, of course, the Jew could not endure. "Every attempt to detach a Jew on grounds of principle from the Law was bound to arouse the unanimous resistance of

Jewry, for the abolition of the law meant the national and religious surrender of Judaism. A Jewry which did not observe the law would necessarily become merged with the other nations. Whoever questioned the validity of the law for that very reason abandoned the eschatological expectation of Israel. An attack on the law of the Jews was lax conception of the law. It was forced to accept the apostasy of individuals; but it had to defend itself with every possible means against an antinomian propaganda."[6]

Schmithals sums up the bearing of this position on the relationship of Paul and James as follows:

> There was already in the early days of Christianity in Jerusalem a party among the primitive Christians who observed the Law, and another which was free from its control. The two were organised separately, which was indeed required by their different attitudes to the Law. We cannot be sure what their relation to each other was like. Even those who clung to circumcision did not observe the Law strictly, and the relationship between Paul and Jerusalem a little later completely disproves open hostility between the two sections of Jerusalem Christians at that time. It is true that their relations were certainly not free from tension. But the persecution of Stephen and the Hellenists was not due to Judaising Christians, but to non-Christian Jews. The Judaising Christians remained unmolested. But this means that the Jewish Christians who did not dispute the validity of the Law for Jews could live in the national community of the Jews, while the Jewish Christian who declared himself on principle to be free from the control of the Law was turned out of the community. *Therefore, for the Jewish Christians in Palestine the question of their attitude to the Law was not only, perhaps not even principally, a theological problem, but a question of their existence as a Church in the Jewish land.*[7]

But we must draw a distinction, lest the word "attitude" mislead. Nothing in their environment could make the faithful Christian Jews doubt or disguise the truth that Christ's redemptive work is above the law, that is, the law as a whole. But faith in Christ did not forbid a faithful Christian Jew to have his son circumcised—not, like some Galatians, to earn merit, but to preserve outwardly his community with his nation and to avoid an enmity and persecution that Christian faith did

6. Schmithals, *Paul and James*, p. 44. The importance of this for the original Jewish church in Palestine was obvious and serious: they could not openly renounce the forms of Judaism; to do so would have been "equivalent to giving up peace . . . equivalent to a war to the knife which official Judaism would have declared against it" (E. Haupt in ibid.).

7. *Paul and James*, p. 36.

not require a person to call down on his head. In our haste we must not damn all tact as hypocrisy.[8]

Schmithals well emphasizes the importance of the threat from the non-Christian Jews in Palestine to the Jewish Christian church precariously existing among them in explaining Paul's anxiety about the contributions he had collected in fulfillment of the terms of the Council of Jerusalem as stated in Gal. 2:10.[9] Pointing out that all the good manuscripts omit "that" *(hina),* interpolated between "and" *(kai)* and "service" *(diakonia)* in the Textus Receptus of Rom. 15:31, he shows that Paul is envisaging not two dangers but one danger with two aspects—the danger from the hostility of the (non-Christian) Jews in Palestine that might (but in the end did not) have the consequence of forcing the Christian Jews there reluctantly to refuse to receive the money Paul brought. In their hazardous existence among the non-Christian Jews, among whom James himself was not long to survive, soon "to be stoned on the charge of having broken the law" (A.D. 62),[10] the Christian Jews might well have hesitated to accept Paul's contributions and thereby risk the charge of being identified with the antinomian gospel that he preached to the Gentiles.

It is worth noting, moreover, that while Acts puts Paul's conversion after the death of Stephen, which is represented as the cause of the spread of Christianity beyond Jerusalem, actually, as Schmithals shows, it must have reached Syria at an early period, and in fact from Galilee. "The Galileans" is well attested as an early name for the Christians, and Paul was persecuting near Damascus when he was converted.

The missions of the Lord's brothers probably started from Galilee. Nowhere in the NT except in 1 Cor. 9:5 is anything said of these missions, but obviously the Epistle of James is related to them as Paul's Epistles are to his missionary activities, and James restricts its address to the Diaspora because of his delicate relations with the home (unconverted) Jews in Palestine: perhaps it was from the Epistle of James that Paul took the pattern of form and structure that pervades all but the most extensive examples of his missionary letters.

8. On the absolute need for the Jews to resist any undermining of their rule and practice of circumcision, see Schmithals, *Paul and James,* pp. 43-45.

9. *Paul and James,* pp. 79f.

10. *Ant.* 20.200. On the possibility that James had too liberal an attitude to the law and on the politico-religious conditions in Palestine that led to his death by Ananus II, see R. P. Martin, *New Testament Foundations,* II (1978), p. 360, n. 10 and p. 361; "The Life-Setting of the Epistle of James in the Light of Jewish History," *Biblical and Near Eastern Studies: Essays in Honor of William Sanford LaSor,* ed. G. A. Tuttle (1978), p. 101, n. 8.

LAW

Let us now consider the second chapter of the Epistle of James. James has already declared that a man's Christianity begins with an act of faith, namely, his accepting the "Word of truth" along with the promise and duty that attend that faith; and he names the Christian law of life "the law of liberty" (1:25) and presently "the royal law, according to the scripture, 'Thou shalt love thy neighbor as thyself' " (2:8). In our view these two verses crystallize the entire doctrine of the Epistle of James on the Old Law and the New Law—the "law of liberty," as James twice calls it in his short Epistle. To be sure, Paul does not use that term, but he does (once) say "law of Christ" (Gal. 6:2) and "the glorious liberty of the children of God" (Rom. 8:21).

How are we to explain James's continued preference for the term "law"; and what are we to make of what seems to be the intrusion of the contrary concept of the law in the very next verses, 2:9 and 10?

We might suggest at least one possible explanation for the comparative ease with which James thinks and speaks of "the law of liberty," whereas Paul must express the same essential thought more explicitly as "the law of Christ" or, without the term *law,* as "the glorious liberty of the children of God." To Paul, more than to James, "law" was a word of some unfortunate associations, the result partly of his revulsion from Pharisaism and partly of the Roman citizenship of which he was justly proud ("But I was born free").

To the Roman the word "law" *(lex statuta)* had for a few centuries sounded most loudly the note of *authority,* the note that holds an empire together (see Lk. 7:6ff.). The Romans had a genius for empire, an empire that in a sense is not yet dead. For the Greeks, notwithstanding Alexander's brief brilliant conquests, empire was an exception: for them the rule was in the comparatively small state, the *polis,* in which the law, *nomos,* retained a strong suggestion of its origin, "custom," as *a way of life.* OT law also began as tribal or racial rather than imperial law, and has so continued. Hence Paul, as a Roman citizen, easily thinks of that status as his freedom, while James no less easily thinks of his Christian way of life as a *nomos,* a real law of liberty; for James, the Galilean in breed and mind, seems less "conditioned" than Paul by the "metropolitan" bias of Jerusalem and Rome.

The Epistle of James itself, especially its origin and circumstances, offers an important clue to James's continued use of "law" in his two terms "law of liberty" and "royal law." The second chapter continues and completes the first of the two sections of the Epistle of James, the section in which (as sometimes in Paul's similarly proportioned

Epistles) theology figures more prominently than in the other. In the first chapter James stresses the importance of faith in a person's relations with God (e.g., in prayer) and with people (e.g., in vv. 22 and 27); in short, he insists that a person's Christian faith must be dynamic. Then, inevitably, he proceeds to consider *how* the Christian faith must operate. It must not merely be "orthonomic"; that is all right so far as it goes, but it does not go far enough. As good manners mean more than etiquette, so religion goes beyond rules. The Christian faith must be what the Greeks would have called "eunomic," an essentially social ideal of our duty to God and to each other, one ideal with these two inseparable aspects in a law under which obedience is freedom.

"Respect of persons" is a common constituent of the world of the wealthy, the sort of world that Jesus and the first Christians so vehemently condemned. James, of course, adapts his argument: he does not, he can not, *immediately* rest it on "the faith of our Lord Jesus Christ," which these offenders can scarcely claim to possess or understand; for, as he indicates in 2:1, one cannot really have that faith and behave as they were behaving.

James can appeal to them only as people who have shown some half-hearted interest in Christianity and who, being Jews, profess to be bound by the OT law, which he adduces against them (Ropes cites as relevant texts Lev. 19:15 and Dt. 1:17; 16:19, which forbid partiality in judgment). Having shown their guilt under the OT law, he reminds them that under that law "whoever shall keep the whole law, and yet offend in one point, he is guilty of all." Then, like a good missionary, he goes on to emphasize the quality of freedom in the Christian law, and, by obvious implication, the spirit in which people must try to obey that law, against which their present attitude to the poor (2:6) is a flagrant offense.

We think the current interpretations of Jas. 2:8-13 are wrong. In 2:12 James expressly contrasts the law of liberty with the pre-Christian Jewish law, where "law" is used in a restricted sense. The same restriction occurs in England where in one kind of juridical context "law" is contrasted with "equity" (which, too, is narrower in this application than in ordinary talk). It is only in this narrower sense that God's law in the OT can be contrasted with his law as a whole, by which latter we mean the sum of his principles in dealing with man (and the rest of his creation). Paul describes this latter aspect of God's law in 2 Cor. 3:17, "Where the spirit of the Lord is, there is liberty"; in contrast is the Mosaic law (vv. 6ff.). The written law condemns to death, but the Spirit gives life. The law, engraved, etc., dispensed death (NEB). So in England equity is above the law (and so is the Sovereign's prerogative of mercy).

James and Paul are in agreement in their teaching of the law of liberty. For in Paul the believer, freely justified by grace, enters into "sonship"[11] and is said to be "transferred to the kingdom of his beloved Son."[12] In James the Christian is brought into the same relationship as an heir of the Kingdom[13] by the regenerating "Word of truth."[14] In both apostles Christian sonship springs from the grace of God freely offered through the gospel of liberty, transforming the whole human concept of law. This fundamental notion of the regenerating Christ explains why the Christians regarded themselves as sons of God in a sense never possible before the incarnation: "For through faith you are all sons of God in union with Christ Jesus."[15]

In Gal. 5:2 Paul discusses the relation of law to liberty. He shows that such liberty is not license, but freedom from legalism—a liberty that issues in deeds of love. Both Paul and James knew, and sought to safeguard against, the potential antinomian tendencies inherent in such an interpretation of the law. Properly followed, however, the law of liberty guarantees an even higher standard of conduct. For James, P. J. Du Plessis says, "the theme of unity of faith and works finds its culmination in the statement that law and freedom stand in no conflict with each other."[16] By virtue of his status as a son the Christian enjoys a unique freedom—"the ability to do what we really wish" (Gal. 5:17; Rom. 7:15ff.)—and at the same time the gift "to desire that which is pleasing to God" (Phil. 2:13). So the new life is "not the copy of a model and not the dead fulfilment of a law, but an original product of the spirit ever welling up anew, springing from fellowship with Christ; a new creation of religious inwardness which draws its laws from its own being."[17]

For James and Paul alike this inward liberty is created by love, which transforms the whole concept of law. This does not mean that love is the final ingredient in the fulfillment of the law, but rather its essence. Love transforms the whole concept of law, and results not only in a new *positive* norm from which legalism (chiefly concentrating on, as it were, "keeping out of court") disappears but also in an infinitely stronger urge toward perfection than was possible under the Torah as it

11. Rom. 8:15.
12. Col. 1:13.
13. Jas. 2:8.
14. Jas. 1:18.
15. Gal. 3:26 (NEB); see also Gal. 4:7.
16. ΤΕΛΕΙΟΣ: *The Idea of Perfection in the New Testament* (1959), pp. 238f.
17. J. Weiss, *The History of Primitive Christianity,* II (1937), 557.

had been previously understood, and not only in a higher standard of ethical conduct but also in greater power to achieve it against the perpetual temptations of the flesh.

This is why Christians are free as people never were free before; and their law, the law of Christ in them, *is a law of free people,* free from bondage to sin and the flesh: it is the law of Christ lived by those who have been freed by Christ. The conflict between the lusts and God is, alas, not just a theological fiction: we know that in our appetites per se there is nothing capable of discriminating what we may or may not do by way of indulging them. *Without Christ,* the lusts of the flesh make it impossible for us to keep God's law (not rules and rituals, but the highest commandments of the Decalogue and the sovereign Law of Love). Free from the law, the Christian is now able to fulfill it, for love is the fulfillment of the law (Gal. 6:2).

JUSTIFICATION

Jas. 2:8-13 is in complete and deliberate agreement with this doctrine as enunciated (but *not* invented) by Paul: James need not, but quite possibly may, have had knowledge of some of Paul's statements of it (see, e.g., Gal. 5:1-6, addressed to Gentile converts who wished for circumcision). When you seek to be justified by way of law, your relation with Christ is completely severed: you have fallen out of the domain of God's grace (see 3:10f., NIV: "All who rely on observing the law are under a curse, for it is written: 'Cursed is everyone who does not continue to do everything written in the book of the law.'" In 2:8-13 James is not seeking to undermine or to confirm, but simply to state, the operation of the law of death and damnation (as Paul calls it in 2 Cor. 3:6f., 9).

James is *not* (as some, perhaps all, unconverted Jews suspected) seeking to abolish the law and practice of circumcision for Jews, the most prized element in the old Jewish law, the "trademark" the Jews—quite rightly, we agree—cherished as indispensable to the preservation of their national identity and existence, and the token of that nation's historic priority in God's education of man. We know, however, that tokens of such priority or superiority are often temptations to snobbish and exclusive vanity and pride. Paul can tell his Gentile converts that circumcision is no good at all to them; it is of no more good, we might say, than a wedding ring to one who is unmarried.

James does *not* deny that circumcision may be good and necessary *for Jews:* he may well have believed in its having for Jews the value we have just mentioned. But James and Paul agree completely on the paramount truth *for Jew and Gentile alike,* that the Jewish law cannot save anyone; any more, we might say, than a wedding ring can make a lawfully married woman a virtuous woman. Jews and Gentiles knew, as we do, that nothing can make a human being perfectly sinless, as the law implacably required. Paul and James therefore entirely agree, and insist, that no man, Jew or Gentile, may rely on the law to save him.

In this letter, which may have been scrutinized by Mosaic Jews from Palestine,[18] it was tactically expedient to demonstrate that James and his Jewish converts in the Diaspora did not reject the law, as Paul's Gentile Christians did. It is obvious that James himself bases his entire gospel of the Christian life on the Christian law of liberty, "the royal law" of *love* (2:8), just as Paul commends the "more excellent way" (1 Cor. 13), where, incidentally, he says that without *love,* "though I have *all faith,* so that I could remove mountains, I am *nothing*" (v. 2).

This leads us to consider the example of Abraham. Both James and Paul use this precedent—both from Gen. 15:16 (when in fact he was still Abram) and James also from Gen. 22:16—but in very different and apparently contradictory ways. But there is no real inconsistency if only we look at the context. Paul employs the example of Abraham for two reasons:

1. Paul wished to attack the idea of salvation by Jewish Torah, particularly important for the admission of the Gentiles. The distinguishing mark of the Jews, as exemplified by Abraham, was neither Torah nor circumcision but faith; and this is the only condition for salvation for *all* men and women.
2. Paul wished to controvert the Jewish belief in meritorious observance of the law; this is no substitute for faith.

Accordingly, both Jew and non-Jew must be justified, not by works of the law, but by faith, namely faith in Jesus Christ and his resurrection. In that Abraham trusted in the God of the resurrection (Rom. 4:17) his faith was of the same quality; and it is by the exercise of this faith, rather than by dependence on the Torah, that we are justified. This idea of justification is uniquely Paul's, almost a "technical formula" *(technische Abbreviatur)* designed to answer the question: How can a sinner be justified before a holy God?

James's purpose, however, is quite different. He is concerned not with the admission of Gentiles but rather with the antinomian tendencies of the early Christian Jews. In effect, James and Paul are waging two different battles, Paul the battle against self-righteous legalism and

18. See Schmithals, *Paul and James,* p. 107.

James against self-righteous complacency.[19] So James must show that true faith issues in works, and in the process of his argument he speaks much more in traditional Jewish terms of Abraham as an example of true faith. Where Abraham's belief was sufficient (Gen. 15:16), there was no room for works. But where belief requires a fulfilling act (and faith lives only by that fulfilling act), Abraham's faith was fulfilled, says James (2:21), much later in the sacrifice of his son Isaac, a sacrifice complete so far as he was concerned and leading God again to confirm the covenant. Jas. 2:22 indicates that Gen. 15:6 was fulfilled by the justification of Abraham, mentioned in Jas. 2:21 and Gen. 22:16-18, after the father's offer to sacrifice Isaac.

Declarative or demonstrative? If declarative, especially at the Last Judgment,[20] justification is by both faith and works; if, as is more likely, the verb is demonstrative, then James means that the offering of Isaac demonstrated an already existing faith and *ipso facto* salvation. "The most natural understanding of the passage," says J. A. Ziesler, "is that if belief is genuine, it will be followed by righteous action, and the man in question will be vindicated, demonstrated as righteous."[21] The solemnity of the language here in Genesis supports James in his view of this as the consummation of all that led up to it, from 15:6 onward. So Abraham was "justified"—not by works of law or even by works themselves—but by *works of faith*. His willingness to sacrifice Isaac showed that his faith was not simply a matter of words (2:16) but of deeds, and thus genuine, being "reckoned to him as righteousness" (2:22).

Abraham's faith is thus vindicated by his works, showing that a man is justified by true faith that includes works of faith and not just faith alone: "so faith apart from works is dead" (2:26). "It is true that James implies," observes Cranfield, "that had there been no works, Abraham would not have been justified; but that would have been because the absence of works would have meant that he had no real faith."[22] According to the record the test ("the practical") is given as required by God. But that is not to deny Gen. 15:6 and say that faith was of no consequence. James does not say that anywhere, and Rom. 4:9 quotes Gen. 15:6. In 4:11 Paul argues that circumcision was given later

19. See C. Brown, "Righteousness" *(dikaiosynē), NIDNTT,* III, 369f.

20. See R. Johnstone, *Lectures on the Epistle of James* (1954), pp. 216f.; also W. Beyschlag, *New Testament Theology,* I (^{2}1896), 362-69.

21. *The Meaning of Righteousness in Paul* (1972), p. 129; also C. Brown, *art. cit., NIDNTT,* III, 370; D. J. Moo, *James,* p. 109, for an excellent discussion of James's view of justification, which he takes in the "declarative" sense.

22. "The Message of James," *SJTh* 18 (1965): 340.

as the seal of Abraham's uncircumcised righteousness, shown by his faith, with a worldwide promise not confined to the circumcised (4:16). But this proves only that faith does avail for righteousness.

James does not deny this (see 1:21; 2:5; 3:17; 5:7f., 15, 17). The only ones who deny it are those whom Paul denounces by implication in Rom. 2:28f., and whom James equally denounces in 1:26f., namely, those who think the letter of the law can save without the circumcision of the heart. In denouncing the works of the letter Paul is not disparaging the works of the heart, on which he constantly lays stress. And the works on which James insists are those of the heart, never those of the letter (see 2:1, 8, 13, 15f.; 3:13).

We conclude therefore that James and Paul are in essential agreement in their ideas of "justification," for though Jas. 2:14-26 seems to contradict Paul's position, certainly "the verbal contradictions in this instance are not real contradictions."[23] Based on his own personal effort and failure to find righteousness by the law, Paul confines the term to the very *beginning* (and continuance) of a soul's Christianity, whereas James uses it as embracing not only that miracle but also the duties and/or the joys flowing from it, and, like other NT writers, of the last justification at the Final Judgment on the basis of works. "Righteousness" in James and Paul reflects both the LXX and Hebrew meaning "to be in the right" more than "to be right," and implies a relationship and a conformity to a norm, that is, a forensic or rather a "moral-forensic" usage. The emphasis on the "moral" and "forensic" varies in Paul and James: whereas James stresses the moral but does not exclude the forensic, Paul's use is primarily but not exclusively forensic.[24]

We may say, with J. Jeremias, that for James justification is "analytical" in that God recognizes the fact of righteousness related to correct conduct, as defined by the law of Christ and expected of his disciples of the New Covenant (see Mt. 5:20); for Paul it is "synthetic" in that God adds something.[25] Or, to put it another way, for Paul, "it is God who declares the believer righteous. In the case of James, it is man's works which declare him righteous by showing that he is a man of faith."[26] What Paul means surely is that faith in God—the faith that operates through love—is necessary to bring a person into a right relationship with God. What James means is that a person's genuineness—whether he be Abraham or anyone else—is vindicated not by mere

23. H. Küng, *Justification* (1964), p. 305.
24. See C. E. B. Cranfield, *The Epistle to the Romans* (ICC), I (1975), 95.
25. "Paul and James," *ExpT* 66 (1955): 370.
26. O. Michel, "Faith," *NIDNTT*, ed. C. Brown, I (1975), 605.

intellectual assent or verbal profession but by what he does: "actions speak louder than words."

Whereas Paul thinks of Christian faith and Jewish works, James thinks of Jewish faith and Christian works. While Paul mainly attacks the Jewish fallacy that human works lead to righteousness, James is concerned with the "practical aberration of a dead orthodoxy which rests on mere confession."[27]

In Judaism faith and works are inseparable; thus we have two types of righteousness, the one from faith *(dikaiosynē ek pisteōs)* and the other from law *(dikaiosynē ek nomou)*, existing side by side in complete harmony (Midr. *Tehillim* 27.13; 94.17). This is the key to the interpretation of Gen. 15:6 in Jas. 2:23.[28] Unlike Paul who, in his new exposition of justifying faith, offers his own exegesis of Gen. 15:6, James takes over the conventional Jewish teaching on faith and works[29] but applies it creatively to the contemporary needs of the Jewish Christians and their special situation. We may say that while faith makes works possible, works make faith justifiable.

Certainly we do not find justification by faith taught in this Epistle as we find it taught by Paul.[30] The fact is that not only James but the majority of Christian writers had little conception of justifying faith in Paul's sense. "James's use of 'righteousness' (1:20; 3:18) and the 'righteous' (3:5; 5:6, 16) shows," Brown points out,[31] "that he is standing in the Jewish tradition (cf. also his address in 1:1). At the same time he is appealing within that tradition to a strand of interpretation which complements rather than contradicts Paul." Here again is proof that James represents "old," and Paul "modern," tradition.[32] Indeed, sometimes James's doctrine of justification, despite crucial differences, seems to be markedly closer to, say, Qumran than Paul.[33] But we do not think that James says anything which is really in conflict

27. F. Hauck, *Die Briefe des Jacobus, Petrus, Judas und Johannes*, NTD, X (1937), 20, cited by H.-C. Hahn, "Work" *(ergon)*, *NIDNTT*, III, 1151.

28. See Dibelius, p. 179; E. Käsemann, *Commentary on Romans* (1980), p. 107.

29. See H.-J. Schoeps, *Paul: The Theology of the Apostle* (1961), p. 203; also C. Brown, *art. cit.*, *NIDNTT*, III, 369f.

30. See F. F. Bruce, "Justification by Faith in the Non-Pauline Writings of the New Testament," *EQ* 2.4 (1952): 76.

31. See *art. cit.*, *NIDNTT*, III, 370; also K. Holl, *The Distinctive Elements of Christianity* (1937), p. 49.

32. See A. Meyer, p. 108.

33. See, e.g., among others, R. H. Eisenman, *James the Just in the Habakkuk Pesher* (1986), pp. 7f., 22f., 36f., 58, 76; also *Maccabees, Zadokites, Christians and Qumran* (1983), pp. xii, 5, 43, 89f.

with Paul or—unless we label him "a consummate blunderer"[34]—that he was deliberately countering Paul's position, represented, for example, in later decadent Pauline communities.[35] We believe rather that both (and the writer to the Hebrews as well) are drawing on stock OT examples of justifying faith to which synagogue homilies were accustomed to refer.

The truth is that James says nothing that Paul would condemn—though Paul says much else that is not in James. We do not think it *necessary* to assume that James would have condemned Paul's other doctrines. However important Paul's doctrine of the atonement may be, Christ's own gospel, till near the end of his three-year ministry, had little to say of it, whereas it had much to say of the new way of life in repentance and belief. J. H. Ropes quite rightly insists that we must not approach the NT in the obfuscation of sixteenth-century (and later) theology.[36] Further, it is doubtful that Paul knew the Epistle of James;[37] but if he did, we may be sure that Paul would have understood what James was getting at and would have approved of it rather than deplored it as "utterly superficial" or inadequate,[38] though he might have phrased it differently. Whether James would have approved of Paul's way of putting it is another question! But they are not opposing each other and would have been surprised to be told that they were!

The faith of Abraham was essentially trust in God's *prima facie* unbelievable promise that Sarah would bear a child. Paul, however, with the guilt of his past murder of Christians on his mind, thinks not so much of Abraham's response to the apparently unbelievable as of God's almost unbelievable *grace* to Abraham, as to Paul himself. Paul never forgot what had been forgiven him—his persecution of the Christians—and in turn seems unable to forget his own prominence in working for other people's salvation; James never even hints that he has done anything for Christ, except in the opening signature and the candid and by no means complacent 3:1. The Epistle itself is silent on details of James's religious experience, for example, the time and manner of his crucial conversion. The impression we have is of a "once born" Christian (Dibelius) who has found God without Paul's inner torment; and

34. "But this is scarcely fair to either. If one of these writers is opposing the other, he has not done a very good job, because neither tackles the central point of the other" (L. Morris, *New Testament Theology* [1986], p. 313); also Davids, p. 21.

35. See E. Trocmé, "Les Églises pauliniennes vues du dehors: Jacques 2, 1 à 3, 13," *StEv* 2 (1964): 660-69.

36. P. 35.

37. See Mayor, pp. xci, xcviiff., 143f.; also pp. 39f.

38. Ropes, pp. 35f.

this agrees well with what we know of James the Lord's brother and his decisive, but probably gradual rather than cataclysmic, conversion.

James must have had a much better balanced mind than Paul ever achieved. However tempting, we do not base our view on Paul's alleged misogyny and supposed deprecation of marriage.[39] James, being predominantly "practical," that is, "concerned with the practice of theory," is also predominantly *positive*. Admittedly, he has spells of minatory, even comminatory, denunciation, for example, in the funeral lament for the rich (5:1-6) and the censure of (largely the same culprits) the worldly *dipsychoi* of 4:1-10, the self-deceivers (forgetful hearers) of 2:22-25, and the respecters of persons of 2:1-13. But James does not show the acute self-consciousness of which we are sometimes painfully, though compassionately, aware in Paul (e.g., Rom. 2:16; 16:15; 2 Tim. 2:8; or 1 Cor. 1:17; 7:40; 9:1-6).

We may contrast the well-balanced gravity of James, the dominant quality of his mind no less than of his style—a quality that appears in his attitude to women, even if their role in the church and family is not discussed.[40] In 2:25 Rahab the harlot, specifically so designated, is honored in company with Abraham; in 1:27 and 2:15 women are included without any patronizing disparagement as prime objects for Christian charity; and (we venture) 2:11 implicitly, and 4:4 expressly, recognize the equality of men and women in sin.[41]

As we said earlier, James clearly bases his entire gospel of the Christian life on the Christian "law of liberty," the "royal law" of love (2:8), just as Paul commended the "more excellent way" (1 Cor. 13), where he says that without *love*, "though I have *all faith*, so that I could remove mountains, I am *nothing*" (v. 2). If faith sometimes seems to bulk more largely in Paul's progress, it is mainly for two reasons.

In the first place, after the Council of Jerusalem it was agreed that Paul should go to the Gentiles, while James and the Jerusalem Church evangelized the Jews. Obviously this has a bearing on their respective emphases on faith and works: the ancestral religion of the Jews should already have brought them to the threshold of the Christianity that James was preaching to them, whereas Paul had to teach his pagans a new faith from the beginning.

39. See 1 Cor. 7:1f., 32-34. On this, see the wise cautionary verdict of F. F. Bruce, *Paul: Apostle of the Free Spirit* (1977), p. 457.

40. Laws, p. 34.

41. F. F. Bruce, in a personal note, however, differs. He says, "I don't think the issue of equality of men and women enters into the use of 'adulteresses' *(moichalides)* here" (Jas. 4:4). On adultery in the OT metaphorical sense, see H. Reisser, "Marriage" *(moicheuō)*, *NIDNTT*, II, 583.

The other, and stronger, reason is that the shattering repercussions of Paul's revulsion from his rabid Pharisaism not only made him speak so bitterly of "the works of the law" but also inclined him to regard even Christian works as always having to be kept in their place in Christian theology. Paul's ethics are theologically conditioned in that he normally takes the line: Because of what God has done for you in Christ, therefore this is how you ought to think (see "therefore" in Rom. 12:2; Eph. 4:1; Col. 3:5, etc.).

SALVATION

The main differences between James and Paul, whose unity in the propagation of the gospel is exemplary, are theological and theoretical. It is as if someone asked a golfer, "Is it the arm or the eye that makes the good driver?" "Success," he might reply, "requires both; and only a rabbinical hair-splitter could ask such a stupid question!" Paul, though shocked out of his Pharisaic confidence that "works of the law" could buy salvation, was not content with realizing that the spirit in which people do a thing is vitally important in giving meaning and value to the deed; even after his conversion he could not shake off his long-ingrained Pharisaic habit of hair-splitting, and now he had to ask himself (as we imagined ourselves questioning the golfer), "Is it the Christian *mind* or Christian *conduct* that is decisive for salvation?" It is a question that does not have much bearing on the Christian life, which (except, e.g., in the special case of imminent death) must have *both*, as James and Paul equally agree and insist.

It is perhaps in his most Pharisaical moods that Paul splits his finest hairs on the relation between faith and works; most plain Christians are satisfied that ordinarily faith and works must go together. Nevertheless, though we may not relish some of his sophisticated argumentation, we must admit that his theory is right. If the question must be answered, it is the inspiration, the Christian mind, rather than the culminating conduct that originates the Christian's personal salvation. In exactly the same way, though in much briefer compass than Paul, James puts godly wisdom before godly works and fleshly lusts before the wars and fightings to which they lead (see Jas. 3:13; 4:10, *et passim*).

Like Paul, for example in Eph. 2, James thus holds that our first step to Christianity is the acceptance of God's universal offer of grace. In 1:15-18 he uses "gift" *(dosis)* and "of his own will" *(boulētheis)* of the divine priority,[42] and in 4:6, "grace" *(charis)* of God's initiative in

42. L. Morris, *The Cross in the New Testament* (1965), p. 312. On the de-

helping, not compelling, us to turn from sin and to find new birth in Christ. This is perfectly consistent with NT doctrine. We must first humble ourselves and open our hearts to the grace freely offered to us, the grace that alone can rescue us from sin (Eph. 2:8). We are not saved by faith through grace; we are saved by grace through faith. It is not of our own doing: there is nothing in this for us to boast about. It is God who has made us what we have thus become, created (we might say, re-created) in Christ for good works "for which God has designed us" (NEB). The Roman Catholic/Protestant and pietist/activist controversies[43] about faith and works have arisen from partisans of Christian faith who seem to have thought that anyone who insisted on the (normal) need for Christian works if a Christian is to be saved was bent on derogating from the function of faith, and even setting up works as a sufficient alternative to it.

It may be helpful to consider briefly the Jewish background of faith and works. In early Hebrew religion, in many pagan religions, there was a prevalent notion that man could buy the favor of heaven, for example, by more or less lavish sacrifices. These "works" came to have a specialized sense in Hebrew, "works of the law" *(miṣwôṯ),*[44] meaning virtuous acts done with the purpose or at least the result of "acquiring merit." In so doing one could, as it were, build up a sort of credit of merit in his account with God, just as he now deposits money to feed his account at the bank. It is a notion from which even Christians are not entirely free; but its error was not unperceived in the OT: "To obey is better than sacrifice, and to heed is better than the fat of rams";[45] "to do what is right and just is more acceptable than sacrifice" (NIV);[46] "The sacrifice of the wicked is an abomination to the Lord; but the prayer of the upright"—of which we hear much in James and the Gospels—"is his delight."[47]

CREDIT/DEBIT RELIGION

Now it is obvious that no idea could be more repugnant to the whole doctrine of grace than this notion of buying God's approval by "works of merit." While we must be careful not to think of Judaism as a religion

cision of the will (here, of God), see D. Müller, "Will" *(boulomai), NIDNTT,* III, 1016f.

43. See C. Brown, *art. cit., NIDNTT,* III, 369, 374ff. with literature.

44. See Käsemann, *Romans,* p. 88; S-B III, 89ff., 160ff.; IV, 559ff.; also G. Bertram, *ergon, TDNT,* II, 646.

45. 1 Sam. 15:22.

46. Prov. 21:3.

47. Prov. 15:8. See Hos. 6:6; Ps. 40:6-8.

of "anxious book-keeping," these "works" fostered formalism and, above all, tended to denude even an otherwise good act of any real religious merit. An unbeliever's genuinely compassionate gift to a hospital is almost divine in comparison with what a professing Christian gives, if the Christian gives solely in order to buy God's favor. Thus we can readily understand why James was anathema to those Christian theologians who suspected him, or indeed condemned him in no uncertain terms, of harking back to the old idea of buying God's favor, here and hereafter, with a treasury of merit.[48]

To that notion James is in fact as hostile as Paul. Grace is not alien but essential to his gospel of God. What more comprehensive scope, or what greater emphasis, could he have given to grace than he does in 1:16-18 and 4:6 where he reminds us that it is grace that cherishes us in the truth, which itself is the gift of grace? The very root of reformed conduct is the act of faith: "Receive with meekness the engrafted Word" (1:21); and the nature of the conduct proper to that faith is made clear, directly and by contrast, in vv. 21, 26ff., and throughout the Epistle.

Moreover, the simpler statement of this duty in the Epistle of James is in no way discordant with the similar but much more abstrusely argued doctrine of Rom. 8:12-23, beginning: "Therefore, brothers, we have an obligation—but it is not to the sinful nature, to live according to it. For if you live according to the sinful nature, you will die; but if by the Spirit you put to death the misdeeds of the body, you will live" (NIV). And we will hazard the statement that on this point too James neither says nor omits anything that is not said with equal or greater force by Paul. In Rom. 1:16-18, 21, 26, 32 faith that is not fulfilled in conduct is denounced as clearly as in the Epistle of James. The wrath of God is visited upon empty faith, on those who believe the truth but live wickedly: "they knew God" (Rom. 1:21) but "did not think it worthwhile to retain knowledge of God" (Rom. 1:28, NIV). Thus they committed, and approved, the whole catalogue of sins given in vv. 24-27, 29-31. The same lesson is taught from the opposite side and with no less force in Rom. 8:1, "who *walk* not after the flesh but after the Spirit."

Rom. 8 is to an astonishing degree parallel to the Epistle of James—in the emphasis laid on the frame of mind (faith) requisite in the Christian (e.g., 8:5), the conduct due from that mind (8:1, 12f.), the adverse experience encountered in the Christian life (8:17f., 22, 26), and the need for patience (8:25). Again, could anything more explicitly

48. Neatly summarizing the differing roles of "good works" in Judaism and Christianity, C. F. D. Moule notes: "In the one they are part of the *means* of 'staying in,' in the other they are a *symptom* of 'staying in'" ("Jesus, Judaism and Paul," *Tradition and Interpretation in the New Testament,* Essays in Honor of E. Earle Ellis, ed. G. F. Hawthorne [1987], pp. 48f.).

deny the absolute, inevitable, exclusive, invariable efficacy of faith for salvation than 1 Cor. 13:2? The next verse, 13:3, we submit, is of cardinal importance for our present subject: it emphasizes that it is not what we do but the spirit in which we do it that matters. Even my feeding the poor will not please God unless my action proceeds not from vanity, for instance, or the desire to win votes, but from the genuine compassion of Christian love.

That, says James also (1:26f.), is the crucial test of our Christianity. Behind both is the authority of Jesus, who gave both the first and the second great commandments (Mt. 22:35-40; see also Mt. 23:1-7 on motives). In Gal. 5:6 Paul is thoroughly in keeping with James, both in doctrine and in language, in saying that in Christ neither circumcision nor uncircumcision avails *(ischyei)* at all, but only *pistis di' agapēs energoumenē,* "faith operating in love." In the NT only here and in Jas. 5:16 do we find the collocation *ischyei energoumenē*. It is hardly necessary to mention how much this truth, that in Christ neither circumcision nor uncircumcision matters at all, owes to the counsel and letter of James in Acts 15. Besides the word *prosōpolēmpsia* common to Rom. 2:11 and Jas. 2:1, we may well ask ourselves whether James anywhere goes further than Paul does in Rom. 2:6: (God) "will pay every man for what he has done" (NEB); see also Phil. 2:12-16: "You must work out your own salvation . . . for it is God who works in you, inspiring both the will and the deed . . . and proffer the word of life" (NEB); Phil. 3:9: "with no righteousness of my own, no legal rectitude, but the righteousness which comes from faith in Christ, given by God in response to faith" (NEB). This last passage gives a clue to the meaning of "works" when used, as often by Paul, with disparagement rather than to describe an operative faith. Himself an old Pharisee, he knew how liable Pharisees were to such insincerities as we see denounced in Mt. 23, and to the temptation to think (so it often appeared) that salvation could be bought by observance of rules and performance of ceremonies without any more regard to the spirit in which that was done than we think necessary in paying our taxes.

As for works, then, they are no less important for Paul than they are in the Epistle of James. In Ephesians, for example, Paul devotes chs. 4 and 5 (about 55 percent of the Letter) to works; and he constantly lays emphasis on the "fruit of the Spirit" and condemns the "works of darkness," as in 1 Cor. 5:1-13, where he threatens excommunication for gross incest. The situation in Corinth with its divisions, immorality, and apparent indifference to Paul's plea for the poor (2 Cor. 8–9:15) offers real parallels to the faults rebuked by James; for example, indifference to the poor, the sins of the rich, false spirituality (Jas. 2:14ff.; 3:13ff.; 5:1ff.) plus an inconsistent spiritual life-style (Jas. 3:1ff., 11ff.). Significantly Paul does not teach justification by faith to the Corinthians but rather the necessity of works.[50] The reason why James and Paul insist on "works" is, as they more than once make clear, that a profession of faith is worthless if it is not sincere. And unless it is a fact that you will die before there is time for you to do any "works," a "faith" that is followed by no sincere effort to make your conduct fit your faith is not genuine faith in God. The nature of the conduct proper to that faith is made clear in Jas. 1:21, 26f., and the rest of the Epistle.

The almost incredible recklessness of Luther's misrepresentation of James on this matter is clear from Jas. 1:21 and 26f. and Rom. 8:12-23.[49] On this matter Moffatt writes as follows:

> So far as the Christian praxis of religion is concerned, James and Paul are at one, but each lays emphasis on different syllables. The *pistis* ("faith") of Jas. 2:14-26 is an acceptance of the divine *nomos* ("law") as an impulse and standard of moral conduct; the caricature of it, which he denounces, is a belief which is divorced from good behavior. Paul could never have used the term *dead faith* (2:26), although he had often in mind the same ethical fruitlessness which roused the indignation of James. Furthermore, what James calls *erga,* Paul describes as *fruits of the Spirit* (Gal. 5:22); to Paul *erga* ("works") are *erga nomou* ("works of the law") and over against them he sets *pistis* ("faith").[51]

There is in fact no difference between James and Paul in their doctrine of the Christian spirit and the Christian life in which it must be expressed except that Paul in his theology is naturally more sensitive about the function of *faith* because he knew how previously he had given the limelight to *works.* For James and Paul alike it is not *sin* per se, but the evidential force of *unrepented sin* that may condemn a person, and it is not the nonexistent *purchasing power* of "good works" per se that may save some of us, but their evidential value, evidence, that is, of genuine Christian effort in life. Jas. 1:21 and 26f. are simply stated but in complete agreement with Rom. 8:12-23.

Further, James and Paul are completely agreed that works without faith cannot save a person.[52] No disagreement is even alleged against them on the doctrine requiring both faith and works in this matter; the allegation is that they differ in their application of the term "save," from which in fact Paul insists on excluding works while James no less strongly insists on including them. The two agree that works, unlike faith, cannot initiate a person's salvation, and also that flagrantly care-

49. See, among others, our remarks on pp. 266ff.; also pp. 392ff.
50. See C. Brown, *art. cit., NIDNTT,* III, 369.
51. *Introduction to the Literature of the New Testament* ([3]1918), p. 465.
52. See Ropes, p. 223.

less and idle faith cannot ultimately secure it unless that faith is revived in genuine—even deathbed—penitence and genuine faith in God's mercy.

If there is a difference between the two apostles, it is not on the necessity of both faith and works but in their estimates of the respective powers of faith and works, and also in their respective situations. There is no reason to believe that James, though he used the same verb "save" of the Christian faith and the actions expressing that faith, both being absolute requirements for salvation (as Paul also agrees), ranked them as equals in status for that combined operation and its accomplishment; and though Paul makes a certain use of the verb "save" of the work of faith, it is a work that, in his doctrine no less than that of James, faith by itself can begin—must be the beginner—but (in the normal human mind and body) cannot finish or even continue without "works."

To repeat, there is no difference between James and Paul in their view of the essence of the Christian spirit and the life in which it must be expressed except that Paul in his theology is naturally more sensitive to the function of *faith* because he knew how previously he had given the limelight to works.

Completing the first section of the Epistle, ch. 2 ends with a formal exposition of the relation of works to faith. It is a passage that some theologians have condemned as not merely worthless but pernicious. It is vitally important to note (1) that vv. 14-26 are not to be isolated from the rest of the Epistle, and (2) that James does *not* present works as a substitute or as an equal to faith in the matter of salvation. He does mean that faith, if not preserved and kept alive by works, perishes, or "is dead" (v. 20).

Some commentators have taken 2:24f. to signify that James is making works an equal of faith in being "able to save your souls" (1:21).[53] But in 2:21-24 James makes it clear that he is *not* making works a rival of faith: his picture of Abraham in these verses is a picture of *faith,* faith in operation—*pistis energoumenē,* if we may imitate the language of 5:16.[54] The statement in Jas. 2:22 could scarcely be clearer: his faith was fashioned by his works, and by works his faith was made perfect; v. 23 expressly merges the act into the belief, saying that this

53. For their views, see W. Nicol, "Faith and Works in the Letter of James," *Neotestamentica* 9 (1975): 7ff.

54. This verse, 5:16, seems to owe something not only, as we have already conjectured, to Ps. 20:4, but also to the pains James has been forced to take to convince the obtuse that an operative life is the only life faith can live. So, too, the anxieties of the Council of Jerusalem evoked from his resources the striking word *anaskeuazontes* (Acts 5:24).

cooperation of faith and deed fulfilled the scripture that said, "Abraham believed God, and it was counted to him for righteousness." Then, more briefly, James adds that Rahab's case was similar: "Likewise also Rahab. . . ." Her faith was expressly acknowledged in old Hebrew tradition, as in Heb. 11:31. We must not wrench 2:24 out of its context: "by works" does not mean "by works alone," but only that works in fulfillment of faith and in conjunction with faith can save—an effect that an inactive faith cannot per se produce.

If we were asked, "Are Christians saved by faith or by works?" we think we would say something like this. We are saved neither by faith nor by works; we are saved by *grace*—God's grace, as Paul himself says. There is no real dichotomy between faith and works: a living faith must work as a living heart must beat, and Christian works are simply Christian faith at work, working for that salvation toward which we believe we are, by God's grace, on our way. Like Paul and James we say, quite excusably, that faith *works* wonders; but strictly faith only *opens the door* to God's grace, which really does the work. To use an analogy, though we say *we* boil the water for our tea, strictly it is the electricity that provides the heat and boils the water. We only fill the kettle, put it on the stove, and turn on the heat—necessary preliminaries, but only preliminaries.

FAITH AND WORKS

Many of the alleged contradictions between James and Paul, therefore, are only apparent, and are explained by the fact that at one place "works" means works without faith and at another it means works of faith, the former being worthless for salvation and the latter being evidence of the faith that, by God's grace, can save.[55] Eulogies of faith are usually earned only by (in Paul's words) "faith operating in love" or "the righteousness which is of God by faith." In fact, James does not overestimate, and Paul does not undervalue, the function of works in Christian salvation; on the contrary, Paul insists on works with no less force and at much greater length than James. No one reading Peter's words in Acts 10:35 can imagine that germinal Christianity substituted dogma for deeds; and neither does Paul, even in the most advanced subtleties of his theology.

For Paul, as for James, faith without works is dead. The works

55. For a further discussion and comparison with Paul, see pp. 400ff.; 411ff.; 31f.; and for a succinct summary of the historic attempt to harmonize the two writers, see Mussner, pp. 148-50.

Paul denounces are the works of the law; James equally denounces the same works in the delusions of the "religious," a false faith in man's ability to buy salvation at a fixed price within the compass of his own resources. The works of Christian faith do not come within this condemnation; rather, they are essential to faith. Nor do they operate or suffice in or by themselves as a legal title to salvation, but by the grace of God working in and over them, as also in the miracles of the Spirit in the apostles. The works that Paul and James reject are insincere "works of the law" by which some thought they could buy salvation without their character and conduct being taken into account (see 1:26; 2:10). The works on which James and Paul insist are works of Christian faith that are genuine and sincere.[56]

One reason for James's great stress on action (works), though he is by no means for "one leg" only, is that his mission and preaching to the Jews (who are also, or are being called to be, Christians) must avoid appearing to reject the Old Law if he is not to rouse their hatred and persecution. We would expect this from James, the leader of the moderate Jewish Christians in Jerusalem, for their concern seems to have been preeminently practical. "Their Late-Jewish emphasis on orthopraxy," writes J. J. Scott,[57] "together with their ingrained distrust for Gentile propensity to idolatry and moral laxity apparently caused the Moderates to emphasize the implications of faith in Jesus for life and conduct." Paul, on the other hand, had to stress the element of faith, since he virtually substituted it for both the law and the old pagan faith. If the pagans were attracted to it, it was for exactly the wrong motives that had brought the law into condemnation in the scribes and Pharisees.

So Paul, though the "other leg" is not by any means ignored, has to stress both the necessity and the sufficiency of faith in Christ. If a Gentile convert of Paul's who had never had anything to do with Jewish or OT law suddenly decided that besides baptism he needed circumcision or the rest of the outward ritual and ceremonial of the Old Law of the OT, Paul was not unreasonable in taking that as a denial of the sufficiency of Christ's grace and redemptive work for salvation. For such Gentiles the law scarcely existed. For some Jews, too, the law for practical purposes scarcely existed.

Extended rabbinic discussions of the respective merits of faith and works show that the problem of antinomianism was not confined merely to the Gentiles but also apparently plagued the Jews. Appropri-

56. On "works," but not necessarily *saving* "works of the law," see E. P. Sanders, *Paul and Palestinian Judaism* (1977), pp. 33-58 *et passim*.

57. "Parties in the Church of Jerusalem as Seen in the Book of Acts," *Journal of the Evangelical Theological Society* 18.4 (Fall 1975): 225.

ating similar rabbinic terminology James seems, as we have seen, to be combating similar tendencies among members and parties of the Jerusalem Church. Whether he was also combating Paul or pseudo-Paulinism we do not know, although it is highly unlikely that James would directly attack Paul. James's entire argument can be explained as a controversy within Judaism and by reference to the rabbinic tradition and terminology—as can the similarities with Paul.[58]

JAMES AND THE JERUSALEM CHURCH

According to this interpretation, James is, strictly speaking, rebuking an overzealous concern with legalist orthodoxy, perhaps by the Pharisaic or Judaizing wing of the Jerusalem Church, and also their failure to realize the moral implications of the gospel. Negligent conduct then would be the only issue.[59] We suspect, however, that the same people would not be slow to welcome and communicate such antinomian versions of Paul's teaching.

We imagine that reports of this startlingly new Pauline emphasis, probably distorted, would soon reach James in Jerusalem; later he would receive it firsthand from Paul himself (Acts 21:17ff.). "It would be gratuitous scepticism," writes James Moffatt, "in view of the polemic in 2:14ff. to doubt that James draws upon the conceptions which Paul had already minted for the primitive church."[60] While we cannot speak with certainty as to the time and manner in which James would receive these reports of Paulinist heresy, it was almost certainly very early;[61] the logical source, in our opinion, would be the Gentile church at Antioch, which not only made no pretense of observing the Jewish Torah but also probably, except for a few significant instances, had little contact with the Jerusalem Church. It is intriguing to speculate on the role of Barnabas, the Jerusalem leaders' commissioner in Antioch, who seems to have stayed there for a considerable time. In Gal. 1:18 Paul tells of his own first brief trip to Jerusalem three years after his conver-

58. See, e.g., Cadoux, pp. 27ff.; Davids, p. 21; Reicke, p. 32; A. Meyer, pp. 107f.; G. Quell and G. Schrenk, *dikaioō, TDNT,* II, 219; J. D. G. Dunn, *Unity and Diversity in the New Testament* (1977), pp. 251f.

59. So, e.g., R. Schnackenburg, *The Moral Teaching of the New Testament* (1965), p. 356.

60. *Introduction to the Literature of the New Testament,* p. 466; see also R. P. Martin, *New Testament Foundations,* II (1978), 362; Kümmel, *Introduction to the New Testament,* pp. 288f.; Beasley-Murray, p. 28.

61. See G. Kittel, "Der geschichtliche Ort des Jakobusbriefes," *ZNW* 41 (1942): 94, 102.

sion. Its purpose was purely nontheological, simply "to visit" Peter.[62] During this time, he tells us, he saw no other apostle, only James the brother of the Lord.

Later (c. A.D. 44-46) on the occasion of the Judean famine prophesied by Agabus, Paul and Barnabas visited Jerusalem with a collection from the brethren at Antioch. Of this mission (which we do not identify with that of Gal. 2:1ff.)[63] we know nothing except that its immediate object was successfully accomplished;[64] we can be fairly certain that both sides had a full and frank discussion. It is significant that after the Antiochene delegation returned from Jerusalem, Barnabas and Paul were sent on their first missionary journey,[65] and having been rejected by the Jews, they turned to the Gentiles, preaching salvation by faith in Christ and not by observance of the law.[66]

On hearing that Paul did not require the Gentiles to observe the Torah before church membership, legalist Jews from Jerusalem accused Paul of preaching a mutilated gospel, and demanded that the Mosaic law be restored, that Jewish holy days and feast days be observed, and that the Gentiles be forced to submit to circumcision for salvation.[67] In Gal. 2:12 Paul speaks of certain persons who came from James and advocated circumcision to Gentile Christians. Acts 15:1 simply says "who had come from Judaea."[68]

All the evidence of Paul's meetings and relations with James himself makes it inconceivable that Paul believed him to be behind the men against whom the bitter, and indeed coarse, tone of Gal. 4:17; 5:7-12; 6:11-13 is used (see 5:12 NEB).[69] If sent by James, it must have been for some other purpose, that is, not with an ultimatum but with a warn-

62. I.e., probably in the sense of "get acquainted" with an authoritative teacher in order to get information (about a tradition?). See G. N. Stanton, *Jesus of Nazareth in New Testament Preaching* (1974), p. 93, nn. 3, 4; G. Howard, *Crisis in Galatia* (1979), pp. 36, 89 n. 114 with literature; F. F. Bruce, *The Epistle to the Galatians* (1982), p. 98; also J. D. G. Dunn, "The Relationship between Paul and Jerusalem according to Galatians 1 and 2," *NTS* 28.4 (1982): 463ff.

63. *Pace*, e.g., G. S. Duncan, *Galatians* (1934), pp. xxiiff., and others there cited.

64. Acts 12:25.

65. Acts 13:1ff.

66. Acts 13:38f.

67. Gal. 2:15–4:11. See F. Watson, *Paul, Judaism and the Gentiles* (1986), pp. 55ff.; F. F. Bruce, *Peter, Stephen, James and John* (1979), p. 92.

68. As already implied, we accept the traditional view, which identifies the visit to Jerusalem in Gal. 2:1-10 with that in Acts 15.

69. See G. Dix, *Jew and Greek*, pp. 43ff., quoted in Schmithals, *Paul and James*, p. 67, n. 12; see also J. B. Lightfoot, *Saint Paul's Epistle to the Galatians* (1865), p. 112.

ing that fellowship between Jewish and uncircumcised Gentile Christians in Antioch and Galatia could provoke non-Christian Jews to persecute the Judean church. Acts 15:24 flatly declares that these were persons "to whom we gave no such commandment."

Acts 15:5 says that, at Jerusalem on the eve of the Council of Jerusalem, "some of the Pharisaic party, who had become believers," described as "zealots for the law" (Acts 21:20), advocated the same policy, but there is no evidence that James incited or supported them. Nevertheless he would be under considerable pressure to set forth the official view of the Jerusalem Church; and what better way was there for him to set the record straight on the relation of faith to works than to write the Epistle of James?

In A.D. 49 the Council at Jerusalem met to discuss the question of admitting Gentiles into the church without observing the law, that is, becoming Jews. According to Acts 15:2, the Antiochene delegation led by Paul and Barnabas conferred with James and the other Jerusalem leaders and elders in a spirit of great harmony and resolved the disputes. It was James, rather than Peter, who now had the confidence of the ordinary member of the Jerusalem Church and was able to lead his Jewish-Christian brethren into a limited rapprochement with the Gentiles. This was because, as F. F. Bruce puts it, James had "not blotted his copybook by fraternizing with Gentiles, as Peter had done, and he continued to enjoy the esteem not only of his more conservative brethren in the Jerusalem Church but of pious Jerusalemites in general."[70] The impression that the account in Acts gives is that the entire question was much more easily settled than that in Galatians would lead us to believe.[71]

Nevertheless James is clearly the undisputed head of the Jeru-

70. *Peter, Stephen, James and John*, pp. 91f.

71. If Luke's version of the conference may be questioned, we cannot, however, go so far as those who assert that "Luke's treatment of the event is only literary-theological and can make no claim to historical worth" (Dibelius, *Acts* [[2]1973], p. 100, quoted approvingly by Schmithals, *Paul and James*, p. 38). Less radical is Hort, who rejected the idea that James played such a decisive role. In his view (see *Christian Ecclesia* [1908], pp. 79ff.) Acts 15:19 is only the expression of a personal opinion, and the letter from the apostles and elders does not mention him. But if James did not actually preside—and we dispute this—he was clearly the key person. If not, it is difficult, perhaps impossible, to explain why Luke cast him in this leading role, or why, in this aspect at least, Paul agrees with Luke (see Gal. 2:9 and above). For an excellent essay on the critical questions, see K. Lake, "The Apostolic Council of Jerusalem" and "Additional Notes" in *The Beginnings of Christianity:* Part 1, *The Acts of the Apostles*, eds. F. J. Foakes-Jackson and K. Lake, V (1920), 195-212, 1-16; S. G. Wilson, *Luke and the Law* (1983); also M. Hengel, *Acts and the History of Earliest Christianity* (1979).

salem Church, under whose guidance the law continues to be observed and the new faith interpreted in terms of the old Jewish dispensation. Not only does James preside and speak with characteristic authority, but he also composes the apostolic decree. All that is known of his attitude before or in that Council is found in Acts 15:13ff., where his sympathy with the needs of the Gentiles, his rejection of formalism, and his reference to the "beloved Barnabas and Paul" confirm James as a leader who loved peace more than faction, spirit more than law, tolerance more than bigotry. Any suggestion that his speech represents any retreat from an earlier attitude or previous speech (not evidenced) in the Council is quite unfounded.[72]

We know from the Epistle of James (even if it is argued—unconvincingly, we believe—that the actual Greek is not his) how devoted he was to Amos,[73] whom he quotes here as his authority and guide—Amos who, in his hatred of hypocrisy and perversion of religion by liberalism and formalism and oppression, is indeed a Paul among the prophets. Peter's speech emphasizes, in effect, Whitsunday as the birth of the ecumenical kingdom, extending (as promised) the "Davidian," but it does not (we think) have a word about the prophets (Acts 15:7-11). James's speech is "nearly all" from the prophets (vv. 15-18): v. 14 is "the previous speaker . . . ," vv. 19 and 20, "My sentence is . . . ," and he cannot even end without v. 21, harking back. The prophets pervade his very style—and in all these aspects, too, we are reminded of the style of the Epistle of James.

From this discussion James emerges as a devout and powerful Christian Hebrew leader, who, while remaining thoroughly Jewish, was neither a zealot for Jewish ceremonial law[74] nor an ally of the

72. G. Schofield, e.g., in his interesting (but not, we think, correct) *In the Year 62* (1962), puts this Epistle very early, before the Council of Jerusalem. He also says that James was the leader of the Judaizers. This last we cannot accept. There is no evidence that James's policy at that Council was reluctant or insincere or that he ever recanted it. James did not fool the Galatians, or Peter at Antioch, though no doubt a faction within James's group at Antioch abused the opportunity of another mission. But we could certainly not refute the early setting: in fact, we see much to commend it. See Bruce, *Peter, Stephen, James and John*, pp. 91ff.

73. Indeed, James has paragraphs that recall the very expressions used by Amos and that are full of the same fiery eloquence and prophetic fervor. "In Amos," observes D. A. Hayes, "the knowledge of God and love to man correspond to 'faith' and 'works' in James" ("The Epistle of James," *The International Standard Bible Encyclopaedia*, III [1930], 1562).

74. *Pace* Hegesippus, *q.v.*; Eusebius, *Hist. Eccl.* 2.23.4; for an evaluation, see Dibelius, pp. 15ff.; Ropes, pp. 64ff.; Lightfoot, *Saint Paul's Epistle to the Galatians*, p. 367; J. N. Sevenster, *Do You Know Greek?* (1968), pp. 17ff.; F. F.

Judaizers. The intention of the oracle is clear. F. F. Bruce summarizes it well:

> The Gentile mission in its present form has been foretold by the prophets of God with his manifest approval; no attempt should therefore be made to turn Gentiles into Jews. No disadvantage will be suffered by Moses: his law is read publicly every Sabbath in synagogues throughout the world, and Gentiles who wish to assume its yoke have every opportunity to do so (Acts 15:21). All that is necessary to avoid giving offence to synagogue worshippers is for converts to Christianity to accept certain social restrictions which will promote smooth relations with Jews and especially with Jewish Christians.[75]

Respected by the Jews of Jerusalem and apparently a strict adherent of the Torah himself, James is nevertheless able to sympathize with the problem of the Gentiles because of his breadth of vision: he resists the proposal to circumcise them and is in every way anxious to help Paul in their evangelization.[76]

By the agreement at the Council of Jerusalem, Paul virtually abandoned any mission to the Jews, leaving that to Peter and James and their helpers. So Paul had to expatiate on faith, for the only faith his Gentile converts had any opportunity to know beforehand would be some pagan faith (e.g., in Jove), and the faith Paul was preaching to these Gentiles was not only entirely new to them but presented as sufficient for their salvation. Philip Sigal thinks that James concentrates on "the triad of faith, works, and grace" (the denominator common to both Judaism and Christianity) because of historical necessity, namely, that the Christian synagogues "were becoming increasingly populated by former pagans who did not have the same attachment to Judaism."[77]

But even more pressing for James, in our opinion, than the problem of former pagans would be that of the Jews, converted and unconverted. James's gospel to the Jews was obviously not so new; yet he does not underrate what Christ *added* to old Judaism. But with the good that come to the Jewish convert from his heritage of Judaism came also the evil, the damage of substituting ceremonial performance for spiritual sincerity—a charge also laid against the scribes and Pharisees, who

---

Bruce, *New Testament History* (1971), p. 350; G. Kittel, "Die Stellung des Jakobus zu Judentum und Heidenchristentum," *ZNW* (1931), pp. 145ff.; J. J. Scott, *art. cit.*, *Journal of the Evangelical Theological Society* 18 (1975): 217ff. See also below, pp. 413ff.

75. *Peter, Stephen, James and John*, p. 94.

76. See Elliott-Binns, pp. 59ff.; Kittel, *art. cit.*, *ZNW* 41 (1942): 71-105.

77. "The Halakhah of James," *Intergerini Parietis Septum* (1981): 344.

tithed mint and cummin. As a result it is not surprising that James had much to say about both sincere religion and sincere performance.

The maintenance of the law outwardly in circumcision was necessary for the preservation of the national existence of unconverted Jews in Palestine, and James had to be careful not to rouse enmity, persecution, and hostility in the neighboring intransigent Jews. And there was no harm in a Christian's respecting, as a Jew, the old traditional religion in its pure aspects (and circumcision is not per se impure), even as Christ himself did. "We must guard against making the word 'Jewish-Christianity' a catchword and a pattern," warns G. Kittel; "Naturally there was a Jewish Christianity which threatened to counterfeit and to Judaize, and thus to corrupt the Gospel; we have sufficient clear traces of this, just as we have of the battle which Paul led against these corrupters of Christianity. But there was also another Jewish Christianity—namely Jewish people who, moved by Jesus, sought to orient their thinking and doing toward him."[78] So James found it necessary to stress the need for sincerity in Jewish Christianity exactly as Christ did in traditional Jewry.

And we see, too, why James sees less danger in addressing a letter to his converts *in the Diaspora:* the agreement at the Council of Jerusalem would more than "countenance" it. Paul *yearned* for the conversion of his Jewish brothers, and in leaving *them* to James and the others, it must be assumed that James and the others would *do* that side of evangelization.

LITERARY PARALLELS

Finally, let us briefly consider and compare James and Paul from a literary standpoint, noting the alleged literary "parallels" between their Epistles.

On this topic we take issue with G. H. Rendall:[79] he at once sharply distinguishes between the literary features of this Epistle and those of Paul's Epistles. "The hand is not that of a skilled or practised writer," and except in ch. 1 (and not always there), we find "no ordered exposition or theme," no "sustained copious flow of words such as we find in Paul, still less any of the cultured rhetoric and Hellenism that distinguish the Epistle to the Hebrews. Transitions of thought are often abrupt, . . . the movement is discursive and undeveloped, and, more and more as the Epistle proceeds, it drops into detached and undeveloped notes of exhortation."

78. Kittel, *art. cit., ZNW* 41 (1942): 104.

79. *The Epistle of St. James and Judaic Christianity,* pp. 86ff.

Rendall's evaluation does less than justice to James's rhetorical powers. The old, attractive myth of the simple unlettered preacher is still being canvassed.[80] The truth is that James and Paul have their own distinctive literary excellence, and Paul's should not blind us to James's. James here is simply not Paul. Paul was a skilled orator, a pleader, a theologian, a forensic type, and a citizen of Rome, claiming, and obtaining, his rights before Caesar's judges; James was not such. We will now try to learn what he was.

Even in his literary composition he displayed several good features. "The style is short and energetic, with a ruggedness resulting from . . . high moral tension . . . but nothing dictatorial: there are over fifty imperatives in the five brief chapters but far more often . . . of appeal than of dictation or reproof."

"The phrasing has a force and pungency" showing "character and conviction," with gifts of illustration and racy observation. In its colloquial turns and interrogations, its dramatic forms of address and second-person appeal (e.g., "brothers" three times in each of chs. 1, 2, and 3, once in ch. 4, and five times in ch. 5), the work is clearly "that of a preacher . . . a preacher of few words intensely felt, having the accent of authority and not as the scribes."

Thus, instead of what he calls Paul's "copious flow of words" and "cultured rhetoric," Rendall finds other worthy literary qualities in James. Adages and maxims occur in 1:19; 2:13, 26; but there is little quotation of more than individual OT words. On the other hand, there is distinguished original power in vocabulary: in five short chapters James has thirteen words not previously occurring elsewhere.[81]

The language of the Epistle of James is correct scriptural Greek, with a Greek vocabulary but Hebraic idiom, as was customary in such bilingualism. There is, as we have seen, no ground for the theory that our Epistle of James is a translation from an Aramaic original: its debt to the LXX is constant and clear, but it almost never draws from an original Hebrew text; on the other hand, there are many notable signs of influence from Hellenic literature and other Hellenic culture.[82]

80. So, e.g., "Unlike the Apostle Paul, James was no urbane man of letters. He was a simple, homespun preacher, perturbed at people who were not living right" ("James," *The Student Bible: New International Version,* Notes by Philip Yancey and Tim Stafford [1986], p. 1079).

81. See Rendall, p. 60; also above, pp. 119ff.

82. The metaphors, says Rendall (p. 37), are more frequent and vivid than in any other of the Epistles, and remind us of our Lord in the Synoptics. They are drawn in part from the prophets and Wisdom literature (1:11; 3:18; 4:6; 5:2, 25), and in part from personal observation of Palestine scenery familiar to James (1:6,

While the focus of the relation between James and Paul is found in James's discussion of faith and words (Jas. 2:14ff.), many other literary parallels have been adduced between their Epistles. These are most obvious in the Epistle to the Romans, especially Rom. 2:1-16 (see, e.g., Rom. 2:1, 3; see also Rom. 14:4 and Jas. 4:11 [on passing judgment on others]; Rom. 2:12 and Jas. 2:12 [judged by the law]; and Rom. 2:13 and Jas. 1:22, 25 [hearing and doing]).[83] There are other less significant parallels in the rest of Paul's Epistles (e.g., 1 Cor. 1:27 and Jas. 2:5; 1 Cor. 10:13 and Jas. 1:3).[84] Typical of the view that literary priority rested with James, G. H. Rendall argued that Rom. 13:8-10 is simply a "Pauline résumé" of Jas. 2:8-11 and that "when Paul was writing to the Romans, the words of our Epistle were fresh in his mind and came glibly from his pen."[85] But it is perhaps better to be less dogmatic, for the parallels, viewed singly and as a whole, are really too brief and fragile to permit a definite judgment, and besides they sometimes reflect stock themes.

We are therefore inclined to favor Parry's more cautious verdict; though assigning priority to Paul, he suggests that the connection need not be direct but due rather to oral reminiscences behind the written passages.[86] This hypothesis is more in line with modern research, which assumes dependence on a common catechetical stock rather than on literary borrowing per se. Especially telling are the verbal congruences found in 1 Pet. 1:6, Rom. 5:3, and Jas. 1:2, which when carefully examined tend to strengthen the theory of a common catechetical source—a point that has already received some attention.[87]

James and Paul were both anxious that their Epistles should be used as resources from which to draw material not only for catechetical primers but also for any other current mode of instruction in the Christian way of life; see Jas. 1, 3, and 4:1-10, where the topics come in much the same order but do not receive such full treatment as in other Epistles. Such coincidences could be due to derivation from an early common stock of Christian ideas and phrases; and we maintain that the Epistle of James as we have it is part of the work James did for the prop-

11; 3:4, 12, 18; 5:7). In 3:12 the "bitter water" is that of the Dead Sea, appearing in the Bible only in that connection.

83. Compare Rom. 2:3 and Jas. 2:20; Rom. 2:5 and Jas. 5:3; Rom. 2:25, 27 and Jas. 2:11; Rom. 5:4 and Jas. 1:3f.; Rom. 7:23 and Jas. 4:1; Rom. 8:7 and Jas. 4:1; Rom. 8:7 and Jas. 4:4; Rom. 13:8-10 and Jas. 2:8-10; Rom. 14:4 and Jas. 4:11.

84. See Mayor, pp. lxxxixff.; Schlatter, pp. 43-67.

85. Pp. 83-87.

86. P. 57. See also W. Sanday and A. C. Headlam, *Romans* (1950), p. lxxix.

87. See above, pp. 65ff.

agation of Christian truth. Paul also draws on this stock of Christian elements, but Paul discusses the *kērygma* as related to the *didachē*, whereas James concentrates mainly, but not solely, on the *didachē*, that is, the kind of conduct the Christian faith requires or forbids in the believer.

Above all, James is not as concerned as Paul to reconcile Mt. Sinai with Mt. Olympus. For James and his Jewish converts to Christ, the coming of Christ reinforced the ancient Jewish code of life and thought (Mt. 5:17); and however Pauline Hellenism had to vary any of the first apostolic conceptions of Christian theology, there was not such a difference between the followers of James and Paul respectively in their notions of Christian ethics as there possibly was in their Christology. The OT gives no indication that the coming Savior would be God Incarnate; but it was not quite so hard for Jesus to proceed from "Love your neighbor" to "Love your enemy," and Jas. 1:19f. is not far short of that paradox which Paul repeats in Rom. 12:19f. on the same basis as James. It is clear from 1 Cor. 15:51ff. that even Paul's creed of resurrection and salvation needed some revision in details, and it is by no means certain that the submission and assumption of 1 Cor. 15:28 are the same as the co-equal Trinitarianism of the fully developed Christian Creed (which the old Jew would consider rank polytheism).

Clearly James is not as Hellenized as Paul. On this matter E. G. Selwyn writes:

> St. James had been the leader of the Jewish-thinking element in Christianity and was reckoned from the earliest times to be one of the "pillars" of the Church. I think it would be difficult to exaggerate the influence of his martyrdom on the minds of the Christians of that day; *for it meant a decisive repudiation of Christianity by Judaism*. Hitherto Christians of Jewish origin had been able to regard themselves as a kind of Jewish sect, and this attitude was shared by many non-Christian Jews; and St. Paul's life and letters shew that the officers of the Roman Empire were prepared . . . generally to extend to the Christians the privileges which the Empire had long given to the Jews.[88]

Paul did not long (if at all) survive A.D. 62, and with the death of James the original link between Judaism and Christianity ended. Though in cast of mind James was as Jewish but less Hellenic than Paul, that was not the reason for the eclipse of the Epistle of James and the reign of Paul's Epistles in the Christian church. As we have said, the reason for the eclipse of James was the crash of Jewish Christianity with the Jews themselves and their city and temple, and the indifference or hatred of even Christian Gentiles in the following centuries.

88. Pp. 57f. (italics ours); also pp. 247-50.

We ourselves believe that, though a parallel to Paul's forensic genius and skill is not to be found in James, a faint but distinct parallel to James does appear not only in ancient Qumran but also, we suggest, even in such modern cases as that of John Milton and the friend he laments in his *Lycidas*. James is an artist, observes D. A. Hayes, and "believes in concrete realities. At the same time he has a touch of poetry in him, and a fine sense of the analogies running through all Nature and all life. There is more of the appreciation of nature in him than in all the Epistles of Paul put together."[89] City-bred, Paul was predominantly forensic and rhetorical, while James in his Epistle and in his Christian office was essentially rural and pastoral; and, in the earlier application of his word, his vocabulary is noticeably pastoral, laden with the scent of hay and breath of cows, as are so many of the Psalms, which we may be sure were as familiar to him as the land of Galilee, then "The Garden of the Earth." The quality of James's style, of which some perceive only enough to disparage it, is pastoral, akin to that of Milton's *Lycidas;* and, I believe, its pastoral knowledge and fervor betoken what the Lord and his brother James were brought up to know and love.

CONCLUSION

Because of the service and sacrifice that James gave to Christianity, and the literary culture and skill to which this Epistle from beginning to end testifies, we would not allow James to be so eclipsed as he too often is by the unique merits of Paul. While it is clear that James did not write his Epistle to combat Paul, nevertheless, as J. A. Brooks wisely points out, "his book functions within the New Testament as a means of balancing and as a means of preventing the misinterpretation and misapplication of Paul's teaching. . . . Therefore James serves as a corrective to the ever-present danger of misinterpreting Paul in such a way that an inadequate concept of Christianity will result."[90] James was not Paul, though both at first were slow to recognize the claims and quality of Jesus. When the time came, however, both died for their faith in him.

How is it that today, when Christianity more than ever needs Christians like James and teaching such as his, the Epistle of James receives little attention and even less respect? That, however, was how he began. Other early Christians died as martyrs; James lost not only his life but his people, and Gentile Christianity has given his Epistle little attention and less affection.

89. "James," *International Standard Bible Encyclopaedia,* III (1930), 1567.

90. J. A. Brooks, "The Place of James in the New Testament Canon," *SWJT* 12.1 (1969): 55.

3. Socioeconomic Background

"In this implacable society where the state uses its power to oppress and money uses its power to possess, God in Jesus Christ calls the Christian to love according to God's will; in other words, to accomplish something truly extraordinary. God never proposes that people collectively should turn society into an earthly paradise, only that individuals, called to very specific tasks, fulfill his purposes in this environment and not some other."

Jacques Ellul, *Money and Power* (1984), p. 27

Like the threads in a piece of cloth, our lives are interwoven with those of our fellow human beings. Thus the pattern of the political, social, and economic conditions of the community to which we belong are vitally important to us. As Christians (as well as non-Christians) we find ourselves dependent on home, food, and clothing in order to maintain our daily lives; we require some form of social and economic order to which we must inevitably adapt—or die.

But the kind of socioeconomic order in which that life must be lived is an order of history, the result of a development wherein people have sought to satisfy their needs; as such it is inseparable from the political order through which they seek to create responsible government, the socioeconomic order always bearing a relation to the political. At the same time the socioeconomic order reveals a development in which nations, classes, groups, even individuals have sought a relatively privileged status. This historical evolution includes good and evil, so that in the resultant socioeconomic situation the will of God is both affirmed and denied. The Christian has the difficult duty of discerning these affirmations and denials.

The writer of the Epistle of James is concerned with the life of the Christian within the prevailing social and economic situation, the external forms of which he must accept. People are called to repent and submit to God; but like his Master, James does not challenge the conditions of labor existing in his society. The Christian is to be patient, to quit grumbling, to persevere in the faithful performance of his duties (5:7ff.). He will recognize the existing order as an order of history, accepting the God-given situation in which he must seek to live as a Christian. James realizes that the final impact of Christianity may change the social and economic situation, but in his approach he accepts the order that exists, addressing his word directly to Christians submitting to that order.[1]

Christianity enjoins us to love both God and our neighbor. But since in neither of these duties can we rely on others (or ourselves) but are taught rather to rely on God's help, we are constantly faced with the problem of the evils that are apt to be fostered not only in our own hearts but also in our environment. So far as by example or persuasion we can at all lessen any of the political or other evils that we encounter, it is of course our duty to do our best to that end. But beyond that, we can normally fight these evils only with the Christian patience to which James in fact gives the opening verses of his Epistle.

In order to understand his attitude, it may be helpful to enlist the method of socio-redaction criticism, examining what James says on the subject of wealth, a study that also throws light on the economic and social background, as well as on the origin and date of the Epistle.

1. See, e.g., C. E. B. Cranfield, "The Christian's Political Responsibility according to the New Testament," *SJTh* 15.2 (1962): 176ff.; C. K. Barrett, "The New Testament Doctrine of Church and State," in *New Testament Essays* (1972), pp. 1ff.; A. Richardson, *The Political Christ* (1973); R. J. Cassidy, *Jesus, Politics and Society: A Study of Luke's Gospel* (1978); S. Liberty, *The Political Relations of Christ's Ministry* (1937); F. C. Grant, *The Economic Background of the Gospels* (1926); T. E. Schmidt, *Hostility to Wealth in the Synoptics* (1987); J. Jeremias, *Jerusalem in the Time of Jesus* (1969); S. Freyne, *Galilee: From Alexander the Great to Hadrian* (1980); R. Scroggs, "The Sociological Interpretation of the New Testament: The Present State of Research," *NTS* 26.2 (1980): 164-79; C. C. McCown, "Palestine, Geography of," *IDB*, III 636; P. F. Esler, *Community and Gospel in Luke-Acts* (1987). For material specifically relating to James, see Mayor, ch. 6; Dibelius, sec. 6, "Poor and Rich," pp. 39ff.; B. Noack, "Jakobus wider die Reichen," *StEv* 18.1 (1964): 10-25; Mussner, p. 76; P. U. Maynard-Reid, *Poor and Rich in the Epistle of James: A Socio-Historical and Exegetical Study* (1981); also *Poverty and Wealth in James* (1987); H. Köster, *Introduction to the New Testament*, I (1982), 326ff., 390ff.; G. E. M. de Ste. Croix, *The Class Struggle in the Ancient Greek World* (1981); M. Goodman, *State and Society in Roman Galilee, A.D. 132-212* (1983).

WEALTH—THE BIBLICAL VIEW

Some of the evils the Christian has to face arise out of his own heart, but many others—and our concern is with these—are fostered by the social and economic conditions of his life. The NT never asserts or implies that it is a sin to be rich; but, unlike the OT, it never tires of warning us of the constant spiritual dangers of wealth, or of condemning some who have given way, or are giving way, to its temptations. Wealth is often represented as a separate personality, a potential snare and a temptation: no man can "serve God and mammon";[2] "the deceitfulness of riches" chokes the Word of God.[3] This strain in our Lord's teaching, reflected elsewhere in the NT[4] and in later literature,[5] emphasizes the need for caution and spiritual detachment. Difficulties of interpretation, however, arise—for example, in Christ's judgment of the rich young ruler[6] and his woes on the rich.[7] They also arise in the Epistle of James.

James is no less persistent than Jesus on this subject. He is addressing both rich and poor, perhaps not all being Christians. Though we can hardly speak of a "recently revitalized pride of the poor,"[8] his sympathies are chiefly with the poorer sort, those who are exposed to hardship and oppression (see 2:6f. on the oppression of the poor). In 5:1-6[9] the rich as a social class, *not* as individuals (witness, "the rich"

2. Mt. 6:24. On this, see J. Ellul, *Money and Power* (1984), pp. 75ff.; also pp. 62ff. on wealth as a "sacrament" in the OT and on its "desacramentation" in the NT. *Economic Justice for All: Pastoral Letter on Catholic Social Teaching and the U.S. Economy* (1986), pp. 26f.

3. Mt. 13:22.

4. E.g., 1 Tim. 6:10.

5. E.g., Hermas, *Sim.* 1; *Vis.* 3.1-13.

6. Mt. 19:23f. See also P. Davids, "The Poor Man's Gospel," *Themelios* 1 (1976): 38; F. Hauck and W. Kasch, *ploutos, TDNT,* VI, 330ff.; M. Hengel, *Property and Riches in the Early Church* (1973); F. Selter, "Possessions" *(ploutos), NIDNTT,* II, 840-45.

7. Lk. 6:24.

8. Dibelius, p. 45.

9. See Mussner, pp. 193f.; also pp. 76-84, 122. Jas. 5:1-6 reminds us of the vehemence and thought of Hesiod on the same subject, e.g., *Works and Days* 201: "And there shall be no defense against evil" (*Hesiod,* tr. R. Lattimore [1959]) (compare Jas. 5:1); again in *Works and Days* 263ff.: "Beware, O barons, of such spirits. Straighten your decisions, you eaters of bribes. Banish from your minds the twisting of justice. The man who does evil to another does evil to himself, and the evil counsel is most evil for him who counsels it. The eye of Zeus sees everything. . . . He is watching us right now, if he wishes to, nor does he fail to see what kind of justice this community keeps inside it" (compare esp. Jas. 5:3 and 5:4a and b). Similarly, *Works and Days* 210 (the Hawk to the Nightingale): "He is a fool who tries to match his strength *(antipherizein)* with the stronger" (compare Jas. 5:6, "he does not resist you"; ibid., "You have condemned").

[*hoi plousioi*] and the vocative with the article), true to the Epistle's basic communal thrust, are denounced with a prophetic, but not necessarily "sub-Christian"[10] or "crude,"[11] invective. "Weep and howl over your coming miseries."

This terrible passage, full of deepest mystery, is related in almost every word to the rest of the Scriptures, especially the Prophets, the Psalms, Qumran, and the patriarchal-pietistic tradition. It is in the context of this agrarian or peasant protest that the Epistle must be understood. The great note of eschatological doom underlies all the misery, reminding us once more of Causse's phrase "le prophète contre la civilisation royale."[12] These rich in ch. 5 are unbelievers;[13] thus James does not waste words calling them to repentance, knowing that they will not heed them anyway. Only judgment awaits them—but constant use of the present tense means "eternity is NOW; judgment is NOW."

For Christians there is "a certain grim comfort in the hardship of poverty,"[14] but James urges on the faithful the same lesson from their trial as at 1:2-4. Nevertheless 2:1-12 proves that in the management of their churches, as in our congregations, some—either the rich or at least those with their footstool (*hypopodion*) above the poor—despised the poor while they favored the rich. Thus even professing Christians, in the house of God itself, are liable to worship wealth (see 2:1-2 on snobbish discriminations even in the place of worship).

The essence of the evil is not in the possession of wealth, but in the pride, greed, and inhumanity to which the rich are characteristically prone. The burden of the charge against the rich, therefore, is their attachment to wealth; neither James nor the early church is Marxist.[15] His

10. Dibelius, p. 49.

11. Hengel, *Property and Riches in the Early Church,* p. 47.

12. Cited by C. C. McCown, *The Genesis of the Social Gospel* (1929), p. 134; see also F. C. Grant, *Ancient Judaism and the New Testament* (1959), pp. 145f. Nor is James ignorant or his readers too poor to know that gold and silver do not rust. He is reminding the rich that "wanting money above all else, they will be joined forever to it. They will be possessed by it, turned over defenseless to it, so that its fate will be their own—rusty money, doomed to destruction" (J. Ellul, *Money and Power,* p. 140).

13. *Pace,* e.g., T. Zahn, *Introduction to the New Testament,* I (1909), 86.

14. Ropes, p. 282; C. S. Dudley and E. Hilgert, *New Testament Tensions and the Contemporary Churches* (1987), pp. 51ff.

15. *Pace,* e.g., K. Kautsky, *The Foundations of Christianity* (1972), p. 329. Scroggs, *art. cit., NTS* 26.2 (1980): 177ff.; Dibelius, p. 43; O. Cullmann, *The State in the New Testament* (1956) and *Jesus and the Revolutionaries* (1970); M. Hengel, *Was Jesus a Revolutionist?* (1971) and *Victory over Violence* (1975); Cassidy, *Jesus, Politics and Society,* pp. 212ff.; see E. Troeltsch's warning in *Social Teachings of the Christian Church* (1931), pp. 44f.

stance is essentially conservative: he is not writing as a revolutionary or doctrinaire socialist. Nor is he necessarily aligning himself with "the radical anti-rich policies of the Zealots."[16] What James is emphasizing is the moral danger of wealth, the sins to which the lust for it leads, the power of oppression that it gives, and that wealth belongs to another, "Mammon," who belongs to someone else, Satan. His blunt observation "You covet and cannot obtain" (Jas. 4:2) is fully realized in the area of wealth.[17] To understand his doctrine here, we must examine the social and other conditions by which it was provoked, a task that resolves itself into a study of James's milieu.

The rich were an old problem in Israel. Amos 2:6 condemns their oppression of the poor.[18] The division between rich and poor, "which had begun as a social distinction in and immediately after the Exile, was reinforced by a religious cleavage between the same classes."[19] G. F. Moore describes this cleavage in the NT period as "a strident note of class conflict. . . . The poor and humble are in their own consciousness the pious; they denounce their adversaries as ungodly."[20] The Scriptures warn the poor to temper their wrath even if the riches of the wicked be ill-gotten.[21] Frequent abuse of power over the poor made "rich" (*'āšēr*) a synonym for "wicked" (*rāša'*) in Hebrew, practically equivalent to our modern "plutocrat" or "capitalist," "with this difference, that the *'āšēr* employed his powers for his own unrighteous purposes" (see Ecclus. 13:17f.).[22] On the other hand, "poor" and "pious" were associated as they seem to be in Hebrew etymology,[23] and the Psalms of

16. H. Maccoby, *Revolution in Judaea* (1973), p. 306.

17. See Ellul, *Money and Power*, p. 95.

18. See Jas. 2:6f.

19. A. W. F. Blunt, *Israel before Christ: an account of social and religious development in the Old Testament* (1924), p. 126.

20. *Judaism*, II (1928), 156f.

21. 1 Sam. 2:7f.; Ps. 113:7f.; Prov. 15:16f.; 23:4f.; Eccl. 5:12f.; Ecclus. 11:18ff.; 20:31; Davids, pp. 41ff.; S. E. Keeble, *The Social Teaching of the Bible* (1909), *passim*.

22. S. Schechter, *Studies in Judaism* (1908), p. 79.

23. The Hebrew words for "poor" *('ānî)* and "pious" *('ānāh)*, so often used in parallelism (e.g., Pss. 68:1f.; 132:15f.), seem to come from the same root. See P. U. Maynard-Reid, *Poverty and Wealth in James* (1987), pp. 24ff.; E. Hatch, *Essays in Biblical Greek* (1889), p. 76; A. Rahlfs, *'Anaw and 'Anawim in den Psalmen* (1892), p. 58; Schoeps, pp. 352ff., esp. p. 351, n. 3; A. Gelin, *Les Pauvres de Yahve* (1953); J. Bonsirven, *Le Judaisme Palestinien au temps de Jésus-Christ*, I (1934), 41ff.; W. Sattler, "Die Anawim im Zeitalter Jesus Christi," *Festgabe für Jülicher* (1927), pp. 1ff.; Dibelius, pp. 39ff.; Mussner, pp. 76ff.; H.-H. Esser, C. Brown, "Poor" *(ptōchos)*, *NIDNTT*, II, 821ff.; Ellul, *Money and Power*, pp. 142ff.; L. E. Keck, "The Poor among the Saints in the New Testament," *ZNW* 56 (1965): 100-29, esp. 116f. on the Epistle of James; E. Bammel, *ptōchos*, *TDNT*,

Solomon,[24] the Book of Enoch,[25] and the Qumran literature[26] ("sinful wealth," "wealth of injustice") clearly testify to the resulting cleavage in Israel. Though not definitely a political party, the common people, the remnant of Israel, led the resistance to the Hellenization that was favored by the rich in the days of the Maccabees. The rich also "despised the law" in their alliance with the Sadducees.

Too few families enjoyed the prosperity that Herod restored and increased after the sack of Jerusalem in 37 B.C.,[27] and along with the prosperity came a great increase of poverty. By farming the taxes,[28] the rich—and many of these were Sadducees[29]—gained control of the collection of the revenue, and with it an opportunity for oppression.[30] The vast army of priests[31] was supported by the various Pentateuchal offer-

---

VI, 885-915, esp. 911; R. Hoppe, pp. 78ff.; Davids, pp. 42-47. "It is beyond dispute that the term *poverty* is here not a purely sociological term but resonates with a religious interpretation of the social condition" (G. Theissen, *The Social Setting of Pauline Christianity* [1982], p. 62, n. 26; also p. 187, n. 17).

24. E.g., Pss. Sol. 1:4ff.; 5:2; 10:6; 15:1; 18:2. See "Psalms of Solomon (First Century B.C.). A New Translation and Introduction" by R. B. Wright, *The Old Testament Pseudepigrapha,* ed. J. H. Charlesworth, I (1985), 643. On the identification of *ptōchos* with *dikaios* (compare Jas. 5:6), see E. Bammel, *art. cit., TDNT,* VI, 896.

25. 1 En. 94ff.; 96:4ff.; 97:8f.; see also 63:10; Ecclus. 13:17ff.

26. On the priestly attacks against the "community of the poor," see, e.g., 1QpHab 12:3ff.; 6QD 6:16ff. (9:13ff.); and for the "poor in spirit" (*'anwê rûaḥ*), as in Mt. 5:3, see 1QM 14:7. See also Mussner, p. 79; Bammel, *ptōchos, TDNT,* VI, 896ff.; L. E. Keck, "The Poor Among the Saints in Jewish Christianity and Qumran," *ZNW* 57 (1966): 54ff.; G. J. Botterweck, *'eḇyôn, TDOT,* I (1974), 27ff.; Esser and Brown, "Poor" (*ptōchos*), *NIDNTT,* II, 821ff.

27. See Cassidy, *Jesus, Politics and Society,* p. 89; also A. H. M. Jones, *The Herods of Judaea* (1938); A. Schalit, *König Herodes: Der Mann und sein Werk* (1969); S. Perowne, *The Life and Times of Herod the Great* (1956) and *The Later Herods* (1958); H. W. Hoehner, *Herod Antipas* (1972); S. Zeitlin, "Herod: A Malevolent Maniac," *JQR* 54 (1964): 1ff.; Freyne, *Galilee: From Alexander the Great to Hadrian,* pp. 190f.

28. G. Vermes, F. Millar, and E. Schürer, *The History of the Jewish People in the Age of Jesus Christ,* I, (1973), 375; O. Michel, *telōnēs, TDNT,* VIII, 94.

29. See Maynard-Reid, *Poverty and Wealth in James,* pp. 20, 30, 107 nn. 22, 23, 110 n. 25, 36, 129 nn. 35-39; L. Finkelstein, *The Pharisees: The Sociological Background of their Faith,* 2 vols. (1938); also "The Pharisees: Their Origin and their Philosophy," *HTR* 22 (1929): 191, 202-21, 232; Jeremias, *Jerusalem in the Time of Jesus,* pp. 95ff., 229ff.; F. Lang, *Saddoukaios, TDNT,* VII, 35ff.

30. See "The Case of the Bankrupt Widow" cited in Shoḥar Ṭob on Ps. 1:1; I. Abrahams, *Studies in Pharisaism and the Gospels,* First Series (1917), p. 80.

31. See Jeremias, *Jerusalem in the Time of Jesus,* pp. 163ff.; G. Vermes, F. Millar, and E. Schürer, *The History of the Jewish People in the Age of Jesus Christ,* II (1979), 244ff.

ings[32] and the half-shekel (Ex. 30:11ff.; Neh. 10:33ff.), a sort of Peter's pence[33] levied on Jews of the Dispersion as well as of Palestine. The temple became virtually "The Bank of Jerusalem,"[34] and the size of the nonproductive portion of the city's population—priests, Levites, and temple servants—was in itself an economic burden.

"Palestine," says Joseph Klausner, "came to possess a class of poor, destitute and unemployed, and landless peasants, side by side with a class of wealthy farmers, great landed proprietors and rich bankers."[35] The poverty was aggravated by overpopulation, always a problem in Jewish territory,[36] and at that time even more serious with the blessing of the *Pax Romana*. The people were also under an alien, Gentile, government: in A.D. 7, immediately after the appointment of a procurator, Coponius, Rome sent Quirinius to Judea to number the people[37] (which the Holy Law forbade[38]) for a poll-tax[39] and to value their land

32. E.g., G. A. Smith, *Jerusalem*, I (1908), 360; Jeremias, *Jerusalem in the Time of Jesus*, pp. 27-30, 147ff.; A. Büchler, "The Priestly Dues and the Roman Taxes in the Edicts of Caesar," *Studies in Jewish History* (1956), pp. 1ff.

33. F. C. Grant, *The Economic Background of the Gospels* (1926), p. 96; see also Mt. 17:24ff.; R. de Vaux, *Ancient Israel* (1965), p. 403.

34. N. Q. Hamilton, "Temple Cleansing and Temple Bank," *JBL* 83 (1964): 365ff.; Vermes, Millar, and Schürer, *The History of the Jewish People in the Age of Jesus Christ*, II, 279-84.

35. *Jesus of Nazareth* (1927), p. 189; on the landless poor, M. Goodman, *State and Society in Roman Galilee*, pp. 37-40, 121f.; 201 nn. 205f.; M. Hengel, *Judaism and Hellenism*, I (1974), 32ff.

36. Grant, *The Economic Background of the Gospels*, p. 86; but see Jeremias, *Jerusalem in the Time of Jesus*, p. 205; Hoehner, *Herod Antipas*, pp. 52f., 291-97; Cassidy, *Jesus, Politics and Society*, pp. 98f.; McCown, *art. cit.*, *IDB*, III, 637; Theissen, *The Social Setting of Pauline Christianity*, pp. 31, 60 n. 17; Goodman, *State and Society in Roman Galilee*, pp. 31ff.

37. Josephus, *Ant.* 18.1-10. See also G. Ogg, "The Quirinius Question Today (Luke 2:1-7)," *ExpT* 79 (1967): 231ff.; Goodman, *State and Society in Roman Galilee*, pp. 146, 260 n. 195; G. Vermes, F. Millar, and E. Schürer, *The History of the Jewish People in the Age of Jesus Christ, Excursus I*—"The Census of Quirinius, Luke 2:1-5," with bibliography, I (1973), 399-427.

38. See 2 Sam. 24:1-15; 1 Chr. 21:1. Yet, as F. F. Bruce rightly points out in a personal note, "the holy law did not forbid the holding of a census absolutely; consider the censuses of Numbers 1:26. What was wrong about David's census is not said expressly. The census of Quirinius was objectionable by Zealot theology, because it was the basis of the assessment of the tribute to be paid to Caesar."

39. On taxation, see Jeremias, *Jerusalem in the Time of Jesus*, pp. 124ff.; Büchler, "The Priestly Jews and the Roman Taxes," *Studies in Jewish History*, pp. 1ff.; Vermes, Millar, and Schürer, *The History of the Jewish People in the Age of Jesus Christ*, I, 373ff., 401ff.; Goodman, *State and Society in Roman Galilee*, pp. 146-48.

or, if they had none, their goods[40] for taxation and the imperial treasury (*fiscus*).[41]

People especially hate paying taxes to a foreign conqueror; what is more, however, the rich farmed out customs, harbor dues, and the like to the *publicani*;[42] and the Jewish religious exactions continued. It is estimated that altogether Roman taxes, customs, etc., and Jewish religious levies took away 40 percent of a person's income,[43] a burden far heavier for the precariously struggling populace of the city of Jerusalem than for the less impoverished peasants of Galilee.[44] Herod sometimes granted the common people a remission of taxes, a trifling alleviation of the added burden of his palatial building schemes.[45] Apart from the economic hardships, the land was filled with resentment against the conquerors in spite of the efforts the Romans made, as usual, to conciliate the inhabitants;[46] note the trials of Jesus and Paul (who, however, was a Roman citizen).

As often happens in history, unrest was worst at some distance from the capital, in Galilee, that notorious hotbed of nationalist unrest,[47] where patriotic and other outrages of robbers and assassins were frequent; and conditions were little better in any other part of Palestine.[48] The root of the trouble lay largely in the feuds within the family of

40. See Josephus, *Ant.* 18.2.26.

41. Mt. 22:17.

42. "At every stopping place by land or sea, some tax was levied" (Pliny, *Natural History* 12.63-65). See also Klausner, *Jesus of Nazareth*, pp. 186ff.; Vermes, Millar, and Schürer, *The History of the Jewish People in the Age of Jesus Christ*, I, 373ff., 401ff.

43. Under Tiberius in A.D. 17 (Tacitus, *Annals* 2.42): "The Provinces of Syria and Judea, exhausted by their burdens, implored a reduction of tribute." See Freyne, *Galilee*, p. 178.

44. See Elliott-Binns, *Galilean Christianity*, pp. 25ff.

45. Jeremias, *Jerusalem in the Time of Jesus*, p. 124; Klausner, *Jesus of Nazareth*, p. 146.

46. See P. A. Brunt, "Josephus on Social Conflicts in Roman Judaea," *Klio* (Berlin) 59 (1977): 149-53; Jeremias, *Jerusalem in the Time of Jesus*, p. 125 for citations from Josephus (e.g., *Ant.* 15.380).

47. See E. Bammel, "The Poor and the Zealots," *Jesus and the Politics of His Day* (1984), p. 114, n. 44; for a careful evaluation of the roles of the rich and the poor in the social conflicts in Roman Judea, especially with reference to James, see P. A. Brunt, *art. cit.*, *Klio* 59 (1977): 152, n. 9; Goodman, *State and Society in Roman Galilee*, p. 148.

48. See the Parable of the Good Samaritan (Lk. 10:30ff.); Jeremias, *Jerusalem in the Time of Jesus*, pp. 52f.; also A. Büchler, *The Economic Conditions of Judea after the Second Temple* (1912), pp. 55-57.

Herod[49] and in the religious hierarchy at Jerusalem, especially that of the Pharisees and the Sadducees.[50] During the life of Jesus things had been relatively quiet. Soon after the Crucifixion, however, disintegration came swiftly, ending in the revolt of A.D. 66 and the destruction of Jerusalem and its temple.

Undeniably some of the first Christians were wealthy, as in Jas. 1:9-11, where they are reminded of the evanescence of riches. Mayor cites Nicodemus, Mary of Bethany, Joseph of Arimathea, and Barnabas,[51] and one could add Zacchaeus[52] and many others, although 1 Cor. 1:26 indicates that comparatively few of the upper classes at Corinth were Christians. As F. F. Bruce observes, however, some of the Corinthian Christians were relatively more affluent than Christians in Macedonia, for example, and Paul is trying to cut them down to size.[53]

How much wealth did rich Christians like Barnabas possess? Usually we cannot speak with any precision of the amount of their capital or income, or its purchasing power. "Rich," "prosperous," and "poor" are elastic terms in the Bible, just as they are today. "Poor" indicates less, "prosperous" something more, and "rich" much, or even immensely, more than a person absolutely needs in order to survive without great anxiety or hardship. Our NT rich, as masters and not mere workmen, seem to have had ample present provision and prospective security for the needs, interests, and pleasures of their lives, and many of them obviously had sizeable capital. Rabbi Tarphon, who could remember the temple services and is a trustworthy witness of NT times, once said that a man was rich *('āšēr)* if he had a hundred vineyards, a hundred fields, and a hundred slaves to work in them[54]—and we need not impugn his standards as exalted even in wealth.

49. Klausner, *Jesus of Nazareth,* pp. 149ff.: Cassidy, *Jesus, Politics and Society,* p. 182, nn. 23f.

50. Jeremias, *Jerusalem in the Time of Jesus,* pp. 265ff.

51. P. 44.

52. Lk. 19:8; see Acts 2:41ff.; 6:7, 10-12; 8:13; 9:40; 10:1; 13:1, 12; 16:14; 17:33f.; 18:8; also 19:19; 20:28ff. This last, and similar invectives in the Epistles, including the Epistle of James, disclose that prominent sections of the Christian community and its fringes were well-to-do rather than well-doing; on this Ropes (p. 145) cites Hermas, *Vis.* 3.6. There is therefore no reason to doubt Ropes's description (p. 40) of the mixed congregations of richer and poorer Christians that James had in mind in addressing the lowly brother and the rich.

53. In a personal note.

54. b. Shabbath 25b. For rich men with detailed references to their wealth we may cite, among others, Bonjos ben Bonjos (b. 'Erubin 86a; riches are assessed here variously as ten or twenty thousand denarii, or a thousand ships and a thousand towns); the corn merchant Nicodemus or Naqdimon b. Gorion (see Jeremias,

James promptly defines the Christian attitude to wealth (1:9-11) for those who have it and for those who do not.[55] The latter, whom he characteristically takes first (v. 9), must conquer the physical and mental pains of their lack of esteem and worldly comforts with the gladdening thought of the heavenly grace and eschatological promise that eclipse all their afflictions in this world. The rich, on the other hand, must rejoice in the equal brotherhood of Christianity, and renounce, not necessarily worldly wealth itself (which can be used for Christian good), but all the pride and the groundless illusion of its permanence and the self-sufficiency that wealth is apt to breed in its *pro tempore* possessors.

Both rich and poor must see themselves in the light of the coming cosmic transformation.[56] The poor Christian can exult that despite his worldly poverty he is as good, per se, as the rich, while the rich Christian must recognize, with a proper and probably quite novel humility, that in God's sight he is, per se, no better for his wealth than his impecunious brothers, who are indeed brothers and, per se, his equals in Christ. James never regards wealth as a sign of God's favor.

As Ropes points out, "brother" *(adelphos)* is to be supplied with "rich" *(ho plousios),* the reference here being to rich and poor classes of Christians.[57] There is here no prediction that the poor Christian will literally have his belly filled or that the rich Christian will literally go bankrupt. James quite plainly makes no promise that the *peirasmoi* of

---

Jerusalem in the Time of Jesus, pp. 96, 225f.); the three Jerusalem merchants, "great men of wealth" (b. Gitt. 65a); the rich man in Antioch under Domitian with twenty thousand drachmas (Philostratus, *Apollonius* 6.39); Justus of Antioch, martyred during the reign of Diocletian, whose immense wealth is itemized in *Corpus Scriptorum Christianorum Aethiopicorum,* ser. II, 28, *Acts of Martyrs,* VII (1907), 73. On the other hand, we may note two men of Judea during Domitian's reign who owned and personally tilled land worth nine thousand denarii (Hegesippus, quoted in Eusebius, *Hist. Eccl.* 3.20.2). Although it is difficult to give a realistic equivalent of these enormous sums in our modern currency, it is perhaps helpful to remember that "a denarius a day" was a standard wage in NT times (see our coming remarks, pp. 241ff.; Jeremias, *Jerusalem in the Time of Jesus,* pp. 26, 28, 98ff., 100, 111; Goodman, *State and Society in Roman Galilee,* pp. 33ff., 196 n. 96, 198 nn. 124f.; see also Mt. 20:2; also Cassidy, *Jesus, Politics and Society,* pp. 108ff.).

55. In the short space of five chapters James mentions "rich" *(plousios)* and "riches" *(ploutos)* at least six times—five times literally (1:10f.; 2:6; 5:1f.) and once figuratively (2:5), but never, according to some commentators, "symbolically," i.e., of the spiritual self-aggrandizement of the Jews.

56. Dibelius, p. 84.

57. In his note on 1:10, with other interpretations. For a careful discussion of this "great reversal," see Maynard-Reid, *Poverty and Wealth in James,* pp. 38ff.; Davids, pp. 76f.; also, for our further remarks, pp. 324f.

any Christian, whether it be the hunger of the poor or the luxury of the rich, shall ever cease in this world; his message is that we must *use* trials as steps to triumph. His outlook is like that of Paul, who writes: For our conversation, our citizenship, our fellowship, is in heaven, from whence we look for the Savior, the Lord Jesus Christ, who will transform the body of our humble state to conform to the splendor of his body.[58] That is the "exaltation" *(hypsos)* of Jas. 1:9,[59] which emphasizes not only God's promise but also its uplifting power in the earthly life of the struggling but faithful Christian.

James, who knows that his own affinities are with the upper class (3:1), does not say that all men who die rich are damned beyond redemption. Nor does the Magnificat (Lk. 1:51-53) say that the Incarnation literally abolishes the pride, power, and wealth of the rich; instead, the Incarnation nullifies all that in quite a different way (Phil. 3:19). So the rich, "whose god is their belly, who glory in their shame, whose minds are set on earthly things," are "heading for destruction"; it is the destruction, however, of their souls, not of their worldly wealth.

So "shall pass away" (*pareleusetai;* Jas. 1:10f.) does not, *pace* Ropes, "describe the *certainty* of loss to the rich" . . ."the *sure* fate of the typical rich man" (our italics). This is simply not true. The risk of such loss should chasten the thoughts of every rich man, even if he is an atheist; but the history of plutocratic dynasties, not to mention the published valuations of "recent wills," refutes the theory that a rich man never, or hardly ever, dies without having previously lost all or almost all his worldly wealth.

First Peter has several passages that are reminiscent of the Epistle of James (see 1:3, 6f., 17, 22, 23-26). Jas. 1:10, like 1 Pet. 1:24, is dependent on Isa. 40:6f.; as Ropes admits, the original comparison in Isaiah relates to human life in general, and not to the rich. Since "shall pass away" *(pareleusetai)* cannot here simply mean "die," "for the rich is no more sure to die than the poor," Ropes has it include the destruction of the rich man's wealth by moth and rust after his death. The whole tenor of James and 1 Peter shows that James here is emphasizing, not the evanescence of human life and human wealth, but the contrast between mortal and immortal life, as Paul does in Phil. 3:19-21 quoted above. Ropes himself describes the humbling of the rich as something "which substitutes real values for transitory ones."[60]

But loss of worldly wealth is not the only key to that humbling of

58. Phil. 3:20f. See H.-H. Esser, "Height" *(hypsoō), NIDNTT,* II, 262f.

59. On the exaltation of the righteous, see D. Müller, "Height" *(hypsoō), NIDNTT,* II, 201.

60. P. 148.

the rich; in the Gospels we read of persons who without that loss had learned that humble faith in Christ and that humble love of their brothers with which, not wealth rightly used for Christian good, but the arrogance that too often springs from wealth is fatally incompatible. Thus Michel Quoist warns: "We can hardly respect money enough for the bread and toil it represents. Money is frightening. It can serve or destroy man."[61]

Each must learn this truth in time. Loyal John Evelyn observed King Charles II a few days before the latter's death and remarked: "I am never to forget the inexpressible luxury . . . as it were total forgetfulness of God (it being Sunday evening) which I was witness of the King sitting . . . with his concubines . . . while about twenty of the great courtiers were at (cards) and a table . . . a bank of at least 2,000 in gold before them. Six days later all was dust."[62]

The exceptionally appalling poverty endemic in Jerusalem has already been mentioned. The early chapters of Acts[63] throw light on the economic (and other) difficulties of Christians in the city, and the generosity of the rich in contributing their wealth for the common maintenance of the brotherhood, pending the expected early return of Christ in glory. It was a temporary expedient limited to Jerusalem, and in no way implies that private property is in itself sinful[64] or that "a religious communism of love"[65] is the only or the best way of discharging our Christian duty to the poor—a duty observed, and naturally abused, by early converts in the Diaspora.[66]

WEALTH—ECONOMIC SUMMARY

We now turn to some of the important economic conditions prevailing in NT Palestine and consider them in relation to three groups—Farmers, Merchants, and Financiers—who, though sometimes overlapped,

61. "Prayer before a Five Pound Note," in *Prayers of Life* (1963), p. 23.

62. *The Soldier's Armoury* (Jan.-June 1975): 28.

63. E.g., 2:44f.; 4:32f.; 11:27ff. (famine).

64. See Mt. 6:4; 10:42; 12:13; 25:35; 1 Cor. 16:2; Gal. 6:10. Apparently Mary the mother of Mark kept her property even in Jerusalem (Acts 12:12). See M. Goguel, *The Primitive Church* (1964), ET by H. C. Snape, p. 544.

65. So E. Troeltsch, *The Social Teaching of the Christian Churches,* I, 62. See also F. J. A. Hort, *The Way, The Truth, The Life,* p. 137; W. L. Knox, *St. Paul and the Church of Jerusalem* (1925), pp. 4ff., who argues (mistakenly, we think) for an elaborately organized communistic system in the Jerusalem administration; Dibelius, p. 43; Jeremias, *Jerusalem in the Time of Jesus,* p. 130, n. 19; and Hengel, *Property and Riches in the Early Church,* pp. 30ff. on "The 'Love Communism' of the Primitive Community."

66. See Acts 17:1-4; 2 Thess. 3:6-13.

possessed wealth, with occasional references, where relevant, to some of the poor.

FARMERS (5:1-6)

1. *Come now, you rich, weep and howl over your coming miseries.*
2. *Your wealth has rotted, your clothes are moth-eaten.*
3. *Your gold and silver is corroded, and the corrosion shall be for evidence against you, and shall devour your flesh like fire; you have laid up treasure in days that are coming to an end.*
4. *See, the wages of the workers that have mowed your fields, which you have withheld from them, cry aloud; and the outcry of the reapers has reached the ears of the Lord of Hosts.*
5. *You have lived on the earth in luxury and wantonness; you have fattened your heart for the slaughtering-day.*
6. *You have condemned and murdered the just man; he does not resist you.*

The commination of the rich in 5:1-6 includes some farmers who do not promptly and punctually pay the wages of men who have been working for them in the fields (v. 4). As Mayor points out, this charge goes deeper than that of the next pericope, 4:13-16, which concerns the illusion of self-confidence and self-sufficiency that rules the mind of godless men whose main interest is naturally the pursuit of wealth.[67] What agitates the mind of James is not so much the failure of the rich to pay wages—bad as that is—but rather the implications of this economic injustice. The crux of the social problem is spiritual, namely, the denial of the hireling's human worth.[68]

Many of these farmers, whether they owned or rented their farms, worked them[69] sometimes with slaves, but more often many others (owning or renting) relied wholly or mainly on hired labor.[70] Profiteering ab-

67. P. 153.

68. For the theological implications, see Ellul, *Money and Power,* pp. 102f.

69. On the less common use of slaves in ancient Near Eastern agriculture, see Goodman, *State and Society in Roman Galilee,* pp. 37, 199 n. 167.

70. Farms of any size at that date were of two main types, those that the owner (commercial farmer) occupied and worked with the help of slaves, and those that (apart from any under his own cultivation) a capitalist rentier leased to one or more tenant farmers. In some instances the arrangement might be combined, the owner farming some of his land and leasing the rest to a tenant farmer. See Mt. 20:1-16; 21:33-41; Lk. 20:9 and parallels. For background material, see F. M. Heichelheim, "Roman Syria," in T. Frank, *An Economic Survey of Ancient Rome* (1940); Klausner, *Jesus of Nazareth,* pp. 174ff.; S. Krauss, *Talmudische Archäologie* (1910-12), 4 vols. in 5; also A. Ben-David, *Talmudische Ökonomie* (1974).

sentee landowners, often foreigners, presented a special problem.[71] The farms were often extensive estates (not small plots of land or "fields," KJV), as the term *chōra* applied to them (5:4) indicates.[72] Agriculture in Palestine was mostly in small holdings;[73] but the drift to the towns,[74] and the hazards and difficulties of agriculture for lean purses, played into the hands of the capitalists, who had ample funds for slave labor,[75] especially in populous and fertile Galilee, and, as James shows, went far toward reducing some free labor to the same status as that of slaves.

The "hirelings" might be hired "by the job" *(ergatai)* or "by the time" *(misthōtoi)*,[76] and some of them were workers who had a holding of their own[77] but at times hired themselves out, sometimes Gentiles to

71. See, e.g., Maynard-Reid, *Poverty and Wealth in James*, p. 87 with notes; G. Theissen, *Sociology of Early Palestinian Christianity* (1978), p. 56; Goodman, *State and Society in Roman Galilee*, p. 33.

72. See Am. 3:9ff.; 2 Macc. 8:6; Lk. 12:16, 21; Jn. 4:35; Ropes, p. 288. For the concentration of power among a few, often corrupt and sometimes unscrupulous, large Palestinian landowners and their harsh treatment of smaller landowners, tenants, and workers, see, e.g., Maynard-Reid, *Poverty and Wealth in James*, pp. 85ff.

73. See Freyne, *Galilee*, p. 166. On their taxation problems and dire poverty, see Hoehner, *Herod Antipas*, p. 79.

74. "In such of the cities as achieve large size and its accompanying prosperity, the result is abundance of population and neglect of the land" ("Letter of Aristeas [Third Century B.C.–First Century A.D.], A New Translation and Introduction" by R. J. H. Shutt, *The Old Testament Pseudepigrapha*, II, ed. J. H. Charlesworth, 20, 108).

75. G. F. Moore, *Judaism*, III, 135ff.; Klausner, *Jesus of Nazareth*, pp. 182ff.; Heichelheim, in *An Economic Survey of Ancient Rome*, p. 165; also J. Jeremias, *Jerusalem in the Time of Jesus*, esp. "Gentile 'Slaves,'" pp. 344ff.; *Slaves and Day Labourers*, pp. 110ff.; *Jewish "Slaves,"* pp. 312ff.; Cassidy, *Jesus, Politics and Society*, pp. 111ff.; see also E. Schweizer, "Zum Sklavenproblem im Neuen Testament," *Evangelische Theologie* 32 (1972): 502ff.; S. Schultz, "Hat Christus die Sklaven Befreit? Sklaverei und Emanzipationsbewegungen in Abendland," *Evangelische Kommentar* 5 (1972): 13ff.; K. Fullerton and J. P. Hyatt, "Slave," "Slavery," *Dictionary of the Bible*, ed. by J. Hastings, rev. by F. C. Grant and H. H. Rowley (1963), p. 924; J. Vogt, *Sklaverei und Humanität* (1972), pp. 20ff., 131ff.; S. S. Bartchy, *MALLON CHRESAI: First Century Slavery and the Interpretation of 1 Corinthians 7:21* (1973); Goodman, *State and Society in Roman Galilee*, pp. 37f.; Freyne, *Galilee*, pp. 179f.

76. *pô'ēl (operarius)* and *śāḵîr (mercenarius)* are the Talmudic and Latin equivalents (see S. Krauss, *Talmudische Archäologie*, II [1910-12, reprinted 1966], 102, 499 nn. 705, 706; Heichelheim, *An Economic Survey of Ancient Rome*, p. 147). According to the Talmud, both the *latifundia* laborers and tenants fell into several categories with correspondingly different arrangements. For details of the less important tenant class, see Klausner, *Jesus of Nazareth*, p. 181.

77. On the peasant small-holders *(oikodespotēs, ba'al habbayiṯ)* see Mt.

Jews and vice versa, for the day *(śakîr yôm)* or a longer period,[78] the maximum contract permitted under Jewish law being six years. F. C. Grant is probably right in taking this reference to hired farm laborers in James as striking proof of the Epistle's Palestinian milieu and origin,[79] and in our judgment is another clear "fingerprint" of the Galilean author, the traditional James.

The OT often speaks of the oppression of the sojourner, the poor, and the hireling.[80] The rich farmers defer payment of the hireling's wages, contrary to Dt. 24:15; Lev. 19:13. His lot was probably worsened by the rapidly rising unemployment,[81] increased, *inter alia,* by imported manpower and slave labor; hence the references in the Talmud and the Gospels to the "rural proletariat," "unemployed *pô'ēl,*" and "the workmen idle all day" (Mt. 20:1-7). Of these J. Klausner writes: the unemployed "waxed poorer and poorer, sinking into mendicancy. . . . If they could not find work, they were reduced to want and beggary—passive victims of grievances . . . , or else imbued with violent rage and the spirit of revolt."[82] The agricultural crisis in Galilee was a root cause of the

---

13:27; M. Baba Meṣi'a; 7.1, 6; Krauss, *Talmudische Archäologie* (1910-12), II, 102, 499 n. 708.

78. M. Baba Meṣi'a 5.10. See Krauss, *Talmudische Archäologie,* II, 102, 499 n. 706; Goodman, *State and Society in Roman Galilee,* pp. 39, 45f.; Heichelheim, *An Economic Survey of Ancient Rome,* pp. 147f. See also our further remarks, p. 243, nn. 84f.

79. *The Economic Background of the Gospels,* p. 76; Cadoux, p. 30; Davids, pp. 32, 33 n. 106.

80. See W. Harrelson, "Law in the Old Testament," *IDB,* III, 77ff.; R. de Vaux, *Ancient Israel* (1965), p. 75. Theoretically at least the Talmud appears to sympathize with the hireling: see, e.g., "For four reasons the properties of landowners *(ba'ᵃlê bāttîm)* pass to the Roman treasury, the first two being deferring and withholding of wages" (b. Sukka 29 ab; Tosefta Sukka 2.5). Other sources show that parts or perhaps the whole is not paid at all. See Klausner, *Jesus of Nazareth,* p. 181; Davids, p. 177.

81. Mt. 20:1-7. See also Jeremias, *Jerusalem in the Time of Jesus,* p. 111.

82. *Jesus of Nazareth,* pp. 182, 189; Freyne, *Galilee,* p. 196; Theissen, *The Social Setting of Pauline Christianity,* p. 30; Goodman, *State and Society in Roman Galilee,* p. 40; 1 Enoch, esp. chs. 6–36, which reflects the plight of the Palestinian agricultural worker at the beginning of the second century B.C. For the late case of Rabbi bar Hana's oppression of his hired carriers, see b. Baba Meṣi'a 83a. Poseidonius tells of a female laborer who left her work to give birth to her baby and came straight back to her work on the same day, since she could not afford to lose her wages (Strabo, *Geography* 3.4.17, p. 113). In Roman times examples are found of wages being withheld from the hired laborer (e.g., Dio Chrysostom, *Orations* 7.11f.). Besides these and other ancient examples, G. E. M. de Ste. Croix cites the seventh-century *Spiritual Meadow* of John Moschus, which tells of the grievance

Jewish revolution.[83] Wages were not controlled by law but only, to some extent, by custom and precedent.[84] The denarius a day in the parable of the vineyard in Mt. 20:2 was probably the standard rate for that work in NT times; and in the case of stoneworkers, secular evidence supports Rostovtzeff's contention that "the average remuneration for technical service" was about a denarius or a drachma a day.[85] But there is the case of a Jerusalem dovecatcher,[86] and also Hillel the laborer,[87] who got only a victoriatus—roughly half a denarius—per day. From this he had to pay the caretaker, leaving only a quarter of a denarius to support himself and his family.

To be unemployed or not to receive one's wages was very serious indeed. The rich farmers in James invite suspicions that they paid their workers even less, if at all. The wage to which he refers is in coin (not in kind),[88] the OT method for such seasonal work, as, for example, in the vineyard of Mt. 20:1ff. It is clear that because of slave competition and other causes, the hireling's wages did not rise much above the poverty level. When in the gathering of his harvest, or because of a bad harvest,[89] the farmer defaulted in the payment of his laborers, the very circumstances underlined the heinousness of the sin and the certainty of judgment,[90] for "the outcry of the reapers has reached the ears of the Lord of Hosts"—a vivid scene that conjures up something like Hierony-

---

of a hired agricultural laborer who worked for a rich man for fifteen years without receiving his wages (*The Class Struggle in the Ancient Greek World* [1981], pp. 187f.).

83. See, e.g., Josephus, *War* 2.118, 433.

84. See the Laws of Hammurabi cited in J. Hastings, *Dictionary of the Bible*, V. The whole subject is thoroughly discussed in the Talmud (see b. Baba Meṣi'a 110a). On the custom of setting aside at least two days' wages per month in the Qumran community, see, e.g., 6 QD 14:14 (18:3). See, too, Bammel, *art. cit.*, *TDNT*, VI, 898.

85. *The Social and Economic History of the Hellenistic World* (1959), p. 1601. See also R. Dussaud, "Comptes d'ouvriers d'une funeraire juive," *Syria*, IV (1923), 241ff. A *sela (sil'ā)* was worth four *dinars* (denarii).

86. M. Kerioth 1.7.

87. b. Yoma 35b. Jeremias, *Jerusalem in the Time of Jesus*, pp. 111, 116; Krauss, *Talmudische Archäologie*, II, 104f., 500f. nn. 721f.

88. E.g., ritual inspection of sacrificial animals could be paid for in asses (M. Berakoth 4.5). See also Mt. 10:10; Lk. 10:7.

89. For ample evidence from both Josephus and the Talmud, see Freyne, *Galilee*, p. 178.

90. On the imminence of the Kingdom and its relation to riches in the early messianic preaching, see M. Hengel, *Property and Riches in the Early Church*, p. 29. See also Lk. 19:20; Acts 16:17; also the cries for help in the Psalms.

mus Bosch's hay cart rumbling to perdition with establishment riders ushering it from behind and poor people scrambling for food.[91] Similarly, in sixteenth-century England Robert Crowley passionately denounced the rich who used embezzled church money for their own gain:

> . . . be you sure, eternal fire
> Is ready for each hell firebrand
> Both for the housing and the land
> That you have taken from the poor,
> Ye shall in hell dwell evermore.

This recalls Josephus's terrible descriptions of the slaughter of the rich in A.D. 70 by the Idumaean Jews. Landless themselves, these desperately poor serfs were recruited by the Zealots. They "may have been equally affected by the exactions of the rich landlords, whose power base was the government of Jerusalem, the seat of wealth."[92] The land-hungry Idumaeans saw in Ananus the high priest all that they hated in the rich and powerful landowners, and were "certainly inspired not so much by hatred of Rome as by loathing of the Jewish upper classes, whom they thought responsible for their oppression."[93] While the rich, in their extravagance, thought they were storing up treasure on earth—despite the solemn warning of Jesus (Mt. 6:19ff.)—ironically, says James, they were really storing up judgment. Nor does James condemn the rich for a particular action; he is opposed to their materialistic mindset and life-style, which are the exact opposite of Christ's teaching.[94] That is why "on a note of majestic pathos" (Tasker) he returns to the plight of their unresisting victims (5:6).[95]

A similar, though not identical, kind of economic injustice described by James was perpetrated by the high priests, led by Ananias (A.D. 59 on), when they sent their men to the threshing floors to rob the poorer priests of their tithes of grain. This shows that "the clergy them-

91. See the editorial "Hay Wain into Hell," *The Economist* 291 (1984): 13 with its cover picture from Hieronymus Bosch's "The Hay Wain" at the Prado in Madrid.

92. Josephus, *The Jewish War* (1982), ed. G. Cornfield, p. 281.

93. G. H. Stevenson and A. Momigliano, ch. 25, "Rebellion Within the Empire," *Cambridge Ancient History,* X (1963), 860; also Vermes, Millar, and Schürer, *The History of the Jewish People in the Age of Jesus Christ,* I, 497f.

94. See J. Eichler, C. Brown, "Possessions" *(thēsauros), NIDNTT,* II, 831, 836 on the consumption of earthly treasure by moth and rust. For the extravagance of the wealthy, see Jeremias, *Jerusalem in the Time of Jesus,* pp. 92ff.

95. This is the usual interpretation, which we prefer to valiant efforts to link 5:6 (after an improbable delay of seventeen verses) with 4:6, making the subject God and not the poor: "God resists the proud . . . does He [God] not resist you?" See L. A. Schökel, "James 5, 2 and 4, 6," *Bib* 54 (1973): 73-76.

selves are divided on the basis of social status and access to the source of wealth."[96] Without the grain, many starved to death. In desperation the poorer priests joined forces with the Zealots and Idumaeans against Agrippa and the wealthy Sadducees; their unwillingness to offer daily sacrifice for the emperor was the immediate cause of the Jewish War, though other factors prevailed.[97]

Regardless of the position taken on the authorship of the Epistle of James, this type of economic oppression provides an appropriate setting for the events leading to the death of James the Lord's brother, at the hands of high priest Ananus II.[98] If it is true that James was a Nazirite and priest who wore the priest's mitre and linen,[99] he would naturally champion the cause of the lower clergy, incurring the wrath of the wealthy hierarchy, who would not rest until he was brought to trial and executed.

Allusions to the Sea of Galilee (1:6), the Sirocco (1:11), the Dead Sea (3:11), the Mediterranean culture of the fig, olive, and vine (3:12), and "the early and the late rain" (5:7) offer the strongest possible proof of a Palestinian or Syrian milieu.[100] Thus, "the early and the late rain" (5:7) was evidently, as Ropes remarks, "a matter of intense interest, an habitual subject of conversation, in Palestine," the special anxiety about these rains being apparently unique in that area, "as distinguished from other portions of the sub-tropical region of the Mediterranean basin."[101]

96. Josephus, *Ant.* 20.180f.; see also Freyne, *Galilee,* p. 284; E. M. Smallwood, "High Priests and Politics in Roman Palestine," *JTS* n.s. 13 (1962): 14-34, esp. 25ff.; G. A. Williamson, *The World of Josephus* (1964), pp. 137f.

97. See Vermes, Millar, and Schürer, *The History of the Jewish People in the Age of Jesus Christ,* I, 455ff.; Jeremias, *Jerusalem in the Time of Jesus,* pp. 118f.

98. See F. F. Bruce, *New Testament History* (1980), p. 349; Theissen, *Sociology of Early Palestinian Christianity,* p. 43.

99. Epiphanius, *Refutation of all Heresies* 29.3-4; 78.7-14 (Migne, *PG,* XLI, 396; XLII, 721); also Eusebius, *Hist. Eccl.* 2.23.3f., especially "James drank no wine or strong drink, nor did he eat flesh; no razor went upon his head. . . . He alone was allowed to enter into the sanctuary, for he did not wear wool but linen." On James as priest and his wearing priestly linen, see S. G. F. Brandon, *Jesus and the Zealots* (1967), p. 122, n. 2; R. H. Eisenman, *James the Just in the Habakkuk Pesher* (1986), pp. 3 nn. 8, 9, 10; 45 n. 32; 70; 92; also *Maccabees, Zadokites, Christians and Qumran* (1983), p. 48, n. 51. For another view, see H.-J. Schoeps, *Paul: Theology of the Apostle in the Light of Jewish Religious History* (1961), p. 67.

100. D. Baly, *Geographical Companion to the Bible* (1963), pp. 34, 141ff.; *The Geography of the Bible* (1957), pp. 47ff., 50f.; Smith, *Jerusalem,* I, 312.

101. P. 295 and p. 45; S-B III, 758ff. This reference to the rains of Palestine, which is unique to James, being found nowhere else in the NT or the early Fathers, is clearly based on personal experience rather than traditional or literary allusion (*pace* Laws, p. 212; so Ropes again, p. 296; Davids, pp. 183f.).

Contemporary sources show that the rich Jews owned *latifundia* in Palestine and employed many hands, and these *latifundia* were sometimes quite extensive,[102] even equipped with workshops to manufacture articles for sale and where they might pursue their capitalist ventures.[103] They were often situated near wealthy urban centers like Sepphoris and Tiberias in the more fertile area of Lower Galilee,[104] which, when wholly under cultivation, seemed like one great garden.[105] In the NT era, the landowners ("men of property" [*'attîrê nik̲sîn* or *ba'ᵃlê nik̲sîn*] in the Talmud) were mainly Herodians or Sadducees.[106] The stronghold of the Sadducees was in Jerusalem, but their temple and family estates, as well as their positions on cult ritual, made them the most influential landowners in Palestine.

If it is remembered that the priests were probably representatives of the landowning aristocracy,[107] James's polemic receives fresh point and power. It is entirely possible, of course, that James is also attacking *Christian* landowners, since some of these belonged to the church in Jerusalem.[108] His language, however—extraordinarily harsh for a pastor addressing his flock—seems to make this less likely.

TRADERS AND MERCHANTS (4:13-17)

13. *Come now, you who say, Today or tomorrow we will go to some particular city, and stay there one year, and trade, and make a profit.*

102. On the land and laborers of the fabulously wealthy R. Gamaliel II, see M. Baba Meṣi'a 5.8; M. Demai 3.1; for the large estate and olive garden worth fifteen and twenty thousand drachmae in Antioch as well as the two brothers with a mansion and estate, see Philostratus, *Apollonius* 6.39; b. Baba Bathra 7a; Goodman, *State and Society in Roman Galilee*, pp. 33, 196 n. 101.

103. b. Baba Meṣi'a 42a.

104. See Freyne, *Galilee*, p. 170.

105. E.g., "It is easier to raise a legion of olive trees in Galilee than one child in Palestine" (Gen. R. 20.6; see also b. Megilla 6a; Josephus, *War* 3.43; 3.516ff.; *Life* 40; *Ant.* 17.318. See as well E. W. G. Masterman, *Studies in Galilee* [1909], p. 17; M. Goodman, *State and Society in Roman Galilee*, pp. 22f.).

106. Klausner, *Jesus of Nazareth*, p. 180; Jeremias, *Jerusalem in the Time of Jesus*, pp. 228ff.

107. E.g., Eleazar b. Ḥarsum; Josephus. On the landed priests of Jerusalem, see Jer. 32; Am. 7:17; 1 Kgs. 2:26; see also Smith, *Jerusalem*, I, 356ff.; Klausner, *Jesus of Nazareth*, p. 180; Jeremias, *Jerusalem in the Time of Jesus*, pp. 99, 228ff. Yet, for cautionary comments, see Goodman, *State and Society in Roman Galilee*, p. 33. For the novel but unlikely view that the rich and poor addressed by James are Christian pastors "whose wealth or lack of it was becoming a bone of contention among them," see Scaer, pp. 48, 122.

108. On estate owners in the Jerusalem Church, see Acts 4:34, 37; 5:1ff.; Jeremias, *Jerusalem in the Time of Jesus*, p. 39.

14. *In fact, you know nothing of tomorrow. (For what is your life? A vapor that shows for a little and then vanishes.)*
15. *What you should say instead is, If the Lord will, we shall live and do this and that.*
16. *As it is, you vaunt yourselves in your bragging: all such vanity is wicked.*
17. *If then a man knows how to do right and does not do it, he is in sin.*

These merchants might include the old Hellenistic traders by sea *(nauklēroi)* or caravan *(emporoi)*, or others whose business was both "at home and abroad" *(pragmateutai)*.[109] James is here rebuking a fault common to all these categories, but with none of the almost personal bitterness of his attack on the farmers in the pericope 5:1-6.[110]

These merchants were the utterly materialistic core of the contemporary bourgeois prosperity; they exemplified those who loved the world *(Weltliebe)* and were divided in heart (see 4:1ff.) (Mussner). In 4:11f. the sin of arrogance was expressed in self-opinionated, self-righteous smearing of others; here it is in the equally godless self-assurance that appeared in the usual trader's mentality and prospectus.[111]

Have these merchants already appeared "as newcomers in James's congregation, with fine faces, gold rings, and smart clothing," and are they simply "industrious and ambitious small businessmen of the first century who are courageously planning future operations as travelling traders"?[112] There is no proof or probable presumption—the omission of "brothers"[113] notwithstanding—that here in 4:13-17, any more than (obviously) in all the rest of the Epistle (except in the peculiarly bitter climax in 5:1-6), the offenders rebuked may not be wealthy[114] and do not include some Christians, who (v. 17) ought to know better. Here, it is plain from v. 15, there is no thought of calling for "charity" (Noack), "reform," or sharp practice, an obvious possi-

109. As an example of the *pragmateutēs*, Heichelheim cites Firmus of Alexandria, who led an uprising in the time of the principate. See "Roman Syria," in *An Economic Survey of Ancient Rome*, p. 205.

110. See, however, R. B. Coote and A. C. Wire, "Alias James," *Pacific Theological Review* 12.1 (1979): 11; B. Noack, "Jakobus wider die Reichen," *ST* 18.1 (1964): 19ff.; Dibelius, pp. 274f.

111. An excellent example of a pagan discussion of this subject is found in Seneca's "On the Futility of Planning Ahead," *Epistles* 101, noted in Maynard-Reid, *Poverty and Wealth in James*, pp. 78f.

112. Coote and Wire, *art. cit., Pacific Theological Review* 12.1 (1979): 11; H. S. Songer, *James* (1972), p. 130.

113. Laws, p. 190.

114. Davids, p. 171; also p. 31, n. 100.

bility, with which James in this passage is not concerned, but only of arrogant self-assurance[115] and the threat of judgment.

Though not the subject of James's present rebuke, the sharp practice of profiteers was prominent enough in and before the early Christian epoch: the merchants of Lydda[116] and John of Gischala,[117] as well as profiteering and oppressive priests like Ananus,[118] were notorious examples of it. The vast ramifications of commerce to which the world had long since advanced are a prominent part of our NT background, and the Scriptures recognize its moral dangers. "How hard it is for a merchant," says Ecclesiasticus, "to keep clear of wrong or for a shopkeeper to be innocent of dishonesty."[119] Concealed theft or adultery is apt to be reckoned more heinous than the same sin done openly. The very name of merchant, with an odor of secret tricks and profits, was a byword in NT times.[120] There was also the question of "status inconsistency";[121] since the merchants worked to obtain their wealth, this, by the values of the (upper) class, was "unpardonable." We need scarcely be told that attempts recorded in the Mishna[122] to control retail prices utterly failed.

James is addressing the Jews of the Dispersion, and the mercantile condition of the Mediterranean and Asiatic and other parts of the

115. Strictly speaking, "braggings," the plural here suggesting the possibility of numerous instances of confidence in one's cleverness, luck, and so forth that brought material gain. See E. Güting, C. Brown, "Pride" *(hyperēphanos), NIDNTT,* III, 31.

116. b. Pesaḥim 62b. See the saying "rain clouds bring 'ill-luck to the profiteers (lit. fixers of market prices)'" (Gen. R. 13.12 on 2.6), cited by Jeremias, *Jerusalem in the Time of Jesus,* p. 122; also J. R. Murray, "Trade and Commerce," *Dictionary of Christ and the Gospels,* p. 739 on the merchant and his profits; see also J. D. M. Derrett, "The Parable of the Talents and Two Logia," *ZNW* 56 (1965): 187ff.

117. Josephus, *Life* 70-73; *War* 2.591.

118. See Josephus, *Life* 38; Eisenman, *James the Just in the Habakkuk Pesher,* pp. 42f., 48f.

119. 26:29, NEB; see also 27:2; 37:11.

120. So R. Jochanan: "Wisdom is not in heaven—that is to say, not to be found among the proud; nor beyond the sea—that is to say, you will not find it among traders and among travelling merchants" (b. 'Erubin 55a). Hardly accurate, however, is F. Delitzsch's statement: "In the whole Talmud there is scarcely a word of honour about trade" (*Jewish Artisan Life in the Time of Christ* [1902], p. 16. See also Jeremias, *Jerusalem in the Time of Jesus,* p. 31 for the opposite view). For classical material, see, e.g., Plato, *Laws* 918d, 919d; Xenophon, *Memorabilia* 3.7.6; Plutarch, *Pericles* 12.

121. Coote and Wire, *art. cit., Pacific Theological Review* 12.1 (1979); 11; also the Sjöberg citation, p. 14.

122. M. Baba Meṣi'a 4.3.

world are relevant to the understanding of his Epistle. Travel and trade were brisk: though not well served by roads, Jerusalem was "rich in trade."[123] Palestine, the bridge between East and West, was well placed for making full use of first-class Roman roads giving access to the remoter vital trade routes of the known world. Besides being a flourishing domestic trade, one of the most remunerative industries in Galilee was the export of pickled and salted fish to quite distant places, not excluding Rome.[124] She also had within her borders several roads available for extensive world trade,[125] for example, the route from Damascus to Acre and that from Damascus to Egypt. Moreover, she produced exports both for her neighbors and for distant lands. So typically Julianus of Egypt speaks of "sea voyages that give profit."[126] Jewish traders flourished not only in Palestine but also to the utmost ends of the Diaspora to which the Epistle was addressed.

By making travel easier and safer, Rome injected fresh life into Near Eastern commerce; and her roads linked up with the caravan routes of the Empire. The merchants who used them slept at night in inns, or by the roadside in specially fortified camps. James's reference (4:13) to a trader's absence for a year on such a venture (not necessarily by caravan) is not without support from the NT, for example, travellers like Aquila and Priscilla, and from the extant sources.[127] The largest trading centers on the Palestine coast were Hellenistic,[128] but there were many

123. Letter of Aristeas 114. See Jeremias, *Jerusalem in the Time of Jesus*, pp. 27ff., 51ff., 58f.

124. Goodman, *State and Society in Roman Galilee*, pp. 24, 192 n. 102; Freyne, *Galilee*, pp. 173f.; Hoehner, *Herod Antipas*, pp. 65ff., especially 67, n. 12 for reservations; M. 'Abodah Zarah 2.6; M. Nedarim 6.4; Herodotus 9.130; Strabo, *Geography* 16.2.45, p. 297; Aelian, *Anecdotes on Various Subjects* 12.9.

125. Masterman, *Studies in Galilee*, pp. 10f.; M. P. Charlesworth, *Trade Routes and Commerce of the Roman Empire* (1941), ch. 3; Jeremias, *Jerusalem in the Time of Jesus*, pp. 31ff., 58ff.; Smith, *Historical Geography of the Holy Land*, pp. 425ff.; "Trade and Commerce," *Encyclopedia Biblica*, IV, cols. 5145-99; Baly, *The Geography of the Bible*, pp. 95ff., 136f., 172, 185, 216; *Geographical Companion to the Bible;* also Goodman, *State and Society in Roman Galilee*, pp. 16ff.

126. *Greek Anthology* 9.446, tr. W. R. Paton, Loeb Classical Library, III (1948), 251.

127. This material is conveniently assembled by Heichelheim, "Roman Syria," in *An Economic Survey of Ancient Rome*, pp. 210f.; see also H. A. Kent, Jr., *Faith that Works* (1986), p. 160; Jeremias, *Jerusalem in the Time of Jesus*, pp. 31ff., 58ff.; Theissen, *The Social Setting of Pauline Christianity*, pp. 11ff.; Goodman, *State and Society in Roman Galilee*, pp. 16f., 61f.

128. See Josephus: "We (Jews) neither inhabit a maritime country nor do we delight in merchandise" (*Against Apion* 1.60); Hengel, *Judaism and Hellenism*, I, 32f.; M. Goodman, pp. 19, 188 n. 8.

Jews in Palestine who had capital to start a lucrative business.[129] Some, like John of Gischala, were laymen;[130] others, such as John Hyrcanus, were priests. The high-priestly caste figured largely in trade. As a lucrative shopowner, the high priest Ananias, for example, was known as the "great procurer of money." "In those days," writes George Adam Smith, "nearly every priest must have been a trader."[131] The prayers of the Day of Atonement included one for "a year of trade."[132]

Trade on all scales flourished in NT Palestine, and market days and markets (*agorai*; see Mk. 6:56), some named after the merchant or his trade, had long been in existence;[133] the shouts of those crying their wares were heard in the streets.[134] To say that trade was the lifeblood of the Jew in NT Palestine is merely a truism. The merchants whom James rebuked for their arrogant self-assurance are not the small retailers but traders on a large scale, who have amassed considerable wealth.[135]

It is clear that the Jews played a key role in the commerce of the Roman Near East; many of them were wholesale traders,[136] keepers of large shops, shipowners, bankers, or contractors.[137] Naval allusions in James are certainly not non-Jewish, and Klausner reminds us that the Jewish sailor was as common a sight as the Jewish donkey driver in NT Palestine.[138]

FINANCIERS (2:6-7)

6. *But you have had only contempt for the poor. Do not the rich use their power to oppress you? Is it not actually they who drag you to court?*
7. *Do they not actually sin impiously with their tongues against the noble names by which you are called?*

Among the rich who oppressed people not rich enough to resist

129. See 2 Macc. 4:9, 19. See also Jeremias, *Jerusalem in the Time of Jesus*, pp. 228f.

130. See Josephus, *Life* 75.

131. *Jerusalem*, I, 366. See Josephus, *Ant*. 20.205.

132. Palestinian T. J. Yoma 5.3.

133. Klausner, *Jesus of Nazareth*, pp. 186ff.; Goodman, *State and Society in Roman Galilee*, pp. 54ff.

134. b. Pesaḥim 116a.

135. See, however, Davids, p. 171.

136. Exodus R. 54.4 on 39.32. See also Jeremias, *Jerusalem in the Time of Jesus*, p. 34 *ad fin*.

137. See J. Juster, *Les Juifs dans L'Empire Romain*, I (1914), 207ff.; J. R. Frey, "Les Communautés Juives à Rome," *Recherches des sciences religieuses* 20 (1930): 291ff.; R. M. Haywood, "Roman Africa," in *Economic Survey*, IV, 44ff.

138. *Jesus of Nazareth*, p. 186.

them successfully (Jas. 2:6) may well have been some from yet another important part of our NT background—the Jewish bankers.[139] The nature of the oppression referred to is somewhat obscure and difficult to interpret. There are grounds for assuming that the oppression was of a purely economic order, inflicted by wealthy Christians on their poorer brothers, the rich perhaps being more easily induced to apostatize than the poor.[140] This view is supported by Ropes, who suggests that this was a "legal action, arising from the ordinary working of social forces in an oriental community."[141] To some extent the context seems to support this position. It could be argued that the oppressors are Christian. James has been deploring the way the rich were treated in church, noting that they did not deserve preferential treatment.

The much varied business of the Jewish bankers included holding deposit funds.[142] Through these they had a supply of liquid capital and commanded a crucial area in the business world of their day—without pretending to be Gentiles so as to escape the Jewish Holy Law forbidding a Jew to lend to a Jew on usury (Dt. 23:20).[143] More probably this oppression, and the blasphemy against the name of Christ, came from non-Christian Jews.[144] The bankers that James may have had in mind, or at the back of his mind, were, of course, not the only blaspheming non-Christian oppressors; nor did the rich necessarily confine themselves to one kind of business for their wealth. The Jews probably still had the old Babylonian interest limit of 12 percent in law,[145] but in fact the interest was often exorbitant, sometimes even 300 percent.[146] Often mortgages went even higher[147] and, as with us today, the mortgagee who

139. For details, see Maynard-Reid, *Poverty and Wealth in James*, pp. 63ff.; Jeremias, *Jerusalem in the Time of Jesus*, pp. 56, 173f.; also preceding, n. 34.

140. See Pliny the Younger, *Letters* 10; Polycarp, *Martyrdom* 9.

141. P. 196; see also Dibelius, pp. 138ff.

142. Klausner, *Jesus of Nazareth*, p. 189; Goodman, *State and Society in Roman Galilee*, pp. 58f.; Jeremias, *Jerusalem in the Time of Jesus*, pp. 18, 33, 48f.

143. Cassidy, *Jesus, Politics and Society*, p. 103.

144. See Ropes, pp. 196f.

145. b. Baba Bathra 60a. See J. Abelson, "Usury" (Jewish), *ERE*, XII, 556-58.

146. See C. H. W. Johns, *Babylonian and Assyrian Laws*, ch. 28, "Loans and Deposits"; also J. D. M. Derrett, *art. cit.*, *ZNW* 56 (1965): 188f.

147. See b. Baba Meṣi'a 61b, where the moneylender is compared to the shedder of blood; also b. Baba Meṣi'a 63a. See also E. Lambert, "Les Changeurs de la Monnaie en du I-er au III-e siècle de l'ére Vulgaire d'après les textes talmudiques," *Revue des Études Juives* 51 (1906): 217ff. and 52 (1906): 24ff., esp. the examples on p. 34. See also Jeremias, *Jerusalem in the Time of Jesus*, p. 56. For the rabbinic discussion of *prozbul*, a device which ensured that outstanding loans continued to be repaid despite an intervening sabbatical year, see J. Neusner, *The Rabbinic Traditions About the Pharisees Before 70*, III (1971), 415 for refer-

did not keep up his payments had to hand over the property involved. Clearly this led to persecution by process of law and the transference of peasant and small farmers' land to bankers and landowners. Josephus tells how the palaces of Agrippa II, Bernice, and Ananias the high priest were burned "to destroy the moneylenders' bonds so as to prevent the recovery of debts, in order to secure the support of an army of debtors and enable the poor to arise with impunity against the rich."[148]

The social conditions reflected in the Epistle of James do not conflict, but rather agree, with our hypothesis that the Epistle was written in first-century Palestine before the fall of Jerusalem when, writes Jacobs, generally speaking, the Jewish dress of Palestine, at least in the cities, "was adapted in large measure from the Romans."[149] Inevitably, the Jews would imitate foreign fashions of costume along with other foreign customs; witness, for example, the sartorial vocabulary of the Talmud, especially Shabbath,[150] where a full list of articles is given with their Greek names. The Talmud also tells us that the *stola* that a Jew wore was a long mantle of fine material girded under the breast, striped, often with gold embroidery, and very costly, priced at one hundred minae.[151]

The reference to the ring and the bright clothing, possibly the Roman toga (Reicke), may also be taken to reflect conditions of the time when the Epistle was written. From the Romans, too, the Jews probably copied the wearing and renting of rings, a symbol of social status or ambition, especially for the newly rich.[152] Martial mentions a sardonyx in an ex-slave's finger-ring. B. H. Streeter thought (wrongly) that our Epistle emanated from Rome since the ring was worn by the Roman equestrian order. Neither the OT nor the NT knows much of the habit.[153] Indeed, apart from the ring given to the Prodigal (Lk. 15:22)—and this is an illustration or parable—the Epistle of James contains the only other reference in the NT.

---

ences; *From Politics to Piety* (1973), pp. 14ff.; Maynard-Reid, *Poverty and Wealth in James*, pp. 89f.; and D. A. Hagner, *The Jewish Reclamation of Jesus* (1984), pp. 174f.

148. *War* 2.426, 427.

149. *JE* IV (1901), 295.

150. b. Shabbath 120a; see also the parallels in the Jerusalem Talmud. See Vermes, Millar, Black, and Schürer, *The History of the Jewish People in the Age of Jesus Christ*, II, 70f.

151. b. Shabbath 128a.

152. *Epigrams* 2.29.2; also Pliny the Elder, *Natural History* 33.25; Seneca, *Hyppolytus* 319 et al.

153. *The Primitive Church*, p. 196; see W. Barclay, *The Letters of James and Peter* (1976), p. 64; see also W. Stegeman, *The Gospel and the Poor* (1981), p. 69, n. 43; Maynard-Reid, *Poverty and Wealth in James*, pp. 59ff., for the view that the rich visitor is probably "a canvassing politician."

James's palpably disparaging reference to "Goldfinger," reminiscent of the pagan satires on the *nouveaux riches*, seems to suggest that the rich visitor was of that sort, possibly a non-Christian, probably a Jew, perhaps a prosperous merchant from the East, with no official Roman status and only his display of wealth to evoke all that servility—and perhaps looking for something to allege as legal grounds for the suppression of Christianity.

It is worth noting that James appears oblivious to the Gentiles. We are thinking of them primarily in connection with the rich and their role in society. But obviously their social and theological roles cannot be separated. Thus it is significant that James is silent on the question of their admission to the church. From this we might deduce that his Epistle is late, certainly later than A.D. 60 when, according to Acts 21:20ff., the issue was still very much alive. In turn this would place the Epistle after the death of James the Lord's brother in A.D. 62.

A better deduction from the evidence is that the Gentile question is not mentioned simply because it had not yet arisen. This would require a date at least contemporary with or earlier than the controversy that followed Paul's first mission to Antioch (c. A.D. 44).[154] The same silence on the Gentiles observable in connection with the church is also evident in connection with society. The oppressors against whom James inveighs were not Roman but Jewish magnates. Many of them were probably drawn from the influential Sadducee-Boethusian party led by Annas and his sons,[155] and had "the confidence of the wealthy alone but no following among the populace."[156]

We have already noticed that the priests belonged to the powerful and wealthy merchant and landowning classes, and we are not surprised to learn that they also operated as bankers. Besides being a religious center the temple was the hub of Jerusalem's trade and commerce, its banking and money-changing facilities being used by rich and poor alike.[157] Since the Romans entrusted the Sadducees with

154. Acts 11:19ff.; see also Gal. 2:1ff.

155. See Klausner, *Jesus of Nazareth*, p. 314; Jeremias, *Jerusalem in the Time of Jesus*, pp. 96ff., 194ff.; P. Gaechter, "The Hatred of the House of Annas," *Theological Studies* 8 (1947): 3ff.; S–B I, 953; II, 569; Cassidy, *Jesus, Politics and Society*, p. 197.

156. Josephus, *Ant.* 13.298. For this and other citations from Josephus, see Cassidy, *Jesus, Politics and Society*, p. 195, n. 19; Vermes, Millar, Black, and Schürer, *The History of the Jewish People in the Age of Jesus Christ*, II, 404.

157. On the economy of the temple, see *Acta Apostolorum* 10.1f. See also A. Edersheim, *Life and Times of Jesus*, I (1903), 371ff.; Heichelheim, "Roman Syria," in *Economic Survey*. For temple accounts see Jeremias, *Jerusalem in the Time of Jesus*, p. 56.

the control of the courts—and this involved the administration of civil cases in accordance with Jewish laws as well as the punishment of crime—it is not difficult to see how the courts might be biased in favor of banker colleagues.

According to contemporary records, the Sadducees were "very boorish"[158] and violent,[159] and this must be taken to refer not only to their own personal conduct but also to that of their independent police force. "Riches and power the new hierarchy had in plenty," wrote J. Jeremias, "but these could in no way make up for their lack of legitimacy."[160] The Sanhedrin sent their police out to arrest the accused and bring him to trial.[161] The description of Christians being dragged before the courts recalls the preconversion activity of Paul, who as the official agent of the Sadducees harassed the church in its early days.

If the traditional view of authorship is correct, this verse in our Epistle has ironical overtones, for such harassment, which began immediately after the death of Christ, culminated in the death of James the Lord's brother, and this was at the hands of Ananus, the leading high priest of the Sadducean-dominated Sanhedrin.[162] We may assume, therefore, that the courts before which the Christians appeared were those of unconverted Jews, the profession of the name of Christ being regarded as inimical to orthodox Judaism. These courts *(kritēria)* or Sanhedrin (Heb. *sanheḏrîn;* Gk. *synedrion*) were everywhere and exercised supreme judicial authority in Palestine and even in the Diaspora;[163] in cases not involving the death penalty, its verdicts were final and without appeal.[164] Through the courts, therefore, the wealthy non-Christian Jew could wage legalized warfare against poor Jews, partic-

158. Josephus, *War* 2.1.66. On the strong-arm methods employed by the chief priests to collect tithes, see *Ant.* 20.8.8; 20.9.2.

159. Ass. Mos. 7:3-10. A Talmud street ballad faithfully reflects the anger of the people and the *clerus minor* against this lawless new hierarchy: "Woe unto me because of the house of Baithos (Boethus). . . ." For the texts and comments, see Jeremias, *Jerusalem in the Time of Jesus,* pp. 195f.; Klausner, *Jesus of Nazareth,* p. 337; Cassidy, *Jesus, Politics and Society,* pp. 120f.

160. *Jerusalem in the Time of Jesus,* p. 198. See also Eisenman, *James the Just in the Habakkuk Pesher,* p. 42 n. 24; 44ff. nn. 30, 31; 48.

161. Mt. 26:47; Acts 4:3; 5:17f.

162. Josephus, *Ant.* 20.200. For a discussion of other possible interpretations, see Laws, p. 106.

163. See Acts 9:2; 22:5; 26:12. See also S. Hoenig, *The Great Sanhedrin* (1953); T. A. Burkhill, "Sanhedrin," *IDB,* IV (1962), 214ff.; Vermes, Millar, Black, and Schürer, *The History of the Jewish People in the Age of Jesus Christ,* II, 199ff., esp. 218ff.

164. Acts 4:2-23; 5:21-40.

ularly Christian Jews, by arraigning them on an ostensibly legitimate ground before their local sanhedrin.

Of course this Epistle knows the need to be tactful; its paramount aim is to resist the imposition of the entire Jewish law on the Jew or (though the case is not quite the same) Gentile who had joined, or is thinking of joining, the Christians. Gal. 2:1 (after 14 years) and then vv. 11, etc. suggest (as we might indeed presume) that the center of propaganda for the retention of the Jewish law by the Christian Jew and the imposition of that law on Gentile Christians was Jerusalem itself. We think that the tone of this letter is just what was to be expected from James, then the leader of the world's Christians, seeking to counteract the Jewish propagandists who have been the source of the troubles such as Paul found among the Christians in Rome, Galatia, and Colosse.

The conditions so clearly revealed in the Epistle are, in our opinion, decisive arguments in favor of its early date.[165] With the outbreak of the Jewish War (A.D. 66-70) and the destruction of the temple, the Sadducees disappeared.[166] The old social cleavage between rich and poor and their traditional identification with the pious and the wicked are still clearly evident in the Epistle of James. But in the era after the Jewish War, the new division is primarily intellectual rather than social, namely, between the *'ammê hā'āreṣ* and the *ḥᵃḵāmîm;*[167] on this and also on the later second-century *Märtyrerproblem*[168] (with its corresponding "martyr theology") the Epistle is silent. After the destruction of the second temple, most of the new aristocracy were killed or sold into slavery and lost their wealth;[169] against such changed social conditions (amply corroborated in relevant Jewish sources) the message of James is unintelligible.

For such conditions in the early church, we must look to the crisis period prior to A.D. 50 and possibly as early as before the fourth decade; therefore, the most likely view is that which dates the Epistle in the immediate neighborhood of that period.

165. See G. Kittel, *art. cit., ZNW* 41 (1942): 72ff. For criticisms of our perception of James's economic situation, see Davids, p. 30, n. 95.

166. "By abolishing the Sanhedrin and the High Priesthood and by forbidding the resumption of the worship of the Temple at Jerusalem, the Romans destroyed the political and religious centre of Judaism" (G. H. Stevenson and A. Momigliano, ch. 25, "Rebellion Within the Empire," *Cambridge Ancient History,* X, 864); see also R. Meyer, *Saddoukaios, TDNT,* VII, 46, n. 69; Jeremias, *Jerusalem in the Time of Jesus,* p. 232.

167. See Moore, *Judaism,* II, 157ff.

168. G. Kittel, *art. cit., ZNW* 41 (1942): 81f.

169. See A. Büchler, *The Economic Conditions in Judea after the Destruction* (1912).

CONCLUSION

From the data presented, it is clear that the rich Christian of the Epistle of James chimes with the description of such wealthy converts as Barnabas, Nicodemus, and others described in the Gospels and the early chapters of Acts. The other three classes, into which the unconverted rich fall, also fit remarkably well into the general picture of the Sadducee-Boethusians and other Hellenized Jewish bourgeoisie found in Palestine before the destruction of the second temple and, says F. F. Bruce, "could provide an appropriate life setting for the New Testament document called the Letter of James."[170] The sources of income are the same: agriculture, trading, and other financial operations. Their personal and social traits coincide.

Again, this study of the social and economic background of the Epistle shows that at first the Christian church drew its public primarily from the economically poor; indeed, James may appear "to be so severe with the rich as to tempt the poor into self-righteousness."[171] Though the rich did figure more prominently than is sometimes recognized, most of them probably belonged to the Jewish *'ᵃnāwîm*. Certainly many of those in the Epistle share a striking affinity with this class. It is as one remembers this milieu of the primitive church, composed of ordinary men and women who in unspectacular ways and despite persecution were true to their Lord, that one begins to understand how the Epistle of James came to be written. From what we have seen, it is highly probable that we are in the presence of traditional Jewish "ethics of poverty" *(Armenethik).*

Most of James's readers were drawn not from the so-called "rich" *(plousioi)* but from "the working classes" *(penētes)* and those who are known in the Epistle simply as "the poor" *(ptōchoi).* This term "poor" had acquired a peculiar meaning by NT times; and this is the meaning that James employs, signifying not merely a social, economic, or material condition but also a certain religious temper. Poverty thus sometimes acquired a moral significance that was reinforced by socioeconomic conditions prevailing at the time. Examination shows that the Aramaic equivalent of the Greek word "poor" would itself, by reason of its current usage, suggest a religious meaning.

James's readers would at once think of the faithful, God-fearing Israelites, mostly literally poor, perhaps because of their strict religious loyalty, but not universally so. Largely neglected in the study of the

170. *Peter, Stephen, James and John,* p. 113. Similarly, Maynard-Reid, *Poverty and Wealth in James,* p. 7.

171. W. Stringfellow, *Count It All Joy* (1967), p. 21.

primitive church are these ordinary but devout souls, the "Messianic pietists," exemplified in Qumran ("congregation of the poor")[172] and elsewhere, who continued the simple OT "patriarchal-pietistic" way of life. While it is hard for us to gauge precisely the composition of the first congregations, yet this is what we must attempt; and when we make the effort, we find it highly probable that they were drawn from this unique group. Neither Pharisees nor Sadducees nor Zealots but the *'ᵃnāwîm,* these simple yet deeply pious folk of the post-Exilic period shunned all political activity, fostering a growing messianic expectation. Such was the spiritual breeding of the Christian congregations found in the Epistle of James.

Moreover, examination of the Epistle reflects two complementary strands of thought, namely, patient constraint and vigorous activism. These are expressed, on the one hand, in concern for the poor and oppressed (2:1ff.; 5:1ff.) and, on the other, in admonitions against violence, anger, or any hasty action (1:20f.; 2:11f.; 3:13f.; 4:1f.; 5:1f.). We sense a certain tension, suggesting perhaps that James is seeking to reconcile two opposing factions. The first may have included the mistreated clergy, both Jewish and Christian, with whom James sympathized; and the second, the divisive, more aggressive members of the church. In this second group, perhaps, were some Zealots, whose violence James, like Jesus, opposed, preferring the way of gentleness and peace.

To encourage the poor and oppressed, James denounces those who hear and do not act (1:10f.), profess much and practice little (2:14ff.); for the wicked plutocrats, on the other hand, he reserves the fiercest diatribe (2:1ff.; 4:13ff.; 5:1ff.), reminding them that the God who is on the side of the humble will resist the proud (4:6f.). But all this requires wisdom, and this God gives freely for the asking (1:5f.).

Yet despite his rejection of revolution, James is neither passively quietist nor blindly fatalistic: he has a vigorous social conscience, is sensitive to all types of discrimination and oppression, and does not hesitate to attack social ills whenever he sees them. At the same time, his approach is pacific and nonviolent: his people must shun useless strife and division and instead channel their energies into tangible brotherly love. It is true that he looks beyond the present hardships to the future for ultimate vindication. "Where shall I find help? Help comes only from the Lord" (Ps. 121:1, 2, NEB).

The cry of the poor has reached the ears of the Lord of Sabaoth, who will right the wrongs inflicted upon them. The Judge is at the door

172. See K. Schubert, *The Dead Sea Community* (1959), p. 138; E. Bammel, *ptōchos, TDNT,* VI, 896ff.; Dibelius, p. 41, n. 144.

(5:9); he will rescue the oppressed and destroy the oppressor. Yet, significantly, these otherworldly hopes tend to strengthen rather than weaken the Christian's obligations in the here-and-now of this world. Unfortunately, an outsider like Ananus II, the object of James's wrath, probably ignored or misconstrued his messianic and pietistic ideals and would hardly appreciate his nonviolent intent. Lumping James together with the Zealots, Ananus contrived his trial and had him legally murdered.

A final conclusion may be drawn. From the data presented, we may safely say that the Epistle of James is clearly one of the earliest documents in the NT, in many ways reflecting attitudes and events of the early chapters of Acts. The readers of the Epistle were being oppressed by the rich, and this, we have seen, probably happened before A.D. 60. Because of the elusive nature of the evidence—partly due to the general character of the Epistle and partly due to the lack of historical and human points of reference—it is difficult to be more specific.

From the cumulative evidence gathered here and elsewhere in our study, we are led to believe that the period described in the Epistle corresponds with what, for Jewish Christians, we may call the "crisis of A.D. 44" and the events immediately before and after it. This points to that period as the probable approximate date of the Epistle. The features of that situation provide an excellent historical background for the Epistle of James and give fresh pertinence to much of its contents.

4. Teaching

"Religion embraces both faith and action. The primary quality is action, for it lays the foundation for faith: the more we do good, the more readily do we grasp the meaning of duty and life and the more readily do we believe in the divine from which stems the good."

Leo Baeck, *The Essence of Judaism* (1948), p. 135

The author of the Epistle of James, a letter distinguished for its passionate commitment to Jewish Christianity, has been dubbed "the Amos of the new Covenant." As a guide to Christian behavior, the letter deals with themes of universal importance, and is excelled by no other NT book (the nearest parallel, surely, is Philippians) as an epitome of the basics of practical Christianity. Among these basics are the nature of God and man, the evils of lust and pride that menace the Christian, the virtues of faith and hope that sustain the believer, and the forces of faith and love. James compares the person whose mind is divided on life's issues to the waves of the sea, agitated by every fleeting gust of wind. His most rigorous rebuke is reserved for those who allow themselves to be possessed by the lure of riches.

The substance and authoritative tone of the Epistle follow the tradition of Elijah and Moses, and the style and diction resemble some of the outstanding qualities of the Psalms and Prophets. Christianity was the culmination of Judaism and shared much of its theory and some of its previous experience. Not until the execution of James and Paul (about A.D. 62) and the fall of Jerusalem (A.D. 70) was the link between Judaism and Christianity irreparably damaged. The decisive breaking of the link is usually taken to be the introduction into the synagogue of the "Benediction against the Heretics" *(Birkaṯ ham-Mînîm)* around A.D. 90.[1] This explains why, after centuries of development of Christian doctrine, the extraordinary Jewish tone of the Epistle of James has led some to deny its Christian origin. That, however, is established, in part at least, by such distinctively Christian passages as 2:8-13 (compare Gal. 3:10-14, 21-26).

James therefore, in addressing Jews, could take much for granted that Paul had to instil *de novo* into his pagans. The Epistle of James contains a long, impressive series of what we think are authentic (rather than imitated) Jewish ideas; indeed, it may be noted that "the religious attitude of the average rabbinical Jew would in most respects well sum up the fundamental ideas of the Epistle of James."[2] His readers knew their OT and strove to obey the precepts of the Jewish Torah, interpreted and consummated now in the life and teaching of Jesus Christ, the long-expected Messiah and Head of the new Israel.

Saturated with the words of Jesus, the Epistle of James partakes of the nature of a primitive Jewish-Christian midrash on the OT, a necessary document for both Jewish converts and Jews who might seek guidance on the ethical and theological significance of Christianity vis-à-vis Judaism in this unique period of transition. As a result James speaks as a converted Jew who stands in the transitional period between legalistic ethics and the ethics of grace and redemption, from a law that enjoins us to a love that is a by-product of a living relationship to Christ and an experience of God's pardon, a free, responsive love evoked by the love of "the Lord of glory."

We will adduce evidence to show that the form of the law reflected in the Epistle of James shows strong affinity with that of the Epistle to

1. On this, see L. H. Schiffman, "At the Crossroads: Tannaitic Perspectives on the Jewish-Christian Schism," in *Jewish and Christian Self-Definition,* by E. P. Sanders with A. L. Baumgarten and A. Mendelson, II (1981), 115ff.; P. Richardson, *Israel in the Apostolic Church* (1969), chs. 1, 2, 3, especially pp. 43ff.; G. Vermes, F. Millar, M. Black, and E. Schürer, *The History of the Jewish People in the Age of Jesus Christ,* II (1979), 462, n. 164; also C. W. Dugmore, *The Influence of the Synagogue upon the Divine Office* ([2]1964), pp. 3ff. The break between Jewish and Gentile Christianity also probably occurred after the Jewish War, perhaps at Antioch. See W. A. Meeks and R. L. Wilken, *Jews and Christians in Antioch in the First Four Centuries of the Common Era* (1978), p. 18; D. A. Hagner, *The Jewish Reclamation of Jesus* (1984), pp. 44f.

2. Ropes, pp. 31, 29f.; Cadoux, pp. 10ff.; A. L. Williams, "The Epistle of St. James and the Jewish-Christians of His Time," *Church Quarterly Review* 123 (1936): 24-32; H. E. Dana, *Jewish Christianity* (1937), pp. 103ff.; D. L. Bartlett, "The Epistle of James as a Jewish-Christian Document," SBL 1979 Seminar/Papers, II, 173-86, argues that two test cases, the use of Abraham as an example of faith and the use of the terms *dipsychos* and *dipsychia,* show that James's Epistle is in large measure shaped by Judaism and by concerns germane to Jewish Christianity.

the Hebrews, and this appears to point to a Jewish and non-Pauline area of origin. We will also find very attractive the suggestion that "law" *(nomos)* in this Epistle has become the messianic Torah. Paul, however, was a radical. Before his conversion he had sought to attain salvation by observance of the Torah. But his experience at the hand of Torah proved hard and bitter, and after his conversion he completely rejected his former method. Thus the Torah becomes a deceiver and a murderer of hope, and we find him stressing the opposition of Torah to gospel.

We find no hint in Paul of the unity and continuity of the old and the new that we find in the Epistle of James. The real antithesis for him, it must be added, was not between ceremonial and moral "works"; nor was it even, as is commonly supposed, between faith and works, but rather, C. F. D. Moule points out, between a salvation earned by "works" ("legalism") and a salvation dependent on God's grace.[3] Paul has experienced a conversion; having broken with his old life, he describes the gospel in contrast to the Torah, for he regards these as totally and mutually exclusive. It is legalism, rather than the law per se, that Paul regards as totally antithetical to the gospel; note his emphatic response in Gal. 2:21 to the question "Is the law against the promises of God?"[4]

The risen Lord's appearance to James must have been as decisive for James (*ōphthē Iakōbō,* 1 Cor. 15:7) as his appearance to Paul was for Paul. James's training, background, and religious experience, on the other hand, have been very different. He, too, draws a contrast between Torah and gospel, but his view of the Torah is much more restrained. Like Paul, James believes in the abrogation of the old law, but he presents this as due not to the fact that the new is radically different from the old, but that the old is imperfect and only a shadow of that which is perfectly realized in what he calls "royal law." He—and, we may add, the author of the Epistle to the Hebrews—does not entirely discard the idea of law as Paul did, but now regards the gospel as a deliverance from the Torah: to James the gospel is the transfiguration of the Torah, the faithful and continued observance of that which finally wins salvation.

In the Epistle of James, the name "Christ" occurs only in 1:1 and 2:1; and these plus the two references to the "Name" itself (2:7; 5:14), his "*onoma*" Christology, are all that he says about Christ.[5] The

3. "James, Judaism and Paul," in *Tradition and Interpretation in the New Testament,* Essays in Honor of E. Earle Ellis (1987), ed. G. F. Hawthorne, pp. 48f. Further, on Paul's break with Judaism, especially the Torah, see *Anti-Judaism in Early Christianity:* I, *Paul and the Gospels,* eds. P. Richardson and D. Granskou (1986), 21ff.

4. See W. Morgan, *The Religion and the Theology of Paul* (1917), p. 85; also C. E. B. Cranfield, "St. Paul and the Law," *SJTh* 17 (1964): 43-68.

5. Some commentators find an oblique reference to Christ in Jas. 1:9-10, on the unlikely grounds of alleged parallels with Paul's christological passages

"Name," interpreted christologically, is closely associated with the title "Lord"; see Acts 2:21, quoting Joel 2:32 and 2:34f.; Ps. 110:1; also Acts 8:16; 9:10-17; 15:26; 22:13-16 and, above all, Phil. 2:9-11. Paul also joins the "Name" and the "Lord"; see 2 Thess. 1:12; 3:6; 1 Cor. 1:2, 10; 5:4; 6:11; Eph. 5:20; Col. 3:17—for two reasons, indicated in Rom. 10:13 (salvation) and Eph. 1:20-22 (sovereignty). It is true that James speaks as Jesus speaks rather than as Jesus is spoken about,[6] and we may be tempted to think that for James Christian ethics eclipsed all interest in the theological meaning of the incarnate being of Christ.

Some critics speak disparagingly of his "theology," especially his Christology,[7] but ironically, as Frank Stagg points out, it is often exactly "the barren stereotyped, transactional and propositional theology today which finds James untheological or theologically deficient."[8] There is more than meets the eye, for most of his teaching is implicit or indirect.[9] This is uniquely true of his Christology, from which, though mostly "assumed" or "indirect,"[10] flows all his ethical and theological teaching. Of paramount importance, however, are the few explicit references, notably to Jesus "the Lord of Glory" (2:1). Here, as Cranfield affirms, "is no theological moralism but a faithful—though, for a special purpose, oblique—proclamation of the gospel of Christ."[11] Having ascribed these supreme titles to Jesus, James can say no more: nothing that Paul is destined to say (in even fuller detail) can match the fullness of James's implicit Christology. According to Scaer, James's christological language means, first, that "it was not Paul who is responsible for a highly defined Christological dogmatic theology in the Church, but Jesus";[12] and, second, that the first Christians were already thoroughly familiar with it apart from Paul.

Kyrios as a title for Jesus is now admitted to be pre-Pauline. Jewish Christian materials show that the designation of Jesus as Lord, in acclamation and not just in common courtesy, followed and was mainly due to the resurrection (see Thomas, in John 20:28, 31). Before that it

---

(Phil. 2:8; 2 Cor. 8:9). See, e.g., Scaer, pp. 48f.; see also his discussion of his "even fuller Christology" (1:12) on pp. 51ff. On the significance of "the name of Jesus," see H. Bietenhard, "Name" *(onoma), NIDNTT,* II, 654.

6. R. Henderlite, "The Epistle of James," *Interpretation* 3.4 (1949): 470.

7. See, e.g., Dibelius, pp. 21f., 48f.; A. M. Fairbairn, *The Place of Christ in Modern Theology* (1893), p. 238.

8. F. Stagg, "Exegetical Themes in James 1 and 2," *RevExp* 66 (1969): 391.

9. For a summary of the teaching *implied* in the Epistle, see Mayor, pp. cxff.

10. See F. Mussner, "'Direkte' und 'Indirekte' Christologie im Jakobusbrief," *Catholica* 24.2 (1970): 111-17; Davids, pp. 39f.

11. C. E. B. Cranfield, "The Message of James," *SJTh* 18.2 (1965): 185.

12. P. 48.

was only a conventional address of respect during his ministry, when they did not yet realize that what they were then witnessing was the fulfillment of the messianic Scriptures (see Jas. 1:1; 2:1; Phil. 2:6-11; Acts 2:36; Jn. 20:28, and, explicitly, Rom. 14:8f.). The fact that James and Paul mention Christ's Lordship almost incidentally is evidence that they are simply reproducing a primitive Jewish Christian belief (see Mt. 28:18-20: "All authority . . . has been given to me . . . go *therefore* and make disciples . . ."). Thus, although clearly perceived upon the resurrection, the Lordship of Jesus was supported theologically and biblically in the minds of the first Christians by their memories of this ministry and of the act itself. Therefore, while the use of *Kyrios* in the LXX for two centuries must have had some effect on Palestinian usage, any correspondence between the first Christians and Greek influences on the point of Christ's Lordship is of secondary significance. The Jewish Christian materials and the letters of Paul show that, though both expressions were used by the early Christians, "Jesus is Christ" was more prominent in early Jewish Christianity but "Jesus is Lord" was more common than the other among those ministering to the Gentiles.[13]

In apprehension and not only in expression there seem to have been differences between James and Paul. For James and the early Jewish Christians it seems that the worship of Jesus had mainly a religious and historical meaning, drawn primarily from their knowledge of his incarnate life on earth and not to any great extent from thought about his relation to the structure of the universe. In addition to Paul's Pharisaic training, the impact of environments of alien ideologies probably extended the concept of Jesus (whom Paul had not known and loved personally as the disciples did during his earthly life) beyond the religious and historical connotations and concerns of his Lordship into the universal realm of cosmology. The title *Christos,* like Messiah, speaks to the heart of man; *Kyrios,* Lord, speaks of sovereignty over man and matter.

We shall return to this topic in our concluding reflections, but in

13. Paul is careful also to avoid any pagan idea that his new doctrine merely amounted to another new god; hence for the Gentiles with their commonly polytheistic past he habitually says, "one God the Father" and "one Lord Jesus Christ." But it also seems to have been Paul who gave the best expression to the nearness of Christ and the Spirit to the Christian in the joys and tribulations of daily life. Paul extended thought about Jesus beyond the dominating religious and historical context, but seems to have taken up the cosmic themes *only* when Christ's supremacy was challenged on speculative and metaphysical grounds. As a result the cosmic supremacy of Jesus was soon acknowledged within Jewish Christianity, as in the Prologue to John's Gospel and Revelation. See R. N. Longenecker, *The Christology of Early Jewish Christianity* (1970), pp. 120ff.; also our remarks, pp. 273ff.

the meantime we suggest that the time is ripe for a radical evaluation of James's theology and especially his Christology. Sometimes we wish he had written at greater length, or even a second Epistle, but this is idle speculation. If James never mentions the resurrection by name (although "the glory" in 2:1 must at least imply Easter "glory"), neither do the rest of the Catholic Epistles from James to Jude inclusively, except 1 Peter.

Commentators have also discussed the novel, if less than convincing, view that James was dealing especially with "gospel-hardened" readers who would be impervious to any full-orbed presentation of the gospel.[14] Possibly James the Lord's brother was too near to Jesus and to his return to feel the need to theologize about redemption as Paul did for the Gentiles.[15] More likely James was writing in a hostile environment and at a time when Christianity was a forbidden religion and proselytizing (or even the hint of it) was unlawful. The restraints placed on Christians in modern Israel offer an illuminating, almost uncanny, parallel well worth further exploration.[16] James's presentation of the Christian faith is restrained, even veiled, for this obvious reason; so much so that his Epistle almost becomes a spiritual cryptogram.

We shall see later that too long we have been deluded, first, by the belief that the Epistle of James is formless from "the least consecutive of writers";[17] and second, that James's version of Christianity is odd and unorthodox. We need no more than 1 Tim. 5:8 and Jas. 2:15ff. to show that Paul and James are at one in the religion of faith at work. James is in harmony with the rest of the NT and cannot be understood apart from it.

* * * * *

Before turning to a detailed examination of the teaching of James, let us glance at the following *Analysis,* which shows that the theme "Faith at Work" is the key to its teaching, and also that every topic tossed out of ch. 1 (there are no new themes in ch. 2) has had some elaboration in ch. 1 or 2, with one great exception—wisdom, which receives little (but that most important) more than a mere mention in 1:5. In our *Analysis* we found that James, like Jesus, employed "the principle of trajectory,"[18] that is, he never communicates his teaching exhaustively, but always with a certain reticence, leaving the reader to interpret, amplify, and apply what he taught.

14. Cranfield, *art. cit., SJTh* 18.2 (1965): 182-93.

15. See Tasker, p. 28.

16. See M. Barth, *Jesus the Jew* (1978).

17. R. A. Knox, *A New Testament Commentary: The Later Epistles, the Apocalypse,* III (1956), 92.

18. See E. Routley, *Into a Far Country* (1962), pp. 20ff.

ANALYSIS

First Section: 1:2-11

1:2-4: Peirasmos *is a testing of faith, and its fruit is constancy in faith.*

1:5-8: *Knowledge of God comes by prayer, and prayer is meaningless without faith. God has no tie of duty to answer the faithless.*

1:9-11: *Christian brotherhood is nothing but a fraternity of faith, with no place for distinctions of worldly status—poor and low, or rich and high.*

Second Section: 1:12-21

1:12: *The reward for God's faithful (that is the meaning of love in this context).*

1:13-21: *We are God's people, not the world's; thus, as his loyal children, we are bound by his law.*

Third Section: 1:22-27

1:22-25: *This continues the thought: the loyal Christian must do his Lord's will.*

1:26-27: *On fraternity and unfaltering allegiance to God. Sincere faith must express itself in conduct and speech.*

Fourth Section: 2:1-13

Faith must live in brotherly love.

Fifth Section: 2:14-26

Faith must live in conduct generally.

Sixth Section: 3:1-6

Sincere faith will guard the tongue.

Seventh Section: 3:7-12

Sincere faith is always consistent.

Eighth Section: 3:13-18

Sincere faith is wise in practice.

Ninth Section: 4:1-10

Doctrine (of faith) must live in peace, purity, and humility.

Tenth Section: 4:11-17

True faith is neither censorious nor boastful.

Eleventh Section: 5:1-6

The judgment of the faithless rich.

Twelfth Section: 5:7-12

Stand fast in constancy of faith and in faithful speech.

Thirteenth and Last Section: 5:13-20

Final duties of faith.

In our *Analysis,* we have tried to show something of the sequence of thought governing the form of this Epistle. Now let us turn to a more difficult question. What is its teaching, and what in the mind of James prompted the feelings and thoughts to which the Epistle gives expression?

a. Faith in Action

"Faith is not the clinging to a shrine but an endless pilgrimage of the heart. Audacious longing, burning songs, daring thoughts, an impulse overwhelming the heart, usurping the mind—these are all a drive towards serving Him who rings our heart like a bell. . . . To rely on our faith would be idol-worship. We have only the right to rely on God. Faith is not an insurance but a constant effort, constant listening to the eternal voice."

A. J. Heschel, *Man Is Not Alone* (1976), p. 174

We have already seen that Luther in some careless talk condemned the Epistle of James as deficient in the power and function of faith. "I think," he says, "that the Epistle was composed by some Jew or other, who had heard of Christ but had not joined the Christians. James had learned that Christians insisted strongly on faith in Christ, and so he said to himself: 'Well, you must oppose them and insist only on works.' And so he does."[1] Elsewhere he writes: "You see, he teaches nothing about faith, only mere law."[2]

We must therefore examine what James says about faith and determine the accuracy of Luther's remarks. In fact, in his five brief chapters James mentions faith at least 19 times—in connection with God (1:6, 13; 2:29; 5:15), Christ (2:1), and Christian virtues such as endurance (1:3), wisdom (1:5f.), prayer, and healing (5:15)—and he insists on faith (and some kindred aspects of the Christian spirit) quite as explicitly and emphatically as Paul.

Faith is at the head of the Epistle (1:2-4), which speaks of the testing of faith and the cultivation of its fruits in Christian conduct; and this, as D. E. Hiebert says, seems to be "the key which James left hanging at the front door, intended to unlock the contents of the book."[3] His

1. *LW,* LIV, 424. See also our previous remarks, pp. 31f.

2. See Dibelius, p. 56, n. 232.

3. D. E. Hiebert, "The Unifying Theme of the Epistle of James," *Bibliotheca Sacra* 135 (1978): 224. Like us, D. J. Moo has compared the Epistle to a symphony or opera, whose several key motifs continually recur. Unlike us, however, he does not believe that these are not dominant enough to serve as organizing heads, or, as we believe *(q.v.),* to be subsumed under the one main theme of faith (*James,* p. 39).

first thought, then, is of faith and its growth in constancy under trial. But of course it must be consummated in action (1:3f.), and it is this constancy in the love of God that wins the crown of life. In the process the Word of truth chimes in with the music of faith.

The "music" of James, so to speak, is an excellent example of the "fugue," a type of writing in which a tiny fragment of a theme, the motif, played off against itself in continued suspension, ends in a unique unity. The motif becomes the subject of endless variations upon which, as a foundation, an elaborate composition is built. The motif, or theme, of the Epistle of James is "faith at work." Though this motif is subject to numerous variations, through them all the motif itself is always heard, and it is the recurrence of the "faith at work" motif that gives unity and coherence to the whole. This motif is the text on which the rest of the Epistle is but exposition and commentary.

THE LIFE OF FAITH

James shows that he has a clearly conceived philosophy of religion (in a nutshell, "Christianity is a life of faith"), and that he has the power to propagate its gospel with the force of rhetorical skill and logical coherence. This theme, "faith realized in conduct" (action, deed, or whatever we care to call the practical outworking of faith), is the key to the Epistle. Nor is faith one work among others. All other virtues such as endurance, sincerity, and humility are comprehended under this one paramount thought, which, in Bengel's phrase, is the *prora et puppis* (literally "from stem to stem") or "lock, stock, and barrel" of the Epistle.[4] Could anyone have emphasized more the fundamental, paramount, indispensable importance of faith? Clearly James is the apostle of faith and his Epistle the Epistle of faith.

Before going further, we must try to see the real logic of 1:5-8. How are we to interpret it? Very simply: the keynote is not "trial" *(peirasmos)* or "constancy" *(hypomonē)* but rather, as Heb. 11:6 puts it: "Anyone who comes to God must believe that he exists and he rewards those who search for him." The word *diakrinomenos* means here "halting between two opinions," like those people in the OT who were divided between God and Baal. It cannot refer, as Ropes suggests, to "constancy (*hypomonē*) in the Christian religion,"[5] for *hypomonē* in v. 4 is not articulated or adhesive to anything in vv. 5-8. We often "do not

4. For a discussion of the comprehensive nature of faith in the light of Bengel's phrase, which he rendered in German "Ein und Alles," "one and all," see G. Eichholz, *Glaube und Werk bei Paulus und Jakobus* (1961), p. 39.

5. P. 140.

see our way" in some matter and realize the need for (higher) wisdom, before or even without being (in any sinister sense) "tempted." Thus a father might desire guidance (to use a simple illustration) on whether he should let his daughter marry X, or try, however hopelessly, to stop her; the latter might just make her all the more determined.

The waverer vacillates over questions like "Will God answer my prayer and grant my petition as I desire, or not?" The one who is praying certainly believes in God but (compare human child and father) is not at all sure that he will get from God what he is asking for. That is equally clear in the parallel, Jas. 5:15. There the "prayer of faith" (adjectival genitive) obviously does not mean "the prayer of a company of elders who fully and genuinely and sincerely profess and practice the Christian religion"; rather it means "the prayer, offered in faith that God will listen to it and it will be granted or (only in God's superior wisdom) denied ('Nevertheless, not my will. . .')."

Clearly, too, the reference to faint-heartedness (*oligopsychia*)[6] does not signify lack of steadfast loyalty to God but lack of confidence in petition. It is because children have a full background of faith in their father, in his feeding and clothing them and training them for life, that they confidently ask him how to "spell out some hard word for them." So it is with Christianity as a whole and Christian prayer in particular. It is rather like the relation between knowing the principle of gravitation and levelling a pendulum clock.

The key word, therefore, introducing and unifying 1:5-8 is "faith" (*pistis*), mentioned initially in connection with *peirasmos* and later with prayer (v. 5, let him ask "in faith"), apparently in contrast to "wavering." James puts faith at the forefront. Wisdom may be given in answer to prayer, but the quality of prayer springs from God's prevenience—from faith. James does not separate faith as God's gift from faith as a human act, or our relationship with God from that with people. He is not interested in analyzing the situation, but merely in stressing the need for unswerving faith. Faith is not a matter only of recognizing and accepting a truth with the mind; the devils also believe. But if it is no more than that, faith is dead.

What is full, living faith? No word or phrase will cover the whole of it, but no one clue takes us further into the truth than the action seen in the case of "perfect" (*teleios*) in 1:4: "that you may be perfect, and complete in every part, lacking in nothing." *Teleios* in 1:4 signifies perfect in intention, in performance, and in wisdom. The case of the person lacking in wisdom comes in only at 1:5. The *teleioi* of 1:4 are, ex-

6. Ecclus. 7:10; cited by Ropes, p. 141.

pressly, lacking in nothing. Therefore the "faith" *(pistis)* of 1:6 must be capable of being possessed by one not yet *teleios,* but wholeheartedly determined to seek to become *teleios*—in fact, the person who has made the first step, namely, "Repent and believe," but yet has much to do and much to learn. Besides, if the petitioner is "perfect," he need not be told not to fear the risk of chiding. The key thought is largely contained in the opening "servant" (*doulos*) in 1:1, namely, that "wholehearted devotion, service, and allegiance" which is implied in *teleios.* The "perfect" man has an undivided heart because he has given himself to God in an allegiance of reciprocal love, loyalty, and service.

THE SINCERITY OF FAITH

The master key to James's thought is sincerity. This explains (as nothing else could better explain) why he, alone in the NT, employed (and, for all we know, invented) the word *dipsychos,* "of divided mind," that is, "insincere," and used it not once but twice in his Epistle (1:8; 4:8). Of *dipsychos* J. H. Ropes says:

> The word is not found in secular literature nor in LXX or N.T. except here and Jas. 4:8. . . . In early Christian writings *dipsychos* and *dipsycheo* . . . are frequent, occurring in Hermas about forty times, especially in *Mand.* IX; Clem. Rom. 11:2 (of persons like Lot's wife; 23:2). . . . In 2 Clem. Rom. 11:2 the same quotation is given as from *ho prophētikos logos,* which Lightfoot conjectures to be "Eldad and Modad." Cf. Didache 4:4, Barn. 19:5; 20:1 (*diplokardia*). 2 Clem. Rom. 19 (*dipsychia*); see Mayor for some later references.[7]

Articles by O. J. F. Seitz and others[8] suggest that *dipsychos* was invented by a translator into Greek from a Hebrew writing dealing with this topic, a phenomenon not uncommon in the OT and derivative literature. Nothing that is not speculative and conjectural, however, has been added to Lightfoot's conjecture on the source of the quotations in Clement of Rome, and we cannot claim any certain knowledge of the lexical history of *dipsychos* before James.

The thought is perhaps most familiar from Mt. 6:24, which Ropes cites, along with parallels from the OT and Apocrypha (e.g., Ps. 12:2 [11:3]; 1 Chr. 12:33; Ecclus. 1:28; 2:12-14; Hos. 10:2). But the writings

7. P. 143. For Bonhoeffer on the "double-minded man" *(anēr dipsychos),* and especially in relation to wisdom and simplicity, see *Ethics* (1962), p. 7.

8. For details see our discussion, pp. 321ff.; Adamson, p. 61, n. 52; also C. Vlachos, "Hē Epistolē tēs Dipsychias," *Deltion Biblikon Meleton* 3.10 (1975): 134-45; D. L. Bartlett, "The Epistle of James as a Jewish-Christian Document," SBL 1979 Seminar Papers, II, 179ff.

from Qumran suggest that the topic of the single/double heart was an issue at that period, as earlier and later. So also *akatastasia,* meaning strife in society and state, is used in Jas. 3:16 as well as in Luke and Paul, while *akatastatos* occurs only in Jas. 1:8, and probably as the better reading in 3:8, where it denotes the internal conflict of inconsistency and inconstancy that is largely covered by the word "insincerity," though other words such as "inconstant" may be more apt for translating a particular sentence. See also 4:4, 8.

Dipsychos is synonymous with *diakrinomenos* (1:6), and *akatastatos* as a description means much the same as the elaborated simile describing the *diakrinomenos* in 1:6, where the point is inconstancy of direction, or being at the mercy of the proverbially shifting winds.[9] So the *akatastatos,* lacking constancy of direction and consistency of purpose, attains nothing, or, as we say, gets nowhere. The antidote to wavering is trust. The waverer does not give himself either to God or the world; he does not, and can not, keep to the way of life. Neither can his asking avail, for without faith it is meaningless, like the prayer: "O God, make me pure, but not today." We cannot desire good (and God has nothing else to give) unless we desire good alone with *all* our mind and (like God's giving) "without reservations" (*haplōs*).

James implies that "to come to God in prayer is to invite criticism upon our desires, which, accepted, will transform them into that with which he can and will co-operate . . . wisdom is the special promise to sincere prayer, there being no true knowledge without supreme desire for him."[10] So the waverer's prayer fails, not because God is unwilling, but because he is not really serious, determined, and single-minded in his prayer. "Lead us not into *peirasmos*" is meaningless if it includes a reservation, "provided we need not renounce evil." Ropes says that the sentence seems to call for a characterization of the person rather than a prophecy of his fortunes. In fact, both are essential to the meaning: his fortunes are the fruit of his character, just as in Phil. 1:9-11 righteousness is the fruit of sincerity and knowledge; 2 Cor. 1:12 is similarly parallel to this passage in James.

Christian faith *(pistis),* therefore, means trusting yourself totally to God. So the Heidelberg Catechism asks: "What is required in the tenth commandment?" "That even the least inclination or thought against any of God's commandments should never enter into our heart; but that with our whole heart we are continually to hate all sin, and to

9. Mussner, p. 71, n. 6. See B. Gärtner, "Distinguish, Doubt" *(diakrinō), NIDNTT,* I, 502f.

10. Cadoux, pp. 60, 64.

take pleasure in all righteousness."[11] You cannot choose God with part of your mind for part of your life, and give part to the world, the flesh, and the devil—that is the essence of double-mindedness. We now believe that the importance of this topic in the apostles' minds is indicated by the emphasis laid on the opposites of *dipsychos* and *dipsychia,* namely, *eilikrinēs* and *eilikrineia.* For *eilikrinēs,* see Phil. 1:10, where, as in James, sincerity is coupled with knowledge, and 2 Pet. 3:1, which describes the proper attitude of the learner to instruction; and for *eilikrineia,* see 1 Cor. 5:8, of moral duty, and similarly 2 Cor. 1:12, which contrasts sincerity with fleshly wisdom, and 2:17, which contrasts sincerity with self-seeking hypocrisy. An *aparchē* ("firstfruits") is holy/dedicated, consecrated, hallowed, sanctified; *therefore* you must not live like the unconverted or like the renegade converts of 1 Cor. 6:8-10, a passage which, like Jas. 1:16, has the warning *mē planasthe,*[12] "Make no mistake about this fact."

It is abundantly clear that the first Christians did not all live up to their faith (Who does?). That is why Paul and James and others are *constantly* preaching the duty of conduct in keeping with faith. This is the logic that pervades the NT and, *mutatis mutandis,* the OT—and not least the Epistle of James. Christian conduct must be *eilikrinēs,* pure, unmixed, unalloyed, and unadulterated, rather like James's words in 1:27, *katharos, amiantos,* and *aspilos.*[13] This essential logic of Christianity is put perhaps most plainly and briefly in 1 Cor. 5:8: "Christ our passover is sacrificed for us. *Therefore* let us keep the feast, *not with* the old leaven of malice and wickedness (NEB . . . of *corruption* and *wickedness;* Gk. *kakia* and *ponēria*), *but with* the unleavened bread of *sincerity (eilikrineia) and truth.*" The etymology of *eilikrinēs* is not known. The NT writers must certainly have taken it (rightly?) as connected with *krinō,* with a meaning similar to that of *adiakritos* (Jas. 3:17), the opposite of *dipsychos* (1:8) and *diakrinomenos* (1:6). So James is quite in line with Paul on this matter: you cannot serve God and sup with the devil.

This theme of unwavering faith (and its opposite) dominates the

11. T. F. Torrance, *The School of Faith: The Catechisms of the Reformed Church* (1959), p. 92.

12. See H. Braun, *planaō, TDNT,* VI, 242-51.

13. Liddell and Scott, s.v., quotes "What kind of thing is most related to truth? *The pure and unadulterated" (to katharon te kai eilikrinēs)* (from Plato, *Philebus* 52d), and Aristotle's statement (*On Colours* 793a) that *eilikrineia* (the word of 1 Cor. 5:8) is the opposite of *mixis* ("mingling"). So in 1 Cor. 5:8 the NEB has "corruption" as the opposite and (very well) in Phil. 1:10 "flawless" for *eilikrinēs.*

entire Epistle: 1:4 (faith at work), 6 (faith in prayer, along with works), 12 (faith, and reward for constancy in conduct therein), 19-21 (faith in conduct), 22-25 (faith, or "word" in conduct), and, in sum, 26f. (faith *is* conduct. So 2:1 contains the Christian law of conduct (social), 8ff. speak of that law, the royal law of love, which will be vindicated in merciful conduct, 13, 14, and 20 are the alpha and omega on Christianity in conduct, and 21-24 and 25-26 are similar. In ch. 3 we cite only vv. 13-17 (though vv. 1-12 are not irrelevant). In ch. 4 on works, we would cite v. 8 ("draw near," etc.) and v. 17. Ch. 5 is nearly all about sin and the Christian way of life. Even the dangerous "faith" of 3:1 has for its corollary in salvation the "work" of 5:29.

One of the chief objections to the Epistle of James is its deficient theology. Its "theology" is simply "You know what Christ would have you do; do it and leave the rest to him. You know his promise." That, in the main, is what James means by faith realized in action. It fills nearly all his thought, so that we cannot understand why some have tried to teach that James "does not state distinctly what he means by faith"[14] or that he is all for works and barely thinks of faith.[15] From first to last, the Epistle of James teaches nothing but that Christianity is a life of faith.

THE DYNAMIC OF FAITH

In the Epistle of James the emphasis is clearly on conduct and the mind that governs conduct: it is an epistle of behavior founded on faith and the crucial test of faith, namely, works. Orthopraxy (right conduct) is more important than orthodoxy (right doctrine). In his teaching on faith James articulates his doctrine of the Word. Faith begins with hearing the Word; the transition from hearing to doing "resembles the movement of God's Word towards mankind."[16] According to 1:16-18 the content of faith is the Word of truth, which by God's grace we believe, and which, as James reminds us in 1:21, alone can save us; but according to 1:22-24, the truth cannot save us if we do not keep it in mind and allow it to guide us in our actions, any more (if we may change the analogy) than food will feed us if we do not remember to eat it. The

14. So Mayor, p. xcviii.

15. See, e.g., T. Lorensen, "Faith without Works does not Count before God! James 2:14-26," *ExpT* 89.8 (1978): 235; W. Marxsen, *Introduction to the New Testament* (1968), pp. 226ff.

16. J.-L. Blondel, "Theology and Paraenesis in James," *Theology Digest* 28.3 (Fall 1980): 255.

denunciation of mere formalism without Christian conduct could scarcely be clearer than it is in 1:26; and 1:27 is in perfect harmony with Paul's dictum in 1 Cor. 13:1f., that without Christian love shown in Christian compassion and aid for the fatherless and widows (Jas. 1:27) the gifts of tongues, prophecy, and faith itself count for nothing. Moreover, there is nothing in 1:22-27 with which even the stiffest orthodoxy could disagree.

The nature of works, like that of faith, may be deduced both positively and negatively, by their presence and their absence (or opposites). This is clearly illustrated in James's pivotal second chapter, where true "faith," by definition, is shown to be not only a dynamic power in Christian life but also a power *that must be applied to our lives in a practical Christian way,* especially in the care of our brothers and sisters. This is the true fulfillment of the royal law, the law of liberty, a law that is violated by toadying to the rich and despising the poor while exhibiting compassion toward the compassionate.

This is brought out clearly in the important verse 2:1 where "faith" and Christ are explicitly linked, for the first and only time, with "the cult of persons." The initial isolated statement[17] "faith in our Lord Jesus Christ"[18] really provides the key to this somewhat complex, enigmatic, and much discussed (see especially 2:14ff.) second chapter. If in addition the reference to the "Glory" *(doxa)*—neither, in our opinion, an afterthought[19] nor a gloss[20]—is taken in closest conjunction with Christ himself *(ipse Christus),*[21] then the rebuke on "respect of persons"

17. *Pace* WH; RV mg.

18. Wrongly, S. Wiersma et al., as subj. gen.: "the faith which Christ has." *Prosōpolēmpsia* cannot be taken to refer to apostolic (esp. between James and John) rivalry (*Gereformeerd Theologisch Tijdschrift* 56 [1958]: 179, answered by J. A. Scheps, ibid. 58 [1958]: 54ff.). Similarly, efforts to connect *doxa* as "opinion" with the distant *prosōpolēmpsia* (Erasmus, Calvin), or even with *pistis:* "faith in the glory of Christ" (Pesh. 69, 173, 206, 1518; so Grotius), strain the Greek even more.

19. So R. A. Knox, *A New Testament Commentary: The Later Epistles, The Apocalypse,* III (1956), 98.

20. Spitta, A. Meyer, and others. Textual evidence (13 Sah.) and Jewish-Christian instances of "the Lord of Glory" (e.g., 1 En. 22:14 *et saepe* [9]; Ps. 29:3; 24:7-10; Eph. 1:17; see also Jas. 5:14) alike are palpably weak—and why, too, should a Christian redactor be content with such a superficial change?

21. As a qualitative (Semitic) genitive (so Brinktrine, "Zu Jak. 2:1," *Biblica* 35 [1954]: 44ff. et al.), with persuasive reference to Hebrew and Aramaic parallels, i.e., "faith in our glorious Lord Jesus Christ" (see Jas. 1:25; 2:4, et al.); or more likely, in direct apposition (but without the additional reference to "Lord" [Knowling]), taking Christ as "the Glory" (Bengel, Mayor, Oesterley, et al.). See also the attractive alternative "Jesus Christ who reigns in glory" (NEB).

(prosōpolēmpsia) achieves fresh significance. We translate, transferring "our" (with some manuscript support) to the end of the sentence and linking it with "glory," "our glory": "Do not try to combine faith in the Lord Jesus Christ, our Glory, with worship of men's social status."[22] Evidently James's approach to Christology—a problem, according to some,[23] even more vexing than that of "faith and works"—is in harmony with the Epistle's strong Jewish caste, through the doctrine of the *Shechinah,* the metonym for the divine Presence,[24] as well as the link between the Old and New Covenants.

As on faith, so on Christ, James's comparative silence is not the result of lack of information; what he says on both speaks volumes. The use of "Lord" *(Kyrios)* and "servant" *(doulos)* in 1:1, in conjunction with the title given by James in 2:1,[25] is highly significant and succinctly summarizes his theology of the Person of Christ in his divine and human aspects, especially in relation to "faith." "James refers to Jesus with equal facility as 'The Lord' and 'the Word,'" writes Henderlite; "The ethic of James, therefore, goes far beyond Judaistic legalism and approaches the supernatural quality of Pauline ethics in that it takes into account the power which is available for man through Jesus Christ."[26] We need not imagine that, though decisive, the conversion of James was as spectacular as that of the Pharisee Paul; but the OT has many records of faithful servants of God to whose hearts he spoke, and who responded to his will.

James's conversion must have been an intensely personal experience, and from that, not from Hellenistic habit, comes the devotion that sounds in the title "Lord" as given to Jesus (1:1 and 2:1), no less than to the Father (e.g., 4:10; 5:11). Jewish-Christian materials indicate that the designation of Jesus as Lord, in the highest sense of that title, followed and was due to the resurrection.[27] For two centuries *Kyrios*

22. For this emendation, see Adamson, p. 104; and for criticisms, see P. U. Maynard-Reid, *Poverty and Wealth in James* (1987), pp. 51f.; Davids, p. 107.

23. See A. M. Fairbairn, *The Place of Christ in Modern Theology* (1893), p. 328.

24. L. Blau, art. "Shekinah," *JE,* XI (1908), 258-60.

25. Unfortunately, as we have seen, the meaning has been much disputed. We believe that it would be doubted much less frequently if we more clearly realized the early date of the Epistle and the markedly Hebrew character of the first great Christian church, the Jerusalem Church.

26. "The Epistle of James," *Interpretation* 3.4 (1949): 471.

27. See Jn. 20:8f., 24-28, 31; 21:15-17; Phil. 2:9-11; Acts 2:36, and explicitly, Rom. 14:8. This title, "the Lord Jesus Christ," is found by far the most frequently in Paul. In the confession of Jesus as "Lord" Paul saw nothing less than the working of the Holy Spirit and the sole condition of being "saved"; the fact that Paul mentions the title almost incidentally shows that he is simply repeating common doctrine. James probably did not even think of all the details of Paul's

had stood in the LXX as the Greek for the Lord (God), no doubt making some necessarily limited impression on and through its readers among the Jews. We must also remember that in the NT *Kyrios* and *doulos* do not signify heartless tyranny and abject slavery; according to Jesus himself (Mt. 6:24), affection was the essence of the relationship. If affection is to be relevant, lack of it will be no bar to serving two lords, and Christ's argument will not stand.

So also when, for instance, James (1:1) calls himself *doulos* of God and the Lord Jesus Christ, he does so in the zeal of devotion and love; he has given himself (as must his readers) to God in an allegiance of reciprocal love and loyalty. Similarly, "take my *yoke* upon you and *learn* of me" (see 1:5). In such a relation, faith and acts are obviously inseparable: action is of the essence of the life of a servant. Thus faith and unfaith have ethical no less than intellectual consequences. The double-minded man is *not* a true "servant" *(doulos)* of Christ; if he were, his commitment would preclude all wavering.

THE TEST OF FAITH

An important key to James's theology of faith is the doctrine of the *Shechinah*. In the NT "glory" is used not merely in thought of the *impression* flowing from Christ before the incarnation, in his life on earth, after the resurrection and ascension, and, in the fullness of time, in his Second Coming, but in recognition of his essential "doxological" nature. James's exalted Christology, like John's, is firmly rooted in the OT, especially in the idea of "the glory *(kāḇôḏ)* of Yahweh," implying exaltation, revelation, and divine eschatological salvation,[28] but also in

---

analysis of the Lordship and redemptive work of Christ; but, as we have seen elsewhere, any sound belief in Christ the Redeemer must recognize how in that function he transcends the old law, however modernized it may be, in the work of each person's salvation. When we remember the meaning of "Lord" to the Hebrews, we will scarcely speak of the poverty of their nascent Christology. From the Lordship of Jesus Christ also flowed far-reaching and practical consequences for the church. "In every expression of its life," notes H. Bietenhard, "the Christian community stands before the *kyrios* who has authority and exercises it over the community (1 Cor. 4:19; 14:36; 16:7)" ("Lord" [*Kyrios*]; *NIDNTT*, II, 517). See, e.g., R. N. Longenecker, *The Christology of Early Christianity* (1970); C. F. D. Moule, *The Origin of Christology* (1977), pp. 31ff., 35ff.; I. H. Marshall, *The Origins of New Testament Christology* (1977), pp. 97ff. See also our previous remarks, pp. 17, 262f.

28. See Heb. 1:3. For references and details, see G. Kittel, *doxa*, *TDNT*, II, 248f.; W. D. Davies, *Invitation to the New Testament* (1966), p. 42; A. M. Ramsey, *The Glory of God and the Transfiguration of Christ* (1949); Davids, p. 107.

the later idea of *Shechinah* (lit. "dwelling"), denoting "the manifestation of God upon the stage of the world, although he abides in the faraway heavens." So the *Shechinah,* the effulgence of God, may make its presence felt anywhere.[29]

We cannot tell how much of the *Shechinah* theology James knew, but it is in the evolution of this idea from Moses onward that the Christianity of James is to be set. "In the Lord Jesus Christ," observes B. B. Warfield, "James sees the fulfillment of these O.T. promises: He is the Jehovah come to be with His people: and, as He has tabernacled among them, they have seen His glory. He is, in a word, the Glory of God, the *Shechinah:* God manifest to man."[30] According to James, therefore, God's glory was revealed supremely in "our Lord Jesus Christ"—in what he was, in the event of his earthly life and death and resurrection, in his promised Second Coming, and in his church, the extension of his incarnation, revealing his glory as the glory of God. Thus James shared the central conviction of the NT *kerygma,* that Jesus Christ is "the republication of the glory of God."[31]

But with the Christian promise and the Christian hope comes the Christian duty. As the *Shechinah,* Christ is the revelation of God, and as God he is never *prosōpolēmptēs*[32]—indeed, his glory ought to bring

---

So it is in the Pauline "the Lord of Glory" (1 Cor. 2:8), as Warfield points out, designating him "to whom glory belongs as His characterizing quality" (*The Lord of Glory* [1907], p. 243). In this use, the primary meaning of "glory" is the radiance of God's invisible glorious nature as shown in the divine character and deeds, especially in the character and deeds of "the Lord Jesus Christ." Personified (e.g., Ezek. 3:23; 9:3; 10:4; 43:2, etc.), the *kāḇôḏ* of Yahweh in the OT was his self-manifestation to all nations (Isa. 46:18). When Moses wishes to know the nature of God, he says, "Show me your glory" (Ex. 33:18). See G. von Rad, *doxa, TDNT,* II, 238ff.; J. M. Lochman, "The Glory of God and the Future of Man," *Reformed World* 34.3 (1976): 97ff.; also S. Aalen, "Glory" *(doxa), NIDNTT,* II, 44ff.

29. A. Cohen, *Everyman's Talmud* (1932), p. 42; J. Abelson, *The Immanence of God in Rabbinical Literature* (1912), pp. 77ff.; M. Kadushin, *The Rabbinic Mind* (^{2}1965), pp. 222ff.

30. *The Lord of Glory,* p. 243.

31. See G. S. Hendry, "The Glory of God and the Future of Man," *Reformed World* 34.8 (1976): 151; F. Mussner, "'Direkte' und 'indirekte' Christologie im Jakobusbrief," *Catholica* 24 (1970): 112; Hoppe, pp. 72ff.

32. See E. Tiedtke, "Face" *(prosōpon), NIDNTT,* I, 587; the LXX expression *prosōpon lambanein* for the pejorative "showing partiality" usually translates the Hebrew *nāśā' pānîm* (sometimes *hikkîr pānîm, hāḏar pānim*) (e.g., Lev. 19:15; Dt. 10:17; Ps. 82:2; Prov. 28:50). Less often the expression is used in a good sense, "be gracious to" (e.g., Dt. 28:50; 2 Kgs. 3:14; Job 42:8f.; Lam. 4:16). See W. D. Davies, *Invitation to the New Testament,* p. 48.

people closer to him.[33] No Christian can practice *prosōpolēmpsia*. The clue to the understanding of this verse is in the traditional Greek philosophic contrast of truth (or, here, true *pistis*) and error, or pernicious discriminations (2:4).

The lively little "synagogue"[34] scene (2:3), even if hypothetical (Dibelius)—which we question—is obviously true to life. The delicate balancing of rich and poor worshipper with the usher's little comment shows James's artistry with words. Whether the term "synagogue" *(synagōgē)*—not necessarily a decisive argument either for the Epistle's early date or for a Jewish destination, but, significantly, found only here in a Christian sense (see 5:14) in the NT—means primarily the building, congregation, or court[35] is not clear. Certainly in Judaism the idea of the *Shechinah* is intimately linked with that of the Jewish synagogue where indeed specific precautions had to be taken to avoid "the glare of the *Shechinah*";[36] the possible reference to seating arrangements[37] (and the usher *[hypēretēs]*?)[38] also seems to suggest a local assembly. Since, however, the local "assembly" was coextensive with (what was now) the true Israel, conditions here—and the terminology of the Scrolls[39] may confirm this—appear to reflect those of the *koinōnia* at

33. On "the assimilative power" as well as the eschatological aspect of God's glory, see Hendry, *art. cit., Reformed World* 34.8 (1976): 151f.

34. Rare in early Christian literature. See, e.g., Epiphanius, *Refutation of all Heresies* 30.18 (both senses); *Synagōgē Markiōnistōn,* Le Bas-Waddington, *Inscriptions Grecques et Latines,* III (1870), no. 2558, p. 852; also Hermas, *Mand.* 11.9. Nor is the LXX helpful, the 215 instances representing mainly *qāhāl* (111) and *'ēdāh* (always translated *synagōgē*), which, like *ekklēsia* and *synagōgē,* are practically synonymous (see K. L. Schmidt, *ekklēsia, TDNT,* III, 518. Apparently *synagōgē* came to have a more local and less purely religious flavor than *ekklēsia.* See also *episynagōgē* (Heb. 10:25); and, in an eschatological sense, 2 Thess. 2:1: every "gathering" was a foretaste of the final "mustering" at the parousia. See T. Zahn, *Introduction to the New Testament,* I (1909), 94ff.; L. Coenen, "Church, Synagogue" *(ekklēsia), NIDNTT,* I (1975), 291ff., 304; also W. Schrage, *synagōgē, TDNT,* VII, 798ff.

35. On the church as a court, see Scaer's Excursus, pp. 78ff.

36. See J. Gutmann, *The Jewish Sanctuary* (1983), p. 18; J. Abelson, *The Immanence of God in Rabbinic Literature,* p. 123; *Jewish Mysticism* (1913), p. 91.

37. M. Megilla 4.21; b. Sukka 51b; Mt. 23:6; also W. Bacher, "Synagogue," *JE,* XI (1908), 639ff.

38. *Apostolic Constitutions* 2.58; *Didascalia* 12; *Statutes of the Apostles,* G. Horner (1904), pp. 195ff. See also Bacher, *art. cit., JE,* XI, 640ff.

39. See T. H. Gaster's interesting, if not completely convincing, interpretation of "seat" *(môšab; mêṯbâ)* and "to stand without" in terms of "status" and "be excluded from society," pointing to the community as a whole *(The Scriptures of the Dead Sea Sect* [1957], p. 25). For a careful discussion of the setting described in this pericope, 2:1-13, see Maynard-Reid, *Poverty and Wealth in James,* pp. 48ff.;

large. In the best traditions of the Greek diatribe, James vividly describes the royal treatment of the "richly clad" *(en esthēti lampra)* and "beringed" *(chrysodaktylios)* stranger (catechumen?—more probably, non-Christian), and the way the usher "fawns upon" *(epiblepō)* him. In sharp contrast he describes, as vividly, the shocking treatment of the poor, unforgettably exposing the essential evil of "respect of persons" (see Lev. 19:5).

Deep down, however, James is not dealing with social snobbery but with spiritual pride, the terrible pride of those who are certain that they are instructors of the ignorant and guides of the blind, and yet are poor and naked before God (Rom. 2:19), and whose arrogance excludes God's presence from the community. We read: "Whosoever is proud of heart causes the *Shechinah* to withdraw" (Mek. Ba-Ḥodesh 9). Jas. 3:1 shows that James had the local "diaspora" instructors (rabbis) in mind; the letter would be sent to them, naturally for the benefit of their flock, and probably read from the *bîmāh,*[40] a focal point in the synagogue from which the Torah was read. Surrounded by benches, the *bîmāh* was probably a rectangular, balustraded wooden platform; or less likely perhaps, as in later synagogues, an elaborate marble structure, enclosed by a wrought-iron fence with doors, reading desk, lamps, and of course with steps to it.

James is not merely thinking of a "dignitary"[41] but the rabbi (don't some ministers stand at the door "receiving the incomers," Christian, non-Christian, wealthy, or otherwise—for a time at least?),[42] and here we conjecture that the *hypopodion* is the same as the Latin *podium*. This should suggest the picture not of a footstool but rather something like the galleries of which Scottish-Presbyterian Churches were rather fond, or at least (more probably) the exalted seats of "dignitaries" or "rabbis" condemned by Jesus (Mt. 23:6 with parallels). It is just as if we told a humble visitor, "Stand at the back, or sit here on the steps of my pulpit, platform, stall." In the same way a cathedral dignitary (canon?) might have said (when cathedrals did not provide chairs), "Stand there, or sit on the steps of (i.e., leading up to) my stall (stall has the same etymology

---

C. H. Felder, "Partiality and God's Law: An Exegesis of James 2:1-13," *Journal of Religious Thought* 39 (1982-83): 51-69.

40. From the Greek word *bēma,* "platform." See Gutmann, *The Jewish Sanctuary,* p. 15 with Plates XLIIf.; also R. Posner, art. "Synagogue," *Encyclopaedia Judaica,* XV (1971), 591f.; G. Vermes, F. Millar, M. Black, and E. Schürer, *The History of the Jewish People in the Age of Jesus Christ,* II (1979), 446, nn. 89ff.

41. As per Ropes, p. 190.

42. *Pace* Davids, p. 109.

as stool)." The two authentic commands, "Will you sit here, please *(kalōs),* sir . . . ,"[43] "Stand over there, you, or sit at my feet on the steps of my stall," serve to stress the two very different types of approach.

Such discrimination recalls the conduct of corrupt judges; the context (see, too, 2:13) and usage suggest a purely legal sense for *diakrinō,* like that of *dialogismos.*[44] A literal translation can hardly catch the elusive play of the Greek: "Did you not deliver judgments on one another, and become judges who corrupt judgment?" A judge's respect of persons is said to cause the *Shechinah* to depart.[45]

True "faith" and "respect of persons" therefore are mutually exclusive. The *Shechinah* and snobbery do not mix: "If you worship the Lord of true Glory, you do not observe worthless social distinctions." By God's grace we all must strive, so far as we can, to "realize" the incarnation in our lives; and we must face up to the ethical duties on which James ever insists.

THE FAITH OF CHRIST

From this glaring example of class discrimination (2:1ff.), James proceeds to an exposition of the new righteousness revealed by Christ, especially in the Sermon on the Mount. In this revised and authoritative ethic from the teaching of Jesus the impact of Christianity on the epistle can perhaps be seen most of all. The vigorous reminder *(akousate)* of the peculiar position of the poor (2:5), their wealth in the realm of faith *(plousioi en pistei),*[46] and their hope of the Kingdom—a promise that perhaps recalls the Hellenistic "faith-sight antithesis" (Dibelius) or Jewish sayings about the reversed lot of poor and rich, but surely is directly inspired by Luke's Beatitude (6:20)—binds the idea of *prosōpolēmpsia* still more firmly to that of the *Shechinah.* Given exclusively to Israel[47] as a mark of Yahweh's election-love *('ahᵃḇāh),*[48]

43. So Ropes, *pace* Mayor, "in a good seat," "comfortably" (see Alciphron, *Epistles* 3.20: Aelian, *Anecdotes on Various Subjects* 2.13; Aristophanes, *Knights* 785). *Kalōs* is perhaps used colloquially, as in Greek comic writers (see LS, s.v.), for polite "please," "pray."

44. See MM, pp. 150f.; BAG, p. 185.

45. See S. Schechter, *Some Aspects of Rabbinic Theology* (1909), pp. 229ff.

46. Correctly Kent comments: "James was probably not stating the content of their wealth as consisting of faith, but denoting the realm in which their riches are to be found, in contrast to the world where their poverty is viewed" (*Faith that Works,* p. 80).

47. b. Sanhedrin 59a; b. Berakoth 7a.

48. On Israel as *'am sᵉgūllāh,* see H.-J. Schoeps, *Aus frühchristlicher Zeit* (1950), pp. 191ff. With her corresponding response (v. 5b) see Schechter, *Rabbinic Theology,* chs. 4f.; N. H. Snaith, *The Distinctive Ideas of the Old Testament* (1944),

the *Shechinah* now rested on the poor, who, as the new Israel, would inherit its splendor in the coming Kingdom.[49]

Yet, in spite of the exalted position of the poor, the readers of the Epistle dishonored them (2:4, 6); equally inexplicable was their exaggerated deference to the rich, for they were precisely the ones *(autoi)* who perpetrated judicial oppression. The courts *(ta kritēria)* in question were probably the local sanhedrin to whom Rome entrusted local government. The application of the two verbs *atimazō* and *katadynasteuō* to readers and rich, both terms associated in the LXX[50] and especially in the prophets with a particular kind of social injustice—and this ("the sighing of the needy"), too, removes the *Shechinah*—places his readers virtually in the same camp as the devil and their enemies, the rich.

The rich are also responsible for "the profanation of the fair Name"—a special type of blasphemy and a capital crime[51] covering irreverence, insincerity, and flagrant moral breaches, which was forgiven only at death.[52] This, too, banished the *Shechinah*,[53] and in Qumran meant banishment from the community.[54] The offense here might be economic (e.g., usury) or, possibly as in the first instances, injustice toward slaves or servants;[55] but more likely the oppression is essentially religious. The "Name," in the sense of revealed work, purpose, and character, probably refers to the (preexistent) Name of the Mes-

---

ch. 6; Davids, p. 111; W. Günther, H.-G. Link, "Love" *(agapaō), NIDNTT,* II, 540; G. Wallis, *'āhabh, TDOT,* I (1974), 104.

49. b. Berakoth 17a. Abelson shows that the Kingdom *(malᵉkuṯ šāmayim)* and the Fatherhood of God are twin concepts "at the root of the mysticism of the *Shechinah*" (*Jewish Mysticism,* p. 85); see also K. L. Schmidt, *basileia, TDNT,* I, 571, *malᵉkuṯ šāmayim* in rabbinic literature.

50. For *atimazō (bûz)* see M. Görg, *bāzāh, TDOT,* II, 60ff. for discussion and examples; e.g., Prov. 14:21; 22:22; Ecclus. 10:23; Acts 5:41; 1 Cor. 11:22; for *katadynasteuō (yānāh)* see, e.g., Ezek. 3:7, 12, 16; 45:8, and for *'āšaq* see, e.g., Jer. 7:6; Mic. 2:2; Am. 4:1; Zech. 4:10; Mal. 3:10; also Wisd. 2:10.

51. See Am. 2:7 *et saepe* (ten times in the OT); also the Mishnah tractate Sanhedrin for trial; I. Abrahams, "Blasphemy," *ERE* (1908), 671-72. See also Sifré on Dt. 32:38 (end): "The Holy One, blessed be he, pardons everything else, but on profanation of the Name he takes vengeance immediately." See H. Währisch, C. Brown, "Revile" *(blasphēmeō), NIDNTT,* III, 342ff.; also W. Dommershausen, *ḥll, TDOT,* IV, 410.

52. b. Yoma 86a.

53. *Sifré debê Rab,* ed. Friedmann (1864), 104a. Also Schechter, *Some Aspects of Rabbinic Theology,* p. 223.

54. 1QS 6:25-27. See M. Newton, *The Concept of Purity at Qumran and in the Letters of Paul* (1985), p. 44.

55. S. H. Blank, "Isaiah 52:5 and the Profanation of the Name," *HUCA* 25 (1954): 7.

siah,[56] with a possible, but not necessary, reference to the baptismal formula "in(to) the name" *(eis to onoma)* (see Acts 8:16).[57] The idea of Israel's dedication to Yahweh[58] is naturally transferred to the new Israel, who are Christ's special possession. To ill-treat the poor, therefore, was to ill-treat the *Shechinah* or Christ himself.

THE LAW OF FAITH

We now have a new and important phase in the attack on snobbery (2:8).[59] The exact function of the Greek connecting particle *mentoi,* ignored by the KJV, is obscure. If concessive, this would form a direct reply to the "excuse" (Ropes) that deference to the rich was simply done in obedience to the law of love. More probably, the correct sense is affirmatory (Hort). So "if (to anticipate any argument) you *really* keep . . . you do well (*kalōs poieis;* contrast 2:19)"—a claim that their partiality disproved, and a further sin against the *Shechinah.*[60] The royal Torah—the anarthrous *nomos basilikos* (Lat. *lex regia*) indicating, not necessarily a quasi-proper noun,[61] but rather the law's essentially messianic, as distinct from Mosaic, character—is the law of love *(Liebesgebot)* contained in Lev. 19:18 (LXX), prominent, even in its positive form, in later Judaism,[62] and finally enunciated by Christ, the royal Messiah, as the transcendent principle of his Kingdom.

Certainly the epithet "royal" *(basilikos)* can hardly be divorced from the previous reference to the Kingdom (v. 5);[63] for the most part, other interpretations[64] are merely derivatives. This view, if correct, fits

56. On "The Invocation of the Name," see K. Kohler, "The Tetragrammaton," *Journal of Jewish Lore and Philosophy* (1919): 19ff.

57. W. Heitmüller, *Im Namen Jesu* (1903), p. 92. For the corresponding rabbinic expression *lᵉšēm,* see H. Bietenhard, "Name" *(onoma), NIDNTT,* II, 650, 655.

58. b. Pesaḥim 54a; Gen. R. 11.

59. Yalḳuṭ on Prov. 20; b. Sanhedrin 58b.

60. "Whoever acts with effrontery towards a King is as though he acted in similar manner before the *Shechinah*" (Gen. R. 94.9; see also b. Sanhedrin 49a; Tanḥuma b. Noah 19b-20a; C. G. Montefiore and H. Loewe, *A Rabbinic Anthology* [1938], p. 254; Cohen, *Everyman's Talmud,* p. 189).

61. Mayor; Ropes; see also C. F. D. Moule, *An Idiom Book of New Testament Greek* (1953), p. 108.

62. See F. F. Bruce, *Acts* (1951), (Gk.) p. 299; (Eng.) p. 312; L. T. Johnson, "The Use of Leviticus 19 in the Letter of James," *JBL* 101.3 (1982): 393.

63. See Windisch; Rendall.

64. E.g., law: as king *(lex rex): nomos pantōn basileus* (Plato, *Gorgias* 484b); for kings (Pseudo-Plato, *Minos* 317c; see also 4 Macc. 14:2; 1 Pet. 2:9; so Mayor, Ropes, Zahn, Dibelius; it creates kings (*quia reges facit;* so D. Thomas). See C. H. Dodd, *The Bible and the Greeks* (1935), p. 39.

in admirably with the Jewish doctrine of the Messianic Torah.[65] But since snobbery deliberately violates (*hamartian ergazesthe* = "*you* work sin") this law, the readers incur its condemnation (2:9). They are therefore "sinners" *(parabatai)*[66] or even, as the context suggests, *rebels*—"rebellion" *(peša')* or presumptuous sin, according to the rabbis, being the most heinous sin, equivalent to breaking the yoke of heaven and being against the *Shechinah*.[67]

The principle of organic unity is introduced to add support to James's argument. Since the royal messianic Torah, like the Mosaic law, is one immutable, indivisible unit—its unity being derived from the love of the Lawgiver, the one true God (2:8, 10a; see 4:12)—a single infraction *(ptaisē)* ("incipient falling," Rom. 11:11 [Hort]) *de en heni* (2:10) means that a person, even though he keeps the rest of its precepts, has become *(gegonen)* guilty of all. Although divided into "light" (easy?) (*qallāh*—i.e., nonessential)[68] and "heavy" (burdensome?) (*ḥ^amôrāh*—i.e., essential) *(corpora legis, gûpê tôrāh)*,[69] the Jewish Torah, even in its separate statutes, was immutable[70] and indivisible.[71] Later tradition,

65. E.g., Yalkuṭ on Isa. 26; see also Gen. R. 98; W. D. Davies, *Torah in the Messianic Age* (1952), p. 74.

66. A reference to the rabbinic idea of a "hedge" or "fence" about the Torah (M. Aboth 1.1), transgression sometimes being interpreted in the light of Eccl. 10:8, i.e.,"the serpent of the rabbis has bitten him" (b. Shabbath 11a). See G. D. Kilpatrick, "Übertreter des Gesetzes. Jak. 2:11," *ThZ* 23 (1967): 433.

67. b. Yoma 36b; Schechter, *Some Aspects of Rabbinic Theology*, ch. 14.

68. E.g., freeing the mother bird (Dt. 22:7; see also Deuteronomy R. 6; b. Kiddushin 39b).

69. E.g., honoring parents (Ex. 20:12). See I. Abrahams, *Studies in Pharisaism and the Gospels*, First Series (1917), 26; W. D. Davies, *Paul and Rabbinic Judaism* (1948), p. 120.

70. S–B I, 244ff.

71. E.g., "He who transgresses a light commandment will end in violating the more heavy one. If he neglected the injunction of 'Thou shalt love thy neighbor as thyself' (Lev. 19:18), he will soon transgress the commandment of 'Thou shalt not hate thy brother in thy heart'" (Lev. 19:17; Torat Kohanim 108b); also "If a man do all, but omit one, he is guilty (*'āšēm;* Gk. *enochos*, a forensic term meaning "subject to"; see also Mt. 5:22; 1 Cor. 11:27; P. Oxy. 275 A.D. 66; BAG, s.v.; H. Hanse, *enochos*, *TDNT*, II, 828; also F. Thiele, "Guilty" *[enochos]*, *NIDNTT*, II, 142) "of all and each" (Midr. Numbers R. 9.12; b. Shabbath 70b; b. Horayoth 8b; also Gal. 5:3; S–B I, 244f.; Schechter, *Some Aspects of Rabbinic Theology*, p. 216). On Augustine see *Letter* 167. *Augustine to Jerome (Spring 415)*. On Jas. 2:10: "Whosoever shall keep the whole law," etc. *St. Augustine, Letters*, IV (165-203), tr. W. Parsons, "The Fathers of the Church," ed. R. J. Deferrari (1955), 32ff. See *Retractations* 2.45. On the (unlikely) possibility of Stoic influence, see Mayor, p. 93; Ropes, p. 200; *pace* M. O'R. Boyle, *art. cit.*, *NTS* 31.4 (1985): 611ff.

however, chiefly due to Akiba and Hillel,[72] was less stringent, so that wearing phylacteries and fringes meant observing the whole Torah[73]—a standpoint radically different from that of James.[74]

An appeal to the seventh (adultery) and sixth (murder) commandments (2:11) further stresses the law's basic unity, local conditions, as well as the LXX version,[75] being responsible for the choice and order of these two ethical directives. Both commandments are given by God: to obey the one and not the other is to transgress the Torah. That adultery was not committed is indeed possible (Hort), although 4:1ff. might suggest a different conclusion.

For James, then, the law is neither "natural" nor "Mosaic" (which like any code of the law suffers from a certain "rigor mortis") but the "law of liberty," the "royal law." It is not a new Torah, but a new interpretation of God's purpose, manifested and mediated through the long-promised Messiah. Christ's claim (in the Sermon on the Mount) to interpret the Torah and the Prophets without "tradition" (which with time becomes as deadening as the code of law itself) rests on the messianic quality of his insight into the true spiritual nature of the law. His unprecedented pronouncements did not abrogate the law but fulfilled it in the true sense.

Qumran has confirmed W. D. Davies's thesis that some elements in Jewish messianic hopes led at least some of them to expect with the Messiah a new Torah. Three points are to be stressed:

1. The Dead Sea community conceived that they were repeating the experiences of their Mosaic forefathers;
2. the activities of the "revolutionary" Messiahs from Hezekiah to Simeon B. Kosebah in marshalling their forces in the wilderness

72. M. Aboth 3.16.

73. Mayor, p. 89; also T. J. Kiddushin 1.10.61a; b. Rosh ha-Shanah 16b, 17a.

74. Bruce, *The Acts of the Apostles*, p. 294; *Commentary on the Book of Acts* (1954), p. 307. We may note in passing that, as with, e.g., "faith" and *peirasmos*, James also uses "law" in a double sense, either as OT injunctions or "the law of liberty." Each must be carefully distinguished. See H.-H. Esser, "Law" *(nomos)*, *NIDNTT*, II, 450.

75. Ex. 20:13, 5 (B): Nash Hebrew Papyrus; Mk. 10:19; Lk. 18:20; Rom. 13:9 (contrast Mt. 5:21, 27 with *ou*, future indicative and in the usual order), with *mē* instead of LXX *ou*. "The prevalence of this sequence in some circles of early Christianity may have been the result of the Egyptian decalogue order, or again it may have simply reflected the instinct that unchastity deserved to be mentioned first in order of importance" (J. Moffatt, "Jesus on Sins," *Studies in Early Christianity*, ed. S. J. Case [1928], p. 196). See also L. T. Johnson, *art. cit.*, *JBL* 101.3 (1982): 393.

show how firmly the concept of a New Exodus was connected with Messiahship;
3. the ease with which NT writers interpreted the Christian dispensation in terms of the Exodus proves that that way of interpretation must have been readily comprehensible.

Likewise the *Preaching of Peter* (according to Clement of Alexandria) and Justin Martyr respectively call Jesus "Law and Word" and "another Law," and the Shepherd of Hermas equates the "Law of God" with the "Son of God." The use of these motifs by the Christians is probably the reason why the Talmud is silent upon them.[76]

There had long been a common Jewish belief that when the Messiah came, he would bring a fresh interpretation of the law, called "the Torah of the Messiah" *(tôrāh šel māšîaḥ)*. Thus Paul of Burgos writes: "The Law thou learnest in this world is vanity compared with the Law of the world to come." Yet the rabbis do insist that the messianic Torah is not essentially different from the Mosaic Torah. The question of the Messiah abrogating the Torah does not arise, for the Messiah not only obeys the Torah but also studies and expounds it.[77] Jesus' fulfillment of the law and prophets did not mean that he fulfilled it as a subordinate

76. See W. D. Davies, *The Setting of the Sermon on the Mount* (1964), pp. 26, 116ff.; also below, p. 381. This doctrine in Christianity is clearest in Mt. 2:13–7:29; Acts 7:17-46; Heb. 3:7–4:11, and notably in John's Gospel (on Jesus as creating a "new covenant" by his life and work), and especially 14:6 and 5:39-47 (in his transcending the [Old] Law). Though Paul, in the main, used the nations' exodus illustratively and based his doctrine chiefly on what Jesus said and did, many of the early Jewish Christians to some extent developed a New-Exodus redemptive typology and a New-Torah Christology; but there was a vital difference between Judaism and early Jewish Christianity in the use of this imagery. Judaism, as Davies (*The Setting of the Sermon on the Mount*, p. 480) points out, came to place more and more emphasis on the Torah and magnified Moses chiefly as the means by which that blessing, the gift of the Old Exodus, came to Israel, and culminates in the Mishnah; the Christian church remembered above all the person of Christ, through whom the New Exodus was wrought, and so climaxes in the Christianity of the Gospels, where all is subject to Jesus as Lord.

77. "Such an assumption is excluded from the beginning by the firmly established doctrine *(Glaubensatz)* that just as the Torah pre-existed in eternity, so it was given to Israel for all eternity, and nobody has the right to add anything to it or subtract from it" (S–B IV, 1; also pp. 878, 883, 918). See also A. D. Nock, *St. Paul* (1938), p. 38; W. D. Davies, *Torah in the Messianic Age and/or The Age to Come* (1952); R. Banks, *Jesus and the Law in the Synoptic Tradition* (1975), pp. 70ff.; A. L. Williams, *Adversus Judaeos* (1935), p. 270; H.-J. Schoeps, *Paul: The Theology of the Apostle in the Light of Jewish Religious History* (1961), p. 173, n. 2.

executive minister of the divinely inspired prophets, or even of their truth.[78]

So Jesus, not in any slavish literal way but uniquely by his dynamic words and self-sufficing, incarnate life, could transcend the Scriptures in fulfilling them.[79] In his life, teaching, death, and resurrection, Christ did not abrogate but perfectly fulfilled the ideal that the law contemplated—an ideal of righteousness and love—and established the true meaning and value of the perfect law. When James speaks of "the perfect law of liberty," it seems fairly certain that he is referring to "the Messianic Torah."[80]

Again the principle of organic unity is invoked to support James's argument, the unity of the law being based on the unity of the one true God. The passage becomes eschatological once more in its reference to the Judgment and to mercy. Like his Master, therefore, James proclaims the supremacy of the law of love, meaning, as we have seen, the comprehensive sovereign rule, the term being used much as in Mt. 22:36 and elsewhere. Mercy has been defined as "the emotion roused by contact with an affliction which comes undeservedly on someone else."[81] In this sense mercy *(ḥeseḏ)* was already prominent in Judaism;[82] so it was written: "May it be Thy will that Thy mercy may subdue Thy wrath."[83] But since the coming of Christ that mercy has flowed with

78. So on the phrase *lᵉqayyēm mah šenne 'ᵉmar,* "to make to stand that which is said." A. Guillaume rightly observes that "it does not necessarily mean to fulfil in the sense that a complete and final significance or function is given to the original text of Scripture which it had until that moment lacked" ("The Midrash in the Gospels," *ExpT* 37 [1925-26]: 394). The verb means "to establish by scrutiny and examination, by exegesis, by obedience to the Spirit as much as to the letter." For rabbinic citations, see A. Guillaume, ibid.; also I. C. Rottenberg, "Fulfillment Theology and the Future of Christian-Jewish Relations," *The Christian Century* 97.3 (1980): 66-69; Hagner, *The Jewish Reclamation of Jesus,* pp. 122ff.

79. See T. W. Manson, *The Mission and Message of Jesus* (1937) on "The Attitude of Jesus to Law" (by H. D. A. Major, T. W. Manson, and C. J. Wright), p. 445; Banks, *Jesus and the Law,* pp. 208f.

80. See Longenecker, *The Christology of Jewish Christianity,* pp. 40f.; Schlatter, p. 153; Rendall, pp. 68ff.

81. R. Bultmann, quoted by H.-H. Esser, "Mercy" *(eleos), NIDNTT,* II, 594; also our remarks, p. 383.

82. See Hos. 6:6; Wisd. 3:9; 4:15; 5:15.

83. See Schechter, *Some Aspects of Rabbinic Theology,* p. 322; see also S–B I, 203ff.; G. F. Moore, *Judaism,* I (1927), 287ff.; Cohen, *Everyman's Talmud,* pp. 16ff. See also K. Stendahl, *Paul among the Jews and Gentiles* (1978), pp. 97-108, who argues that judgment and mercy are not to be balanced against each other nor is God's judgment tempered by his mercy; rather, judgment is an integral part

royal extravagance;[84] for James mercy is the main ingredient of "the law of liberty."[85] In 2:12f. James teaches the general principle that mercy should govern conduct; similarly, Paul, for whom "unmerciful" "is the lowest rung in the downward ladder of Rom. 1:29-32 and so the completest negation of the knowledge of God."[86] Ultimately, all conduct (*houtōs . . . houtōs* is emphatically inclusive, perhaps even a catechetical echo [Dibelius]) will be judged by this inexorable law of liberty, which, as v. 13 shows, brings both condemnation and acquittal.

Expanded, this difficult ellipse (v. 13)—made even more difficult by the lack of particles—seems to mean: The unmerciful man will be judged by his own standard of pitiless justice. His ill-treatment of the poor (vv. 6ff.), and especially his partiality (v. 4), is a sin against the *Shechinah,*[87] and this, as the rabbis believed, "weakens the Power of the Above[88] and turns the attribute of mercy into that of strict justice."[89] The merciful man may well hope in God, since mercy (impartial love)[90]—rather than strict justice—is the essence of the messianic Torah as well as the prerogative of the divine Judge. So "mercy has the laugh over *(katakauchatai)*[91] judgment"—the latter referring surely, in the first instance, to divine rather than human judgment.

---

of God's mercy. On the divine right to mercy, see A. Richardson, *A Theological Word Book of the Bible* (1963), p. 119.

84. See 1 Jn. 2:1f.

85. H.-H. Esser, "Law" *(nomos), NIDNTT,* II, 449.

86. H.-H. Esser, "Mercy" *(eleos), NIDNTT,* II, 599.

87. He who helps (blesses) Israel, helps (blesses) God (Mekilta on Beshallaḥ [ed. Friedman, 1870], 39; (Tanḥuma on *wayᵉḥî*). Similarly, "he who rises up against Israel rises up against God; hence the cause of Israel is the cause of God" (Mekilta on Beshallaḥ, 39). Again, he who opposes (hates) Israel, opposes (hates) God (Sifré Num. 22b). Also, he that strikes the cheek of an Israelite, strikes, as it were, the cheek of the *Shechinah* (b. Sanhedrin 58b); for, indeed, the *Shechinah* suffers with those who suffer.

88. Sifré debé Rab, ed. Friedman (1864), 136b, 137a.

89. Gen. R. 33.3; Tanḥuma B. 3.55a; Yalḳuṭ Machiri to Isaiah, p. 7; Schechter, *Some Aspects of Rabbinic Theology,* pp. 239f.

90. *Pace anileōs* (TR), for Attic *anilaos,* see Herodianus, *Epimerismoi* 257; G. W. H. Lampe, *A Patristic Greek Lexicon* (1961), p. 145 (NT *hapax legomenon*); see also Test. Abr. 12:1, 10 *(anileōs)* and 16:1 *(aneleos)*; from many kindred Jewish sentiments, see "Be careful not to be unmerciful, because he who keeps back his compassion from his neighbor is to be compared to the idolater" (Sifré debé Rab 98b; according to the rabbis, mercy is distinctive of Israel; S–B 1, 203ff.). Also Mt. 6:14; 7:1; 18:28ff.; 25:4; Jas. 1:27; 2:15ff. The article in *hē krisis* has demonstrative force, referring to *krinesthai* (2:12b) and contrasting with v. 4.

91. Indicative (B א) rather than subjunctive (*katakauchasthō;* so A. See Ropes, p. 202, for other, inferior readings; see also Jas. 3:14; Rom. 11:18), without

True to the prophets,[92] then, James tackles and solves the problem of justice and mercy[93]—perhaps personified here as Judgment *(middat̠ ḥārôn)* ("Elohim") and Merciful *(middat̠ hāraḥᵃmîm)* ("Yahweh"?)[94]—by emphasizing the rule of mercy. This is not achieved at the expense of justice, for justice must still be done.[95] As "Judge" in the sense of "Vindicator" or "Champion"[96] God offers his grace or "mercy,"[97] that is, something more than justice, to the downtrodden and disadvantaged.[98] So in his righteousness, justice and mercy are joined in perfect union. Genuine love will mean that the "poor" and the "rich" will be treated exactly alike, since each has exactly the same relationship to God. The unmerciful man will be judged by his own standard of pitiless justice. His oppression of the poor, and especially his dis-

---

any particles. The connection with the previous discussion is obvious. R. A. Knox, influenced by the Vulg. *(superexaltat),* has in his NT translation "give an honourable welcome," although in his *Commentary* he has "Pity—true Christian pity—makes short work of uncharitable judgments," i.e., human rather than divine judgment (in contrast to v. 4).

92. So also the Jewish commentator Rashi (1040-1105). On this and the eleemosynary element in *ṣedeq* and its cognates, tending toward the meaning of benevolence, and reaching beyond strict justice to salvation, see Snaith, *The Distinctive Ideas of the Old Testament,* pp. 70ff., 77, 120; Dodd, *The Bible and the Greeks,* pp. 44-65. Also Shakespeare, *The Merchant of Venice:* "And earthly power doth then show likest God's when mercy seasons justice" (4.1.176f.).

93. On the eternal conflict in Judaism between justice *(absoluta)* and mercy *(ordinata),* see Cohen, *Everyman's Talmud,* pp. 16ff., e.g., "Even while God is preparing to inflict punishment, God's compassion is bestirring itself" (b. *Pesaḥim* 87b); Philo, "And not only does this mercy follow His judgment but it also precedes it. For mercy with Him is older than justice" (*The Unchangeableness of God* 76). On justice and love, see E. Brunner, *Justice and the Social Order* (1945), pp. 114ff.; E. Sellin, *Theologie des alten Testaments* (1936), pp. 30f.; W. Dyrness, "Mercy triumphs over justice: James 2:13 and the theology of faith and works," *Themelios* (1981): 12f.

94. Gen R. 32.3; 12.15.

95. W. Eichrodt, *Theology of the Old Testament,* I (1961), 124; *pace* A. Ritschl, *Die Christliche Lehre von der Rechtfertigung und Versöhnung,* II (1882), 107; L. Diestel, *Die Idee der Gerechtigkeit* (1860), p. 188.

96. P. Volz, *Prophetengestalten des alten Testaments* (1938), p. 91; W. F. Lofthouse, "The Righteousness of Jahweh," *ExpT* 50 (1938-39): 343.

97. On his right to mercy, see H. Cremer, *Die Paulinische Rechtfertigungslehre* (1900), p. 24; *pace* L. Köhler, *Theologie des Alten Testaments. Neue Theologische Grundrisse* (1936), pp. 16ff.; W. Schneider, "Judgment" *(krima), NIDNTT,* II, 366; F. I. Andersen, "Yahweh, the Kind and Sensitive God," pp. 44ff. in *God Who Is Rich in Mercy,* Essays presented to Dr. D. B. Knox (1987).

98. E. Sellin, *Introduction to the Old Testament* (1923), pp. 83ff.; J. H. Ropes, "The Righteousness of God in the Old Testament and St. Paul," *JBL* 22 (1952): 216; H.-H. Esser, "Mercy" *(eleos), NIDNTT,* II, 596.

crimination, is a sin against "our Lord of Glory" (2:1, 4, 6ff.), whereas God's judgment of the merciless is "merciless."

The merciful man, says James, may well hope in God, since mercy (impartial love)—rather than strict justice—is the prerogative of the divine Judge. As the defender, the rescuer, the champion of the oppressed, he is, says C. S. Lewis, "more like Jack the Giant Killer than like a modern judge in a wig. The knights in the romances of chivalry who go about rescuing distressed damsels and widows from giants and other tyrants are acting almost as 'judges' in the old Hebrew sense: so is the modern solicitor who does unpaid work for poor clients to save them from wrong. . . . We are all in the same boat. We must pin our hopes on the mercy of God and the work of Christ, not on our own goodness."[99] Here again we see the impact of Jesus' teaching; see especially the beatitude on mercy (Mt. 5:7); the forgiveness petition in the Lord's Prayer (Mt. 6:12, 14f.); the parable of the unmerciful servant (Mt. 18:23-35); and Mt. 25:31-46.

There is no inconsistency here with the doctrine of justification by grace, for this, as Cranfield observes, is "but a salutary reminder that the absence of compassion for one's fellow men is conclusive proof that one's professed faith is counterfeit, while mercy shown—though certainly not to be thought of as a meritorious work putting God under an obligation—may be an evidence of genuine faith."[100] "If indeed," says James, "you fulfill the sovereign law, according to the scriptures, 'Thou shalt love thy neighbor as thyself,' you do well." But to violate this law by showing "respect of persons" is ultimately to be judged by the pitiless OT *lex talionis* (2:13a). Likewise to slander a fellow Christian is equivalent to slandering the law, and the one who judges another risks the inexorable and final verdict of the one who is both lawgiver and judge (4:12).

THE FRUITFULNESS OF FAITH

The main ingredient of the law of liberty, then, is mercy (2:13) expressed in deeds of kindness. These are the proof of true faith, the moral fruitfulness of faith being the natural corollary of the law of love. The remainder of 2:14-26 is spent in proving and illustrating the thesis that true faith issues in works. Indeed, it can be argued that while we have a self-contained pericope in Jas. 2:14-26, it continues the thought of vv. 1-13, to which it refers back now and then. Thus the "works" of v. 14

99. *Reflections on the Psalms* (1966), pp. 17f.
100. "The Message of James," *SJTh* 18 (1965): 193.

are those dealt with in vv. 1-13. The *tis* who makes the "objection" in v. 14 is perhaps a recent convert who has received insufficient instruction along the lines of v. 12.

This central section recalls the essential purpose of the Epistle. James was written not to cause us to see something, but to act on what we have already seen—that is, in one saving word, *Do*. He assumes that most Christians are bone lazy and will seek to get to heaven by (pardon the expression) "loafing on the Holy Spirit." For Paul, notes Brown,[101] "faith signifies implicit trust and works man's attempt to procure favour with God by his own merits. With James the contrast is between holding something to be true without acting upon it and acknowledging a truth which is worked out in daily life." Hence the question "What is the use of a man claiming *(legē)* to 'have faith' [in our Lord Jesus Christ, 2:1] if it is without works? Can this kind of faith *(hē pistis)*[102] save him?" (2:14). While "save" here almost certainly has a full soteriological and eschatological content, the "faith" described in the second question is emasculated and negative (interrogative *mē* expecting "no": "Surely faith cannot save him")—the sort of "faith" that is without "works." Such "works," defined in the following verses, that is, caring for the hungry and the needy,[103] are somewhat similar to the rabbinic *gᵉmîluṯ ḥᵃsîḏîm (Liebeswerke)*[104] but essentially different from the ceremonial *miṣwôṯ* attacked by Paul.[105] They are also one of the three pillars on which the world, or social order, rests, associated,[106] and even identified, with the *Shechinah*. James has not forgotten the ill treatment of the poor (2:6), and returns to it now.

101. "Righteousness" *(dikaiosynē), NIDNTT,* III, 37.

102. Article of previous reference, perhaps even more specific—"*his* faith"—if *auton* is emphatic (Moule, *Idiom,* p. 111).

103. See also 1:25, 27; 2:8.

104. Cohen, *Everyman's Talmud,* pp. 224ff.; S–B IV, 559ff.

105. Schechter, *Some Aspects of Rabbinic Theology,* p. 214; also for the three (Greek, Jewish, and Christian) types of "good works," especially with his *caveat* on the General Epistles, see W. C. van Unnik, "The Teaching of Good Works in I Peter," *NTS* 1 (1954-55): 92ff. Whereas "Paul's contrast was a novel one, viz. between the works of an old and abandoned system and the faith of a newly adopted one, James is led to draw the more usual contrast between the faith and works which are *both* deemed necessary under the *same* system" (Ropes, p. 205). See also M. Aboth 1.2.

106. "How great is the virtue of charity! If a man gives only one coin to a poor brother, he becomes worthy to receive the Face of the *Shechinah*" (Yalḳuṭ on Ps. 17); "Even the evildoers, provided they have given alms to the poor, will have the merit of receiving the Face of the *Shechinah*" (ibid.); "Greater is the reception of wayfarers than the reception of the *Shechinah*" (b. Shabbath 127a).

A simple illustration (2:15f.) makes the point clearer. Suppose a fellow Christian (lit. "brother or sister"), possibly a bereaved spouse but especially a widow or an orphan (1:27), is found, perhaps even in church,[107] in rags and starving,[108] and instead of being clothed and fed—for only so is it possible "to walk after the *Shechinah*"[109]—he is peremptorily dismissed with "Good luck to you" *(hypagete en eirēnē)*[110] . . . "warm and feed yourself" *(thermainesthe kai chortazesthe).*[111] "It is easy enough," wrote Thomas Merton, "to tell the poor to accept their poverty as God's will when you yourself have warm clothes and plenty of food and medical care and a roof over your head and no worry about the rent. But if you want them to believe you—try to share some of their poverty and see if you can accept it as God's will for yourself!"[112] It is inconceivable—or is it?—that this heartless Christian is a church

107. On feeding the poor in the synagogue, see art. "Charity," *JE*, III (1901), 667ff.

108. See Kent, *Faith that Works*, p. 91. Lit. "naked" (*gymnos;* Heb. *'ārôm;* e.g., Gen. 2:25; 3:7, *et saepe*), sometimes "without an outer garment" (*chitōn;* see Jn. 21:7) and lacking "a day's supply of food" *(ephēmerou trophēs).* The meaning of *ephēmeros (ephēmerios, epameros), hapax legomenon,* is difficult to determine, depending on whether it is taken as "that which is on day" or "that which has day upon it" (see H. Frankel, *Transactions of the American Philological Association* 77 [1946]: 131ff.). The use of *hyparchō* for *eimi* to translate "is naked" is a delicate and intentional touch—probably "a backward look to an antecedent condition which has been protracted into the present" (M. Vincent, *Word Studies in the New Testament,* I [1873], 743).

109. "What means the text, 'You shall walk after the Lord your God' (Dt. 13:4)? Is it, then, possible for a man to walk after the *Shechinah* of which it is written, 'The Lord the God is a devouring fire' (Dt. 4:24)? But the meaning is to follow the attributes of the Holy One, blessed be He: as He clothed the naked (Gen. 3:21), so do you clothe the naked: as He visited the sick (Dt. 18:1), so do you visit the sick" (b. Soṭa 14a). Similarly, "he who welcomes his fellowman is considered as though he had welcomed the Shechinah" (Mekilta, tractate Amalek 3).

110. Sometimes futurive with *eis* (Mk. 5:34). See Heb. *lᵉḵî lᵉšālôm* (Jub. 18:6 *et saepe*); Lk. 2:29 (*Nunc Dimittis;* likewise *Pax Vobiscum*). See also S–B I, 138. According to E. F. F. Bishop, *Apostles of Palestine* (1958), p. 185, beggars outside synagogues in Jerusalem are still so addressed today. On the phrase "to greet" *(šā'al bᵉšālôm),* see H. Beck, C. Brown, "Peace" *(eirēnē), NIDNTT,* II, 779.

111. The former is found frequently in the OT, especially in reference to warm clothes (e.g., Hos. 7:7) but also in the NT (e.g., Mk. 14:54), along with secular instances, e.g., B. Galen, *On the Simplicity of Medical Men* 2; also Plutarch, *Table Talk* 6.6), the latter meaning literally "gorge oneself" like a ravenous beast, especially cattle (see *chortos*), as well as references in the classics (LS, s.v.). See Mk. 14:20; 15:37, *et saepe.* The passives (the middle would need a reflexive pronoun [Ropes]) stress the irony of continuous and willful evasion of responsibility.

112. *New Seeds of Contemplation* (1961), p. 179.

leader[113] who is appealing here to some precept of Jesus (e.g., Mt. 6:25ff.).

But words in themselves, even those of Jesus, without clothes and food,[114] are worthless.[115] "Christ told us to judge by results," warned C. S. Lewis; "A tree is known by its fruit; or, as we say, the proof of the pudding is in the eating. When we Christians behave badly, or fail to behave well, we are making Christianity unbelievable to the outside world."[116] So faith, unless backed by deeds, is absolutely[117] dead. If the faith that tolerates respect of persons[118] is suspect, so also is a faith that is content with mere words,[119] sentiment,[120] or orthodoxy.[121] In Christianity, the one who loves his neighbor, observes Barbara Ward, "is quite simply the man who feeds him, shelters him, clothes him and heals him. It is all very direct and physical and lacking in 'spiritual' overtones. Yet the food given to the least of the little ones is given to God himself."[122] The activity of love is always to be preferred to the orthodoxy of faith, for without works faith may call itself "faith," but it is faith in name only.

Is James thinking of two *kinds* of faith?[123] The distinction is, of course, very good and up to a point perfectly permissible and in line with his habit of attaching different meanings to the same word (see *peirasmos* and *peirazomai,* 1:2, 13). James was as much aware of the dual nature of faith as were Calvin, Luther, and the church throughout

113. For the unlikely view, however, that James here—and almost throughout his Epistle—is thinking exclusively of Christian clergy, see Scaer, pp. 88, 35, and elsewhere.

114. *Ta epitēdeia, hapax legomenon,* "necessities."

115. "If thou draw out thy soul to the hungry (Is. lviii.10)—if you have nothing to give him, comfort him with words. Say to him: 'My soul goes out to you because I have nothing to give you'" (Lev. R. 3.15; see also Cohen, *Everyman's Talmud,* p. 224).

116. *Mere Christianity* (1952), p. 172.

117. *Kath' heautēn; in semetipsa* (Vulg.; *pace* KJV). For a careful analysis of possible translations, see Kent, *Faith that Works,* pp. 93f.

118. 2:1ff.

119. 2:14.

120. 2:16.

121. 2:19. On the vital relation between faith and works, see A. C. Thiselton, *The Two Horizons* (1980), pp. 422ff.

122. Cited in *The Four Gospels.* The Armoury Commentary (1973), p. 95.

123. See W. Nicol, "Faith and Works in the Letter of James," *Neotestamentica* 9 (1975): 7ff.; C. H. Powell, "'Faith' in James and its Bearing on the Date of the Epistle," *ExpT* 62 (1951): 311ff.; W. H. P. Hatch, *The Idea of Faith in Christian Literature* (1925), p. 65.

history. Faith alone saves, but if it is genuine faith, then by its very nature it will express itself in works of the Spirit. Since faith has a dual character, as is evident from the NT, there is always the danger that undue emphasis will be given to one aspect in preference to the other. So it does appear that James is thinking of two kinds of faith, condemning the one (workless) and praising the other (that which produces works). But we think that James is more nearly comparing true faith with that which is really nothing at all.

Ironically, the finest exposition of James's doctrine of faith is given by none other than Luther himself when he describes a living faith *(fides viva)*. We quote this important passage in full:

> Faith is a living, daring confidence in God's grace, so sure and certain that the believer would stake his life on it a thousand times. This knowledge of and confidence in God's grace makes men glad and bold and happy in dealing with God and with all creatures. And this is the work which the Holy Spirit performs in faith. Because of it, without compulsion, a person is ready and glad to do good to everyone, to serve everyone, to suffer everything, out of love and praise to God who has shown him this grace. Thus it is impossible to separate works from faith, quite as impossible as to separate heat and light from fire. Beware, therefore, of your own false notions and of the idle talkers who imagine themselves wise enough to make decisions about faith and good works, and yet are the greatest fools. Pray God that he may work faith in you. Otherwise you will surely remain forever without faith, regardless of what you may think or do.[124]

James has his own rich doctrine of faith, which is not merely a negative reaction to that found in Judaism, Paul, or anyone else. It is certainly very different from the sub-Christian "faith" that someone "claims" to have (2:14). We see here a *vital, internal,* or *grammatical connection* between faith and works because for James true faith by its very nature must express itself in works. Apart from a dynamic act of will that produces works, workless faith remains "dead in itself" and does not *exist*. It remains a potentiality but not yet a vital force.

Similarly, without faith, works may be called "works," but they are works in name only. Paradoxically modern Christians—unlike James's readers—may need to be reminded of this valid converse truth, namely, that works without faith are dead. It is possible to be so busy with good works that faith is neglected. Unless inspired and linked with faith, such works, like works of the law, are dead "in themselves" (see

124. *LW,* XXXV, 370f. See P. Althaus, *The Theology of Martin Luther* (1966), p. 246, especially his footnotes, for a valuable discussion; also G. W. Forell, *Faith Active in Love* (1954), pp. 87ff.

Jas. 2:17). The test of genuine faith is its power to produce works, a power that must be applied to life, and applied in the Christian way, that is, in Christian love. This is the true fulfillment of the royal law, the law of liberty, a law that has room for compassion toward the compassionate but is completely broken by toadying to the rich and despising the poor. Paul himself in 1 Cor. 13:2 emphatically declares that faith is quite nugatory unless expressed in Christian love,[125] and in the next verse Paul points out that the work itself ("though I bestow all my goods to feed the poor") is nothing without the Christian spirit of love to animate it: belief in some purchasing power in relation to God, to be acquired ipso facto by an action per se, is nothing but an empty delusion.

Christian love of others is the work of Christian faith: it is the fulfilling of the law of Christian life, the life that *implements* the Christian faith.[126] When James writes "I will show you my faith by my works" (2:18), he is not arguing for the efficacy of works per se; his point is that a faith not operating in action is dead. Verse 17 means, in effect, "*Faith* that is not expressed in corresponding *conduct* is simply *not alive.*"

So someone who *genuinely* has Christian faith may say to a man of that type:[127] "You claim to have Christian faith;[128] I do Christian actions. I challenge you: I will prove *my* Christian faith by the Christian things I *do; how* will *you* prove your Christian faith without being able to mention (or produce for inspection) anything you have done (or suffered) accordingly?"

The opponent retorts: "Certainly I will prove it—I accept the *Shema'* (Heb. *šᵉma'*, "hear") (lit. I 'believe that' *[pisteuein hoti]*[129] God is one)." To recite the *Shema'*,[130] the essence of the Torah[131] and the

125. See 1 Jn. 3:17f.

126. See Rom. 13:8-10.

127. *Erei tis*, i.e., a genuine Christian. For this technique, often used by rabbinic preachers, see, e.g., *'m 'mr lk 'dm*, A. Marmorstein, "The Background of the Haggadah," *HUCA* 6 (1929): 192; Wessel, "The New Testament," *Wycliffe Bible Commentary* (1971), p. 953; *ISBE*, II, 962.

128. *Sy pistin echeis*. *Sy* is of the opposite type; and here *echeis* has no more force than "Let us suppose . . ." or "You claim to have. . . ." See also above, pp. 126f.

129. *Pisteuein hoti* (Heb. *he'ᵉmîn kî*), i.e., "to believe that God exists," instead of *pisteuein* plus dative (Heb. *he'ᵉmîn bᵉ*), i.e., "to trust God," emphasizes *intellectual* acceptance (C. H. Dodd, *The Bible and the Greeks* [1935], p. 66).

130. "Hear O Israel: YHWH *'ᵉlōhēnû* YHWH *'eḥāḏ* (lit. Yahweh our God Yahweh one)" (Dt. 6:4 and, later, 11:13-21; Num. 15:37-41). Further, see Windisch, p. 18.

131. T. W. Manson, *The Teaching of Jesus* (1935), p. 192; W. Mundle, "Hear" *(akouō)*, *NIDNTT*, II, 177.

daily confession *(Bekenntnis)*[132] of the pious Jew, was equivalent to accepting the yoke of the Kingdom. By reciting the *Shema'* R. Akiba, who died as a martyr with a long drawn out "one" *('ĕḥāḏ)* on his lips, received "the yoke of the kingdom."[133] Indeed, the *Shechinah* is said to stand in the synagogue at the time when the Jew enters it to read the *Shema'*.[134]

"Well done *(kalōs poieis; 'ahsant)*"[135] is the crushing response; and then he proceeds to describe the result of this "faith": "so do the demons, and this makes their hair stand on end (numinous *phrissein*)." Strange "works" indeed!

Let us pause for a moment to consider this further example of worthless faith (v. 19). Arguing after the fashion of some rabbis[136] that the *Shema'*, and even the paper on which it is written, is holy (Oesterley), E. Peterson suggested (*pace* Dibelius) that B's monotheistic "there is only one God" *(heis theos estin)* instead of the other readings' "God is one" (i.e., unique) emphasis may well be that of the apotropaic formula, not that of the Christian *kerygma;*[137] but that is debatable.[138] It is further suggested that the numinous *phrissein* theme, common in Judaism,[139] but especially linked with that of diaspora syncretism that blended the one God with *Aiōn,* may be a pointer to this sort of background.[140]

132. I. Elbogen, *Der jüdische Gottesdienst in seiner geschichtlichen Entwicklung* (1924), pp. 28ff.; S–B IV, I, Ex. 9, *Das Schema,* pp. 189-207.

133. *Qibbaltā 'ôl malᵉkûṯ šāmayim* (Dt. R. 6.4). See b. Berakoth 61b; T. J. Berakoth 2.4a, cited by K.-H. Bartels, "One" *(Heis), NIDNTT,* II, 720.

134. I. Abelson, *The Immanence of God in Rabbinical Literature* (1912), p. 123.

135. Normally a term of approbation: "We can almost hear the accents of the Jerusalemite James saying, as he would today, *'ahsant*" (Bishop, *Apostles of Palestine,* p. 186)—but surely here, brilliantly ironical!

136. E.g., b. Berakoth 5a. For the exact and meticulous rules to be followed in reciting the *Shema'*, see the Tosefta tractate *Berakoth,* pp. 1-43 in *The Tosefta, First Division* (1986), eds. J. Neusner, R. S. Sarason; also C. Brown, "Prayer" *(proseuchomai), NIDNTT,* II, 864ff.

137. *Eis Theos: Epigraphische, formgeschichtliche und religionsgeschichtliche Untersuchungen* (1926), p. 295, n. 3. See, too, M. Dibelius, "Die Christianisierung einer hellenistischen Formel," *Neue Jahrbücher für das Klassische Altertum* (1915), pp. 224ff.; R. A. Horsley, "Gnosis in Corinth: 1 Cor. 8:1-6," *NTS* 27.1 (1980): 35f.

138. See B. M. Metzger, *A Textual Commentary on the Greek New Testament* (1975), p. 681.

139. Job 4:15; Dan. 7:15; 4 Macc. 14:9.

140. See P. Paris 33.3.17; also G. A. Deissmann, *Bible Studies,* tr. A. Grieve (^{2}1903), pp. 42ff.

On the other hand, W. L. Knox, who notes that the theme is inscribed on a certain amulet but ignored by Strack and Billerbeck, believes that this may indicate Hellenistic (possibly even universalistic [Oesterley?]) affinities, or "it may be due to the disappearance of the Kerygmatic form of exorcism from orthodox Judaism in the face of Christian competition."[141] It is possible that James is merely using a stock Orphic phrase for casual illustration;[142] but more likely the *Shema'* may well have been an important catechetical article, especially among early Jewish Christians;[143] if so, to recite the *Shema'* was for the Christian still synonymous with "taking the yoke of the Kingdom" (Jas. 2:5), whose inevitable ethical corollary was love for the brotherhood (Jas. 2:8).[144]

James's opponent is prepared to accept the *Shema'*, but merely mechanically and without its moral demand, like Stephen Leacock's character who declared he had "learned the motions of swimming" but when he fell overboard he "found the motions hard to put into practice";[145] or like the hopefully mythical "professional theologian" who, though perhaps thoroughly acquainted with the Bible's social principles, may neglect to apply these to, say, *apartheid* or the plight of that starving child in Bombay or Pittsburgh.[146] To learn the motions of religion is not enough. This kind of faith is shared by the demons, who tremble; and this lip service adds to their condemnation because it is precisely this amount of "faith" that forms the purchase, as it were, for their undying enmity.[147] The fact that this so adds to their condemnation can have only one meaning, namely, that the "faith" of demons is God's own gift turned back against him in precisely the same way that

141. "Jewish Liturgical Exorcism," *HTR* 31 (1938): 194, n. 5.

142. E. Langton, *Essentials of Demonology* (1949), pp. 198ff.

143. R. A. Knox, *A New Testament Commentary,* III (1956), 101. In due course, the Romans were to restrain both Jews and Christians from reciting the *Shema'*, though later "naturally the *Shema'* could not be recited in its Jewish form by Christians without a complete denial of the pre-eminent place held by Jesus, so soon at least as they began to think out the relationship of the Father to the Son" (C. W. Dugmore, *The Influence of the Synagogue upon the Divine Office* [^{2}1964], p. 103; also pp. 16ff.). While not conclusive, this seems to be another sign of our Epistle's early origin.

144. Sifré Dt. 6f. See K. Kohler, art. in *Journal of Jewish Lore and Philosophy* 1 (1919): 264; J. H. Hertz, *Sermons and Addresses* (1938), p. 7.

145. S. Leacock, *Humor and Humanity* (1938), p. 208.

146. See J. R. Fry, *The Great Apostolic Blunder Machine* (1978), p. 152.

147. On the moral nature of demons, especially in the NT (Mk. 1:24; 5:7; Mt. 8:29), see L. de Grandmaison, *Jesus Christ,* III (1928), 128ff., 268ff.; S–B IV, 501ff.; H. Bietenhard, "Demon" *(daimonion), NIDNTT,* I, 453.

the human heart turns God's law back against him—that the "exceeding sinfulness of sin" may be clearly revealed.[148]

THE PRACTICE OF FAITH

Resuming the dialogue, James (2:20) now appears to lose patience with his opponent, brusquely asking, "Don't you realize *(gnōnai,* punctiliar aorist conveying asperity), blockhead *(ō anthrōpe kene),*[149] that 'faith' lives by works; without works 'faith' is sterile?" Although apparently, as in later Jewish literature, the "emptiness" of the opponent is primarily intellectual, this has serious ethical implications on the doctrine; see 2:26, where James speaks of the body without the spirit as (not a man, not even half a man, but) merely a motionless corpse, a carcass.[150] So

148. For patristic references, see J. Beumer, "Et Daemones credunt (Jac. 2:19). Ein Beitrag zur positiven Bewertung der fides informis," *Gregorianum* 22 (1941): 231ff.

149. An address (Pesh. *ḥ^a lāšā' :* "weak"; Vulg. *inanis;* Corbey MS *vacus)*—supposed by Schammberger, Weinel, et al. to be a Gnostic attack on Paul *(sic)*—common to the diatribe ("fool that you are, wretched man"; *mōre ō talaipōre; stulte, miser,* et al.); R. Bultmann, *Der Stil der Paulinischen Predigt* (1910), p. 14; rarely of people (MM, p. 340); akin to if not identical with NT *Raca* (Mt. 5:22; see Mayor and Knowling *pace* Oesterley), OT *rêq* (Judg. 9:4; 11:3; 2 Sam. 6:20, *et saepe*), and esp. Aram. *rêqā',* "empty." See also T. W. Manson, *The Sayings of Jesus* (1949), p. 156; T. Sorg, "Rhaka" *(raka), NIDNTT,* I, 417f.

150. This metaphor is sound (see Latin proverbs such as *vita hominis sine litteris mors est* ["The life of man, without literature, is death"]; also Q. C. Rufus, *History of Alexander* 10.6.19; Plutarch, *Advice on Keeping Well* 27 [*Moralia* 2], p. 137; see also Ropes, Dibelius) and requires no emendation (*pace,* e.g., Spitta who suggests *kinēma* for *pneuma*) provided it is remembered that (a) *pistis* is used in the non-Pauline sense of a body or *corpus* of opinion; that (b) *sōma* represents the Hebraic monistic (rather than Gk. *sōma–sēma* dualistic) view of the total, essential person (see 1 Cor. 15; rightly, it is observed, *soma–pneumatos* reflects "a typical Jewish Christian anthropology" [Davids, p. 133]; "The body is the soul in its outward form" [J. Pedersen, *The History of Israel* (1926), pp. 170ff.]); for the Greek view, see E. Käsemann, *Leib und Leib Christi* (1933), pp. 23-59; that (c) the primary effect of *pneuma,* like the OT *rûaḥ* ("spirit" or "breath"? [see Mayor]), is life. Breath or spirit *(rûaḥ)* makes the body a living soul *(nepeš),* as in Gen. 2:7, and it departs at death (see A. B. Davidson, *The Theology of the Old Testament* [1904], p. 203; M. S. Enslin, *The Ethics of Paul* [^{2}1962], pp. 120ff.); that (d) the *tertium comparationis* is the essential deadness of both "body" *(sōma)* and "faith" *(pistis)* apart for the vital principle *(pneuma)*—works being equivalent to the spirit or breath of life; and that (e) probably, as R. A. Knox thinks, this illustration is his opponent's "From some kind of native obstinacy, St. James insists on using the *same* illustrations, but turning them inside out. He is saying, in effect, 'No, it is not works without faith that should be compared to a corpse; it is faith without works'" (Knox, *A New Testament Commentary,* III, 102f.). On the idea of motion

faith without works is not even half Christianity, but merely dead thought, cold abstraction, like the opinion correctly enough held by demons (v. 19). To say that faith alone gives value to works ("Also sind die Werke ohne Glauben todt"—Luther) is beside the point, which is that only works give life to faith: faith does not qualify works but works give life to faith.

Religious faith, living faith, is belief energized by activity, and life (especially for James, a master, not a tiro, in Greek) is essentially activity. Faith cooperates with works; that is how faith lives. All this is in perfect agreement with what Paul and John have said, that faith without works is a sham. Only inspired by the Christian love that fulfills is the Christian law genuine. So let our view of the Epistle of James not be clouded by misunderstanding.

The Example of Abraham

With two very different OT illustrations, James continues with his theme of faith in action. The nature of faith is exemplified first by righteous Abraham (2:20), that obvious "type of faith"[151] and "outstanding hero of faith,"[152] "the father of the faithful,"[153] whose name is also closely linked with the *Shechinah*.[154] He is a crucial example in synagogue discussion, probably already cited by the opponent of 2:19, and later possibly a prime article of Jewish-Christian catechisms. The rabbis attached importance to faith. But their faith was a species of intellectual belief rather than the basic Christian idea of "trust," and it was

---

as a vital sign, see "James," *The Student's Bible: New International Version*, Notes by Philip Yancey and Tim Stafford (1986), p. 1079.

151. "Der Typus des Glaubens" (W. Eichrodt, *Theology of the Old Testament*, II, 24); see also E. Käsemann, *Romans* (1980), pp. 106f. with references; Hoppe, pp. 112f.; Bartlett, *art. cit.*, SBL 1979 Seminar Papers, II, 173ff.

152. A. Meyer, pp. 135ff. See Philo's long eulogy *On Abraham* 262-76, concluding "himself a law and an unwritten statute" *(nomos autos ōn kai thesmos agraphos); Who is the Heir?* 90-95; *On the Virtues* 216; *On the World* (Pseudo-Philo) 1; also b. Sanhedrin 11a et al. See also S–B III, 186ff.; A. Meyer, pp. 135ff.; Dibelius, pp. 157ff.; W. Vischer, *The Witness of the Old Testament to Christ*, I (1949), 20: "Søren Kierkegaard sank down at the thought of Mount Moriah. None was so great as Abraham. Who can understand him?"

153. A. Marmorstein, *The Doctrine of Merits in Old Rabbinical Literature* (1920), p. 38—a possible, but not inevitable (Rom. 4:16ff.; 1 Clem. 31:2), proof of Jewish-Christian origin.

154. Abraham received (Gen. R. 14.2.6) and restored (Num. R. Naso. 13.2) the *Shechinah*, which was tabernacled in Israel for his sake. See C. G. Montefiore and H. Loewe, *A Rabbinic Anthology* (1938), p. 84.

regarded as itself one of many meritorious works.[155] He who exercises it acquires merit before God. The "binding of Isaac" (*'Aqēdat Yiṣḥāq*) (Gen. 22:9), his tenth and greatest trial of faith[156] in which he glorifies the divine Name,[157] shows that faith is not merely a work[158] but also an energy, namely, love[159]—which is the source of all works (Jas. 2:8). His righteousness,[160] therefore, was conditioned by obedience. Instead of being merely one particular meritorious work[161] in Abraham's justification, faith, too (2:22), is vitally linked to works, although neither is unduly stressed and both are carefully balanced.[162]

That for James faith and works are "two distinct entities"[163] is true only in the sense that there was a kind of faith known to his opponents that had no works—a dead, fruitless tree.[164] They are one or two in the same way that a tree may be regarded as one or two (see v. 26). Body

155. S–B III, 186.

156. M. Aboth 5.3; 1 Macc. 2:52; b. Sanhedrin 89b; H.-J. Schoeps, "The Sacrifice of Isaac in Paul's Theology," *JBL* 65 (1946): 385ff.; P. R. Davies and B. D. Chilton, "The Aqedah: A Revised Tradition: History," *CBQ* 40 (1978): 514ff.; P. H. Davids, "Tradition and Citation in the Epistle of James," p. 115 in *Scripture, Tradition, and Interpretation,* eds. W. W. Gasque and W. S. LaSor (1978); Dibelius, pp. 168ff.; sometimes taken as equivalent to the Greek tradition of the labors of Hercules: see M. E. Andrews, "Peirasmos—A Study in Form Criticism," *ATR* 24 (1942): 235. See also F. F. Bruce, *The Epistle to the Hebrews.* NICNT (1964), p. 309, n. 142.

157. Tanḥuma Wayerah, in answer to Ps. 8:5 (Schoeps, *art. cit., JBL* 65 [1946]: 387).

158. "He was found faithful" (Ecclus. 44:19-21); "to be faithful" (1 Macc. 2:52). S–B III, 186, show that, according to the rabbis, Abraham is reckoned righteous on account of his works, and that his faith, equated to some extent with faithfulness to the Torah, revealed at Sinai (Midr. *Tehillim* 16, 17), acquired a meritorious power, proceeding from this unfinished deed, which was already active at the Red Sea (Mekilta Ex. 15 [30a]) and was only one kind of "work." See Käsemann, *Commentary on Romans,* p. 107.

159. "When Abraham, without any questioning, obeyed God's order to sacrifice his son Isaac, he was inspired by his love to God" (Sifré Dt. 6.5, 32, 73b bottom; Jub. 17:18). See also A. Büchler, *Studies in Sin and Atonement* (1928), pp. 126ff.

160. Tanḥuma f.30a (ed. Buber), I, 115. See also A. Marmorstein, *The Doctrine of Merits,* p. 8; Jub. 23:10; Prayer of Manasseh 8; Apoc. Bar. 58:1; Gen. R. 49.2; Ex. R. 15.10; b. 'Abodah Zarah 8b, et al. On righteousness and the *Shechinah,* see R. Simeon b. Yohai: "Whithersoever the righteous go, the *Shechinah* goes with them" (Gen. R. Wayesheb 86.6).

161. See Käsemann, *Romans,* p. 107; S–B III, 186ff.; B. Lindars, *New Testament Apologetic* (1961), p. 225.

162. Ropes, p. 219; Davids, p. 128.

163. Dibelius, p. 179.

164. Kent, *Faith that Works,* p. 105; Mayor, p. 104.

and spirit are one or two depending on how one happens to consider them. Body without "spirit" is body in the sense of corpse, dead. Body as seen in action is *alive,* vivified only by "spirit." James is actually using *synērgei* as such, and the way the Greeks used *energei(tai):* the *syn* element explains the reference to "friend" in v. 26, while the remaining *ērgei* is a play on *argē*[165] (v. 20), a statement rather than a question (KJV). "Faith" cooperated with (or in) (*synērgei,* iterative; impf.) works, and by works "faith" was made perfect *(eteleōthē),* that is, was consummated, or expressed and fulfilled itself. Faith operates in conjunction with works, not otherwise.

The *'Aqēdat* is now said "to fulfill" *(plēroun)* the text in Gen. 15:6:[166] "And Abraham believed God, and it was imputed *(elogisthē)*[167] unto him for righteousness" (2:23).[168] This "fulfillment" is probably to

165. For the play on *argē,* with variants, see, e.g., Kent, *Faith that Works,* pp. 100f.

166. Unlike Paul, who, in the interests of his theory of justification by faith, breaks fresh ground by isolating Gen. 15:6 from Gen. 22:1ff., James, in support of his thesis that justification is by works and not by faith alone (see Ps. 106:30f. [Phinehas]), was content to follow a Jewish exegetical convention at least 150 years old (1 Macc. 2:52) and combined them (see W. R. Farmer, "The Patriarch Phinehas—a note on 'It was reckoned to Him as Righteousness,'" *ATR* 44 [1952]: 26ff.). See also Dibelius, pp. 172ff.; Käsemann, *Romans,* p. 107; G. Howard, *Paul: Crisis in Galatia* (1979), pp. 54f.; Davids, pp. 129f.; O. Michel, "Faith" *(pistis), NIDNTT,* I, 604f.

167. So "the habit of belief in Yahweh, He reckoned to Abraham as righteousness" (BDB, s.v. *ḥāšēb* II.3); "it was reckoned [Ger. *anrechnen;* Gk. *logizomai*] to him for righteousness" (Gesenius-Bühl, *Hebräisches und Aramäisches Handwörterbuch über das Alte Testament* [[17]1921]); "something is transferred to the subject (person) in question, and reckoned to him, which he for himself does not have . . . it is accounted to the person *per substitutionem,* the object present (here, Abraham's faith) takes the place of what it counts for (righteousness), it is substituted for it" (J. Eichler, "Reckon" *[logizomai], NIDNTT,* III, 824f.). See Dt. 24:13; 6:25; Prov. 27:14; S–B III, 199ff.; H. W. Heidland, *logizomai, logismos, TDNT,* IV, 284ff. See also Dibelius's (p. 179) useful analysis of the different interpretations of Gen. 15:6: *episteusen A. tō theō kai elogisthē autō eis dikaiosynēn.*

Judaism	A. believed God	and this belief was counted to him as a work "for righteousness."
Paul	A. believed God	and this belief was reckoned to him instead of works.
James	A. believed God	and his faith and works were counted to him "for righteousness."

168. A (א, B missing) reads *kai episteusen A. tō theō, kai elogisthē autō eis dikaiosynēn* (LXX), containing, against the MT, *Abraam* and the passive *elogisthē* to avoid the name of God, for the active Hebrew without *Lamed* ("unto").

be understood not merely in terms of isolated "prophecy,"[169] but rather, as the Talmudic root suggests, "as establishing by obedience to the spirit as much as to the letter."[170] The *'Aqēdat,* therefore, may be said "to establish" and "interpret" Gen. 15:6, and this is a divine, "suprahistoric" verdict delivered on Abraham's whole life. As a copartner *(šuttāp)* with God, he (his faith) is reckoned "to be righteous."[171] This righteousness is neither in the narrow classical nor in the purely Pauline sense, but in the sense of a right covenant *relationship (Rechts-Pflichts-Verhältnis),*[172] expressed here in the highest terms of friendship.[173] So the Abrahamic title friend of God (*philos Theou;* see Isa. 41:8)[174]—once (but no longer)

Apart from the opening *episteusen de,* James concurs (see Rom. 4:3; 1 Clem. 10:6; Justin Martyr, *The Dialogue with Trypho* 92; Philo, *On the Change of Names* 177: "and it was accounted to him for righteousness").

169. Mayor; Ropes. See also Guthrie, *New Testament Theology,* p. 975, n. 47.

170. "To establish, to interpret, to perform; to ratify or identify as genuine; to establish by scrutiny and exegesis, by obedience to the spirit as much as to the letter." On *l^eqayyēm mah šenne '^emar,* "to make to stand that which is said," see A. Guillaume, "The Midrash in the Gospels," *ExpT* 37 (1925-26): 394; Hagner, *The Jewish Reclamation of Jesus,* pp. 122f.; also above, p. 285, n. 78.

171. "Every judge who administers justice in perfect truth, even for one single moment, is regarded by the (Holy) writ as if he were a *šuttāp* (a copartner) with the Holy One, blessed be He, in the work of creation" (b. Shabbath 10a; Mekilta Ex. 18.14).

172. Schrenk shows that the basic Hebrew roots (*ṣedeq,* n. 1; *ṣ^edāqāh,* fem. n.; *ṣaddîq,* adj.; *ṣādaq,* qal; *hiṣdîq,* Hiphil) represent the idea of relationship: "A man is righteous when he meets certain claims which another has on him in virtue of relationship" (G. Schrenk, *dikaiosynē, TDNT,* II, 195). "Something in the instinctive Hebrew attitude to life," says Dodd, "caused *ṣedeq* always to tend away from the more abstract and intellectual Greek conception of Justice, in the direction of something warmer and more humane" (*The Bible and the Greeks,* p. 45; *Romans,* pp. 9ff., 51); B. Przybylski, *Righteousness in Matthew and His World of Thought* (1980), pp. 11f.; W. Eichrodt, *Theology of the Old Testament* (1961), pp. 240ff.; Snaith, *The Distinctive Ideas of the Old Testmaent,* pp. 51ff. On interpretations of "justification" in James, see Hoppe, pp. 112f.; W. Beyschlag, *New Testament Theology,* I (1896), 362ff.; Davids, pp. 127f.

173. See L. T. Johnson, "Friendship with the World/Friendship with God: A Study of Discipleship in James," in *Discipleship in the New Testament,* ed. F. J. Segovia (1985), pp. 173f.

174. "To the formation of such a covenant there might go all sorts of motives, as in the case of Aristotle's *philia;* for the give and take which was looked to for the security of some personal advantage, to pure friendship and affection" (W. F. Lofthouse, "Chen and Chesed in the O.T.," *ZAW* 20.1 [1933]: 33f.); M. Weinfeld, *b^erîṯ, TDOT,* II, 258ff.; G. Stählin, *philos, TDNT,* IX (1974), 167-70; E. Peterson, "Der Gottesfreund: Beiträge zur Geschichte eines religiösen Terminus," *ZKG* 42 (1923): 161-202; F. I. Andersen, *art. cit.,* pp. 43ff. in *God Who Is Rich in Mercy* (1987).

held to be a play on the name "Abraham"[175] but more likely reflecting a non-LXX, special biblical,[176] wisdom,[177] or Jewish tradition,[178] known also to Islam *(Ibrahim al-Khalil),*[179] foreshadowed in Plato,[180] and finally consummated in the ideal friendship offered by Christ[181]—is a verdict (ein "Spruch") in the full sense of the word.

Clearly, then, in this context faith and works are both necessary for justification, faith alone (emphatic *monon*—so KJV *pace* RV) being useless without works (see v. 14). Of this relationship between faith and works Melanchthon said: "Faith alone justifies, but faith is never alone." A similar collocation of ideas is found in the Scrolls. Thus, "God will save those Jews who are Law-Doers from the House of Judgment because of *their works ('āmālam) and their faith* in the Righteous Teacher" (1QpHab 8:2). "Here there can be little doubt," comments R. H. Eisenman,[182] "that we are in the typically 'Jamesian' milieu of

175. *'aḇrāhām: rāḥam; philos.* "Very doubtful," says Hort (p. 65)—he could have ruled it out altogether.

176. For the idea in the Bible, see 2 Chr. 20:7 (*'ōhaḇᵉḵā; ho ēgapēmenos;* Vulg. *amici tui*); Isa. 41:8 (*'ōhᵃḇî; hon ēgapēsa*); Dan. 3:35.

177. E.g., "Age after age wisdom enters into holy souls, and makes them God's friends and prophets" (Wis. 7:27, NEB); cf. Wis. 2:6-20. See U. Luck, "Der Jakobusbrief und die Theologie des Paulus," *Theologie und Glaube* 61 (1971): 161-79 and Mussner's stringent criticisms (pp. 249f.) of Luck's thesis that the wisdom theme underlies 2:14-26 and that that theme, especially of Abraham as the wise man, is continued through ch. 3, even though Abraham is not mentioned by name. So by the *'Aqēḏaṯ* Abraham is said to be the one who "showed his works in meekness of wisdom" (*ta erga autou en praÿtēti sophias*) (Jas. 3:13), reaping "the harvest of righteousness" (Jas. 3:18), all of which, it is believed, is in line with the Wisdom tradition, e.g., Ecclus. 3:17, "My son, perform your task in meekness *(en praÿtēti ta erga sou diexage).*"

178. E.g., Philo adds *tou philou mou* to Gen. 18:17 (*On Sobriety* 56); rabbis (e.g., b. Soṭa 31a; M. Aboth 5.4; see also Jub. 19:9; 30:20; Ecclus. 6:17 [Gk. Heb.]; Test. Abr. *passim;* 4 Ezr. 3:14); and Church Fathers (1 Clem. 10:1; Tertullian, *An Answer to the Jews* 2; Irenaeus, *Against the Heresies* 4.16.2): "A. was made (?) a friend. . . . Isaac and Jacob were recorded as friends of God." See also B. I. Reicke, "The Jewish 'Damascus documents' and the New Testament," *Symbolae Biblicae Upsalienses* 6 (1946), A. I. IIIf., p. 10. On the possible underlying Jewish idea of "celestial tablets" and its connection with "justification" (Jub. 30:19f.), see Dibelius, p. 173; also Zahn, *Introduction to the New Testament,* I, 120; Deissmann, *Bible Studies,* pp. 167ff.; Hoppe, pp. 116f.; O. S. Wintermute, "Jubilees (Second Century B.C.)," *The Old Testament Pseudepigrapha,* ed. J. H. Charlesworth, II (1985), 40, 113.

179. E.g., Qur'ān 4.124.

180. Plato, *Symposium* 212a; see also Xenophon, *Memorabilia* 2.1.33; Cicero, *On the Nature of the Gods* 1.43.121.

181. Jn. 15:9-17.

182. *James the Just in the Habakkuk Pesher* (1986), p. 40.

works-righteousness," and where these and the issue of "faith" are concerned, as in the case of "Jews who were Law-Doers," the *pesher* would appear to have been framed with the express position of "the Enemy" in mind, that is, a man is not saved by his "faith" alone, but by "works" working with "faith." The covenant, as the trial of Abraham showed, involves not only a necessary initial act of faith but also a continuous confirmatory manifestation;[183] in other words, each person has his *Recht* and *Pflicht*. Nor is this position—even though lacking the distinctive Pauline insights—"false" (*falsum:* Luther) to Paul's essential message. Indeed, we may say that Abraham was justified by faith (Paul) in that he trusted God and obeyed his voice in respect of his son Isaac. He may be said to be justified by works (James) because his trust and obedience led him to take Isaac—that is, to do something.

The Example of Rahab

The same point is now clinched by a very different example *(homoiōs de),* namely, Rahab (2:25). Rahab was a typical Gentile (woman), a proselyte, and in addition a prostitute,[184] said to have been converted through the report of miracles,[185] married to Joshua, welcomed into a Jewish family,[186] and the ancestress of eight prophets[187] as well as of Christ,[188] who was also said to have been visited by the Holy Spirit.[189] Her faith, assumed here, too,[190] was vindicated by her deeds, and she

183. Ropes, p. 218.

184. *kai Rhachab hē pornē: hazzônāh,* connected by Rashi et al. with *zûn* "to feed," and hence given the unlikely meaning of "innkeeper" *(pûndāqiṯā')* (Targ. Jon. on Josh. 2:1). Further on etymology, see S. Erlandsson, *zānāh, TDOT,* IV, 99. Rahab, according to the rabbis, was one of four women of surpassing beauty, whose name inspired lust (b. Megilla 15a; b. Ta'anith 5b), and who had the opportunity of approaching God, but was debarred through unworthiness (Num. R. 3.2: "Rahab is a kind of saint for later Judaism"; see also Heb. 11:31; Jas. 2:25; 1 Clem. 12:1; also Mt. 1:5; G. Kittel's footnote, Ger. tr.). Dante, in *Paradiso* 9.112ff., places her in the Third Heaven. For rabbinic material, see S–B I, 20ff. See also D. J. Wiseman, "Rahab of Jericho," *Tyndale House Bulletin* 14 (1964): 8-11; Bruce, *The Epistle to the Hebrews,* p. 328, n. 228.

185. Ex. R. 27.4; see also Josh. 2:9-11.

186. Josh. 6:23; Midr. Ruth 2.1.

187. b. Megilla 15a.

188. Mt. 1:5.

189. Sifré Dt. 1.24.

190. Cassiodorus: *quae non fide tantum, sed opere justificata cognoscitur* ("which is known to be justified not by faith alone but by works") (Dibelius, p. 157, n. 1); F. Manns, "Jacques 2,24-26 à la lumière du judaïsme," *Bib Or* 26.3 (1984): 143ff.

was considered to be righteous;[191] in other words, justifying faith is *operative*. As one who was "brought near,"[192] Rahab the proselyte might especially appeal to Jewish Christians. Whereas Abraham was prepared to sacrifice his son, she gave the scouts *(tous angelous)*[193] hospitality,[194] helping them escape *(ekbalousa)*.

Not surprisingly (*pace* Dibelius), James's treatment of Rahab is slight, hardly offering evidence, as Bacon thought,[195] of a progressive doctrine of faith. Here again much is assumed; but the point is that faith operated in and cooperated with works. Like Abraham, Rahab was justified, but not by "faith" alone.

These examples of Abraham and Rahab both show that faith produces works, and these in turn attest the genuineness of faith. Correctly James suggests that Abraham was saved not by faith per se but by faith in action. Faith was an attitude that moved Abraham to take his son to Moriah—an act of obedience whose motive, according to the rabbis, was love.[196] Indeed, the patriarch is a model, for "he was found faithful and a lover of the Lord." This also tells us what James means by works, a term that he uses much more frequently than Paul—ten times to be exact, mostly in 2:14-26—and that he uses differently from Paul's "works of the law."

James has no truck with works that are divorced from faith; that is clear from, for example, 2:22. And in the next example, Rahab's action was not without faith; unless there was faith alongside the action of Jas. 2:25, that verse can have no bearing on 2:26. Besides, James of course knew that in Josh. 2:9-13 Rahab expressly declares faith in the God of Israel—"The Lord your God, he is God in heaven above and in

191. Eccl. R. 5.1.

192. Num. R. Bemidbar 3.2; see also Midr. Ruth 2 (126a), cited by Davids, pp. 132f.; *art cit.*, pp. 116, 124 n. 13.

193. *Pace kataskopous*, read by a few minor MSS, perhaps influenced by Heb. 11:31. The use of *angelos* here may suggest (Hort) that in receiving the messengers she was in fact receiving angels (Gen. 32:3, 6 *et saepe;* Mt. 11:11). *Ekballō* is used, not pejoratively (see Jn. 9:34), but simply to emphasize the difficulties of escape, e.g., the different route.

194. "Great is hospitality: greater even than early attention at the House of Study or than the reception of the *Shechinah*" (b. Sanhedrin 103b; b. Shabbath 127a).

195. On the Holy Spirit (see n. 189 above) and the *Shechinah*, see B. W. Bacon, "Doctrine of Faith in Hebrews, James and Clement," *JBL* 19 (1900): 12ff. See Justin Martyr, *The Dialogue with Trypho* 111; Irenaeus, *Against the Heresies* 4.20.12.

196. b. Soṭa 31a; Tosefta Soṭa 6.1. See also J. Bowker, *The Targums and Rabbinic Literature* (1969), pp. 210, 222f.

earth beneath"—and confirms her faith in God by her action and by cannily exacting the two men's oath by that God before she released them (v. 21). R. B. Ward is correct when he shows that these works as "works of mercy *(eleos)*" are the unifying theme in ch. 2, although we think it is a mistake to confine works to "hospitality."[197]

But while James neither defines nor develops what he means by "works," he does insist on their necessity. Obviously he is talking of Christian works in the widest sense of Christian conduct; and he does not feel, as Paul sometimes does, that circumstances necessitate an elaborate proof that you cannot do a really Christian work unless you have a Christian faith or that you cannot have a Christian faith without doing some Christian works, though James does give some, probably adequate, attention to the latter. The "works" of which James speaks are never "duties to God" or Pharisaic righteousness, but simply, as in the Sermon on the Mount, "works of love" *(Liebeswerke)* such as caring for the orphan and widow, feeding the hungry, and clothing the naked. As such they are somewhat similar to Qumran's "suffering works," sometimes translated "works with soteriological effect."[198] Works of this sort, in the nature of the case, have nothing to do with ceremonial Torah.

This important rabbinic distinction between *Liebeswerke (gᵉmîlûṯ ḥᵃsîḏîm)* and "the law of goodness" *(ḥᵃsîḏûṯ)*[199] shows us the kind of

197. Moo, *James,* "Additional Note: Works in Paul and James 2:14," p. 201ff.; Ward, *art. cit., HTR* 61 (1968): 283ff.; see also H. Chadwick, "Justification by Faith and Hospitality," *Studia Patristica,* IV, pt. 2 in *Texte und Untersuchungen* 79 (1961): 281.

198. Eisenman, *James the Just in the Habakkuk Pesher,* p. 40; also *Maccabees, Zadokites, Christians and Qumran* (1983), p. 43, n. 24.

199. See Jub. 17:18; cf. also Büchler, *Studies in Sin and Atonement,* pp. 126ff., 142 with our comment on Jas. 2:21; S–B IV, 559ff.; also G. Bertram, *ergon, TDNT,* II, 647; Cohen, *Everyman's Talmud,* pp. 224ff.; C. J. Montefiore and H. Loewe, *A Rabbinic Anthology,* pp. 279ff. on *kawwānāh* and *lišmāh.* As examples of such *Liebeswerke* we may cite such simple acts of kindness as visiting the sick, burying the dead, giving to the poor, entertaining strangers as having nothing to do with ceremonial Torah. To clothe the naked and to visit the sick is to imitate God: "As he clothed (Gen. 18:1) the naked (Gen. 3:21), so do you clothe the naked: as he visited the sick (Gen. 18:1), so do you visit the sick" (b. Soṭa 14a). Elsewhere we read: "Greater is the reception of wayfarers than the reception of the *Shechinah*" (b. Shabbath 127a). Again R. Simlai once said: "The Torah contains works of love at its beginning and at its end. At its beginning, as it is written: 'And the Lord God made coats for Adam and Eve his wife' (Gen. 3:21); and at its end, as it is written: 'And He buried (Moses) in the valley'" (Dt. 34:6) (b. Soṭa 14a). See S. Schechter, *Some Aspects of Rabbinic Theology* (1909), p. 214, for a careful study of the development of the "law of goodness"; also T. W. Manson,

righteousness James has in mind. If commentators had remembered this, the "works" of James would hardly be seen either as a "new legalism" or as a post-Pauline "relapse into the righteousness or good works of Judaism."[200] This distinction between these two types of righteousness illustrates the dilemma within Judaism itself. The tension between prophetic and Pharisaic righteousness is so strong that in NT times we may speak paradoxically of almost two Judaisms.

THE ETHIC OF FAITH

Significant in this connection is the implication of Mt. 5:20, where Christ seems to distinguish between an actual and an ideal Judaism: "Except *your righteousness* shall exceed the righteousness of the scribes and Pharisees, you shall in no case enter into the Kingdom of Heaven." The righteousness of the scribes and the Pharisees—in essence "the works of the law" *(miṣwôṯ)*—was the righteousness of empirical and legalistic Judaism of which Christ despaired.[201] Such a distinction is also implicit in the concluding verse of the Sermon,[202] where the two kinds of righteousness, Christ's and the Pharisees', are apparently contrasted. "Your righteousness" (the righteousness of ideal Judaism), which was different in kind rather than degree ("not *allo* but *heteron*"),[203] is expressed through the "works" of practical benevolence. Essentially this was the OT prophetic position in contrast to that of legalistic Pharisaism, whose preoccupation with "works of merit" roused Paul's wrath.

Clearly the kind of righteousness enjoined by James is "not *allo* but *heteron*," a prophetic righteousness whose works are simply works of charity. That which constitutes obedience to the "royal law"—a law based on Christ's own teaching—is the new righteousness,[204] which, as Bacon notes, does not busy itself in acquiring meritorious good works but is involved in "an inward renovation which makes them flow from

---

The Sayings of Jesus (1949), p. 348, Additional Note, 153; J. Jeremias, "Die Salbungsgeschichte Mc. 14:3-9," *ZNW* 25 (1936): 78; V. P. Furnish, *The Love Command in the New Testament* (1972), pp. 175ff.

200. See, e.g., H. A. A. Kennedy, *The Theology of the Epistles* (1919), pp. 227f., 243f.; also Van Unnik's valuable analysis of Greek, Jewish, and Christian "good works" in "The Teaching of Good Works in 1 Peter," *NTS* 1 (1954): 92-110.

201. "But seek first his kingdom and *his* righteousness" (Mt. 6:23, NIV).

202. See Goguel, *Life of Jesus*, pp. 585f.

203. See W. F. Lofthouse, "The Righteousness of God," *ExpT* 4 (1939): 442. See also Gal. 1:6.

204. See Mt. 5:16; also Mt. 23:3; Jn. 3:20.

the heart as naturally as vine and fig trees bear their fruit."[205] By "works" James is thinking of the good deeds enjoined by Jesus,[206] and also by Paul,[207] acts of practical morality somewhat akin perhaps to what the rabbis called *lišmāh*[208] and Qumran "suffering works" *('āmāl)*[209] but quite different from the works of the ceremonial law *(miṣwôṯ).*

Like his Lord, James is faithful to the prophetic rather than the Pharisaic idea of righteousness—in effect exalting what William Manson[210] called the "unmeasured" element. This is the key to James's ethics and especially to what he means by "works." Apparently, the latter are simply deeds of generous, uncalculating love, the product of single-minded faith, inspired no doubt by what the Christian learned of God's grace in Christ, rooted in an "ethic of filial righteousness" (an "ethic of sons") and ultimately in the doctrine of the *Imitatio Dei.*

So this crucial second chapter ends with a powerful description of the required relation of Christian faith to our deeds and words and thoughts—in short, to the life by which that faith is or is not fulfilled. "Deeds do not reinforce faith," comments Moffatt; "they are or ought to be the outcome of that relation to the regenerating Word, which implies submission of life to the royal law of love" (2:8f.).[211] Faith alone cannot save; nor can works alone save. It is vitally important to note that James does not present deeds at any time or in any way as a substitute for Christian faith; he holds that, if it is not maintained by Christian exercise in an active Christian life, faith, like many activities, perishes in a sort of parasitic paralysis. "If a Church produces no living acts of charity for the community as a whole," wrote E. Brunner, "it is

205. See B. W. Bacon, *Studies in Matthew* (1930), pp. 339f.

206. E.g., Mt. 5:16; 7:21; 25:31ff.

207. See, e.g., Rom. 2:6ff. C. E. B. Cranfield aptly comments: "The *ergon agathon* is not regarded as constituting a claim upon God, but as the expression of faith and repentance. The good work no more earns salvation than does the evil work. The difference between them is the difference between evidence of openness to God's judgment and evidence of the persistence of a proud and stubborn self-righteousness" (*The Epistle to the Romans,* I [1975], 153).

208. Literally meaning "for its name," i.e., for its own sake, *lišmāh* expresses the great rabbinic idea that an act has ethical value only if it is performed from disinterested motives. Regarding Prov. 31:26, "on her tongue is the law of kindness," e.g., the question is asked: "Is there, then, a law not of kindness?" and the answer is given: "Law studied *lišmāh* is a law of kindness" (b. Sukka 49b). See C. J. Montefiore, *Rabbinic Literature and Gospel Teachings* (1930), p. 188.

209. See above, n. 198.

210. *Jesus the Messiah,* p. 84; for a comparative study of "the imitation of Christ" and "the imitation of God" in Paul and Christ, found in Matthew, see, e.g., R. Mohrlang, *Matthew and Paul* (1984), pp. 76ff. See also our remarks, p. 363.

211. P. 44.

impossible to avoid suspecting that she is sick unto death."[212] When James writes, "I will *show* you my *faith* by what I *do*" (2:18), he is not *divorcing*, but *marrying*, principle and practice in Christian life. And at the end of this chapter, he says conclusively: "As the *body, without respiration—that is, not breathing at all—is dead, so faith,* without *action,* is dead also" (2:26). It has been well said that "we are not Christians because we do good works; we do good works because we are Christians."

CONCLUSION

The Epistle of James emphasizes the inescapable relationship between ethics and faith. James was certain that sound doctrine and creative living go hand in hand. One must believe right in order to do right: the one without the other is useless. In essence, the book is an exposition of the verse in Proverbs: "As a man thinks in his heart, so is he" (Prov. 23:7).

Few have been more faithful to this challenge to practical faith in their lives, both in word and in deed, than one who left her convent to help the poor, feed the hungry, and minister to the dying, selflessly producing on the streets of Calcutta "living acts of charity for the community as a whole." Mother Teresa has written:

> If sometimes our poor people have had to die of starvation, it is not because God didn't care for them, but because you and I didn't give, were not instruments of love in the hands of God, to give them that bread, to give them that clothing; because we did not recognize him, when once more Christ came in distressing disguise—in the hungry man, in the lonely man, in the homeless child, and seeking for shelter.
>
> God has identified himself with the hungry, the sick, the naked, the homeless; hunger, not only for bread, but for love, for care, to be somebody to someone; nakedness, not of clothing only, but nakedness of that compassion that very few people give to the unknown; homelessness, not only just for a shelter made of stone, but that homelessness that comes from having no one to call your own.
>
> To show great love for God and our neighbor we need not do great things. It is how much love we put in the doing that makes our offering something beautiful for God.[213]

212. *The Divine Imperative* (1937), p. 554.

213. Mother Teresa of Calcutta, *A Gift for God: Prayers and Meditations* (1975), pp. 24f., 69.

b. Trial and Temptation

Outside the Bible *peirasmos* seems to occur only four times in secular Greek.[1] One refers to doctors' experiments with drugs,[2] and another—"There is *peirasmos* in land and sea"[3]—reminds us of Hesiod, "The earth is full of evil things and the sea is full of them."[4] The verb *peirazō,* however, is more common outside the Bible, and means simply "to try," "to make trial of." The meanings "tempt" and "allure" are also developed, as in Jas. 1:13f., where the two participles, *exelkomenos* and *deleazomenos,* are used practically as synonyms. In the NT the noun *peirasmos* is used some 21 times,[5] usually, we are told, in the neutral sense of trial or test, and by definition applied only to the believer.[6] Unbelievers, standing outside, are not in the state of *peirasmos;* contrast the meaning "crucible" *(maṣrēp),* notably in Qumran,[7] where the wicked are tested by fire and consequently destroyed (see also Mal. 3:2ff.).

TRIAL

For the moment, let us accept "testing" as the dominant meaning of *peirasmos.* The Hebrew verb *nāśāh* seems to imply primarily "a testing of the partner in the covenant to see whether he is keeping his side of the agreement."[8] But, as has been pointed out,[9] there is one vital distinction: God's testing is *benevolent;* God hopes that, like Abraham or Job, we shall pass the test.[10] "My son, if you aspire to be a servant of the Lord, prepare yourself for *peirasmos.*"[11] Successfully tested, the

1. See Hort's excellent discussion (pp. 4f.); also H. Seesemann, *peira, TDNT,* VI, 24ff.; W. Schneider and C. Brown, "Tempt, Test, Approve" *(peirasmos), NIDNTT,* III, 798ff.

2. Dioscorides, *Materia Medica,* Preface, 5. See Ropes, p. 133 *ad init.*

3. Cyranides, 40, 24. See also Syntipas, pp. 124, 18; Test Jos. 2.7; BAG, p. 647, s.v. *peirasmos* 2b.

4. *Works and Days* 101.

5. See Hort, p. 4.

6. K. G. Kuhn in *The Scrolls and the New Testament,* ed. K. Stendahl, pp. 96f.

7. See CD 20; 1QM 17.1, 9; also A. R. C. Leaney, *The Rule of Qumran and its Meaning* (1966), p. 126. On the trial of the wicked, see, e.g., 1QSb 3:23; 1QM 16–17.

8. B. Gerhardsson, "The Testing of God's Son (Matt. 4:1-11 and Par.): An Analysis of an Early Christian Midrash," *Coniectanea Biblica* 2.1 (1966): 26f.

9. See Hort, pp. 4f.

10. See 1 Macc. 2:52; Ecclus. 44:20 on Gen. 22:1; see also Job (Jas. 5:11).

11. Ecclus. 2:1, NEB; also v. 5 and 33:1; also Jub. 8:25.

"happy warrior" emerges a maturer soul, stronger in faith, more constant in endurance, and finally vindicated. Asks Robert Browning:

> "Why comes temptation, but for man to meet
> And master and make crouch beneath his foot,
> And so be pedestaled in triumph?"[12]

From a very different point of view, people have made trial of God, as the Israelites did in the wilderness,[13] and as children often "try" their parents. Satan also makes trial of us with sinister intent, hoping that we shall fail. For this reason, *peirazō* or *peirasmos,* though it always means "test," has other shades of meaning, depending on whether it is God or the devil that is doing the testing. Satan tempts people so that they may sin. God tries people with peirastic and paideutic intent, so that, being tested and thereby trained, they may be saved. This reminds us that, like other NT writers, James's view of the Christian life is essentially optimistic. The present life is all a probation for the next.[14] This, however, is not the end of the matter. "The whole group of words *peirasmos* and, e.g., *peiraō* and *peirazō,*" says Ropes, "is also said to refer to temptation to sin, since that, primarily an assault, is at the same time a test."[15]

An important key to understanding the Epistle of James, therefore, presents itself, for the *peirasmos* theme explains the Epistle's origin, pervades its thought, and dictates its pattern. It is also important to remember that this term is filled with eschatological (already–not yet) tension, for the present struggle of the Christian is part of the final testing at the end of the age. This struggle will soon be over, for the end is near.[16]

The Nature of Trial

This eschatological note is struck in the Epistle's opening verses. James reveals at once his genius in faith and art by beginning his Epistle with

12. *The Ring and the Book* (1904), bk. X, 1. 1185.

13. Ex. 17:7; Dt. 6:16; 9:22; Ps. 95:9.

14. This appears throughout the NT; see, e.g., 1 Pet. 4:12, "do not be surprised at the painful trial you are suffering" (NIV) *(tē . . . pyrōsei pros peirasmon hymin genomenē);* Heb. 12:5-8; 1 Pet. 5:8-10; also Heb. 4:15. Even using *thlipseis* (Acts 20:23), Paul shows that he is thinking of them as one on probation in all but words; in the next verse he says that he will not be tempted thereby to abandon his duty. See also I. H. Marshall, *Kept by the Power of God* (1975), p. 155.

15. P. 133.

16. On the importance of "inaugurated eschatology" for James, see Mussner, pp. 207ff.; Schlatter, p. 36; Davids, pp. 38f.

peirasmos, the common and critical experience of the Redeemer and the redeemed. Dispensing with preliminaries, he plunges "into the midst of things," urging his converts to deem their ordeal an occasion for pure joy. His language recalls the suffering and heroism of the Maccabean martyrs. While he does not necessarily imply that he is writing in a similarly stirring period of persecution, his aim, as Dibelius shows, is "to revive again the heroic sentiment of the epoch in the midst of the present 'various trials.'"[17] He also reminds them that ultimately the Christian's struggle will not go unrewarded, "for he will receive the crown of life" (1:12).

The crown, headwreath, chaplet, or circlet was the victor's prize in the Greek games.[18] Paul and others often use the figure of the race and the crown,[19] but he carefully points out one difference between the runners' effort and reward and that of the Christian life: they all run, but only one receives the prize.[20] Certainly the Christian is not competing against his fellows as the athletes do; yet the image was felt to be, and is, relevant. The clue to understanding the image is in Heb. 12:1. There we have a crowd of spectator-witnesses, the past heroes of the faith, and the stripping off of encumbrance, as it were of clothes, for the race. It is the race of *hypomonē;* and the model of *hypomonē,* and the founder and perfecter of the faith that we must maintain by *hypomonē,* is Jesus. Whereas the athletes have human competitors, the Christian's adversaries are the powers of darkness, trying to push him off the course and rob him of his crown.

James mentions no other part of the agonistic metaphor; but his constant reference to the theme of *peirasmos* brings with it the thought of the constant struggle against evil, a struggle well likened to that of an athlete. But there is another difference between the Christian life and the Greek athletic contest: whereas the Greek judges were impartial, dispassionate, and detached, the Christian's judge is God; and the crown, it seems, is rewarded on the great day of Christ's return.[21] A further clue to James's concept of the crown is found in Jas. 2:5, where, as Mayor notes, what is here said of the crown is repeated of the Kingdom[22] (sometimes crown and Kingdom are synonymous in Jewish thought, suggesting that the idea of kingship is also present).[23]

17. P. 71.

18. For a catalogue of its uses, see Ropes, pp. 150-52; also Dibelius, pp. 88f.

19. E.g., 1 Cor. 9:24f.; 2 Tim. 4:8; Heb. 12:1; 1 Pet. 5:4.

20. 1 Cor. 9:24.

21. See 2 Tim. 4:8; 1 Cor. 9:25; Jas. 5:7-9.

22. P. 49.

23. See M. Aboth 4.13; Sifré Num., sec. 119.4.

In the Epistle of James the concept is fundamental: the reference to inheritance and promise shows that, like the parousia, the Kingdom is very near and is promised to those who fulfill the required conditions—the promise itself being "implicit in the very concept of the kingdom."[24] As Ropes suggests, "the Kingdom" almost certainly means "the reign of God" and is practically equivalent to salvation or eternal life, and "the crown of life" consists in eternal life, suggesting that, unlike the chaplet of leaves, this does not fade[25]—in short, it is the joy of immortality in the heaven to come.

Salvation usually suggests the thought of a crisis of peril, as in war or the like; in the germinal Christianity of the NT it regularly implies *krisis,* a judgment, as in court before a judge to whom we must give account (see Jas. 2:12f.). "To assert the accountability to God of every individual man," notes Cranfield, "is to assert his inalienable dignity; and it would be difficult to think of any other single thing that has done as much in the last half-century to degrade human dignity as the weakening of Christian conviction at that point."[26] The first Christians did not concern themselves much with Christ's return as an assurance of their own personal rising from the grave; it is clear that in general they did not expect to die, but obviously expected Christ to return very soon, in their lifetime. As time passed, however, the question of those who had accepted Christ but died before his return became urgent, as in the case of the Thessalonians; and Paul also has the Christian dead in mind in 1 Cor. 15. But germinal Christianity is based on Christ the Judge, as they thought he would soon be, of the still living generation in which the gospel was first proclaimed.

The point we are now pressing is the supreme importance of the character of Christ as Judge in the eschatology of the Epistle of James. James is almost entirely concerned with the expected early return of Christ, with judgment, and with Christian duty in the time of waiting and working for the Christian reward. Here again we note how *relevant* James is: eschatology for him is much more than "speculating on the future and building prophecy charts; it meant realizing that coming judgment was imminent and thus living and evaluating all of life from that perspective, for 'the Judge stands even at the door.'"[27] No doubt this intensified his sense of responsibility as "teacher" (3:1) and his anticipation of the reward (soon to come, as he thought), the note on which he ends (5:20). Witness Jas. 5:7-11, a section replete with love, theology,

24. Ropes, p. 195.
25. P. 194.
26. "The Message of James," *SJTh* 18 (1965): 192.
27. P. H. Davids, "So What?" *New College Berkeley Notes* 5.2 (1982-83): 1.

encouragement, and warning—and, above all, strongly eschatological, recalling the article of the Creed, "from thence he shall come to judge the quick and the dead." (By implying all of the Creed before and after this point, this article gathers up all the threads of theology woven elsewhere. Here is maximum concentration of truth.) The purpose of Jas. 5:7-11, however, is not to set forth, for example, the nature of the resurrection body or to elaborate these truths, but to encourage those who believe them in a time of testing and trial.

The first generation of Christians expected the early return of Christ, the "second Advent" (parousia); this is the climate of expectancy to which the Epistle of James belongs.[28] The coming of Jesus and the Kingdom is no more, and no less, an imminent reality to the Epistle of James than it is to 1 Cor. 7, for instance, or to 1 Thess. 4:13–5:11. In 2 Thess. 2:1-12 the reality is no less, though the nearness of the event is not so definitely suggested; but in 1 Cor. 7 Paul clearly expects the end in the lifetime of the current generation: his wish that all people, or even only Christian men and women, might be without children would be blasphemously sinful if he contemplated a longer postponement of the crisis. The thoroughly Jewish tone and language of 5:1-8 have led some to equate "Lord" in the phrase "coming of the Lord" *(parousia tou kyriou)* with God in the "the coming of God,"[29] that is, "the Lord of Sabaoth,"[30] although it is apparently not found in this sense in pre-Christian Jewish literature.[31]

Unless we are prepared to accept a pre-Christian patchwork approach to the Epistle[32] (which we are not), we see no reason for assuming that the parousia has here a meaning other than Christian. James is using "parousia" in the technical theological sense of the coming of

28. We accept Huther's view, in Ropes, p. 166, middle, small print, that "us," with "firstfruits" (1:18), means the first generation of Christians. We think that the author of the Epistle of James definitely assumes that his days are the last days and that the Apostolic Age is to be the last (see Rom. 8:22-25; Heb. 10:36f.; 11:39f.; 13:20f.). Many other texts could be cited. Similarly Kittel, "The end of time stands not merely before the door but is right on the threshold" ("Der geschichtliche Ort des Jakobusbriefes," *ZNW* 41 [1942]: 83).

29. On the two "comings" of God, the one to bless (2 En. 58:1) and the second to judge (2 En. 32:1; 42:5), see F. I. Andersen, "2 (Slavonic Apocalypse of) Enoch (Late First Century A.D.)," *The Old Testament Pseudepigrapha,* ed. J. H. Charlesworth, I (1983), 182, 154, 168 with notes; also A. Meyer, pp. 159ff.

30. So Windisch, p. 31; see also Test. Jud. 22:2; 2 Pet. 3:12.

31. See A. Oepke, *parousia, TDNT,* V, 865; G. Braumann, C. Brown, "Presence" *(parousia), NIDNTT,* II, 900f.

32. For this and the influence of Jewish eschatological thought on Jas. 5:1-11, see Oesterley, pp. 30ff.; Davids, pp. 182f.

Christ in messianic glory at the End (much as some, e.g., supposed a purely Jewish application of "the Day of the Lord" at the historical judgment of the people of Israel; e.g., Isa. 22:5, 25; Jer. 46:10, 21). This event, which is supernatural in origin, will occur in the near future with catastrophic results when—as the martyr James foretold—the Son of Man will come on the clouds of heaven—perhaps a significant allusion if James wrote this Epistle.

There is no sign of delimitation, doubt, or disappointment over any delay (as in the later Epistles; e.g., 2 Pet. 3:4); on the contrary—and this, coupled with the Epistle's uniquely Jewish stamp, is another strong argument for an early date—the readers seem to be in a mood of high expectancy because the Judge is at the door. This suggests, as we noted earlier, the eschatological imagery of watching and waiting, for the End is near (Mt. 24:33, 45ff.; Mk. 13:29, 34; Lk. 12:42ff.; Rev. 3:3, 20). "It is an expectation," writes Sevenster, "which as yet does not rely on a broad apocalyptic portrayal of the future but refers concretely and vitally to the immediate, practical situation."[33] Unlike those of later eschatology, James's beliefs are refreshingly simple, clear, unspeculative, and unapologetic,[34] essentially reflecting the twofold ethical development of the post-Exilic period.[35]

First, ethics is linked with eschatology; thus in 5:7 the parousia is specifically given as the reason for endurance: the theme is "Patience to the end, for the Lord, the Judge, is very near." So James "makes the unconscious impatience of primitive Christianity a basis of his exhortation to conscious patience."[36] With patience there is hope, and this in turn brings peace, for as J. A. Bengel finely says,[37] "Joy in the Lord brings forth true peace of mind." The parousia, therefore, is of immense *practical* importance.

Second, the gentler qualities are emphasized; hence the example of the patient farmer (5:7). Turning from his attacks on the wicked rich, James bids Christians, among others, to emulate the prophets—was he thinking, perhaps, especially of Jeremiah (Jer. 20:2; 38:6)? They must meet their sufferings with endurance, trusting, like Job, in the mercy of

33. *Do You Know Greek?* (1968), p. 6; see also A. L. Moore, *The Parousia in the New Testament* (1966), pp. 149f.; but for a differing interpretation, see Laws, pp. 29, 35f.

34. J. Sevenster, ibid.; see also G. Kittel, *art cit., ZNW* 41 (1942); 83; and "Der Jakobusbrief und die apostolischen Väter," *ZNW* 43 (1950-51): 54-112, 68ff.

35. C. J. Barker, *The Way of Life* (1946), p. 28.

36. Plummer, p. 290; Moo, pp. 43f. On the circular nature of this reasoning, see J. T. Sanders, *Ethics in the New Testament* (1975), p. 103.

37. Cited by K. Barth, *The Epistle to the Philippians* (1962), p. 121.

God. James does not mean they they are to endure evil that can be righted or that they can expect others to do so. Some things must be endured, and for them the prerequisites are faith and prayer.

So there is no hint of redress or, as Hauck suggests,[38] of the righteous themselves taking swords, as in 1 Enoch,[39] to avenge themselves. As in apocalyptic literature, James sees in humility "the eschatological attitude to which the promise of the reward and the help of God are addressed." We may add that here as elsewhere James and Paul complement each other. In his high mood Paul can write "Rejoice in the Lord always" (Phil. 3:1); but we must note a difference between James and Paul (at least in some places) in their common apocalyptic conviction that the present world has all but come to its end (Jas. 5:3, 8f.; 1 Cor. 7:29). Contrast this last cited verse of Paul, prescribing iron rations for hard times ("the impending distress"), a sort of Lenten abstinence in preparation for the advent of Christ the Judge, with the spirit of James, sounding clear in the very first words of his Epistle: "Count it all joy."

Unlike some current philosophies that embrace *Nirvana* as the answer to all life's ills, James urges vigilance and work, saying in effect: "The best way to prepare for the coming end is to bend every effort and grow more and more fond of work—the work of righteousness and peace." We think that both James's final words of exhortation and admonition (5:7-18) and his Epistle as a whole are consciously directed toward that crisis, and are deliberately designed to present Jewish Christianity with a short but sufficient synthesis and synopsis of the essentials of thought and conduct required by both the old and above all the new elements in their religion (2:1).

The Epistle is something like a student's plan of preparation for an important examination. Since James believed that the date of the parousia was very near, the aim of the Epistle is to give the best plan for preparing for that Day. Key to the success of this plan is "endurance" *(hypomonē)*, a theme with which he opens his Epistle and to which, characteristically, he returns at the end. *Hypomonē* is still pre-eminent (5:11); with it, however, he links *makrothymia*. Though allied in meaning, we note that, unlike *hypomonē*, *makrothymia* in the NT is used of

38. Hauck, p. 18; *pace* A. Feuillet, "Le sens du mot Parousie dans l'Évangile de Matthieu: Comparaison entre Matth. xxiv et Jac. v. 1-11," in W. D. Davies and D. Daube, eds., *The Background of the New Testament and its Eschatology* (1956), p. 276, n. 1.

39. E.g., 91:12; 98:12; 104:3. See E. Isaac, "1 (Ethiopic Apocalypse of) Enoch (Second Century B.C.–First Century A.D.)," *The Old Testament Pseudepigrapha,* ed. J. H. Charlesworth, I (1983), 9, 78ff. Contrast Jas. 5:6: "You have condemned and murdered the just man: he does not resist you."

God as well as of the Christian. Christian patience *(makrothymia)* is a way of life, an expression of active, disinterested love (1 Cor. 13:4), something which prompts us to meet our neighbors halfway and to share our life with them.[40] To inculcate patience, then, is clearly a paramount purpose of the Epistle. The apparently disjointed topics of patient restraint in mind and speech, and prayer for each other's afflictions (ch. 5:7-11, 12, 13-18), are united—together with the warning to the rich (vv. 1-6)—by their common relation to that Judgment Day (5:9).

Most commentators drift along without any serious belief, and often with positive disbelief, that there is any unity of plan, design, purpose, argument, or exhortation in the Epistle as a whole or in the development of any one theme or paragraph in the Epistle in itself or in its relation to any other part or to the whole. Here it is pertinent to observe the plan of 5:1-11, which, it has been noted, links two aspects of patience, namely, "that extended to our fellows and that which is needed to cope with all the trials and tribulations of this world until the parousia."[41] Clearly the pericope 5:1-6, apart from its function in relation to the Epistle as a whole, also has a definite function as the basis of 5:7-11; the prophecy in 5:1-6 is the basis of the comfort of 5:7-11 in the same way that it is exemplified in the analogous Ps. 58. However it may be paragraphed, 5:7-11, which is a response to 5:1-6, forms a unity, compacted by *(inter alia)* the last sentences of vv. 8 and 9, and by the theme of "patience" *(makrothymia)* in vv. 7 *(bis)*, 8, and 10, the practically synonymous "do not grumble" *(mē stenazete)*[42] in v. 7, "suffering" *(kakopatheias)* in v. 10, "those who endured" *(hypomeinantas)* and "endurance" *(hypomonēn)* in v. 11, and the prophets and Job as examples of patient endurance to the end in vv. 10 and 11. The better text omits the article with *kyrios* in v. 11, just as it omits the article with *kyriou* in vv. 10 and 11. Ropes[43] is right in his interpretation of *telos*. I would, however, stress that in saying "his troubles" we must above all realize that the Epistle of James ends as it began, with the thought of *peirasmos*, and that the Book of Job is itself a story of *peirasmos* (1:8-12 [cf. v. 22]; 2:3-6 [cf. v. 10]; 9:14f.; 10:13-15); see also the end of the Book of Job cited by Ropes from the LXX.

40. See U. Falkenroth, C. Brown, "Patience" *(makrothymia)*, *NIDNTT*, II, 770.

41. U. Falkenroth, C. Brown, *art. cit.*, *NIDNTT*, II, 770; see also L. T. Johnson, "The Use of Leviticus 19 in the Letter of James," *JBL* 101.3 (1982): 396ff.

42. On the meaning of *stenazō* as inner sighing rather than open complaint, see T. M. McComiskey, "Lament" *(stenazō)*, *NIDNTT*, II, 423; also J. Schneider, *stenazō*, *TDNT*, VIII, 603.

43. P. 299.

Ropes, quoting Mayor, rightly rejects the view that *telos* here means the death of Christ, or his resurrection. We also reject the view that "the end" is an eschatological term, like the Hebrew *qēṣ,* referring to the Messiah's parousia, the Christian equivalent of the Jewish Exodus.[44] We would add that these would give a meaning completely unrelated to the sense and unity of this whole passage. It is a typical example of the incoherent improvisations that flow from the belief that James is just "a wayward gabbler." "The end of the Lord" means "the end granted by the Lord" after *peirasmoi* such as the prophets and Job in their day endured, and we in turn must likewise endure.

What is that end? Instead of a noun, such as "mercy" or "pity," James uses a "that" clause—"that the Lord is merciful," along with two adjectives (see also Ps. 103:8). The first occurs nowhere else in the Bible and is translated by Ropes as "very kind." Literally it is a Hebraic locution, "having a lot of bowels (of compassion)," expressing the strongest feeling of mercy.[45] We speak (if we do) of "guts" in another connection, but the Hebrew could use the word in speaking of the opposite of what we call "heartless." It is another example of James's force and boldness of style. The second adjective also illustrates both his force and his Hebraic affinities. James began this section (vv. 7-11) with an assurance that their reward was near; he concludes with an assurance of the quality of that reward.

The Purpose of Trial

In a spirit of urgency and expectancy James continues, as he began, with the paradox of effort and comfort that is the essence of the Christian life (1:3). Rejoice in the enemy's ingenious assaults; constancy in withstanding them will win God's approbation in the end. K. G. Kuhn,[46] who deals with the background of this verse, says that in the NT the believer is in constant danger of attacks by Satan, and of falling under his assaults. He illustrates the ordinary NT view of the devilish origin of assaults of evil by texts such as 1 Cor. 7:5; 1 Thess. 3:5; Mk. 4:3; Lk. 8:13; Rev. 2:10, besides 1 Tim. 6:9 and Jas. 1:13. He also shows admirably that our current *peirasmoi* and the final cataclysmic battle are all part of the one great war in which the Christian is engaged. *Peirasmos* is rooted in the imagery of a war between God and Satan. The believer is

44. See R. P. Gordon, "KAI TO TELOS KYRIOU EIDETE (Jas. V.11)," *JTS* 26 (1975): 91-95; S–B I, 671; III, 416; R. Schippers, "Goal" *(telos), NIDNTT,* III, 63.

45. See H.-H. Esser, "Mercy" *(oiktirmos, splanchna), NIDNTT,* II, 598f.

46. In K. Stendahl, *The Scrolls and the New Testament* (1958), p. 97.

God's soldier. There is no discharge from that war, which is the testing place for the world to come; but the prize for the Christian warrior is eternal life.

Having already spoken of the duty of Christian joy (1:2), James next discusses the basis of this joy, appealing to the fruits of experience. He wishes to instruct as well as to inspire. Ordinarily, as John Calvin says, tribulation "provokes a great part of mankind to murmur against God, and even to curse Him."[47] But James here is thinking of the Christian who has a strong faith in God. The essential purpose of *peirasmos* is probationary, purifying the soul like a refiner's fire, burning up the impurities, and leaving behind that which is tested and approved, *dokimeion,* that is, "the genuine element of true character."[48] Steadfastness, but only steadfastness, in resisting the enemy will win this approbation. "Steadfastness" is a good translation for the noun *hypomonē;* even better is "constancy in endurance" or "endure with constancy" for the verb *hypomenō.*[49]

47. *The Epistles of Paul the Apostle to the Romans and to the Thessalonians,* tr. R. Mackenzie (1961), p. 106.

48. To avoid the improbable assumption that *dokimeion* here is not the same as in 1 Pet. 1:7 and to bring v. 3 more in keeping with the Epistle's thought in general—for his main point surely is that constancy in endurance wins final approval—we emend 1:3: "You must realize that your approbation is accomplished by constancy in endurance." This also brings v. 4 uninterruptedly in line with all the assaults of evil of v. 2, and v. 4 in line with v. 3, with constancy at work in both. It is the same "perfect work" as that which "works out" in v. 3, the adjective "perfect" and the noun "work" corresponding respectively to the perfective force of the preposition *kata-* and the idea of the *ergazetai* verb. "Perfecting" is not really different from achieving "approbation." "Your approbation is accomplished ('worked') by 'constancy in endurance,' so let constancy 'have its full work' or, perhaps more colloquially, 'make a complete job of it,' that is, do its work fully, namely, bring you to 'approbation' or 'perfection.'" 1:4 now becomes both clear and forceful. "But let constancy in endurance have her perfect work (i.e., perfect her work) and that you may be perfect." Her work is the work of accomplishing your approbation or perfection, as stated in our new emended text, v. 3. Exactly so, "endures" in v. 12 indicates the means to becoming "approved" *(dokimos)*—not merely, as in the KJV, "tested." "Having passed the test," says the NEB correctly. See H. Haarbeck, "Tempt" *(dokimos), NIDNTT,* III, 808ff.

49. *Pace* Hort, p. 5, the verb *hypomenō,* common enough (in the sense we are considering) in Classical Greek, comes in Aristotle and others later; for the noun earlier Classical Greek has *karteria.* The verb *kartereō* is very common in Classical Greek, being found in simple forms as well as compound, e.g., *dia-; en-.* *Karteria* is found in the NT only once, but in one of the most famous passages, Heb. 11:27. The corresponding Latin word *patientia* is defined by Cicero: "Patience is a willing and sustained endurance of difficult and arduous tasks for a noble and useful end" (*On Invention* 2.54.163, H. M. Hubbell's Loeb translation [1949]). See

At bottom *hypomonē* is "firmness of faith"; it is "not passive patience, but that gallant spirit which can breast the tides of doubt and sorrow and disaster and come out with faith still stronger on the other side";[50] and as James says, it is *hypomonē* that brings faith (in the fullest sense) to approval (1:3). The root words are *menō,* "to stay, remain, stand firm," and *hypo,* "under pressure, attack, difficulty, hostility"; thus the essential meaning is to stand fast without shrinking from what comes against or upon one. "If you lay stress on submissiveness (i.e. the *hypo-* of compound *hypomenō*)," says Schneckenburger, "you will find expressed in this word patience and endurance of ills, but if (you lay stress on) the *menō* (of the compound), i.e. constancy and steadfastness, (you will find expressed in this word) perseverance and unshaken fortitude in bearing misfortunes (calamities) and refusing temptations (snares, enticements)."[51]

To put it succinctly: *hypomonē* means to stand fast *(menō)* under *(hypo)* assaults of evil. That is the Christian sense. Elsewhere it is used of soldiers standing fast under hostile assaults of the military sort, and, especially of the Hebrew word *qāwah,* "await," "hope" in the LXX, of "nerving oneself . . . to hold fast to God and not to mistake his power and faith . . . fulness,"[52] especially in "the last days." *Hypomonē* in itself means a sort of persistence in something in spite of influences to something else, and can acquire eschatological overtones. In the NT, very naturally, it means such persistence in the Christian faith. As contrasted with *hypostolē* (i.e., "withdrawal," Heb. 10:39), or *aphistantai* ("defection," Lk. 8:13), *hypomonē* can be used with the emphasis on the notion of *persisting.*

Again, very naturally, *hypomonē* is mentioned with express or tacit reference to the assaults of evil we resist. Since these are all devilish, and have that unity of origin, we need not essay the hard, and indeed futile, dichotomy "external," "internal" *(exterius, interius)* of Bede and other commentators. But the question does not affect Jas. 1:4, for which we must consider another use of the word; it is often used with the emphasis not on our *persistence* but on the *faith* that we persist in, that is, not on our *refusal* to give up our faith but on the *faith* that we refuse to abandon—in short, on our *continuing faith.*

U. Falkenroth, C. Brown, "Patience," *NIDNTT,* II, 767f. on *kartereō* and 772f. on *hypomenō.*

50. Barclay, *The Letters of James and Peter,* p. 125.

51. See, for the Latin quotation, Huther, p. 44, n. 1. Our translation.

52. F. Hauck, *menō, TDNT,* IV, 583f.; U. Falkenroth, C. Brown, "Patience" *(hypomenō), NIDNTT,* II, 772.

When faith is thus in the foreground of the meaning, faith is naturally associated with work. So it is in one of the oldest and greatest parables (the first in Mark); in Luke's version we read "by persevering produce a crop" (NIV) *(karpophorousin en hypomonē)* (8:15). See also Rom. 2:7 ("by *hypomonē* in well-doing"), 2 Cor. 12:12, and Col. 1:9-11, the last of which resembles James in the concatenation of wisdom, good works, *hypomonē,* joy, and the final reward; really those verses expand the previous Col. 1:4-6. (The "rondo" form of James is good, recognized technique, and often appears in, e.g., Paul.) Similarly, the lesson to be drawn from the heroes of faith in Heb. 11 is *hypomonē* at work ("let us run with perseverance" *[di' hypomonēs trechōmen]*, Heb. 12:1, NIV). Again, in Rev. 2:19 we get *hypomonē* and works, and in 14:12 *hypomonē* and keeping the commandments. In Rom. 5:3f. the absence of any mention of works can only mean that that activity is implied with *hypomonē;* for Paul cannot be imagined to mean that "approbation" can be won without works (see, e.g., Rom. 5:21–6:23).

Ropes gives some valuable hints of the truth. *Hypomonē* is "active": "We must see that it produces . . . fruits"; "This is closely similar to the characteristic Pauline doctrine of faith working itself out . . ."; "This inclusive and fundamental thought well fits its position at the opening of the tract."[53] Ropes, however, seems to confine the thought too closely to lists of "other virtues," as in Rom. 5:3f. and 2 Pet. 1:5-7. But it is not a question of "further fruits" added to one fruit, *hypomonē,* already acquired; rather, it is a question of a governing principle, that faith must live by works.

The parable in Mt. 19:16-22 illustrates how "works" *(erga)* bring a man to perfection and its reward, eternal life. There one act was needed to complete all the good work done in keeping the commandments—vv. 17, 19, and finally 21, "if you wish to be perfect, . . . sell," etc. Perfection is not just the "completeness of character" mentioned by Ropes but that character, that is, that faith, doing its full work. If we may adapt a vernacular saying, "Perfect is as perfect does." *Hypomonē* is a distinctively Hebrew virtue—indeed, for Philo,[54] "the queen of virtues"—exemplified by Abraham[55] as well as the later Jewish martyrs,[56] and "no-

53. P. 137.

54. *On the Change of Names* 197.

55. Ecclus. 44:20; 1 Macc. 2:52, *et saepe*. See also Ropes, p. 136.

56. E.g., "For the tyrant Antiochus, observing intently their heroism in virtue and their endurance under torture, publicly held up their constancy as a model for his soldiers" (4 Macc. 17:23, "4 Maccabees" [First Century A.D.]. A New Translation and Introduction by H. Anderson, *The Old Testament Pseudepigrapha,* ed. J. H. Charlesworth, II, 563).

where more fully exhibited than in the history of the Jewish race,"[57] but supremely in the life and death of Jesus. Declares the writer to the Hebrews: "In bringing many sons to glory, it was fitting that God . . . should make the Pioneer of their salvation perfect through suffering."[58]

Mayor[59] correctly embraces both the so-called external and the so-called internal assaults of evil, and avoids the entirely false suggestion that *hypomonē* has anything merely passive in it. The palmary examples of turning the other cheek, going the second mile, etc. illustrate the active effort involved in patient endurance through faith. Constancy is a moral quality, the quality of persistence. In itself "keeping on" has no fruits; the farmer (5:7) does not win his bread by *hypomonē* in all the hardships and difficulties in the field, but by the digging, plowing, and other works in which, under difficulties, he persists. So salvation is not the fruit of *hypomonē,* but of the faith in which one endures. This makes the Christian life an effort, indeed a ceaseless battle—a thought magnificently captured in John Bunyan's "To Be a Pilgrim":[60]

> Who would true valour see,
>   Let him come hither:
> Here's one will constant be,
>   Come wind, come weather.

The Rewards of Trial

James constantly keeps the effort and reward in mind. The Christian must not be satisfied with showing constancy in endurance only to a limited extent, on some occasions, and in some matters, but to perfection, that is, always. *Hypomonē,* practice under difficulties, consolidates our faith, not by extending it but by assuring our hold on it; every victory over *peirasmos* lessens the danger of a lapse from the standards of faith in life. We all know we have yet further to go in wisdom, or, as James calls it, the knowledge or law of God. That is why James has no sooner written 1:2-4 than he proceeds to v. 5 on wisdom. Of course, any further wisdom we get by prayer must thereafter, as previously, be made secure

57. Oesterley, p. 421. On Rebekah and Jacob as symbols of "suffering unto perfection" (1:2-4, 12), see Meyer, pp. 270ff.

58. Heb. 2:10, NIV. For a discussion of the perfecting of Christ through suffering, and linguistic analysis of the idea of perfection in the entire NT, including the Epistle of James, see D. Peterson, *Hebrews and Perfection* (1982), pp. 49ff., 21ff., 41.

59. Pp. 184ff.

60. *The Poems,* ed. Graham Midgley, in *The Miscellaneous Works of John Bunyan,* gen. ed. Roger Sharrocks, VI (1678), 160.

by *hypomonē;* and *hypomonē* in faith is not static but at work. If we let *hypomonē* do its work in full, we will come to (we mean "toward") perfection, that is, full Christianity perfectly assured against lapse.

In the important phrase "perfect work" (1:4), there is an analogous notion of totality, completeness, or wanting nothing that is actually expressed in the accumulated synonyms attached to "perfect," which describes the complete product of "constancy in endurance." Hort says this work "must not be suffered to cease prematurely."[61] True, and his use of that word shows the irresistible approximation of the notions, premature and incomplete. We may also say that that work must make us completely inured and constantly vigilant against, not some or many, but all the wiles and assaults of evil. Constancy in endurance is related to faith—it is its lifeblood (would one say?) or its backbone.

Faith and works are an inseparable unity, for faith exists by working; thus *hypomonē* exists in its exercise.[62] James says that the exercise of *hypomonē* must not be defective or we shall be defective; rather, it must be practiced, and so expert, against all assaults of evil. If this is achieved—as nearly as we, by grace, can achieve it—then we shall have every Christian virtue and each in perfection—as nearly as we, by grace, can attain thereto. If we realize that *peirasmos* in 1:2 is comprehensive,[63] the argument in "perfect work" becomes clear; especially with our emendation, we keep *hypomonē* at work also in v. 3.

Carelessly used, such doublets as "perfect" and "complete in every part" (1:4) are perfunctory; but James uses such accumulation of near synonyms to give weight, emphasis, and balance, not as a mere cliché. Here is another example of the unity of the Epistle of James and its "rondo" recurrences; for in "perfect" and "complete in every part," he is thinking along the same lines as in 1:18: "firstfruits," like every other offering to God, must be perfect and unblemished.

His repeated use of *teleios* ("perfect")—it occurs at least six times[64]—is a measure of the importance James attaches to this idea of completeness or wholeness. Like *holoklēros* ("complete in every part"), *teleios* in the OT has cultic associations, especially of ritual fitness; it also has a wide personal qualitative sense[65] and (unlike *holoklēros*) is commonly so used. Thus OT characters like Noah (Gen. 6:9), Abraham

61. P. 5.

62. A. H. McNeile, *New Testament Teaching in the Light of St. Paul's* (1923), p. 97.

63. See below, pp. 343ff.

64. 1:4 (bis), 17, 25; 2:22; 3:2. See also G. Delling, *teleios, TDNT,* VIII, 75; R. Schippers, "Goal" *(teleios), NIDNTT,* II, 267.

65. E.g., Gen. 6:9; 17:1; Dt. 18:13, *et saepe.*

(Gen. 17:1), and Jacob (Gen. 25:27) are called "perfect" *(tāmîm)* not because of their moral perfection but because of their right relationship with God, that is, "righteousness" (see 1QH 1:37; 7:12). If the idea were that of sinless perfection (1QH 14:17), this was in fact unattainable (1QS 5:24), for "the way of man is not established except by the Spirit which God created for him to make perfect a way for the children of men" (1QH 4:32; see also 1QH 7:17).

The "perfect man" (Jas. 3:2), therefore, is single-minded, obedient, and dedicated in life and conduct, that is, "righteous," but his righteousness springs from grace (Jas. 1:16f.). Here we see clearly the influence not only of the OT,[66] the rabbis,[67] and Qumran,[68] but supremely of the teaching of Christ, especially in the Sermon on the Mount: for example, "You must be perfect—just as your Father in heaven is perfect" (Mt. 5:48, GNB); again, "No one can be a slave to two masters . . ." (Mt. 6:24). That is also why James lays such stress on the undivided heart, for only the single-minded person can face and pass the test (*dokimos;* 1:12).

Here again, as in Qumran,[69] *teleios* has eschatological overtones, meaning one who is both tested and finally approved. Perfection, therefore, as Davids finely says, is a tension which encompasses both the possible and impossible, present and future, which "in its realizable form is focused on copying God and Christ and thus needs divine revelation and human obedience."[70] For James, as for Matthew (e.g., 5:48)

66. E.g., Ps. 12:2; 1 Chr. 12:23 (indecision in battle); Ecclus. 2:12-14, to be studied carefully in full with Ropes, p. 143 *ad fin*. By contrast see 1 Chr. 29:9 (NIV): "their leaders had given freely and wholeheartedly (lit. with a full or whole heart [*en kardia plērei*; Heb. *bᵉlēḇ šālēm*]) to the Lord."

67. On the rabbinic doctrine of the two *yēṣers* and the divided heart, especially in prayer, see S. Schechter, *Some Aspects of Rabbinic Theology* (1909), p. 255 with note.

68. For a similar type of dualism in Christian and Jewish literature, including Qumran, see, e.g., W. I. Wolverton, "The Double-minded Man in the Light of Essene Theology," *ATR* 38.2 (1956): 165-75; O. Wernberg-Møller, "A Reconsideration of the Two Spirits in the Rule of the Community (1Q Serek 3:13–4:26)," *Revue de Qumran* (1961): 413-41; an important series of articles by O. J. F. Seitz; Laws, pp. 58ff.; S. Marshall, "*Dipsychos:* A Local Term?" *StEv* 6 (1969) = *TU* 112 (1973): 348-51, perhaps hinting at a Roman locale? See also Adamson, p. 61, n. 52; see above, pp. 268ff., for a fuller discussion; B. Gärtner, "Simplicity" *(haplotēs), NIDNTT,* III, 572.

69. See E. P. Sanders, *Paul and Palestinian Judaism* (1977), pp. 288f.; A. R. G. Deasley, *The Idea of Perfection in the Qumran Texts* (Unpublished Ph.D. thesis, Manchester, 1972); Davids, GNC, p. 21.

70. GNC, p. 20.

and the Dead Sea Scrolls, the goal of perfection is likeness to God *(imitatio dei)* as he is revealed to us by "the Lord Jesus Christ, our glory." By inference, on the other hand, the person of divided heart, of two minds, who is distracted by the world, the flesh, and the devil, and obviously the antithesis of "the perfect person," will not pass the last test. The dualism here is practical rather than Gnostic and metaphysical.[71] Like Tennyson's Sir Bedevere, hesitating, "this way and that dividing the swift mind in act to throw," and repeatedly failing to act, the *dipsychos* person gets nowhere and ends up a lost soul (5:19f.). So James says, "But let him ask in faith, with no halting between two opinions. . . ." Like God, who gives unreservedly, the Christian must pray without reservation, the single-mindedness of the giver being matched by the single-mindedness of the suppliant.

The exact meaning of this strange word *dipsychos,* as we have seen, is determined in part by the word itself and in part by its context. Ropes is not wrong in his translation "with soul divided between," but we would avoid "double-minded" and prefer "the person of divided mind" or "you of divided mind"—split mind, in fact moral "schizophrenic." We get the full force of Jas. 1:8 and 4:8 if we remember Christ's word in Mt. 6:24: "No one can serve two masters. You cannot serve God and Mammon." "Double-minded" seems to smell too much of formations like "bigamy" or "bimetallism," and indeed (in etymology and in meaning) of "duplicity"; we want an odor of "dilemma" or the like. The road to salvation is beset with bifurcations, and the first thing we have to learn—a thing so obvious that many never see it—is that we cannot go down both forks at the same time. So we have to fork "right"; if not—as poor "Christian" found ere he had scarce begun his pilgrim way—there will be Satan to pay.

Jas. 1:6 shows that the point is doubt or lack of faith; inasmuch as it is directed against hope and confidence and conflicts with the gospel, such doubt is essentially eschatological.[72] There is also the idea of confusion and instability (1:8), but with no thought of duplicity (which might be inferred from the term itself). This meaning is confirmed in its later use (4:8) and by Hermas, where it does not mean *dolosus,* "guileful, cheating," but obviously, again, "of two minds" in the sense "of divided mind," a kind of "demonic instability," like Bunyan's "Mr. Facing-Both-Ways." Here the mind is distracted by lusts and temptations, all of which should lead the doubter to doubt himself, that is,

71. See Dibelius, p. 83.
72. B. Gärtner, "Distinguish, Doubt" *(diakrinō), NIDNTT,* I, 505.

his own credibility.[73] Chapter 4 makes that clear, from its first verse onward. (Is it too fanciful to conjecture that James, in part, may be combating the alleged syncretistic tendencies of the Hellenists?[74])

A glance at the evidence suggests that the topic of the single/double heart is found in OT, rabbinic, Qumran, and other literature.[75] It is possible that James found the word already in use; it is (in the absence of contrary evidence) also possible, and no less probable, that the Epistle of James originated this term and the use of *basilikos* in 2:8;[76] at any rate, its meaning is clear enough, namely, the *uncommitted* doubter, leading us to pray with poet Antoinette Bourignon:

> "Henceforth may no profane delight
> Divide this consecrated soul."[77]

Of necessity trial is no respecter of persons and the common lot of the Christian regardless of status. The poor believer of course suffers most, but he should regard it as a privilege and find compensation in spiritual elevation; likewise the rich brother,[78] stripped of his wealth, must rejoice in his humiliation, discovering its benefits. James does not here speak to Christians collectively, and say, for instance, "Carry each other's burdens" (Gal. 6:2, NIV). After the necessarily collective opening allocution in 1:2-4, he adopts the individual approach in v. 5, "if anyone," and continues it (Who will say it is not best?) in every verse up to the 15th, which is not really an exception; it recurs in vv. 19, 20, 23, 24, 25, 26, and 27. Speaking of communal behavior, he naturally uses the plural in 2:1ff.; but the singular is noticeable in the argument of 2:14ff. In 1:9f., as elsewhere, the individual approach lends added weight to the message. Here the point is appreciating the blessing of Christian brotherhood in the pursuit of the Christian ideal. This pursuit, in the face of *peirasmos,* is the leading theme of the chapter and of the Epistle.

To be sure, James was aware of the Jewish "piety-poverty equa-

73. B. Gärtner, *art. cit., NIDNTT,* I, 505.

74. For the view that the Hellenists were Jews of syncretistic bent, see, e.g., O. Cullmann, "The Significance of the Qumran Texts for Research into the Beginning of Christianity," *JBL* 74 (1955): 213ff.

75. See nn. 64ff. above.

76. If our author was the inventor, then he correctly formed it according to the analogy of similar neologisms like *dichonous,* "double-minded," and *diglōssos,* "speaking two languages." See Ropes, p. 143, for further examples.

77. See Ropes, p. 146.

78. For the other view, that the rich man is not a Christian, see Kistemaker, Davids, and others; also our previous discussion, p. 237.

tion"; but to say "Poverty is real wealth"[79] only obscures the train of thought—which is the happiness and joy of Christian faith and life. Happy are they who encounter trying assaults of evil and withstand them, making progress toward their ideal. If they have faith, they will receive wisdom generously and without chiding, and (to anticipate) by constancy in endurance win the crown of life. Happy also is the brother of low financial status, for in the brotherhood he is exalted, as 2:5 confirms; and he shares the eschatological reward of 1:12. Happy, too, is the wealthy man who has learned humility in Christ and so has won an everlasting treasure.

In Judaism the undulating fortunes of the rich and poor is a cause for rejoicing,[80] their rise and fall being likened to a revolving wheel, and their happiness to be found only in death.[81] The lot of the poor will be reversed in the life to come.[82] On the revolving wheel the poor ascend and the rich descend, and this is God's will.[83]

This "exaltation" and "humiliation" in James are also both eschatological rather than ethical. Brotherhood is an aid and joy in the pursuit of the ideal, and is similarly named in 2 Pet. 1:5-9, in a catalogue of the things a Christian must not lack if he is not to be "unfruitful in the knowledge of our Lord." The help of the brotherhood in resisting the assaults of evil is beyond doubt; as here, near the beginning, so at the end James mentions it (5:16, 19f.). The same is true in the context of prayer, which seems naturally to suggest the fellowship of the faith, as in the case of illness (5:14f.).[84]

Such examples of poverty and wealth further illustrate the nature

79. So Ropes, p. 4.

80. Ecclus. 10:14f., 25; 11:21; 21:4; also Lk. 1:51-53.

81. Ecclus. 11:28.

82. Apoc. Bar. 70:3f. See *The Syriac Apocalypse of Baruch,* tr. R. H. Charles, revised by L. H. Brockington, p. 883; also *The Apocryphal Old Testament,* ed. H. F. D. Sparks (1984), p. 837.

83. "This is the path to the Torah," says the Mishnah, "a morsel of bread with salt you must eat; and water by measure you must drink; you must sleep upon the ground the while you toil in the Torah. If you act thus, 'Happy shalt thou be and it shall be well with thee' (Ps. 128:2)—happy shall you be in this world, and it shall be well with you in the world to come" (M. Aboth 6.4).

84. Building on the works of J. B. Souček, R. B. Ward, and others, P. H. Davids, GNC, p. xxvi, e.g., draws a parallel with the ethic of Qumran and stresses the Epistle's "communal concern," arguing correctly that "it is wrong to read the epistle with an individualistic focus." While we are in substantial agreement with this thesis, what we have written above and on pp. 116f. ought to remind us again that the Epistle does have an *individual* message—a truth which must be held in firm juxtaposition with the Epistle's obvious communal thrust.

and purpose of trial. They concentrate not so much on the circumstances attending trial, but on the Christian himself under trial and the caliber of his faith. In every example that James cites in connection with trial he refers to Christian experience. In the words of G. Kittel:

> In our document it is apparent that these men live in the tradition of the Word of Jesus—at the same time that they intend to stay in the shadow of the end, waiting for the return of the Lord, yet that this eschatological knowledge did not result in apocalyptic speculation, but rather requiring obedience to the demand of Jesus for love, for honesty, for brotherhood, for mercy, for a truly authentic social ethic and for a practical Christianity. One may perhaps simply describe these men, insofar as the Epistle allows us to see them, thus: that they strive to conform themselves to the word of their Lord, and wait on his coming.[85]

Although sin is mentioned at least once (5:13-18) in connection with suffering, God is never associated in any way with sin or suffering. If, unlike Paul, James for his own reasons does not appeal to the sufferings of Christ as an aid to endurance, it is significant that as a Hebrew Christian he finds congenial examples in Job and the OT prophets. At the same time, he is able to baptize afresh into the Christian faith familiar Jewish ideas such as joy in trial[86] and its educative purpose,[87] and the reward for "those who love him" (1:12).

Now we must make another more relevant and important point. In early OT battles against idolatry, and likewise in the eschatological atmosphere of the NT, including James, with its ever present sense of the powers of evil at war with God and believers, "those who love him" gains much of its force from the choice of allegiance a person must make: "Under which King?" To Christians of James's age, the pressing choice was not between belief in God and unbelief, between religion and atheism, or between revelation and reason, but, quite starkly, between good and the devil (see Jas. 4:4; 2 Tim. 4:10 [Demas]). This is what gives force to "those who love him," and to all the passages about divided minds and the Christian war with the world. This sounds, too, in the term "slave" (1:1), God's person, in that struggle. And faith, be-

85. *Art. cit., ZNW* 41 (1942): 105.

86. See S–B III, 751f. For suffering in the OT generally, see J. Scharbert, *Der Schmerz im Alten Testament* (1955); and for suffering in Qumran in particular, see J. Carmignac, "La Théologie de la Souffrance dans les Hymnes de Qumran," *Revue de Qumran* 3 (1961): 368ff. Also A. R. C. Leaney, "The Eschatological Significance of Human Suffering in the Old Testament and the Dead Sea Scrolls," *SJTh* 16 (1963): 286ff.

87. See G. F. Moore, *Judaism*, II (1927), 248-56; see also C. G. Montefiore and H. Loewe, *Rabbinic Anthology* (1938) on "Suffering"; also Davids, pp. 35f.

sides its connotation of belief, also carries the idea of loyalty, reciprocated faith, a loyalty like that of a serf to his feudal lord, trusting that his Lord will not fail him at the end of the day or in the hour of need.

TEMPTATION

Besides laying stress on trial from external suffering, Judaism speaks much of inner testing, especially by the "evil inclination" *(yēṣer hārā')*. "The *yēṣer,*" writes Davids,[88] "is simply undifferentiated desire, striving for whatever it sees. It is not the self or *ego* of the person (it fits more closely Freud's *id*), but unless it is limited by the Law or Torah (in Judaism) or some other counterforce, it will control the *ego.*" Clearly the *yēṣer* plays an important part in James's doctrine of *peirasmos,* not only in 1:13ff., where he specifically describes its activity, but also, as we shall see, in the preceding section, starting with the opening greeting of 1:2. In keeping with his Jewish heritage, James has a keen awareness of sin.[89] That sin constitutes a break between man and God and, consequently, between man and man, is seen in the calls for purity[90] and confession.[91]

James's caution against unclean living (1:21) is common in the NT, which seems regularly to represent pagans as wallowing in sin. There is plenty of evidence that many of them did; but not all. The evidence of the NT also shows that a host of Christians were no better. The testimony of James in this *Deponentes* section underlines this truth. "Dirt" *(ryparia),* found only here in the NT and not in the LXX, may mean, as, for example, in Plutarch, *Moralia* 60d, "sordid avarice";[92] or, linking *ryparian* with *kakias,* this whole phrase may equal "all evil filth" *(pasan kakian ryparian).*[93] With Calvin, however, we take it by itself,

88. GNC, p. 25. For texts and details, see, e.g., W. Hirsch, *Rabbinic Psychology* (1947), pp. 227ff.; Schechter, *Some Aspects of Rabbinic Theology,* pp. 256ff.; S–B IV, 466ff.; J. Hadot, *Penchant mauvais et Volonté libre dans la Sagesse de Ben Sira* (1970); J. Marcus, "The Evil Inclination in the Epistle of James," *CBQ* 44.4 (1982): 606-21.

89. See L. Morris, *The Cross in the New Testament* (1965), pp. 310f. His vocabulary is limited to the usual *hamartia* (1:15 *[bis]*; 2:9; 4:17; 5:15, 20); see also *hamartōlos* (4:8; 5:20) and *ponēros* (2:4; 4:16), the latter being almost equivalent to *hamartia.* So Ropes, p. 281. James also uses two other words, *adikia* (3:16) and *parabatēs* (2:9), but not *parabasis.* See also G. D. Kilpatrick, "Übertreter des Gesetzes, Jak. 2, 11," *ThZ* 23 (1967): 433.

90. 4:8.

91. 5:16.

92. See further Mayor, p. 64; Dibelius, p. 113.

93. E.g., by Wiesinger.

with the meaning *akatharsian* (see Col. 3:5), "wickedness," which includes "hypocrisy and contumacy, and the whole range of corrupt desires."[94] Oesterley[95] shows that Heb. *tô'ēḇāh* ("abomination"), like Syr. *ṭanpûṯâ* ("pollution"), is associated in the OT with idolatry (e.g., Ezek. 44:6) and in later literature, especially Proverbs, with unchastity.[96]

The next phrase, *perisseian kakias,* means the same as *kakian perisseuousan.* So in Rom. 5:15 we have "its effect is vastly exceeded by the grace of God and the gift that came to so many" (NEB) *(hē dōrea en chariti . . . eis tous pollous eperisseuse),* and in v. 17 "those who receive in far greater measure God's grace" (NEB) *(hoi tēn perisseian tēs charitos . . . lambanontes).* Here a specific object of compassion is mentioned (one man's sin and its results): "God's act of grace is out of all proportion to Adam's wrongdoing" (Rom. 5:15, NEB). So also Jas. 4:6, *meizona didōsi charin,* that is, stronger than our innate propensity mentioned in the preceding verse. Salvation, like any other victory, requires not mere parity of grace with its adversary, sin, but a margin of superiority. In 2 Cor. 8:2 and many other places, the standard of comparison is unspecified and the meaning is often like "to an impressive and remarkable degree"; in 2 Cor. 8:2, the NEB gives "exuberantly happy" and "lavishly open-handed," the NIV "overflowing joy" and "welled up," for *perisseia* and *eperisseusen,* respectively.

"Abundance" usually serves to express an overflowing fullness of good. Where the profusion is reprehensible, as in prolixity, we sometimes speak of "redundancy." By pruning away the redundant we may preserve the good; but where the whole thing is undesirable, for example, vice, it is hard to find an English word that is both literal and idiomatic. The quaint KJV "superfluity of naughtiness" is open to the same objection, for, as Mayor rightly says, "This would seem to make the writer guilty of the absurdity of supposing a certain amount of malice to be proper for a Christian."[97] In Lk. 6:38, overflowing fullness, *hyperekchynomenon metron,* is *mensuram superfluentem* in the Vulgate. So the Dictionary quotes from Cicero, *supra fluentis iuvenili quadam dicendi impunitate et licentia,* that is, running to extravagant lengths.[98]

94. P. 272. So, too, J. I. Packer, "moral filthiness," art. "Dirt" *(rhypos), NIDNTT,* I, 479.

95. P. 432.

96. See L. E. Elliott-Binns, "James 1:21 and Ezekiel xvi. 36: An Odd Coincidence," *ExpT* 66.9 (1955): 273. See, too, Schechter, *Some Aspects of Rabbinic Theology,* p. 233, n. 5; C. G. Montefiore and H. Loewe, *A Rabbinic Anthology* (1938), p. 306.

97. Pp. 64f.; see also BAG, p. 397.

98. "Excess of my style, which was marked by a youthful impetuousness

But "extravagance of vice" is open to misunderstanding; it might seem to mean that a certain amount of vice is right. "Enormity of vice" is a little better. In the parallel phrase in 1 Pet. 4:4 (clarified by vv. 2f.), the KJV and the RV have "excess of riot"; the NEB "reckless dissipation"; and BAG, s.v., "all the evil prevailing (around you)." We can think of nothing better for "lavish indulgence of profligacy" in Jas. 1:21a than *prodigality of vice*.

Having spoken of the need for repentance, James goes on in 1:21b to urge meek acceptance of the implanted Word that is able to save the soul. So repentance is followed by the reception of the gospel, and this in turn (1:22ff.) is to be accompanied by good deeds. A somewhat similar pattern is found in Judaism, where repentance, Torah, and good works are said to be effective weapons against the *yēṣer*.[99] Conjoined with repentance, therefore, is the Torah, the Jewish equivalent of what James designates the "perfect law" or "the implanted Word." The Torah is the best weapon against the *yēṣer:* "If God has created the *Evil Yēṣer,* he also created the Torah as spice (remedy) against him" (b. Baba Bathra 16a). Good works also help to fight the *yēṣer* (1:22ff.).

Equally essential, says James, in the Christian's battle with evil and especially with his hostile lusts (1:13ff.; 4:1ff.) are the weapons of repentance, the gospel, and good works. We must resist lust, bring forth the fruits of repentance, and heartily welcome the implanted Word of truth. By God's grace, therefore, we shall overcome the assaults of evil and win the salvation of our souls.

The Source of Temptation: Human Desire

As to the origin of the malady of sin itself James says nothing; nor does he observe the distinction between sin as a principle and an act; instead, he dwells on the origin, growth, and result of human sin (1:14f.). "The vivid imagery," writes Leon Morris, "pictures sin as a thing of power and force and life."[100] His purpose, however, is remedial, not speculative, and his concern is with the human heart, not with a list of the temptations it may meet. He does not even mention the example of solicitation of others as a *peirasmos*, powerful as these were even before the age of television.

---

and lack of restraint" (*Brutus* 91.316, ed. G. L. Hendrickson [Loeb Library, 1962], p. 274). See *Oxford Latin Dictionary*, ed. P. G. W. Glare (1983), p. 1028, no. 4, s.v. *licentia*.

99. See Schechter, *Some Aspects of Rabbinic Theology*, p. 313.

100. *The Cross in the New Testament*, p. 310.

The claim in 1:13 rests on this truth, that God in creating our appetites, for example sexual libido, neither sins nor incites us to sin. The appetites can be sinfully indulged, as the rabbis taught about the *yēṣer;* but as the rabbis taught[101] and Paul says in 1 Cor. 10:13, to meet the temptation God provides the "way of escape" or *ekbasis*. Exactly so James: if we truly seek God and his righteousness he gives us the grace to overcome the appetite when to indulge it would be sin.[102] The rabbis testified that "Satan and the *Yēṣer* and the Angel of Death are one"[103]; in the same way Jas. 1:15 traces "death" ultimately to "desire" in a way that recalls the Pauline connection between death and the flesh, especially "the body of death."[104]

The ground for denouncing the flesh is that it knows no righteousness; other things being equal, it finds the sin of 1 Cor. 6:18 as attractive as the duty of 1 Cor. 7:5. And so it is with all our carnal appetites; indeed, "stolen fruits are sweet." Further, whereas the appetites are indifferent to sin, the devil, who tries to make use of them (see Mt. 4:2f.; 1 Cor. 7:5), is content only with sin: from him, not from God, comes incitement to sin by yielding sinfully to an appetite that should be resisted. The whole logic of Christian moral theology is that acceptance of the Word (Jas. 1:21; Eph. 4:17-29; 1 Cor. 6:9-20; and throughout the NT) imposes the duty, and the gift of grace (Jas. 4:6-8; see also Phil. 2:13 and throughout the NT) provides the means, to resist our appetites, if and when right so requires; in Jas. 4:7 the choice between the Captain of Good and Evil is plain and imperative.

Commentators on Jas. 1:14 rightly cite verses in ch. 4; we must realize, however, that, in line with James's customary circling style, 4:1-12 is *essentially* a second handling of the themes of 1:19-21, and the two passages must be interpreted together, both in turn being interpreted by the prior notion of "the double-minded man" *(anēr dipsychos)*. We note the occurrence of *dipsychos* in 4:8 as in 1:8, the futile prayer of the *dipsychoi* in 4:3 as in 1:6f., and cleansing in 4:8 as in 1:21. Most importantly, we must understand and then relate the "pesher" in 4:5 (and 6), which we translate: "Or do you suppose it is an idle saying in the Scriptures that the spirit that has taken its dwelling in us is prone to envious lust?"

Does the "spirit" here refer to the Spirit of God, or the human spirit? A vital clue to this notorious *crux interpretum* is furnished by the

101. See Schechter, *Some Aspects of Rabbinic Theology*, ch. XVI.

102. Jas. 4:6.

103. b. Baba Bathra 16a.

104. Rom. 7:24. Compare also Rom. 8:13; Gal. 6:8. See A. C. Thiselton, "Flesh" *(sarx)*, *NIDNTT*, I, 681.

emphatic introductory *pros phthonon,* a phrase that apparently can only be taken adverbially[105] in the sense of *phthonerōs,*[106] that is, "enviously," "spitefully," or "maliciously."[107] This accords, too, with the basic meaning of *phthonos* itself as "malice" or "ill-will."[108] *Phthonos,* as R. C. Trench showed, ought to be clearly distinguished from *zēlos.* "*Zēlos,*" he writes, "is a *meson,* while *phthonos,* incapable of good, is used always and only in an evil signification."[109] Trench's verdict, which has recently been impressively reinforced by L. T. Johnson,[110] who flatly declares: "*phthonos* is *always* a vice," may be tested by reference to the classics[111] or the LXX,[112] particularly the latter, as well as to Ex. 20:5, where the jealousy *(qānā')* ascribed to God is, significantly, not *phthonos,* but *zēlos* (see also Jas. 3:14), a difficulty that advocates like Mayor and others cannot explain. Yet this is as expected, and is the reason why

105. Dibelius, p. 224, n. 89; Hort, p. 95; KJV mg. *pros bian,* that is, *biaiōs,* by force, forcibly (Plato, *Critias* 16.10d; Philo, *On the Special Laws* 3.3: "and ceased not to pull me down violently"). Similarly, *pros orgēn, pros epithymian.* To avoid attributing *phthonos* to God, Wesley, e.g., tried unnaturally to take *pros* with its usual NT force (see Gal. 5:17). See also Mitton, p. 155, n. 1.

106. E. Preuschen, *Griechisch-Deutsches Wörterbuch zu den Schriften des Neuen Testaments und der übrigen urchristlichen Literatur . . . von Walter Bauer* ([2]1925-28), p. 1140.

107. A point of some importance, if accepted as a principle of interpretation. Thus Bede, e.g., knows at least three meanings of *phthonos:*

(1) *adversus invidiam.* So Luther: "The Spirit's desire is opposed to hatred."

(2) *ad invidiam.* So Calvin: "Is the Spirit of God disposed to envy?"

(3) *ad invidiam usque.* So von Soden: "He loves the Spirit to the point of jealousy."

On these, with full patristic references, see Mayor, pp. 142f.

108. See Liddell and Scott, s.v.

109. *Synonyms of the New Testament* ([10]1886), p. 87; see also Ropes, p. 263.

110. "James 3:13–4:10 and the *Topos Peri Phthonou,*" *NovT* 25.4 (1983): 327-47, esp. 335.

111. E.g., "envy is base and characteristic of base men" *(to de phthonein phaulon kai phaulōn)* (Aristotle, *The "Art" of Rhetoric* 2.11); "jealously disposed and harmful" *(phthonerōs kai blabēros)* (Plato, *Phaedrus* 243c); "since foster mothers must be jealous" *(phthonein gar phasi mētryias teknois)* (Euripides, *Ion* 1025; see also *Alcestis* 306; *Iphigenia in Taurus* 1268). Also Plato, *Symposium* 213d; *Philebus* 47e; *Laws* 679c; *Menexenus* 242. See further LS; BAG, s.v. *phthonos, phthoneros,* and *phthoneō,* p. 718 states: *pros phthonon,* prob.: *phthonerōs,* jealously.

112. For Jewish and biblical usage, see Wisd. 2:24 *(phthonō de diabolou);* 6:25; 1 Macc. 8:16; Tob. 4:7, 16; Test. Sim. 4:5; Test. Benj. 8:1; Philo, *On the Life of Moses* 1.2; Josephus, *Life* 80; 122; 204; also *Corpus Hermeticum* 13.7. The term occurs five times in NT vice lists (Rom. 1:29; Gal. 5:21; 1 Tim. 6:4; Tit. 3:3; 1 Pet. 2:1) and three times elsewhere (Mt. 27:18; Mk. 15:10; Phil. 1:15)—always pejoratively.

no Jew could attribute *phthonos* in its true Greek sense (i.e., a god's spiteful envy of humans)[113] to Yahweh. "Lack of envy" or "generosity" *(aphthonia),* on the other hand, was regarded as a divine attribute, and this fits in well with Jas. 1:5; 4:6. Nor, again, can *phthonos* possibly stand for a lover's or husband's jealousy.[114] In fact of such evidence, therefore, the attempt to construe *phthonos* with the Spirit of God appears misguided and indefensible.

If not the Holy Spirit, then, does the "spirit" mean the human spirit? Light is shed on this point by certain important parallels in Hermas, particularly *Mand.* 3.1, where the thought of James is reproduced almost word for word: "the spirit which God has settled in this flesh of yours" *(to pneuma ho theos katōkisen en tē sarki tautē).*[115] Though somewhat obscure and baffling, the spirit referred to here is not the Holy Spirit,[116] but the spirit implanted in humans, originally pure and truthful, but capable of becoming darkened *(episkotoumenon)* and "contaminated by bitterness" *(miainomenon hypo tēs oxycholias).*[117] The constant conflict that rages between the spirit of anger, bitterness, and lust[118] on the one hand, and the spirit of truth and longsuffering[119] on the other, corresponds psychologically to the struggle between man's good and evil ego.

Against such a background, James's concept of the divinely implanted spirit in us *(to pneuma ho katōkisen en hēmin)*[120] becomes clear,

113. "The jealousy of the gods" *(theōn phthonos)* (Aeschylus, *Persians* 362; *Agamemnon* 947); "may no god of your bliss be jealous" *(phthonos mē genoito tis theōn)* (Euripides, *Alcestis* 1135). For other examples, see LS, s.v., who note that while *zēlos* is a neutral word, *phthonos* is always used in a bad sense and is never employed in the LXX where the Hebrew word *qānā'* is to be expressed in reference to God or men. See I. Abrahams, *Studies in Pharisaism and the Gospels,* Second Series (1924), pp. 167f.; also D. H. Field, "Envy" *(phthoneō), NIDNTT,* I, 558, who, after stating "Jas. 4:5 may provide the only example of *phthonos* used in a good sense," cites the linguistic difficulty, and notes that NEB gives *phthonos* "its more usual bad sense of envy." For *aphthonia* ("lack of envy") see L. T. Johnson, *art. cit.,* "James 3:13–4:10," *NovT* 25.4 (1983): 337.

114. See Ropes, p. 263; *pace* Mayor.

115. See also *Mand.* 5.2.5; 10.2.5;10.3.2.

116. For valuable remarks on this and the entire subject, see Dibelius, pp. 223ff.

117. See *Mand.* 5.1.2; 3.2.

118. For the terms "passion" *(thymos),* "anger" *(orgē),* "malice" *(mēnis),* "bad temper" *(oxycholia),* and "bitterness" *(pikria),* see Mand. 5.2; 10.1; 5.1; also Dibelius, p. 223.

119. *Mand.* 3.4; 5.2.3.

120. Reading the better-attested *katōkisen,* "caused to dwell" (RSV, GNB, NIV after **p**[74] ℵ B Ψ 049 1241 1739 *al*) against *katōkēsen,* "dwells," taking the aorist, "he dwelt," to mean "has taken up his dwelling" (KJV after **PM** sy (p)). See B. M. Metzger, *A Textual Commentary on the Greek New Testament* (1975), p. 683.

probably reflecting a similar type of pre-Christian or Jewish dualistic "demonological ethic."[121] If, in turn, as Hort believes, this doctrine may be traced ultimately to the human creation in Gen. 2:7,[122] there is a strong possibility that his immediate source is some rabbinic variant of this story.[123] We are inclined to take "spirit" in the sense of a pure spirit given by God originally at creation that we must keep clean. Accordingly, it is particularly tempting to see a reference here to the Jewish idea of the two *yēṣers*,[124] "the spirit which enviously yearns" being simply a veiled reference to his evil *yēṣer*.

James has already alluded to this struggle in 1:14, and takes up this theme again when he describes the passions that war within the soul (4:1ff.). The context shows that he has in mind the non-Christian Jewish community, not the individual. Indeed, it can be argued that James is using the *topos* on envy "to give substance to his conversion call."[125]

121. Dibelius, p. 224.

122. See Gen. 6:3 (backed by Targ. Onk. and Syr.); Job 27:3; 33:4; 34:14; Wisd. 12:1; *Sib. Orac.* frag. 1.5; also Seneca, *Moral Epistles* 41.2. See also A. B. Davidson, *Theology of the Old Testament* (1904), p. 193. In a personal note C. F. D. Moule draws my attention to the eighteenth-century commentator, Matthew Pole, who has a very long Latin note beginning cheerfully: "No passage in the N.T. is more difficult or capable of more varied interpretations." He proceeds to give *plaustra* ("cart-loads," I suppose) of interpretations, all turning on "spirit" meaning "the Spirit of God"; then toward the end he deals with "spirit" as the spirit of man. Apart from their general interest and their lively awareness of the difficulty of Jas. 4:5f. his comments show that Pole, writing in 1712, knew of the "human spirit" interpretation and thought it was related to Gen. 6, which he took as a stock biblical passage for building the *yēṣer hā-ra'*. In fact, the excursus in S–B IV, 1, on *Der gute und der böse Trieb* (pp. 466-83) shows that Gen. 8:21 is the stock one.

123. The rabbis taught that the soul, as given originally by God, is pure at birth (b. Shabbath 152b; Eccl. R. 12.7; see also b. Niddah 30a). Prayer must be said daily for its purity (b. Shabbath 32b; b. Baba Bathra 16a) and on death it must be returned pure to God (b. Baba Meṣi'a 167a; T. J. Berakoth 2.3.14a; see also Philo, *Who is the Heir?* 22; Wisd. Sol. 20). Similarly, in Test. Naph. 10.9, man is exhorted not to sully the holy spirit lodged in him by God, but to return it, pristinely pure, to his Creator. For full references and discussion, see Hirsch, *Rabbinic Psychology*, pp. 150ff., 215ff.; Dibelius, pp. 223ff.; and E. Schweizer, *pneuma*, *TDNT*, VI, 446f.; all of these take *pneuma* in James in this sense, that is, as a pure spirit given by God that we must keep clean. For references to Hermas also, see H. Weinel, *Wirkungen des Geistes und der Geiste* (1899), p. 159.

124. On Gen. 2:7, the rabbis took the two *yods* in *wyyṣr* as evidence that God had created man with both a good and evil *yēṣer* (Gen. 64.7; b. Berakoth 61a). For these and other examples, see Schechter, *Some Aspects of Rabbinic Theology*, p. 264.

125. See L. T. Johnson, *art. cit.*, "James 3:13–4:10," *NovT* 25.4 (1983): 327-47; also "Friendship with the World/Friendship with God: A Study of Discipleship in James," *Discipleship in the New Testament*, ed. F. F. Segovia (1985), pp. 167ff.,

Two types of struggle are going on simultaneously—one in the individual and the other in the community—and the latter is the result of the former. People make war with their fellows because they are not at peace within themselves, and outward division is the manifestation of an inner disharmony.

The allusion to peace (3:18) leads paradoxically to an abrupt, characteristic question on the origin of wars and fightings—two terms, the one broad and the other narrow in meaning, used metaphorically and somewhat loosely, like our "trouble and strife," to describe "the chronic and acute hostilities in the community."[126] A further question shows that such conflict has its source in the pleasures that lie entrenched in their "members" *(melē),* that is, "flesh" or, better, "personality," another reference probably to the work of the *yēṣer.*[127]

In 4:2f., where this theme is pursued, we have to deal with the so-called "intolerable anticlimax" of the Gk. *phoneuete kai zēloute.* Psychologically we might expect the sequence to be reversed, murder following rather than preceding envy, and in our commentary on *James* (NICNT), pp. 167f., we proposed the emendation "covet" *(phthoneite)* for "kill" *(phoneuete).* We now believe the usual explanations (a corrupt text,[128] a political reference to Zealotism,[129] a case of hendiadys,[130] or faulty punctuation[131] merely substitute one anticlimax for another.

---

who argues that the apparent contrast between war and peace is controlled by the more basic subject of envy. Also Schlatter, p. 240.

126. Ropes, p. 253.

127. See p. 372, n. 33. On "pleasure" and "desire," see G. Stählin, *hēdonē, TDNT,* II, 909-26; E. Beyreuther, "Desire" *(hēdonē),* I, 458-60.

128. *Phthoneite,* first suggested (followed by Erasmus, Spitta, Mayor, Moffatt, Windisch, Dibelius, Phillips, et al.) perhaps by Oecumenius, who originally wrote *phoneite,* and later corrected to *phoneuete* (Mayor), in his text (not comment), but without manuscript authority. For a like collocation, see Test. Ben. 7:2 (where R. H. Charles reads *phonos;* see also the Orthodox Church Version); 1 Pet. 2:1b; Gal. 5:21; Ps.-Cl. *Homilies* 2:11; also 1 Macc. 8:16; Test. Sim. 4:5 (see also 2:7 and 4:7); 1 Clem. 3:2; 4:7, 13; 5:2. For emendation with rare Sophoclean *phonate,* see Dibelius, p. 200.

129. See Rendall, p. 114; B. I. Reicke, *Diakonie, Festfreude und Zelos* (1951), pp. 341ff.; M. J. Townsend, "James 4:1-4: A Warning against Zealotry?" *ExpT* 87.7 (1976): 211ff. True, Josephus uses the noun *zēlōtēs* in this technical sense, but never the verb; on this see Plummer, p. 96.

130. I.e., taking the phrase, impossibly (Bengel et al.), as "you murderously envy."

131. So Mayor (Ropes, Hort, WH mg, Knowling, et al.), who inserts a colon after *phoneuete,* translating: "Unsatisfied desire leads to murder (as in the case of Naboth); disappointed ambition leads to quarreling and fighting." Yet two major difficulties remain: the intrusive *kai* before *zēloute,* which makes the Greek diffi-

The best solution is found if, reading *kai ouk echete dia,*[132] we set the verses down in a series of theses and antitheses, thus preserving the fine symmetry of the original Greek parallelism:

epithymeite	—*kai ouk echete*
phoneuete kai zēloute	—*kai ou dynasthe epitychein*
machesthe kai polemeite	—*kai ouk echete dia to mē aiteisthai hymas*
aiteite	—*kai ou lambanete, dioti*

We may interpret this reasoning as follows: *You desire*—in the broad, literal, evil[133] (possibly sexual?)[134] sense of "you set your heart upon" *(epi-thymeite)—and yet you do not have (kai ouk echete;* see also 1 Jn. 5:15). So frustrated, *you desire to destroy and possess (phoneuete kai zēloute),* taking *phoneuete* not in the literal sense,[135] but in the ethical or metaphorical sense of "cherish murder in your heart," that is, a hyperbole of "hate,"[136] or perhaps even pick a quarrel,[137] and almost certainly reflecting the saying of Jesus on "murder" (Mt. 5:21ff.).

James's statement "you murder" *(phoneueis),* as Kittel notes, "is, so to speak, set in quotation marks: 'you murder'—namely, if you do

---

cult and harsh; also the reference to murder, which compels Mayor, significantly, to revert to the further expedient of emendation.

132. א P Ψ minn. vg[cl] sy[bo] rather than the shorter *ouk echete dia* (A B M vg[st] sa), or the Received *ouk echete de dia.*

133. See 1 Cor. 10:6; see also Jas. 1:13ff. On envy leading to war, with tests, see L. T. Johnson, *art. cit.,* "James 3:13–4:10," *NovT* 25.4 (1983): 336.

134. See Mt. 5:28; also Xenophon, *Anabasis* 4.14.

135. *Pace* evidence (e.g., Acts 9:23; 20:3; 23:12ff.; 1 Pet. 4:15; Did. 3:2; 1 Clem. Rom. 4:7, 9) submitted by Ropes et al. Is it entirely likely that, in the next breath, James should proceed to instruct such murderers in the art of prayer? Nor is it clear why *machesthe kai polemeite* should not be taken equally literally. In any event, such an interpretation merely accentuates the "anticlimax."

136. D. W. Burdick, *James,* the *Expositor's Bible Commentary,* ed. F. E. Gaebelein, XII (1981), 193; also Hiebert and others. Found in Jas. 5:5 and other places in the OT and NT, e.g., Dt. 24:6; also Ecclus. 34:21f.; Mt. 5:21f.; 1 Jn. 3:15. Somewhat similarly, Oecumenius and Theophylact interpret "hate" as "moral suicide."

137. According to E. F. F. Bishop (*Apostles of Palestine* [1958], p. 182) some increased form of the Semitic root Q-T-L may underlie the Greek, for the Arab. *fa'ala* (3rd form) means "to make war on someone" and often in modern Palestinian Arabic "to pick a quarrel with." So he thinks that *phoneuete* may have been employed "to render an Aramaic word having the same connotation as the Arabic Increased Form. In fact in ordinary speech people use *qaṭala* where they should use *qāṭala,* which means 'try to kill' with the consequent extension of 'quarrel.'" It is interesting that the Arabic MS CUL 2621 in Cambridge University Library so translates *phoneuete,* and that there is also a Quranic parallel.

the thing that the Lord has called 'murder.'"[138] *Zēloute* would then point to the purpose of such "murder," namely, the hope of economic or social gain[139] . . . *and (yet) you are not able to obtain (kai ou dynasthe epitychein)*. Still balked, *you fight and struggle (machesthe kai polemeite)*,[140] unfulfilled desire inevitably issuing in conflict not simply with man—a stock idea of ancient ethics[141]—but here fundamentally with God . . . *and (yet) do not have (what you desire) because you do not claim it as yours (kai ouk echete dia to mē aiteisthai hymas)*, the point being that since the objects of their desire—unspecified, probably deliberately—are a legitimate object of prayer that ought to be so claimed.

You ask and do not receive because you claim it wrongly in order that you may spend it on pleasures (rather than on God), implying that when they did pray they did so from a wrong motive, that is, self-gratification (see Jas. 1:7). But is there—as we have suggested here—a distinction between the active and middle of "ask" *(aiteō* and *aitoumai*), described variously as "hypothetical" (Dibelius), "interchangeable" (Moulton, Dibelius, Windisch, BAG), "arbitrary" (B1-D), "an extinct subtlety" or "freak" (Moulton), or a subtle signal that this is a reference to a saying of Jesus (Mussner)? Ineffective distinctions have been drawn on the basis of (1) loan and gift (Ammonius Hermiae, c. 5th century A.D.; T. Magister); (2) personal and business (official) affairs;[142] and (3) asking a person for a thing (Hort: "St. James could never mean to say that they did *aitein* though they did not *aiteisthai*"[143]).

138. Kittel's important explanation deserves fuller quotation: "In the word of Jesus, indeed Mt. 5:21ff., the commentary and inner significance of the 'murder commandment' is given; that is, his 'But I say to you': the murder commandment in actuality means, on the one hand, avoidance of the transgression of the command to love and, on the other hand, the demand of the attitude of love. But with this we obtain precisely the sense which our approach to the dependency of James demands. The command of love is the one, the royal, chief commandment; whoever keeps the sixth commandment, but transgresses the fifth—that person is guilty of breaking the whole law" ("Der geschichtliche Ort des Jakobusbriefes," *ZNW* 41 [1942]: 87).

139. Hort thinks that the use of *epitynchanō*, that is, "attain" rather than "obtain" (see *Berliner Griechische Urkunden* 1.332.6) favors the latter, which he translates "sordid and bitter personal ambition." Yet, perhaps, here as elsewhere (e.g., Hesiod, *Works and Days* 23: "The neighbor envies the neighbor who presses on toward wealth" [*zēloi de te geitona geitōn eis aphenos speudont*]) the two ideas merge.

140. A clear echo of preceding nouns; but see Dibelius, p. 201n.

141. For examples, particularly Philonic, see Ropes, pp. 257f.

142. See G. Stählin, *aiteō*, *TDNT*, I, 194; H. Schönweiss, "Prayer" *(aiteō)*, *NIDNTT*, II, 856. See also MM for papyrus examples.

143. P. 91.

Nearer the truth is Mayor, who regards the middle as "subjective" or "dynamic," the active therefore suggesting "outward action" as opposed to inward feeling.[144] Thus *aiteō* means "prayer of the lips, as contrasted with prayer of the heart." In support he appeals to classical[145] as well as other biblical examples, citing, too, Favorinus, who takes *aitoumai* as the request (*meth' hikesias* or *meta paraklēseōs*) of an inferior to a superior. Yet this, too, is unsatisfactory—for how can one "ask evilly" *(kakōs aiteisthe)* in the spirit of prayer?

A better solution is furnished by Liddell and Scott, s.v., who define *aitoumai* as "to ask for one's own use, claim," that is, *claim as one's own* or *appropriate*. In this sense it is practically equivalent to the Lat. *sibi vindicare,*[146] clearly brought out in Mk. 6:22-25, where Salome *claims* (not only asks for) the head of John the Baptist (v. 25). Like Salome, James's readers claimed "evilly" (*kakōs—not* "amiss," KJV)—probably a reference to the *yēṣer*[147] since they wished to spend it[148] on their pleasures. The use of the preposition *en* with *dapanaō,* "spend" (instead of the usual *eis*), is significant, for thereby the two spheres of pleasure (Jas. 5:5) and God (see Mt. 6:32) are set in contrast, implying that to choose pleasure means to reject God. Accordingly, such "evil," selfish, lustful prayer must go unanswered.

In view of the obvious reference here to Mt. 7:7ff. (Lk. 11:9f.), the problem of unanswered prayer may have agitated some of James's circle,[149] and it may well be, as Kittel thought, that we have here a hidden (negative) allusion to a word of Jesus:

> . . . in the Greek tradition of Jesus-sayings which was familiar to him, the active was given. He shapes the proposition and speaks for himself with the middle form: "You do not have because you do not ask . . . you ask wrongly"—both times *aiteisthe;* but between the two the saying of Jesus intrudes: "You ask and do not receive," and here the

144. P. 133.

145. E.g., Thucydides 3.59.2ff.; 4.18.

146. See Cicero, *The Republic* 1.17.27. See also *Oxford Latin Dictionary,* ed. P. G. W. Glare, s.v. *vindico.*

147. See W. F. Lofthouse, "Poneron and Kakon," *ExpT* 60 (1948-49): 264. See also Wisd. 14:19, 30; 4 Macc. 6:17; Jn. 18:23 (*kakōs* contrasted with *kalōs*); Jas. 1:5; 5:16; L. T. Johnson, *art. cit.,* "Friendship with the World/Friendship with God," *Discipleship in the New Testament,* p. 169.

148. See also *Berliner Griechische Urkunden* 1.149.5; Lat. *consumere in re.*

149. For rabbinic teaching on wrongly inspired prayer, see M. Berakoth 9.3; M. Sanhedrin 10.6b. See also S–B I, 396-426; I. Abrahams, *Studies in Pharisaism and the Gospels* (Second Series) (1924), ch. 11, "Some Rabbinic Ideas on Prayer," pp. 72ff.

aiteite word of Jesus "ask and you shall receive" is stamped with an active.[150]

Such conduct amounts to apostasy and must be denounced. Hence the harsh apostrophe, "adulteresses" (4:4), is to be interpreted, as the following rhetorical question shows, in the figurative[151] rather than the literal, OT prophetic sense of idolatry—in this case, "friendship with the world." These two words "friendship" and "world" epitomize the dualism, ethical rather than metaphysical, which pervades the Epistle, "world" *(kosmos)* in this instance also ethical and spiritual, standing for the world of evil rather than that of nature or people. From the general idea of "friendship" and "enmity," James proceeds to show precisely how this choice of the world constitutes personal and deliberate hostility toward God. Idolatry and adultery were the two great passions on which the *yēṣer* fed,[152] and both of these were apparently in James's mind.

Victory over Temptation: By God's Grace

Having spoken of the corrupt, sinful activity of the human spirit, James then proceeds to the utterly *gracious* activity of God: "But God gives greater grace in view of the greater requirement" (Ropes). The requirement in this case springs from the need to resist the human spirit of envy. Our interpretation is once more in accord with good rabbinic doctrine. To the humble, God gives a greater degree of "grace" *(charis)*, that is, to resist the *yēṣer*. While insisting that man had the power of choice, the rabbis also affirmed that those who made the right choice receive "grace" as divine help; and they quote *(inter alia)* Prov. 3:34 to support their view.[153]

"Grace" in James, then, is to be interpreted not in the original non-theological sense of Prov. 3:34, "divine acceptance and favor." His idea is thoroughly Christian, far outstripping the highest Jewish theological notions of "grace," almost equivalent to the Holy Spirit; to him grace is, as Mitton observed, "similar to that which is characteristically Pauline, of God's generous, active, effective help to man, far beyond anything the man deserves or can rightly expect."[154] Both in his doctrine of

150. *Art. cit., ZNW* 41 (1942): 89.
151. *Pace* Oesterley, Hort, and others.
152. Schechter, *Some Aspects of Rabbinic Theology*, p. 250.
153. G. F. Moore, *Judaism*, I (1927), 455f.
154. *Some Aspects of Rabbinic Theology*, p. 156; see also Davids, p. 163.

phthonos and in his use of *charis* as *victorious* grace James is characteristically Greek (as usual beyond all the rest of the NT); as in Pindar, *charis* quite commonly means "victory."

Words take on overtones or associations from the situations in which they are used. Thus *charis,* which among other things means "favor," often means the favor of the gods in Greek. We must always remember that the Greeks did believe in a Supreme Being. Pindar's mind (in his Victory Odes) was filled with God and Victory; so it was only natural that he sometimes used *charis* for that manifestation of heaven's favor which was most relevant, namely, victory in the games. Such victory was highly prized, and Pindar constantly reminds his patrons that they owe it entirely to the gods. The same is true of the Hebrew mind in the OT. Theirs was a world at war: they never had rest (for very long) from their enemies. They started with a notion of a tribal god whose business it was to save them from those enemies, and salvation and saving became so colored by circumstances that "salvation" is often used to mean "victory."

James (need we say?) views life as a battle against the assaults of evil *(peirasmoi)* and for the crown of joy and victory. That is why we think that in this verse, *charis,* "grace," has a tinge of the meaning "victory." This is especially so because it is used with *meizona,* "greater," that is, "conquering," "prevailing over the innate vice." Thus 4:7 carries on the metaphor of battle and victory (over the devil; see also 1 Jn. 4:14). This is all basic NT doctrine; the ideas of grace, faith, and victory are found, for example, in Rom. 4:16; Eph. 2:5; Jn. 5:4f. (compare Jas. 4:4); and 1 Cor. 15:54-57, where vv. 57 and 58 might be an epitome of James.

We think that at the beginning of ch. 4 as at the beginning of ch. 2 James is addressing sinners of whom some at least seem *not to know* that they are sinning. Ps. 37[155] shows that even fairly well-meaning people are tempted to imitate the (for the present) prosperous ungodly (e.g., vv. 1, 7f., 16, 27, and the end, 35-40). In the same way the Christian Jews of Jas. 2:1-13 and 4:1-10 are yielding to the temptations of snobbery (wealth) and greed. This interpretation gives clear cohesion to vv. 5 and 6. *Pros phthonon* then indicates the natural, proud, unregenerate mode of human yearning, that is, envious (or spiteful), covetous, and thus rounded strife.

155. See also Ps. 19:12. As usual, the Prayer Book version is almost right; but for "secret faults" we should read "unconscious sins" (note, for example, the pedestrian I injure without even knowing my car has touched him, and the sins I do not even know are sins).

The adultery here refers not to sexual immorality but to apostasy, and the phrase *pros phthonon,* "prone to envious lust,"[156] reverts not to the "adulteresses" of 4:4 but to the lusts of 4:1-3. Its meaning is not far from "covetousness," the mother of many sins: envy of another's fortune usually combines grudging spite (the basic meaning of *phthonos*) with covetous (and, 4:12, pugnacious) desire. *Epipothei,* lit. "yearns," in the Vulg. is (rightly) *concupiscit,* the word also at the beginning of the Tenth Commandment in Ex. 20, *non concupisces.* Adam's sin, and our own experience, show that the spirit God breathed into man (Gen. 2:7) was not God's own infallible spirit of wisdom, righteousness, and truth; the human spirit, as we know too well, has appetites (lusts, in the ambivalent, nonmoral sense of that word) that, properly indulged, are necessary and valuable but otherwise lead to sin. It would have been futile for God to create man and food without creating in man the appetite for food; but the appetite so necessarily created in man has nothing in its own nature or power to keep man to the proper indulgence of it.

Appetite for food, drink, sex, and the rest is no measure of right or sufficiency. To eat as much and as pleasurably as we can is at least gluttony, and may be theft (if unlawfully I eat another's food); appetite in itself knows no righteousness, and to be a slave to appetite is sin. As James roundly asserts (1:13f.), it is false to say that God made appetites to be indulged freely. Appetites are necessary, but so is discipline. Like every other virtue, according to James and all Christian teachers, appetites can be conquered only by God's help (4:6).

The influence to evil comes from the appetite of the body (part of "the world of iniquity," 3:6) in which we are living. The "flesh" and the "world" *(kosmos)* are in the spirit of Satan, and the law of the "flesh" (uninhibited indulgence of the appetites) is evil and is at war with the law of God and of good. Some Greek philosophers (e.g., Heracleitus)[157] thought that the substance of the *kosmos* was fire. Considering some NT, especially Christ's, remarks (Mt. 25:41) about hellfire,[158] not least the words of Jas. 3:6, we think James is visualizing the world of iniquity as a world consisting of fire. The tongue is fire, the world of sin, set on fire by hell and setting on fire the cycle of our mortal birth (and life)—our mortal creation—being set among the members of the body that frames

156. See our remarks, pp. 330ff.

157. See, e.g., H. Bietenhard, "Fire" *(pyr), NIDNTT,* I, 654; also below, pp. 370f.

158. On "Gehenna" as an eschatological place of fire, with references, see J. Jeremias, *Geenna, TDNT,* I, 657f.; H. Bietenhard, "Hell" *(gehenna), NIDNTT,* II, 208f. On hell also as Satan's abode, see Dibelius, pp. 198f., with citations, n. 87.

a person's mortal existence. The appetite beckons to our mind, and we feel "the pull of its distraction and the enticement of its bait."

James's metaphors are those of a fisherman, probably based on his Galilean fishing experiences. Like a harlot who entraps her lover, "desire," writes Davids,[159] "has used her wiles, succeeded, been fertilized, and now carries within her a conceptus. Yet, 'no one need know,' she whispers to her illegitimate lover. The inner defection from the life of faith and trust need never be seen by others. But the womb of the heart cannot hold the illegitimate thing forever; desire's child comes to birth, and its name is sin." We note the force of the present tenses, indicating no more than the effort by the forces of evil, not—so far—their success. If we yield to it, our desire conceives, and in due course bears sin; this "unwanted, parthenogenic, bastard monstrosity" then grows up, and when full-grown causes death to the soul. Persistence in evil carries with it the perversion of the will (Isa. 5:20), rendering the sinner powerless to do right (Jer. 13:23)—and that spells spiritual death. Aristotle pointed out that at first sin may be voluntary but that, after sinning, virtue may become impossible (*Nicomachean Ethics* 3.7.111.4a).

The stages of the metaphor are thus paralleled in the human act. We yield to lust; conceive (design) the sin, commit it; one sin leads to another, and more, and in time a sinful disposition is established that spells death to the soul. Briefly the sequence is: lust, sin, death. God, on the other hand, is the giver of life rather than death. "He chose to give us birth through the word of truth, that we might be a kind of first-fruits of all he created" (1:18, NIV). By origin, nature, and destiny, these two "families" are set in sharpest contrast.

If, unlike Paul,[160] James is silent on Adam, preferring to concentrate on sin's direct and immediate link with death, their teaching is essentially the same. "The New Testament," notes Leon Morris, "contains no more forthright statement of the connections between sin and death."[161] Here, as in 5:20, James is thinking of salvation as membership in the covenant and death as exclusion from it,[162] that is, spiritual (eternal) death. James's fraternal appeals, however, are in sharp contrast to the remorseless, intolerant attitude of Qumran to the erring.[163]

159. Davids, GNC, pp. 11f. See also G. W. Barker, W. L. Lane, and J. M. Michaels, *The New Testament Speaks* (1969), pp. 329f.

160. See Rom. 7:13a, 24.

161. See also our later discussion on the Jewish covenant and "covenantal nomism" (pp. 416f.).

162. *The Cross in the New Testament,* p. 310; G. C. Bottini, "Correzione fraterna e salevezza in *Giacomo* 5,19-20," *Studii Biblici Franciscani Liber Annuus* 35 (1985): 131ff.

163. 1QS 2:5–3:6.

Since such exclusion is irrevocable, the meanings of spiritual and eternal death often merged, the former sometimes being called, especially in Revelation, "the second death."[164]

Commentators used to quote Jewish and classical Greek statements that God or the gods make a man or woman sin.[165] But James may well be doing more than simply denying that theory. Qumran has opened our minds to the thought of that epoch, the thought sometimes found in the usual references to the Essenes.[166] It seems to us that James would have looked with disfavor on at least some interpretations of Paul's doctrine (perhaps the doctrine itself), voiced also in the Epistle to the Hebrews, about God's chastisement of men and women. But certainly James would agree with Paul, and Qumran, that "the flesh" is evil. "The background of James's use of *epithymia*," says Ropes, "is currently popularized conceptions of Hellenistic philosophy."[167] No doubt James thoroughly understood these conceptions, but we think that, like Paul and Qumran, he went further and regarded "the flesh" as essentially evil.[168]

James never forgets, much less minimizes, the unity of good in God, or the unity of evil in the Prince of Darkness; and, as we shall see, he does not discard or forget Satan, any more than Paul in his diatribes against the flesh. The flesh and the sinful world are in Satan's spirit; the law of the flesh is evil, and, like Satan and all inspired by him, is at war with the law of God and of good. Paul says all this very plainly (e.g., Rom. 7:2-25), as do John (e.g., 1 Jn. 5:19, RV) and Qumran.

We have thought it advisable to emphasize James's actual view of the flesh; we think he agrees with Paul. In 1:15 the question is not really urgent: "each one is tempted" *(peirazetai)*, v. 14, introduces here a sentence about lust that the mind (in the case meant to be contemplated) has a duty to disobey. Only the apparent attempts to dissociate lust and the body from Satan make these remarks necessary.

If it seems strange that James is silent about Satan,[169] we suggest

164. See Rev. 2:23; 6:4, 8; 8:9; 9:18; 21:8. Abrahams, "The Second Death," *Studies in Pharisaism and the Gospels* (Second Series), pp. 41ff.

165. E.g., "Lead my foot not into the power of sin. And bring me not into the power of iniquity. And not into the power of anything shameful" (b. Ber. 60b). See Ropes, p. 165.

166. See Ropes, p. 155; also T. H. Gaster, *The Scriptures of the Dead Sea Sect* (1957), pp. 24-27, 43. E.g., "If I stagger because of the sin of flesh my justification shall be by the righteousness of God which endures for ever" (1QS 11:12). See H. Seebass, "Flesh" *(sarx)*, *NIDNTT*, I, 673.

167. P. 156.

168. See Thiselton, *art. cit.*, "Flesh" *(sarx)*, *NIDNTT*, I, 678ff.

169. See Hort, p. 24.

that the reason for his omission, though presently he mentions the lusts, is simply that James shares strongly the view of Paul, and Qumran, that the flesh is evil, like the rest of the present world of sin: in the body the Prince of Darkness has already set his snares. The dualism of the Clementine Homilies, mentioned by Hort,[170] is not surprising, now that we know from Qumran so much about the theological atmosphere—not actually Christian—of the epoch. But the contrast between Satan as an external power and the lusts as a third factor subject to man's own mastery is dangerously misleading, and ignores James's own fundamental doctrine. A person's fleshly lusts are no more, and no less, subject to his own mastery than Satan himself is (see Jas. 4:5-7). A person can master his lusts, and Satan, if he submits himself to God, whose overcoming grace gives him the mastery over lusts and the devil. James does not say only that the present *afflictions* of the faithful will be compensated by bliss in the world to come (and for James it was indeed a world to come, very soon, another creation, not this present world of sin and present cycle of creation, 3:7). He also says that for the faithful there is already victory over evil, victory during this life, victory over all *peirasmoi,* whether painfully deterrent to or pleasantly seductive from the faith. No evil can happen to a person except to *be* evil: and for the faithful God's grace keeps evil from affecting or infecting the soul.

CONCLUSION

We are now in a better position to answer the question, What are the *peirasmoi* of Jas. 1:2—trials by "affliction" or by temptation to sin, or both? The commentators[171] explain them as a variety of *adversities,* such (no doubt) as the ills of which Hesiod speaks. Nevertheless, especially if we have learned to expect some cohesion in the Epistle of James, we must give weight to the context: the nature of the *peirasmoi* in vv. 12-15 is obvious—"lust"; in v. 10 it is the morally chastening worldly misfortunes of the rich; v. 6 is a warning against the sin of doubt and wavering.

We suggest, therefore, that in this context it is not only better but necessary to interpret *peirasmos* in 1:2 as at least including temptation to sin. In 1 Cor. 10:6-15 and the sequel, 14-22, connected by "wherefore," *peirasmos* in v. 13 cannot be taken as a solitary reference to "afflictions," but must refer to evils like those in the rest of the context. Against these evils the previous verse, 12, gives the warning: "If

170. P. 24.
171. Notable exceptions are Oesterley and Parry.

you think you are standing firm, be careful you don't fall" (NIV). Similarly, in 1 Tim. 6:9 *peirasmos* indisputably means moral temptation, leading men to "ruin" *(olethros)* and "destruction" *(apōleia),* a temptation arising out of "love of money" *(philargyria)* (v. 10).

Ropes cites 1 Pet. 4:12 (where *peirasmos* signifies an expected cataclysm) and says, "The people here [i.e., in the Epistle of James] addressed are not a missionary outpost among the heathen";[172] but at least many of the Jews of the Diaspora lived in a pagan environment. Ropes continues: "They appear to be largely poor and struggling people, subject to the hardships of the poor, 1:10, 2:1ff., 5:8"; and he concludes, "note the prevalent eagerness to have, implied in 4:1-3." If that were so, that is all the more reason (though we needed no more) for believing that in his Epistle James would be no less alive to the moral temptations of poverty than Paul, who said in 1 Tim. 6:10, "Love of money is the root of all evil." Even a priori, is it at all probable that a Jew, not to say a rabbi, brought up on his nation's constant if sometimes faltering battle for the righteous life, and addressing Jews living amid pagans, would be confining the thought of the first verse of his message to all but *moral* dangers?

Indeed, we would hazard this conjecture: there is a strong possibility that James is thinking chiefly but not solely of moral dangers and difficulties, and that in 2:1 he is recalling not only the temptations but also the hardships of human life, for example, poverty, which brings both. It would be characteristic of his power and freedom in Greek if he ventured to combine in his *peirasmoi* both of the meanings of the word that are established in the NT, here primarily connoting "moral temptations" but also including "the ills and hardships of life." So seen, "various" *(poikilois),* 1:2, is no ornamental literary epithet, but gets full force, deliberately emphasizing the scope of meaning intended here in *peirasmoi.*

Two trivial points need scarcely detain us. Nobody expects the Christian to enjoy (say) the pain of torture on the rack; the ground for his rejoicing is rather the opportunity for endurance and the ultimate approval its actual exercise may help to win. This joy the Christian can get no less from wrestling with sin than with bodily pain, and it is expressly promised in 1:2: "Happy [or blessed] is the man who masters the temptations of his lusts." This refutes those who invented a distinction between "external" and "internal" *peirasmoi,*[173] and, ignoring 1:12,

172. Pp. 186f.

173. See Ropes, pp. 40, 133; Mayor, and some others. See also 1 Pet. 2:11f.; 5:8-11; 1 Jn. 2:16 for a comparable comprehensive use of *peirasmos.*

say that moral temptations spring mainly from within and "could not be a subject for rejoicing."

Peirasmos in the Epistle of James has a single meaning throughout, that is, a trying (testing) assault of evil, by which the various manifestations of the powers of evil, especially evident in the *eschaton* or "the last days," try to shake a person in and from his Christianity. We can find only this cumbrous periphrasis to indicate James's constant meaning in the widely varying sentences; "test," "trial," and "temptation" are all too wide or too narrow to cover the meaning, and to choose one of them would be to invite dangerous ambiguity. Such assaults of evil are to be greeted with joy, and when endured and resisted can be overcome by God's grace.

c. God

"The mystery of evil is very difficult when we believe in a good God, but the problem of goodness seems to us impossible when we do not."

Harry Emerson Fosdick, *Living under Tensions* (1941), pp. 215f.

Rather than dwelling on the origin of temptation, James expounds the royal goodness of God; and he cautions against error about God's nature and his relation to sin. "Against this false theology he sets a strong theodicy," writes F. Stagg, "negatively denying that God is behind temptation and sin and positively tracing all good to God."[1] It is axiomatic that God is good, nothing but good, the sole giver of good, and the giver of nothing but good.[2] No one, when he is tempted, is ever to make excuses and blame God for his solicitation, for sin can make no appeal to God, who is "invincible to the assaults of evil" *(apeirastos kakōn),* nor can sin originate in him; therefore "he himself tempts no man" (1:13).

We take "evil" *(kakōn)* to mean moral evil (see Rom. 1:30; 1 Cor. 10:6) rather than "afflictions."[3] Nobody can seriously say that this means only that God does not, for example, get AIDS or cancer, or suffer

1. "Exegetical Themes in James 1 and 2," *RevExp* 66.4 (1969): 396. See also Mussner, p. 90.

2. 1:16f. See Mt. 19:17; Mk. 10:18; Lk. 18:19. See also W. Grundmann, *agathos, TDNT,* I, 15.

3. So von Soden; see Mayor, p. 50, n. 1. Mayor classes *kakōn* under "genitive of the sphere," "an extension of the inclusive ('partitive') genitive"; we prefer to call it "genitive of separation." See also Ropes, p. 155.

other such afflictions. That notion looks like the fruit of taking *peirasmos* too narrowly; but even that error is not usually carried into 1:13ff. If we remember that *apeirastos* means "invincible to assaults of evil," this should remove this and similar difficulties of interpretation. Pain (say, AIDS) and pleasure (say, sex) are really indistinguishable as instruments of evil in the flesh (being merely two species of one genus), and are only potentially dangerous to the spirit; whether one actually succumbs to the danger is a matter of the spirit. So we can truly say that God cannot be overcome by any assault of evil (of deterrent pain or seductive pleasure) without in the least impugning the "temptations of Jesus" or Isa. 63:9: "In all their afflictions he was afflicted."

GOD IS HOLY

To interpret *apeirastos* correctly we must remember that the Greek present tense quite regularly gives an unfinished effect to statements of activity, especially when the verb stem indicates a tentative activity.[4] Just as *atherapeutos*, for example, signifies that you may *therapeuein* but you will not succeed in effecting a cure,[5] so *apeirastos* says that you may *peirazein* but you will not succeed. Here Ropes, very wisely, contents himself with expressing a preference for "incapable of being tempted"[6] rather than "inexperienced in."[7] Which then fits best here? Rightly Ropes says, "In favour of the meaning 'untemptable' is the sharp verbal contrast then afforded to 'tempts no one' *(peirazei oudena)*."[8]

Mayor puts the same truth more clearly: "The meaning of the rare word *apeirastos* must be determined . . . especially from the following

4. See *ereunaō, heuriskō, diaphtheirō, iaomai, akeomai, therapeuō, sbennymi:* I try, or busy myself, searching, discovering, corrupting, healing, curing, treating, or quenching. The negative verbal compound ending in *-tos*, when virtually a negatived gerundive, does not mean that the activity in question cannot be tried or begun, but that it cannot succeed; *anereunētos*, past searching out; *aneurētos*, not to be discovered; *adiaphthartos*, incorruptible; *aniatos, anēkestos, atherapeutos*, incurable; *asbestos*, inextinguishable. *Peirazō*, like *ereunaō* or *therapeuō*, for instance, has an obvious conative sense.

5. Thucydides 2.51.2 is very illuminating on topic and tenses, but not essential.

6. P. 155.

7. These two translations arise as possibilities because *peirazō* and *peiraō* tend to be used as synonyms, meaning "to try," "attempt," and even "assault," and *peiraomai*, the middle, often means "to experience something"; thus *apeirastos* may be employed normally to negate *peirazō* but sometimes to negate the middle *peiraomai* in its sense of experiencing something.

8. P. 155.

clause, which is evidently intended to be its exact correlative in the active voice (is incapable of being tempted, and himself tempts no one)."[9] Hort is also helpful up to a point.[10] He understands *peirasmos* in 1:2 as affliction and the later *peirazomai* as indicating temptation by, for example, lust; and he thinks *peirasmos,* affliction, is sometimes sent by God. We deny both this distinction and the ascription of affliction and temptation to God. Hort goes on to show that *peirazō* and *peirasmos* came to signify a hostile menace, not an (immediate) instrument directed by God; he says the same of the word in the Lord's Prayer.

Then Hort takes up the meaning of *apeirastos:* the essentials of his comment are these: (a) *Apeirastos* as incapable of tempting to evil, *pace* Origen (*Homilies on Exodus* 15:25), lacks sufficient authority in actual literary use and would be saying the same as "and does not tempt any man." (b) As passive *apeirastos* means either "not attempted" as in Clement,[11] or "incapable of being tempted" as in Pseudo-Ignatius: "How are you to tempt him who is invincible to temptation?"[12] and "For he who tries to tempt *you* is trying to tempt the untemptable."[13] Here we add, from Mayor, Photius, ". . . to the Sadducees, essaying to tempt him who is untemptable,"[14] from the ninth century with reference to Mt. 4:7.

Hort concludes, "In this way we gain a forcible antithesis to the following clause, but with the loss of causal connexion with the preceding (clause)."[15] He says this because he sees that "God is not temptable" has in itself no immediate bearing on "God does not tempt you"; and this is all that Hort has against the meaning "untemptable." But his objection vanishes if we perceive the connection of the first half of the verse with the second (which second half does bear directly on the preceding "God does not tempt you"). We may therefore dismiss Hort's desperate attempt to make *apeirastos* here equal to *apeiratos.*[16]

9. P. 50.

10. Pp. 22ff.

11. *Stromateis* 7.12. For this use, possibly in secular Josephus, *War* 7.262, see P. H. Davids, "The Meaning of *Apeirastos* in James 1:13," *NTS* 24 (1978): 388, n. 4; *pace* H. Seesemann, *peira, TDNT,* VI, 24. See further G. W. H. Lampe, *A Patristic Greek Lexicon* (1961), p. 179 for the triple meaning, with patristic references.

12. *To the Philippians* 11 (to the Devil). For text and comment, see Dibelius, p. 92, also n. 127.

13. *Acts of John* 57. See E. Hennecke, *New Testament Apocrypha,* II (1963), 242f.

14. *Against the Manicheans* 4.25 (Migne, *PG,* CII, 234).

15. P. 23.

16. I.e., "unversed in" or "without experience in evils" *(apeiratos kakōn),*

The relevant half of the sentence, therefore, is the second. The first adds balance in form and confirmation in reason: the invariably good is ipso facto incapable of leading men into evil—is not consistent with God's nature. Here we have "a statement about the nature of God which we do not find elsewhere in the Bible";[17] see Jas. 1:17; 3:10-12 on the argument from natural consistency. We should realize that the idea of the consistency of the nature of God and the universe so far as it partakes of him and not of the devil is akin to the doctrine of the Logos propounded by Heracleitus and adopted and developed by the Stoics and others.[18] In language it gave rise to the philosophy of etymology.[19] Indeed, Mimnermus (c. 630 B.C.) said: "Truth is the most righteous of all things." Now perhaps, if we remember this background, we may grasp the force of the argument in Jas. 1:13.

The second half of this verse is the important half,[20] the half that is immediately and directly relevant; thus "Don't say God tempts you"; "God tempts nobody." That is what is of primary relevance. I don't need to say that God is never tempted; that in itself does not directly bear on your claim that God is tempting you. It simply adds force, in balance and reasoning, to the essential statement, that God tempts nobody. In the present context (*peirasmos, peirazomai, peirazomenos*), *apeirastos* is related to *peirazō* in its usual sense and not in the occasionally permissible sense of having experience; that is, it must mean "invincible to temptation [or 'enticement'] to evil" or, as we prefer, "invincible to assault of evil."[21] So God is intrinsically holy and righteous, untainted by evil.

GOD IS GRACIOUS

In 1:5 James has already described God as the One who gives "simply" or "unreservedly" *(haplōs)*, with no *arrière-pensée* or hidden condition.

---

apparently almost a proverb (e.g., Plutarch, *Moralia* 119f). See also Hort, p. 23; R. A. Knox, *New Testament Commentary*, III (1956), 94.

17. H. G. Seesemann, *peira*, *TDNT*, VI, 29.

18. See Moffatt, p. 18.

19. See P. B. R. Forbes, "Etymology," *The Oxford Classical Dictionary* (^{2}1970), 411f.

20. Mayor, p. 50, points out (and he cites W. E. Jelf, *A Grammar of the Greek Language* [1843], sec. 797, as well as Jas. 2:2, 11) that "the relation of the two clauses would have been more clearly marked if *men* had been added after *apeirastos*." This is correct. The insertion of *men* to mark balance is usual but not compulsory; yet it is possible to get balanced clauses with it.

21. See Mayor, pp. 48f.; Ropes, p. 155; also P. H. Davids, "The Meaning of *apeirastos* in James 1:13," *NTS* 24.3 (1978): 386-92.

Wisdom then is available for every Christian in *peirasmos*. But as important as the gift is the attitude of the Giver—and here James is clearly echoing our Lord, for example, "Ask and it will be given to you" (Mt. 7:7f.; Lk. 11:13); "If your eyes are good *(haplotēs)*, your whole body will be full of light" (Mt. 6:22)—as well as plenty of human parallels. David, for example, is said to have given his gift to God "in singleness of heart" *(en haplotēti kardias*, Heb. *bᵉyōšer lᵉḇāḇô* [1 Chr. 29:17; cf. Lev. 1:3]). Using the analogy of the bride and her love for only one man, Paul illustrates the idea of total dedication of the believer to Christ *(haplotēs eis Christon)* (2 Cor. 5:14-20). The occurrence of *haplōs*, found only here in the NT, and which we translate "singly," "simply," or "unreservedly," Janus-like, looks back and forward, almost certainly arising—although we cannot prove our point—by psychological association (by contrast) with the previous (v. 2), "in various trials." Liddell and Scott, s.v., show how often "various" *(poikilos)* is used in contrast (express or tacit) to "singly" *(haplōs)*. On the other hand, we believe that *haplōs*, describing the single-minded generosity of God, is implicitly contrasted with the *dipsychos* or divided human nature (1:8). True, these two ideas, the human disunity and the unity of God, are never spelled out; rather, they are set in implicit contrast (see Dt. 6:4f.). "That God is one" (2:19) is expressly affirmed and its ethical implications are everywhere implied in the Epistle (e.g., 4:2).

The unity of God is also the motive for adherence to the whole law, since he who said "'Thou shalt not commit adultery' said also 'Thou shalt not murder'" and since there is one lawgiver and judge. "It is tempting to associate these two similar themes, of the singleness and consistency of God, and the doubleness and inconsistency of man," writes Laws, "and to suggest that underlying James's condemnation of the latter and his exhortation to singleness is the idea of ethics as the imitation of God."[22] The singleness of God is reflected in his giving, which consists of a giver and a gift (besides a recipient): a *gift* given *haplōs* (i.e., with *haplotēs*) is given simply as a gift—of sheer bounty, of sheer kindness and goodness, without prior or ulterior motive of self-interest, without condition or restriction, penalty or encumbrance.

James had to say all that in one word. The KJV rendering "liberally," which seems to depend on the Vulg. *affluenter* (ff. has *simpliciter*) and suits *haplotēs* as "generosity," would be the best translation[23] if we

22. Laws, p. 30.

23. Hort, p. 9; see also Mayor, Appendix; C. Edlund, *Das Auge der Einfalt* (1952). O. Bauernfeind concludes that "the meaning might well be 'kind' or 'generous' yet the sense of 'wholehearted' is perhaps nearer the mark" (*haplous, haplotēs, TDNT*, I, 386). When used of giving between persons, that is, as a qual-

could preserve exclusively its proper ethical sense; but, as it is, "liberally" smacks too much of *profusely. Graciously,* linked as it is with "gives," is perhaps the best available word. Now "bounty" (occurring in Hort)[24] was once *bonitas* (2 Cor. 8:2), and that recalls the OT "goodness" (i.e., kindness, benevolence) of God. In Rom. 2:4—and James seems to contain echoes of the beginning (at least) of Romans—*tēs chrēstotētos* and *to chrēston* represent this OT quality, the grace and goodness of God (in giving good and withholding punishment); the NIV says "kindness," and at 1 Cor. 13:4 even the KJV for the cognate verb *chrēsteuetai* has "is kind." So, for example, in Gen. 24:49 *ḥeseḏ* is "kindness" (NIV), and often it means "lovingkindness" (see Col. 2:13). Of course, this is not the same word as *haplōs,* but *haplōs* and *haplotēs* are clearly very near to *chrēstos* and benevolent goodness or grace in giving as we have described it. The worldly wise would call that goodness "simple" (idiotic, imbecile) and "silly."

James further stresses the unconditional character of the divine intention. God gives his wisdom not only freely but also without chiding. The thought may refer to the petitioner's previous ignorance, or perhaps even to his misapprehension of the purpose of his ordeals. The person who blames God for sending evil assaults (1:17f.) might well expect "upbraiding." There is no evidence here of the current pagan belief in the gods' jealousy of humankind.[25]

J. H. Ropes argues that James is thinking of human beings, who are apt to do a person a good turn and then keep casting it up to him.[26] So Bunyan wisely writes: "It appeareth that He (Christ) is free, because He giveth *without* Twitting: He gives to all Men Liberally, and upbraideth not; Jam. 1.5."[27] Thus James says that God gives freely and "without twitting" (taunting, rebuking)—does not hold it against you with chiding words. Hort points out that the contrast is clearly to "graciously" *(haplōs)* rather than "gives"[28] and shows that Classical Greek

---

ity of the heart (Test. Iss. 3:8), *haplotēs* can mean "goodness," "kindness" (e.g., Josephus, *Ant.* 7.332). See B. Gärtner, "Simplicity" *(haplotēs), NIDNTT,* III, 572.

24. P. 7.

25. See W. Barclay, *The Mind of Jesus* (1960), p. 109.

26. P. 140. On the proverbial contrast between human grudging and God's generous giving, see, e.g., Sextus, *Sentences* 339; Pss. Sol. 5:15f. cited by Laws, p. 56.

27. "There are some," says Bunyan, "that will not deny to do the poor a pleasure, but they will mix their Mercies with so many *Twitts,* that the persons on whom they bestow their charity shall find but little sweetness in it" ("Come, and Welcome, to Jesus Christ" [1678], *The Miscellaneous Works of John Bunyan,* ed. Richard L. Greaves, VIII [1979], 389).

28. P. 9.

often uses *oneidizō* in the sense of reproachful giving.[29] Here Ecclus. 41:22 is relevant: "Be ashamed of reproaching your friends, or following up your charity with a lecture" (NEB).[30] Better still is a letter in Arthur Bryant's collection of letters to a younger brother at Oxford, 6 April 1700:

> George: You will easily please me if you would but do three things for yourself, viz: In the first place fear and serve God sincerely. . . . In the next place by applying yourself closely to your study which you have hitherto been exceeding negligent of. And in the third place by being a better husband of the money allowed you than you have hitherto been. If you lead a godly and a studious life, frugality and good husbandry will follow of consequence, so I shall judge of your devotions and study by the balance remaining in your hands each quarter for the future. You may draw a bill on me for £25 payable at one day's sight.
> And by doing as aforesaid you may retain me. Your loving brother.
>
> P. Shakerly.[31]

Having spoken of the corrupt, sinful activity of the human spirit (4:6), James compares the utterly *gracious* activity of God: "But God gives greater grace." We take "greater" here to mean not "greater grace than the world gives" (Bede), but "greater grace in view of the greater requirement" (Ropes), although the requirement in this case springs from the need to resist the human spirit of envy.[32] Our interpretation is

29. E.g., Aristotle, *The "Art" of Rhetoric* 2.6.10; see also *On the Crown*, sec. 269.

30. See further, E. Kutsch, *ḥrp, TDOT,* V, 215.

31. *Postman's Horn* (1936), p. 50.

32. Mayor (pp. 141ff.) links it unnaturally with the demands of the divine Spirit. Equally unsatisfactory is Mitton's attempt (p. 156) to paraphrase the phrase on the basis of the RSV, namely, "though God's jealous concern for complete obedience is a most pressing concern, yet His grace is even 'more'; His mercy outstrips even His righteousness." Undoubtedly James believed this; but that is not what he means here. We take *meizona* to mean "greater grace in view of the greater requirement" (Ropes, p. 265; J. Marty, p. 160; also Selwyn, pp. 234ff.; 417f.), although the requirement in this case springs from the need to resist the human spirit of envy. This interpretation suggests that the increasing demands on the Christian are met by a corresponding divine endowment, perhaps implying, too, that the soul that makes use of its privileges received them from God's hand in ever-increasing measure (see Mt. 25:29; Jn. 1:16). Our interpretation is more in accord with rabbinic teaching, for they taught (W. Hirsch, *Rabbinic Psychology* [1947], pp. 224ff.) that for the righteous, life was a prolonged conflict with the *yēṣer,* which must be daily resisted (Gen. R. 22; b. Berakoth 16b). Although man himself is ultimately responsible for the removal of the *yēṣer* (Num. R. 15), the rabbis, like James, taught that divine grace is promised in this struggle (S. Schechter, *Some Aspects of Rab-*

once more in accord with good rabbinic doctrine. To the humble God gives a greater degree of *charis* so that they may resist the *yēṣer*. While insisting that a person had the power of choice, the rabbis also affirmed that those who make the right choice receive "grace" as divine help and they quote *(inter alia)* Prov. 3:3 to support their view.

"Grace" in James then is to be interpreted not in the original non-theological sense of Prov. 3:34, "divine acceptance and favor."[33] His idea is thoroughly Christian, far outstripping the highest Jewish theological notions of "grace"; it is indeed, as Mitton observes, "similar to that which is characteristically Pauline, of God's generous, active, effective help to man, far beyond anything the man deserves or can rightly expect,"[34] possibly tantamount here to the Holy Spirit.[35] Both in his doctrine of *phthonos* and in his use of *charis* as *victorious* grace James is characteristically Greek (as usual, beyond the rest of the NT). So in Pindar, as we have seen, *charis* quite commonly means "victory."

After a brief parenthesis the awaited (4:5a)[36]—but already anticipated—quotation from Prov. 3:34 (LXX) is now resumed:

> Scoffers *(lēṣîm)* he scoffs at,
> But to the pious he shows favor.

Whereas God gives the converted true grace, he ranges himself against the scornful, that is, not merely the boasters (see *alazonia*, 4:16) but the arrogant, those whose self-righteousness is associated with the wealth and friendship of the world (see Lk. 18:10ff.). The rabbis taught that God "cannot live in the same world as the proud and arrogant" (b. Soṭa 5a) and that "whosoever is proud of heart causes the land to be defiled

---

binic Theology [1909], p. 278). Prayer (b. Berakoth 16b, 17a) and Torah (b. Baba Bathra 16a; Makkoth R.15) give help. Thus R. Lakish said: "Every day the *yēṣer* strives to overpower man and kill him. Were it not for God's help, it would not be possible to withstand him" (b. Sukka 52b). Elsewhere we read: "The door is opened to him who seeks contamination, and help is given to him who desires to be pure" (b. Shabbath 104a).

33. So J. Moffatt, *Grace in the New Testament* (1936), pp. 315-18.

34. P. 156.

35. See Davids, p. 164.

36. *Pace* most commentators who, having assumed that v. 5a refers to the words immediately following, trace the supposed quotation variously to the LXX, practical rendering of Ex. 20:5 (Ropes) and Gen. 44:19 (God; A. Meyer); to the NT (by Bengel and others) (Mt. 6:24; Rom. 8:7; Gal. 5:7; 1 Jn. 2:15; also de Wette, who strangely takes 4:5a with the preceding verse; but see Oesterley); to some lost Hebrew gospel (Resch) or apocryphal book (Dibelius) or, lastly, to a corrupt text (Erasmus and others). So this scripture that James quotes from Proverbs contains both a threat and a promise.

and the *Shechinah* to withdraw" (Mek. Ba-Ḥodesh 9). But the humble, who had already been contrasted with the ungodly rich (1:9), recognized their dependence on God. While the arrogant *(hyperēphanoi)* were doomed, the humble through God's grace would win spiritual exaltation and victory (1:9ff.).

The admonition against slander (4:11f.; the echo of 1:26; 2:12; 3:10) is to be applied to all—not simply to teachers—and especially the proud (4:10), who compromise with the word (4:1ff.) in the matter of speech. The sin of slander ("the third tongue"; *lišān tᵉlitai*), roundly condemned by the rabbis and the Covenanters, and absolutely by Christ (Mt. 7:1), is almost a *terminus technicus* in the early Christian vice catalogue (Dibelius). When committed against a brother (see Hermas, *Mand.* 2.2),[37] according to James, it is equivalent to transgression of the Christian (not Jewish; so Oesterley et al.) Torah, since the interests of the two are identical.

Parry explains that James "regards the brother who is slandered, that is, whose life or action, in reality truly Christian, is regarded as un-Christian, as, in his degree, embodying Christian law."[38] If the Torah is so personified, any slander or judgment of a brother not only implies an active disregard of Torah but also an attitude of superiority reserved solely for God, who is the all-powerful Lawgiver and Judge. H.-H. Esser sees[39] in the double use of "one" for the divine name with the predicate "who is able" *(ho dynamenos)* an indication that the "lawgiver" *(nomothetēs)* is both the Father and the Son. On the characteristically Jewish doctrine of God's supreme sovereignty, the final source of judicial authority, see, for example, Dt. 32:29; 1 Sam. 2:6; 2 Kgs. 5:7; Ps. 75:8; 1QS 10:18; Midr. R. Ex. 31:3: "One He casts down and the other He raises up." See also the striking rabbinic saying, cited by Dibelius, Mekilta, tractate Amalek 1 on Ex. 17:9. The unanswerable "And who are you that you pass judgment on your fellow?" clinches the point.

In saying that God's gifts are "from above" James is simply following a common Jewish thought of God, as in Isa. 57:15: "For this is what the high and lofty one says—he who lives forever, whose name is holy: 'I live in a high and holy place, but also with him who is contrite and lowly in spirit' " (NIV). God's gifts are good, not because of his su-

37. "Do not speak against anybody, and do not listen readily to a slanderer" (*The Shepherd of Hermas,* tr. J. M.-F. Marique, *The Apostolic Fathers,* "The Fathers of the Church," gen. ed. R. J. Deferrari, I (^{3}1962), 261. Slander has always been viewed with extreme gravity, likened sometimes to leprosy and, as in Qumran, often punishable by excommunication. See 1QH 5:24f.; 1QS 7:16f.

38. P. 30. See also W. Mundle, "Revile" *(katalaleō), NIDNTT,* III, 346.

39. "Law" *(nomos), NIDNTT,* II, 450.

perior elevation ("from above"),[40] but because of his nature: they come from One who is nothing but good. There is no need for James to repeat this or to state the corollary that God does not give bad gifts,[41] or for us to take *pas* to mean "only," "nothing but," instead of "every"—a perfectly normal use. James wishes to show that the goodness of God precludes any such notion of his temptability. One need only cite Gen. 1 ("it was good"), references to "goodness" in the Psalms (e.g., 25:8; 73:1), or the frequent rabbinic formula *haṭṭôḇ wᵉhammēṭîḇ* ("he who is good and does good") based on Ps. 119:68 (M. Ber. 9.1) to show that James is following the typical Hebrew confession of God (1 Chr. 16:34; 2 Chr. 5:14). The well-known saying of R. Ḥaninaḥ is similar: "Nothing evil descends from above."[42] James firmly denies God's responsibility for people's sins and sufferings and places the blame on them as clearly as many Greeks do, from Homer, *Odyssey* 1:322ff., onward.

Here James deliberately corrects the misguided notion, due possibly to a misunderstanding of "the temptation clause" in the Lord's Prayer,[43] that God sends the *peirasmos* that in fact originates from man's own "desire"—in this context probably the *yēṣer*. We have a notion that James is consciously denying a doctrine common enough in other writers, including those of Qumran,[44] that God deliberately and directly sends afflictions to try people (and those writers often distinguish afflictions such as oppression from the seductive allurements of the passions). Along with the evil *yēṣer*, which in itself was said to be "good" (see Gen. 1:31), God created the "good" *yēṣēr (yēṣer ha-ṭôḇ)* identified with Torah or Wisdom; and since "every good and perfect gift" points to the "good" *yēṣer*, this suggests that God is responsible for the good inclination in man but excludes "the belief that the *yēṣer hā-ra'*,

40. *Pace* Ropes, p. 160. To avoid the awkward implications of James's Hebrew cosmogony, Hort (p. 29) substitutes, unnecessarily, "from the beginning" for "from above"—a stock rabbinic phrase. So R. Ḥaninah: "Nothing evil comes from above" *(millᵉma'ᵃlāh)* (Gen. R. 51 on 19:24); see also Tanḥuma *mᵉṣôrā'* 9.43; S–B III, 752; Schlatter, p. 132; F. Büchsel, *anōthen, TDNT*, I, 378.

41. Ropes, p. 159; Dibelius, p. 99, n. 151.

42. Gen. R. 51 on 19:24; S–B III, 752; F. Büchsel, *anōthen, TDNT*, I, 378; Schlatter, p. 132.

43. See J. Jeremias, *The Prayers of Jesus* (1967), p. 104; W. Schneider, C. Brown, "Tempt" *(peirasmos), NIDNTT*, III, 803; J. Carmignac, *Recherches sur le "Notre Père"* (1969), pp. 287f.; *The Lord's Prayer and Jewish Liturgy*, eds. J. J. Petuchowski and M. Brocke (1978), p. 97; *pace* Dibelius, p. 92; Davids, p. 81.

44. E.g., "Remember me and forget me not and lead me not into situations too hard for me" (11QPsᵃ, col. 24.11). "Neither let pain nor the evil inclination take possession of my bones" (11QPsᵃ, col. 19.15f.). J. A. Sanders, *The Psalms Scroll of Qumran Cave 11* (11QPsᵃ) (1965), p. 71.

whereby men were tempted, came from God."[45] So James firmly rejects the popular heresy that God sends the *peirasmos* that in fact originates from man's own desire, *epithymia:* God can neither tempt, nor be tempted to sin.

Ronald A. Knox has pointed out that the phrase "to tempt God" is found often in both the OT and the NT, and that God is said to "tempt" man as can be seen in the use of the word "tempt" in describing the relations between God and man.[46] He then cites the cases of the Israelites tempting God in the desert and God tempting Abraham. Yet it is difficult to see the force of this reasoning, and the result (as Knox himself admits) is "obscure." The Israelites' tempting of God, "Is the Lord among us or not?" (Ex. 17:2, 7), is not relevant to the issue here. Theirs was not an attempt to entice God to evil, but to do what they thought they knew better than God to be right.

Exactly so, many generations have asked for a sign; indeed, that is the meaning of the temptation in Mt. 4:6. The Israelites' tempting was a crime of violence—setting their judgment above God's, affecting to be wiser than he; and it provoked God to just anger. Nor is the case of Abraham, that is, of a man who, when feeling tempted to evil, says that God is enticing him, relevant here. If, being tempted to evil, a person thinks his case is like Abraham's, he may rest content: he will not sin, and God will stop him, as he stopped Abraham, in time. If not, it was not God but the devil that was working in him. But Abraham's case is no argument for committing sin—under the alleged authority of God, or at all.

Of all the aspects of the goodness thus ascribed to God, a Hebrew most emphasized his love of humankind, especially as shown in the gift of his law, in salvation. "He [God] *of his own wish* begot us by the Word of truth" (1:18). The Christian's regeneration is the result of God's gracious initiative. "Good" in the OT has a redemptive significance,[47] is bound up with personal faith in God, and is used especially of God's gift of the Torah (or Wisdom, 3:17); there is a rabbinic saying: "The good simply means the Torah,"[48] observance of which leads to goodness. This is the thought connecting God's benevolence and our re-

45. Oesterley, p. 411.

46. *New Testament Commentary,* III, 94; also P. H. Davids, *art. cit.,* "The Meaning of *Apeirastos* in James 1:13," *NTS* 24.3 (1978): 389; *James,* pp. 82f.

47. *ṭôḇ ṭôḇāh;* e.g., the Exodus (Ex. 18:19; Num. 10:29ff.; Hos. 8:3; 14:3); also Jer. 32:39, 42; Isa. 52:7, of *messianic* salvation. See further I. Höver-Johag, *ṭôḇ, TDOT,* V, 311ff.

48. M. Aboth 6:3; see Mic. 6:8. See also S–B I, 809; III, 238; W. Grundmann, *agathos, TDNT,* I, 14; E. Beyreuther, "Good" *(agathos), NIDNTT,* II, 101f.

generation in 1:17f., where, says Scaer, James brings together ideas like "incarnation, duty, completion, and overabundance."[49]

God's goodness is revealed supremely in the gift of new creation by Jesus Christ and ultimately in messianic, eschatological redemption. This is the point of "from above" (*anōthen,* 1:17; see also 3:17) and "begot" (*apekyēsen,* 1:18), the latter carefully chosen, we believe, to emphasize the Christian's sonship with "the Father of lights," who would otherwise be a far-off, transcendent God. The "Word of truth" means the gospel, although the context may suggest "that what is at issue is that God acts reliably and consistently. God does not tempt men to sin (vv. 13-16). With him is no shadow due to change (v. 17). His word is, in this sense, the word of truth."[50] We can—and the Hebrew did—say that God made us; but the only begotten Son was not "made"—consider Acts 8:37 and the host of Christian references to Jesus Christ, the Son of God, or "Jesus Christ His only Son our Lord" (the Apostles' Creed). Now he who accepts Christ is thereby born again: he becomes a new person with Christ in him. Hence *apekyēsen* seems the right word for God's bringing the Christian to birth in Christ, in kinship with the only begotten Christ, supervening upon the old kinship with Adam who was created.

The argument touching both the goodness of God and the Christian's regeneration therefore must be set in the context of redemption. While it is certainly true that God is active in all of life and that we are personally accountable to him, yet essentially, as Leon Morris points out,[51] "James sees God as the compassionate Deity who has provided for our salvation." So we reject an interpretation of 1:18 as expounding a doctrine of people at large (for there were no Jews till Abraham), for such an argument is not properly Christian. As interpreted on that basis 1:16-18 could be addressed by a non-Christian to non-Christians. The perfect goodness and blessing of God are accepted in the non-Christian Jewish belief from Abraham till today; but that does not impel a Jew to be a Christian, nor is the perfect goodness and blessing of God *in itself* the reason for a Christian to live a clean life and resist *peirasmoi.*

The Christian's reason for believing in the perfect goodness and blessing of God, the reason for a Christian *as such* to live righteously and fight *peirasmoi,* is, in a word, Christ. We maintain that that is all that is meant in Jas. 1:16-19, the entire chapter, and indeed the whole

49. P. 59.

50. See "Truth" *(alētheia), NIDNTT,* III, 888; W. Bieder, "Christliche Existenz nach dem Zeugnis des Jakobusbriefes," *ThZ* 5 (1949): 111; Mussner, p. 91, n. 7. See also our discussion, pp. 393ff.

51. *New Testament Theology* (1986), p. 315.

Epistle. The relevance of the Christian Torah in this call to righteous living will (it is hoped) be made clearer elsewhere in the discussions of law and wisdom.

GOD IS UNCHANGING

In the phrase "Father of lights" (1:17), "Father" is used for Creator in conjunction with "light," as often in Jewish literature. In the Testament of Abraham, for example, the archangel Michael is linked with "the Father of lights."[52] On the use of "father" for Creator, Ropes very effectively cites Philo's constant use of "the father of all" *(ho patēr tōn holōn)* in the sense of "Creator";[53] the citations that follow the phrase "Father of lights" are also noteworthy. The belief in God as Creator of *(inter alia)* lights, celestial and (probably) spiritual, is typical not of pagan astrological fatalism (e.g., "besouled stars") nor of the Greek concept of the universal fatherhood of God[54] but of Jewish religion from its early stages.[55] With it was associated the idea of God as dwelling in the heavens above, as was the notion of all blessings descending thence upon men, like the sun and the rain; but James emphasizes that, unlike the lights, God suffers no change.

The sequence of thought is clear: to say that temptation comes from God is a lie (1:13), for temptation comes from lust (1:14), lust produces sin, and sin brings forth death (1:15). "Take it from me," says James: "God is good, nothing but good, and all his gifts are good and perfect" (1:16). They come down from him who is invincible to assaults

52. M. R. James, *Texts and Studies,* II, no. 2. See also Ps. 136:7; Job 28; 32; Jer. 4:23; Mal. 2:10; Apoc. Mos. 36:3; CD 7.19; S. Schechter, *Doctrines of Jewish Sectaries,* I, 5; S–B III, 752. The *'abbā' d'nahire,* Ephraim the Syrian, *Opera* V, col. 489, "Polemic Sermon," 23 may echo James's phrase (BAG, p. 641).

53. P. 160.

54. On the two main types of astrology, universal and individual, see W. Carr, *Angels and Principalities* (1981), pp. 16ff.; also H. Conzelmann, *phōs, TDNT,* IX, 356, as well as the entire article; also H.-C. Hahn, "Light" *(phōs), NIDNTT,* II, 440ff.; E. E. Ellis, *The Gospel of Luke* (1974), pp. 166f.; Moffatt, p. 19; O. Hofius, "Father" *(patēr), NIDNTT,* I, 621.

55. Thus the first of the Jewish daily benedictions reads: "Blessed art Thou, O Lord, creator of the luminaries" (M. Berakoth 8.5). For the belief in God as Creator of the luminaries, see Gen. 1:14; Ps. 136:71; Jer. 4:23; also Parry, p. 38; Mussner, pp. 91f., which in turn recalls the Platonic association of light and goodness *(Republic* 507e-509b); and there with God and salvation, see H.-C. Hahn, *art. cit., NIDNTT,* II, 490f.; also for the biblical view of God and the stars, see J. H. Charlesworth, "Treatise of Shem (First Century B.C.)," *The Old Testament Pseudepigrapha,* ed. J. H. Charlesworth, I (1983).

of evil. The paramount revelation or achievement of Jewish religion was their creed that God is good in righteousness and love. In Jewish thought God is often likened to, though not, as in pagan thought, identified with the sun.[56] Commenting on Ps. 27:1, "The Lord is my light and my salvation," Philo says[57] that God is not only light, but is also the archetype—and higher than the archetype—of every light. One rabbi wrote: "The Holy One, blessed be He, enwrapped Himself in light like a garment, and the brilliance of His splendour shone forth from one end of the universe to the other."[58] This leads to the affirmation that all light is from God.[59] Clearly the sun, with its beneficent influence, was well suited to represent God, the source of all good.

So James likens God to the sun but shows that unlike it he knows no change or obscuration. Since God is constant and unchanging, his care and love are constant and unchanging. Like his Son, God is "the same, yesterday and forever" (Heb. 13:8); but unlike us, God is no fickle creature of moods; his care never falters and his love never fades. We may be faithless, but he remains faithful; we may forget him, but he never forgets us. God cannot deny himself: he must act in accord with his character, and his character is one of gracious and redeeming love.

Because God is what he is—good and nothing but good—the gifts that he gives are also good and nothing but good. "Witness," writes A. J. Gossip, "that wonderful metaphor of the hush of high noon with the sunshine flooding every chink and cranny in a shadowless splendour of warmth and golden glory—so God too is always at His zenith, giving all He has and all He is in an immeasurable and unstinted liberality."[60] To see what James is saying, we now quote Ropes (slightly emended):

> The affirmation is that to send good gifts belongs to God's unvarying nature. In this he is unlike the sun, which sends now the full light of noon, now the dimness of twilight, and which at night sends no light at all. God's light ever shines.[61]

Also relevant are the following citations: Isa. 60:19f.; Wisd. 7:29f.; Heb. 7:13-18; Philo, *Allegorical Interpretation* 2.33: "even as unchangeableness is the property of God"; Clement of Alexandria, *Stromateis* 1.24

56. Mal. 4:2; Isa. 60:1, 19f.; Ps. 84:11. For rabbinic ideas, see b. Ḥullin 5a, b; Tanḥuma (ed. Buber) 2.98; Midr. Ḥagigah (ed. Schechter) 8af. See also H. R. Engler, *Die Sonne als Symbol. Der Schlüssel zu den Mysterien* (1962).

57. *On Dreams* 1.75.

58. Gen. R. 3.4.

59. Num. R. 15.5; see also Jn. 8:12.

60. *The General Epistles*. The Study Bible (1930), p. 5.

61. P. 161.

(p. 418). In Philo we note, "All else turns, but in him alone there is no turning," and in Clement of Alexandria, "stedfast," "abiding," "without turning." Now in his note Ropes inserts, "from him proceeds no turning shadow";[62] that is, for Ropes (and other commentators) the shadow is simply an indicator of turning, and for them this is just James's way of saying God is "without turning" *(atreptos)* etc., as in Clement of Alexandria just quoted.

We believe that, as in 1:6 and 3:6, James's most stylized expressions are fully forcible and relevant to a fundamentally simple meaning. We don't need a shadow to impress on us the fact that the sun (unlike God) rises, reaches its zenith, and sets; the whole point of the sun's circling is that for about half its circle it leaves us in the dark (or at any rate the night), without even the shadow that can mark its turning. The most important and emphatic mark of the "turning" *(tropē)* of the sun is the night that follows day.[63] There is no need to assume a technical sense, for example, *parallax* for *parallagē,* here only in the NT.

"Variation" (RV) is better than "variableness" (KJV) since an actual change, not an abstract quality, seems to be implied.[64] So NIV translates well: "who does not *change* like shifting shadows." The prime reference is to the light of the sun which varies from hour to hour and at night disappears altogether. In force and essential lucidity *parallagē tropēs* seems to be quite proper to the Greek of the Epistle of James for signifying the variation of an object in constant orbit.[65]

We assume no recondite meaning for *aposkiasma,* here only in the NT. Plutarch uses the cognate *aposkiasmos* for the shadow on a sundial—a reference that Ropes excludes from the present passage. The light of the sun may be blocked, for example, by some material object, so as to cast a shadow; indeed, for a time, in an eclipse, the direct light of the sun (or moon) may be shut off from the observer. Not so God as the eternal, perfect Sun: he does not "turn," does not vary his position, and does not cast a shadow at all, being a perfect Light that illumines everything, everywhere.

62. P. 161.

63. See Isa. 60:19f. So it is with the other alterations of nature (e.g., Gen. 1:4; 8:22; 45:6). See Hort, p. 31. On later superstitions connected with the "turnings of the sun" *(t^eqûpôt),* see J. Trachtenberg, *Jewish Magic and Superstition* (1939), p. 257. *Tropē,* a NT *hapax legomenon,* can be used in a technical sense (but not here) for the solstice (so Eng. "tropic") (e.g., Dt. 33:14; Wisd. 7:18), and can stand for the path taken by the celestial bodies after they have gone down in the West (1 En. 72:35; 41:8).

64. Hort's note (p. 30) is good, especially on Emperor Severus.

65. Ps. 19:6; the KJV and RV "circuit" and the Vulg. "occursus" represent the Hebrew noun *qûp,* i.e., *tropē.*

Nothing can block God's light, nothing can interrupt the flow of good from him, and nothing can put us "in shadow" so that we are out of the reach of his radiance. It is not necessary to confine "shadow" to eclipses or any other specific sort of shadow.[66] God's light or radiance lets nothing stop it.

Light of the world, undimming and unsetting
O shine each mist away;
Banish the fear, the falsehood and the fretting;
Be our unchanging day.[67]

We read *aposkiasma,* not the genitive, and we think Hort's conjecture was right, namely, that it was followed by "he" *(autos)* in earlier manuscripts.[68] We also think that "he" *(autos)* is right, and should be restored to the text as the first word of 1:18, properly and emphatically taking up the "Father of lights" of 1:17.

We have concluded, too, that no sense can be made (though we confess we have tried) of any current text. We suggest that *ē* (ἢ) is misplaced and should come after *tropēs,* reading: *par' hō ouk eni parallagē tropēs ē aposkiasma autos boulētheis*[69]—"from the Father of lights, whose nature suffers neither the variation of orbit nor any (occluding) shadow. He, of his own wish. . . ." This fits the manuscript confusion, and makes the quoted "parallels" given above really parallel.[70] For *par' hō* see Eph. 6:9; Rom. 9:14; Mk. 10:27; Rom. 2:11. *Para* with the dative is used of persons, in a local or almost local sense; often, too, of kings and courts.[71] So "with God" there is no respecting of persons, no unrighteousness, nothing impossible.

Hort's phrase about an "instinct of reverence" may be nearer the

66. For examples, see Davids, p. 87.

67. H. Bonar (1808-89). For the full text, see the *Church Hymnary* (1927), p. 171. For references to the unchangeableness of God, see Dibelius, p. 103, n. 176; also p. 177; 1QS 3:15-17.

68. Ropes, p. 163, line 9. For discussion of Jas. 1:17, see B. Metzger, *A Textual Commentary on the Greek New Testament* (1975), pp. 679f.

69. We take *eni* (i.e., *enesti*) here to mean inherent nature rather than inherent possibility; but it really doesn't matter. On their respective uses, see J. B. Mayor, *Further Studies in the Epistle of St. James* (1913), pp. 33f.

70. Isa. 60:30; Wisd. 7:29f.; Ecclus. 17:31; Ropes, p. 161.

71. E.g., *para kyrō,* in Cyrus's presence or entourage; sometimes to state a "concomitant." So Sophocles, *Oedipus Tyrannus* 612; *ton par' autō bioton,* "To cast away the life in his own bosom" (Jebb); Xenophon, *Anabasis* 1.7.4: *ta par'emoi,* "My circumstances." So, in another sense, *par'emoi, me iudice:* "In my judgment (or eyes)" (Herodotus 1.32).

truth than he ever knew[72]—for we believe that it may be used of God exactly because it was so normally used of judges, kings, and various magnates. That is very apt in the light of James's references to God, the only Lawgiver and Judge, able to save and to destroy (4:12; 5:1ff., 9), as well as to kings (2:9).[73] This "instinct of reverence" is perhaps best illustrated in the name "Lord of Sabaoth" (5:4), which refers to Yahweh as the God of Hosts *(YHWH sᵉbhāôth)*,[74] the One who combines majesty and transcendence, who defends the poor and punishes the rich, attributes best known to us through Luther's hymn "A Mighty Fortress."

The *Shechinah*, a term for the Divine Presence and Fatherhood, is usually associated with light, sometimes more particularly with the sun, but there is no ground for asserting that James had this usage in mind here. In 2:1, however, "glory" almost certainly stands for the *Shechinah*. The mental association of light with joy and good, as in Ps. 36:9 (cited by Ropes) or Ps. 97:11, is familiar in the OT, the rabbis, and Philo, as well as in some modern hymns:

> Great Father of glory, pure Father of Light,
> Thine angels adore Thee, all veiling their sight;
> All laud we would render: O help us to see
> 'Tis only the splendour of light hideth Thee.[75]

But it is hard to deny that, in the use of this figure here, as in Eph. 5:8; 1 Thess. 5:5; 1 Pet. 2:9; 1 Jn. 1:5-7 (which last is extremely apposite to our Jas. 1:13ff.), we can see the influence of a contemporary train of thought (illuminated and indeed dominant in Qumran), in which "the Prince of Lights" is said to control all who practice righteousness and walk in ways of light.[76] Reference to the battle between the Prince of Lights and the Prince of Darkness (light and darkness typifying the

72. P. 30; see Ps. 36:10; 130:7; Job 27:11 for the Hebrew's preference for "with," "to," and "in" when speaking of God.

73. See Rom. 9:14 and 2:11 (Lev. 19:15 is juridical, as are Dt. 1:17 and 16:19; see also Ropes on Jas. 2:9). Mk. 10:27 (see also 10:23-26) is on God as Judge and King (see "Kingdom").

74. This intensely Jewish phrase, used in the OT of the remnant (Isa. 1:9; also Rom. 9:29), may be taken, we believe, as further strong proof not only of the Epistle's Judaic texture but also of its Jewish origin, authorship, purpose, and probable destination.

75. Walter Chalmers Smith. See b. Sanhedrin 39a; see also J. Abelson, *Jewish Mysticism* (1913), p. 83; *The Immanence of God* (1912), p. 82. On the Messiah and light, especially at creation, see Pesiḳta Rabbati 159b; 1 En. 45:4; S–B I, 67, 151, 161; II, 428.

76. Hort, p. 29. For St. Bonaventura on this thought, see F. D. Maurice, *Medieval Philosophy* (1962), pp. 205ff.

powers of good and evil) can be found without difficulty, showing that James shared many of the ideas of Qumran.[77]

CONCLUSION

The purpose of Jas. 1:17ff. is not (in our view) to prove that God is perfectly good. That was axiomatic[78] for pre-Christian Jews, for non-Christian Jews even in our day, and for all Christians, Jewish or Gentile. No intelligent person could imagine that it is proved by anything in this *locus vexatus,* 1:16-19; these are just the "given" premises from which the Christian argument flows in 1:19 onward—really to the end of the Epistle. 1 Jn. 2:6 puts it all in 13 words. Its purpose is supremely practical: negatively, to show that God by his very nature cannot tempt the Christian to evil; and, positively, to hold up God's perfect nature as an example for the Christian to imitate. In a striking parallel, Philo reasons that the wise man who turns to God, the perfect One, rejects that which is imperfect. Instead of change and mutability, which is the essence of imperfection, he finds in God's unchangeableness true stability and unchanging peace.[79] Besides contrasting this peace with the "war in peace" of society and in man,[80] Philo links doubleness and speech, and affirms that contemplation of the one God alone brings stability.[81]

In our opinion, therefore, the contribution of Jas. 1:17f. is not to prove a theological point but to provide a theological rationale for Christian conduct. James's ethical teaching is inseparable from his teaching about God's unchanging sovereign goodness. Thus, if God created man in his own image, then cursing and all forms of anger directed against another human being are grievous sins (3:1-12). While never explicitly linked, the two ideas of the unity of God and the disunity of man are implicitly juxtaposed. "If God is one, and man should be one," writes Laws, "it is obvious that man's aim is the imitation of God. If this is admitted then it can be said of other N.T. authors that his ethical teaching has a theological basis."[82] Like Jesus, and the other NT writers, James

77. See 1QS 3:20; Hymns 4:6; 18:29. See also T. H. Gaster, *The Scriptures of the Dead Sea Sect* (1957), p. 25; Dibelius, p. 100.

78. By *axiomatic* we mean that the perfect goodness of God is outside proof. It is a fact that God taught the Jews by act and word; from him they learned all they ever knew about good or what is good.

79. *On the Giants* 45-49, cited by Laws, p. 31.

80. Ibid. 51.

81. Ibid. 52.

82. P. 32. For a fuller treatment, see, e.g., S. Laws, "The Doctrinal Basis for the Ethics of James," *StEv* 7 (1982): 299-305; R. A. Wild, "Be Imitators of God," in *Discipleship in the New Testament,* ed. F. J. Segovia (1985), pp. 127-43. For the

is following the OT holiness code (Lev. 19:2), the holiness of God being reflected in holy conduct.[83]

Thus James states: "He of his own wish begot us by the Word of truth, for us to be a kind of firstfruits of his creation." In other words, he (God) is the author of our Christian being and purpose, which is to be holy, as firstfruits. For the Christian, therefore, obedience to God's perfect will is paramount (4:15). In contrast to man's desire which results in double-mindedness (1:8) and begets spiritual death (1:13ff.), God's single, deliberate, purposive will is gracious, initiating and begetting new life. This experience of the new birth will show itself in conduct. "Wherefore, my beloved brothers . . ." (1:19ff.).

Theologically, therefore, the imitation of God *(imitatio Dei)* is for James both the supreme incentive and the final goal of Christian ethics, and indeed of all our striving, leading us to pray the prayer of Erasmus:

> O God of love, you are the true sun of the world, evermore risen and never going down. We pray you to shine in our hearts: that the darkness of sin and the mist of error being driven away, we may this day and all our life long walk without stumbling in the way you have prepared for us, which is Jesus Christ our Lord, who lives and reigns with you in the unity of the Holy Spirit, one with God in glory everlasting. Amen.

d. Wisdom

"For do not the words on 'the wisdom from above' read like James's veiled picture of the gentle Heart of Love that, many a time beside the bench, refused to be provoked by his bitter tongue?"

J. A. Robertson, *The Hidden Romance of the New Testament* (1920), p. 237

The paramount consideration of James—as of Paul and the other NT writers—was not persecution but sin. This is why even though he

---

Jewish background, see A. Marmorstein, "The Imitation of God *(Imitatio Dei)* in the Haggadah," *Studies in Jewish Theology,* eds. J. Rabbinowitz and M. S. Lew (1950), pp. 106-21; I. Abrahams, "The Imitation of God," *Studies in Pharisaism and the Gospels,* Second Series (1924), pp. 138-82. See also W. Bauder, "Imitate" *(mimeomai), NIDNTT,* I, 491f. For a different view, see B. Lindars, "Imitation of God and Imitation of Christ," *Theology* 76 (1973): 394-402.

83. See L. T. Johnson, "The Use of Leviticus 19 in the Letter of James," *JBL* 101.3 (1982): 391f.; 393ff.

believes that the end is near James is concerned about Christian conduct and fills his Epistle with eschatological ethics. Living in the last days calls for special skills in Christian conduct. So he strikes the keynote at the beginning: "If any of you is lacking knowledge [of God's way and will], let him ask of God." Now if the testing in Jas. 1:2 is both tribulation and temptation, "wisdom" in Jas. 1:4 falls into place at once; for, just as ignorance[1] is the mother of sin, godly wisdom[2] (certainly not here Greek philosophy but rather Jewish *praktische Lebensweisheit*)[3] is the key to the virtuous life. So 1:5 says, in effect, "If any man finds himself falling into sin [and who does not? "for we are all guilty of many sins"] as in the days of his 'ignorance,' let him pray for 'godly wisdom' to withstand temptations."[4]

Faith is the prerequisite to achieving wisdom. God's generous gift of wisdom is only for the single-minded: the double-minded can expect nothing. And the connection between 1:5, 17f., 21, 25 is that briefly indicated in 1:3-5: "assaults," "endurance," "wisdom," "work," "perfect," and "joy" ("blessed"; 1:12, 25). When lust is resisted by "wisdom" and "endurance" it is abortive (1:14); but when it is not resisted it conceives sin (1:15). "Light" in 1:17 looks back to "wisdom" in 1:5 and forward to "the Word (of truth)" in 1:18, 21.

THE EPISTLE OF CHRISTIAN WISDOM

The Epistle of James may be described as the Epistle of Christian Wisdom, applied to the concerns of everyday living. Wisdom is a divine gift, the prime moral virtue, the root of the Christian life.[5] Like Qumran and later Jewish Wisdom writers,[6] James finds this the one comprehensive source from which flow all the other ethical exhortations, for "underlying his thoroughgoing ethicism, James has an idea of an inner power, 'a wisdom that is from above' (3:17), a subtle, diffusive, presumably irresistible life, revealed most clearly in its fruits";[7] indeed,

1. Ignorance *(agnoia)*—Acts 3:17; 17:30; Eph. 4:18; 1 Pet. 1:14.

2. Wisdom *(sophia)*—Jas. 3:17; 1 Cor. 3:18; 2:6-16.

3. J. Schneider, *Die Briefe des Jakobus, Petrus, Judas und Johannes*. NTD, X (1961), 6-26.

4. See C. Spicq, "*AMETAMELĒTOS* dans Rom. XI, 29," *RB* 67 (1960): 210ff.

5. On wisdom *(ḥoḵmāh)* in Judaism as the gift of God, see G. Fohrer, *sophia, TDNT*, VII, 493; Dibelius, p. 108.

6. See Fohrer, *sophia, TDNT*, VII, 486. See also 1QS 4:22 where God gives "true insight into the knowledge of the Most High and the wisdom of the heavenly sons"; Davids, pp. 52ff.

7. A. C. Zenos, *The Plastic Age of the Gospel* (1927), p. 132.

wisdom and ethics are so closely linked that the wise and the righteous[8] (or "the perfect man")[9] are practically synonymous.

The Christian *mind*—not of human origin, and not without God's guidance—animates the Christian *life*. But the great pioneers of the Christian religion tend to emphasize one aspect of that divine inspiration; thus Paul regularly thinks much of Christian faith, but in 1 Cor. 13 even more of Christian love. To James "wisdom is what faith is to Paul, hope to Peter, love to John—the essence of the Christian life."[10] There is hardly a commentator who would not agree with this judgment and recognize the crucial position wisdom occupies in the thought of James, though, especially in the light of Qumran studies, we can no longer speak of the Epistle as a "NT wisdom book."[11] It is also probably too much to claim that wisdom is the Epistle's theological ground plan ("weisheitstheologische Grundstruktur").[12]

Such, then, is the goal toward which faith must strive. In keeping with the cast of thought prominent in the Epistle of James we may say that as the Torah (taught by "the wise" *[ḥᵃḵāmîm]*, e.g., in the Scrolls[13] and identified with wisdom in Prov. 13:14, where the law of the wise is the fountain of life) was to the Jew the essence of the life devoted to God, so wisdom, God's guiding (not compelling), implanted (not imposed) instruction, is for James what faith, hope, or love is to some of his great contemporaries—the essence of the Christian life; hence the command: "Receive the implanted Word" (1:21).

THE TEACHER OF WISDOM

It can hardly be surprising that the true teacher of wisdom is identified

8. See Job 28:28; Prov. 14:16. For the wise–righteous equation in the Scrolls, see 1QH 34ff.; CD 4:3f. (6:3ff.); see U. Wilckens, *sophia, TDNT,* VII, 504f.

9. See 1QS 4:20-22. For a full discussion, see A. R. G. Deasley, *The Idea of Perfection in the Qumran Texts* (unpublished Ph.D. thesis, University of Manchester, 1972).

10. F. B. Clogg, *An Introduction to the New Testament* (1937), p. 151. See Mayor, p. 36; also D. A. Hubbard, *The Book of James* (1980), who claims that "wisdom that works" is the master theme of the entire Epistle.

11. For the older approach see, e.g., R. G. Moulton, *The Literary Study of the Bible* (1896), pp. 292ff. See also B. R. Halson, "The Epistle of James: 'Christian Wisdom?'" *TU* 102 = *StEv* 4 (1968): 308-14; Davids, p. 51. Also above, pp. 101f.

12. U. Luck, "Der Jakobusbrief und die Theologie des Paulus," *Theologie und Glaube* 61 (1971): 172.

13. See CD 4:3f. (6:3); also U. Wilckens, *sophia, TDNT,* VII, 505; Oesterley, p. 422.

with the Wise Man *(sophos)*, the official description of the teacher (3:1), a title greatly coveted by the Jews,[14] frequently in Qumran, especially of the Teacher of Righteousness,[15] and, of course, applied supremely to Jesus as the new Moses (Mt. 12:36; see also 23:8; Jn. 11:28).[16] Nor is it too difficult to see in this warning an implicit reference to the example of Jesus, the supreme Teacher. Since James's church, like Paul's, was "a church of the Spirit,"[17] it is entirely possible that at this early date there was no definite office of teacher to which people were ecclesiastically appointed, but, as with the prophets, a charismatic ministry that people occupied by virtue of the appropriate gifts (see Rom. 12:6f.).[18] On the other hand, the evidence of the Scrolls may suggest a special class. In Qumran "the wise" came immediately after "the heads of the fathers of the community" in the eschatological hierarchy.[19]

Those claiming to be teachers without proper qualification were a constant problem, leading to self-assertion, confusion, acrimony, and disputatiousness (see Acts 15:24; 1 Cor. 14:26ff.; 1 Tim. 1:6f.; 6:3; 1 Pet. 2:1; 1 Jn. 3; Hermas, *Sim.* 9.22.2f.). Jesus warns against teachers who aspire to positions which properly belong to God: "But you are not to be called 'Rabbi,' for you have only one Master and you are all brothers. And do not call anyone on earth 'father,' for you have one Father, and he is in heaven. Nor are you to be called 'teacher,' for you have one Teacher, the Christ" (Mt. 23:8ff., NIV). Later Origen[20] used James's warning most effectively against those who hanker after a bishopric, since, he says, "it's good for a man not to rush into dignities,

14. E.g., R. Eleazar b. Shammua said: "Let the fear of thy teacher be as the fear of Heaven" (M. Aboth 4.12). See Dibelius, p. 183, 12, 14, 15; Davids, p. 136; also GNC, p. 64; F. W. Weber, *Jüdische Theologie* (1897), pp. 125ff.; A. Richardson, *A Theological Word Book of the Bible* (1963), p. 148; U. Wilckens, *sophia, TDNT,* VII, 505; K. Wegenast, "Teacher" *(didaskalos), NIDNTT,* III, 766ff.

15. See Wegenast, *art. cit., NIDNTT,* III, 766; R. H. Eisenman, *James the Just in the Habakkuk Pesher* (1986), pp. viiff. and throughout; also *Maccabees, Zadokites, Christians and Qumran* (1983), p. xv and throughout.

16. See R. Mohrlang, *Matthew and Paul* (1984); W. D. Davis, *The Setting of the Sermon on the Mount* (1964), pp. 418f., 422ff.; *Beginnings,* I, 492ff.; C. K. Barrett, *The Gospel According to St. John* (1955), p. 331; Wegenast, *art. cit., NIDNTT,* III, 767; also K. Rengstorf, *didaskalos, TDNT,* II, 156.

17. See Davids, GNC, p. 53.

18. For a short, judicious study of NT prophets and teachers, see M. E. Boring, *Sayings of the Risen Jesus* (1982), pp. 78-80; also A. A. T. Ehrhardt, *The Apostolic Succession in the First Two Centuries of the Church,* pp. 83ff.

19. See 1QSa 2:16; also 1:28; 1QS 4:3-6. See also Wilckens, *art. sophia,* for Qumranic parallels.

20. See Ehrhardt, *The Apostolic Succession in the First Two Centuries of the Church,* p. 144.

prelacies, and ministries of the church, for they all come from God," and "he who is the bishop of a Church and does wrong, will have the greater punishment."

The sincerest teachers and even the finest saints too often succumb to such temptations: witness Jerome's asperities against Augustine. The Christian teacher therefore must always be acutely aware of his accountability: "Greater responsibility means heavier judgment" (3:1). "The sentiment," writes R. A. Knox, "is interpreted as meaning that people in important positions will be more severely judged (Lk. 12:48). But we are not told that; we are told that if we become teachers we shall be punished more severely than ever, like the scribes and Pharisees who profess piety while they wrong their neighbors (Matthew 23:14)."[21]

Certainly, like that in James, the latter passage contains the word "judgment" *(krima)* while the other does not; but even a cursory reading of Lk. 12:41-48 shows that no word of judging as such occurs. It is all about rewards and punishments, and only in the last sentence, by implication and in stating the principles of judgment, does the trial itself come into the picture. The words "important positions," though true as far as they go, as an interpretation of the latter half of v. 48 must not blind us to what goes before it: "And that servant who *knew* his Lord's will shall be beaten with many stripes. But he that *knew not* . . . shall be beaten with few stripes." The text says nothing about important positions; it speaks of those to whom much, or little, is entrusted; and the responsibility of more or less knowledge could not be more plainly stated. This, too, is the meaning of Jas. 3:1 and 4:17. There is therefore no substance in the distinction Knox seeks to draw between his passages from Luke and Matthew. Knowledge is an important trust, and it has a particular relevance in discussing teachers, the sort James had in mind. Jas. 1:5 ("chides not") and 3:1 ("we are all guilty of many sins") have some relevance here.

It is important to distinguish the two sets (here as always) in James's "audience," that is, the sincere and the pretenders (if we may so succinctly call them). James constantly differentiates these two sets in his sympathy for the one and his castigation of the other. In saying "be not many of you rabbis, knowing that we shall receive greater damnation" (3:1), James is telling the genuinely faithful that few of them should aim at being *didaskaloi;* and he means, so far as we can judge, just what, say, the zealous pastor means when he tells his (quite admirable) young people: "Don't many of you go in for the Ministry; the

21. P. 103.

standard of righteousness is such that few can hope to approach (and none can reach)." This seems to be the meaning—a quite definite, apt, and forceful meaning—of "many" *(polloi)*.[22]

Ropes's comment is to the point: "The main thought in vv. 1-12 is the greater responsibility of teachers and the extremely dangerous character of the instrument which they have to use. In vv. 9-12 the noble possibilities of the tongue are presented as a motive for checking its lower propensities. This passage naturally connects with 1:19f., 26; 2:12."[23] And *polloi* has its ordinary meaning, "many." "Do not many of you be rabbis"; in other words, James does not want many of them to become rabbis. There is no irony here. James is in dead earnest about the dangers and responsibilities of a rabbi. Even if we understand James's anxiety, we may be tempted (are we not?) to think that his diatribe, like the parallel diatribes in Qumran on the so-called "Spouter of

22. Accordingly, the persistent attempt to emend *polloi* (see Ropes, p. 226; Dibelius, p. 183, n. 9) or to evade its plain meaning seems not only inapposite in v. 1 but also ruinous to the passage on the tongue as a whole. We are thinking particularly of R. A. Knox's strange translation "voluminous teachers" (*A New Testament Commentary,* III [1956], 104). For a predicative use of *polys* see LS, which shows it with a finite verb: *polys tois symbebēkosin enkeitai,* "he is severe (presses hard) upon" (W. W. Goodwin, *A Greek Grammar* [1883], p. 308; Demosthenes, *On the Crown,* sec. 199). So LS, which Knox was obviously consulting, gives "(Themistocles) broke into a passionate speech" *(p. ēn en toisi logoisi)* (Herodotus 8.59); one from Polybius, with *pros* plus the dative; one from Diodorus, with *epi* plus the dative; also *p. ēn tois epainois* (Aeschines). "In most of these cases a sense of repetition is joined with that of Degree," says the Lexicon. "He was urgent in his entreaties," says LS (small edition), p. 575. A. W. Spratt, *Thucydides* (1912), p. 194, on 4.22.2 quotes Sallust, *The Jugurthine War* 84.1—*multus atque ferox instare* ("to attack persistently and boldly"). Now we note that in the singular *polys* so used is not ambiguous if this meaning were possible in the plural; and, as we see, the examples given are all in the singular. No Greek would write or understand James's words as having Knox's meaning—Be not "voluminous teachers"—or as being pertinaciously or extensively didactic; *polloi* could not mean that, nor could *didaskaloi.* It is idle to play with the English word "didactic," even if it ever did (does it ever?) mean censorious. James knows how to express himself on the censorious (4:11f.); he does not use *didaskō, didaskalos* for *krinō, kritēs,* as we can see six times in two verses. "It is a defiance of grammar because it is a defiance of logic," says Knox; but grammar often defies logic, e.g., in Greek "relative attraction" or in the English "than *whom* there is none better." The point is immaterial; but Knox, too, "is not at all grammatical." "Don't many of you become teachers" seems to us perfectly possible English. "The form of your sentence embraces a whole group of human beings, while the message it conveys is only meant for a portion," says Knox; but partitive apposition is common in Greek.

23. P. 226.

Lies,"[24] on the tongue approaches too near to extravagance; but if we fail to sense the real depths of his feeling about his own function as a rabbi, a feeling probably shared by Qumran's Teacher of Righteousness and certainly by Paul in a similar function (1 Cor. 9:23-27), these words of James (and many others of Paul) must appear inexcusably extravagant.

THE POTENTIAL OF THE TONGUE

James proceeds (3:2) to justify his warning on the office of teacher with a series of "almost psychedelic portraits of the evil of the tongue,"[25] the explanatory "for" and the plural "we" indicating the continuity of the theme.

(1) The first of several—seven in all—well-chosen metaphors, namely, bridle and horse, rudder and ship (vv. 3-5a), portrays *the influence of the tongue,* one of the most potent instruments alike for good and evil. The control of the tongue represents the final achievement of the perfect man. To say that this is "superficial," since "an accomplished hypocrite's works may be irreproachable, although belied by his thoughts," is surely itself "superficial."[26] An accomplished hypocrite's words can be irreproachable only in the ears of those thereby deceived. The hypocrite who utters the words cannot be said to bridle his tongue, since bridle in this context can only mean bridle for good; it does not include technique in sin, either by word or by deed.

In men and women anything "perfect" is the consummation of an almost certainly long course of progress, and James begins his epistle on that very note in his treatment of *endurance*. In the ordinary sense, "perfect" is applied rather to that which lacks no proper good quality or is marred by no bad quality. God is, and always will be, perfect. Human beings, on the contrary, become perfect, if at all, only by a process leading from greater to less imperfection; to them, *not* to God, "perfect" applies in some of the old sense of the Lat. *perficio,* "I work at making something until it is thoroughly, and thoroughly well, made, 'til it is 'finished to perfection.'" The Gk. *teleios* in its original sense contains the same notion of progress from an immature, unripe, inchoate

24. For a discussion of the "Liar" or "Spouter of Lies" with references, e.g., 1QpHab 2.1ff.; 10.9-13; see Eisenman, *James the Just in the Habakkuk Pesher,* pp. 22f., 33ff., 70ff., 91f.; *Maccabees, Zadokites, Christians and Qumran,* pp. xii, 35, 50, 90; also U. Becker, H.-G. Link, "Lie" *(pseudomai), NIDNTT,* II, 471f.

25. Davids, GNC, p. 56.

26. Easton, p. 47.

state to a perfect, mature, ripe, complete, and completing "finish" or *telos*[27]—where *telos* signifies not just where something stops but where it has attained the consummated fullness of growth or progress in the attributes and qualities that lie with the nature of its species. We may say with a little laxity that an individual is honest or sober, or has perfect technique in painting or another art or profession; but in ethics, *teleios* must mean "perfectly righteous," or "perfectly skilled in righteousness." James so describes the man who bridles his tongue, never sins in what he says, and is therefore "a perfect man."

That James really believes there is such a man is, of course, a different story. It is certainly true and relevant that Orientals give vent to speech more freely than we are prone to do; but we cannot think of one of us who does not find it easier, in general, to keep his other members from sin than it is to keep his tongue from sin, especially since to the sincere Christian all uncharitable talk is sin. Nothing is more trite, and true, than that we find it harder to avoid sinning in words than in deeds, but we cannot believe that James is endowing the tongue with a separate personality. Nor is he saying that *by* controlling our words we *thereby* control the rest of our body, for that is not consistent with his statements about lusts. We think the obvious meaning is simply that if a person can control the most recalcitrant of his members, he can also control his other members.

(2) Further, the tongue is said to be *capable of great mischief*. Its recurrent evils are like a revolving wheel of nature that goes *ad infinitum* in all the changes of life. "In many primitive rituals," observes J. H. Moulton, "a wooden wheel is rapidly rotated on a wooden axle to produce fire. The image here is that of a flame spreading from the centre down all the radiating spokes."[28] Isaiah speaks of "wickedness burning as the fire; it shall devour the briars and the thorns, and kindle in the thickets of the forest" (Isa. 9:18). The image of the tongue as flame is common enough in Jewish and other writings. Thus, "the tongue has no power over the god-fearing; they cannot be burned in its flames" (Ecclus. 28:22). But the thrust in James is eschatological, for James is thinking of the "end time." The mischief spreads in ever-widening circles. The wrong use of the tongue engenders all kinds of wickedness. Language as an instrument of evil, and like fire, undeniably brings immense harm to people and through people to things.

At one time we should probably have excepted the great works of nature from this statement; today we are not so sure of even our own

27. See R. Schippers, "Goal" *(telos), NIDNTT,* II, 59ff.
28. "James," *Peake's Commentary* (1931), p. 905.

earth. But here in James we may fairly take world and creation in their human reference, humanity living in this present evil age; worldly people with their thoughts and deeds are the world of sin, and the circling course of creation means people born or to be born until the period of this present age comes to its imminent end. So in Mk. 16:15 *ktisis* really means humanity, and in Col. 1:23 "in the whole creation" means the whole world of people, "all humanity."[29]

The power of the tongue is seen in the mischief it can do—a mischief out of all proportion to its size. "A hasty argument kindles a fire" (Ecclus. 28:29, NEB). James was drawing on his experience of the devastating forest fires in Palestine. The Talmud tells of summer fires fanned by the evening breeze and spreading so fast that it was difficult to determine if the cause was arson.[30] A tiny spark may set on fire a great forest and lead to vast destruction: think, for example, of a lighted cigarette tossed away by a careless smoker.[31] "So, too, the tongue is a little member of the body vaunting great power. See how much brushwood a little fire sets alight. The tongue, also, is fire; the sinful world (is) wood." (The thought here is of sinful people, as, since the Fall, *all* humanity has been, is, and will be sinful.) "Thus the tongue stands among our members, defiling the whole body and setting fire to the cir-

29. See H. Sasse, *kosmos*, *TDNT*, III, 868ff.; also J. Gurth, "Earth" *(kosmos)*, *NIDNTT*, III, 524f.

30. M. Goodman, *State and Society in Roman Galilee,* A.D. 132-212 (1983), pp. 21, 190 n. 41. See W. Barclay, *The Letters of James and Peter* (1976), p. 85.

31. "Sparks"

"How great a matter a small fire kindleth";
And a still smaller spark kindleth the fire.
Ask the firefighters of California,
Small things count;
They may be decisive.
A virus fells a human genius.
Had Cleopatra's nose been shorter,
"The whole aspect of the world would have been altered."
An atom split can blot out mankind;
A little kindness may turn a human life from crime
To saintliness;
Witness Jean Valjean
A wooden cross reveals the divine heart;
From it flows a redemptive stream
Through centuries.
Bigness is not all;
Despise not the day of small things.

Robert Worth Frank, *Monday Morning* 42.20 (1977):1.

cling course of creation, and being set on fire by hell" (3:5f.). But though James does not say this, the opposite is also true:

> It only takes a spark to get a fire going,
> And soon all those around can warm up in its glowing.
> That's how it is with God's love. . . .[32]

Like a spark (or bit or rudder), the tongue is only a small part of the whole; nevertheless it exercises an inordinate power, one that is certainly out of all proportion to its size. The tongue is said (v. 6) to be able to defile or corrupt the whole body just as a defective part in an automobile engine could bring the whole vehicle to destruction. The person who can control his tongue can also do what is easier, that is, control his body; the more difficult includes the less difficult. Mastery of the tongue also shows mastery of the body—a reference perhaps to the *yēṣer,* which is said to be "king over its two hundred and forty-eight organs"[33]—and shows that the person in question has nothing more to learn or remedy in the relevant matter, namely, moral self-discipline for good in speech and action. If, therefore, we find a person who can control his tongue perfectly, we will also find that that person can achieve the comparatively less difficult task of controlling the rest of his members. But, as James indicates, such an ideal person does not exist, for he has already said that no person is perfect in righteousness: "we are all guilty of many sins" (3:2).

(3) Like Qumran, James uses strong, and what might seem to be exaggerated, language about the tongue. He now proceeds to justify it by describing the tongue's *intractability.* Whereas wild animals can be tamed, the tongue cannot be tamed; it alone is intractable and beyond our control. "Words which we think are our slaves and instruments," wrote Dean Church, "may become our masters and tyrants."[34] Of the variant readings, "irreducible to order" *(akatastaton)* and "unruly" *(akatascheton),*[35] in 3:8, we have adopted the former. As Ropes[36] indicates, Bengel's valuable principle "The more difficult reading is stronger" *(lectio difficilior, lectio potior)* favors "irreducible to order" as likely to come in by error for "unruly" than the latter by error for

32. Kurt Kaiser, copyright 1969 by Lexicon Music, Inc.

33. See, e.g., 1QS 4; Aboth R. Nathan 16; also A. Cohen, *Everyman's Talmud* (1932), p. 89; Davids, GNC, pp. 65, 77.

34. "Strong Words" (Sermon 15), p. 259 in *Pascal and Other Sermons* (1896).

35. *akatastaton* is read by ℵ A B K P 1739 *pc* latt. sy^{p}? sa? bo and *akatascheton* by C Ψ M Syr^{h}; Hier^{pt} Spec.

36. P. 241.

akatastaton. Also, that feature of style so common elsewhere in James, the "rondo" or "closing circuit," favors *akatastaton.* If we accept it in the opening of the paragraph, that is, in vv. 7f. (which two verses form a unity), we find it duly "rounded off on the same note" at the end of the paragraph from *ou chrē* etc. in v. 10 to the end of v. 12.

Another aspect, we think, of James's complaint against the tongue is its baffling *inconsistency.* The tongue, says James, is an evil irreducible to order, to a consistent character of disciplined obedience to righteousness. It is the tongue itself, not only its misuse, that is condemned.[37] In plain and perhaps not too free English: "The tongue is a monster of inconsistency—or even better, a monster of caprice—full of deadly venom" (3:8). While every kind of beast has been tamed by mankind, the tongue remains "a restless evil, full of deadly poison" and quite untamable. But does this not make nonsense of the fact that humans are made in "the image of God" (Gen. 1:26),[38] for how can one "pretend to bless the person (God) and logically curse the representation of the person (a human)?"[39] This should not be (3:10)!

Though we have subdued much of the world around us, our own nature remains untamed. We can bridle and break a horse, but we cannot govern our own tongue. In the circus, says Isocrates, we see bears behaving more humanely to their trainers than some people to their benefactors.[40] To anticipate, we may say here that the word for "peaceful, or peaceable, tempters" is that of 3:13, where the KJV has "meekness," the NIV "humility," and the NEB "modesty." The word means the opposite of the strife mentioned in 3:14 and elsewhere. So here Isocrates contrasts "gentleness" *(praotētas)* and "savageness" *(agrio-*

37. So M. Aurelius, *Meditations* 6.41; also O. Michel's remarks in *ios, katioomai, TDNT,* III, 335.

38. Jas. 3:9. See N. H. Snaith, "The Image of God" (with references), *ExpT* 9.1 (1979): 20.

39. Davids, p. 146; also GNC, pp. 52f.; 66f., on cursing and Jewish references employing the image of God against cursing. See E. Beyreuther, G. Finkenrath, "Like" *(homoios), NIDNTT,* II, 505.

40. This passage, denouncing some who disparaged education of the sort we used to call "humane," is rarely if ever cited by the commentators. We quote in full: "Although every year they see in the circuses lions that are more gently *(praoteron)* disposed towards their keepers than some men are towards their benefactors, and bears rolling and wrestling and imitating our skills, these disparagers cannot even from this perceive the value of education and training, or that these would much more quickly benefit our nature than that of those animals. I find it hard to say whether one might more justifiably marvel at the peaceful tempers instilled into the fiercest of animals or the wild natures that exist in the minds of men (who think) like that" (*Antidosis* 213). For other illustrations, see Dibelius, pp. 199f.

tētas). May we suggest that here James is thinking partly, perhaps mainly, of the educative aspect of our dominion over animals; for he was no doubt well aware of the wild animals of the Jordan Valley. Even a well-trained bear may at some time forget itself; but with it its trainer is not really on tenterhooks every moment of the day. With the tongue, however, you are, even if you are a fine professing Christian.[41]

(4) Finally, James returns to the theme of double-mindedness (1:8), speaking now of *the ambivalence of the tongue* (vv. 9-12), showing how it can destroy our relationship with God.[42] If "ambivalence" is, as defined by the dictionary, a "simultaneous attraction toward and repulsion from a person, object or action," it is hard to believe that this happens in religion—but it does. The same tongue that blesses and praises God may also curse and blaspheme.[43] In this ambivalence it contradicts even the elemental laws of nature where each element produces its own distinctive kind.[44] Nature knows no duplicity. It is unthinkable,

41. On the point of domesticated animals, it may be relevant to remark that the rich denounced by James regarded and treated the poor workers as cattle; we think that it is a fair deduction from what James says of the rich. The once common American slogan "free, white, and twenty-one" may also remind us that the original U.S. Constitution denied slaves their equality (U.S. Constitution, Art. 1, Sec. 3).

42. On the ambivalence of the tongue, compare Ecclus. 5:13: "Honour or shame can come through speaking, and a man's tongue may be his downfall" (NEB)—*Doxa kai atimia en lalia kai glōssa anthrōpou ptōsis autō*. The Greek itself chimes with Jas. 3:2 in word as well as in thought. We need scarcely point out that *ptōsis,* "fall," in Ecclesiasticus comes from the same etymological cradle as *ptaiō,* found twice in Jas. 3:2; see also *paraptōmata,* "trespasses," elsewhere. And only three verses above, Ecclus. 5:10 (like James deploring the tongue's inconstancy), after condemning the *diglōssos,* says strongly and clearly: "Be steadfast, *estērigmenos,* in thy understanding; let thy *logos* be one" (RV), i.e., not *diglōssos* but *heis.* Later we read: "Blow on a spark to make it glow, or spit on it to put it out: both results come from the same mouth" (Ecclus. 28:12, NEB). On the tongue, good and also bad, see Midr. Vayyiqra R. 33 on Lev. 25:1 and other illustrations given by Dibelius, pp. 201f., nn. 102f.; Davids, pp. 145f.; GNC, pp. 59, 66f.

43. On the Jewish blessings, "The Holy One, blessed be He," "Blessed art Thou" in the *Shemoneh Esreh,* the Jewish Eighteen Benedictions and Jewish Cursings and their later Christian equivalents, among others, e.g., Rom. 12:14 (NIV): "Bless those who persecute you; and do not curse," see Dibelius, pp. 202f.; H.-G. Link, "Blessing" *(eulogia), NIDNTT,* I, 206ff.; G. Vermes, F. Millar, M. Black, and E. Schürer, *The History of the Jewish People in the Age of Jesus Christ,* II, 455ff.; also J. Scharbert, *brk, TDOT,* II, 279ff. for blessing; B. Wiklander, *zā'am, TDOT,* IV, 107 for cursing; and B. Otzen, *ṭal, TDOT,* V, 325 for blessings and curses.

44. See R. Hooykaas, *Natural and Divine Miracle: The Principle of Uniformity in Geology, Biology and Theology* (1963). On the Stoic view of nature's orderliness, interrelation, and interdependence, see Dibelius, p. 204; also G. Harder, "Nature" *(physis), NIDNTT,* II, 656ff.

therefore, that the same fountain can send forth both salt water and sweet, or that a fig tree or vine can yield alien fruit. The offering such a person makes to God is tainted. For if he blessed God one moment and the next moment uses his tongue for cursing, where is such a person's integrity? "The good mind," we read, "has not two tongues, of blessing and of cursing—but it has one disposition, uncorrupt and pure, concerning all men" (Test. Benj. 6:5).

Such things ought not to be, says James. His condemnation and his repudiation of the suggestion of amoralism in God are in the strongest Greek he can find—*ou chrē,* only here in the NT.[45] The tongue's ambivalent defiance of any uniformity of character and behavior (1:13 and 3:7-12) is completely contrary to nature. James's phrase is rather like our "It's not right," uttered with all the force of protesting condemnation. The control of the tongue, therefore, is a paramount concern of the Christian.

THE TONGUE AND THE OATH

In the final verses of his Epistle James returns to the tongue, this time in connection with the oath (5:12), which seems to signal the close of his letter.[46] We have already discussed the connection between the saying of James here and that of Jesus in Mt. 5:33ff.[47] But equally clear is the connection of both with the practice of Qumran, which, with a few exceptions, forbade all oaths, teaching instead the importance of plain speaking.[48] The Covenanters were well aware that one of the first and apparently most enduring lessons religion teaches is to back one's assertions with an oath. In early law the oath is a great menace, both as a generator of formalism and as an impediment to juridical progress. Before people learned to use documents or their friends to attest transactions, they were accustomed to call on the gods—who must always

45. See W. L. Lane, "Want" *(chreia), NIDNTT,* III, 958.

46. On James's probable knowledge of this device in Greek letters, see Davids, GNC, p. 92.

47. See pp. 182ff.

48. Of the Essenes Josephus says: "Every word they speak is more binding than an oath; they avoid swearing as something worse than perjury among other people, for they say a man is already condemned if he cannot be believed without swearing by God" (*War* 2.135; also 139, 142 for oaths of initiation; and CD 9:9f. before judges). On the oath, with literature, see H.-G. Link, "Swear" *(omnyō), NIDNTT,* III, 737ff.; also Mussner, pp. 213ff. For our purposes, the Essenes are identified with the Qumran Community; see M. Newton, *The Concept of Purity at Qumran and in the Letters of Paul* (1985), p. 121, n. 1; Vermes, Millar, and Schürer, *The History of the Jewish People in the Age of Jesus Christ,* II, 555ff., esp. 583f.

have been rather unsatisfactory witnesses. In the absence of testimony for commercial dealings, or where evidence is lacking, the oath comes into use.

The oath, like the other forms of ordeal, is an appeal to the judgment of heaven, especially in the absence of the testimony of men. In this light we may understand what Homer means when he says that Autolycus, grandfather of Odysseus, "excelled all men at thieving and making oath." Ropes begins his note on 5:12: "Do not break out into oaths. . . ."[49] The exhortation relating to oaths appears parallel with *mē stenazete*. "Do not put the blame for your hardships on your brothers; do not irreverently call on God in your distress." Vv. 12-18 all relate to the religious expression of strong emotion.

But James does not even mention God. Further, Ps. 22:1f. is not irreverent; if Job in his distress had found fault with God or cried his name in reproach without faith, that would have been irreverent, but it would be neither *omnymi* nor *horkos*, neither "swearing" nor an "oath." In Greek these words do not themselves express an ejaculation of joy, sorrow, or other emotion. A Greek said "Herakles!" just as Shakespeare has "Angels and ministers of grace defend us!" but that is not swearing an oath, the essence of which is the express or implied invocation of God to punish the speaker if his words are to prove to be false (see Gen. 26:28-31 for a covenant and 1 Kgs. 19:2 for Jezebel's wrath; and such must have been the oaths with which Peter denied his Lord—perhaps like this: "God's curse on him; God slay me if I know him").

Of course, like the Covenanters, James was against frivolous swearing of oaths in conversational extravagance ("the requirement here is simplicity and sincerity of conversation"—Bengel); but perhaps he would have thought it superfluous to say so. We are sure that his warning does not stop at that. No doubt, too, he was against Christians swearing oaths in pagan law courts; he and the Christians he was addressing were living under the Roman empire. Roman law, under the classical Republic and under the empire, especially before Constantine, did much to keep the oath out of court. But in actions for a stated sum, and some others, the plaintiff could challenge the defendant to settle the dispute by swearing a conclusive oath (like Autolycus); and the defendant might reverse the challenge. James (2:6) mentions that the rich haul Christians before the courts, and he may well have had this circumstance in mind when he wrote his warning about oaths.

But we think that his chief concern was the promissory oath, that is, the use of the oath to confirm serious statements or promises such as

49. P. 300.

arise in making or fulfilling business agreements, or in disputes and complaints of loss, injury, or other wrong in these and many other relations and transactions in daily life. Everybody understands the promissory oath, "By the gods I will do or pay, etc." James must have known the long and sinister history of the oath in such connections; and like the writer of Prov. 30:8f. (who takes us back to Autolycus's thieving and false swearing), he was aware of its temptations: "lest you fall under condemnation" *(hina mē hypo krisin pesēte)* (5:12). So, too, Mt. 5:33-37, which has been held to be aimed at the hypocrisy and fraud of Jews who thought they escaped the sin of perjury if in their oaths they avoided using the name of God. Note the rabbinical saying: "As heaven and earth shall pass away, so passeth away the oath taken by them."[50] Religion is not to cloak the false promise or any other lie. It is hard for the modern reader to see this matter in true perspective. The promissory (and conclusive) oath flourishes only in a world that believes in God, as the ancient Jew and the early Christian did, and as our modern world does not.

THE GIFT OF WISDOM

The teacher, as Ropes rightly says, was "One who has a knowledge of God. The words of James relate to the ideal to be maintained by a professional Wise Man and teacher, not merely to the private wisdom of layman."[51] James next considers 3:13–4:17, the quality and duty of Christian wisdom. Sincerity is essential (3:13, 17); but as 1:5 was followed by castigation in 1:6-8, so 3:14-16 begins a castigation that continues throughout ch. 4. As usual, sincerity goes with humility and "good works," and insincerity with worldliness—pride, lust, greed, envy, disputing, backbiting,[52] and bragging. Chs. 3 and 4 aim their censures at those whose knowledge of God adds to their sin.[53] These passages, among countless others in the NT, illustrate the disease endemic in all early, and perhaps not only early, Christianity. But Jas. 3 and 4 are not pastoral like 1 and 2 Timothy and Titus, which are directed to the duties[54] and risks of teachers.

50. See S–B I, 321ff.; also J. Schneider, *omnyō, TDNT,* V, 178.

51. P. 244.

52. See 2 Cor. 12:20; W. Mundle, "Revile" *(katalaleō), NIDNTT,* III, 346, who sees this and the other apostolic injunctions as proof of the outworking of Jesus' love-commandment in the Christian church.

53. 3:1; 4:17; see also Rom. 1:21-32, and throughout the Bible; e.g., 1 Tim. 1:3f., 19f.; 2:2; 4:1f.; 6:3, 5, 17-19; 2 Tim. 1:15; 2:16-18; 3:2-8, esp. 5-8; 4:3f.; Tit. 1:10-16; 2:11-14.

54. So Scaer, pp. 97ff.; also W. Lock, *The Bible and Christian Life* (1890), p. 227.

James is addressing a general congregation, and Paul (probably quite consciously) follows James's pattern in one of his earliest Epistles, 1 Cor. 1:7–4:21. Like Jas. 3 it begins—and this should be verified by reading, favorably, 1:7-10, 30, 51—by addressing the brotherhood, as in 1:10. But at 1:11 Paul turns to censure, just as James does. In contrast to the Pastoral Epistles, Paul in 1 Corinthians, like James in the Epistle of James, is not, as it were, addressing a bishop on an episcopal vocation but Christians on a Christian vocation; and Paul, like James, finds a multitude of impostors.[55] Since James is addressing Jews, the evidence of Tit. 1:10, 14 is noteworthy. "In Jewish usage," Ropes adds, "the teacher is one who has a knowledge of practical moral wisdom, resting on a knowledge of God."[56] James says: "The prayer of a righteous man is mighty in operation" (5:16) and "We are all guilty of many sins" (3:2). Does it not follow that no one is righteous? Strictly, we suppose, that is so; no one is perfect. But there is a sort of person to whom the term "righteous" can be applied in a definite though limited sense. We mean the person who genuinely believes that there is such a thing as right, as contrasted with wrong, and is genuinely determined to make every effort to do the right.

"Where is the wisdom we lost in information?" asks T. S. Eliot; "Where is the understanding we have lost in knowledge? . . . Where is the life we have lost in living?"[57] A great number of people, perhaps without knowing it, simply do not believe that there is such a thing as right, and of course do not believe that there is a God. Such folks may know how many beans make five in a worldly sense and how to get worldly gain, "the quick-witted, take-it-or-leave-it, worldly wisdom of the salesman rather than the compassionate time-consuming wisdom of the godly counsellor."[58] Wisdom is not just the sum of factual knowledge, such as historical dates or the location of an untapped oil well: "Knowledge comes, but wisdom lingers" (Tennyson). The wisdom of a pastor, we suppose, consists not in his skill at amassing information, but, for example, in the wizardry with which he can get the most and best out of his flock.

In short, the meaning of wisdom is well indicated by its opposite, which is folly, not ignorance (see Eccl. 2:12-16, esp. v. 13: "Wisdom is better than folly, just as light is better than darkness" [NIV]). The path

55. E.g., 1 Cor. 3:3; 4:6-8, 19f. (1 Cor. 4:20 is much like Jas. 3:13).

56. P. 244.

57. "Choruses from 'The Rock,'" *T. S. Eliot: The Complete Poems and Plays, 1909-1950* (1972), p. 96.

58. So C. Kent, cited in K. Lawson, *The Soldier's Armoury* (January-June 1987): 39.

of wisdom is the path to freedom. For the wise, therefore, wisdom is the perfect law of freedom (Jas. 1:25). "The true beginning of wisdom is the desire to learn, and a concern for learning means love towards her; the love of her means the keeping of her laws" (Wisd. 6:17, NEB). To keep her laws is to submit to wisdom's yoke, which brings relief and joy (Ecclus. 6:23ff.). Wisdom is essentially a quality of spirit (as is obvious in any really good teacher); thus the Bible often speaks of God's Spirit and God's Wisdom in almost the same sense, and we speak indifferently of his hand or his arm to denote his power. But we must remember that the terms are not exactly synonymous: wisdom is only one activity of his Spirit.[59]

This leads us naturally to inquire whether James entertained some kind of Wisdom Christology. Discussing this question, A. C. Zenos recalls that "before the synthesis of the primitively Hebrew concept of wisdom with the Stoic 'word' *(logos)* which took place in Alexandria, the term designated the divine energy (spirit of God) which operates in creation, revelation and providential protection of the chosen people."[60] It may be, especially in view of the relation of the Holy Spirit to the *Shechinah* in Jewish literature,[61] as well as the later equation of Spirit and Wisdom, that James also identified the Spirit with Wisdom, or at least equated Wisdom with the *fruit* of the Spirit—possibilities that have been canvassed from time to time. "If some works have a wisdom Chris-

59. Thus in Gen. 1 "the Spirit of God was moving upon the face of the waters," and in Ps. 33:6 the heavens were made "by the word of the Lord . . . by the breath of his mouth"; see also Job 34:14; Ps. 104:30. In Prov. 8:22-31, however, no less prominence is given to Wisdom; see also Wisd. 7:22; 8:6; 9:17f.: "Whoever learnt to know thy purposes, unless thou hadst given him wisdom and sent thy holy spirit down from heaven on high? Thus it was that those on earth were set upon the right path, and men were taught what pleases thee; thus were they preserved by wisdom" (NEB). Texts like these, which could easily be multiplied, show that, though not identical, the Spirit and Wisdom are often presented as playing similar roles or, as in the last quoted text, a joint role, in creation and salvation. So in the Midrash it is stated that Solomon's wisdom was the Holy Spirit who was guiding him (Genesis R. 85). So the Divine Wisdom takes the role of the pillar of cloud and of fire in the Exodus from Egypt (see Wisd. 10:17); in Isa. 63:14, however, it is "the Spirit of the Lord" that "gave them rest." So in Ex. 15:8 the waters were piled up by "the blast of thy nostrils" (KJV).

60. *The Plastic Age of the Gospel*, p. 132; see also U. Luck, "Weisheit und Leiden zum Problem Paulus und Jakobus," *ThLZ* 92.4 (1967): 253ff.; Hoppe, pp. 44ff., 98.

61. On James's *Shechinah* theology, see our interpretation of the divine "glory" (Jas. 2:1), pp. 275f.; also on the rabbinic interchanging of the word *Shechinah* and the Holy Spirit, a notion with which James was probably familiar, see, with references, Newton, *The Concept of Purity at Qumran and in the Letters of Paul*, p. 133, n. 27.

tology," says P. H. Davids, for example, "James has a wisdom pneumatology, for wisdom in James functions as the Spirit does in Paul."[62] Admittedly, however, this is difficult to establish.

By contrast, Zenos thinks that the context points rather more vaguely to "a complex of mental and emotional energies constituting an urge toward an ideal,"[63] and that that urge is ambivalent in both origin and nature. In his anxiety to show that James in 1:5, 3:13, 15, 17 is using "wisdom" as a code word, practically equivalent to "Spirit," implying a Palestinian setting for the Epistle, J. A. Kirk adopts (for us) a confessedly extraordinary translation of 4:5f.[64] The congruent Spirit/Wisdom texts are useful but have long been common knowledge, and James got even them from previous writers.

The voice of a common tradition sounds in the verbal congruences in Jas. 3:17 and Wisd. 7:22-24, but even more significant is the community of thought in the two writers. It is from the Hebrew OT, and more particularly the thought reflected in the Dead Sea Scrolls, especially 1QS 4:1ff. but also 1QS 3:13–4:26, however, that James drew his example for a more practical application of the thought of God's Torah than we find in that passage from the Book of Wisdom.

The entire bent of the Epistle of James is practical and communal.[65] Wisdom comes down from the throne of God in heaven to dwell among us, helping us to endure *peirasmoi* (1:5), teaching us the divine truth (3:1), and training us to be worthy members of the Christian fellowship. But in James, so mindful of the OT, we shall not expect much theoretical advance toward the later identification of Wisdom with the Holy Spirit.[66] "While the Gospel is pre-eminently the divine gift of wisdom,"says B. W. Bacon, "wisdom is not personified in the Epistle of James, but (like, we may add, the Torah) is conceived primarily as a system of humanitarian ethics"[67] (see also 3:13–4:17). This

62. Pp. 55f.; also pp. 152, 154.

63. *The Plastic Age of the Gospel*, p. 132.

64. "The Meaning of Wisdom in James: Examination of a Hypothesis," *NTS* 16 (1969): 24-28.

65. See R. B. Ward, "The Works of Abraham," *HTR* 61 (1968): 283-90, where, as in his unpublished thesis (see p. 290), James's significant emphasis on communal concern is noted. See our remarks on p. 235, n. 84.

66. See Kirk, *art. cit., NTS* 16 (1969): 24-28; Cadoux, p. 69; Windisch, p. 26; W. Bieder, "Christliche Existenz nach dem Zeugnis des Jakobusbriefes," *ThZ* 5 (1943): 111ff.; R. Obermüller, "Hermeneutische Themen im Jakobusbrief," *Biblica* 53 (1972): 237; also J. D. G. Dunn, *Christology in the Making* (1980), pp. 134ff.

67. *Encyclopaedia Britannica*[11], XV, 146. See U. Wilckens, *sophia, TDNT,* VII, 498ff.

concept of wisdom is most nearly like that of Proverbs and Ecclesiasticus, recalling also a rabbinic notion of redemptive wisdom "coming down from the Father of lights" as "the Word of truth" and producing "a kind of firstfruits of his creation." This idea of heavenly Wisdom, equated with the Messianic Torah of perfect liberty, is paralleled in the Wisdom Hymn of Baruch 3:29ff., in particular v. 37, where we read, "wisdom appeared on earth and lived among men" (NEB). In later Jewish literature, including Qumran[68] and Paul (see 1 Cor. 2:4-6), wisdom is also linked, sometimes eschatologically, with perfection. Here we detect a certain tension between wisdom as a gift to the "wise" (righteous)[69] in the present age and its full realization in the Messianic Age.

But James shows no knowledge of Paul's concept of the heavenly redemptive Wisdom as the preincarnate Spirit of Christ, who for Paul is both Wisdom and Word.[70] Though the "Word" in James is not the same as that of Greek thought, an easy transition is possible once the "Word" has been equated with the heavenly Wisdom. Bacon shows that the description of Christ, according to Clement of Alexandria in that primitive product of the Syrian Church, *Preaching of Peter,* as the Word and Law, the logical end of James's Christology, illustrates how these two terms, applied in the Epistle of James to the Christian revelation, opened the door to such developments in Christology, perhaps very early on in the Jerusalem Church, linking it eventually with the Word in John.[71]

Yet even if Wisdom is never philosophically identified with Christ or the Spirit in the Epistle of James, we may speak of a functional or ethical identification, for some congruence does appear in their activities; thus, for all practical purposes, James's "works of wisdom" and Paul's "fruit of the Spirit" are the same. For James, as for Paul, wisdom is Christian wisdom and Christ is in a real sense the "Wisdom of God";[72]

68. See, e.g., 4 Ezra 8:52 (NEB), "For all of you, Paradise lies open, the tree is planted; the age to come is made ready . . . goodness and wisdom are brought to perfection." For other examples, with Dead Sea parallels, see U. Wilckens, *art. cit., TDNT,* VII, 503f.; Davids, GNC, p. 20.

69. U. Wilckens, *art. cit., TDNT,* VII, p. 503, n. 258.

70. For the notion of the preexistent Christ/Spirit/Wisdom in the NT as a whole, see R. G. Hamerton-Kelly, *Pre-Existence, Wisdom, and the Son of Man: A Study of the Idea of Pre-Existence in the New Testament* (1973); M. J. Suggs, *Wisdom, Christology and Law in Matthew's Gospel* (1970).

71. "The foundation is seemingly 1 Peter 1:23-25, adopted in James 1:18, 21; but the outcome is a Logos doctrine widely different from that developed in Asia under the influence of Paul" (Bacon, *Encyclopaedia Britannica*[11], XV, 146). See also our remarks on the Messianic Torah, pp. 283ff.

72. Bacon, ibid.; L. Dewar, *An Outline of New Testament Ethics* (1949), pp. 263f.

James's distinctive claim to authority rests on his devotion to the *verba Christi,*[73] especially the "wisdom sayings," emanating from Christ the Divine Wisdom, and his distinctive message is his exposition of the Christian ethic in terms of the wisdom of the messianic Torah.

TRUE WISDOM

Now if all true wisdom is the servant or ally of our aim to live according to God's will, it is self-evident that the attributes and qualities of true wisdom will be the same as those of the godly life. It is therefore not surprising but inevitable that James's panegyric of true wisdom should be nearly identical with the vocabulary of the many NT descriptions of the Christian life. Of a host of passages we mention only Gal. 5:22f.; Eph. 4:2; Phil. 4:8; Col. 3:13f.; 1 Tim. 6:11; 2 Tim. 2:25; and Tit. 3:2; and we find somewhat similar catalogues of virtues outside the Bible, for example, in the Scrolls (see 1QS 4).[74] In contrast to the false wisdom that is "of the earth, of this life, of the devil," James describes "the wisdom from above." Like love, this wisdom is not so much a single virtue as the bond that unifies many virtues, and, unlike the false wisdom, also unifies the community. The thought of wisdom, mentioned in 1:5, resumes in ch. 3 and reaches its climax in this panegyric.

Like Paul's Hymn of Love in 1 Corinthians, James's Hymn of Wisdom is integral to the entire Epistle and is certainly composed with equal skill, displaying symmetry and many other similarities. But there are also significant differences:

1. The two words with identical endings *(hagnē . . . eirēnikē),* both in contrast to the false wisdom and recalling (as do all the adjectives) qualities associated with Christ, namely, spiritual purity (1 Jn. 3:3) and robust, creative pacifism (Mt. 5:9);[75] contrast the results of zeal and partisanship, division, strife, and murder (4:1).
2. Then there are two words with another ending, similar in rhythm and sound *(epieikēs . . . eupeithēs)* and meaning "humane," yielding from strength (not weakness) to the wisdom of others, and also "con-

73. Rendall, p. 51. "Could it be," asks B. R. Halson, "that in one school of catechists a 'Wisdom-Christology' was preserved by casting the ethical teaching of Jesus in the mould of the Wisdom tradition, and that we discover this school in the Epistle of James?" ("The Epistle of James—Christian Wisdom?" *StEv* IV = *TU* 102 [1968]: 308-14). So, too, H. Preisker, "At any rate 'the wisdom from above' *(hē de anōthen sophia)* is a christological phrase, and the attributes mentioned all refer to Christ as depicted in the Gospels . . ." (art. *epieikeia, TDNT,* II, 590, n. 4).

74. See, e.g., the table in Davids, p. 54, with a list of "community-preserving virtues" in Jas. 3, 1QS 4, Mt. 5, and Gal. 5.

75. Clogg, *An Introduction to the New Testament,* p. 28, n. 5.

ciliatory," yielding in this instance to proper persuasion—twin qualities foreign to the false wisdom.

3. Then, too, there are adjectival phrases rather than straight adjectives and not a couple of rhyming nouns but a rhythmical balance, "full of compassion and good fruits" *(mestē eleous kai karpōn agathōn);* and the carefully chosen "good," linked with only the second noun. Whereas the false wisdom is narrow and restrictive, true wisdom is marked by a compassion or "lovingkindness"[76] that is catholic and all embracing[77]—of all the Beatitudes the fifth is surely supremely characteristic of Christ (Mt. 5:7). The mention of "good fruits," which is essentially compassion in action, reminds us that wisdom, like faith, is practical and useless unless it issues in deeds of love and peace.
4. Finally, there are the two similar long adjectives *(adiakritos . . . anypokritos),* both of which imply the prevalence of opposites: "undivided in mind" is James's way of reprobating "the man of divided mind" (1:6; see Christ's demand for "the single eye," Mt. 6:22f.), while "untainted with hypocrisy" rebukes sham and partiality, reiterating once more the need of sincerity, as exhibited especially by our Lord.

Evident also is the consummate artistry of the nine-word sentence (3:18) that crowns the preceding eulogy, namely, three three-word phrases, the first suspending the other two and the two being linked by "peace" at the beginning and end respectively. The art of the composition is such that it could almost be an independent literary unit, but examination shows that each element is directly related to a definite situation, to the entire Epistle, and most of all to Jesus Christ, "the Wisdom from above."

FALSE WISDOM

The dualistic description of the false wisdom as "earthly, natural, and demonic" and of its devastating consequences leaves no doubt as to the kind of wisdom James has in mind.[78] To be sure, it was clever and resourceful, debilitating in controversy, devastating for the community, employing all the tricks of the skilled debater to win its point and defeat its opponent.[79] The outstanding fact that emerges from the foregoing

76. R. Bultmann, *eleos, TDNT,* II, 483; also H.-J. Zobel, *ḥesed, TDOT,* V, 45ff.

77. Contrast, e.g., Judaism; see also W. Bousset, *Die Religion des Judentums* (1903), p. 189; S–B I, 205.

78. See 1QS 3:13–4:26 for striking Qumranic parallels.

79. Oesterley's masterly characterization (p. 455) may be quoted in full:

description is the emphasis placed on the unethical nature of this so-called wisdom. It is on this rather than on the minutiae of its teachings that James dwells. Is it possible that James is recalling and contrasting his own preconversion type of wisdom with the "Incarnate Wisdom" of the One with whom he worked at the carpenter's bench?[80]

A few writers have tried to maintain that the Epistle was specifically written to combat a late Gnosticism. For example, Schammberger sought to prove that the Epistle was a carefully unified anti-Gnostic polemic, of which he found what he calls "the clearest proof of Gnosticism" in the description of the false wisdom that, unlike the true, is said "not to descend from above."[81] Using late and, in our opinion, mostly inapposite parallels from post-apostolic books like Clement of Rome and the Shepherd of Hermas coupled with quotations from Jude, notably v. 19, Titus, and certain Pauline epistles, Schammberger fastens on the three epithets "of this earth" *(epigeios)*, "of this life" *(psychikē)*, and "of the devil" *(daimoniōdēs)* used to describe the false wisdom in Jas. 3:15, as well as other Gnostic slogans *(Schlagwörter)* like "empty" *(kenos)*, "from above" *(anōthen)*, which he thinks show James is acquainted with and is attacking the Gnostic doctrine of a superior divine *(anōthen)* wisdom. A good example of the use of an inapposite parallel is Schammberger's citation of 1 Clem. 38:2 in connection with Jas. 3:13, mostly dealing with criteria for recognizing the difference between true and false prophecy.[82]

In our opinion, naïve and unquestioning use of such parallels is unfortunate. Questions of literary indebtedness and mutual dependence (especially in the case of Hermas) need to be settled before conclusions on date and situation may be reached. Further, in the light of recent study on pre-Christian Gnosticism, it is difficult to understand why Schammberger ignores the possibility of a much earlier Gnostic *Sitz im Leben* and fails to mention parallels from Sirach, the Rabbis,

---

"The wisdom referred to—acute argument, subtle distinction, clever conversational methods which took small account of truth so long as a temporary point was gained, skilful dialectics, the more enjoyed and triumphed in if the poisonous shaft came home and rankled in the breast of the opponent—in short, all those tricks of the unscrupulous controversialist which are nonetheless contemptible for being clever—this was wisdom of a certain kind."

80. See J. A. Robertson, *The Hidden Romance of the New Testament* (1920), p. 237.

81. *Die Einheitlichkeit des Jakobusbriefes im antignostischen Kampf* (1936).

82. With Tit. 1:16, on which see Ropes's careful evaluation and rejection (p. 244 *ad fin.*). See p. 35 for numerous quotations (e.g., *Mand.* 9.11; 11.3, 4, 6, 8, 11, 13, 17).

Philo, and other Jewish writers (and now Qumran) that are certainly not attacking late "libertine Gnosticism."[83]

In later years Hermas and others were to employ James's invective in their battle against Gnosticism, yet this was a corrective to doctrinal heresy while James speaks of ethical wisdom. At this period of church history doctrinal dispute is dormant. James is not particularly interested in purely theological concerns, nor does he attack doctrinal error *(Irrlehre)*. Conduct is his prime concern. We think that all those Greek philosophical adjectives in Jas. 3:13ff. *are* related to a particular contemporary situation affecting James. Classical Greek from Plato onward has "of the earth" *(epigeios)* in the literal sense[84] (contrast, e.g., "marine" biology);[85] good instances of *epigeios* are Jn. 3:12 and (very much in point) Phil. 3:19.

Here, once more, Paul and James are complementary. We are sure that Phil. 3:19, which also uses *epigeios* (found only six times in the NT), is again directly aimed at those "sect-propagators" "whose glory is in their shame, whose aims are *earthly,*" just like the boasting and comprehensive evil of Jas. 3:14f. In Classical Greek *psychikos* means "pertaining to the *psychē,*" that is, life, not (of course) the Christian soul.[86] Here in James it means "pertaining to mere life as common to men and (other) animals." It is the opposite of *pneumatikos,* "spiritual," and so, oddly enough, has much the same force here as would have been conveyed by "carnal," namely "sensual" (KJV) or "animalis" (Vulg.).

Though apparently unknown in prior Jewish literature,[87] this quasitechnical term is introduced in a way that shows that the readers would know what it meant. Now Ropes cites *(inter alia)* 1 Cor. 2:14. Once more Paul and James are complementary. 1 Cor. 2:13 has another slap at "human wisdom," as does 1 Cor. 1, which we have already discussed. In 1 Cor. 2:13 human wisdom is contrasted with *ta pneumatika* (spiritual); and 1 Cor. 2:14 describes the professor of "human wisdom" (the "sect-propagator") as *psychikos,* the same adjective James uses in

83. See Schoeps, pp. 344f., and Windisch, p. 148, for a partial endorsement of Schammberger's view. Further, see Dibelius, p. 212; Mussner, p. 171; Schneider, *Die Briefe des Jakobus,* p. 26; also U. Wilckens, *sophia, TDNT,* VII, 525; Schlatter, pp. 234ff.

84. E.g., *The Republic* 8.546a; R. Morgenthaler, "Earth" *(gē), NIDNTT,* I, 518.

85. See LS, s.v.

86. See E. D. Burton's classic discussion *Spirit, Soul and Flesh* (1918), p. 50; also BAG, s.v. *psychikos;* Dibelius, pp. 210ff.; A. T. Lincoln, *Paradise Now and Not Yet* (1981), pp. 40f.; B. A. Pearson, *The Pneumatikos-Psychikos Terminology in 1 Corinthians* (1973); C. Brown, "Soul" *(psychē), NIDNTT,* III, 676ff.

87. See S–B III, 329.

3:15, reminding us of the modern pseudo-intellectual who, despite a usually moral character, is quite unspiritual.

Thus two of the epithets James employs are demonstrably associated with the contemporary situation, the "sect-propagators." After pointing out that the ending *-ōdēs* denotes (1) fullness and (2) similarity, Hort waters down the rendering "inspired by demons."[88] But James is not mealy-mouthed and this attempt is unjustified. It is axiomatic in the NT that demonic forces are responsible for all kinds of evil, even rebellion against God, and that this activity will increase in the last days.[89] So much for the lexicography of *daimoniōdēs*.

We would add, however, that no less than the first and second epithets it belongs to the campaign against the "sect-propagators." Their wisdom is the negation of the true, *anōthen* wisdom, and James feels so strongly about them that he uses here the strongest word he can think of to mark the contrast, the almost unique "demonic" *(daimoniōdēs)*.[90] He also says they are "false to the truth" (3:14), which may refer to a false estimate of their capabilities. More likely, he is warning his readers that "selfish ambition and arrogance lead people to put considerations about their own status even above those which concern the truth."[91] His vehemence is enough to convince me at least that he is condemning not just possibilities or probabilities but actualities. Of course, adjectives such as "pure" and "peaceable" in an account of wisdom might perfectly well be addressed to good Christians (see Gal. 5:22f.)[92] or to many other sorts of sinners than "sect-propagators."

This account of true wisdom, however, is expressly contrasted with false wisdom, and James is deliberately and expertly[93] using these epithets by way of contrast and rebuke to the "sect-propagators." In fact, we go further than Beasley-Murray:[94] we think it is more than "plausible," even obvious and demonstrable, that in 3:13-18 James is castigating actual "sect-propagators" of the sort that draw Paul's fire in 1 Cor. 1:10ff., discussed elsewhere in our comments on *eritheia*[95] and described (with

88. P. 84. See H. Bietenhard, "Demon" *(daimonion)*, *NIDNTT*, I, 450ff.

89. See 2 Thess. 2:9; 1 Tim. 4:1; Rev. 6:13f.; W. Foerster, *daimōn*, *TDNT*, II, 19.

90. Ropes, p. 248.

91. See A. C. Thiselton, "Truth" *(alētheia)*, *NIDNTT*, III, 888.

92. See W. Bieder, *art. cit.*, *ThZ* 5 (1943): 112 for a chart giving parallels between Jas. 3:17 and Gal. 5:22f.; also E. Kamlah, *Die Form der Katalogischen Paränese im Neuen Testament*. Wissenschaftliche Untersuchungen zum Neuen Testament 7 (1960), pp. 39ff.

93. *Pace* Dibelius, pp. 253ff.

94. *The General Epistles*, p. 33n.

95. See Adamson, p. 151.

rigorous penalties) in the Scrolls (1QS 5-6, 7, and 9). In 3:15, as we have also shown, it is even clearer that James's words are related to precisely the same situation of "sect-propagation."

We have mentioned previously that James and Paul are often complementary to each other.[96] Jas. 3:16, excellently interpreted by Hort, is another example:

> St. James has just used strong language respecting the professed wisdom of these teachers, and the reasonableness of his language did not lie on the surface, but had to be explained. *Hopou* and *ekei* express presence. Though wisdom is God's gift, it is also an energy of the human mind and heart. If jealousy and rivalry are present there, these other things inconsistent with a truly divine wisdom must be present there likewise.[97]

James, as we have said, here complements Paul's message in 1 Cor. 1:10-31, especially vv. 13-15, where Paul says that because of kindred dangers and consequences abhorrent to him (and, we should say, not primarily relevant in Jas. 3) he deliberately shunned the danger of even seeming to succumb to a danger that James—but not Paul in this place—calls *eritheia*.

Paul's passage shows that even the innocent teacher's name could be dragged into his converts' sectarian self-glorification. This fault, which experience of politics as well as religion shows to be a natural counterpart of a sectarian leader's vanity in collecting adherents, though no doubt present in the Christians of the Epistle of James, is not relevant to Jas. 3, which is expressly and primarily concerned with the true and the false "rabbi"; but the complementary relation of the passages in Paul and James is surely obvious and interesting.

This esoteric wisdom brings with it (says James) "unrest and every evil work," a phrase that might admirably sum up the activity of that "worldly wrangling crew," the Corinthian teachers:[98] the somewhat unfamiliar[99] *phaulos* means "worthlessness,"[100] while *akata-*

96. Perhaps the most important case is that of Christian liberty and the Old Law as found in Jas. 1:25; 2:12 complementary to Rom. 8:21; 1 Cor. 10:29; 2 Cor. 3:17; Gal. 2:4; 5:1, 13. Again, Gal. 2:10 provides a parallel to the high concern for the poor that is so clear in the Epistle of James.

97. P. 85.

98. See Moffatt, pp. 53f.

99. See Rom. 9:11; 2 Cor. 5:10, where some manuscripts and later Fathers read *kakon*.

100. So, e.g., the papyri, where the reference is to bad wine, not so much to moral evil. See J. H. Moulton and G. Milligan, *The Vocabulary of the Greek Testament* (1930), p. 665.

stasia[101] (see 1:8; 3:8) stands for any kind of unsettlement, as, for example, the disorders from the disputatious discussions in his churches. "The meaning here," observes Hort, "seems to be that the presence of jealousy and rivalry implies a disorderly state of mind leading to disorder of spiritual vision, so that everything is seen in a distorted and disarranged light, the true mark of wisdom being to discern the inward order of things."[102] Divorced from its usual political associations,[103] "anarchy" may best sum up James's idea here. It appears to represent the confusion produced by jealousy and rivalry, and is the opposite of that peace which is the mark of true wisdom.

The office of teacher, however, could readily be abused, for, as Ropes also points out, "It was plainly possible for a man who believed himself competent for the work to put himself forward and take up the activities of a teacher."[104] False pretenders to the name obviously abounded in the Apostolic Age; and the same is undoubtedly true in every age. Especially in the last century, any quack might call himself "Reverend," "Professor," or "Doctor." The thought certainly fits the construction—especially if we take *praÿtēti sophias* as a Hebraism meaning "a wise meekness."

The person who is "wise and understanding" must do something to show it (i.e., the fact that he is wise). His virtuous behavior (and his) will in this matter must be seen in his deeds. The test of wisdom is not knowledge but conduct. These deeds will be done in the spirit of meekness, and this—not arrogance or argument—is the mark of true wisdom.

"Overbearing pride and arrogance unfortunately often characterize the so-called educated person," notes Robert Mounce; "Superficial learning is proud that it has mastered so much, but true wisdom is humble both because there is so much yet to learn and because God is so much more than a computer-stocked answer man."[105] Meekness (not weakness) is the absence of contentiousness, self-control rooted in the confidence that, with God's help, truth will prevail, the virtue that courageously cares for truth and those who differ from us more than our own self-interest.

101. See A. Oepke, *akatastasia, TDNT,* III, 446f.; H. Beck, C. Brown, "Peace" *(eirēnē), NIDNTT,* II, 776ff.

102. P. 85.

103. See the citation from E. Hatch, *Essays in Biblical Greek* (1889), p. 4 in Ropes, p. 249.

104. P. 227.

105. "The Marks of an Educated Person," *Christianity Today* 33.25 (1979): 24; also, with examples, L. T. Johnson, "Friendship with the World/Friendship with God: A Study of Discipleship in James," in *Discipleship in the New Testament,* ed. F. J. Segovia (1985), p. 183, n. 66.

Genuine wisdom, then, is essentially practical, exemplified in the virtuous life, never rude and harsh, and always "peaceable." The Jews were notoriously zealous (Acts 21:20), and this, as Jas. 3:14 shows, sometimes produced harmful results; indeed, if the letter were addressed to *unconverted* Jews, this might be its main purpose, namely, to awaken them from a blind unbelief based on "party spirit."[106]

In the NT *zēlos,* depending on its motive, may have a good or an evil sense. Classical authors generally do not use it in the evil sense,[107] but Jas. 3:14 does: "But if you have contentious zeal and the accumulation of adherents in your heart, do not boast and lie against the truth [but repent]."[108] "Contentious" (or, here, controversial) is not a bad literal translation of *pikron* (contentious, as contrasted with peaceable, gentle, and "unquarrelsome"); and along with the epithet James here adds to make it clear that, as in the Acts and Paul, he is using *zēlon* pejoratively (see Jas. 3:16), "zeal" will be adequate. If wisdom includes "striving after the best ends, as well as the using of the best means . . . and mental excellence in its highest and fullest sense" (Trench), then "contentious zeal" proves its absence.

With "zeal" James combines "ambition" *(eritheia)* in a way that recalls Paul's similar combination to describe the intrigues of the Judaizers (Gal. 5:20; see also Rom. 2:8; 2 Cor. 12:10; Phil. 1:17; 2:3). The word came to be used not merely for securing support by bribery, but for seeking to have a following with which to advance one's glory, pride, profit, pleasure, or any other personal interest or ambition.[109] "This all points," writes Hort, "to the personal ambition of rival leader-

106. See J. H. Moulton, *art. cit., Peake's Commentary* (1931), p. 904.

107. See Hort, p. 81; A. Stumpff, *zēlos, TDNT,* II, 881; H.-C. Hahn, "Zeal" *(zēlos), NIDNTT,* III, 1166f.; L. T. Johnson, "James 3:13–4:10 and the *Topos Peri Phthonou,*" *NovT* 25.4 (1983): 333ff.

108. Since we consider it more important to make ourselves clear in too many words than less than clear in the right number, we offer, in addition to this almost literal version, the following: "But if zeal for triumph in controversy and if ambition to accumulate adherents rule your heart. . . ." On the antithesis of truth and lie see U. Becker, H.-G. Link, "Lie" *(pseudomai), NIDNTT,* II, 473.

109. In Homer *erithos* means a hired laborer, e.g., agricultural, and later "women servants spinning wool." Aristotle shows a further development, saying, in *Politics* 5.2.9, that constitutions may change without factious strife *(aneu staseōs),* owing to election intrigue *(dia . . . tas eritheias),* as at Heraea," where apparently they changed from election to lot (as a method of appointing councillors and the like) because, before this change, they had been in the habit of selecting *tous eritheuomenous,* i.e., those who had secured support by bribery or other ways of currying favor. So Suidas equates *eritheuō* with *dekazesthai,* the common word for political bribery. See Hort, pp. 81f.; Dibelius, p. 209; F. Büchsel, *eritheia, TDNT,* II, 660f.

ships. . . . There is no real evidence for 'party spirit,' 'faction', etc., i.e., for the vice of the followers of a party: *eritheia* really means the vice of a leader of a party created for his own pride: it is partly ambition, partly rivalry."[110] So James may be envisaging these careerists, Judaizing pretenders who worked against Paul, possibly even those of the so-called "James party":[111] far from serving the truth their disputatiousness simply denied it. This bragging and lying, which James calls "this wisdom," is the very antithesis of wisdom.

CONCLUSION

To James the authentic Christian life-style is the way of true wisdom, which yields "the fruit of the Spirit." This is the antithesis of the false wisdom, which is "earthly, natural, and demonic." Unlike the wisdom from above that is intrinsically good, the false wisdom is evil in its nature, resulting in demonic division, unrest, and every evil work. To deduce a late date for the divisiveness of this church, however, is quite unsound. Paul was faced with precisely the same problems at Corinth as were the Covenanters at Qumran, who, as we know, had their own problems, especially with the "Wicked Priest" and the "Spouter of Lies."

Indeed, according to W. L. Knox, the situation described in the Epistle of James corresponds precisely with that in the early church at Jerusalem.[112] In regard to these Jerusalem factions, it is impossible, despite recent studies,[113] to reach unquestioned conclusions. It is sufficient to note with F. F. Bruce that "there is much that must be read between the lines of Luke's account."[114] We cannot agree with Ropes, on 3:15 *ad fin.*, ". . . not the substance but the temper. James is not attacking systems of false teaching." We would not quibble about what is or

110. P. 82.

111. Gal. 2:12; 2 Tim. 3:6. See also Davids, p. 153 *sub fin.*

112. "It is only as the expression of the attitude of the primitive Church at Jerusalem that the Epistle of St. James becomes intelligible. It stands for extreme and sometimes rather formal piety, of which we have no trace elsewhere in the New Testament. No document is more vigorous in denouncing sin (cf. 4:4-8; 5:1-6), yet the sins denounced in it amount to no more than anger, respect of persons, quarreling, presumptuousness (conceived in a very formal manner), riches and swearing" (*St. Paul and the Church of Jerusalem* [1925], p. 21, n. 44). See also Rendall, p. 45.

113. See, e.g., with references, J. J. Scott, Jr., "Parties in the Church of Jerusalem as seen in the Book of Acts," *Journal of the Evangelical Theological Society* 18.4 (Fall 1975): 217-27.

114. *Peter, Stephen, James and John* (1979), p. 99.

is not a "system"; but from what we have said it must be clear that James and Paul are attacking both what the "sect-propagators" are saying and the personal vanity and ambition that Ropes calls "temper."[115] Indeed, it is axiomatic in James and Paul (and some others) that that "temper" cannot see or tell the truth; 2 Tim. 3:8, "they cannot pass the tests of faith" (NEB) *(adokimoi peri tōn pistin),* complements Jas. 1:6a, "in faith" *(en pistei),* and 1:3.

The faults condemned are those of professedly religious people, and the only disquieting thing is the attempt to shift responsibility for their failure on to God.[116] Not discernible is late speculative Gnosticism, although an incipient Gnosticism is most probable;[117] worldly possessions, not "knowledge," are destroying the brotherhood. Nor are there those warnings against false teachers found in some other NT books; Jas. 5:19f. almost certainly applies to ethical, not intellectual lapses. Strife seems to be rooted in personal jealousy, perhaps in the desire to become "teachers," and not in doctrinal differences. The sins here denounced—snobbery, oppression, strife, hypocrisy, greed—do not flatter this church. This objection has been satisfactorily dealt with by Mayor, who cites the unhappy moral record of other congregations in the early church as proof that the experience of James's readers was not exceptional.[118]

Quite unwarrantable, therefore, is the assumption that James's description of such disputatious wisdom implies a late date for our Epistle. His condemnation of the esoteric wisdom as "earthly, natural, and demonic" strikes at the root of its evil—not only its worldly aims and its exploitation of human weakness and folly, but also its devilish selfishness. James dwells on this (3:13; 4:9) rather than on any minutiae of its doctrines or technique.

e. Salvation

"In the final analysis, being a Christian can never be described as a form of living; one must have trust in the Word from Christ that produces Christian existence, to be sure, trust only in the evident and concrete Word. James knew that basically too; this became clear finally in his astonishing word about the judging of the Law (4:11f.). Thus, in

115. See 2 Tim. 3:8f.
116. Jas. 1:13ff.
117. See Adamson, p. 21.
118. Pp. cxxviiiff.

spite of the empirical focus of his parenesis, James belongs quite justifiably to the New Testament."

L. Goppelt, *Theology of the New Testament,* II (1982), 211

We propose to show that there is no conflict, no controversy, no contradiction, and no incompatibility between James and the rest of the church on the subject of faith and works in the life of the Christian. Are works of a certain kind indispensable for salvation? No.

Between the stirrup and the ground
Mercy I asked, mercy I found.[1]

The traditional Christian doctrine on faith and works, sin and salvation, is that even if I have committed murder, *if I repent,* though only at the foot of the scaffold, it will suffice—if both my repentance and my faith in God's mercy are genuinely sincere. We do not think it can be denied, except perhaps by Luther, that Paul holds this view and that it is shared by James. Luther condemned James as contradictory to Paul on the power and duty of faith, on which (according to Luther) Paul had learned that Christians strongly insisted, and so (according to Luther) he does.

Here Luther's allegations are plainly disproved by Jas. 5:14-16, where, though confession is not expressly mentioned until v. 16, probably confession and certainly penitence are implied in the situation; at any rate, the remission of sins (which Paul more emphatically than anyone else declares to be the essence of salvation) mentioned in v. 15 is not conditional on the sick man's past or prospective performance of any works. About 55 percent of Eph. 4–6, for example, is devoted to "works." Faith is no less important—in fact, *vital*—for James than it is for Paul: a person's Christianity begins with an act of faith, namely, his acceptance of the Word of truth and the promise of salvation, along with the duty of conduct that attends that faith (see, e.g., 2:1ff. or 3:13-18).

CHRIST'S NEW CREATION

True Christianity is from our first submission to God until our death "faith operating in love" (Gal. 5:6). We think that this and other passages (e.g., Phil. 2:12f.; Col. 1:27; 1 Thess 1:3; 2:13) contain embry-

1. From William Camden, 1551-1623, "Remains. Epitaph for a Man Killed by Falling from His Horse," *The Oxford Dictionary of Quotations* ([3]1979), p. 128, no. 5.

onic elements of the idea that in its fuller development figures so notably in the discussion of the Word in Jn. 1:1-5, 14. We certainly agree that James was "a theologically minded person,"[2] for too hastily we dismiss James as "no theologian."[3]

Jas. 1:21-25 shows the same perception as Paul's 1 Thess. 1:13, that the *logos* is not only a message but also an activating Spirit. As Rachel Henderlite puts it, "The Word is not one who merely speaks. He is one who in speaking empowers. The Word, being dynamic, cannot be professed by the believer unless in the believer this profession is embodied in action. For a word not accompanied by action is obviously not the Word of God."[4] The meaning and force of James's "implanted" *(emphyton)* must be taken into account. It is not a bit of otiose tautology, duplicating "receive" *(dexasthe);* rather, it is dynamic and looks forward to the specification "which is able to save your souls."

The cryptic brevity of Jas. 1:18 is charged with the common doctrine of the apostles. "For by 'the Word' James evidently means him who reveals the will of God," notes Henderlite; "but he obviously means also him who brings salvation. The Word is dynamic. His very revelation was by an act. He did not merely speak to man. He became man and lived an active life among men."[5] This verse is closer to Johannine thought than the NEB seems to indicate: "Of his set purpose, by declaring the truth, he gave us birth to be a kind of first fruits of his creatures"; thus we must interpret it in harmony with our belief that James was writing for Christian Jews, that 1:1 and 2:1 are not spurious, and that when, in common with the apostles who use the term, James speaks of this "begetting," he is not thinking of human creation in Genesis or of the Jews as God's "first fruits," but of the Christian's regeneration by his reception of the truth in Christ.[6]

Yet the theory of some commentators that Jas. 1:18 refers to the

2. L. Morris, *New Testament Theology* (1986), p. 315.

3. See Scaer, pp. 15, esp. 60f., whose high view of James's theological prowess is similar to ours. See also our previous remarks, pp. 78f.

4. R. Henderlite, "The Epistle of James," *Interpretation* 3.4 (1949): 471.

5. P. 471.

6. The conflicting view is, of course, maintained by those who hold that the Epistle of James is a non-Christian or even pre-Christian document, e.g., Spitta and Meyer (who also sees a tribal reference to Reuben in *aparchē* [pp. 76, 268]; on this see Ropes's most effective reply [p. 166]); but it is also shared by distinguished advocates of the Christian origin of the Epistle, e.g., Hort, Rendall, Cadoux, and Elliott-Binns. Preferring a mythical cosmological setting, C. M. Edsman found three creation motives *(Schöpfungsmotive)* in 1:18: (1) act of will; (2) birth; (3) deed of a mediator ("Schöpferwille und Geburt Jac. 1:18. Eine altchristliche Kosmologie," *ZNW* 38 [1939]: 44).

creation of humanity needs some attention. Properly understood, it is said to give a clear, coherent argument, with an obvious relevance in "firstfruits"; and *pace* Ropes, there is, it is also said, a close connection "between the verse and Philo's figure . . . of the generative word of God."[7] In 1:17 the perfection of God's gifts and the constancy of his nature embrace all mankind in his benevolence; so, it is argued, does the specific example.

He begot us by the Word of truth. Ropes quotes a scholiast's remark on Euripides, *Orestes* 96, that *aparchē* (Heb. *t^erûmāh*), "firstfruits," a figure, he says, not very common in Jewish thought but with Greek writers more frequent in a figurative sense, "was not merely of that which was first in order but of that which was first in honour."[8] Human beings have this priority in honor, shown (a) in the metaphor, "begot," making us children of God, and (b) in the gift of truth, by the Word of truth. So we might say that God made lions and tigers "by the word of strength," or "by the word of his power" *(to rhēmati tēs dynameōs autou)*. Christ is the strength and stay of all creation (Heb. 1:3).

God created us with reason and the animals with instincts only. Reason is essentially the perception and coordination of truths; truth is beyond the scope of instinct. So James would certainly have held. The power of appetite for truth that God has given to us and not to the rest of his creation is a prime example of his good gifts to us, carrying with it, as James says, a primacy of honor over the rest of creation.

James continues, in effect: "Therefore [having this power and appetite and duty for truth, having this faculty bestowed on you in your creation], be swift to hear, slow to speak. That obviously is the way to get to know more and more truth: you must not be loquacious." And he adds, "Do not get involved in angry controversies, as so many professors of wisdom are prone to do" (3:13-18). Angry controversies do not foster (the truth of) God's righteousness. (Truth, wisdom, and righteousness overlap each other greatly in this sort of thought.) So, opening your ears, as I urged you, "accept the implanting of the Word [used proleptically of OT and NT truths], which is able to save your souls."

As to the arguments for man's creation, briefly:

(1) Moule's explanation of the omitted article with "Word of truth" is conclusive.[9]

7. P. 167.

8. P. 167.

9. *An Idiom Book of New Testament Greek* (1953), pp. 115, 117. Hort's statement (p. 32) that James "never indulges in lax omission of articles" should be read in the light of his own explanation of the article absent from Jas. 1:1 (see p. 1); also Mayor, *Appendix: Further Studies in the Epistle of St. James* (1913), p. 17.

(2) The objection to "creations" *(ktismatōn)* for men *(anthrōpōn)* instead of the created world has even less force: in the NT this verb "create"[10] is used of the general creation, but it is also used of the first creation of humans (1 Cor. 11:9; possibly Col. 3:10). In these two places, there is no express mention of both "the old man" and the new; and the word is apt, being normally associated with the creation of "the old man" but inspired with new meaning when applied to the new. This deepening of meaning is explicitly marked by *kata theon* in Eph. 4:24, and by *en Christō Iēsou* in Col. 2:10; in Col. 3:10 the marks of the new creation are again explicitly mentioned, in contrast to the old. In Eph. 2:15, *ktisē* is not used of regeneration, but echoes *ho poiēsas* of the previous verse: "who has made the two [Gentiles and Jews] one."

Another excellent example of the combining of the old and the new is Rom. 8:19ff., where Paul pictures the whole creation *(ktisis)* groaning and travailing in expectation of the revealing of the sons of God. In Eph. 2:10 *poiēma* is the proper sequel to *ergon;* it will be clearer in Latin than English if we may alter the Vulgate for this purpose: *non ex factis . . . ipsius enim sumus factura* ("Our works are not to *our* credit; for we are *his* work"). So the product of a machine tool is not to the credit of the tool but of those who made the tool. Even so, the author adds "in Christ Jesus" to the "created" that runs on from *poiēma.*

By "firstfruits" *(aparchē)* James means, like Paul in Rom. 16:15 (see also 1 Cor. 16:15; Rev. 14:1), that God with the Word of truth, the gospel, has given life to us free Christians (unlike the sin-bound men and women of the sinful world), to be the firstfruits of his creation, the true Israel, a *chef d'oeuvre* of the whole creative process. The term "firstfruits," frequently used of God's choice of Israel (Jer. 2:3; Ecclus. 36:20),[11] implies priority in quality as well as in time; and in the Greek writers (for the custom was not only Jewish) the figurative use of the word is far commoner than in Hebrew literature.[12] Windisch points out that since we were created last,[13] we could hardly be the firstfruits. The church is now the heir to Israel's prerogative and is the firstfruits of an offering that will be the whole of the redeemed universe,[14] "a temporary

10. BAG, s.v. *ktizō.*

11. "As the stack stands ready for the priest to come and take from it his Terumah, even so has the Holy One, blessed be He, made the world stand ready as a stack and lifted Israel out therefrom" (Ex. R. 31.9; see Philo, *On the Special Laws* 2.180).

12. Mayor, p. 64; *Further Studies,* pp. 16f.

13. Philo, *On the Creation of the World* 77, cited by Windisch, p. 10, and noted but not adequately answered by L. E. Elliott-Binns, "James 1:18: Creation or Redemption?" *NTS* 3.2 (1957): 153.

14. See C. E. B. Cranfield, *The Epistle to the Romans,* I (1975), 417f. for

down payment to be followed by the remaining members of the species."[15] Martin Luther frequently used Jas. 1:18, which the Vulgate translates "a kind of beginning of his creation" *(initium aliquod creaturae eius)*. So he says: "We are the firstfruits of creation only so far as we receive and have the firstfruits of the Spirit in this life."[16]

(3) The principle of coherence by which Hort tries to establish his case is sound,[17] and compels us to circulate "the Word of truth" (1:18) with hearers (v. 14), Word (vv. 21-23), and law of liberty (v. 25) rather than take it as an isolated reference to the word of God in the original creation of humans. Hort's objection is not consistent with a proper view of the sequence of thought in the whole of this passage, the logic of which, and the phraseology seen in this and the other *apothemenoi* parallels, is definitely as Christian as anything in Paul (e.g., Rom. 11:36 immediately preceding 12:1).

Certain consequences flow from the Word of 1:18, as is shown in the following verses, which also form part of the context. The Word is to be listened to, rooted in the heart, done and not only heard, and identified with the perfect law. "The law of which James speaks is the law of liberty, the royal law," comments Henderlite; "Like the Mosaic law it comes from God himself, who is Creator and Ruler of the world. But unlike the Mosaic law it is revealed and mediated through Jesus Christ."[18] It is difficult to see why, in speaking to Christians, James would suddenly introduce human creation.

More likely this verse contains one of the few more obviously distinctive Christian ideas in the Epistle. Ropes is right in emphasizing as "decisive," against the view of Spitta and especially Hort, that "the figure of begetting was not used for creation (Gen. 1:26 does not cover this)."[19] In fact, human knowledge of good and evil, which is tantamount to the gift of truth, came through another channel (Gen. 3:22), "whereas 'begetting' came early into use with reference to the

---

an excellent lexical discussion; G. Delling, *aparchē, TDNT,* I, 485f.; also H.-G. Link, C. Brown, "Sacrifice" *(aparchē), NIDNTT,* III, 416ff.

15. Dibelius, p. 106.

16. See P. Althaus, *The Theology of Martin Luther* (1966), p. 237, nn. 67, 68.

17. P. 32.

18. *Art. cit., Interpretation* 3.4 (1949): 471.

19. P. 166. See also K. H. Rengstorf, *gennaō, TDNT,* I, 669ff.; W. L. Knox, *Some Hellenistic Elements in Primitive Christianity* (1944), pp. 61f., 90ff.; S–B II, 421; E. Sjöberg, "Creation and New Creation in Palestinian Judaism," *ST* 4 (1950): 44-85; N. A. Dahl, "Christ, Creation and the Church," *The Background of the New Testament and Its Eschatology* (1956), pp. 422ff.

Christians, who deemed themselves 'sons of God.'" This idea of divine begetting in a person's existence has its roots in Greek, not in Jewish, thought.[20] We have already noticed that no NT author is more Greek than James.

THE DIVINE WORD

Decisive here, too, is the fact that "the Word of truth" is a *terminus technicus* for the "good seed" or the gospel,[21] acceptance of which leads to regeneration. James sees salvation as God's (not man's) work, observes Stagg, not as "deterministic" but as a possibility of a new kind of existence, a certain firstfruit of his creatures, opened up to those who will receive his "perfect gift."[22] We believe that "the Word of truth" in James (as in other NT writings)[23] is based on the ideas that Philip Carrington has tentatively assigned to a primitive Christian "catechism" for use in the instruction of early Christian converts for baptism.[24] It is hard to understand those who believe that this refers to humanity as "the crown and promise of the original creation" and that James knows nothing of any new "creation" in Christian theology;[25] that was "later." Are we therefore to assume that James did not know as much as Paul (e.g., Eph. 2:10) or as the Fourth Gospel ("above" in Jas. 1:17; compare Jas. 3:3—an odd coincidence?)—that, in short, he worked and thought in a theological vacuum and was a kind of early Christian oddity? We cannot see that it reflects any epoch except that of primitive apostolic Christianity.

"The Word of truth," like the perfect law of liberty (1:25; 2:12) and the royal law of love (2:8) with which, along with "the implanted Word" (1:21), it is to be identified, is the Christian gospel. For James "truth" means "Word" or "Torah," which are essentially synonymous. The Torah, like the Word, is the effective coefficient of the new cre-

20. So Clement, *Stromateis* 5.2. Cited by Ropes, pp. 166f.; also G. W. H. Lampe, *A Patristic Greek Lexicon* (1961), p. 199.

21. Mayor, p. 63. See also above, pp. 355f.

22. F. Stagg, "Exegetical Themes in James 1 and 2," *RevExp* 64.4 (1969): 396; see also Mussner, p. 103.

23. E.g., Rom. 10:13-15; Col. 1:15; Eph. 1:13; 2 Tim. 2:15; 1 Pet. 1:23. See also Selwyn, pp. 150f.; Moffatt, p. 21. For similar Jewish expressions, see, e.g., Test. Gad 3:1; Ps. 119 (118):43; Neh. 9:13; see also 4 Ezr. 19:13; Mal. 2:6; Prov. 22:21; Eccl. 12:10.

24. *The Primitive Christian Catechism* (1940), pp. 82ff., where we find *(inter alia)* mention of the personification of good and evil forces in the universe. See also Scaer, p. 60.

25. See, e.g., Elliott-Binns, *art. cit., NTS* 3.2 (1957): 150.

ation.[26] We may say that *logos* tends to mean a law of being and thinking, and *nomos* a law of conduct. Like the Greeks, James tended to have a functional view of virtue. The "truth" is the truth revealed by Christ in his life and teaching, especially in the Christian Torah of love. When we say that "the Word of truth" is the gospel, we mean, not the mere narrative of Jesus' sayings and doings, but the statement of the truth of God, of the truth in and flowing from God, the truth that makes us free, of which Christ said: "I am the way and the truth and the life. No one comes to the Father except through me" (Jn. 14:6, NIV).

As in the rest of the NT (as well as the OT), the end of James's logic is the *reward:* "Accept the implanted Word; *for that is able to save your souls*" (1:21). 1 Thess. 1:5f.; 2:13 illustrate the meaning of effective acceptance. It is the difference between *receiving* the gospel and *accepting* it as truth on which to act. Calvin's attempt to make *emphytos* proleptic is unnecessary. Possibly James is referring to the Parable of the Sower (Mk. 4:20; 8:13). Mayor is right in saying that we must take *emphytos logos* as "the rooted Word," that is, a word whose property it is to root itself like a seed in the heart (see Mt. 13:3-23; 15:13; 1 Cor. 3:6), which, in Christ, "opens a hope and a history."[27] Though *emphytos* often means "natural"—in contrast, say, to the "taught" (*didaktos;* e.g., Plato, *Eryxias* 398), the "extraneous," or the "acquired"—it may also connote "deep-rooted" as opposed to "superficial."[28]

The implanted Word is dynamic and saving, in activity and result

26. So Mt. Sinai is called "the Mother of Israel," for by "the precious instrument of creation" given there, God created Israel "sons of God" (M. Aboth 3.15). Again, we learn that God is said to have created the world by and for the sake of Torah (Ex. R. 47.3; Gen. R. 12.2), all souls, even those still to be created, being present at the revelation on Mt. Sinai (Ex. R. 28.6); called "my mother" because "there Israelites were made, infants a day old." Using the Song of Solomon 5:6, Rabbi Levi interprets: "my soul departed as he spoke." "He" means heard God's word (based on Dt. 5:21). At this impact "my soul departed . . ."; they died. As proof he cites Song 5:6. The Torah then pleaded with God to restore them to life and God did so. They were "reborn." His prooftext is Ps. 19:8, "God's Torah is perfect, restoring the soul," i.e., renewing life (Shemot [Exodus] Rabbah 29.4). Corresponding to the Torah given at Sinai is the perfect Torah, the messianic "law of liberty" given by Christ, the Sermon on the Mount, or, as it is called here, "the word of truth," the divine instrument of regeneration.

27. P. 66; J.-L. Blondel, "Theology and Paraenesis in James," *Theology Digest* 28:3 (Fall 1980): 255.

28. Polybius, *History* 2.25. See Ropes, p. 172. Ropes's other comment on *dexasthe* (p. 172, lines 2-5) would be apt and true if amended thus: "Thus *(dexasthe)* refers (like *dexasthe eis tēn kardian sou* in Dt. 30:1) not to the mere initial acquaintance with the gospel, preached and heard (see *emphyton*), but to effective acceptance of the gospel truth."

recalling John's *logos* and even, in some respects, Paul's *en Christō*. "Thus, as with Paul, so with James," writes Henderlite, "the ethical demand rests on an indwelling power which enables one to live rightly. Paul, whose experience has been with the eternal living Christ, finds power from a mystic union with him; James, whose experience has been with the man Jesus, finds power in the dynamic conviction that God is as Jesus knew him to be, and that life must be lived in obedience and trust."[29] The Torah is said to be a fruitful seed that, when sown in the heart (Ezr. 9:31; see also 8:41), strikes deep as a root, spreading in all directions (Eccl. 12:11; Num. R. 14.4).[30] The Jews also regarded the Torah as saving and life-giving, the "spice" against the *yēṣer* (b. Baba Bathra 16a). By virtue of its messianic origin the law of liberty possessed a unique redemptive quality.

Later (v. 25) James goes on to speak of the law in a way that again suggests he regards "Logos" and "law" as synonymous. Whether Logos or law—and inevitably the source and substance of revelation seem to merge in James's thought—behind every concept lies the redeeming power of Jesus Christ: only he can save the soul. James may not mention Christ by name but this conviction is cardinal. Christ's Saviorhood, if not explicitly elaborated in the Epistle, is ever implied.

"SALVATION": A WORD STUDY

Words differing from each other in meaning often tend to merge or overlap at some points of their respective ranges of use; thus "liberty" may merge with "trespass," as when you say one has taken a liberty with you: "innocent" may mean "not sinful," or "not quite sane." I suggest that before going further we try to clear away some of the confusion that too often obscures the functions of "faith" and "works" in the Epistle of James in the matter of our salvation; and that we begin by examining the use of the word *sōzō* (and its derivatives) in Greek, and in its contrast with the word *asphalēs* (and its derivatives).

The primary (and usual) meaning of *sōzō* etc. (e.g., *sōtēria*) points to danger escaped—in a word, *deliverance;* but *asphalēs* and its derivatives nearly always denote the exclusion or absence of risk and

29. *Art. cit., Interpretation* 3.4 (1949): 472. Compare C. Vaughan's similar view: "To receive the word in the fullest sense is to so open the inner self to the influence of God's Word that its truth is transfused into the heart" (*James: A Study Guide* [1969], p. 36).

30. More implausibly, Oesterley, p. 433, suggests that *emphytos* may refer to the Jewish Torah, which was implanted, like wisdom, in God from the very "beginning" (*rē'šîṯ*).

danger—in a word, *security.* In Mt. 27:64-66 *asphalizō* and in Acts 16:23f. *asphalōs* and *ēsphalisato* by no means indicate salvation but the exclusion of risk, here of the removal of Christ's body and of two prisoners' escape.[31]

In contrast we get some notion of the meaning of *sōzō* and its derivatives from the pictures drawn, for example, in Ps. 69 (NIV), as a whole and particularly in vv. 1, 13, 14, 18, 29, 35, and 36 (see also Ps. 70:1, 4, 5 and 71:2, 4, 12, 18, 20, 23). I think we can safely *(asphalōs)* say that, although it sometimes indicates protection from the risk of possible danger (perhaps tomorrow), *sōzō* and its derivatives primarily and usually connote *rescue,* desired or achieved, from actual danger, in contexts like those of the Psalms just cited. In Tit. 3:5 *esōsen* is usually and correctly enough translated "He saved us"; but it might be more helpful if we said "He rescued us."

Paul himself never forgets (if we may use the Psalmist's metaphor) that he was near drowning in a sea of sin and was spectacularly rescued by Christ's appearing to him outside Damascus; and, however confidently he may allow himself to speak (he sometimes seems to border on the smug self-complacency with which, at one time at least, some well-meaning evangelicals used to ask a stranger, "Are you saved?"—as if they were certain that they were *asphalēs* and that a place was irrevocably booked for them in heaven), nevertheless Paul does not really forget that although a man has been rescued from a sea of sin it is not impossible, but rather dangerously possible, that he may fall into it again, with fatal results.

1 Cor. 9:27 conclusively proves that Paul recognizes that any rescue ("salvation") from sin vouchsafed to converts to Christianity, on their first or any other penitence, is during their lifetime only conditional—conditional on their making every possible effort to maintain, and not lapse from, their Christian faith, and on their utmost possible (though, alas, never perfectly successful) efforts to match that faith with their conduct. There is all the difference between (as one evangelist put it) "knowing how to be saved" and "how to *do* it."[32] If by "Are you

31. "To be made secure," "make it secure," "made the grave secure," "keep them under close guard," "he . . . secured their feet in the stocks" (NEB). So in Acts 2:36 *asphalōs* means, not "with assurance of salvation" but "with assurance that this is true and that there is no risk of its being a lie"; "Let all Israel then accept as certain that . . ." (NEB). So in Phil. 3:1 *asphales* does not mean "leading to salvation" but "eliminating any risk that you may misunderstand or doubt my teaching therein"; "it is a safeguard for you" (NEB) or "a safe course." See C. Brown, "Firm" *(asphaleia), NIDNTT,* I, 663f.

32. See E. W. Hayden, *Preaching through the Bible* (1964), pp. 148f.

saved?" we mean definitely and irrevocably booked for heaven, Paul here plainly indicates that no one is "saved" until he is dead. For even if I never commit murder, theft, or adultery, how many days do I live completely without sinning, in thought, word, deed, or omission? Even in Ps. 69:35f. the rescue and rebuilding of Zion will have effect only so long as the next generations of inhabitants remain loyal to God.

The author of the Epistle to the Hebrews is equally explicit about this. In 5:9 he calls Christ "the source of eternal salvation for all who obey him" (NIV). We prefer, however, to make the meaning undoubtedly clear: "that continue to obey him." Then (6:1) he mentions the initial moment of the convert's Christianity, "the foundation of repentance from acts that lead to death, and of faith in God." But in vv. 4-8 he recognizes (with despair) the case of those who "have once been enlightened, when they have had a taste of the heavenly gift and a share in the Holy Spirit" (NEB) (compare the *emphytos logos* of Jas. 1:21 and the exordium of the gospel of his fellow disciple, John) and afterward "fall away," who "crucify to themselves the Son of God afresh" and whose "end is to be burned."

Except in deathbed cases, then, salvation is inchoate; this, of course, is clearer in Greek than in English. In 1 Cor. 1:18, the present tense of both *apollymenois* and *sōzomenois* is aptly used to express this limitation of meaning in the description of the two classes present at Christian homilies, namely, "those on their way to ruin" and "us who are on the way to salvation" (NEB). Note that in both cases the process is incomplete: the former class *may yet* repent and be rescued from their present servitude to sin, the latter *may yet* "fall away" (Heb. 6:6). In 1 Cor. 15:2 this limitation of meaning is marked not only by the present tense of *sōzesthe,* "You are in the process of being saved" ("which is now bringing you salvation," NEB), but also by two expressed conditions, "if . . ." and "unless. . . ."

Likewise in 1 Cor. 1:21 the aorist infinitive *sōsai* is synonymous with "rescue," and in 1 Tim. 1:15 exactly the same part of the same word, *sōsai,* is used to state that Christ Jesus came into the world to rescue sinners "of whom," says Paul, "I am chief. Howbeit . . . [*ēleēthēn,* v. 16], I obtained mercy"—"I was mercifully dealt with" (NEB). We hardly need mention Jas. 3:1 and 5:20—both in regard to the Judgment at which alone our final salvation or damnation will be determined, and the word *sōsei,* "will be rescuing his soul from death" (NEB).[33]

33. Only in Eph. 2:5 and 8 does Paul (assuming he was the author) use the perfect passive of *sōzō*. In v. 5 the three words *chariti este sesōsmenoi* are thrown parenthetically into the statement about God's action in rescuing them from their

Accordingly, salvation in the Epistle of James is conceived of in the fullest sense.[34] The OT speaks of "saving," but not much of saving souls.[35] The phrase in James, a Hebraism, appears already in the Gospels in a quasitechnical way (Mk. 8:35; Lk. 9:24; see also 1 Pet. 1:9). Although James might have written simply "save you" (1:21), it is unlikely in view of his solemn language in v. 20, and "here also he is emphasizing the thought of a salvation with external issues" (Mt. 10:20; 16:26).[36] Here, as elsewhere in the Epistle of James, the point of *sōsai* is to save in view of the rapidly approaching "Day of Judgment"[37] (see Acts 17:30f.).

This eschatological urgency is no less prominent in Paul, whose Christianity is a religion of conversion, which is simply the Hebrew word for repentance. The "moral achievement here and now" is not to be misunderstood as the achievement of moral conduct but of moral *purpose,* which, however frustrated by the flesh, is accepted by grace for salvation. The law gave us nothing to enable us to keep it; grace, no thanks to ourselves, makes good the defects of success if, like Paul, we sincerely try to do our best, and keep on trying. We believe that Paul

---

servitude to sin (see Eph. 2:1-22) and bringing them to life with Christ. We quote now Eph. 2:8-11 since we think it gives the Pauline philosophy of Christian salvation in a nutshell: "For it is by his grace you are saved, through trusting him; it is not your own doing. It is God's gift, not a reward for work done. There is nothing for anyone to boast of. For we are God's handiwork, created in Christ Jesus to devote ourselves to the good deeds for which God has designed us. Remember then your former condition." Neither in v. 5 nor in v. 8 does Paul contradict the doctrine of his statements elsewhere; he is not saying that these Ephesians are irrevocably booked for heaven. He is using the perfect exactly as it is used, e.g., of the woman in Mt. 9:22 or the man in Acts 4:9f.—of their rescue, bringing complete deliverance from their past disease. He is saying to the Ephesians that all that sinful past has ended; but he does *not* imply that their eternal salvation has been finally accomplished, any more than the perfect tense, *sesōstai,* and the adjective *hygiēs* in Acts 4:9f. exclude the possibility of subsequent illness. On the contrary, Eph. 2:10 shows what is yet to be done, and v. 11 reminds them of their recent miserable state. Furthermore, in v. 22 Paul is careful to indicate to them that the process of their salvation, however striking, is yet incomplete: "in him you too are being built together to become a dwelling in which God lives by his Spirit" (NIV). Similarly, in Acts 9:31 the NIV expresses the force of the tenses more clearly than the KJV: "Then the church . . . enjoyed a time of peace. It was strengthened; and encouraged by the Holy Spirit, it grew in numbers."

34. *Pace,* e.g., Ropes.

35. See C. Brown, "Redemption" *(sōzō), NIDNTT,* III, 208f.; also our discussion on the Jewish doctrine of the covenant and "covenantal nomism" (pp. 416f.).

36. Knowling, p. 30.

37. See J. Schneider, "Redemption" *(sōzō), NIDNTT,* III, 216.

would say (and virtually does say, 1 Tim. 5:8): "If you do not genuinely *try* to live rightly, you have not *begun to be saved.*" Apart from the sense of physical healing, the perfect of *sōzō* occurs in the NT only in Eph. 2:5 and 8. We think that the force there is anticipatory and that in any case it may be an argument for those who do not consider Paul to be the author of Ephesians; no view of these two verses is valid that tries to derogate from the plain force of Eph. 5:5.

All requisites of human conduct in this world are *pre*requisites; for salvation is not completed before the Judgment. Acquittal does not come before trial, and Paul, no less than James, is aware of that (1 Cor. 9:27). No game is won or lost until the final whistle blows. No soul is finally saved until the Last Judgment; hence James's gospel of faith continuing at work in hope of that final approbation (1:3, as emended). "Salvation is thus not propositional, transactional, or forensic," says Frank Stagg; "it is essential. It is renewal, transformation, or a new creation, brought about by a release within one of God's dynamic words, made possible through the channel of faith, i.e., trust or openness to God and to his people."[38] Dynamic faith, expressed in action—*magna efficacia,* Bengel calls it—puts the power *(dynamis)* of the divine Word into human life, so that the soul is saved at the Last Judgment.

THE LOGIC OF GRACE

The moral logic of God's philanthropic grace that we find here in the Epistle of James is the same throughout the OT as well as the NT.[39] By associating the idea of holiness with the idea of righteousness, the

38. Stagg, *art. cit., RevExp* 66.4 (1969): 402.

39. The moral logic of Christianity finds clear, but rather more sophisticated, expression in Heb. 10:11-31, the leading verses of which are 14, 19f., 24, 26; indeed, it is covered by v. 26 (NEB): "If we persist in sin after receiving knowledge of the truth, no sacrifice for sin remains: only a terrifying expectation of judgment and a fierce fire which will consume God's enemies." After ch. 11, the great chapter on faith exemplified in deeds of the past heroes, the rest of the Epistle (except the three last—personal—verses) goes on to exhort to Christian conduct. Notice 12:1-11, on *hypomonē;* 12:18-29, on the perils of recalcitrance; and 12:12-17, on the duty of peaceable and pure living. Note also the detailed rules of 13:1-19, and the conclusion, saying in effect: "May God, who gave his Son to die and rise again to make you his, make you perfect in every good work to do his will by the power of Christ." "Divinity" and "practice" are inseparable. The same moral logic is elaborated fully in Colossians. Ch. 1 and 2:1-15 state the work of Christ and the duty of faith, and barely mention the duty of conduct (2:6). 2:16-23 is against rules merely observed. Then 3:1-5 sets forth the true Christian standard, and 3:5–4:6 gives a code of Christian moral conduct; the rest of Colossians is personal.

eighth-century prophets, for example, gave the idea a new ethical content.[40] The holiness of God demands that all who are "holy," that is, belong to God, express his holiness in sound conduct (see Isa. 5:16; 6:1-5); failure to do this is viewed by Amos, for example, as profanation of God's holy name (Am. 2:6-8; compare Jas. 2:7). Righteous (just) dealing and living is an attribute of God in the OT as well as the NT, and *therefore* must also be displayed in man. Similarly, the Greeks, but according to their own lights, said that in man alone God planted "justice" *(dikē)*.[41]

In the same way, says James, God plants "the Word of truth" in those who hear the gospel; in such converts truth and righteousness are almost synonymous. Sin is a repudiation of grace (see Heb. 10:29, 31; 12:15, 22-25). Now every Christian sins. But the genuine Christian strives to resist sin, and by grace often succeeds. Furthermore, when we sin, we gain mercy by repentance. Other people sin and neither wish nor try to avoid sin or resist it; nor, having sinned, do they listen to God's call to repentance. Church congregations are full of such people. Christian renegades who revert to such love of sin excommunicate themselves (1 Cor. 6:8-11; 5:9-11). It is these renegades who come under the condemnation of Heb. 10:26, for they exclude themselves from the benefits of Christ's sacrifice (see v. 12) and make themselves enemies (see Jas. 4:4) whom he is waiting to destroy (Heb. 10:13).

The author of this Epistle was, we think, the Lord's brother, a Christian Jew of the first epoch of Christianity. At that time there was yet no full and final divorce between Christian Jew and Jewish non-Christian, and even Paul circumcised Timothy—in deference to the Jews (Acts 16:3). How then is the Christian James to be judged? By the discrepant company he keeps in the temple where he worships; by the OT he uses and, like Jesus, may quote; and by the Ten Commandments he observes? Or by this Christianity—which has created the discrepancy? The answer is obvious. Then is not his a "newly adopted" faith?

40. See, e.g., N. H. Snaith, *The Distinctive Ideas of the Old Testament* (1944), ch. III, "The Righteousness of God," pp. 51ff.

41. E.g., "You, Perses, should store away in your mind all that I tell you, and listen to justice, and put away all notions of violence. Here is the law, as Zeus established it for human beings; as for fish, and wild animals, and the flying birds, they feed on each other, since there is no idea of justice among them; but to men he gave justice, and she in the end is proved the best thing they have. If a man sees what is right and is willing to argue it, Zeus of the wide brows grants him prosperity. But when one, knowingly, tells lies and swears an oath on it, when he is so wild as to do incurable damage against justice, this man is left a diminished generation hereafter, but the generation of the true sworn man grows stronger" (Hesiod, *Works and Days,* 274-85, tr. Richmond Lattimore [1959]).

Are his "works" in that faith "the works of an old and abandoned system"?[42]

He who runs may read:

1:22. *But be doers of the Word and not merely hearers of it, deluding yourselves.*

23. *For if anyone is a hearer of the Word and not a doer of it, he is like a man observing the face of his mortal, physical birth (created being) in a mirror.*

24. *For he observes himself, and is gone, and immediately forgets what he was like.*

25. *But he who has bent over to look into the perfect law of liberty, and has stayed by it, since he has not been a hearer who forgets but a doer who acts, he shall be blessed in his doing.*

26. *If anyone among you thinks he is devout, and does not bridle his tongue but deludes his own heart, this man's devoutness is vain.*

27. *Devoutness pure and undefiled in the sight of God the Father is this, to visit the fatherless and widows in their affliction, and to keep oneself unspotted from the world.*

2:10. *For whoever observes the entire Torah but contravenes a single commandment becomes guilty of all.*

11. *For he who said, "Thou shalt not commit adultery," said also: "Do not kill." If you do not commit adultery but do kill, you become a transgressor of the law.*

12. *So speak and so act as those who will be judged in accordance with the law of liberty.*

We may summarize the sequence of thought so far as follows: v. 13 mentions certain false relations between God, man, and sin. Vv. 14 and 15 correctly connect man to sin. Vv. 16 and 17 correctly divorce God from sin. V. 18 connects the sinless God with Christians. Vv. 19ff., resuming the thought of v. 12, discuss the Christian's relation to God, the gospel, fellowmen, and sin. The exhortation of a previous verse to receive (hear) and not merely speak the Word is now safeguarded by the further contrast between hearing and doing.

HEARING AND DOING

Once more we have the moral logic of James. Like "faith," "hearing" the Word is a privilege that involves the responsibility of "works."[43] The

42. See Ropes, p. 205.

43. See G. Kittel, *akouō, TDNT,* I, 218; also W. Bacher, *Die exegetische Terminologie der jüdischen Traditionsliteratur,* I (1899), 189ff.; II (1905), 219ff.

OT is full of the contrast, expressed or tacit, between hearing and listening, between having the commandments and keeping them (see Dt. 5:27ff.; also Qumran, e.g., 1QS 2:25–3:12). The Talmud also asks: "Why were the Israelites compared to an apple tree? To teach you just as the fruit of the apple tree precedes its leaves, so did the Israelites give precedence to *'we will do'* over *'we will hearken.'*"[44] To hear the Word was not enough, for "merely hearers" (we prefer *akroatai monon;* here, as sometimes elsewhere, Bff. are right) had not really received the implanted Word, which can only grow in the soil of obedience. "Act on the Word, instead of merely listening to it" (Moffatt).

The Word is dynamic and finds valid expression only in action. "The conviction of God's power and righteousness," says Henderlite, "is given to man by the Word, who in the very act of revelation takes hold of the heart of man and gives him power to live the same righteousness."[45] The person whose religion allows him to hear without doing may seem devout, but in reality he is deluding himself. His religion is vain (see 1:26). Although "delude" *(paralogizomai)* can mean "deceive wilfully" (of others), here it means unwitting self-deception, that is, making a mistake. The OT also has the case of the person who hears God's Word but rejects it (e.g., Ps. 81:8-13)—like the parishioner of questionable character who confided his theological problems to John A. Hutton: "I have great difficulty about the deity of Christ." Replied Hutton: "But are you not a little weak, also, on the Ten Commandments?"[46]

James begins with the simple yet basic assumption that what he says is true, and that which is true must be practiced; indeed, for James "truth" is never academic, but practical and existential, and, like "the word of truth" itself, essentially redemptive. Respect for truth, therefore, is crucial. So James attacks self-deception, for as Jesus himself said: "The last shall be first, and the first last." His Epistle, like the rest of the Bible, is full of such antitheses: those in trial are to count themselves supremely happy; the humble man is to know that he is exalted; doers, rather than hearers, of the gospel are saved; the snob has "to begin with shame to take the lowest seat"; the poor in the eyes of the world are rich in faith; faith without works means death, not life; disputatious wisdom must give way to gentle peacemaking; the riotous rich are to mourn, weep, and howl; the judge is to become a lover; the wealthy are to become poor; the fattened cattle are to be slaughtered; sufferers, like Job, are to remember the end of the Lord. The individual in James hears,

44. b. Shabbath 88a.
45. *Art. cit., Interpretation* 3.4 (1949): 471.
46. Cited by F. Coutts, *The Four Gospels* (1973), p. 157.

but, as in the parable of the man and the mirror, forgets, ignores, and thus flouts it in his life; so in the end he is very much like the man of Ps. 81.

Here again the sequence of thought is simple. 1:25: Receive (hear) the Word. 1:22: But do it, too; otherwise you deceive yourself (see 1:26) and get nothing more than a glimpse of your face in the mirror. The parable of the mirror illustrates the nature of the Christian's self-deception. He who hears and does not do is like a man who observes *(katanoeō)* the face of his created being in a mirror. In *katanoeō, kata-,* as in many other verbs, expressly conveys the inceptive force often attached to the simple verb. By inceptive force we mean the force distinguishing "I become aware of this" from "I am aware of this"; this distinction can often be made in the simple verb by using the appropriate tense, for example, the imperfect of "have" for *I had,* the aorist for *I got.*

Like *noeō, katanoeō* often means mental perception of truths and ideas. These, of course, are not visible to the senses. In philosophy both of these words have developed with some subtlety. Often, however, as in Jas. 1:23f., *katanoeō,* like *noeō,* signifies seeing the visible with at least that degree of attention which must be implied in the word "perceive" in the sense of notice, note, or observe, words that, of course, are not confined to visible things and in which the degree of attention implied must be gauged from the context. Thus Thucydides 2.3 and 3.66: *noticing* (observing) that the Thebans were not numerous; 3.59: *observing* (noting) the dreadfulness of the fate we shall suffer; and 2.102: Alcmaeon, in his perplexing search for a home, *noticed* the sediment of the river Achelous and decided that it satisfied the terms of the oracle he was hoping to fulfill. Or, again, Acts 27:39: "They *noticed* a bay with a sandy beach" (NEB).[47]

47. In Lk. 12:24, 27, surely spoken out-of-doors, Jesus' words are "Observe the ravens" and "Observe the lilies," that is, "Look at them"; not "Consider" (KJV), much less "Think of" (NEB). The modern weakness for an intellectual interpretation is obvious in Lk. 6:41: *ou katanoeis* is rightly "perceivest not" in the KJV, but "never a thought for" in the NEB. In the next verse Luke, we should have thought, has made the meaning of *ou katanoeis* clear by adding the synonymous *ou blepōn,* "When thou beholdest not" (KJV), for which the NEB gives "when you are blind to," no doubt deliberately, to match "never a thought," though it could have stood quite well with the proper translation of the proper verse, as in the KJV or, more colloquially, "don't notice." The old reading (KJV) of Rom. 4:19 is probably correct, meaning, in effect: "Strong in faith, he did not stop to take notice of his age." In the same way Cylon (Thucydides 1:126, where the same Greek word is used) did not stop to notice which feast of Zeus the oracle meant. On *noeō* and *katanoeō,* see G. Harder, "Reason" *(nous), NIDNTT,* III, 123ff.; J. Behm, *katanoeō, TDNT,* IV, 973f.; D. J. Moo, *James,* p. 83.

THE PARABLE OF THE MIRROR

So in James we have a man who "notices" or "observes" his face in a mirror; but the degree of attention given to it is clear from the sequel, including the instantaneous perfect: at once he is gone, and immediately he forgets what his face was like.[48]

In discussing "the face of his creation"—or, as we prefer, "birth"—sometimes *genesis* means the created world, including humans, and sometimes it means coming into being, birth, creation (Ropes). So we have to choose between "the face, or his face, related to the created universe" into which (what Ropes calls) "nature" sent him,[49] and "the face, or his face, related to his coming into the universe." We think it is only the current doctrine of "the wheel of nature" in Jas. 3:6, as propagated by the commentators, that brings nature into his verse (1:23).

This is the same "genesis" as in 3:6.[50] We suggest that there we have not the created universe but the cycle of time, in course of which people and things come (and have come) into being in the universe of created things. So in 1:23, we would interpret this phrase as "the face related, not to the cosmos and cosmic law, but to the engendure, birth, creation, coming into being, or whatever we may like to call it, of the man."

The Greeks had a notion of a destiny attached to a person by the stern Spinsters at his birth, and the Romans had a like idea of the *genius natalis*. We feel that a thing as personal as our face is more naturally and immediately associated with the notion of our personal incarnation, *ab initio,* than with the notion of the cosmos, undeniable though this latter association is. Ropes, in the same sentence to which we have just referred, says: "The meaning of 'birth' . . . is hardly adequate, since a man sees in the glass not merely the gift of birth but also the acquisitions of experience."[51] This is absurd. Whatever time and experience have done to our face, even if we have grown a beard and lost an eye or ear, not to mention all the lines of wisdom, or debauchery, our face is still the only one we ever had, the face that came with us into the world: age does not efface our identity.

48. Commenting on Plato, *The Republic* 375d, J. Adam notes: *enoēsamen . . . physeis:* "We did not notice that there are. . . ." Here *noein* is not *putare,* nor—we think—*perpendere,* but simply *animadvertere,* "notice," as is often the case. Such a meaning is peculiarly appropriate with (the aorist) *idoi* (i.e., *idoi men an tis* . . . : "One might observe this in other animals, and especially in the dog").

49. P. 176, beginning of last sentence of first small print.

50. Ropes, p. 235.

51. P. 176.

We can scarcely say "the face of his nativity," but that is about what the expression literally means.[52] "The face of nature" is impossible Greek for "his natural face," and "his natural face"[53] is simply not good English for the meaning intended here. What would we understand by "my natural foot"? "The face of his birth" is hard enough, but as a Hebraism it falls in line with "a hearer of forgetfulness." If the latter means a hearer who forgets, a forgetful hearer, the former can, with difficulty but nevertheless, be taken as the face with which he was born—however it has changed since. So we translate "the face of his created being" with a tacit hint of its character as seen and temporal, and sinful and imperfect, as if James had said "the face of his earthly incarnation."[54]

Perhaps James is contrasting the dim, fleshly image in the mirror with the perfect picture of truth in the gospel (law of liberty). We must remember that "genesis" has a rather sinister, worldly connotation in James, like "flesh" in some other NT passages and in Jas. 3:6. Its correlative is *phthora,* "destruction" or "corruption." So the "natural face" is in antithesis to the "perfect [eternal] law" of God (Rom. 8:21); it is the face that is part of him in this mundane existence into which he was born.

Ronald Knox points out that "the difficulty of verses 23-25 is singularly unremarked by the commentators. St. James embarks on a formal comparison; the mere listener is compared to a man who looks in a looking-glass, the practical Christian is compared—to what?"[55] Knox begins his answer to this question much as we do. The man who sees his face in the mirror "catches sight of the face of his birth" (the face with which he was born); "bends down to get a good view of that perfect law we are meant to live by."

So far, good; but no farther. The contrast is *not* between a casual look and a careful look at the same thing (a polished silver bowl, he suggests) but between a casual look and a careful look at two different things, that is, a casual look into a mirror and a careful look into the law. There is indeed, as Knox says, no question of two mirrors; but his way of finding "parity of matter" by making both men look into the same thing, which is not a mirror at all but only a mirror by accident, does hopeless violence to the plain Greek, or English, word "mirror" ("in a

52. Ropes calls it (preferably) a genitive of attribute, meaning evidently what is more often called a genitive of description (or definition). Moule, *Idiom Book,* p. 38 gives as examples Mammon of unrighteousness, the body of sin, an instrument of choice (a chosen instrument), and others.

53. So Dibelius, Davids, and others.

54. See Ropes, p. 176.

55. P. 96.

mirror"). The two men, listening, he says—though there is no need or warrant for stating their experience within such narrow limits—"to the same sermon," do "react differently." One is like a person giving his face a casual glance in a mirror, "for he observes himself, and is gone, and immediately forgets what he was like."

The tenses are important. The two aorists "observes" and "forgets" are gnomic, and refer, as Ropes says, to something that happens naturally, normally, or repeatedly.[56] The gnomic aorist occurs only in the indicative; hence "noticing" (*not* "looking at," *pace* Ropes) in 1:23 is a present participle with the same force as the gnomic aorist in 1:25. He *catches sight* of himself, and *(at once) is gone,* and forthwith *forgets* what he was like (in the mirror).

Modern men, constantly using shaving mirrors, may be surprised at this statement; but even a good artist might hesitate to do a self-portrait from memory. And James is speaking of people of the normal sort who do not care much about remembering their faces: he does not say *all* people are equally forgetful in this matter. The other man is like one *not* confronted with a looking-glass (that is why, as Knox says, he sees no reflection of himself at all), *but* carefully studying the Word or Law. Today's jargon uses "image" much as the Elizabethans used "mirror" *(A Mirror for Magistrates).*

So here James is thinking of the Word/Law presenting in words (as of sermons and other such instruction) a picture of the righteousness prescribed by God for us to live by and fulfill with his helping grace. The one, hearing the Word/Law, lets it go in one ear and out the other, with no more effect than a fleeting glance at his face in a mirror; the other, hearing the Word/Law, gives it close and sustained attention—the word denotes *penetrating absorption*[57]—not only at the time of hear-

56. P. 176.

57. So W. Michaelis, *parakyptō, TDNT,* V, 815, n. 13. "The word *parakypsas* often implies 'a rapid, hasty, and cursory glance,'" Ropes rightly observes (p. 177), "but that shade of meaning seems here excluded by the latter half of the verse." Certainly "that shade of meaning" is absent in Jn. 20:5 where the disciples' look is not rapid, hasty, or cursory. Neither was Mary's look (vv. 11-14) momentary (witness the conversation) nor uninterested. It is difficult to square these texts with Hort's quite dogmatic statement: "The notion of a steady gaze has been imported into the word from the context, and prematurely. It seems never to have any such meaning. . . . When used figuratively, as here, it seems always to imply a rapid, hasty, and cursory glance" (p. 40). J. B. Mayor, *The Epistle of St. James and Further Studies in the Epistle of St. James* (1913), p. 22, quotes with approval Westcott's view that "the idea conveyed is that of looking intently with eager desire and effort at that which is partially concealed." He also notes that Epictetus (*Dissertations* 1.1.16) mentions travelers detained by adverse winds as "continually

ing but also in trying to carry it out in his life, just as if he were poring over God's design for living and trying to fulfill it in thought, word, and deed.

THE CHRISTIAN IDEA OF WORD/LAW

The Christian concept of Word/Law is related both to the religious history of the Jewish nation from its origin in Abraham, and to the thought that descended into that history from the previous period of prehistoric religious myth. From the former comes the notion of God's people; from immemorial tradition comes the notion of some divine love of humans and of some divine law in the universe. Among God's people the concept of God's law was often obscured, not least in the century of the incarnation.

The sons of Adam, before no less than after Abraham, are sons of God. But while they are prone to break that relationship by sin (see Acts 7:9, 17, 25, 35-39, 43, 51-53), God is ever eager to repair it by his grace, a voluntary gift (Jas. 1:18, *boulētheis;* and 1:17, *dosis*) specially promised to Abraham and his seed 430 years before the law was first given to Moses. The contrast between that law and the Christian law of liberty consists not in the defects of the Torah and abuses of it such as Jeremiah denounces (5:31)—not to mention literalism, legalism, and mere outward self-interested compliance—but in the contrast between the law *without Christ* and the law *with Christ* and with God's grace offered redemptively through him to all people. The Christian must ever look beyond his own sin to God's mercy revealed in Christ.

---

looking to see" *(parakypsas synechōs)* what wind is blowing. Also Ecclus. 14:20-23 (NEB): "Happy the man who fixes his thoughts on wisdom . . . the man who contemplates her ways and ponders her secrets. . . . The man who peers in *(parakypton)* at her windows." In 1 Pet. 1:12 also we have no casual look (again *pace* Hort). *Katanoēsen,* "notices," is often used for observing things we were not looking for (e.g., a dogfight) or, as James says, our face as we pass by a mirror (incuriously as we usually do). But *parakypsas* implies a deliberate intention to look, sometimes frivolously or cursorily, but in this context with serious attention (see H. A. Kent, Jr., *Faith that Works,* p. 68; Mayor, p. 69); *katanoeō* implies no such deliberation. Ropes, p. 177, says: "The figure is of looking ["peeping," "glancing"] into a mirror, and is brought over from the simile in 1:21." But the fairly small hand-mirror—usually made of bronze or polished metal—was the sort most familiar to the ancients; and we venture to say that here *parakyptō* has *not* "lost all trace" of stooping (or rather, here, bending over) to look and suggests no "peeping" or "glancing" or even mere "noticing" as in a mirror, as in 1:23f. 1:23f. is clearly not a case of a man deliberately seeking a mirror and concentratedly examining, say, a pimple on his nose, but of a man catching sight of his face in a mirror as he goes about his house intent on other things.

So the gospel is a mirror that "reflects not only our own miserable selves, but also the glory and love of God."[58] By continuing to look into that mirror, we experience an inner freedom and growth in Christian character. This is the same point made by Paul: "We all reflect as in a mirror the splendour of the Lord; thus we are transformed into his likeness, from splendour to splendour" (2 Cor. 3:18, NEB). That is the liberating gospel, "the perfect law of freedom."

The Christian holds that it is our duty to obey God's law, but that our breach of it can be repaired. This fact rests, not on any distinction between our moral and our ceremonial obligations under God's law, but on the principles mentioned in our discussion of faith and works in James and Paul. Fundamentally it is a distinction between spirit and form, between justice and the formalism in religion that is one of the greatest threats to righteousness in life, as it always has been to justice in courts of law. Thus in cases of debt and detinue in England, ordeal by oath, whereby a shameless defendant possessor could win his case without more ado by a false oath, endured till 1833, the last case being *King* v. *Williams* in 1824.[59]

In our discussion of faith and works we should not construe works as essentially different from *law;* but at the same time we must not fall into the sin of those Pharisees whose notion of both law and works deadened the spirit of their religion (see Lk. 11:37-52). In his distinctive insistence on faith *and* works James, like Christ, reflects and defines the teaching of both the OT and later Judaism, where faith usually means obedience to God, fidelity, and "devotion to the law" *(Gesetzfrömmigkeit);*[60] the same is true of Qumran, where "faith is doing the law,"[61] implying, as in James, the necessity of both faith and works. The righteous are called "the doers of the Torah." For James, too, faith is doing, not merely hearing, "the Word," except that "the Word" in this instance is the Christian, not Jewish, Torah; and paradoxically twice also in connection with his conviction that the Word

58. D. M. Baillie, *Out of Nazareth* (1958), p. 127.

59. See P. B. R. Forbes, "Hesiod v Perses," *Classical Review* 54 (1950): 82-87.

60. See 4 Ezr. 9:7; 13:23; B. M. Metzger, "The Fourth Book of Ezra (Late First Century A.D.)," *The Old Testament Pseudepigrapha,* ed. J. H. Charlesworth, I (1983), 544, 552. See also A. Meyer, pp. 125, 137; H.-J. Schoeps, *Paul* (1961), pp. 202f.; O. Michel, "Faith" *(pistis), NIDNTT* I, 597; also R. Bultmann, *pistis, TDNT,* VI, 199-202.

61. See 1QpHab 8:1-3; also Michel, "Faith," *NIDNTT,* I, 598. On the "doers of the Torah," see R. H. Eisenman, *James the Just in the Habakkuk Pesher* (1986), pp. 35ff., 68ff.; also *Maccabees, Zadokites, Christians and Qumran* (1983), pp. 41ff., 70.

should be done and not merely heard (1:22) he describes this as "the law of liberty."[62]

The origin of the phrase is not known, though the adjective "perfect" *(teleios)* (1:25) probably points to a Jewish background (see Ps. 19:7). The idea, however, is by no means exclusively Palestinian; it is found not only in the OT (e.g., Ps. 51:12; 119; Jer. 31:33) and the rabbis ("not a burden but a glory," "the joy of the commandments")[63] but also in both Stoicism[64] and later Judaism (e.g., Philo[65] and Qumran[66]). James's attitude to the law is that of a sincerely devout Jew, freed from literalism, who is devoted above all things to "the royal law" of Christ. This law is not a new Torah but a new interpretation of God's purpose set forth and fulfilled in the long-promised Messiah. Whether late or early, the doctrine of the Epistle of James is thoroughly Christian; but we would like to mention other circumstances that support the ascription of its authorship to James the Lord's brother.

Gal. 2:12 illustrates the attitude of early Christian Jews toward their Gentile fellow-Christians, and vv. 16, 17, and 21 indicate its basis, namely, the value Christian Jews (those "from James") laid upon OT law. Paul had the same grave problems with the Christians of Rome, and took it very seriously in his Epistle to them (see, in epitome, 3:21-24).

Those who "came from James" (Gal. 2:12) did not, we are con-

62. 1:25; 2:12.

63. M. Aboth 3.5, 8; also 6.2. See also S. Schechter, *Some Aspects of Rabbinic Theology* (1909), pp. 148ff.; Montefiore, "The Spirit of Judaism," *The Beginnings of Christianity,* Part I (1920), eds. F. J. F. Jackson and K. Lake, pp. 59ff.; R. T. Herford, *Pharisaism: Its Aims and Methods* (1912), p. 94; A. Meyer, pp. 154ff.; W. Gutbrod, *nomos, TDNT,* IV, 103ff.; R. Fabris, *Legge della Libertà in Giacomo,* for a definitive study; see especially bibliography, pp. 266ff.

64. C. H. Dodd, *The Bible and the Greeks* (1935), pp. 39ff., clearly demonstrates close analogies between Greek and biblical ideas on law, citing parallels from Philo, Xenophon, and the Platonic corpus. See also Dibelius, pp. 111f.; Hoppe, pp. 95f.

65. On Philo's considerable use of the Stoic term "ensouled law" and the general Stoic concept, "all whose life is regulated by law are free," see *Every Good Man is Free* 45. See also W. L. Knox, *Some Hellenistic Elements in Primitive Christianity* (1944), pp. 32f.; also Dodd, n. 64 above. For the unlikely view that James is employing a Gnostic catchword, see H.-J. Schoeps, p. 344.

66. See E. Stauffer, "Das 'Gesetz der Freiheit' in der Ordensregel von Jericho," *ThLZ* 77 (1952): 527-32 *pace* F. Nötscher, "'Gesetz der Freiheit' im NT und in der Mönchsgemeinde am Toten Meer," *Biblica* 34 (1953): 193f.; P. B. R. Forbes, "The Greek View of Law," *Juridical Review* 64 (1952): 214-28. For the term *lex insculpta,* another possible parallel to "the law of liberty," see W. Nauck, "Lex insculpta in der Sektenschrift," *ZNW* 46 (1955): 138-40. Nauck equates *lex insculpta* ("engraved law") with the *ḥōq ḥārûṯ* mentioned three times in 1QS 10:6, 8, 11.

vinced, take their views on that point from him, and this does *not* prove that James was a rabid ritualist and zealot for the Jewish law;[67] on the contrary, we think the chief aim of his Epistle was the same as that of Paul in Colossians, Galatians, and Romans, that is, to save Christianity, the gospel of grace, from being undermined by the rule of ordinances (see Col. 2:16-20). We agree with the view that "James understood Paul's gospel better than Peter and in fact was closer to Paul in theology than Peter."[68] In contrast to Peter and "those who came from James," James himself invoked the law of liberty, as Paul similarly rejoices in his liberty in Christ.

This, we submit, gives better, and better-related, answers to more questions than any other theory yet advanced on the nature and origin of this Epistle. There is no better, and almost no other, explanation of why it was written, or to whom, or by whom, or when, or where, or with such genius and power, or in such good Greek. "It indeed is the 'most un-Pauline book in the New Testament,'" Rendall rightly remarks, "but because it is pre-Pauline, not because it has forgotten and outlived the Pauline inspiration";[69] and, if we may hazard the conjecture, the clouded history of the early years of the Epistle would find a plausible explanation in the (perhaps not remarkable) animosity of the early Gentile Christian church to the first Jewish Christians and their memory.

We must also remember that in their Epistles the apostles had to vary their themes somewhat according to the varying needs of the occasion. It seems clear that too many Jewish Christians (this Epistle was addressed to them), in their progress from the old law, were failing to realize that their practical duties and the Christian law of liberty were more serious than ever before. However theological his Epistles might be, Paul himself regularly concluded with something to *do,* recalling, we might add, Luther's own words:

> O, it is a living, busy, active, mighty thing, this faith. It is impossible for it not to be doing good works incessantly. It does not ask whether good works are to be done, but before the question is asked, it has already done them, and is constantly doing them. Whoever does not do such works, however, is an unbeliever. He gropes and looks around for faith and good works, but knows neither what faith is nor what

67. *Pace,* e.g., A. Meyer, p. 110; Dibelius, p. 14. On this see, e.g., J. B. Lightfoot, *Saint Paul's Epistle to the Galatians* (1865), p. 110; G. Howard, *Paul: Crisis in Galatia* (1979), p. 41, n. 131; p. 79, n. 267; F. F. Bruce, *Commentary on Galatians* (1982), pp. 120ff.

68. Howard, *Paul: Crisis in Galatia,* p. 79; also p. 40, n. 129 *ad fin.*

69. P. 83.

good works are. Yet he talks and talks, with many words, about faith and good works.[70]

Alexander Whyte, the Scottish divine, calls James "half a Pharisee to the very end," and adds "if ever he was a bishop at all, he was the bishop of a half-enlightened Jewish ghetto rather than of a Christian church." Here Whyte—and others—appears simply to reject postcanonical traditions about James and his alleged Nazirite legalism.[71] It has been doubted whether the view of law in the Epistle of James could have been possible for James the Lord's brother.[72] Some have even held that in the sphere of law James and Paul represent two entirely different attitudes. But in our remarks on faith and works in James and Paul we have argued to the contrary, holding that there is no discrepancy between their attitudes to the Torah. Paul's bitterness is not against the Torah devoutly followed, but against the perversions and abuses of it prevalent among the Jews of his day, perversions of which Paul was the more sensitive for having once lived in them.

THE LAW OF LIBERTY

We would venture to explain James's use of the pagan philosophers' term "law of liberty" as only one of several signs, even in his style, that James had done more of his thinking than Paul in Greek; and we defer to Kittel's wise judgment: "The theory that a term 'Law of Liberty' is not possible from the mouth of a Palestinian Christian is therefore not tenable."[73] Elsewhere we have noted how, after his death and the sub-

70. *LW,* XXXV, 370. See again Althaus, *The Theology of Martin Luther,* p. 246.

71. *Bible Characters,* II (1962), 144. For evidence, see especially J. J. Scott, Jr., "James the Relative of Jesus and the Expectation of an Eschatological Priest," *Journal of the Evangelical Theological Society* 25.3 (Sept. 1982): 326, n. 12; R. B. Ward, "James of Jerusalem," *Restoration Quarterly* 16.3, 4 (1973): 179; J. Munck, "Jewish Christianity in Post-Apostolic Times," *NTS* 6 (1960): 103-16; P. U. Maynard-Reid, *Poverty and Wealth in James* (1987), p. 102. See above, p. 20.

72. Dibelius, p. 17: "The decisive argument against James as the author arises from the position of our document with regard to the Law." See also K. Aland, "Der Herrenbruder Jakobus und der Jakobusbrief," *ThLZ* 69 (1944): 97-104; O. J. F. Seitz, "James and the Law," *StEv* 2 (1964): 472-86; Laws, pp. 36f., 40f.

73. "Der geschichtliche Ort des Jakobusbriefes," *ZNW* 41 (1942): 71-105; confirmed also by his posthumous "Der Jakobusbrief und die Apostolischen Väter," *ZNW* 43 (1950-51): 54-112. See also Dibelius, p. 118: "Only too easily do we fall into the error—which, to be sure, is fostered by the character of the materials preserved from the early Christian period—of thinking that Paul had influenced every branch of early Christianity"; also C. Moody, *The Faith of the Early Christian Converts* (1920), chs. 1, 2; Davids, p. 40.

sequent extinction of his (Palestinian) church on the fall of Jerusalem, the Gentile Christian tradition, as represented in Acts, appears to show little interest in the memory of both James and his office and his church. It is with this Palestinian church that both the Epistle of James and the Epistle to the Hebrews are in obvious agreement,[74] whereas Paul's quite perceptible agreement is apt to be overshadowed by the traumatic repercussions of his supernatural conversion from the hostile extremes that he lived to detest, aggravated as these were by attacks from Jews in Asia and elsewhere.

For the Jew the covenant is the principal vehicle of salvation. While membership in the covenant brought salvation, continuing obedience to the commandments ensured one's place in the covenant. "In covenantal nomism," writes E. P. Sanders,[75] "the focus is not on the individual's quest for salvation. God's salvific promises extend to the

74. Like James, the writer to the Hebrews is thoroughly un-Pauline in that he is either consciously supplementing Paul's view of law (see A. Nairne, *The Epistle of Priesthood* [1913], p. 152; J. Moffatt, *Hebrews* [1924], p. 135; F. B. Clogg, *An Introduction to the New Testament* [1937], pp. 138ff.) or in that he is possibly expanding a more primitive and influential view of the Gospels (H. Windisch, *Der Hebräerbrief* [1931], p. 65) and one most certainly familiar to the Jerusalem Church, although this does not necessarily imply that the views of Paul and Jesus are mutually incompatible (see A. M. Hunter, *The Unity of the New Testament* [1952], p. 83; W. L. Knox, *St. Paul and the Church of the Gentiles* [1939], p. 96n.; F. F. Bruce, *The Epistle to the Hebrews* [1964], p. 145). Though the atmosphere of the Epistle to the Hebrews differs palpably from that of the Epistle of James, their basic attitudes to the law are significantly similar. Sharing a common moral tone (see Jas. *passim;* Heb. 10:19ff.; 12:1ff.) and linked with the further notion of each having been initiated into a new experience by Christ (see Jas. 1:25, 27; Heb. 8:10-13), both reveal a deep reverence for the Jewish heritage—the one prophetic, the other priestly—as well as for the Torah. For James the old law is apparently supplemented and superseded by the Messianic Torah and this must be given practical obedience (Jas. 1:25ff.); for the writer to the Hebrews the contrast between the old and new is even more marked, fulfillment in this instance being achieved through patient endurance in divine service (Heb. 10:19ff.; 12:1), the old covenant having been completely replaced by the new (see W. L. Knox, *St. Paul and the Church of Jerusalem* [1925], ch. 1). Christianity as law appears in the Patristic Fathers, which may also indicate that James and Hebrews are reproducing a tradition older than that in either, in greater agreement with Jesus than Paul, reflecting gospel rather than Pauline inspiration, and in turn suggesting an earlier and more Jewish Palestinian Christian source with which the authors of both James and Hebrews were familiar. See also A. C. McGiffert, *History of Christianity in the Apostolic Age* (1897), p. 448n., 446.

75. "The Covenant as a Soteriological Category and the Nature of Salvation in Palestinian and Hellenistic Judaism," *Jews, Greeks and Christians. Essays in Honor of William David Davies,* eds. Robert Hamerton-Kelly and Robin Scroggs, p. 42.

group as such. The individual's responsibility is to remain a member of the group in good standing (although he will also have a personal relationship with God)."

The primary aim of the Jewish religion was not so much the salvation of the individual soul as the survival of the Jewish race, with its unique solidarity and characteristics, a survival that has already been almost a miracle of history, and has required, and produced, an astonishing excellence in the general ethical standards and practice of the Jews. But the doctrine of the Sadducees, denying as it did the immortality of man's soul, emphasizes the paramount importance of the nation, as contrasted with that of the individual, in Jewish religion.

The Jews have always been conspicuous, and have won respect even from Gentiles, including both the Greeks and the Romans, for their faithful observance of their law (see, e.g., circumcision, or the Sabbath). They have always recognized that such religious features in their life, peculiar (in sum) to themselves, are essential to the preservation of their race, which otherwise would lose its homogeneity and become unidentifiably merged with other peoples of the earth, or perhaps perish altogether. Indeed, like some of their other laws, that against unclean food was not a matter of theology or morals but of bodily life and health and, literally, of vital importance for the survival and increase of the nation; even for Gentiles it was not always as safe to eat pork as it is now.

Thus, since their law was in a very real sense the life of their nation, it is not surprising that a school arose among them—the Pharisees (the Purists)—that scrupulously multiplied and elaborated the rules of that law: G. H. Rendall points out that the Pharisees had 248 rules of things that must be done and 365 rules of things forbidden.[76] Their (thoroughly patriotic) aim was to strengthen the Holy Law as a preservative of the Jewish racial character and existence. It is only fair to remember that idolatry was a frequent sin of the Israelites (see Ezek. 14:5 and other texts); thus "adulterous," meaning estranged from God, is often used by the prophets to signify the defection of the Israelites from Yahweh (see Mt. 16:4; Isa. 57:3 and that whole chapter).

The Pharisees, therefore, are not to be blamed simply for their enthusiasm for the law, any more than the author of that *tour de force*, Ps. 119, for his; see v. 97 (NIV): "Oh, how I love your law! I meditate on it all day long." The Pharisees cannot all have fallen within the condemnation pronounced by Jesus in Mt. 16:4. But in Hebrew and Greek and other ancient life generally, law is essentially *a way of life*, neither needlessly arbitrary nor obnoxiously superfluous. Any true law justifies its

76. *The Epistle of St. James and Judaic Christianity* (1927), p. 74.

existence by its social value, that is, by its obvious value for the life of the citizens and the city; for example, even the arbitrary "Keep to the right" or "Keep to the left" is justified in various communities as they severally think fit. Thus the ethnic zeal of the Pharisees for the plenitude of formal observances they considered necessary for the perfection of their holy racial law often seriously obscured their apperception of the paramount meaning and value of law as a guide for life.

It is common knowledge that all of us, even the best, sometimes fall short of God's ideal standards for us, sometimes deliberately and consciously, sometimes (see Ps. 19:12) without intending or even knowing it. Our concern here is not with the mysteries of the incarnation, death, and resurrection of Christ for the redemption of humans but only with the question whether there is any discrepancy between the place that James and Paul assign or do not assign to human conduct and human faith as relevant to a person's salvation. To this question we have already spoken in our discussion of "James and Paul." We hope that here a shorter summary will suffice, based partly on our previous discussion.

We return to Luther's verdict:[77] "I think that the Epistle was composed by some Jew or other, who had heard of Christ but not joined the Christians. James had learned that Christians insisted strongly on faith in Christ, and he said to himself: 'Well, you must oppose them and insist only on works'. And so he does." This is utterly false; in fact, James insists on faith (and some kindred aspects of the Christian spirit) quite as clearly and strongly as Paul.

For James faith is no less important than it is for Paul. In Jas. 1:21-25, and elsewhere in the Epistle, James makes it unambiguously clear that Christian faith is always the indispensable foundation of Christian conduct, and (apart, we may assume, from exceptional cases like deathbed conversions) Christian conduct is the equally indispensable fruit of Christian faith (see Jas. 2:12-25, esp. vv. 13, 14, 17, 18, 20, and 24). There is absolutely no discrepancy between the statement in the Epistle of James on the Christian's duty of Christian conduct as the fruit of his Christian faith and the same but far more abstrusely argued doctrine of Rom. 8:12-24: neither James nor Paul is trying to give a full exposition of Christian theology and practice in a single Epistle.

We have already emphasized the two faces of Jewish law: one, its elaboration by the Pharisees to the detriment of its spiritual force as a guide for life; and the other, the higher morality of the Jews generally in comparison with the Corinthians, for example, or the sinners of Rom.

77. See p. 266 above.

1:18-32. But the emphasis of the Epistle of James on the Christian duty of moral conduct shows how James, in his view of the Mosaic law and that of Christ (which in Gal. 6:2 Paul expressly calls the law of Christ in one of its aspects as the Christian law of love), regards the law of Christ not as a total repudiation of the Mosaic law but as an improvement in the efficacy of the Mosaic law as a rule of conduct, an improvement resulting from the superior efficacy of its foundation, the redemptive death of Christ, as Paul expressly states, for example, in Rom. 10:2-4, and even more forcibly in Rom. 3:31 (NIV): "Do we, then, nullify the law by this faith? Not at all! Rather, we uphold the law."

CONCLUSION

How then can a person hope to be saved? The old Jew knew that as well as the new Christian. In the last analysis the key to James's doctrine of salvation is the OT, baptized by Christ and epitomized especially in the prophets and their demand for true righteousness. To obey God in one's life, as Samuel indicates in 1 Sam. 15:22; to do as Isaiah directs in 1:17: "Cease to do evil, learn to do well ("do well" is an expression James uses twice in this passage, 2:8 and 19): seek judgment, relieve the oppressed, judge the fatherless, plead for the widows"—that is what is desired, not soulless performance of ceremonies and sacrifices by willing servants of sin.

No one can fail to recognize the Christian message of the Psalms (and of Job and Proverbs): see notably the whole of Ps. 101 or 51. It is worth noting that Ps. 51:16f. and, in contrast,[78] v. 19 show plainly the place of ritual, sacrifice, and the like in Christianity. Like Paul in 1 Cor. 13:3, the Psalmist points out the worthlessness of the act (of sacrifice) without the spirit, and shows the value of the same act when it is a natural fruit of the spirit of devotion and gratitude. In his regard for the poor, in the Epistle of James and in Gal. 2:10 James chimes perfectly with the Psalms, where the thought is expressed almost 30 times, apart from passages like Ps. 101:5 (NIV): "Whoever has haughty eyes and a proud heart, him will I not endure."

Ps. 3:8 (NIV) declares: "From the Lord comes deliverance" ("salvation," KJV). How then can we hope to get it? According to Ps. 130:3 (NIV), "If you, O Lord, kept a record of sins, O Lord, who could stand?"; v. 4, "But with you there is forgiveness"; v. 7, "O Israel, put your hope in the Lord, for with the Lord is unfailing love and with him is full re-

78. In Ps. 51, vv. 16 and 17 express the prophetic view; vv. 18 and 19 were added when the psalm was adapted to the sacrificial cult of the Second Temple. I owe this note to F. F. Bruce.

demption"; v. 8: "He himself will redeem Israel from all their sins" ("iniquities," KJV). We, therefore, must genuinely strive to do our—however imperfect—best, and leave the issue to the mercy of God as revealed in Christ.

"So speak and so act as those who will be judged in accordance with the law of liberty. For to him that has not shown pity, judgment [of God on Christians after death] is without pity; but where pity is [if it has been done by the Christian in his life], it triumphs over [legalistic] judgment" (Jas. 2:12f.).

The charge, therefore, that James contains "no Gospel" is clearly false.[79]

79. F. E. Gaebelein, *The Practical Epistle of James* (1955), pp. 10, 48; M. J. Evans, "The Law in James," *Vox Evangelica* 13 (1983): 29ff.

III. VALUE

"THE EPISTLE OF JAMES—FOR GOOD NEWS, TURN ELSEWHERE. Some such signpost seems to have been placed at the head of this Epistle by scores of commentators through the ages. Symbolic biblical road maps and atlases point to the friendly terrain of the gospels, but then faintly suggest a detour around a few of the writings, including this one. Embarrassed scholars and spiritual guides hint that at best James should be put up with or dealt with curiosity. . . . Enough. Not every author has to cover the same subject. In the little library or collection that we call the Bible books have to be allowed to supplement and complement each other. . . . The careful reader can come to cherish James, if he or she already knows Christ. The Church would be poorer without this little manual."

Martin E. Marty, *Good News in the Early Church* (1976), pp. 60f.

Value

Long neglected and rejected by its critics, especially Luther, the Epistle of James has nevertheless had a steady stream of enthusiastic admirers. C. F. D. Moule, my dear friend and supervisor, once shared a moving personal, spontaneous tribute to the Epistle. He simply said: "I love him (James)!"[1] Similarly, R. V. G. Tasker writes: "As part of the New Testament, the Epistle has a permanent message both for the Church as a whole and for each individual Christian—it may well be that few books are more relevant to the contemporary situation."[2] "From the literary point of view," notes F. E. Gaebelein, "the Epistle is a masterpiece."[3] D. J. Moo values the book for "James's genius," which, he says, "lies in his profound moral earnestness; in his powerfully simple call for repentance, for action, for a consistent Christian life-style."[4] "A golden book," testifies J. H. Moulton, "whose quality has been approved not by the weight of other people's judgments, but by the irresistible appeal of an authority which I at any rate find it impossible to gainsay."[5]

Changing the metaphor but in the same vein, Paul L. Maier calls the Epistle "a rare looking glass into the fledgling Church under duress, for which the author has provided the clearest and strongest lens to date."[6] Asserting that James as a theologian "places the early Church's problems within the context of a vibrant Christology and a meaningful doctrine of justification," and in his own way is every bit as capable as Paul, David P. Scaer goes on to suggest that "he is also unsurpassed by

1. In a personal note.
2. *The General Epistle of James*, pp. 10, 11.
3. *The Practical Epistle of James* (1955), p. 13.
4. *James*, p. 9.
5. *Ex* 4 (1907): 45; see also J. A. Robertson, *The Hidden Romance of the New Testament* (1920), pp. 221f.
6. D. P. Scaer, *James, the Apostle of Faith*, p. 12.

any other Epistle writer in using the language style of Jesus in addressing the problems of the early church."[7] Certainly as a pastor, James is at least in the same class as Paul.

These examples of glowing testimony by both well-known and ordinary Christians could easily be multiplied. It was no error or accident, for instance, that the Epistle gained the attention and respect of another Lutheran, Søren Kierkegaard;[8] we know that he took an increasingly negative view of Luther's criticism and became an ardent lover of James, quoting him often in his writings with telling force. Another impressive witness; Adolph Schlatter,[9] believed firmly in the integrity of the work, and even argued that the church, by its studied neglect of the Epistle, has done itself grave harm. For F. J. A. Hort also James held an important place and office in the NT, declaring that "its very unlikeness to other books is of the greatest value to us, as showing through Apostolic example the many-sidedness of Christian truth."[10]

Happily, such views of the Epistle of James are not rare; and indeed, as many Bible expositors will readily testify, interest in, and demand for, its message may be at an all-time high. Interpretations of that message are almost as varied as its readers. Some have treated it as a set of ethical axioms based on natural law, a throwback to legalism,[11] and thus outside the main Christian stream. Others, especially "second stage" Christians[12] who have refused to read the NT exclusively through the eyes of Paul, have found in its brief chapters practical help to everyday living, a powerful plea for vital Christianity,[13] and almost a standard exposition of the Christian faith.[14]

Recently some have gone even further, declaring perhaps with the pardonable rhetoric of enthusiasm that, barring the Second Coming, the Epistle is "the key to the survival of the faith into the 21st century," suggesting also that its doctrine of activated faith ("I will show you my

7. Pp. 15, 42.

8. See G. Eichholz, *Jakobus und Paulus, Ein Beitrag zum Problem des Kanons* (1953), pp. 17ff.; Tasker, pp. 10f.; and *A Kierkegaard Anthology,* ed. Robert Bretall (1951), p. 282. See also, e.g., R. A. Sider, *Rich Christians in an Age of Hunger* (1977); G. Gutiérrez, *The Power of the Poor in History* (1983).

9. Cited by C. E. B. Cranfield, "The Message of James," *SJTh* 18 (1965): 183f.; also B. M. Metzger, *The Canon of the New Testament* (1987), p. 281, n. 29, with comment.

10. P. ix.

11. E. W. Bauman, *An Introduction to the New Testament* (1961), p. 151.

12. Tasker, p. 11.

13. W. Wessel, "The Epistle of James," art. "The New Testament," *Wycliffe Bible Commentary* (1971), p. 944.

14. R. Henderlite, "The Epistle of James," *Interpretation* 3.4 (1949): 464.

faith by works") is "the only hope of Christian evangelism."[15] Granted that some of these, and other, claims are clearly exaggerated, yet their positive thrust is refreshing, preferable by far to the view that the Epistle, like the faith it condemns, is altogether worthless. James has rightly been seen as the spokesman for a section of the church for whom conduct rather than doctrine is paramount;[16] and from time to time they, like others, have discovered that this deceptively simple Epistle enshrines such profound insights and eternal values that they, too, have been led to call it "a golden book."

What then is the value of the Epistle of James? As we near the end of our study, we wish to share our impressions of the quality of the Epistle. In so doing, we shall confine ourselves to a few of its most outstanding features. Of necessity our evaluation cannot cover every aspect of the Epistle. Yet we believe that enough topics will be discussed to show that the Epistle of James reflects many high qualities, making it one of the most valuable books in the entire Bible. If we are accused of bias in favor of James, we readily admit it. On this point, of course, the reader must be the judge.

THE STAMP OF AUTHORITY

Evidence for the value of James has, of course, been seen in some of our previous chapters; specifically, those on Purpose, Style, and Message. Here we are chiefly concerned with a matter of supreme importance: the role, authority, and permanent significance of the teaching of James. The significance of the Epistle of James depends at least in part on the authority of its author and in turn on his relation to the authority on whom he relies. In any assessment of the Epistle of James, it is essential to remember that he was the Lord's brother, that he was first and foremost a Christian Jew, and that these two Jewish and Christian strands are interwoven throughout his Epistle.

James thought, spoke, and wrote both in Hebrew and in Greek. That fact is indisputable and, if he was a "teacher" or "rabbi," not surprising. No Greek type of composition "explains" him; the attempt to identify him exclusively with any one of the literary forms we have discussed is a mistake; he is not to be pigeon-holed with the diatribe or any other Greek or Hebrew type of literary form. Hebrew and Greek together have contributed to molding the Epistle for the purpose for which

15. R. Goetz, "Evangelism by Works Alone," *The Christian Century* 102.9 (1985): 261ff.

16. See Dibelius, p. 180.

it was intended, for a new faith, and for the governing circumstances of the new service of worship used by Jewish Christians.[17]

As in Jewish, rather than Greek, literature, the readers are addressed as "brothers" *(adelphoi).* This not only suggests "the homiletical style of the synagogue . . . brought thence into Christian hortatory language,"[18] but it also reinforces our view that our Epistle was designed to be read aloud in church and, in terms of length and divisibility, takes the form evidently found to be adapted to the Christian service of worship. We believe that James intended his message to be read in all Jewish synagogues. The synagogue provided the apostles with an obvious vehicle for Christian propaganda when they participated in their religious services.[19] Later, of course, Christians built their own synagogues (e.g., the "Synagogue of the Nazarenes") and developed their own liturgy and style of preaching.[20]

The Epistle of James, more than any other NT document, bears the unique stamp of Jewish Christianity and is the sole literary product of its synagogue. If too much has sometimes been made of James's use of "synagogue" (1:2) as a decisive argument for the primitive origin of the Epistle, nevertheless it is significant that of all the NT authors James alone uses it instead of the usual *ekklēsia.* The synagogue practice of inviting comment on the Scriptures is apparently still observed by readers of the Epistle[21]—but also apparently abused.[22] The form of

17. See P. B. R. Forbes, "The Structure of the Epistle of James," *EQ* 44/3 (1972): 147-53. Similar circumstances evidently governed most of Paul's Epistles to the Gentiles.

18. Ropes, pp. 15, 132; also A. Marmorstein, "Synagogue Sermons," *London Quarterly Review* (1916): 238ff.; M. Taanith 2.1; b. Megilla 23b *et saepe.*

19. I. Elbogen, *Der jüdische Gottesdienst in seiner geschichtlichen Entwicklung* (1924), p. 252.

20. F. J. F. Jackson and K. Lake, eds., *Beginnings of Christianity,* I (1920), 304; see also M. Dibelius, *From Tradition to Gospel* (1971), pp. 15ff.

21. In his discussion of this question in the light of the synagogue preaching of Jesus (Mt. 4:23; 9:35; Mk. 1:39) and Paul (Acts 9:19ff.; 13:5), Marmorstein ("Synagogue Sermons in the First Three Centuries," *London Quarterly Review* [1916]: 228f.) rejects M. Friedländer's hypothetical division between Hellenistic and Pharisaic synagogues (*Synagoge und Kirche in ihren Anfängen* [1908], pp. 213ff.), drawing a distinction, instead, between the *official* or halachic part of the sermon, which could only be delivered by an ordained rabbi, and the *logos tēs paraklēseōs* (Acts 9:19ff.; 13:15; compare Lk. 2:46; 4:16f.; also Elbogen, *Der jüdische Gottesdienst,* p. 196), which could be given by any layperson. Rabbinic custom (e.g., b. Soṭa 40a; Gen. R. 78.16) seems to confirm this distinction. See I. Abrahams, "The Freedom of the Synagogue," *Studies in Pharisaism and the Gospels* (First Series) (1917), pp. 4ff.

22. Jas. 3:1ff. See H. E. Dana, *Jewish Christianity* (1937), p. 104.

the work suggests an informal setting for its reading, namely, a primitive Christian "assembly" or "synagogue." The early date of this Epistle allows us to glimpse the simple organization of the primitive church. There was no sophisticated structure; the Christians were united by a common faith, hope, and love. While we reject Arnold Meyer's view[23] that the Epistle is merely a slightly Christianized Jewish "midrash," we think it may well have been designed as "the word of exhortation" *(ho logos tēs paraklēseos)*[24] to be read in the local synagogue. Such, then, may have been the original setting of this primitive Christian letter, although it would also be read privately by anyone who could borrow a copy.

James has no sole progenitor in any piece or type of composition in any language. His Greek is eminently good both in grammar and in the style and power with which he uses the language; and his mind is not untinged with Greek thought. But both in his short-sentenced, grave, forceful style and almost entirely in his mind and soul he is a Hebrew of the Hebrews. He speaks like a prophet, often in tones of scarcely controlled contempt, biting sarcasm, and harshest denunciation. He may be called the Jeremiah of the NT, though his links are rather with the pungent and stubborn realism of a prophet like Amos (e.g., 5:7-13), Zechariah (7:9; 8:17; 12:10f.), or Malachi (2:9, 17; 3:5f.). Describing James as "the Amos of the New Testament," D. A. Hayes[25] also points out his likeness to other OT prophets and lawgivers: James exemplifies "the vehemence of Elijah and the assured meekness of Moses. . . . He belongs to the goodly fellowship of the prophets and of the Apostles." He goes on to say that James speaks with "the authority of both," confirming our belief that the closest literary analogy to our Epistle is not the rabbinic homily but the rhythmical oracles of prophetic discourse.

"If God will" (4:15) illustrates the blend of Greek and Hebrew thought,[26] and "encounter manifold *peirasmoi*" (1:2) the author's rhetorical skill in Greek. But for all James's skill in Greek,[27] we must remember that he was a Hebrew scholar (rabbi or not), as learned in the Hebrew Bible as in the Septuagint. Our Epistle is full of Hebrew thought, and its style (e.g., its gravity, brevity, and constant balance) owes much to the Hebrew Bible—a debt that outweighs all others. Its

23. See above, pp. 106ff.

24. See above, p. 426, n. 21.

25. "James, Epistle of," *The International Standard Bible Encyclopedia,* III (1929), 1562.

26. On this, with references, see C. E. B. Cranfield, *The Epistle to the Romans,* I (1975), p. 78, n. 5.

27. See our remarks on *Style,* pp. 119ff.

literary parentage in thought, style, subject, and form is to be traced, not to the pagan diatribe, but to the Psalms and the Prophets. From these he derives his short-sentenced gravity, "completing the circle"; and, among other things, his homely, forceful, colorful language, including metaphors (or similes). On this last item compare the prophets in 2 Kgs. 21:12f., especially the end of v. 13.[28] For "completing the circle," we may cite from a wealth of examples including Isa. 35:1, 2, 6b-10. So the first two and last two verses of Jer. 5 complete a circle; note also the refrain in vv. 9 and 29; also the "cage full of birds" in v. 27, a figure with which James was surely familiar.[29]

In the large limited liability company from which the stock of his pedigree is issued (as he might have said in one of his metaphors), the governing director is Ezekiel. The Epistle of James has no prototype; the nearest approach to one is Ezek. 33 and 34. Ezekiel, of course, shows strongly the divine intoxication of the spirit of prophecy; James burns no less ardently with the spirit of the gospel, but his utterance is homiletic and evangelic, not (unless exceptionally) intoxicated. Even so, James the evangelist more than once verges on the divine intoxication of the prophet: Jas. 5:1-6 rivals anything in the possessed *enthousiasmos* of Ezekiel or the other prophets; and in 1:10-11 and 17; 2:2-13; the whole of ch. 3; 4:1-10 and 13-17, for example, James well matches the factual rather than prophetically intoxicated recriminatory prelude of Ezek. 34:2-8 and other such passages in Ezekiel and other prophets. There, and in no Greek diatribe, is the ancestry of the brevity, force, balance, and sincerity that are conspicuous in the Epistle of James.

We can see from Acts that, if reliably reported, James was a good speaker, *ex tempore* and *viva voce*, and that, if he was, as we believe, the author of the Council's letter in Acts 15:23f., he was a good letter writer. The Epistle of James shows that he was also good (and, we think, better) when he was at his desk, composing studied prose after the model of the Psalms and Prophets and conveying, like them, a message of counsel, comfort, and rebuke to his nation and the promise of Christian salvation for those who would hearken. Like Thucydides James composed the Epistle of James in the form of a harangue, oration, speech, or oral directive; and like Thucydides (or very likely Demosthenes) before he went into court or assembly, or a minister before going into the pulpit, he composed it at his desk, "on paper."

Moreover, James designed his Epistle expressly as a message to his nation, to be read in all its Christian congregations (Query: in all its

28. Also Isa. 28:20; 29:28 and throughout the prophets.

29. See also v. 24 and Jas. 5:7. See Schlatter, pp. 84f.; also Ropes's note (p. 295), citing Joel, Zechariah, and Deuteronomy as well.

synagogues) as well as privately by any who could get a copy of it in writing. As the volumes of Cicero's letters show, postal services worked well enough already in his day;[30] and the Jews, from the Babylonian Captivity and earlier, developed a sense of national and religious solidarity that the modern Christian cannot realize in imagination, much less in actuality.[31] Certainly long before James or Paul, who also employed this method, the chief rabbis sent letters (circulars) by messengers *(šᵉlûḥîm)* to the synagogue and its rabbi in many a distant place—at New Year's Day, the Passover, Pentecost, or other special occasions. In our opinion James preceded Paul in writing epistles to his converts; and we venture to believe that James was probably not inventing a new form but was merely following the example of generations of chief rabbis and the like.

In our view, the structure of the Epistle of James places it in the same period as the Epistles of Paul. In later times, including our own, the structural affinity between the Epistle of James and those of similar length by Paul has rarely been perceived; the custom has been to deny that the Epistle of James has any structure at all. This period, too (before the fall of Jerusalem), is the only one in which primitive Jewish Christianity could write with such authority, guiding, comforting, and sternly rebuking the Jewish Christians of the Diaspora. It was, therefore, almost inevitable that the Epistle of James should reflect, as it does in 2:5-13, the early Jewish attitude of the first apostolic age, a time when, as in Acts 11:3; 15:1-5 (and in the Council that followed), there was a strong move to prejudice Christianity into Judaism. Paul also had to contend with this move, as in the Epistle to the Galatians.

Although the Epistle of James itself gives us no explicit details of the author's history, we believe that it is essentially autobiographical in the sense that the style is the man and that—and this is, as A. J. Gossip remarks, one of the oddest things in literature—while Paul's immensely vivid portrait has grown blurred, James "unconsciously has

30. Available classical evidence shows that fifty Roman miles a day was the average rate of the imperial couriers. A Roman mile is about eleven-twelfths of an English mile. See, e.g., C. W. J. Eliot, "New Evidence for the Speed of the Roman Imperial Post," *The Phoenix* 9 (1955): 76-80.

31. See S. K. Stowers, *Letter Writing in Graeco-Roman Antiquity* (1986); W. Doty, *Letters in Primitive Christianity* (1973); J. White, ed., *Studies in Ancient Letter Writing* (1982); M. P. McGuire, "Letters and Letter Carriers in Christian Antiquity," *The Classical World* 53 (1960): 185; also M. L. Stirewalt, "Paul's Evaluation of Letter-Writing," in *Search the Scriptures: New Testament Studies in Honour of R. I. Stamm* (1969), p. 188; C. J. Hemer, "The Address of 1 Peter," *ExpT* 89.8 (1978): 239, 242 n. 4; L. Casson, *Travel in the Ancient World* (1974); H. Koester, *Introduction to the New Testament,* II (1982), pp. 52ff.; D. E. Aune, *The New Testament in Its Literary Environment* (1987), p. 180.

painted himself in colours that remain as fresh as the day they were first laid upon the canvas."[32] We do not know at what point in his life he became a Christian; but the impression the entire Epistle gives is that, after his decisive conversion, he grew gradually into the new religion, beholding the old illuminated before his eyes as he came to appreciate the significance of Jesus. Martin Dibelius, as we have seen, thinks of James as a "once born" Christian, one who has found God without such an inner torment as Paul experienced. This chimes with what tradition teaches us about James the brother of the Lord, whose discipleship seems to have been no sudden revolution but a gradual process.

From the Epistle of James we learn that its author likewise is an evolutionist, one who harbors no antagonism toward the Torah but rather reverences its commandments. As a result James, emphatically but briefly relating the Christian life to the Christian faith, can devote himself more comprehensively to the sins and sorrows, the virtues and joys, the wisdom and folly, that may come into that life. Except for the fact that the first Christians expected an almost immediate end of the present world, hardly anything in the Epistle of James is not applicable to Christianity today.

The importance of identifying our James as the author of the Epistle of James can hardly be exaggerated.[33] However "tradition-mongers" may have exaggerated the truth, nothing can surpass the direct evidence of an actual eyewitness to the earthly life and teaching of Christ. Christianity, at least Protestant Christianity, has been, and is, very slow to believe that the Epistle of James is by our James. "Every shred of understanding for the Christian situation as that of 'betweenness' is lacking here," wrote Bultmann; "The moralism of the syr agogue has made its entry."[34] Sometimes the Epistle of James is regarded as nothing more than a pseudonymous document of some-centuries-old Christianity, concocted perhaps by "a first-century Christian legalist and moralistic prig";[35] and James himself is thought of as little more than a modern bishop or religious functionary (and not one of the greatest or best at that). As a result, most Christians entirely miss the dawn of Christianity; and, equally, they miss the "allusions" that vitalized the birth and boyhood of Christ and Christianity.

32. *The General Epistles*. The Study Bible (1930), p. 2.

33. See Scaer's considered judgment: "The search for the earliest connections with the earthly Jesus would be resolved partially if the epistle were written by the uterine brother of Jesus" (*James, the Apostle of Faith*, p. 23).

34. *Theology of the New Testament*, II (1955), 163.

35. See R. Goetz, "Evangelism by Works Alone," *The Christian Century* 102.9 (1985): 261.

Those pioneers in Christ believed in him and his works; and one of his works can be studied in Jas. 5:1-6, with its climax in 5:7f. and its code of conduct in the sequel. When those "allusions" faded, the Christian was bound to think comparatively less (in time and satisfaction) of the rewards (in and after earthly life) for himself and to give more and more thought and work to the laudable goal of social revolution. Rightly, this occupies much of our thinking today, especially with the current ideological assault on the poor.

SOCIAL DOCTRINE

Certainly James would make short shrift of such absurdly blatant rationalizations izations as "in order to succeed, the poor need most of all the spur of their poverty."[36] Yet—and this may be an uncharitable and certainly an unpopular thought—we are deeply concerned that in all that very virtuous, urgent, and necessary clamor about today's social oppression and our Christian duty to fight against it, we may inadvertently be missing the wealth of the dawn of Christianity in Christ. "His ethics, which are an extension of his Christology," notes C. J. S. Millar,[37] "were intended to preserve the community and not to evangelize non-believers. Furthermore, James did not plan to offer any program for reforming society. We should not then be disappointed when we do not find such a program in James." Schemes of social reform, or the conversion of sinners to righteousness, do not figure forcibly in the Epistle of James for the plain reason that James and his contemporary Christians did not expect them to be necessary, since sinners were soon to be destroyed in cataclysmic damnation.

The attitude of James toward the socioeconomic order is conservative yet radical. While interpreting the later OT ideas of poverty and wealth in terms of the gospel, he still thinks of each primarily in a moral rather than an economic context; the poor and the rich as classes are really synonymous with the *'ᵃnāwîm* and the wicked respectively. James would have the Christian accept the existing economic order and live as a Christian within the God-given framework. As far as possible the Christian must accept the present social situation, cooperate with his employer, and apply Christ's principles to daily life. Absent also from James is any teaching concerning the relation of the individual to the secular powers. He has nothing corresponding to Christ's great saying

36. See the excellent article by G. Chauncey, "People and the Current Economic Crisis," *Monday Morning* 47 (1982): 19f.; also *Economic Justice for All: Pastoral Letter on Catholic Social Teaching and the U.S. Economy* (1986), pp. 95f.

37. *The Primitive Christology in the Epistle of James* (1971), p. 56.

"Render to Caesar" (Mk. 12:17), which surely "has deeply influenced all subsequent relationships of Church and State."[38]

Yet when one has stated James's conservative stance, the last word has not yet been said. For if James does not deal directly with the economic problem, the whole tone of his teaching points the way to its solution. Allowance must be made for the full force of the radical spiritual principles basic to James's theology. Applied on a larger scale, his high Christology linked with his emphasis on individual worth (2:1ff.) could not fail to revolutionize the old social order and establish the new. Moreover, he denounces the sins that would harm any community at the same time that he recognizes a corporate responsibility for the care of the poor and the needy, the suffering and the oppressed.

On these and other sins the Christian attitude in the age of James must be distinguished from that of later times: the first Christians exulted in anticipation of an imminent overthrow of sin; some today seem to give programs of moral reform on a large scale the same weight as the early damnation of the wicked in Jas. 5:1-8. James implies that the task of the church in the social and economic order is to create a fellowship in which both rich and poor, employers and employees, express their Christian oneness. If Paul could say that in Christ Jesus there is neither bond nor free, James with similar conviction can say that there is neither rich nor poor. The Christian doctrine of the nature of God and each individual must lead ultimately to the transformation of the entire social and economic order. Thus, even at this early stage, the church under James's guidance is preparing to fulfill its crucial ecumenical function.

James's teaching deals almost exclusively with the social and practical aspects of Christianity and is the richest in the NT. "By his stern insistence upon practice, by his healthy contempt for all shams, by his forthright condemnation of all religion which sets mere orthodoxy before a faith which flows in lovely deeds," says A. M. Hunter, "James provides a wholesome antidote to all evangelicalism that would save its own soul while it lets a brother go his way to perdi-

38. See V. Taylor, *The Gospel according to St. Mark* (1952), *ad loc.;* C. H. Giblin, "The Things of God" in the question "Concerning Tribute to Caesar (Lk. 20:25; Mk. 12:17; Mt. 22:21)," *CBQ* 33 (1971): 510ff.; L. Goppelt, "The Freedom to Pay the Imperial Tax (Mk. 12:17)," *StEv* 2 (1964): 183ff.; L. Goppelt, "Der Staat in der Sicht des Neuen Testaments," *Christologie und Ethik* (1968); J. D. M. Derrett, "Peter's Penny: Fresh Light on Matthew 17:24-27," *NovT* 6 (1963): 1ff.; H. M. J. Loewe, *Render unto Caesar: Religious and Political Loyalty in Palestine* (1940); E. Stauffer, *Christ and the Caesars* (1955); S. G. F. Brandon, *Jesus and the Zealots* (1967); S. Kennard, *Render to God* (1950).

tion."[39] His call for personal commitment is real enough, but far from obscuring social obligation it becomes the very basis of his social doctrine; indeed, "if James was opposed to pious withdrawal from the world, he was equally antagonistic to those who ignored the sovereign will of the transcendent God."[40] He is concerned with the benign piety of the person who seems to be religious but does not bridle his tongue and thus deceives himself (1:26). It is because James saw so clearly what personal commitment involved that he gave such involvement so much prominence in his thought.

Like Jesus, James never makes a statement that would warrant the separation of the individual from the social aspects of life. He urges believers to apply their Christianity to every area of life, believing, as did Martin Luther King, that "any religion that professes to be concerned with the souls of men and is not concerned with social conditions that cripple them is a dry-as-dust religion."[41] Faith is useless if it is not socially fruitful.[42] Thus James enjoins kind and considerate action to all without discrimination. In particular, Christians should be alert to relieve poverty and need whenever possible.[43] James quotes with approval the summary of the law in terms of loving one's neighbor as oneself[44] and gives attention to many aspects of life that are socially related. The dangers of poverty and wealth with the corresponding problems of discrimination, affluence, currying favor with the rich, and the right use of money[45] are recurring subjects of instruction.

James sees the relevance of Christianity to trade, to business ethics, to wages and hours,[46] to self-control in speech,[47] to apartheid and racism,[48] to temptation,[49] to distress and doubt,[50] to pessimism,[51] and even to sickness.[52] He lays down the great principles for the dialectic

39. *Interpreting the New Testament* (1951), p. 120.
40. F. Greeves, "God Willing," *ExpT* 70.3 (1968): 91.
41. *Stride toward Freedom* (1958), p. 36.
42. 2:14ff.
43. 1:27; 2:13, 15f.
44. 2:8.
45. 1:9f.; 2:1ff.; 5:5ff. For Paul's different emphasis here, see C. S. Dudley and E. Hilgert, *New Testament Tensions and the Contemporary Churches* (1987), pp. 54f.
46. 5:4; 4:13ff.
47. 3:1ff.
48. 2:1ff.
49. 1:13ff.
50. 1:6.
51. 5:13.
52. 5:14.

of Christian existence[53] and for the expression of truly Christian relationships in all spheres of society: the religion of James is real and dynamic and applicable to the present day. In the light of so many clear indications, James undoubtedly regarded friendly and helpful relations with one's fellows as indispensable for the Christian.[54] We are normally rather self-centered about our rights and relatively cooperative in meeting our civic obligations; James, like all serious Christians, stresses the ancient Jewish ideal, "Thou shalt love thy neighbor as thyself" (Lev. 8:19). Faith builds brotherhood, and its genuineness is tested in the reality of brotherly living.

James and his fellow Christian Jews grew up with the philosophy of the ancient Jewish religion. Then, as today, that philosophy was not one in which theory was allowed to eclipse practice, as we see very markedly in the lives of our own Jewish friends. To this inherited tradition of national worship and national fellowship, Jesus, James and his converts believed, by his atoning death *added* the fulfillment of the salvation promised to Jew and Gentile. On that side of the matter, the converted Jew had passed both the first and the second stages in his religious instruction.

That is why James has so little to say about the theoretic aspects of Christianity. The Christianity of James (and Paul) is only the culmination and expansion of Judaism; indeed, it might even be said that the two disciples ultimately divided not on a doctrine but on a practice—circumcision. But that would be too simplistic, for the division is not concerned with the practice as such, but with the practice undertaken as a legal obligation, that is, with the doctrinal implications of the practice. Paul in his letters emphasizes three times that circumcision per se is neither here nor there (Gal. 5:6; 6:15; 1 Cor. 7:19), and he shows this by his circumcision of Timothy for a prudential reason (Acts 16:3). It was against circumcision viewed as a means of acquiring righteousness in God's sight that he set his face. The Jews practiced circumcision as a matter of course, as Paul himself did when he circumcised Timothy to regularize his status.

GOD: MASTERING EVIL

The emphatically Jewish tone of the Epistle of James is not alien but native to infant Christianity; and inevitably that Christianity is not pri-

53. See T. Lorensen, "Faith without Works does not Count before God! James 2:14-26," *ExpT* 89.8 (1978): 234.

54. 5:13ff.

marily something to argue about, as in too many of the divided Christian churches of today, but a godly code by which to live and die. In theory both Jew and Christian have the same fundamental doctrine, that God, the supreme Power in the universe, is eternal and eternally good, never evil, and never the author of evil; while evil originates in the imperfections active in man since he first yielded to its power. This leaves the Jew to puzzle over the origin of evil in the person of Satan; but our aim here is only to state the position of James on the matter.

Sin, says James, comes about through a person's yielding to his "desire"; this is evidently a strong tendency in human nature, but its origin and function are left unexplained. That the NT does not hold *epithymia* itself sinful is plain from, for example, Lk. 22:15, Col. 3:5 ("evil" is necessarily added), and 1 Cor. 7:2, 5; in the last verse we see that satisfaction of an *epithymia* may be not only right but a positive duty. In Jas. 1:14 *(epithymia)* and 4:2 *(epithymeite),* the context proves that James is speaking of *epithymia* sinfully indulged. In 1:14 "his own" is inserted to place the blame squarely where it belongs, on us rather than God; here, and in the next verse, *epithymia* is personified, but by way of rhetorical figure only.[55]

As was often the case in such omissions, James and the Jews to whom the Epistle is addressed would think of some relevant current Jewish doctrine, here that of the *yēṣer,*[56] a fruitful source of rabbinic speculation[57] and apparently familiar in Qumran.[58] It often signified or included the sexual libido, "lust," which may be good or evil since it works within or outside of marriage but in itself is indiscriminating in impulse and activity.[59] Like Jesus, James ignores the Fall, for he is not concerned with the origin of sin except to deny that it can come from God: James here is concerned with our *peirasmos* and present battle with sin. So, in contrast both to the dualistic concept of evil and to the doctrine (not unknown to the rabbis) of original and hereditary sin,

55. See Mussner, p. 88.

56. See, e.g., Mussner, p. 88; also noted by Rendall, Hort, Carrington, Schlatter, Windisch, Büchsel, et al.

57. See above, pp. 330ff.

58. See 1QS 3.12–4.26, esp. 3.13-21; also R. E. Murphy, "*Yeṣer* in the Qumran Literature," *Bib* 39 (1958): 339.

59. The sexual urge, the rabbis said, having been created by God to secure the propagation of children, is good; like other passions, e.g., for eating, drinking, and getting money, it becomes evil only in its improper use. The sin is not in the desire as such but in our yielding to the desire in a wrong case, as in copulation without marriage. Without the ambivalent desire virtue would have no field of choice in which to exercise itself, as it does by the guidance of God's Torah.

James stresses human free will and responsibility; and, as Ropes well reminds us,[60] this passage "has no doctrinal purpose other than to warn the readers against resorting to a current excuse for sin."[61]

If, however, it is erroneous to restrict *peirasmos* in Jas. 1:12 to (say) affliction, it is no less serious to find (as some do) a difference in kind between "external" and "internal" temptations. There is no essential difference between a Nero and a Jezebel. The Epistle of James (and not only James) was written with a *pastoral* mind and must be interpreted with a *pastoral* mind; academic learning, indispensable as it is, must be an adjunct (if it is not to be an impediment) to that mind. The neglect of this truth seems to have created much of the difficulty, especially the false dichotomy, regarding Jas. 1:2 and 12. Pagan philosophy did teach virtue, in theory and quite appreciably in practice.

Some of our commentaries hark back to (or were actually written to) an age in which Christianity was dominant. If we look at our world now, we can see the enormous difficulties and temptations of the Christian in a godless environment. The persecution of a Nero, a Marcus Aurelius (the best and wisest man among the emperors and at the same time the worst persecutor of the Christians), or magistrates instigated by the Jews against Jesus and Paul (see Jas. 2:6?), the afflictions of poverty, illness, and the like—all these are far less prominent (though they are present) to James or Paul than the difficulties of the incessant battle for the "good life" in an environment of wickedness. The NT is full of evidence of that wickedness and of its disastrous effects on hosts of Christian converts at Rome, Corinth, and elsewhere.

James does believe in the devil (4:7), but he sandwiches him so between God and God (note the front and rear protection in the OT) that

60. P. 153. Certainly James does not put it as explicitly as Ecclesiasticus; but free will is just as important to James's thought as in Homer, *Odyssey* 1.34: "By their own sins they have of themselves sorrows beyond the necessities of their lot" (cited by Ropes, p. 154).

61. Of the three great characteristics of the Epistle of James, namely, Apocryphal, Apostolic, and Apocalyptic, the first-named is plain throughout the Epistle. On 1:13, Ropes (p. 154) rightly cites Ecclus. 15:11-20; but he perhaps misses one important point. A parallel thought is found not only here in Ecclesiasticus; we think it is almost certain that James had this passage in mind when he wrote 1:13-18. Not only is "Let none say, etc." of James similar in form and sense to "Do not say, 'The Lord is to blame for my failure'" (NEB) of Ecclus. 15:11, but the point of Ecclus. 15:14, the creation of man with moral power and responsibility: "When he made man in the beginning, he left him free to take his own decisions," is also taken up by James, not as a slavish copyist, but with the characteristic slant of Christian thought. This can be seen from Ropes (p. 167) on 1:18: "But the figure does not seem very common in Jewish thought. With (pagan) Greek writers the word is more frequent in a figurative sense."

he almost disappears: "So enlist under God; fight the devil and he will flee from you." The context almost makes possible the equation: pride = the devil. No one stands so near to teaching that the devil is impersonal as does James. In his discussion of temptation the devil is neither mentioned nor even implied. He gives a masterly analysis of temptation without in the least diminishing its spiritual seriousness and reality.

Modern Christians need to tackle the problem of the personality of the devil. They have shirked a controversial issue, and have made real temptation appear often ludicrous. As a tool, the personality of the devil is, and always will be, immensely useful to preaching; but crude literalism serves only to complicate rather than solve the problem, and can be most misleading. It has been pointed out,[62] for example, that "we have so moralized Satan that we failed to see that the most satanic temptation of all is to become someone other than ourselves." In any case, "the world, the flesh, and the devil" form a trilogy, implying that the constitution of all three terms must be the same, that is, impersonal, or otherwise personal. Belief in a personal devil certainly does not help us in the battle against temptation; indeed, the reverse is often true, leading us (as James saw) to blame the devil ("the devil made me do it") and avoid our responsibility and capability in resisting evil.

If it is true that the admonition to resist the devil unveils James's underlying theology, namely, that "behind the evil impulse lies the devil; suprapersonal forces of evil are behind personal evil,"[63] it is equally true that the doctrine of the devil per se does not offer a satisfactory philosophical explanation of the origin of evil. *Peirasmos* comes not from without—from Satan—but from within. So by virtue of his "desire," "each man is his own Satan" (St. Bernard) and must bear full responsibility. In any case, if the devil is personal, redemption (as such diverse spirits as the ancient Church Father Origen and the Scottish poet Robert Burns, both hinted)[64] *must* apply to him, nor do we believe that the seriousness of sin, evil, and eternal judgment is furthered by stressing belief in a personal devil.

But if God is good, why does evil exist? How the devil, nuclear warfare, earthquakes, the cholera germ, hunger, or AIDS fits in with this idea is a big question. James must have had clear views on it, for nobody could be more aware of the evils of this life and world. Yet

62. W. Wink, *Unmasking the Powers* (1986), p. 18.

63. Davids, p. 166. See C. Brown, "Satan" *(diabolos), NIDNTT,* III, 471.

64. See 1 Cor. 15:48; Rom. 8:18, 22. On this occurrence of *kosmos* (3:6) and the other two (1:27; 2:5), see L. T. Johnson, "Friendship with the World/Friendship with God: A Study of Discipleship in James," *Discipleship in the New Testament* (1985), pp. 172f.

James does not consider this a serious problem. For him the devil is there; the world is evil *(ho kosmos tēs adikias),* and that means not only humankind and living creatures but even the earth and the stars.[65]

In interpreting James it is necessary *not* to obscure the difference between God's overall purpose, which permits evil for a time, and the specific actions of the devil, or us. There is no easy solution to the problem of evil. "It is true," notes Frank Stagg, "that it is God who opens up the possibility of evil, for as soon as he opens the way to good the way to evil is also opened. There can be good without evil, but there cannot be the possibility of good without the possibility of evil. Were it not possible to distrust, there would be no such thing as trust."[66] If we are thinking of the overall purpose of God, we can believe that he permits the existence of evil, and permits it with good intent: if there were no evil there would be no moral effort, for there would be no moral choice, and no free will, for there would be no will to exercise in this sphere. But that is not the same as saying that God directs and orders and instigates the devil to do all or any of his devilish work.

To be sure, God has a "moral responsibility" to allow the devil to exist and work evil. God escapes culpability for the devil's existence and actions because the devil cannot harm us if we put our faith in God, as James and all Christian authorities teach; and this is true whether the devil is attacking by pain, as in adversities, or by pleasures, as in lusts. But that is not to say that God required the devil to do any particular act of evil; it is obvious that anyone who thinks he is being tempted by God in the manner of Abraham or of Dt. 13:3 must at once realize that in that case the sin contemplated must *not* be committed.

James is obviously addressing himself to the case of a person who does not think he is in the place of Abraham or of Dt. 13:3, but thinks, or is in danger of thinking: "This is a sin; God is instigating me to commit it, and so I need not scruple to commit it." That the overall purpose

65. On Origen, see Wink, *Unmasking the Powers,* pp. 34, 180 n. 75. On Robert Burns, see his "Address to the Devil," *The Poetical Works of Robert Burns* (n.d.), ed. Robert Ford, p. 117:

> "But fare-you-weel, auld 'Nickie-ben!'
> O wad ye tak a thought an' men'!
> Ye aiblins might—I dinna ken."

The original Scottish flavor cannot be captured in translation, but roughly the meaning is:

> "But fare-you-well, old Devil!
> O would you take a thought and mend!
> You perhaps might—I do not know."

66. "Exegetical Themes in James 1 and 2," *RevExp* 66.4 (1969): 396.

of God is no excuse for the sinner could not be plainer than it is in Mk. 14:21 (see also Matthew and Luke). We do not think that anyone can mistake the purpose or the meaning of the words of James.

Now those of us who still regard, for instance, stealing and adultery as sins usually ascribe them to the influence of the powers of evil, compendiously named the devil; and so we regard oppressors and persecutors as doing his work, and in this case, as also when we fall ill, we think that God has sent us affliction to try us. James, we are sure, would reject this. God's providence, says Thomas Manton,[67] "is conversant about sin without sin, as a sunbeam lighteth upon a dunghill without being stained by it." God is absolutely good, in every sense of goodness. Once more this truth has practical and pastoral (rather than theoretical) significance, since this doctrine of God means "we can have confidence in the goodness of God *now*."[68]

James's solution to the problem of evil, therefore, is essentially practical rather than philosophical. Here then is a double mystery: "that of God as good in relation to evil, that of God as Providence in relation to human responsibility" (Hort). James will have no truck with the sentimental fatalism that causes us to blame God for failure. Human sin can never be laid at his door.[69] James says expressly that God tests no one with evil. "Don't think that temptation comes from God and so need not be resisted."[70] (The theme of the chapter is the need for that resistance.) For the time being, at least, God allows the devil to tempt us to evil, as he allowed Satan to tempt Job and as he allowed Christ to be crucified. But God does not *want* us to sin, nor the devil to tempt us.

We may ask (and perhaps even conjecture an answer), Why, in that case, does God ever allow the devil to exist and sin to be rampant, and this present world to be evil?[71] But James says nothing about that; he simply says (with the Schoolmen), "God is simple" *(Deus est simplex)*—God is nothing but good and never proposes sin to us, even by way of a test. We must, therefore, put away all our modern talk that God sends evil to try us. We must recover the NT sense of living in a world of sin. Tyrants, war, earthquakes, poverty, disease—all these are parts

67. *An Exposition of the Epistle of James* (1693; reprinted 1968), p. 90.

68. See P. H. Davids, "So What?" *New College Berkeley Notes* 5.2 (1982-83): 1.

69. See Moffatt, p. 21. Islam, on the other hand, with its notion of the absoluteness of God, is not concerned to probe the matter: "God leads astray whom he pleases and guides where he pleases" (Qur'an 74.34).

70. James's language in 1:13 is exact and significant: "I am tempted *from* God"; *apo* rather than *hypo* is chosen to express, more remotely, source rather than instrument, origin not agency. See Hort, p. 21.

71. Gal. 1:4.

of the evil of this world; they never come from God, only from the mystery of iniquity, the powers of evil, which God will destroy today, or tomorrow, or at least very soon. That is paramount in James's parenetic. But Christian principle has not been changed by the visible delay in the destruction of evil; we simply must understand James better, along with his teaching of constancy in endurance.

How do we tackle—and overcome—these *peirasmoi?* The answer is to be found in the opening greeting: "Count it pure joy" (1:2). Life in this world brings constant temptations; welcome them. They are good training in resistance, and when they are overcome by endurance, they bring us nearer the Christian ideal. How are we to overcome them? Not by ourselves: God shows the way and gives strength to all who have the humility to ask for it and the faith to make the prayer effectual; and he helps us if we do not cut ourselves off by pride of class or wealth. Thus his doctrine of suffering *(Leidenstheologie)* helps James "show people how to transcend their present suffering, see the poor as rich, and the rich as desperately poor"; and correctly Davids adds, "If that is not relevant theology, I don't know what is."[72] We agree.

And what is the reward of endurance? Eternal life, for those who give their love to God, not to the world. Must we resist temptations? Yes, always. The mystery of evil is beyond our understanding, but we do know this, that God is against it, and that he is always at hand to help us: that is the theology of the Epistle of James.

To the Jew, God's goodness appeared above all in his love of humankind as shown in his gift of the law and messianic salvation; these two are linked by the rabbis and no less by James in 1:17. As a Christian, he saw the Messiah in Jesus, but he says not a word to elucidate the mystery of iniquity undeniably present in this world of sin, for his prime concern is how to *live* the Christian life "in this world of sin." For this, James, pious Jew turned Christian, needs the law. To James, like every good Jew, religion is essentially *a way of life,* a life of faith in God's law as revealed to man, a life of effort under the guidance of that law, and a hope that is not a mere aspiration but a conviction, as certain as any principle of mathematics, that truly there is a reward for the righteous.

THE PASSION FOR CONDUCT

We have been warned of "a modern Jesus-olatry" whose deity demands that everything in Christianity must be tied directly to Jesus.[73] The point

72. *Art. cit., New College Berkeley Notes* 5.2 (1982-83): 1.

73. P. Perkins, "Expository Articles: James 3:16–4:3," *Interpretation* 36:3 (July 1982): 286.

is well taken. We must never forget that Jesus himself built on the foundation of the OT and that the NT is not a new testament but only a codicil to the OT. It is probable that Jas. 1:26f. is a conscious reminiscence of passages in the old prophets like Isa. 1:13f. and its own context: "If anyone among you thinks he is devout, and is one who does not bridle his tongue but deludes his own heart, this man's devoutness is vain. Devoutness pure and undefiled is this, to visit the fatherless and widows in their affliction, and to keep oneself unspotted from the world."

"Devout" and "devoutness" clarify the meaning of the rare *thrēskos* (adj.) and *thrēskeia* (noun) better than "thinks he is a worshipper" and then "worship" twice in 1:26. Ropes correctly says that both these words "have the sae considerable range of meaning as the English word 'worship' with reference to the inner and external aspects of religious worship."[74] So in Jn. 4:22, the first "worship" and to a lesser extent the second are defective, in comparison with "worship" in the next two verses. Since the so-called "worshipper" thinks his "worship" is the full and true religion, the KJV can withstand criticism.[75]

If "pure" and "undefiled" implies a ceremonial *thrēskeia,* this may suggest a time when Jewish Christians, still joined in the temple worship,[76] were inevitably subject to the peculiarly Pharisaic emphasis on cult ritual, and some of them tended therefore to construe worship primarily in terms of "the washings and purification of late Judaism, multiplying Levitical ordinances" (Hort). The relation of ceremonial to practical duties was a fruitful subject for Jewish debate. Some held, for example, that the cultus was more important than good works.[77] The temptation in late Judaism, with its emphasis on the negative, external, and casuistic, was "to reckon worship as a substitute for sanctity."[78] But James, like the OT prophets, took the opposite view and attacked the cultus as a form of idolatry—though perhaps not the obvious variety that worships Moloch or some heathen god, this is no less real. On

74. P. 181. See also K. L. Schmidt, *thrēskeia, TDNT,* II, 155ff.

75. "Deceiving his own heart." This is quite rightly in the protasis, but not in the apodosis. After the extended and studied balance of the protasis, the short, crisp, monophrastic apodosis has fuller force in itself, and gives fuller force to the epanalepsis, with contrasting epithets, of "worship" at the beginning of v. 27 (we mean epithets contrasting with the preceding "vain").

76. On Philo's reference (*On the Embassy to Gaius* 232, 298) to the Jewish ancestral cultus (and its apparent rabbinic equivalent *hā'ᵃḇôḏāh*), with its implications for the early dating of the Epistle of James, see W. L. Knox, "The Epistle of St. James," *JTS* 46 (1945): 11; see also Davids, p. 102, for other possible interpretations.

77. See b. Sukka 49b; also Sifré on Dt. 3.20.

78. But see W. L. Knox, *art. cit. JTS* 46 (1945): 12.

"vain" *(mataios),* here often used in the LXX for the variety of idols, see Isa. 29:13; Jer. 10; also Eccl. 1:2.

Vain worship, which must be distinguished from true worship, is an "abomination to the Lord."[79] James protests, says W. F. Lofthouse, against "one of the most inveterate weaknesses of human nature—a weakness which dates from primitive ages, which thought of God, or the gods, as non-moral, and requiring to be kept propitious by the regular performance of ceremonial acts. His protest . . . will be of value so long as there are human beings primitive enough to be religious with moral rectitude and love to their fellow men."[80] In line with the traditional prophetic emphasis that true worship is ethical and practical, James believes that caring constitutes the true cultus, and that "good works" are more important than good profession. So he mentions controlled speech—contrast the self-deluded slanderer (1:21f.)—and care of the widow and orphan, whose affliction or trial (1:2) is always a special concern. The strongest expression of responsibility for the widow is found in James, "where all outward veneration of God is contrasted with it."[81] The religion that is genuine before God, therefore, is also pure. "To keep oneself unspotted from the world" is simply another illustration of the way in which the NT gives a new religious and moral content to originally cultic concepts[82] and is just a variant of putting off all filthiness (1:21). On the notion that piety is the true form of purity, we may cite good parallels from the OT (e.g., Isa. 1:16f.; Ps. 82:3) and the NT (e.g., Lk 11:41; Mt. 23:26).[83]

Of course, "this is not a definition of religion"; rather, as Ropes rightly explains, it is a description or statement (by an apparent contradiction, an oxymoron) of what is better than external acts of worship. Ropes cites good parallels, but Rom. 12:1 is most helpful here. As usual, in spite of his wrongly alleged "antinomianism," Paul is James's best interpreter.[84] "Both Paul and James agreed with their proto-rabbinic tradition," observes Sigal, "that not inquiry or study, 'hearing' the word, is what is fundamental, *hā'iqqār* [the important thing], but the doing of it, *he-ma'aśeh* (M. Aboth 1.17)."[85] In James, as in Paul, Christianity is *word (logos)* plus *deed (poiēsis). Thrēskeia* is what I *do* to please God—"wor-

79. See C. E. B. Cranfield, "The Message of James," *SJTh* 18 (1965): 189.
80. *Ethics and Atonement* (1906), p. 6.
81. S. Solle, "Widow" *(chrēma), NIDNTT,* III, 1074.
82. A. Oepke, *aspilos, TDNT,* I, 502.
83. See W. L. Knox, *art. cit., JTS* 46 (1945): 11.
84. See E. Käsemann, *Romans* (1980), pp. 325ff. with bibliography; also Sigal, "The Halakhah of James," *Intergerini Parietis Septum* (1981), p. 340.
85. Sigal, ibid., p. 340; see also p. 341.

ship" or "service"; and if I don't do it outside church and similar observances, I am not doing it at all. The idea of Christ as the *poiētēs,* the *doer* of the word and the law (Jas. 1:22ff.; Rom. 2:13), as F. Thiele notes,[86] "is in sharp contrast with, say, quietistic Epicureanism or the Buddhist ideal of inaction." *Latreia* in Rom. 12:1 is another word for it:[87] and there, as in James, it means the *deed (poiēsis)* of the *word (logos),* that is, of the *logos* that, as James says, is implanted in the Christian by God. Hence Paul very accurately and deliberately calls that *deed (poiēsis)* "your reasonable service" *(logikēn latreian)*—not just a "churchy" *thysian,* "sacrifice," but a living *thysian,* a *thysian* made by a way of thinking and living. Here the NEB is quite good: "I implore you by God's mercy to offer your very selves to him, a living sacrifice, dedicated and fit for his acceptance, *the worship offered by* mind and heart."

James's doctrine of the *poiēsis* of the *logos* is exactly the same; and its foundation, 1:18, is the same as Paul's foundation in the last verse of Rom. 11. It is not a definition of religion, but rather a characterization (not so much a definition of Christian conduct as the *poiēsis* of the Christian *logos*). Worship and *latreia* and *thrēskeia* can properly be done in the narrower sense of these words, but unless they are part of the full scope as in Heb. 9:1 and 6 where these words are used in their all-embracing sense, they are nothing.

Underneath all this thought lies the ancient Jewish insistence on the duty of conduct. In James and the NT this is expressed in terms of speaking, listening, and doing. The Christian is created for good works (Eph. 2:10), is urged to bear fruit in good works (Col. 1:10), and to strive to do good to all (Rom. 15:2; 16:19; Gal. 6:6, 10; 1 Thess. 5:15). In James's Jews, this emphasis was new in its Christian fulfillment of Jewish prophecy; and it was even newer in Paul's Gentiles. The ethical propaganda of the Wisdom literature and epoch, and the immorality or amorality or indifference to ethics in conduct that many seem to have thought compatible with their baptism as Christians, notwithstanding the emphasis seen even in Pliny's account of early Christian worship, leads James, like Paul and the rest, to preach the importance of moral behavior in the Christian religion.

Ecclus. 1–7 is generally acknowledged to be one of the two main sources of inspiration of the "Wisdom" affinities in James and the rest

86. "Work" *(poieō), NIDNTT,* III, 1155.

87. For a careful discussion of *latreuō, latreia,* and *thysian,* see C. E. B. Cranfield, *The Epistle to the Romans,* I, 76f.; II (1978), 599ff.; also K. Hess, "Serve" *(latreuō), NIDNTT,* III, 549; H. Strathmann, *latreuō, latreia, TDNT,* IV, 65; M. Newton, *The Concept of Purity at Qumran and in the Letters of Paul* (1985), pp. 70ff.

of the NT (see Ecclus. 2:5 on the purifying of gold and of men; and on Jas. 1:22 see esp. Ecclus. 3:1: "Listen . . . and do . . . ifyou wish to be safe" [NEB]). James says: ". . . save your souls." So Prov. 6:7 has: "Listen to me and do not ignore what I say" (NEB). The moral duty of the Christian as expressed in the formula of hear, obey, and do, is of the essence of Christianity in the NT. Witness the peroration of the Sermon on the Mount (Mt. 7:24-26). Again, we note the highly advanced rhetorical skill of the Epistle of James, illustrated here in the expression of the familiar thought of hearing and doing.[88]

THE DEMAND FOR RIGHTEOUSNESS

Like the rest of the NT, the Epistle of James is dominated by the demand for righteousness—the kind enunciated, epitomized, and enjoined by Jesus. James's ethics, like all Jewish ethics, was one of obedience to the Torah, in this case the Messianic Torah, a new kind of law which in its turn led to a new kind of righteousness. This idea of righteousness, which is there from the beginning and implicit throughout the Epistle, is first mentioned by name in 1:20, where we read that "a man's wrath [or 'anger'] does not express in action the righteousness of God."

This key verse, which we have not yet discussed, is important for our present purpose and deserves to be studied with some care. Previously we were inclined to take *dikaiosynē* to mean "justice," that is, the penal judgment by God as Judge on sinners, making this an injunction to Christians to help themselves to revenge or recompense when wronged.[89] God's vengeance on sinners is one of the oldest motifs of many religions.[90]

We now think that this interpretation is too narrow; we prefer "righteousness" both for that reason and as more in keeping with the

88. See W. Mundle, "Hear" *(akouō), NIDNTT,* II, 176ff.

89. For other possibilities, see Moo, pp. 78f.; Davids, p. 93.

90. For pagans, see Sophocles, *Ajax* 390, "avenging Justice" *(telesphoros Dikē)* or the Maltese in Acts 28:4, *hē dikē;* for Hebrews, see Ps. 58 *ad fin.* where there is just recompense for the good and the evil. In Rom. 3:4 God in his vengeance is called *ho epipherōn tēn orgēn.* Human self-help by revenge is forbidden in Rom. 12:19 as in vv. 17, 21. On this, see the comment of Cranfield, *The Epistle to the Romans,* II, 646f. That lesson the early Greek cities also had to learn (see Aeschylus, *Eumenides*). This notion is not in itself inapposite in the Epistle of James. The eschatological urgency of the NT springs from the conception of God as Judge (e.g., Acts 17:30f.), and this is the dominant idea of God throughout James, from 1:2 to 5:20. See D. N. Freedman and J. R. Lundbom, *ḥarṭōm, TDOT,* V, 176, on the destructive effects of human anger; also H.-C. Hahn, "Anger" *(orgē), NIDNTT,* I, 107f.; U. Falkenroth, "Punishment, Vengeance" *(dikē), NIDNTT,* III, 96f.

habitual rotary ("rondo") structure of James's exposition. The latter development of 1:20 is not in 4:11f., which deals only with censoriousness, not "wrath" (1:19f.). The development of 1:19f. is in 3:13-18; 1:19f. exhort to meekness and peace, and 1:21 to purity; such also is 3:17 where "pure" reverts to 1:21a and "peaceable," "humane," "yielding to persuasion," and "full of mercy" elaborate "slow to wrath" in 1:20 and are almost identified with God's righteousness (or justice).

Righteousness (or justice) is the opposite of strife, which is also a lie against the truth (Jas. 3:14), as is vice (Rom. 2:2). "Undivided in mind" (with "untainted in hypocrisy") returns to 1:6. The epitomizing conjunction of righteousness and peace in 3:18 is accordingly best taken as similarly connected in thought with 1:20. In 3:18 *dikaiosynē* obviously means not the judgment of God but a way of life that, in keeping with James's usual rotary manner, reverts to the opening verse (3:13) of the section, "by his way of life" *(ek tēs kalēs anastrophēs),* which in turn means *dikaiosynē* in the sense we gave it in 3:18.

3:13-18 is a renewed treatment of the main points in 1:5-21. 1:19-21 in particular describes the mind needed if we are to *hear* and hearken to the Word; 3:13-18 describes the mind (and, of course, it is the same mind) needed if we are to *do* accordingly. At 1:22 James turns from "the mind to hear" to "the mind to do." So at 4:1 he turns from "the mind to do" to the mind "that knows how to do right and does not do it" (4:17), that is, the "double-minded" (4:8). The repetition of "double-minded" from 1:8 is but one mark of the conscious care with which James constructed his Epistle (in his characteristic rotary manner).

Notice also that 4:1-10, like 3:13-18, harks back to the beginning (1:14f., 21), and has the same message as in 1:21, that of repentance and purity and meekness (4:8-10). This last theme leads naturally to its reverse, pride (4:11-16), after which the early theme of *dikaiosynē* (1:20f.), exemplified in the conduct of both Abraham (2:23) and Rahab (2:25) and repeated in 3:13-18, is balanced by a concluding invective against its reverse, namely, injustice and opposition by the powerful rich.

It is virtually impossible to find one word (just[ice]/right[eous]-[ness]) for *dikē* or *ṣeḏeq* and their derivatives, and no English word conveys all the meaning of the Greek or Hebrew.[91] The NEB is much addicted to "justice" (even as a certain way of life), obviously because "righteousness" is little used in modern English. In Jas. 1:20 "the righteousness of God," or God's righteousness, flows from God into our lives if we genuinely accept the "implanted Word," and is exhibited by "peace" and "(sexual) purity." Both "peace" and "purity" are aspects of

91. For a full discussion, see, e.g., Cranfield, *The Epistle to the Romans,* I, 91ff.

sanctification by the new birth (Jas. 1:18 and, e.g., Col. 3:9f.; 1 Cor. 6:11 [note, by the Spirit of our God]), while lust is the enemy of both peace and purity (Jas. 1:14f.; 4:1-3). James mentions "peace" before "purity" (1:19 and 21); the Decalogue (Commandments 6 and 7) and Jesus (Mt. 5:21-26 and 27-32; see also Heb. 12:14) do the same.

J. H. Ropes cites Mt. 6:33 to show that Jas. 1:20 refers to "righteousness which God approves."[92] But in Mt. 6:33 righteousness, like the Kingdom of God, is not something to be approved, but to be a participant in. It is something (in a sense) to *get,*[93] and so is properly contrasted with the food and drink and raiment that we normally consider imperative. What we need to get is participation, as members of his "Kingdom," in the righteousness he alone gives by his Spirit to those who have genuinely accepted him. That God is not the mere approver but the source of all our righteousness (and wisdom, and truth) is a fundamental truth of Scripture. Our business is to accept it meekly, and *express it in our works* ("works righteousness") (see Jas. 3:17).

THE GRACE OF HUMILITY

James is a "teacher" *(didaskalos)* (Ropes, p. 227, on Jas. 3:1).[94] But Ropes's "with special insistence on the liability to opinionated disputatiousness, 3:13-18," though quite true, must be read with care. There was much opinionated disputatiousness in early Christianity (see 1 Cor. 1:10-12; 3:3f.). But the NT presents this not in isolation as merely a disagreeable intellectual fault (possibly not unmixed with good, as we may sometimes find some good in "pugnacity") but as tainted with the deepest sin, pride. Paul, who is James's best interpreter, presents it thus (e.g., Phil. 2:2-4, q.v.), and so does James himself.

The key to James's thought is sincerity; and in James, as in Paul, the first step in sincerity is humility. James stresses the need for humility by implication in the mention of sincerity (1:6-8); he refers to it expressly in 1:10f. in his picture of the vanity and pride of worldly wealth. Note the word *tapeinōsis* ("abasement"), which does not mean stripping oneself, or being stripped, of wealth. The loss of wealth through persecution, as in the anti-Semitic policy under Gaius at Alexandria (Philo, *On the Embassy to Gaius* 18; see also Hort and Ropes), is not

92. Pp. 169f.

93. See J. A. Ziesler, *The Meaning of Righteousness in Paul* (1972), p. 170; but see B. Przybylski, *Righteousness in Matthew and His World of Thought* (1980), pp. 89ff.

94. See below, pp. 468ff.

what James means. Nowhere in his Epistle (or elsewhere in the NT) is poverty praised per se. The convert does not have to empty his coffers; rather, he has to empty his mind of the vain pride of wealth. As Joseph bar Hama says: "When he exalts himself, God humiliates him, but when he repents, He exalts him" (b. Ned. 55a); also Hillel: "My humility is my greatness and my greatness my humility" (Lev. R. 1).

The lesson to be learned from the goodness of God and his purpose for us (1:12-18) is humility (1:19-21). Obviously, Christian humility can only be learned from Christ, and has been well defined as "the extension of Christology into living."[95] "Receive with meekness" the saving Word. Meekness and pride are mutually exclusive; but though on opposite sides of the moral line, they are not exact opposites. The antithesis of pride is humility; of meekness, pugnacity. The proud person often disdains to contradict a false statement he hears (quite apart from motives of courtesy and charity); but the person who lacks meekness often declines to be corrected as to what he says or does. Ropes well uses *receptive* with *meek*[96] and goes on to say, "The emphatic word is 'meekness'" *(praÿtēti)*. This is not incorrect, but it may be clearer to say that in the Greek the emphasis of order in the two parts of the sentence is quite regularly on the beginning, or "putting off" *(apothemenoi)* and "in meekness" *(en praÿtēti)* respectively. But there is scarcely less emphasis on "all filthiness" *(pasan ryparian)* and "receive" *(dexasthe)*, an emphasis obviously strengthened by the semantic contrast with the noun and the verb respectively in the earlier part of the antithesis.[97] This multiplication of emphasis (though without the Greek resources in order) is common in English.

To take root, thrive, and grow, the implanted seed needs the proper soil. This is why the gospel must be received "with meekness," which is the fruit not of human effort but of repentance, a sign of salvation, of "calling" (Eph. 4:2), election (Col. 3:12), the work of the Holy Spirit (Gal. 5:22f.)—and a necessary condition for receiving the Word.[98] "Only as the divine Word was received humbly," says Moffatt, "and allowed to root itself in good soil, cleansed from spitefulness and arro-

95. Scaer, p. 49.

96. On 1:21, p. 170, line 18.

97. The reference is to "all" (1:12-20), and *ryparian, kakian, dexasthe, sōsai, psychas,* and *apothemenoi* are all emphatic. For Aristotle (*Nicomachean Ethics* 11.7.10), for example, meekness is the mean between excessive anger and excessive "angerlessness." The person who is meek is described as "imperturbable, and not led away by passion" (ibid. 55.5.3). See also W. Bauder, "Humility," "Meekness" *(praÿs) NIDNTT,* II, 257.

98. W. Bauder, *art. cit., NIDNTT,* II, 259.

gance, could the saving work be accomplished and Christians be first fruits for God."[99]

Except by the Jews, however, the virtue of meekness was not respected by the ancient world.[100] The classic biblical paragon is Moses, who was "very meek, above all men that were on the face of the earth."[101] The word "meek" does not mean "spiritless," but "submissive to God and lawful human authority, and gently considerate of the rights and feelings of others." Meekness is not weakness but (like tamed wild animals) has reserves of disciplined strength (see Mt. 5:5). Contrasted with "anger" *(orgē)* (v. 20), "meekness" *(praÿtēs)* (v. 21) signifies "a meek and humble readiness" to be taught the Word of God without flaring up against the teacher.

Gentleness is a mark of the true righteous who are inspired by divine wisdom (2:13, 17); it "stands in pleasing contrast to bitter zeal and contentiousness (3:14)."[102] The quality is constantly praised by the rabbis ("the Scriptures teach that he who is humble will as a result make the *Shechinah* dwell with man on earth"),[103] and humility is one of the forty-eight qualifications necessary for the proper reception of the Torah.[104] Significantly it is said that Moses received the Torah because he was meek.[105] Sin and pride must be stripped off before the gospel can be effectively received. This is the doctrine to which James is faithful when he insists on the necessity of a cleansed, repentant, and receptive spirit if the gospel is to take root in our souls.

Sincerity must work in our conduct (1:22-25); and sincerity cannot coexist with pride. "Pure religion . . ." (1:26f.) completes the lesson begun in 1:21 (indeed, 1:10, *tapeinōsis*). The conjunction of 1:26f. with 1:22-25 rests on the thought of self-deceiving pride and illusion of righteousness, the marks of the person who thinks he has a private understanding with God and has no love for his brothers and sisters. Obviously, the well-to-do man or woman who considers the poor and needy must have learned the lesson of humility; thus for the Greeks the cardinal sin is "pride" *(hybris)*.

99. P. 25.

100. F. Hauck and S. Schulz, *praÿs, TDNT,* VI, 645.

101. Num. 12:3.

102. Hauck and Schulz, *praÿs, TDNT,* VI, 650.

103. Mekilta de Rabbi Ishmael (ed. Friedmann, 1870), 77a.

104. M. Aboth 6.6. See also "Blessed be the man who is free from transgression and possesses no sin or fault, but is devoted to good actions, to the study of the Torah, is low of knee (meek) and humble" (*Seder Eliyyahu,* p. 104; S. Schechter, *Some Aspects of Rabbinic Theology* [1909], pp. 232ff.).

105. See A. Cohen, *Everyman's Talmud* (1932), p. 216.

James also has something to say about arrogance. We hold that "bridles not his tongue" (1:26) is not a general reference to the many evils that are done with the tongue, but is written with the specific thought of prideful talk, the pride that goes with the illusion of righteousness and other forms of self-confidence, as in 4:11f. and 13-16, or as in the case of the Pharisee in the temple. This last example illustrates how insidious the temptation is even in the person who in general is probably upright and even amiable.

The sin of 2:1-13 is pride (see v. 6). The vanity of 2:14-16 (*kenē,* v. 20) is obvious, and is a sort of pride (see also "vain conceit" *[kenodoxia]* in a similar context in Phil. 2:3, cited above). In 4:1-5 James denounces lust and its fruits; at v. 6, with no change of thought, he speaks of the "proud"; and vv. 7-10 enjoin humility ("Submit yourselves, humble yourselves"). Carnal pride, or "confidence in the flesh" (as in Phil. 3:3), is well reprobated in the NT. The conjunction of carnal lust and carnal pride is part of James's thought: in the NT the word "boasting" *(alazoneia)*[106] comes only in Jas. 4:16 and 1 Jn. 2:16, where the similarity of context is most striking. In Jas. 5:1-6 the rich who thus live in carnal pleasure and arrogance are not even professing Christians (see 2:6f.). The epilogue (5:7-19) completes the circle in its encouragement of the sincere to endurance and prayer.

THE ENERGY OF PRAYER

The reference to the "prayer of a righteous man" (5:13, 14f., 16, and 17f.) is a further reminder of the practical thrust of James's teaching: everything is possible in the sphere of those who pray. In all these cases James is emphasizing the connection between faith and works, the action of praying and the difference that that action brings or has brought about. "Faith," Laws comments, "is that attitude to God which is expressed in prayer, *but is also necessarily issuing in action*" (italics ours).[107] That latter emphasis is important for a true understanding of James's doctrine of prayer.

Judaism anticipated the teaching of psychosomatic medicine.

106. See above, p. 248, n. 115.

107. P. 27. "A man may pray," writes George A. Buttrick, "but prayer will not plow his field. Even so, the field will not be plowed in honor unless he prays. 'Faith without works is dead' (Jas. 2:20), but not more dead than works without faith—and perhaps less evilly contagious. Likewise, faith without prayer is dead" (*Prayer* [1942], p. 155).

Healing must therefore be for both body and soul (see Mt. 9:1-8). On James and prayer, we now quote H. Schönweiss and C. Brown:[108]

> On the one hand, it is laid down that a Christian's whole life, the good times as well as the bad, should be lived in an atmosphere of prayer, i.e. that the Christian should lay before God everything that happens to him, so that each new experience is suffused with prayer. On the other hand, in cases of sickness, prayer is to be accompanied by the laying on of hands, anointing and confession of sins. Here the laying on of hands (implicit in the phrase "let them pray over him") and the anointing with oil, being outward actions, are considered to be tangible, readily intelligible expressions of prayer for the benefit of the sick individual, while confession of sins is made in order to remove any hindrances to prayer.

For James briefly then the elements required in the healing of physical sickness are: (1) the whole church represented by its elders, "the highest Faculty of Medicine of the Church" (Bengel); (2) the invocation of the name of the Lord; (3) the prayer of faith; (4) forgiveness of sins; (5) confession of sin within the church fellowship; and (6) fervent prayer by righteous people. But the exercise of any or all of these powers is not a magic talisman. Over the entire process we must write: ". . . nevertheless not my will but Yours be done." Those provisions were given for a church in which the powers of the Holy Spirit were clear and active, and where there had not yet been "the great falling away" (see 2 Thess. 2:3).[109] In v. 15, "The prayer of faith shall *save* the sick," the verb is *active* both in form and meaning, and for a similar reason in v. 16 is semantically *active* (rather than passive): "the prayer of faith works powerfully," "is powerful in its working," like the voice of the Lord (we think the word here is "voice") "mighty in operation."

In the highly eschatological 5:16b-18, Elijah, representative of the OT prophets and precursor of the Messiah, is only human like us, but he *prays* that it might not rain, and see what he *effects* thereby. Again three years later he prays, recalling the apocalyptic period of disaster (Dan. 12:7; Lk. 4:25f.; Rev. 11:2). Interestingly, later tradition also makes James a rainmaker, linking him in turn with the eschatological "rain" imagery of Elijah.[110] James's choice of Elijah rather than Jesus

108. "Prayer" *(proseuchomai)*, *NIDNTT*, II, 875.

109. See J. Wilkinson, "Healing in the Epistle of James," *SJTh* 24 (1971): 326-45; D. Müller, "Heal" *(hygiēs)*, *NIDNTT*, II, 171f. for further reading.

110. See Epiphanius, *Refutation of all Heresies* 78.14 (Migne, *PG*, XLII, 721); also R. H. Eisenman, *James the Just in the Habakkuk Pesher* (1986), pp. 34, 60f., 75f.; also *Maccabees, Zadokites, Christians and Qumran* (1983), pp. 48, 54f., 74.

indicates perhaps that "already Christological categories are setting the example of our Lord apart from the rest of us. But what can happen to Elijah, James is arguing, can happen to any other man of like stamp, if he will find a dynamic faith as effective as his."[111] The same kind of faith which will restore the sick is also effective in the spiritual realm.

James is concerned that his readers realize the potentialities of this inner *dynamis*. The primitive character of this type of faith is plain, reminiscent of the kind in the Synoptic Gospels, thereby forging another important and impressive link with our Lord's view of dynamic faith. The prayers of ordinary people have an effect on national history. These predictions are all as *active* semantically as that in v. 15, where the prayer saves the sick man by what the Lord does for him. the reference to the efficacious intercession of the righteous is a further reminder of James's doctrine of faith at work.

POWER OF LANGUAGE

Some may think that James greatly exaggerates the terror of the tongue, that is, the power of language. One quarter of his Epistle (1:26; 3:1-18; 4:1-12; 5:1-12), as we have seen, is preoccupied with this problem; but we do not know the situation he faced. It may be too fanciful to suggest that James is reflecting, in the first instance, on his own intemperate manner of speech as a member of the family at Nazareth.[112] Was it James perhaps who declared Jesus "mad" (Mk. 3:21)? It may be that his memory returns to haunt him as he formulates his apostolic rebuke to his churches. We can only conjecture; yet, if language did not exist, how far would our mind, or body, reach into the world, to the minds and bodies of others? This would make an enormous difference; and modern inventions such as printing, radio, and TV have greatly enlarged the "power of the tongue," for good and for evil.

Moreover, modern thinking tends to regard language as a department of science, not of magic or even nature. We can scarcely understand the attitude that perpetrates such absurdities as the statement of some scholiasts or grammarians that there are seven vowels in Greek because there are (as they once thought) seven planets. To the ancient Greek and Hebrew (among others) this interest in the tongue is colored

111. See P. H. Davids, "Tradition and Citation in the Epistle of James," in W. W. Gasque and W. S. LaSor, eds., *Scripture, Tradition, and Interpretation* (1978), pp. 119ff.; also *James* (1982), p. 197.

112. See Robertson, *The Hidden Romance of the New Testament*, pp. 236ff. For an excellent discussion of the entire subject of "Language and Meaning in Religion," see A. C. Thiselton, "Word" *(rhēma)*, *NIDNTT*, III, 1123ff.

by their deep sense of what they considered the mystery and magic of language: to the Jew it was a sin to pronounce the personal name of God. We could wish that in his discussion of speech James were not so sophisticated; but we must make allowance for his age, in which such diatribes were not uncommon. Even for us, and perhaps even more for us than for James, language as a power for evil is a thoroughly frightening subject to contemplate.

The metaphors and similes describing the tongue's centrality are drawn from many sources,[113] both Greek and Hebrew, but this is secondary. Why, we may ask, is the tongue such a supremely ambivalent and "poisonous" member? After all, a hand and arm can save or kill, unlike the spring that, as a rule, does not arbitrarily and unpredictably shoot forth fresh water and salt. According to the prophet Jeremiah, "The heart of man is deceitful above all things and desperately wicked." The meaning of that statement has not changed, except that it becomes clearer if we say "mind" for "heart." How much of our thinking do we do without word? We even talk in our sleep.

The unique wickedness of the tongue is that it is not just a member of the body but a sort of "audible mind." In a sense, all our actions speak our mind; but obviously we are more apt to make unkind remarks about the preacher's sermon than to give him a slap or a kick for it. Evil speaking is diabolically easy. Besides, even with the best intentions, it is far harder to be sure of speaking the right word and no other than it is to play the right shot and no other in golf. And even if we speak the right word rightly, the danger is not stilled, for words—and the way they are spoken—can too easily be misinterpreted.

Paramount here is James's view of the human personality as a "Gestalt," a whole. The human personality is an organism, and therefore in a vital sense one member of the organism *is* the organism. So the "tongue" is a little member, but expresses the boast of the whole organism. If the tongue is perfectly controlled, then the whole organism is also perfectly controlled. If this is not pragmatically obvious, it is due not only to natural shortsightedness, but also to our too narrow interpretation of the term "tongue," which is to be taken in the broadest sense of "inward" tongue (silence is no less an act of the tongue than speech is). Since we cannot think without the use of symbols such as alphabets and words, the "tongue" here means the whole inward world of human thinking—in effect, *speaking within*. We now know that thinking is accompanied by minute movements of the vocal chords; indeed, we often

113. See the commentaries, e.g., Dibelius, pp. 185ff.; Moo, pp. 122f., and others.

cannot bear the shutting up of inward speaking ("the tongue") and resort to the relief of "talking to ourselves." Far from being madness, this inward speaking is present in every conscious thought.

The tongue, obviously, is not alone among our members in inconsistency; the hand also, to name only one other member, is liable to sin, for example, murder or assault. But the difference, even if only in degree, is big enough to excuse, if we may not say justify, the treatment of the tongue as something unique in its inconsistency. Like the ancients, especially in the East, we are very apt to express evil thoughts and wishes about neighbors and others. The thought comes out in words more readily, even irresistibly, than in deeds. If our unkind words were as rare as (we may justly say) our unkind deeds, many a conscience would be more at peace with itself; but try as we may, the tongue remains like a half-broken horse, a demon of caprice, ever liable to bolt. What would we think of an automobile that sometimes responded to steering and just as often or oftener went off the road? And what if, unlike a horse or even a bear, it were irreparably "wild"? See also Ecclus. 22:27 and 23:7-15.

The point of the vituperation of the double-minded man *(dipsychos)* is that you "cannot have it both ways." You cannot serve God and Mammon, and James is here denouncing not strictly those who serve the devil but those who think they can combine the unworldly life and a half-hearted (insincere) orthodoxy with the worldly advantage of an insincere orthodoxy. The subject was not merely relevant but highly important for James's purpose, namely, to caution the sincere from going in for teaching without thinking hard about its responsibilities and about the question of their qualification to bear those burdens. In the rest of ch. 3 he turns to castigating people who profess the vocation without either sincerity or qualifications.

But we must never forget the difference, well stated in Jas. 3:15ff., between worldly and genuine wisdom. The first part of genuine wisdom is to know God; we must begin with a conviction of God with which there is inevitably joined a conviction of right (see Jas. 1:12-19). The Christian has a different set of values from the non-Christian, being energized by a different Spirit and a different wisdom—"the wisdom from above." "Wisdom," writes J. L. McKenzie, "is viewed too narrowly when it is viewed as wisdom literature. It is also a way of thought and a way of speech which was by no means limited to the schools and the writings of the sages."[114] God's Wisdom has two paramount fea-

114. Cited by J. A. Kirk, "The Meaning of Wisdom in James: Examination of a Hypothesis," *NTS* 16.1 (1969): 32.

tures. The first, which we will only mention here, is its invariable ethical perfection (one aspect of his infallibility); the other is its wizardry. The miracles of Jesus are unforgettable marks of his character. Moreover, our Christian Bible begins with the miracle of creation; indeed, the affinity of its story with the earlier pagan myth of the Six Great Gods who made the world for a wager reminds us that miracles are one of the oldest ingredients of theology. In addition, the personified Wisdom that figures in parts of our OT and Apocrypha is akin to the familiar spirit that still attends the witch or wizard in many of our traditional tales.

Then comes the second part: Knowing God. Even knowing the "rules" he has given us for our guidance, we have to study at every juncture and decide how to apply those principles and rules to the particular questions of conduct that present themselves from time to time in our lives. We must decide for ourselves how we will approach those questions. But the Jewish rabbi, like a wise pastor, can often help in clarifying the issue; as ever, there is no such thing as teaching, only learning.

The devout passion for conduct that distinguished the Jewish religion is liberated and illumined by what James found in Christ. It can scarcely be doubted that the Epistle of James owes much of its inspiration to the teaching of Jesus in the Sermon on the Mount (Mt. 5:7) and the Sermon on the Plain (Lk. 6:20ff.) on the value of trials and temptations, and of good works, and on certain false ideas of the right way to make our faith operative in our actions and conduct in life. He who obeys Jesus' perfect law is freed from bondage to OT legalism.

Many tend to think of the Epistle of James as just a diatribe on Faith and Works (Action), a diatribe long superseded, we assume, by better disquisitions on this subject by more modern thinkers and theologians. Even without his Epistle we should find no difficulty in believing that our James emphasized the duty of *agapē* ("love") in his teaching of Christianity. Nowhere in the NT, and nowhere in the record of Paul, is the paramount Christian ideal, *agapē,* described more forcibly or more eloquently than in 1 Cor. 13, a chapter that magnificently crowns Paul's application of the same noble principle to the otherwise prosaic problem of eating or not eating certain meat (1 Cor. 8).

It seems only reasonable that James must have had his part (Gal. 1:19) in fostering this cast of thought in the tiro's mind; the same trilogy as that in 1 Cor. 13:13 had already appeared in Paul's earliest Epistle: "your works of faith, and labor of love, and patience of hope in our Lord Jesus Christ" (1 Thess. 1:3). "Faith" for James, notes Ronald Goetz, "is being so touched by God's love—which is, after all, the essence of the

Good News—that the believer longs, heart and soul, to show God his or her gratitude by living a life consistent with love."[115] In truth, the essence and value of the Epistle are the same as that of the great chapter on love, 1 Cor. 13. We would venture to sum up the Epistle of James with the last verse of 1 Cor. 13 (NIV): "And now these three remain: faith, hope and love. But the greatest of these is love."

To mitigate the shock of such a statement, it is imperative to remember that chs. 1 and 2 comprise the first installment of the Epistle of James, and that an installment as such has a close. The real close, however, is disguised by an appendix (2:18-25), the last verse of the chapter (2:26) repeating, in effect, 2:17. But it is clear that in 2:14-17 we have a rhetorical peroration, which is partly nullified (as a peroration) by the appendix. But suppose that after v. 16 we found, not our v. 17 but the last verse of 1 Cor. 13; can we honestly doubt that that "Corinthian" verse could have been hailed as a sublime close of the first installment and apt, beyond all possibility of improvement, to the immediately preceding verses and indeed to all the previous verses in these two chapters?

On making faith operative in our life we are content with Rom. 13:10, "Love is the fulfilling of the law," and Gal. 5:6 (NIV), "faith expressing itself through love." And though we see the direct influence of Jesus (see Mt. 5:16, 20) in James's insistence on works, it is indisputable that James does not, and could not, go further in that much maligned insistence than Paul himself in 1 Cor. 13:13, just cited, or in the second verse of the same chapter; in fact, we hope to show that the Epistle of James, no less than Paul's teaching, is founded on the three great inextricable forces, Christian faith, Christian hope, and Christian love.

We all know that James stresses Faith and Works. But since James does not use the noun *elpis* ("hope") we imagine that he has no thought of "hope." The fact is that James feels strongly enough about hope; but being more direct and concrete than Paul, he expresses himself in the more direct and concrete mention of the reward or end that we hope for. In 1:5, 9, and 10, the rich man is plainly hoping to escape the usual lot of the rich; v. 12 contains an indisputable promise and hope; v. 18 gives our hoped-for end; and vv. 21 *ad fin.*, 25 *ad fin.*, 12, and 13 likewise promise mercy in the hope at which we are to arrive. We would also quote from the second installment—4:17; does not that speak to us of hope? Is not hope prominent enough in James's mind and writing here to make that Pauline verse apt for James's climax? The same is true of works. James uses the word "works" so often that

115. *Art. cit.*, *Christian Century* 102.9 (1985): 261.

many of us fail to see what it means in its application to Christianity. In a word, it means LOVE: notice that, and purity from worldly lusts, in 1:27; also works/compassion (mercy) in 2:1, 4, 8, 13-16, just at the point where we sense that Pauline verse as a proxy for 2:17.

There is one changeless law that must govern all the personal and social relationships of all Christians, says James, the royal law of love (2:8). Love is the foundation of brotherhood. Witness his hardly accidental, repeated, unique, unparalleled expression "my beloved brothers" *(adelphoi mou agapētoi)* (1:16, 19; 2:5).[116] Over and over this stands in the foreground of the ethical teaching of this Epistle. Love implies reverence for the human personality; hence his rebuke of the toadies to the rich (2:1ff.). As believers in a Lord who is "the Glory" they ought not to make unfair discriminations; so James condemns snobbery very rightly, with feeling and force. But he is *not* preaching "spiritual communism" (2:1-13), namely, "You see we are all the same before God: we have all sinned and fallen short, etc.; differences in wealth and position and culture are of no account. Humble yourselves and put yourselves on a par with those in whose group you really belong—the poor and needy. . . ." He is saying, in effect:

> Understand, you high up ones, just how high up you really are, and that God has put you there, not to haul you down, but to give you *the function of kings* (see vv. 1, 5, 8), that is, the great prerogative of descending without becoming inferior, condescending without becoming patronizing, putting yourself in your subjects' place and remaining king all the time! Remember, you are kings and Jesus reigns in glory. *Be* kings!

Here we have a powerful statement of James's convictions on brotherhood, though in his Epistle he is writing primarily of *the brotherhood of Jewish Christians.* But if not very explicit in his Epistle, he could scarcely have expressed his abhorrence of such a thing as race discrimination among Christians more clearly and forcibly than he does in Acts 15:13-21, 23-29. The spirit of the circumcision bar that menaced the infancy of Christianity in the church is not remotely dissimilar from that of racism, *apartheid,* "Jim Crow" laws, the color bar, or all those other barriers of social, tribal, or monied exclusiveness that are anathema to Christianity. The OT Jewish religion is far from ignoring the Jew's human duty to the Gentile; but there were at least some Jews who some-

116. While "beloved" *(agapētos)* in the NT is used primarily of the love of Christians for each other, Cranfield correctly notes that "it is probably true to say that where it is so used the thought of the love of God for sinful men, which is the basis of the love of Christians for each other, is not far away" (*The Epistle to the Romans,* I, 68f.). See also L. Morris, *Testaments of Love* (1981), p. 206.

times spoke of "the uncircumcised" as contemptuously as at one time some persons used the term "nigger." It is scarcely possible to overestimate our debt to James for supporting so decisively the idea of *comprehensive* brotherhood in Christ. But we must remember that even tolerant condescension is no substitute for genuine brotherhood in matters of color, culture, or Christianity.

Following Christ,[117] James, as we have seen, acknowledges the supremacy of the law of love, which he terms "the sovereign law," meaning, we believe (*pace* Ropes), the comprehensive sovereign rule or law, much as the term is used in Mt. 22:36 and elsewhere. It is important to notice that "Mercy triumphs *over* judgment" (2:12f.), that is, the relation of mercy to judgment is not paradoxical. Grace and law are paradoxical: they stand intact over against each other in an irresolvable tension. To sacrifice one destroys the other, for law sacrificed results in antinomianism and no grace, and grace sacrificed results in the righteousness of God's act of justification sacrificed and no law.

But mercy and judgment are not thus set in tension. Where mercy is gone there is nothing but judgment; where judgment is gone there is nothing but mercy. Mercy is a very solemn word; to presume on it is finally fatal. Mercy is deeper than grace, for where there is no grace there can still be mercy, but where there is no mercy there is no grace. Christians rejoice too much in God's grace, and tremble too little before his mercy. James redresses the balance of truth. The law of love was part, and is quoted by James as the sum, of the Jewish law. Mercy was already prominent in Judaism.[118] "There is scarcely a passage which refers to God's capacity as judge," remarks Cohen,[119] which does not also allude to his attribute of compassion." "Even in the time of His anger He remembers mercy."[120]

On this liberating gospel of the mercy of God, rather than any right strawy moralism, James delights to dwell, ranking his Epistle with the most evangelical in the NT (including Paul's). It is crucial to grasp this thrust of James's message: to do so, as Donald Baillie says, is "to realize that the Christian way of life is not simply to see ourselves as we are, to see our faults and concentrate on overcoming them, to set our teeth and doggedly cultivate our characters and so save our souls. That method is not successful; it does not make good Christians, but at best,

117. And in company with Paul. See Gal. 6:2, quoted *in vacuo* by Ropes, p. 178. On the centrality of love in Paul, see, e.g., R. Mohrlang, *Matthew and Paul* (1984), pp. 101ff.

118. See above, pp. 285ff.; F. I. Andersen, "Yahweh, the Kind and Sensitive God," pp. 41ff. in *God Who Is Rich in Mercy,* eds. P. T. O'Brien and D. G. Peterson (1987).

119. A. Cohen, *Everyman's Talmud* (1932), p. 17.

120. b. Pesaḥim 87b.

self-righteous Pharisees."[121] All of us sin. The difference between the Christian and the unconverted is not that the Christian does not sin (for we do, as Paul and James confess), but that we are not content to sin. We know that by faith in God's grace we may hope to resist sin; and when we do fall, we know that if we genuinely repent we may repair the sin by God's grace through Christ.

James's theory of sin (1:14f.) parallels that of Paul, and the same antithesis between sin and Christ is found in Jas. 1:18-21 as in Rom. 7:24 and 8:1-4. James is so concise in his theology that some have doubted his conformity with the fundamental views expressed by Paul in his elaborate theology. Clearly James in 1:18-25 is thinking of Christ as the incarnation of the law of liberty; notice "he of his own wish begot us," the reference to Christ by name that follows at once in 2:1. (We have noted more than once that the only other mention of the name of Jesus in his Epistle is in 1:1). So, too, in using the word "heirs" in 2:5 James implies as much as Paul does in Rom. 8:19-25; Paul's is a more detailed statement of the eschatological concepts of freedom, firstfruits, constancy, and probation that are equally important for James.

James ignores ceremonial law; he does not, however, imply that performance of ceremony can never have spiritual value. Who would deny that our ceremonies such as marriage, confirmation, and Holy Communion can have spiritual value? But even if essential, ceremony is a relatively subordinate element in a person's religion, even in the sacraments. And we must remember that James was addressing *Jews*, who scarcely needed much telling about the importance of ceremony, and that his entire Epistle emphasizes the paramount importance of the spirit in religion, including, of course, ceremony. Further, in Deuteronomy, the Prophets, the Psalms, and the like, Hebrew religion constantly told too often unheeding ears that the essence of piety was simply loving obedience.

This concept of the Torah in the Epistle of James was still alive in the piety of "the quiet of the land"; the Pharisees, for whom the Torah, with all the multitude of rabbinic refinements, alone led to righteousness, were in a minority.[122] Moreover, though the Jerusalem Christians attended the temple and remained good Jews, we cannot reasonably suppose that they put their hopes of salvation in the Torah more than in Christ. Like James and Paul, they placed a certain value on the

121. *Out of Nazareth* (1959), p. 127.

122. See Acts 15:5. On the religious diversity in late Judaism, see, e.g., E. P. Sanders, *Paul and Palestinian Judaism* (1977); also C. J. G. Montefiore, *Judaism and St. Paul* (1914); *Rabbinic Literature and Gospel Teaching* (1930); et al.

Torah, as we do on "Thou shalt not steal"; but, like James and Paul and ourselves, they must have set the highest value on the overriding moral and spiritual principles of the Christian life. James's doctrine of the Messianic Torah is not different from Paul's, and has only been isolated from his through the common failure to realize that Paul does not condemn the Torah (nor, e.g., "Thou shalt not steal"), but is perhaps a little too obsessed with (quite rightly) condemning those who make use of or abuse the Torah for their own personal purposes.

James's collocation of law and liberty therefore presents an ideal of law identical with that of the Greeks, later Judaism, and Qumran, the opposite of implacable rigidity or mischievous formalism, an ideal that marries law with justice. It is an ideal of which law in its narrower development falls short, yet for which law in the stricter sense is socially and historically indispensable; and with all his enthusiasm for the law of liberty James gives no hint of antagonism to the Torah. As we have pointed out elsewhere, the passage in 2:8-11 is highly significant: far from repudiating the Torah, he positively uses some of it (vv. 1-11) as a foundation for the advance to mastery of its comprehensive spirit in the sovereign law (v. 8), the law of liberty (v. 12).

ACTIVE FAITH

We rightly exalt the value of "faith"; but Christian faith is not only a matter of theology, as Luther is sometimes held to imply. We should rather think humbly and gratefully of God as indeed "our Father," and not let his children be tempted to think that "faith" requires us to equal him in our understanding of his theology. So it is in our homes: children necessarily have limited understanding of what is in their father's mind, and with the greatest respect we think we do well to recognize the limitations of even Luther's theology on the point in question.[123]

Luther was, of course, engaged in a life-and-death struggle, with the inevitable result that he exaggerated a great deal. He also had a warm, ebullient temperament, quite unlike that of the cool Calvin. Like all his contemporaries of the period, he used extreme and, to us, coarse language, and his generation was not in the least shocked. Further, the canon in those days was not yet as fixed as it is now, and a doubtful book was considered fair game. The crux of the issue was, of course, the *sola fide* taught by the Reformation divines. Strictly, too, they were right, for *meritorious* works and faith cannot be mixed. They do not

123. See D. O. Via, "The Right Strawy Epistle Reconsidered," *JR* 49.3 (1969): 253; also W. Joest, *Gesetz und Freiheit* (1961), p. 135.

form the legitimate poles of a paradox, to be kept together in tension, they are absolutely incompatible, and they can only battle to the death.

The idea that works of love could be meritorious is quite repugnant. The Reformers therefore included the actions of love and obedience under the one rubric of faith—faith works by love (obedience). "Oh, how I love your law! I meditate on it all day long" (Ps. 119:97, NIV). Owing to the dreadful impositions of the Dark and Middle Ages (You are wicked and therefore cannot judge what is right; the church tells you what is right; God's grace will assist you; do it, or else), it was necessary for Luther to shatter the fettered minds and consciences of his contemporaries, and this shattering could not be done by a delicate choice of exact ideas expressed in precise words. Unfortunately, human nature is very glad to hear that we are saved by faith alone, since human nature cannot know what faith is because it is God's gift and cannot be known prior to the act of revelation. Accordingly, a practice of faith largely without works began to characterize Lutheranism and its allies, and Western capitalism is partly a result.

The Epistle of James, in sum, insists that true faith issues in works: if faith without works is dead, by the same token works without faith do not live. James is not interested in the question "Can we be saved by faith *plus* works or by faith *alone*?"[124]—the question of the Reformation *in the context* of the debacle of the medieval church—but in another, namely: "How is faith to be *seen* to be saving, or not saving?" James is interested in the *demonstration* of faith, and to his question he gives the following answers and comments: In itself (1) faith is absolutely invisible; (2) faith can be known only by its results, that is, after it has acted; (3) faith that has no visible results has to be taken as nonexistent; (4) faith that has visible results that may be tested at the bar of historic revelation (prophets, apostles, Jesus Christ) may be accepted as genuine; (5) by implication, therefore, faith does not mean mental assent to dogmatic propositions. "Much of the recent controversy over the effectiveness of the born-again believer," writes David Poling, "centers on the style and expression of Christian ethics. Faith is not the point of difference, rather it is the ethical translation of this new religious experience into the life stream of the world."[125] Faith begins with submission to God, but the (reciprocal) allegiance must be maintained in faith; infidelity or double-mindedness is treason, and brings not approval but condemnation.

The apostolic notion of the Christian's faith is a notion of *loyalty,*

124. See Kent, *Faith that Works,* pp. 90, 100; R. C. Sproul, "Is a Life of Faith a Vacation from Works?" *Eternity* 39.2 (Feb. 1988): 60.

125. *To be Born Again* (1979), pp. 132f.

that is, of *fidelity* and its *inseparable duty of service*, loving service, as, perhaps on a lower plane, in the medieval man's allegiance to his *liege lord*. We will not dwell further on this here but we do wish to emphasize that in trying to understand the Epistle of James, and especially its value, we must free ourselves from the pervading shibboleths faith and works and all the jejune controversy about that, especially its fancied antagonism to Paul. We must read James not just with sight but with insight. We have tended to concentrate somewhat on the first installment; but if we wished, we could show that in spite of all the old or subtle variations of topic or treatment in the second installment, what we have already deduced holds true for the entire Epistle. James really has the same message of faith, hope, and love as Paul; and we personally do not think James is any worse in his thinking or in his Epistle for his predominantly direct and "concrete" way of expressing his thought.

RADICAL RELIGION

This virile interpretation of religion contrasts vividly with the view that the Christian gospel differs little from the highest modern humanistic social ideals and aspirations. Yet while deeply concerned with our present material conditions, James's inspiration clearly springs from sources that are essentially spiritual and eternal. Thus when he speaks of "faith" he does not mean humanistic belief but trust in God—an undivided commitment. This faith then imitates God's compassion by caring for the poor and the dispossessed. Thus the *imitatio Dei/Christi* is the key to all his social thinking. His social philosophy is real and significant, for no one in the NT is more concerned with the pragmatic implications of the gospel for society. Indeed, many of his themes are precisely those agitating the church in the world today. His hatred of all injustice, oppression, and discrimination burns with a volcanic passion. This is particularly seen in his attitude toward the rich and the poor, reminding us that the chasm between these two classes is still as deep today—if not deeper—as when James first tried to comfort the afflicted and to afflict the comfortable. If, like the poor, the rich are always with us, the question of the social responsibility of the affluent must be raised and honestly answered, even at the risk of being accused of "meddling."

What is the duty of the wealthy in our present-day society? F. W. Robertson urgently addressed this question in a sermon entitled "The Message of the Church to Men of Wealth." His words are curiously reminiscent of those of our Epistle:

> For three long centuries we have taught submission to the powers that be, as if that were the only text bearing on the relations between the ruler and the ruled. Rarely have we dared to demand of the powers that

> be, justice: of the wealthy man and titled, duties. We have produced folios of slavish flattery upon the Divine Right of power. Shame on us! We have not denounced the wrongs done to weakness: and yet for one text in the Bible which requires submission and patience for the poor, you will find a hundred which denounce the vices of the rich . . . and woe to us in the great day of God, if we have been the sycophants of the rich, instead of the redressers of the poor man's wrongs.[126]

These fiery words of rebuke, originally directed at laissez-faire Victorians, are uniquely relevant to those engaged in the contemporary struggle with Marxist Communism for the soul of the Third World, and indeed to all Christians who, when seeing the scandal of excessive wealth alongside grinding poverty, fail to protest but keep an indifferent or cowardly silence before this evil. "Indeed, to omit to do good is an actual wrongdoing," according to Pelagius,[127] "for, if a man sees his neighbour in danger of starvation, is he not himself guilty of murdering him, if, having abundance, he does not give him food . . . ? For whoever is able to succour someone who is in danger of dying of want (whatever sort of want it may be), if he does not relieve him, murders him." James says the same thing much more succinctly: "Anyone, then, who knows the good he ought to do and doesn't do it, sins" (Jas. 4:17, NIV).

To all who seek to obey the will of Christ in these matters, the Epistle of James offers wise guidance and deserves careful study—and above all fearless application. Irrespective of wealth or social status, our duty is clear—to care for the poor and to feed the hungry. With half the world's population going to bed hungry at night and droughts and famine raising the specter of human suffering and starvation around the globe, the problem of hunger is horrendous. The Food and Agriculture Organization is begging nations to provide each hungry person with emergency rations consisting of a pitiful 14 ounces of corn, 1.4 ounces of pulses (peas, beans, or lentils), and seven tenths of an ounce of oil *PER DAY*. The command of Christ "Give them to eat" is invested with fresh urgency, and to fail to do so, stopping short with good intentions and fine words, is to be faced once more with James's scornful, unanswerable question: "What good is it?" (2:16). It is also worth noting in passing that the conditions of farm laborers today are little better than those of James's day. Farm workers are the only laborers in the United States today not given protection and rights under the National Labor Relations Act. Despite the media exposure of living and working con-

126. *Sermons on Religion and Life* (1912), p. 31.

127. A. Souter, *Pelagius's Expositions of the Thirteen Epistles of St. Paul* (Texts and Studies 9.2) (1926), II, 104.

ditions, the charity and service of churches and voluntary agencies plus occasional protective legislation directed at those whose labor provides Americans with a rich and varied diet, the oppressive conditions in which farm workers exist have not changed significantly over the past thirty years.

One of the strangest modern paradoxes is our obsession with materialism in spite of the fact that the uncertainty of possession is obvious. The wider national conflicts, moreover, may be traced to the inner impulses that war within each of us (4:1). James's concept of a "law of liberty" (1:25; 2:12) recalls and resolves the modern conflict between the two notions of authority and freedom, summarized admirably by Martin Luther: "A Christian is a perfectly free lord of all, subject to none. A Christian is a perfectly dutiful servant of all, subject to all."[128] James thinks of God's law as a "law of liberty," but he combines belief in Christianity as a divine law of human liberty with an even older thought of a divine law pervading the entire universe.

Profession and performance must square: James insists that the essence of true Christianity is its insistence on the vital difference between merely formal adherence and an honest, though imperfect, effort in the imitation of Christ. This problem, like all others, is set within a transcendent frame of reference: namely, the reality of the Fatherhood of God with its corollary of the brotherhood of man and, especially, the unique worth of each individual (2:1f.). Above all, the Epistle is pervaded with that quiet spirit of patience and fortitude which is linked with the demand that faith should be expressed in deed rather than in word alone.

Compared with other NT writers, James appears to exhibit little of the mysticism found in Paul, for example, in his doctrine of union with Christ. No evidence of passionate, lyrical outbursts marks his Epistle; yet his personal ardor as "a bond slave of God and the Lord Jesus Christ" (1:1) is firmly stamped not only on its opening signature but also on the entire Epistle. For him, proof of union with God is found primarily in the realm of the practical rather than the charismatic, emotional, or mystical. Although we cannot say on the basis of his short Epistle that he did not appreciate these other elements, all that we know of James from the rest of the NT tends to confirm this.

Noting its strangely modern appearance and deploring the suspicions "most evangelical and reformed Christians" have about the Epistle, Frederick Greeves is very sound on James's insistence "that religion which is not concerned with everyday matters of personal and

128. *The Freedom of a Christian* (1520), *LW*, XXXI, 344.

corporate behavior is 'vain,'" and that "like Paul, but with his own distinctive emphasis, James denounced religion that is not active in love,"[129] blasting those who regard their discipleship as an "escape"—a sham or superstition[130]—in Bonhoeffer's phrase, "cheap grace." In our colleges and elsewhere, we have met "agnostics" and "atheists" who very often led more "Christian" lives than many "professing" and "practicing" Christians.[131] In modern days, we are engulfed with a more deadly "atheism," an ignorant and arrogant "atheism," an atheism that is not really atheism at all. In one of his letters John Calmann, for example, quotes with approval the opinion of an Oxford don who told him that idleness was an integral part of education and admits that he distrusts people who forsake "the indefinite practice of humanism" for "the armament of causes and ideologies." Upon which the reviewer[132] trenchantly comments: "This is fine and true up to a point, but without the spice of commitment it produces the arid cerebral attitude of an enlightened man, for whom nothing is worth getting excited about." James could hardly have put this better himself! Too often modern man is not an atheist; he *deifies* himself. Our Epistle is obviously not of the kind to furnish William James with materials for his *Varieties of Religious Experience.* But if there is no ecstatic "vision," certainly we have a steady determination to persevere in the service of God in ordinary life; and this may well be the highest evidence of genuine religion.[133] We suspect that James would have heartily approved of the Christianity of William Temple, in whom, it is said, they could find "no trace of a dual personality: no mask was put on and off. . . . Nor was he a perpetual battleground of repressions and frustrated desires. He had an inner harmony of the soul which no discords of the world, the flesh or the devil could break. He grew into a wholly integrated personality. . . ."[134] Most attractive, too, in this connection, is James's calm tone of authority and complete absence of fanaticism.

129. "God Willing," *ExpT* 80.3 (1968): 90, "James would probably have understood (better than many of us do) the contemporary attempt to distinguish 'secularity' from 'secularism'—when the latter is another name for atheism."

130. "There is also the superstition," writes Greeves, "involving descent into magic, which leads men to worship their own power and to claim the right and ability to manipulate nature (including human nature) without regard to God" (*art. cit., ExpT* 80.3 [1968]: 90).

131. A. E. Housman was an example. His verses "For My Funeral" are full of a sense of a higher power—"Nature" or "Cosmic Law"—than man himself.

132. "A Fatal Lack of Passion," *The Letters of John Calmann 1951–1980* (1986), reviewed by Brian Masters, *The Sunday Times,* 22 June 1986, p. 51.

133. See Isa. 40:21.

134. F. A. Iremonger, *William Temple* (1948), p. 499.

AN ADULT CHRISTIANITY

The Epistle of James is absorbed with relating the Christian ethic to its readers' personal conduct in their specific situation. If his Epistle *seems* theologically inadequate—a point we do not accept, for we firmly believe that an adequate theology *is* present—its vigorous concentration on the active exercise of Christ's ethic fulfills the primary object of the gospel, "to furnish us with rules of life and not food for reason."[135] "In his reinterpretation of new situations, in his insistence on the right practice of prayer and charity, and in his appeal to the nature of man and the nature of God in established rules for conduct," observes Laws, "the author of the epistle deserves a continued hearing."[136] We agree with this verdict. From a careful study of the Epistle, the conviction has gradually but steadily grown within us—and here we differ from Dibelius[137]—that we *are* in the presence of "the boldest and greatest mind" rather than a tantalizingly vague "Mr. Pseudonymous." This is hardly surprising when we remember that the mind belongs to James the Lord's brother.

In our opinion, even a casual reading confirms this impression, for this Epistle, springing clearly from a first-class intellect, certainly comparable to Paul's, speaks eloquently to us today in words of the greatest power; and when taken seriously, its message is capable of influencing the life of an individual, as well as that of society,[138] in the profoundest way. Certainly, it is true that gradually, over the centuries, leaders like James learned to review and to deal with the duties of daily life in a Christian manner, thus "paving the way for the Christianization of a society of good citizenship and their corresponding duties."[139]

As for its purpose, the Epistle of James is concerned, not with the foundations of Christian theology, but rather with the expression of Christianity in the life of professing Christians. It is a practical guide to what Jesus taught his disciples during his earthly ministry. The letter is a challenge to translate into deeds those things that Jesus taught. We might call this the "upper division" gospel course, a kind of "manual of Christian conduct which assumes a foundation of faith on the part of the readers."[140] It is now time to give credence to faith through action. That faith is what was learned through the Gospels, and now it is time

135. A. Westcott, *Life and Letters of Brooke Foss Westcott*, I (1903), 161.
136. P. 2.
137. P. 180.
138. See Via, *art. cit.*, *JR* 49.3 (1969): 267.
139. Dibelius, p. 182.
140. So R. H. Gundry, *A Survey of the New Testament* (1970), p. 343.

to have some guidelines as to how to make it work in daily life. The book deals with almost every segment of life, ranging from the taming of the tongue to who sits in which pew. This is a literature of timeless ideas and ideals filled with practical living not only for Jewish Christians but also for all Christians for all time who have passed the first course, as it were. James is clearly a step beyond.

The Jewish Christians had one great advantage: as Jews their religion had brought them far on the way to Christ, far beyond the progress (not always contemptible) that pagan religions might have made in that direction. To this fact the Epistle of James owes not a little of its unique value as compared with the Epistles (Corinthians, Ephesians, and the like) written for Christian converts from paganism, who had first to learn to believe in Yahweh before being able to know the Son (contrast Heb. 1 *ad init.*).

It is important to remember that the form of preaching to the Gentiles had to be very different from the form of preaching to the Jews; the Epistle of James belongs to the latter, as does the Epistle to the Hebrews, which gives a *theological* basis to James from a Jew's point of view. Is it entirely coincidental, we may ask, that James and Hebrews deal similarly with subjects like law, testing, and perfection or that the two OT examples of living faith employed by James—Abraham's sacrifice of Isaac and Rahab's care of the spies—are also found in the Epistle to the Hebrews? Indeed, the Epistle of James cannot be properly understood unless taken along with Hebrews. Similarly, it is quite inconceivable that Paul could or would have written any letter such as this one by James. The gospel of Christ as preached to the Gentiles had to have a unique form, not suited for the Jews of the Diaspora (see Rom. 2:16; 16:25; 2 Cor. 4:3; 2 Thess. 2:14; 2 Tim. 2:8). If one (Paul, James, or another) wanted to talk about faith and hope to Jews reared in belief in God, he could not give "the first principles" suitable for congenital pagans new both to Christ and to Yahweh. He would have to start from the beginning, verse 1, which the author expects his readers to take in their stride.

James could also have written in this way to his Hebrew Christians in the Epistle of James. And they could have taken it. But the situation being what it was, James thought it required, not a lecture on the nature of their religious assets faith, hope, and love, but on the *investment* of those not unfamiliar assets in the new and only profitable security available, the Christian life of love. We must of course remember the circumstances, the persecution and dispersal of these Christian Jews. That is why James stresses the importance of their investment, the Christian life. And we must also remember that James prizes to their full value the assets of Christian faith and hope: his opening (1:2-18) leaves no shadow of a doubt about that.

There is an adult quality in the Christianity propagated by the Epistle to the Hebrews and the Epistle of James. The separation of faith and works which continued to be such a problem in later Christian theology was never really urgent, as Qumran shows, in Judaism. For the Jew, the crucial question is neither what is correct action nor what is correct intention, but what is correct living. Abraham Joshua Heschel[141] finely reminds us: "Faith is not a silent treasure to be kept in the seclusion of the soul, but a mint in which to strike the coin of common deeds." James's Jewish convert to Christ was already halfway there—in his Jewish, pre-Christian training. For that reason James is better able to concentrate on the *fruits* of the Christian faith, on behavior, including some of the philosophy of conduct, as in the relation of faith and works. "As a permanent contribution to the life of the church," notes E. F. Harrison, "the epistle accents performance rather than profession and keeps the ethical imperative in a position of such prominence that it cannot be ignored."[142] As a result the Epistle of James, being an epitome of the essentials of the Christian life from the perspective of Jewish Christianity in preparation for the Second Advent, is also valuable—more obviously, we think, than any of the other Epistles, even Ephesians—for our new converts or, better, for our young Christians, who in childhood have absorbed the rudiments of Christianity in the tutelage of church and home but now face the responsibilities and the prospects, good and evil, of the adult world into which they are almost grown up. When they ask for a "How-to-Do-It" book on guidance, the Epistle of James is a very good modern answer.[143]

CONCLUSION

We return to the same question with which we began: Who is the author? Though it cannot be answered with absolute certainty, this question has, in our opinion, one simple and satisfactory answer. The only man in the early church capable of composing an Epistle like this was James the brother of the Lord and the first "Pope" or "Bishop" of Jerusalem. We take it that he wrote the Epistle and also the letter in Acts 15, especially v. 24 (the picture there "in making a displenishing havoc in your souls,"

141. *God in Search of Man* (1955), p. 295.

142. *Introduction to the New Testament* (1971), p. 393.

143. For a helpful example of the "How-to-Do-It" approach of James, see P. A. Cedar, *James, 1, 2 Peter, Jude* (1984), pp. 5, 11ff.; also L. J. Ogilvie, *Making Stress Work for You* (1984).

we have noted more than once, almost bears the fingerprint of his powerful vividness of style).

What we have said of the construction and thought of the Epistle of James can scarcely leave any doubt as to the quality of its author. The emphasis on the poor in Gal. 2:10 is perfectly in keeping with the Epistle of James, and in the previous verse James retains the priority of mention that only the inferior texts there give to Peter. We would now call attention to Ropes's good note on Jas. 3:1:

> *didaskalos* means rabbi . . . , and the teachers here referred to, if in Jewish Christian churches, would naturally have occupied a place not unlike that of rabbis in the synagogues. This would apply both to the dignity of the position and to a part of the duties of the rabbis. Among Christians the term was used both for a teacher resident in a Church (Acts 13:1, Antioch) and for a travelling missionary (Didache 11:1f., 13:2, 15:2). Nothing in the text indicates whether James's reference was limited to one or other of these classes. The position of teacher was the function of a specially gifted person, not a standing office, and it was plainly possible for a man who believed himself competent for the work to put himself forward and take up the activities of a teacher. James is himself a teacher (*didaskalos,* 3:1) and points out the moral dangers of the teacher's life, with special insistence on the liability to opinionated disputatiousness (3:13-18).[144]

We would like to interject here that a teacher like James, not likely to be snared by self-conceit and contentiousness, is more apt to feel the stings of (perhaps overconscientious) self-criticism and his sense of duty to other souls, for whom he is never quite sure he has really done his best.

We believe that James, like Jesus,[145] was a teacher, one who had probably been a Jewish rabbi or proto-rabbi, "officially" or otherwise, long before he became a Christian one. If James were a "proto-rabbi," then he was one of the *ḥᵃḵāmîm,* that select group of lay experts in law *(hᵃlāḵāh)* who taught before A.D. 70.[146]

144. P. 226.

145. See Jn. 1:38 on Jesus as "rabbi"; also Mt. 26:25; Mk. 9:5; 11:21; Jn. 3:2; 4:31; 9:2; 11:8, et al. See also L. Goppelt, *Theology of the New Testament,* I (1981), p. 163, n. 3; K. H. Rengstorf, *didaskō, TDNT,* II, 152; *pace* Oesterley, p. 29; also Laws, pp. 140ff., especially her discussion of the role of the Jewish teacher as "guardian" *(mᵉḇaqqēr)* or "master" *(maśkîl)* as instructor and interpreter of the tradition shared with a community like Qumran (see CD 13:7f.; 1QS 9:12-20; and other references in G. Vermes, *Dead Sea Scrolls in English* [[2]1975], pp. 19ff.).

146. P. Sigal, *The Emergence of Contemporary Judaism* (1980), I, pt. I, p. 4.

The merits of this observation are obvious and neither few nor unimportant. This would help explain, in part at least, the possibility of his swift and evidently undisputed advance to the position of Bishop of Jerusalem after the Ascension, why he got the mastery he shows in Greek, including Greek poetry, which he quoted (1:17) as easily and aptly as Paul on the Areopagus, and his familiarity with Greek philosophical ideas, as in his treatment of the tongue as anomalous to cosmic law (3:7-12, where he is, if anything, too rabbinical for our tastes). The theme and its treatment here cannot be put down to the scribes, however such authors depended on them in that age. It would help to explain further how he was so well versed in *Shechinah* theology (2:1), how he knew the story of human creation (4:5), and how he learned of a Scripture not known to our Bible (4:5).

We see no reason to wonder that a carpenter/builder's son from Galilee, a great center of Hellenism, should have become a bilingual Jewish rabbi, and afterward a Christian rabbi. Nor is it absurd that a former Jewish rabbi should know and esteem the LXX, which obviously was made by men of that stamp, whoever they were, or that writing in Greek he should quote Isaiah from the Septuagint. Moreover, his rabbinic training and profession would make his Greek style different from but not inferior to that of Paul or Luke; for another significant sign of his familiarity with Greek, see Ropes on "If God will" (4:15), a "not Hebrew but Greek way of talking."[147] This might also help to explain why James says so little on Christology. In 2:1 he speaks not only as a Christian but as a Christian Jew to Christian Jews: "The faith of our Lord Jesus Christ, our Glory." Here his words are nearly similar to those of Simeon in his song (Lk. 2:32): "To be a light to lighten the Gentiles; and to be the glory of thy people Israel." Even before Jesus was born, such devout Jews knew, and expected other Jews to know, what the Messiah was to be and do and suffer as Savior. When Christ came, the true Jew, as contrasted with the ordinary Gentile, had little to do but recognize and accept him as the Christ, to hold fast, and to work in that faith; Acts 2:14-47, esp. v. 36, is instructive in this respect. If James were a former Jewish rabbi, it would help to explain not only how James became at once the first Pope or Bishop of Jerusalem but also why Paul so respected (and, perhaps, somewhat feared) him, and why at first, for a short time, the unconverted Jews in Jerusalem did not desire, or dare, to meddle much with James and his flock of Jewish Christians (see Acts 5:34–6:1).

James speaks of a rabbi's life not as one new, just out of college,

147. P. 279.

but as one more than halfway through his career and for a long time inured to it. This may be only conjecture, except for the evidence of James's Christian rabbinic office and his obvious rabbinic learning; but it offers some sense on points on which little explanation is usually given. For example, this would help to explain his links with Qumran, as well as his mastery of the art of rhetoric (in the technical sense of that ambiguous term); and it goes a long way toward explaining both the Greek and the Epistle's general excellence, as well as its general rabbinic content, corroborating the view that "every sentence of it could have been written by a proto-rabbi. . . . One can follow James verse by verse and discover allusions to proto-rabbinic and rabbinic literature."[148] In Acts 4:13, Peter and John are called "unlearned and ignorant men"; no one could say that of James.

Even if we had no more evidence than we have of James's quality, if we assign the Epistle of James to this period of Christianity we believe he would be the only possible answer to the question: Who wrote the Epistle of James? It would not be strange if a Jewish rabbi became a Christian at that time. So did many of the Jerusalem priests (Acts 6:7). If we give the Epistle of James such an early author and date we escape the difficulties which none of the commentators has been able to resolve, even to his own genuine satisfaction, of interpreting the dispersion of 1:1. We think that there it is most easily and naturally taken to refer to the dispersion of Acts 8:1; and we submit that the Epistle of James was written for Jewish Christians of that dispersion, and not very long after it, and 1 Peter was addressed to Gentile Christians of the same dispersion at about the same time (1:1 and 4:7; compare "at the door," Jas. 5:8 and 9), when the return of the risen Christ is yet momentarily expected. He has all that early assurance that the parousia is to be expected any day now. And surely he is writing not long after the Resurrection and Ascension, and not on the verge of the fall of Jerusalem.

In view of the persistent tradition that associates the author with James of Jerusalem and the evidence that we have marshalled in its favor, we conclude that the Epistle of James is of no later date than the proto-apostolic age and the author is indeed to be identified with the Lord's brother, "one of the masterminds of that unique company through whom God literally recreated the spirits of men and the life of human society."[149] To James belonged the distinction of writing the church's first official "epistle" at a significant moment in its existence. James wrote between Jesus and Paul at the dawn of the NT; but, as Scaer

148. Sigal, *The Emergence of Contemporary Judaism*, pp. 424f.
149. Parry, p. 97.

points out, "the dawn lasts for only a short time. His epistle is a window to what that dawn looked like."[150]

Emanating from James the Head of the Church of Jerusalem, and later preserved by his school, this Epistle, we believe, was circulated in its original form in a period of quiet before the missionary needs called for in the evangelical note of the gospel. In spite of all difficulties and obscurities, we submit that the Epistle of James is indeed "a magnificent literary monument to the moral sensitivity and concern of the early church,"[151] which, rightly approached and understood, takes us, better than any other NT book, back to the infancy of the church, the purple dawn of Christian enthusiasm, and the first glow of Christian love.

150. *James, the Apostle of Faith,* p. 137.

151. H. S. Songer, *James.* The Broadman Bible Commentary, XII (1973), 100.

IV. CONCLUDING REFLECTIONS

"The Epistle of James is one of the most exciting parts of the New Testament. It has a hard-hitting punch and a reality-oriented attitude that catch readers unaware and astound them, while also offering them practical guidelines for life. Yet at the same time it is a neglected book. . . . The result has been that the work has been pushed aside, so that it is only in the last two decades that a significant number of commentaries and studies on James have begun to appear. One now sees that the ugly duckling is indeed a swan, the neglected stepchild the true heir, for nowhere does the voice of Jesus speak more clearly to the church than in James."

P. H. Davids, *James,* Good News Commentary (1983), p. xv

Concluding Reflections

How then shall we summarize our findings? We have tried to deliver the Epistle of James from four serious misrepresentations too common among the critics. Writers on our epistle have usually labored under at least four handicaps.

(1) *COHERENT.* First we are told the Epistle is diffuse, repetitious, and rambling, with neither unity nor coherence. "There is no order or method in the Epistle," says Luther.[1] "Now he discusses clothing and then he writes about wrath and is constantly shifting from one to the other. What a chaos." Not true. In Part I, Ch. 3, "Plan," we showed that the Epistle of James is an integrated whole with a single unifying theme, which is "Faith realized in conduct."[2] "Rondo" or "fugal" is not an inappropriate description of the mode of construction of the Epistle, with the recurrence of its themes of trials, endurance, wisdom, faith, sincerity, works, etc., connected by "capping dicta," for example, prayer (1:5-7; 4:2f.; 5:13-18) and poor/rich (1:9-11, 27; 2:1-13; 4:1-10; 5:1-6).

There is nothing fragmentary about this Epistle; all is coherent and as complete as the (competent) writer wanted it to be. Whereas many writers construct their train of thought in a more-or-less linear fashion: thus . . . , therefore this . . . etc., James tends to present his thoughts in related circles, but not in terms of a developed argument each segment of which depends on and develops the preceding segment.

Over a century ago J. T. A. Wiesinger with fine perception noted the Epistle's twin characteristics. First, the *sententious form*—it is composed of short, detached sentences. Second, and perhaps even more important, the *concentric structure*—its sentences are linked into unitary "circles," which are again skillfully linked with each other. He writes:

1. *LW,* LIV, 425. See K. G. Phifer, "Expository Articles: James 2:1-5," 36.3 (July 1983): 278.

2. See our discussion on *Faith in Action,* pp. 266ff.

> The *practical* moral tendency of the author can be recognized in the sententiousness of his statements, but even more from the way in which he always steps straight *in medias res;* the first sentence with which he opens any passage (an imperative or a question) states at once, and completely, what he has in his mind, and almost throughout the first words of each passage could be taken as its title. The further development gives, regressively, an increasing elucidation and proof of the opening sentence, and then ends with one summarizing maxim which takes us back to the first sentence again; so that indeed the close of one discussion already prepares for the opening of the new, and usually supplies the theme as well.[3]

Those who expect to find James incoherent will scarcely allow themselves to be disappointed. On the other hand, we are convinced that James is eminently coherent, balanced, and structured—in short, a model of literary artistry. We are happy to note that a spate of modern studies tend in part to support our views. Far from being a string of disconnected moralisms, the Epistle is said to be best appreciated as "a serious theological document with predetermined form, recognizable organization, and literary merit."[4] As a summary of our position, this statement could hardly be improved. We believe that for the first time in centuries of comment we can prove those twin truths—that the Epistle of James has (a) a structure and (b) a style.

(2) *ORTHODOX.* Its conception of Christianity is said to be peculiar and unorthodox. This has moved at least one critic to call for "an evangelical criticism of James, not of his practical sayings, but of *his form of theology (seiner theologischen Gestalt)*" (italics ours).[5] One outstanding problem of the writing is neither its attribution to James nor its intended class of leaders but that it never mentions the life or the gospel of Christ, the grace of God in Christ, the cross, the resurrection, or the Holy Spirit, subjects that are held to be quite indispensable to the primitive Christian kerygma and a complete Christian theology. Above all, why does James say so little of Christ, mentioning him but twice (1:1; 2:1)? Does this suggest a primitive "theopractic" or even a dimin-

3. H. Olshausen, *Biblischer Kommentar,* VI, 1 (1854), 44. See also H. J. Cladder, "Der formale Aufbau des Jakobusbriefes," *Zeitschrift für katholische Theologie* 28 (1904): 296ff. For exposition and examples, J. L. Martyn, *Notes for Use in Studying the Letter of James* (1962), p. 6. For what Martyn calls "generic statements" as closure markers, see J. O. Ekstrom, *The Discourse Structure of the Book of James* (1975), pp. 2ff.; L. Cranford, *James Diagramed* (1984), pp. 45ff.

4. Scaer, p. 22.

5. P. Althaus, "Die Gerechtigkeit des Menschen vor Gott," p. 46 in *Das Menschenbild im Lichte des Evangeliums,* Festschrift for E. Brunner (1950), cited by W. G. Kümmel, *Introduction to the New Testament* (1975), p. 292.

ished "Ebionite" Christology?[6] Is his Epistle really a nonapostolic "oddity" with (as Luther thought) "no tang of the gospel in it";[7] and, if so, is his Christianity "superficial and undeveloped" compared with that of others?[8] He speaks of the sufferings of Job and the prophets (5:10f.); on the Passion of Christ, however, he is silent. His sayings on oaths (5:12) parallel those of Jesus (Mt. 5:34ff.), but he does not mention Jesus himself.

By way of contrast, though this is sometimes overlooked, Christ's Second Coming pervades the Epistle's entire theology. James *appears* to challenge the view of Paul that faith without works can save, though he does not mention Paul by name. But if he does not mention these subjects explicitly, this does not necessarily mean that our Epistle is "less rich in theology," "incomplete," "nongenuine," or "less valuable."

"It is impossible to conclude from the contents of the epistle," says G. E. Ladd, "that he was not interested in theology; a theologian can write practical homilies."[9] The truth is that his Epistle has a rich theology, complete, genuine, and distinctive. We say "distinctive" because in relation to Christianity the Epistle is sometimes said to bring nothing distinctive. On the contrary! The Epistle not only makes a distinctive contribution, but also (we further insist) brings much that is distinctively *Christian.* Nor is this "distinctively Christian" element measured simply by Paul (as though he had worked out some idiosyncratic scheme of his own), but by all the evidence, collectively, of what launched the Christian movement, and what necessitated a distinction from Judaism: in short, the difference (to use the old terms) between the faith *of* Jesus and faith *in* and faith *about* Jesus. If a distinctively Christian stance (or condition or faith or creed) is not merely acknowledging and trying to live by the teaching of Jesus, but confessing Jesus Christ as the risen Lord of Glory, faith in whom provides a radically different drive and direction for life—then, Luther notwithstanding, James *is* incontrovertibly and distinctively Christian and shares the post-resurrection faith, common to the whole NT. We are sure that those first Hebrew Christians who read this letter for the first time found it *distinctive*—refreshingly radical and quite revolutionary in every way, ethically, spiritually, and, above all, christologically. Here James reminds us, as do Paul and the other NT writers, that Christology and

6. See A. J. Hultgren, *Christ and His Benefits* (1987), p. 64; C. F. D. Moule, *The Birth of the New Testament* (1981), p. 165.

7. *LW,* XXXV, 396.

8. See Laws, pp. 1, 3; F. E. Gaebelein, *The Practical Epistle of James* (1955), p. 10.

9. G. E. Ladd, *A Theology of the New Testament* (1974), p. 589.

ethics are crucially connected.[10] If for James Jesus were simply a teacher and no more, his ethic would consist merely of didactic moralisms; if, however, Jesus is actually the *Shechinah*, the divine presence incarnate, then divine also—in nature and origin—is his ethic, thus showing that the influence of James's *Shechinah* Christology on his ethics as well as his entire theology can hardly be overestimated. To those who demur at James's lack of interest in theology (do they make the same complaint about the Sermon on the Mount or the Gospels?), we say we do *not* accept the premise that practice is inferior to doctrine: each is important and we beg leave to point out that James should not be judged because he happens to emphasize the one and not the other. "The believer does not live by theology alone," observes Martin E. Marty,[11] "and James lives by theology hardly at all. His book is a reminder, without being critical of the intellect, that one is not saved simply by its use." Furthermore, we must remember that the Epistle was written for a practical purpose, namely, to strengthen struggling Christians; thus to see it as a string of moralisms with no theology is to distort its basic purpose and meaning. The Epistle has been rightly described as "a serious theological work for suffering Christians" that "at all points revolved around a Christology centered on the sufferings of Jesus."[12] The truth is that James is a theologian of the highest order.

That we have failed to recognize this is due mainly, we are sure, to the brevity of his Epistle. The careful reader, however, will soon find out that this brevity, cryptic at points, is not simply a matter of length but of style. "James's theological and literary genius and uniqueness," as David Scaer well reminds us, "lie in his ability to blend theology into the immediate application. He does not first have to lay down theological principles from which he draws applications. Like Jesus, James in stating the application is at the same time putting forth the theological principles."[13] The importance of this statement can hardly be exaggerated. So, personally, we do not find James either "untheological" or "incomplete"; in fact, we have always been impressed by the wide

10. On this see G. M. Styler, "The basis of obligation in Paul's Christology and ethics," in *Christ and Spirit in the New Testament*, eds. B. Lindars and S. S. Smalley (1973), pp. 186f.

11. *Good News in the Early Church* (1976), p. 63. Equally to the point, though from another angle, is C. E. B. Cranfield's contention that "a good many Protestants have put far too little emphasis on Sanctification, and some have even seemed inclined to frown on the appearance of moral earnestness as though it must necessarily be evidence of a weakening loyalty to the doctrine of *sola fide*" (*The Epistle to the Romans*, I [1975], 95).

12. Scaer, p. 13.

13. Scaer, p. 60.

range, the almost encyclopedic scope of the topics in the Epistle. Indeed, it might be profitable to draw up a table of topics and compare it with one that included a "complete" list, considering the amount and quality of the discussion contained, and that omitted.

The Epistle of James is said to be absolutely essential to Christianity because it seeks to preserve "the solidarity of the life of the community" vis-à-vis "the danger of a mere internalization of faith," thus showing that he has "something decisive to say to a Christianity which in some respects exhibits the same degenerate 'faith' which he attacked."[14] We do not think for one moment that James can replace Paul, John, and the others; but we do believe that he focuses on "aspects of Christian life that have faded from church consciousness."[15] So our Epistle should not be judged by its length but by its function within the NT.

We are convinced that no other Epistle (except Philippians) is more complete, has more wide-ranging discussion, or is a worthier production as an adequately (though not completely) comprehensive Manual of Christian Life. In Jas. 1:3f. we have the first statement of the theme of his religion and his Epistle—"faith" *(pistis)*, "endurance" *(hypomonē)*, and "work" *(ergon)*, leading to perfection, to approbation, and to the final reward. There is indeed more *theology* in Paul and others than in James or in the gospel preached by Jesus, but they all hold the same *religion*, the one James preaches in brief but full simplicity. If James never mentions the death and resurrection of Jesus, neither do the rest of the Catholic Epistles from James to Jude, except 1 Peter and 1 John.

It does seem strange that some Christians prize the First Epistle of John as one of their best books and tend to ignore James as barely Christian at all or at best a NT aberration or innovation. But John's Epistle is as severely practical as James's and his gospel is the same, namely, brotherhood and righteousness (e.g., 1 Jn. 2:3-6), the vanity of theory without practice (which Paul equally denounces), etc.; see also 1 Jn. 3:7f. where John, like James, mentions that coy name, "the devil." 1 John chimes with James, as both do with 1 Cor. 13:2, on the insufficiency of "faith" *(pistis)* per se and the paramount claims of "love" *(agapē)*, which pervades James (e.g., 1:27) even though he does not name it as such. Indeed, the famous 1 Jn. 4:7 is just another way of saying what James says in effect: "The works prove the faith."

Moreover, the fact that the Epistle of James seems singularly or uniquely sparing in theology, especially in its so-called "archaic" Christology, can be taken as a strong testimonial to its authenticity in the

14. W. G. Kümmel, *Introduction to the New Testament* (^{2}1975), p. 292.

15. J.-L. Blondel, "Theology and Paraenesis in James," *Theology Digest* 28.3 (Fall 1980): 256.

dawn of "the Way." S. G. F. Brandon suggested that the Palestinian messianic concept of the Jesus of history was to be contrasted with the Pauline, christological doctrine of an incarnated Savior God.[16] If he is correct, this contrast and the early triumph of the latter might have been one of the main causes for the long eclipse of the Epistle before its ultimate emergence and acceptance into the canon. At first sight, this view is attractive, but it must finally be rejected since we do not see any such contrast or conflict between James and Paul in their respective "assessments" of Jesus. Indeed, we submit that, except for varying degrees of emphasis and development, the Christologies of the two coincide in a remarkable way and are essentially the same, and certainly in this respect—that they both center on the cross and the resurrection. Thus James, like Paul, faithfully preaches a suffering and risen Lord, though never as "a theology of glory for the Church," but rather as "a theology of empiricism,"[17] and always as a challenge to practical faith.

In the realm of Christology, therefore, James is succinct but significant. It has been thought that NT Christianity was at first keyed to faith in the imminence of the parousia, and that disappointment at its delay forced a series of gradual adjustments of doctrine. Now, however, the evidence is that neither the parousia nor its delay was the key to the first Christian faith and its Christology, but the resurrection of Jesus, which opened the eyes of the first Christians to the true character of their Master as they had seen and known him on earth, that is, as the Messiah. From this flow the major christological titles given to him in the Jewish Christian church, and this is the focal point in all thought about Jesus in the Epistle of James. Scarcely less fundamental was the thought of "Jesus is Lord"; but the prominence of the first in early Jewish Christianity, together with the fact that the second is almost confined to the evangelization of the Gentiles, shows that the Messiahship was at least the first decisive criterion of Christian belief, and then Lordship received like emphasis.

Despite its few references to Christ, this Epistle, like the Epistle of Paul, is filled with intense Christian devotion, again reinforcing the truth that this work is intrinsically Christian rather than pre-Christian, Jewish and slightly Christianized. A simple illustration may help here. Suppose we wrote a book describing the way Winston Churchill governed wartime Britain, never mentioning Churchill's name in the writing, and then claiming that the book was a biography of Churchill in that period. We are sure that the book would be rejected. We could claim that the book was "Churchillian" to the end, but without frequent

16. *The Fall of Jerusalem* (1951), pp. 78-84.

17. So L. Goppelt, *Theology of the New Testament,* II (1982), 199f.; also Scaer, p. 15.

use of his name it would not be recognized. What is needed is more than a surface reading. The same is true of the Epistle of James. The name of Jesus is seldom mentioned and there is no account of his life except for a few quotations from his teaching. But if we read the book carefully, we shall see that it is thoroughly inspired by Christ's teaching, spirit, and person—in short, it is completely and genuinely christological from start to finish.

We conclude, then, that James's concept of Christianity is neither peculiar nor unorthodox; his religion is that of the NT, including that of Paul. We cite only 1 Cor. 8:6: "We have one God, the Father, of whom are all things . . . and one Lord, Jesus Christ." Early Jewish Christian theology was almost exclusively Christology,[18] centered above all upon the redemptive activity of the one true God, in whom as both Creator and Redeemer their belief was axiomatic. "James proclaims," wrote Thurneysen, "Jesus Christ, his cross and his resurrection, the power of forgiveness and the obedience of faith, and nothing else. He proclaims that but in his own way."[19] James should not, and cannot, be understood in isolation, but rather in the entire context of the NT. The Epistle itself shows that James no less than Paul resisted the entanglements of the Jewish assessments of Jesus that had figured so perniciously in Colossian, Galatian, and Roman professions of Christianity.

(3) *TRADITIONAL.* The third ground alleged against ascribing this Epistle to James the Lord's brother is the assumption, based on internal evidence, that he could not have had enough Greek or enough culture or enough prestige in Judaism or Christianity to have been able to write an epistle of such literary excellence. The solution to this problem will depend partly on the kind of letter that this ability would permit him to write.

Jewish or Hellenistic? In answer to this question, some have argued that its good Greek and Hellenistic affiliations point to extra-Palestinian Hellenistic sources but not to James the leader of the Jerusalem Church. To say otherwise, says B. S. Easton,[20] is to indulge the wildest imagination. Years ago von Soden expressed the same view: "It is remarkable indeed but only accidental that the author bears the name of James. It is moreover quite obvious that he cannot have been the brother of the Lord. How could such an one have written Greek so good and so completely unaffected by his Semitic mother-tongue! How could he have acquired his familiarity with the literature of the Greeks and Romans!"[21] Recent discoveries, however, notably the Dead Sea

18. O. Cullmann, *The Christology of the New Testament* (ET 1959), p. 3.
19. *Der Brief des Jakobus* (1941), p. 5.
20. *The Epistle of James*, p. 3.
21. *The Books of the New Testament* (1907), pp. 467ff.

Scrolls, the Murabba'at documents, ossuary inscriptions, and others, have shown that this position is untenable. New evidence from the pseudepigrapha, for example, provides excellent confirmation of our findings. After careful research J. H. Charlesworth, for example, shows[22] that the newly-translated ethical tracts, philosophical writings, and wisdom books in *The Old Testament Pseudepigrapha,* namely, 3 and 4 Maccabees, Pseudo-Phocylides, and Syriac Menander, "illustrate impressively the highly-developed, universalistic, and surprisingly different moral ideas prevalent among Jews in the first century." He concludes: "There is absolutely no compelling reason to date James after 70; we may now have reasons to date it prior to the destruction of Jerusalem."

We have seen that by the time of James Hellenism had penetrated far into Palestine, reaching not only the rabbis, most of whom taught Greek, but also the middle and even the lower and rural classes,[23] who knew the Greek language and culture. But we do not need to be told that, for whatever intimacy he had with other cultures or languages, the typical Jew remained thoroughly a Jew; and to NT writers such as Paul and James, the most powerful influence, literary not less than religious, would be the Jewish OT.

It seems entirely possible—and indeed almost certain—that a leader like James the Lord's brother had some facility in Greek, the *lingua franca* of the Diaspora. Common sense would indicate that this man of necessity would be bilingual, even trilingual,[24] possessing the ability to communicate by speech and pen to all the members of his church; and these members would include Jews and Hellenists both in Jerusalem and throughout the Diaspora, including the Jewish Greek-speaking pilgrims who thronged Jerusalem. Further, we have found that if the problem of James is to be solved and his thought understood, we must begin and end with the fact that the author is a Jew and this is the key that unlocks the so-called "riddle"—a point made many years ago by J. H. Ropes when he complained of that lack of rabbinic material so indispensable to a sympathetic interpretation of this thoroughly Jewish Epistle.[25] But thanks to the work of rabbinic and NT scholars like Strack

22. *The Old Testament Pseudepigrapha and the New Testament* (1985), p. 86.

23. See, e.g., our previous discussions, pp. 35f. and elsewhere; also S. Freyne, *Galilee* (1980), p. 140. For an illuminating discussion of teaching, learning, and education in Palestine at the time of James, see R. Riesner, *Jesus als Lehrer* (1981).

24. Kümmel, *Introduction to the New Testament,* p. 291.

25. P. vi. For a modern appraisal of the Judaic context of early Christianity, see J. Lightstone's study in *Anti-Judaism in Early Christianity:* II, *Separation and Polemic* (1986), ed. S. G. Wilson, 103ff.

and Billerbeck, W. D. Davies, E. P. Sanders, and others, the essential Jewishness of James is now virtually unchallenged.

(4) *AUTHENTIC*. But the final—and greatest—handicap is the failure to recognize the Epistle's integrity. The Epistle of James should not be called a "fake" just because it does not neatly fit the predilections of any and every scholar, critic, or commentator. To regard it as "the first-recorded reaction to the proclaimed Christ-event in the early community" may be "beyond belief" or "a theological misuse of the Scripture."[26] Yet we believe, for the reasons stated, that the Epistle of James is an authentic document of undeniable authority and originality, which rightly belongs in the first stage in the religion of Jesus in the Jerusalem Church. That is why it is addressed only to Jews. Who but James would have addressed it to the Diaspora?

A sirloin of beef, or a shoulder of mutton or pork, has a definite, recognizable anatomical structure; but however optimistic one may be about its ingredients, who would look for the anatomical structure of a sausage? The structure of James is obviously inconsistent with a theory of conglomeration and a late date. As one who once warmly embraced the recently revived "two-tiered hypothesis," I recognize its fascination, though by no stretch of the imagination can it be called "simple"![27] Yet no redaction process like that postulated in such a theory could have produced anything like our Epistle of James unless it had finally been rewritten entirely and anew by one man, a redactor, a genius, and a saint like James; and the difficulties of such a theory, for example, double author (who?), double date (when?), and double material (which?), are obvious and invincible. To contend (as we once did) that such material was simply "transmuted" is to beg the question, raising more and more problems, until we are left with a vague, ill-defined, and unsatisfactory solution. We might be prepared to concede that the Greek represents a "careful revision" by a faithful scholar,[28] but even this is hardly necessary.

I suggest, therefore, that we think of the Epistle of James not as the outcome of an author's urge to fulfill himself by his own composi-

26. See J. A. Fitzmyer's remarks, and the Kümmel-Marxsen quotation, in a review in *Interpretation* 32.3 (1978): 312f.

27. See P. H. Davids, p. 12; repeated in his GNC, p. xx. For trenchant criticisms of this solution, dubbed "fudged and unclear," with other points, see C. S. Rodd's editorial, *ExpT* 94.9 (1983): 258. Similarly, D. J. Moo, "We may question whether Davids' theory is necessary. The inconsistencies that Davids cites are not of a type that require the hypothesis of two different stages of composition. . . . That James may have utilized his own sermons in writing the letter is not improbable in itself. But evidence for an earlier literary stage is not compelling" (*James*, pp. 30f.).

28. F. F. Bruce, *Peter, Stephen, James and John* (1979), p. 115.

tion or by a miscellaneous conglomeration of unrelated sections, but as an authoritative pastoral letter, like Paul's (see 1 Cor. 11: "I hear from Chloe . . ."; 5:1: "I hear reports that . . ."; or 7:1: "Concerning the things whereof you wrote to me . . ."). Often students of our Epistle do not realize how centripetal the religion of Israel was (then and not only then), and how the Jews everywhere sought to keep in touch with Jerusalem, regularly going there, for example, at sacred feast times. Aptly described as "a cosmopolitan man who tried to keep his hand on the pulse of world Jewry"[29] and whose influence extended far beyond Jerusalem to "all the Jews, who lived among the Gentiles" (Acts 21:21, NIV), James, as the first Christian "Pope" or "Archbishop" or "Bishop" of the new "Israel," did not always need to travel to see his Jewish Christians and guide them; they came to him from all corners of his "diocese."

That, I am sure, is one reason why the forthright and strikingly comprehensive Epistle of James was written, namely, that they might take it with them when returning to their perhaps distant homes, possibly in Spain, Italy, Rumania, or North Africa.[30] The Jews had learned much during their captivity in Egypt and Babylon and elsewhere, times that had only strengthened their passionate devotion to the land of Israel (read Ps. 137). The English Prayer Book translation best conveys something of the music and the misery of the original.

> How shall we sing the Lord's song
>   in a strange land?
>
> If I forget thee, O Jerusalem,
>   let my right hand forget her cunning.

The letter of James is addressed to the observed and reported needs of his Christian Jews, wherever they might be, and it is no concern of James that these needs must partly coincide with those of other men and women—whoever they are. This is the encyclical of a NT pastor bent on the improvement of a not altogether satisfactory flock.

THE HIDDEN JEWEL

We find James extraordinarily wonderful, but also extremely frustrating. He is Jewish to the bone. "In the nineteenth century Karl Marx and,

29. G. W. Barker, W. L. Lane, J. M. Michaels, *The New Testament Speaks* (1969), p. 326.

30. For the Jerusalem "tourist season" and evidence for visitors from the Diaspora and beyond, as well as from within Palestine, see J. Jeremias, *Jerusalem in the Time of Jesus* (1969), pp. 58-84; G. Vermes, F. Millar, M. Goodman, and E. Schürer, *The History of the Jewish People in the Age of Jesus Christ,* III, 1 (1986), 1ff.

later, his heirs retrieved," as M. E. Marty reminds us, "Aristotle's old notion of *praxis* and made it common in today's usage. . . . *praxis* holds that because something is true it will work—but it must be worked out. Action and reflection are bonded, webbed, and wedded. James thinks similarly. The perfect law that sets men free is 'true,' but it is true for us when we enact it in our lives."[31] Active and pragmatic rather than mystical and intellectual, James uses short, sharp, terse periods and seems to leap bewilderingly from one idea to another. There is nothing simple about the Epistle of James. That is why we cannot say that it has "a single message" for today. Almost every sentence is a message, yet there is no explicit picture of a person, as in the Gospels. But for all its apparent incoherence, we do discern a secret unifying pattern—the pattern of the faith of Jesus, the brother of the writer. Indisputably, "James says less about the Master than any other writer in the NT, but his speech is more like that of the Master than the speech of any one of them."[32] This faith of the man Jesus, the Lord of Glory, and the perfect life that was one with that faith, is the key to the book's underlying unity.

We look in vain for any explicit or extended exposition of the great theological matters of the faith. All this, and more, is doubtless implicit in the book, but so deeply buried as to remain undiscovered without the help of the rest of Scripture. We do not find "the gospel" in James, any more than we find a foundation when we walk into a house; but reposing in the secret depths—exactly as it was "preached" to Abraham (Gal. 3:8) and "beneath" the Jew all through the dispensation—the gospel jewel is hidden in the "right strawy epistle."

This is not to denigrate James but rather to underline the fact that the book is a mystery; indeed, every page shines with the glory of Christ, whose name is only twice mentioned explicitly. Of course Martin Luther, engaged in doctrinal controversy over the whole spectrum of theology and philosophy, called it "strawy." What else could he do? Luther, however, was not a Jew of the Diaspora, nor for that matter a swearing sailor in the Oakland docks, but a theological professor, and for such a person do we not need to exercise special patience? "The juice, the strength, the passion, the fire" which Luther found in the Psalms are all there in the Epistle of James, if only he had eyes to see them. It is a pity that such weight was so long ascribed to Luther's insistence that in the Epistle of James the normal practical requirements of Christian life and Christian conduct as evidence of genuine Christian faith bastardized all the doctrine of James on Christian salvation; it seems to me that Luther's

31. *Good News in the Early Church*, p. 78.

32. D. A. Hayes, "James, Epistle of," *The International Standard Bible Encyclopedia* (1929), III, 1562.

point here is as idle as a debate whether it is the solid foods or the liquids that ordinarily keep a person alive. Dying conversions, like some other extreme cases, make bad law. Concludes Kittel:

> If someone should be amazed that consequently in an authentic document of the earliest apostolic time there is so little addressed to the theological problems of Christology and soteriology, then it would be well to answer that here stands a man for whom everything is comprehended in the phrase, "a servant of God and of the Lord Jesus Christ," and for whom the whole sense and yield of all Christological and soteriological foundations stands on the same point from which his Lord has spoken: "Not everyone who says to me, 'Lord, Lord' shall enter the Kingdom of Heaven, but rather they who do the will of my Father in Heaven."[33]

The real rub is that this brusque but bracing book "finds us," drives us from the balcony to the road, and hounds us out of intellectualism, mysticism, and dogmatism into a real, living, existential world where, with a hand on our throats, we are hurled into the moment of decision. Why is this? The answer must be the closeness of Jesus to each one of us, in our sorrow, pain, loneliness, darkness and tempest, temptation, hunger and thirst, disappointment, sin and rejection. James parcels up for us the vitals of our earthly existence with Jesus Christ.

The Epistle of James reflects the tendencies of Palestinian Christianity. Among the characteristics that indicate a primitive Christian viewpoint is the unselfconsciousness of the author. He does not try to argue for a point of view, to retell the gospel story, which must still have been most vivid, or to elaborate a systematic theology around the person of Jesus. He speaks of "Law" in the unique, distinctive, Christian rather than Jewish or early Catholic sense of "the imperative of the gospel that corresponded to the indicative."[34] Jesus is the promised Messiah and the giver of an ideal law to Israel, and the teaching throughout is that of an exalted ethic that aims at the fulfillment of the Mosaic law. With certain reservations—and these were embodied in the so-called "apostolic decree"—James and the Jerusalem Church recognized the force of Paul's arguments. Henceforth the Gentiles would be admitted into the church without circumcision.

The decision of the Council in accordance with the proposal of James must have satisfied Paul and Peter. But we must not overlook the significance of Acts 15:21: the law of Moses is not to be prejudiced *among the Jews* by this resolution of the Council for Gentiles. That law

33. "Der geschichtliche Ort des Jakobusbriefes," *ZNW* 41 (1942): 105.
34. Goppelt, *Theology of the New Testament,* II, 207.

lives on, says James, and it is clearly his thought that it shall live on, *among the Jews,* in the weekly liturgy of the synagogue. Certainly James is contemplating the retention of Mosaic law, including circumcision, for Christian Jews, and in this Paul agrees with James.

Similarly, the author of our Epistle contemplates no fundamental revolution in religion. His injunctions are intended not to set aside, but to develop, the existing religious system. The law is not to be spoken against nor judged, but to be cherished and reverently obeyed. As far as we can gather, his hope for the nation was that it should continue under the law, only with a greater and truer spirit of dedication. The period in which the Epistle was written was that of nascent Christianity, and in it we feel the birth pangs of a church struggling to be born.

Why do we persist in approaching the Epistle of James with *a priori* considerations, comparing it with Paul whose Christianity is the yardstick with which James, and all other NT writers, are to be judged?[35] This is doubly misleading, for it assumes that Paul's is the only and definitive norm of a multi-faceted NT Christianity, and also that James's Epistle is reduced to a few prooftexts from 2:14ff. where for most the Epistle begins and ends. Much time has been spent and ink spilt on the relation of the two, especially on the question of faith–works–salvation. Occasionally James's entire Epistle has been construed as a sustained polemic against Paul's personal character, conduct, and missionary motives as well as his theology.[36] Doubtless this will continue with mixed results. We are convinced, however, that this is ultimately an exercise in futility, for the work of each writer must be judged as a whole on his own considerable merits. Whereas Paul represents his own important, but not exclusive, type of Christianity, James represents his own—not Pauline, Johannine or Petrine, but uniquely Judaic or "Jacobean," going back to the Jewish Synagogue and the Jerusalem Church, as well as, however indirectly, to Qumran.

Understandably most scholars usually dote without limit on Paul, and never tire of disparaging the Epistle of James, of which we firmly believe James was the author. But the leadership of James in the early church is an insuperable fact, which even Acts cannot and does not try to hide. In the years immediately after the resurrection, James was the leader of the Christians (and was faithfully respected as such by Paul); there may, however, be some truth in the excuse that James was not a believer during the life of Jesus. But the Epistle of James itself speaks

35. See L. T. Johnson, *The Writings of the New Testament* (1986), p. 453.

36. See, e.g., M. Hengel, "Der Jakobusbrief als antipaulinische Polemik," in *Tradition and Interpretation in the New Testament,* Essays in Honor of E. Earle Ellis, ed. G. F. Hawthorne (1988), pp. 252ff.

for its authorship by its very address to the "Diaspora." When could it have been composed, by James or any other serious author, except in the dawn of "the Way"? And would any late forger have used the author's name as a label,[37] "pasted it on," and then addressed the result to the "Diaspora"? The late acceptance of the Epistle of James and the few copies of it available in (say) the second or third century are so much in tune with the view of a depreciatory *tendenz* in the Gospels and even in Acts (apart from the report of the Council) toward James's status that we have argued that here we have positive evidence for the genuineness of the Epistle of James as essentially the work of our James; and, as we have seen, the importance of identifying our James as the author of the Epistle of James can scarcely be exaggerated.

We see no reason why James should not have written an epistle before Paul, and as readily as Paul, which would make the Epistle of James "the first Epistle to Christians." That was in the early stages of Christianity, in the days when there was a sort of projected engagement between Judaism and Christianity, an engagement that (as engagements sometimes do) stopped short of marriage. Nobody *knows* why the Epistle of James was so late in getting into the canon; but we venture to guess that the reason lies in the singularly unfavorable conditions, which were bound to tell most against a letter written in that brief, short-lived, and, as it proved, ill-fated period. To Jews like Paul and James the strongest literary influence would be that of the Jewish OT; but when James and his Christian gospel perished out of Jewry, it is no wonder that his Epistle had some difficulty in surviving, as it providentially has done. No wonder it was so late in getting into the canon! "The inclusion," it has been well said, "represented a victory for the mature, well-balanced view of Christianity. The inclusion insured that a proper concept of Christianity would include a practical orientation which would be relevant to all ages."[38] The experience and the testimony of almost two thousand years of church history combine to show that the early church was absolutely correct in admitting this modest but rich and apparently timeless document into the canon. Ultimately the Epistle of James triumphed!

37. Kümmel, *Introduction to the New Testament*, p. 286.

38. J. A. Brooks, "The Place of James in the New Testament Canon," *SWJT* 12.1 (1969): 55. "But even if, as some scholars continue to insist, the Epistles of Paul and James cannot be amalgamated theologically," B. M. Metzger concludes, "it is a fact that each writer in his historical individuality has served to guard the other against the extremes of misinterpretation. Thus, both writers have proved themselves indispensable to the health of the Church universal" (*The Canon of the New Testament* [1987], p. 281).

V. FURTHER READING

C.-B. Amphoux, "A propos de Jacques 1,17," *RHPR* 50 (1970): 127-36.

C.-B. Amphoux, "Langue de l'Épître de Jacques, Études structurales," *RHPR* 53 (1973): 7-45.

C.-B. Amphoux, "Vers une description linguistique de L'Épître de Jacques," *NTS* 25.1 (1978): 58-92.

C.-B. Amphoux, "Une relecture du chapitre I de l'Epître de Jacques," *Bib* 59 (1978): 554-61.

C.-B. Amphoux, "La parenté textuelle du sy^h et du groupe 2138 dans l'épître de Jacques," *Bib* 62 (1981): 259-71.

C.-B. Amphoux, "Systèmes anciens de divisions dans l'épître de Jacques et composition littéraire," *Bib* 62 (1981): 309-400.

C.-B. Amphoux, "L'emploi du coordonnant dans l'Épître de Jacques," *Bib* 63 (1982): 90-101.

C.-B. Amphoux, "Quelques témoins grecs des formes textuelles les plus anciennes de l'Épître de Jacques: le Groupe 2138 (ou 614)," *NTS* 28 (1982): 91-115.

C.-B. Amphoux and B. Outtier, "Les leçons des versions géorgiennes de l'épître Jacques," *Bib* 65.3 (1984): 365-76.

D. E. Aune, *The New Testament in Its Literary Environment* (Philadelphia, 1987).

J. D. Awoniyi, *The Classification of the Greek Manuscripts of the Epistle of James* (Unpublished Th.D. Thesis, Andrews University, 1979).

E. Bammel and C. F. D. Moule, eds., *Jesus and the Politics of His Day* (Cambridge, 1984).

A. E. Barnett, "James, Letter of," *IDB*, II (E-J), 794-99.

D. L. Bartlett, "The Epistle of James as a Jewish-Christian Document," SBL 1979 Seminar Papers, II, 173-86.

Bede, the Venerable, *On the Seven Catholic Epistles,* tr. D. Hurst (Ann Arbor, 1985).

W. Bieder, "Christliche Existenz nach dem Zeugnis des Jakobusbriefes," *ThZ* 5 (1949): 93-113.

J. L. Bird, *Faith that Works* (Ann Arbor, 1965).

J.-L. Blondel, "Theology and Paraenesis in James," *Theology Digest* 28.3 (Fall 1980): 253-56.

M.-É. Boismard, "Une Liturgie Baptismale dans la Prima Petri II—son Influence sur L'Épître de Jacques," *RB* 65 (1957): 161-83.

G. C. Bottini, "Correzione fraterna e salevezza in *Giacomo* 5,19-20," *Studii Biblici Franciscani Liber Annuus* 35 (1985): 131-62.

G. C. Bottini, "Sentenze di Pseudo-Focilide alla luce della lettera di Giacomo," *Studii Biblici Franciscani Liber Annuus* 36 (1986): 171-81.

M. Bouttier et C.-B. Amphoux, "La prédication de Jacques le Juste," *EThR* 54 (1979): 5-16.

J. W. Bowman, *The Letter of James.* The Layman's Bible Commentary 24, eds. B. H. Kelley et al. (Richmond, 1962).

M. O'R. Boyle, "The Stoic Paradox of James 2:10," *NTS* 31.4 (1985): 611-17.

S. G. F. Brandon, *The Fall of Jerusalem and the Christian Church* (London, 1951).

S. G. F. Brandon, *Jesus and the Zealots* (Manchester, 1967).

S. G. F. Brandon, "The Death of James the Just. A New Interpretation," in *Studies in Mysticism and Religion,* presented to G. Scholem (Jerusalem, 1967), pp. 57-60.

R. G. Bratcher, *A Translator's Guide to the Letters from James, Peter, and Jude* (London, 1984).

J. A. Brooks, "The Place of James in the New Testament Canon," *SWJT* 12.1 (1969): 41-55.

C. Brown, ed., *The New International Dictionary of New Testament Theology,* 3 vols. (Exeter, 1975-78).

F. F. Bruce, *New Testament History* (London, 1971).

F. F. Bruce, *Peter, Stephen, James and John* (Grand Rapids, 1980).

F. F. Bruce, "Justification by Faith in the Non-Pauline Writings of the New Testament," *EQ* 2.4 (1952): 66-77.

C. Burchard, "Gemeinde in der strohernen Epistel," in D. Lührmann and G. Strecker, eds., *Kirche* (für G. Bornkamm) (Tübingen, 1980).

C. Burchard, "Zu Jakobus 2, 14-26," *ZNW* 71 (1980): 27-45.

G. M. Burge, "'And Threw Them Thus on Paper', Recovering the Poetic Form of James 2:14-26," *Studia Biblica et Theologica* (1977): 31-45.

A. Cabaniss, "The Epistle of Saint James," *JBR* 22 (1954): 27-29.

A. Cabaniss, "A Note on Jacob's Homily," *EQ* 47.4 (1975): 219-22.

P. Carrington, *The Primitive Christian Catechism* (Cambridge, 1940).

K. L. Carroll, "The Place of James in the Early Church," *BJRL* 44 (1961): 49-67.

B. S. Childs, *The New Testament as Canon: An Introduction* (London, 1984).

E. P. Colson, *The Practical Message of James* (Nashville, 1969).

R. B. Coote and A. C. Wire, "Alias James," *Pacific Theological Review* 12.1 (Fall 1979): 10-14.

C. E. B. Cranfield, "The Message of James," *SJTh* 18 (1965): 182-93, 338-45.

P. H. Davids, "Themes in the Epistle of James Which Are Judaistic in Character" (Unpublished Ph.D. Thesis, University of Manchester, 1974).

P. H. Davids, "The Meaning of *Apeirastos* in James 1:13," *NTS* 24.3 (1978): 386-92.

P. H. Davids, "Tradition and Citation in the Epistle of James," in W. W. Gasque and W. S. LaSor, eds., *Scripture, Tradition and Interpretation* (for E. F. Harrison) (Grand Rapids, 1978), pp. 113-26.

P. H. Davids, "James, Epistle of," *The Illustrated Bible Dictionary* (Wheaton, 1980), II, 732f.

P. H. Davids, "Theological Perspectives on the Epistle of James," *Journal of the Evangelical Theological Society* 23.2 (June, 1980): 97-103.

W. D. Davies, *The Setting of the Sermon on the Mount* (Cambridge, 1964).

G. E. M. de Ste. Croix, *The Class Struggle in the Ancient Greek World* (London, 1981).

C. N. Dillman, *A Study of Some Theological and Literary Comparisons of the Gospel of Matthew and The Epistle of James* (Unpublished Ph.D. Thesis, University of Edinburgh, 1978).

C. E. Donker, "Der Verfasser der Jak. und sein Gegner. Zum Problem des Einwandes in Jak. 2:18-19," *ZNW* 72 (1981): 227-40.

J. D. G. Dunn, *Unity and Diversity in the New Testament* (Philadelphia, 1977).

C. M. Edsman, "Schöpferwille und Gerburt. Jac. 1.18," *ZNW* 38 (1939): 11-44.

C. M. Edsman, "Schöpfung und Wiedergeburt: Nochmals Jac. 1, 18," *Spiritus et Veritas* (Festschrift Karl Kundsin) (1953), pp. 43-55.

G. Eichholz, *Jakobus und Paulus* (Munich, 1953).

G. Eichholz, *Glaube und Werk bei Paulus und Jakobus* (Munich, 1961).

R. H. Eisenman, *James the Just in the Habakkuk Pesher* (Leiden, 1986).

J. O. Ekstrom, "The Discourse Structure of the Book of James" (International Linguistics Center, Dallas, 1975).
J. H. Elliott, *A Home for the Homeless* (Philadelphia, 1981).
L. E. Elliott-Binns, *Galilean Christianity* (SBT 1/16) (London, 1956).
L. E. Elliott-Binns, "James i.18: Creation or Redemption?" *NTS* 3.2 (1956-57): 148-61.
L. E. Elliott-Binns, "James i:21 and Ezekiel xvi:36: An Odd Coincidence," *ExpT* 66.9 (1955): 273.
L. E. Elliott-Binns, "The Meaning of *hylē* in Jas. III. 5," *NTS* 2 (1955): 48-50.
M. J. Evans, "The Law in James," *Vox Evangelica* 13 (1983): 29-40.
R. Fabris, *Legge della Libertà in Giacomo* (Supplementi alla Revista Biblica, Paedeia, Brescia, 1977).
C. H. Felder, "Partiality and God's Law: An Exegesis of James 2:1-13," *Journal of Religious Thought* 39 (1982-83): 51-69.
A. Feuillet, "Le sens du mot Parousie dans l'Évangile de Matthieu," in W. D. Davies and D. Daube, eds., *The Background of the New Testament and its Eschatology* (Cambridge, 1956).
P. B. R. Forbes, "The Structure of the Epistle of James," *EQ* 44 (1972): 147-53.
F. O. Francis, "The Form and Function of the Opening and Closing Paragraphs of James and 1 John," *ZNW* 61 (1970): 110-26.
M. Gertner, "Midrashic Terms and Techniques in the New Testament: the Epistle of James, a Midrash on a Psalm," ed. F. L. Cross, *StEv* 3 = *TU* 88 (1964): 463.
M. Gertner, "Midrashim in the New Testament," *JSS* 7 (1962): 267-92.
A. S. Geyser, "The Letter of James and the Social Condition of His Addressees," *Neotestamentica* 9 (1975): 25-33.
A. S. Geyser, "The Letter of James in Rome," short paper read at a meeting of SNT in Rome, 1981, pp. 1-7.
L. G. Gieger, *Figures of Speech in the Epistle of James: A Rhetorical and Exegetical Analysis* (Unpublished Ph.D. thesis, Southwestern Baptist Theological Seminary).
R. P. Gordon, "KAI TO TELOS KYRIOU EIDETE (Jas. V, 11)," *JTS* 26.1 (1975): 91-95.
H. Greeven, "Jede Gabe ist gut, Jak 1, 17," *ThZ* 14 (1958): 1-13.
D. Guthrie, *New Testament Introduction* (London, [3]1970).
D. Guthrie, "The Development of the Idea of Canonical Pseudepigrapha in New Testament Criticism," *Vox Evangelica* 1 (1962): 43-59.
E. Haenchen, *The Acts of the Apostles* (Philadelphia, 1971).
B. R. Halson, "The Epistle of James: 'Christian Wisdom?'" *StEv* 4 = *TU* 102 (1968): 308-14.

F. M. Heichelheim, "Roman Syria," in T. Frank, ed., *An Economic Survey of Ancient Rome* (Baltimore, 1938), IV, 121-257.

R. Henderlite, "The Epistle of James," *Interpretation* 3.4 (1949): 460-76.

M. Hengel, *Was Jesus a Revolutionist?* (Philadelphia, 1971).

M. Hengel, *Poverty and Riches in the Early Church* (London, 1974).

M. Hengel, *Judaism and Hellenism*, 2 vols. (London, 1974).

M. Hengel, *Jews, Greeks and Barbarians* (London, 1980).

M. Hengel, *Between Jesus and Paul* (London, 1983).

M. Hengel, "Jakobus der Herrenbruder—der erste 'Papst'?" *Glaube und Eschatologie*, eds. E. Grässer and O. Merk (1985), pp. 71-104.

M. Hengel, "Der Jakobusbrief als antipaulinische Polemik," in *Tradition and Interpretation in the New Testament*, Essays in Honor of E. Earle Ellis (Grand Rapids, 1988), pp. 248-78.

D. E. Hiebert, "The Unifying Theme of the Epistle of James," *BibSac* 135 (1978): 221-31.

D. E. Hiebert, *The Epistle of James* (Chicago, 1979).

R. Hill, "Overview of James"; "James 3-5"; "Displays of Paragraph Constituent Level for James 3–5" (International Linguistics Center, Dallas, 1978).

Z. C. Hodges, "Light on James Two from Textual Criticism," *BibSac* 120 (1963): 341-50.

R. Hoppe, *Der theologische Hintergrund des Jakobusbriefes*. Forschung zur Bibel 28 (Würzburg, 1977).

I. Jacobs, "The Midrashic Background for James II, 21-23," *NTS* 22.4 (1976): 457-64.

J. Jeremias, *Jerusalem in the Time of Jesus* (London, 1969).

J. Jeremias, "Paul and James," *ExpT* 66 (1954-55): 368-71.

B. C. Johanson, "The Definition of 'Pure Religion' in Jas. 1:27 Reconsidered," *ExpT* 84 (1973): 118-19.

L. T. Johnson, "The Use of Leviticus 19 in the Letter of James," *JBL* 101.3 (1982): 391-401.

L. T. Johnson, "James 3:13–4:10 and the *Topos Peri Phthonou*," *NovT* 25 (1983): 327-47.

L. T. Johnson, "Friendship with the World/Friendship with God: A Study of Discipleship in James," *Discipleship in the New Testament*, ed. F. F. Segovia (1985), pp. 166-83.

P. R. Jones, "Approaches to the Study of the Book of James," *RevExp* 66 (1969): 425-34.

E. Kamlah, *Die Form der katalogischen Paränese im Neuen Testament*, Wissenschaftliche Untersuchungen zum Neuen Testament 7 (Tübingen, 1964).

E. Käsemann, *Commentary on Romans* (Grand Rapids, 1980).
L. E. Keck, "The Poor Among the Saints in the New Testament," *ZNW* 56 (1965): 100-129.
L. E. Keck, "The Poor Among the Saints in Jewish Christianity and Qumran," *ZNW* 57 (1966): 54ff.
F. X. Kelly, *Poor and Rich in the Epistle of James* (Unpublished Ph.D. Thesis, Temple University, 1972).
H. A. A. Kennedy, "The Hellenistic Atmosphere of the Epistle of James," *Ex* 2 (1911): 37-52.
G. D. Kilpatrick, "Übertreter des Gesetzes, Jak 2:11," *ThZ* 23 (1967): 433.
J. A. Kirk, "The Meaning of Wisdom in James," *NTS* 16 (1969): 24-38.
S. J. Kistemaker, "The Theological Message of James," *Journal of the Evangelical Theological Society* 29.1 (1986): 55-61.
G. Kittel, "Der geschichtliche Ort des Jakobusbriefes," *ZNW* 41 (1942): 71-105.
G. Kittel, "Der Jakobusbrief und die apostolischen Väter," *ZNW* 43 (1950): 54-112.
G. Kittel, *Die Probleme des palästinensischen Spätjudentums* (Stuttgart, 1926).
G. Kittel, "Die Stellung des Jakobus zu Judentum und Heidenchristentum," *ZNW* 30 (1931): 145-57.
G. Kittel, *"ton trochon tēs geneseōs," ThLb* Beilage, I, 141-68.
W. L. Knox, *Some Primitive Elements in Hellenistic Christianity* (1944).
H. Köster, *Introduction to the New Testament,* 2 vols. (Philadelphia, 1982).
H. H. Kramm, *The Theology of Martin Luther* (London, 1947).
W. G. Kümmel, *Introduction to the New Testament,* rev. ed. (London, 1975).
S. S. Laws, "The Doctrinal Basis for the Ethics of James," *StEv* 7 (1982): 299-305.
S. S. Laws, "Does Scripture Speak in Vain? A Reconsideration of James IV.5," *NTS* 20.2 (1974): 210-15.
J. G. Lodge, "James and Paul at Cross-Purposes? James 2.22," *Bib* 62 (1981): 195-213.
E. Lohse, "Glaube und Werke—zur Theologie des Jakobusbriefes," *ZNW* 48 (1957): 1-22.
R. N. Longenecker, *The Christology of Early Jewish Christianity* (London, 1970).
J. W. MacGorman, "Introducing the Book of James," *SWJT* 12 (1969): 9-22.

J. McGovern, "Letters to James, Peter, John and Jude," 3 cassettes (Columbus, c. 1969).

E. W. Male, "'Divine Healing' According to James 5," *Grace Journal* 1.2 (Fall 1960): 23-30.

F. Manns, "Jacques 2,24-26 à la lumière du judaïsme," *Bib Or* 26.3 (1984): 143-49.

F. Manns, "Confessez vos péchés les uns aux autres. Essai d'interpretation de Jacques 5,16," *Revue des sciences religieuses* 58.4 (1984): 233-41.

G. Marconi, "La struttura di Giacomo 2," *Bib* 68.2 (1987): 250-57.

J. Marcus, "The Evil Inclination in the Epistle of James," *CBQ* 44.4 (1982): 606-21.

S. S. C. Marshall, "*Dipsychos:* A Local Term?" *StEv* 6 (1969): 348-51 = *TU* 112 (1973).

R. P. Martin, "The Life-Setting of the Epistle of James in the Light of Jewish History," *Biblical and Near Eastern Studies,* ed. G. A. Tuttle (Grand Rapids, 1978), pp. 97-103.

R. P. Martin, *New Testament Foundations,* I (Grand Rapids, 1975); II (1978).

W. Marxsen, *Introduction to the New Testament* (Philadelphia, 1968).

P. U. Maynard-Reid, *Poor and Rich in the Epistle of James: Socio-Historical and Exegetical Study* (Unpublished Th.D. Thesis, Andrews University, 1981).

P. U. Maynard-Reid, *Poverty and Wealth in James* (1987).

A. H. McNeile, *Introduction to the Study of the New Testament* (1953).

H. G. Meecham, "The Epistle of James," *ExpT* 49 (1937): 181-83.

M. Meinertz, *Der Jakobusbrief und sein Verfasser in Schrift und Überlieferung,* B.S.F. 10.1-3 (Freiburg, 1905).

B. M. Metzger, *The Canon of the New Testament* (Oxford, 1987).

B. M. Metzger, *A Textual Commentary on the Greek New Testament* (London, 1971).

J. Michl, "Der Spruch Jakobusbrief 4, 5," in *Neutestamentliche Aufsätze. Festschrift für Prof. Josef Schmid,* ed. J. Blinzler et al. (Regensburg, 1963), pp. 167-74.

C. J. S. Millar, *The Primitive Christology in the Epistle of James* (Unpublished Thesis, Graduate Theological Union, Berkeley, 1971).

L. Morris, *1 Timothy—James.* Scripture Union Bible Study Books (London, 1969).

C. F. D. Moule, *The Origin of Christology* (Cambridge, 1977).

F. Mussner, "'Direkte' und 'indirekte' Christologie im Jakobusbrief," *Catholica* 24 (1970): 111-17.

F. Mussner, "Die Tauflehre des Jakobusbriefes," Hansjorg auf der

Maur/B. Kleinheyer, eds., *Zeichen des Glaubens—Studien zu Taufe und Firmung*. F. S. Balthasar Fischer zum 60 Geburtstag (Zürich, 1972), pp. 61-67.
B. Noack, "Jakobus wider die Reichen," *ST* 18.1 (1964): 10-25.
W. Patrick, *James the Lord's Brother* (1906).
L. G. Perdue, "Paraenesis and the Epistle of James," *ZNW* 72.3-4 (1981): 241-56.
P. Perkins, "Expository Articles: James 3:16–4:3," *Interpretation* 36:3 (July 1982): 283-87.
O. Pfleiderer, *Primitive Christianity,* 4 vols. (1906-11).
K. G. Phifer, "Expository Articles: James 2:1-5," *Interpretation* 36:3 (July 1982): 278-82.
J. B. Polhill, "The Life-Situation of the Book of James," *RevExp* 66 (1969): 369-78.
W. K. Prentice, "James, the Brother of the Lord," in P. R. Coleman-Norton, ed., *Studies in Roman Economic and Social History* (for A. C. Johnson) (Princeton, NJ, 1951), pp. 144-51.
D. J. Roberts, "The Definition of 'Pure Religion' in James 1:27," *ExpT* 83 (1972): 215-16.
A. T. Robertson, *Studies in the Epistle of James* (First published as *Practical and Social Aspects of Christianity* [1915], revised and edited by H. F. Peacock [Nashville, 1958]).
J. A. T. Robinson, *Redating the New Testament* (London, 1976).
J. A. T. Robinson, *Can We Trust the New Testament?* (London, 1977).
C. Rountree, "Further Thoughts on the Discourse Structure of James" (International Linguistics Center, Dallas, 1976).
E. P. Sanders, *Paul and Palestinian Judaism* (Philadelphia, 1977).
J. T. Sanders, *Ethics in the New Testament* (London, 1975).
D. P. Scaer, *James, the Apostle of Faith* (St. Louis, 1984).
W. Schmithals, *Paul and James,* SBT 1/46 (London, 1965).
J. J. Schmitt, "You Adulteress! The Image in James 4.4," *NovT* 28.4 (1986): 327-37.
R. Schnackenburg, *The Moral Teaching of the New Testament* (London, 1965).
J. Schneider, *Die Briefe des Jakobus, Petrus, Judas and Johannes*. NTD X (Göttingen, 1961).
H.-J. Schoeps, *Theologie und Geschichte des Judenchristentums* (Tübingen, 1949).
L. A. Schökel, "James 5, 2 and 4, 6," *Bib* 54 (1973): 73-76.
W. Schrage, *Der Jakobusbrief* in *Die katholischen Briefe*. NTD X (Göttingen, 1973).
E. Schürer, *The History of the Jewish People in the Age of Jesus Christ*

(175 B.C.–A.D. 135). A new English version rev. and ed. by G. Vermes, F. Millar, M. Goodman, and M. Black. Literary ed. P. Vermes, organizing ed. M. Black, vols. I, II, III, pts. 1, 2 (Edinburgh, 1973, 1979, 1986, 1987).

J. J. Scott, Jr., "Parties in the Church of Jerusalem as Seen in the Book of Acts," *Journal of Evangelical Theological Society* 18.4 (Fall 1975): 217-27.

J. J. Scott, Jr., "James, the Relative of Jesus and the Expectation of an Eschatological Priest," *Journal of the Evangelical Theological Society* 25.3 (September 1982): 323-31.

O. J. F. Seitz, "Afterthoughts on the Term 'Dipsychos,'" *NTS* 4 (1958): 327-34.

O. J. F. Seitz, "Antecedents and Significance of the Term *DIPSYCHOS*," *JBL* 66 (1947): 211-19.

O. J. F. Seitz, "James and the Law," *StEv* 2 (1964): 472-86 = *TU* 87 (1964).

O. J. F. Seitz, "The Relationship of the Shepherd of Hermas to the Epistle of James," *JBL* 63 (1944): 131-40.

O. J. F. Seitz, "Two Spirits in Man: An Essay in Biblical Exegesis," *NTS* 6 (1959): 82-95.

E. G. Selwyn, *The First Epistle of St. Peter* (London, 1947).

J. N. Sevenster, *Do You Know Greek? How much Greek could the first Jewish Christians have known?* Supplements to *NovT* 19 (Leiden, 1968).

M. H. Shepherd, "The Epistle of James and the Gospel of Matthew," *JBL* 75 (1956): 40-51.

J. S. Siker, "The Canonical Status of the Catholic Epistles in the Syriac New Testament," *NTS* 38.2 (1987): 311-40.

H. S. Songer, "The Literary Character of the Book of James," *RevExp* 66.4 (1969): 379-89.

H. S. Songer, *James*. Broadman Bible Commentary XII (Nashville, 1972).

F. Stagg, "Exegetical Themes in James 1 and 2," *RevExp* 66 (1969): 391-402.

H. Thyen, *Der Stil der jüdisch-hellenistischen Homilie* (Göttingen, 1935).

K. Torakawa, "Literary-Semantic Analysis of James 1–2" (International Linguistics Center, Dallas).

M. J. Townsend, "James 4:1-4: A Warning Against Zealotry?" *ExpT* 87.7 (1976): 211-13.

M. J. Townsend, "Christ, Community and Salvation in the Epistle of James," *EQ* 53.2 (1981): 115-23.

E. Trocmé, "Les Églises pauliniennes vues du dehors: Jacques, 2, 1 à 3, 13," *StEv* 2 (1964): 660-69.

F. Valentine, *Where the Action Is* (Waco, Texas, 1969).

W. C. van Unnik, "The Teaching of Good Works in I Peter," *NTS* 1 (1954-55): 92-110.

D. O. Via, "The Right Strawy Epistle Reconsidered," *JR* 49.3 (1969): 261-62.

R. Walker, "Allein aus Werken. Zur Auslegung von Jakobus 2, 14-26," *ZTK* 61 (1965): 155-92.

R. B. Ward, "James of Jerusalem," *Restoration Quarterly* 16.3, 4 (Third and Fourth Quarter, 1973): 175-90.

R. B. Ward, "Partiality in the Assembly: James 2:2-4," *HTR* 62.1 (1969): 87-97.

R. B. Ward, "The Works of Abraham: James 2:14-26," *HTR* 61 (1968): 283-90.

J. Weiss, *History of Primitive Christianity,* 2 vols. (1937).

G. von Weizsäcker, *The Apostolic Age of the Christian Church,* II (1895).

W. W. Wessel, *An Inquiry into the Origin, Literary Character, Historical and Religious Significance of the Epistle of James* (Unpublished Ph.D. Thesis, University of Edinburgh, 1953).

W. Wessel, "The Epistle of James," in *The New Testament and Wycliffe Bible Commentary* (New York, 1971), pp. 943-64.

W. Wessel, "James, Epistle of," *ISBE,* II (Grand Rapids, 1981), 959-66.

A. Wifstrand, "Stylistic Problems in the Epistles of James and Peter," *ST* 1 (1948): 170-82.

A. Winter, *The Catholic Epistles* (London, 1959).

R. Wolff, *The General Epistles of James and Jude* (Contemporary Commentaries) (1969).

W. I. Wolverton, "The Double-Minded Man in the Light of the Essene Psychology," *ATR* 38.2 (1956): 165-75.

R. C. Worley, *Preaching and Teaching in the Earliest Church* (Philadelphia, 1967).

F. W. Young, "The Relation of I Clement to the Epistle of James," *JBL* 67 (1948): 339-45.

T. Zahn, *Introduction to the New Testament,* 3 vols. (1909).

J. A. Ziesler, *The Meaning of Righteousness in Paul* (Cambridge, 1972).

VI. INDEXES

1. Principal Names and Subjects

2. Principal Authors

3. *Scripture References*

4. Hebrew, Aramaic, and Arabic Words

ARABIC

5. Greek Words

6. Rabbinic Literature

MIDRASH

7. *Jewish Apocrypha and Pseudepigrapha*

8. Dead Sea Scrolls

9. Principal Classical and Hellenistic Writers

10. Selected New Testament Apocrypha and Church Fathers

11. Selected Later Christian Writers

Printed in the United States
203837BV00001B/1-18/A

9 780802 801678